Fodor's 2nd Edition

Naples, Capri, and the Amalfi Coast

Fodor's Travel Publications • New York, Toronto, London, Sydney, Auckland
www.fodors.com

CONTENTS

MAPS

Circled letters in text correspond to letters on the photographs. For more information on the sights pictured, turn to
the indicated page number (A) on each photograph.

DESTINATION NAPLES, CAPRI, AND THE AMALFI COAST

Not all of Paradise was lost. A luxuriant dollop of it—the Bay of Naples and the Amalfi Coast—lingers on here in southern Italy. Erstwhile pleasure dome to the Roman emperors, this region is stuffed with luxurious resorts, fabled ruins, fantasy islands, and sapphire-shaded lagoons. Along the sinuous Amalfi Drive, the towns of Positano, Amalfi, and Ravello entrap the senses, while the petrified mysteries of Pompeii beckon beneath sleeping Mount Vesuvius. Across the bay from seductive Sorrento lies Capri, spiritual capital of *la dolce far niente*, Italy's legendary "sweetness of doing nothing." Naples, the city at the center of it all, quickens pulses as well, and not just because of its whirling traffic—its great art, scenic streets, and endearingly warm people add up to one thrilling operatic scenario.

NAPLES

(A) > 67

"See Naples and die" proclaims the famous anthem, but you're better advised to forget this age-old caveat and simply live life—as the locals do—to the fullest. Ranking rulers stacked Naples with stately palaces and provoking monuments, and it's against this grandiose and theatrical backdrop that Neapolitans go about the extraordinary business of being vibrantly Neapolitan. The marble-clad vastness of the (E)**Galleria Umberto I** proves a handy refuge to observe

(B) > 23

these masters of spontaneity without fear of being clipped by a speeding car. But sooner or later your quest to experience the essential Naples leads you to its heart: ©**Spaccanapoli,** the historic quarter where rainbow rows of laundry flap next to gorgeously gilded churches such as the Ⓓ**Duomo di San Gennaro.** Here the feast day of the city's enshrined patron saint is celebrated with true Neapolitan flair on September 19, when, with luck, his holy blood liquefies in its silver reliquary, a portent of good fortune for the city in the coming year. Frequent as such dramatic moments are in Naples, living well here really comes down to embracing life's simple pleasures. This is, after all, a city where the culinary high point is no more elaborate than a delicious pizza at Ⓐ**Trattoria Brandi,** and where the best show in town, a thunderously beautiful vista of the Ⓑ**Bay of Naples,** is usually awaiting you around the next corner.

AROUND THE BAY

Reminders of Campania's volcanic underpinnings can be found in both directions from Naples, which sits midway along the northern shore of the turquoise Golfo di Napoli. To the west the earth steams and bubbles at the sunken volcanic crater

Ⓑ 126

Solfatara, the focal point of the ©**Campi Flegri,** the Phlegrean Fields. Here, at the Sibyl's Cave in Cumae, ancients once consulted the all-powerful Oracles and believed the portal to Hades lay in the nearby Lago d'Averno. Among spirits you may meet in Pozzuoli are those of St. Paul, who first stepped ashore in Italy here; and of the Roman emperors who built the Ⓐ**Anfiteatro Flavio,** the town's massive amphitheater; even of a real-life goddess— Sophia Loren, a native daughter of the town. East of Naples are Pompeii and Herculaneum, the best-preserved cities of classical antiquity, and their nemesis, now-dormant Vesuvio. It's easy, at Pompeii's ⒷVia dei Sepolcri, to fall into the rhythms of everyday life that ended so abruptly with the massive AD 79 eruption, and, in the frescoes of

the ⒹVilla dei Misteri, to get a glimpse into the voluptuous tastes of the residents of the era. Many years later, in the 18th century, Bourbon aristocrats built the gilded ⒺPalazzo Reale in nearby Portici, the better to witness the famed volcano's hijinks. Will you be present when it awakens from its long sleep?

Sooner or later, one of the three legendary islands off the coast of Naples may lure you to their shores. You'll be in good company, since emperors, poets, Hollywood divas, European nobles, and legions of mere mortals have been answering their siren call for centuries. If the forbidding Ⓐ**Castello Aragonese** on Ischia once did a pretty

Ⓐ 171

CAPRI, ISCHIA, AND PROCIDA

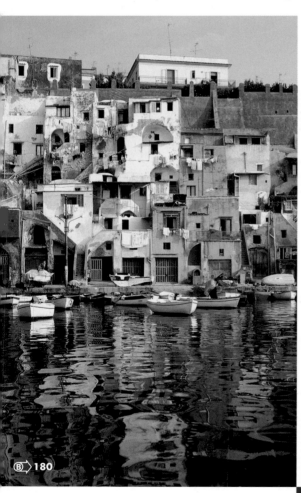

Ⓑ 180

good job of discouraging newcomers from coming ashore, islanders there now readily welcome visitors to their inviting beaches, volcanic slopes, and idyllic spas—you can take your pick of more than 100 thermal baths. Or set sail for Ⓑ**Procida**—although it's a short trip, just 2 miles from the mainland, this little volcanic outcropping incredibly retains much of its picturesque Mediterranean charm, a fact that accounts for a disproportionate number of easel-toting visitors. As for Capri, you must come here at least once in your life: to experience its special mix of jet-setter glamour and understated charm, take a stroll along one of the paved paths perched high above the sea, explore the copious evidence of the hedonistic lifestyle of Tiberius and other Roman emperors, and rub elbows with

Ⓒ 158

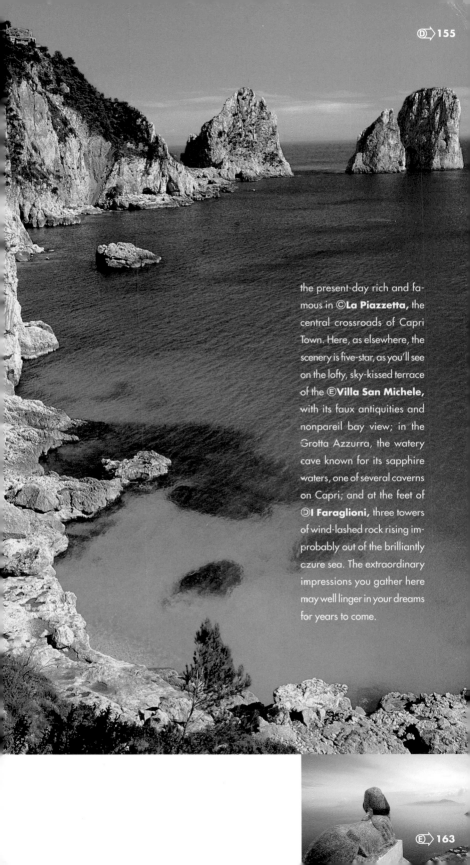

the present-day rich and famous in ©**La Piazzetta,** the central crossroads of Capri Town. Here, as elsewhere, the scenery is five-star, as you'll see on the lofty, sky-kissed terrace of the Ⓔ**Villa San Michele,** with its faux antiquities and nonpareil bay view; in the Grotta Azzurra, the watery cave known for its sapphire waters, one of several caverns on Capri; and at the feet of Ⓓ**I Faraglioni,** three towers of wind-lashed rock rising improbably out of the brilliantly azure sea. The extraordinary impressions you gather here may well linger in your dreams for years to come.

Ⓐ▷ 214

SORRENTO AND
THE AMALFI COAST

Ⓑ▷ 246

An unfolding panorama of color piled on color, Italy has no shortage of natural and man-made beauty. But nowhere do these ingredients blend together as satisfyingly as on the Sorrento Peninsula and along the Amalfi Coast. Don't be surprised if you find yourself bewitched by this surfeit of watery blue vistas, pastel-hue villages, and fragrant lemon groves. The first glimpse

Ⓒ▷ 198

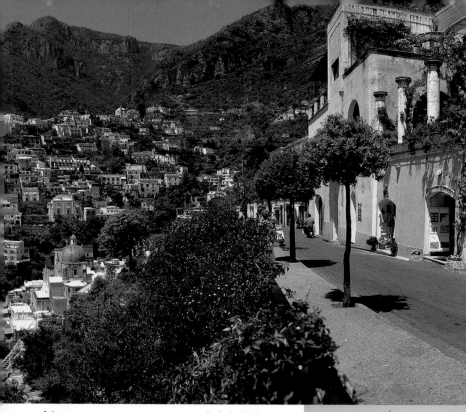

of ©**Sorrento**—Campania at its genteelly faded belle epoque best—conjures images of warbling waiters and throbbing mandolins. In Ⓐ Ⓔ**Positano,** dwellings tinted in sunrise colors climb the mountainside above the sea, and clichés like "heaven on earth" come to mind. The trip south from here on the breathtaking Amalfi Drive is likely to leave you speechless —a good thing, too, because you'll want to concentrate on the twists, turns, and dizzying drops to the sea. Save the superlatives in your vocabulary for what lies ahead. Tiny Conca dei Marini, a village favored by beachcombers and billionaires, is an idyll. The town of Amalfi, tucked into a seaside gorge, would be alluring even if its main square weren't crowned with a cathedral right out of *The Arabian Nights,* the Ⓓ**Duomo di Sant' Andrea.** Finally, like the maraschino cherry on a sundae, there's the hilltop town of Ravello, whose palmy gardens and dreamy villas, including the Ⓑ**Villa Rufolo,** seem an otherworldly vision, floating between sea and sky.

Ⓓ235

Ⓔ214

13

FODOR'S
CHOICE

Even with so many special places in Campania, Fodor's writers and editors have their favorites. Here are a few that stand out.

MAGICAL PLACES

Historic Quarter, Sorrento. Adorned with belle epoque palazzi, Victorian streetlights, and joyously festive crowds, this sector of town is pure vacation magic. Buy a rose and carry it through the streets, for the pure pleasure of the moment. ☞ p. 199

Spaccanapoli, Naples. An unforgettable Punch-and-Judy show, the most picturesque neighborhood of Naples is a 24-hour parade of great people watching. Towering tenements jostle with grand palazzi, amid the district's swirling baroque architecture. ☞ p. 36

Ⓑ **The Temples of Paestum.** Inspiration to countless artists, these noble Greek ruins are best seen at daybreak or dusk, when their grandeur can be fully absorbed. ☞ p. 258

Ⓕ **Villa Cimbrone, Ravello.** Is this the most beautiful spot in southern Italy? To decide for yourself, tour its breathtaking garden—its roses once warmed Greta Garbo's chilly soul—then gape at its sky-touching Belvedere of Infinity. ☞ p. 247

Villa San Michele, Capri. Join the cast posed for an Alma-Tadema painting at this villa of ancient design. Make a wish standing on the Sphinx Parapet, high atop Anacapri. Then, when you return by bus, be extra nice to the driver—you're 2,000 ft above the Bay of Naples on this road. ☞ p. 163

SPECIAL MOMENTS

Dawn Concert at the Villa Rufolo, Ravello. Suspended between sea and sky, this hilltop village is home to the Festival Musicale di Ravello. Experience its extraordinary evening concerts and *concerto all'alba*—a concert that serenades the rising sun beginning at 4 AM (early August). ☞ p. 246

Ⓓ **Festa di San Gennaro, Naples.** Everything in Naples comes to a boil twice a year—on the first Saturday in May and on September 19—when the Liquefaction of the Blood of San Gennaro is celebrated at the city duomo. If you want to "assist" at *Il Miracolo,* arrive as early as 7 AM. ☞ p. 39

Twilight, Positano. The utter tranquillity of Positano at sunset is a balm to the soul. Whitewashed houses tumble down to the azure sea, shimmering under a blood-orange sky. Reserve an alfresco table at a café and let it all soak in. *This* is why you came to Italy. ☞ p. 214

DINING

Ⓐ **Don Alfonso 1890, Sant' Agata.** Lovers of fine food know the road up to mountaintop Sant'Agata is the *strada* to culinary glory: a table at Don Alfonso, southern Italy's finest restaurant. Try *gamberi crude al caviale blue con sucito di limone,* or red shrimp with blue caviar—it's also Prince Rainier's favorite. $$$$ ☞ p. 211

Villa Pompeiana, Sorrento. Here, on the site of the seaside villa where Emperor Augustus once dined on moray eels fattened on human flesh, Lord Astor built a tiny villa set with Pompeiian murals and a stone terrace worthy of a Caesar. Now it's the restaurant of the Hotel Bellevue Syrene, and you can dine here on fine delicacies like Li Galli lobster with melon pearls. No moray eels, however. $$$$ ☞ p. 205

Trattoria Brandi, Naples. Since Pavarotti considers this an obligatory stop when in Naples, why shouldn't you? The birthplace of *pizza Margherita,* it's adorably cozy with full-blast Neapolitan charm. $$ ☞ p. 67

O' Guarracino, Positano. Just maybe the prettiest pizzeria anywhere, this tree house overlooks the cliffs, the sea, and Torre Trasìta. $–$$ ☞ p. 219

HOTELS

Ⓒ **Excelsior-Vittoria, Sorrento.** Magnificently set overlooking the Bay of Naples, this is a belle epoque dream come true, with elegant salons, stunning gardens, and a romantic terrace alive with Cole Porter and Puccini. $$$$ ☞ p. 205

Ⓔ **Le Sirenuse, Positano.** As legendary as its namesake sirens, this exquisite 18th-century palazzo shimmers with glamour. Modigliani-sleek odalisques grace the stunning pool terrace at lunch; for dinner, the restaurant is the best on the Amalfi Coast (and certainly the priciest). $$$$ ☞ p. 220

Punta Tragara, Capri. Pity the billionaire who thinks his ship has come in but has never stayed at this spot built by Le Corbusier over the rocks of I Faraglioni. The beauty of the arbored poolside restaurant stops conversation. $$$$ ☞ p. 166

Caruso Belvedere, Ravello. With regal Empire-era salons and terrace gardens offering spellbinding views of the blue Bay of Salerno, it's no wonder authors like Virginia Woolf, Graham Greene, and Tennessee Williams adored this genteel aristocrat of a hotel. $$$–$$$$ ☞ p. 249

Cappuccini Convento, Amalfi. Like Richard Wagner, you may be tempted to abandon your room and camp out under the stars on this hotel's legendary cliff-top veranda. Southern Italy's most sublime hotel comes with views so picturesque you practically click your camera for you. $$$ ☞ p. 240

Soggiorno Sansevero, Naples. Set in the former palazzo of the Princes Sansevero, right on the most charming square of Spaccanapoli, this tiny pensione can't be beat for the location—or the price. $ ☞ p. 82

1 NAPLES

A kinetic gust of 3-D garlic-and-basil aromatherapy for the soul, Naples is a destination no one ever forgets. The most operatic of cities, it blasts you with a heady mix of beauty, chaos, and a glorious past. If your eye is greedy for splendor, many treasures beckon—the world's finest museum of classical antiquities, opulent palaces, and bravura Caravaggio altarpieces—but the greatest treasure of all is the Neapolitan people themselves. Today, Vesuvius may slumber nearby, but Naples itself is erupting in a renaissance of cultural identity and pride.

By Gregory
W. Bailey

Updated by
Mark Walters

B UILT LIKE A GREAT AMPHITHEATER around her beautiful bay, Naples is an eternally unfolding play acted by a million of the best actors in the world," Herbert Kubly observed in his *American in Italy.* "The comedy is broad, the tragedy violent. The curtain never rings down." Is it a sense of doom from living in the shadow of Vesuvius that makes many Neapolitans so volatile, perhaps so seemingly blind to everything but the pain or pleasure of the moment? Poverty and overcrowding are the more likely causes. But whatever the reason, Naples remains the most vibrant city in Italy—a steaming, bubbling, reverberating minestrone in which each block is a village, every street the setting for a Punch-and-Judy show, and everything seems to be a backdrop for an opera not yet composed. It is said that northern Italians vacation here to remind themselves of the time when Italy was *molto Italiano—really* Italian. In this respect, Naples—Napoli in Italian—doesn't disappoint: Neapolitan rainbows of laundry wave in the wind over alleyways open-windowed with friendliness, mothers caress children, men break out into impromptu arias at sidewalk cafés, street scenes offer Fellini-esque slices of life, and everywhere contrasting elements of faded gilt and romance, rust and calamity, grandeur and squalor form an intoxicating pageant of pure *Italianità*—Italy at its most Italian.

From the moment you arrive at swirling Piazza Garibaldi, the city blasts you with its confounding mix of beauty, chaos, and a glorious past. The piazza, which is home to the Stazione Centrale, the main railroad terminal, seems at first glance a battered place—crowded, polluted, and inhospitable, with Fiats and scooters careening insanely around poorly landscaped traffic islands. Along with the standard complement of street sharks and souvenir-hawkers, the piazza has recently become the meeting-point for immense numbers of eastern Europeans; thanks to its age-old traditions of tolerance and hospitality, Naples is a welcome destination for increasing numbers of guest-workers. Once you get away from Piazza Garibaldi, first impressions begin to mellow: The pace changes, and your point of view along with it. Naples unfolds as a cornucopia of elegant boulevards, treasure-stocked palaces, the world's greatest museum of classical antiquities, the stage-set neighborhood of Spaccanapoli, and hundreds of historic churches. For the serious-minded, walking, cathedral-visiting tourist, Naples becomes *Napoli la bella,* a city centuries of romantics have deemed one of the most beautiful in the world, a designation that owes much to its location on the breathtaking Bay of Naples, plus an immense past attested to by its historic and grand monuments and a mode of life that never fails to fascinate.

Despite these attributes, by the 1970s a different, rather seedy image had emerged: *Napoli la terribile.* Horror stories abounded about the *scippatori,* Vespa-riding muggers who yanked purses from sightseeing strollers; hospitals so terrible that patients were said to dial 113, the emergency number, from their bedsides because they despaired of ever seeing the ward nurse; and the juvenile *scugnizzi,* the street children who would pry off your license plate at one traffic light only to sell it back to you at the next. Unemployment reached 30%, the infrastructure was rotting (government subsidies were simply being *mett'in tasca*—"put into pocket,"—as the local phrase had it, by the Camorra, the Neapolitan version of the Mafia), while the threat of earthquakes and ever-present gridlock turned sectors into an Italian Los Angeles.

By the early 1980s Neapolitans had had enough. Baroness Mirella Barracca mobilized the city's rich and powerful into Committee Naples

Ninety-Nine, an organization whose mission was to uplift both the city's historic structures and its public image. When Antonio Bassolino became mayor in 1992, he jump-started the city's economic development, cleared up the streets, and crowded more policemen than travelers into the main railway terminal. By the time global leaders like Clinton and Yeltsin convened in the city in 1992 for the G7 summit meeting, many palaces had been restored, churches reopened, conferences held; the Camorra was out and art—many city museums were refurbished—was in. Today, a decade later, it is Naples that has erupted in an unending flow of cultural excitement while Il Vesuvio (Vesuvius) slumbers: Artists have taken up residence near the Capodimonte Palace, site of the city's new modern art collection; a renaissance of southern Italian cooking is making headlines around the world; and more and more travelers with a been-there, done-that take on Rome, Florence, and other capitals of northern Italy are setting a southward course. Only a few years ago, Naples was a "don't," and almost all the thousands who entered the city's Stazione Centrale only did so because it was the gateway to Pompeii, Sorrento, Capri, and the Amalfi Coast. Since then, the thousands arriving in the city are discovering that Naples is much more than a railway station—it is a civilization.

The origin of Naples, once called Parthenope and later Neapolis, can be traced to what are now the nearby ruins of Cumae, the earliest Greek colony in Italy, founded around 750 BC. Greek civilization flourished for hundreds of years along this coastline, but there was nothing in the way of centralized government until the Roman Empire, uniting all Italy for the first time, surged southward and, with little opposition, absorbed the Greek colonies in the 4th century BC. The Romans were quick to appreciate the sybaritic potential of the region, and wealthy members of the empire flocked here to build palatial country residences. Generally, the peace of Campania was undisturbed during the centuries of Roman rule.

Naples and Campania, with the rest of Italy, decayed with the Roman Empire and collapsed into the abyss of the Middle Ages. In 1130 the Norman king Roger II, King of the Two Sicilies, made Naples the capital of his Norman empire, until Henry VI of Hohenstaufen captured it in 1194; his enlightened son, Frederick II, endowed the city with a university that attracted many scholars and poets. By now the popes had an eye on Naples, and together with the French king Louis IX and Charles of Anjou, their French Angevin government conquered the Hohenstaufen forces in 1268. Charles of Anjou and Robert the Wise sponsored the construction of several important buildings, including the Church of Santa Chiara, which introduced the style of Provençal Gothic to the city. Aragonese rule arrived in 1442 with the siege of Alfonso I of Aragon, but his line was driven from the city in turn by the alliance between King Louis XII of France and Ferdinand of Spain. The nobles who served under the Spanish viceroys in the 16th and 17th centuries, when their harsh rule made all Italy quake, enjoyed their libertine pleasures, resulting in the flourishing of taverns and gaming houses, even as Spain milked the citizenry with burdensome taxes. During this time Naples became Europe's second-largest city, after Paris (and also its most densely populated—to accommodate the crowds, tenements rose as high as seven stories).

After a short-lived Austrian occupation, Naples became the capital of the Kingdom of the Two Sicilies, established by the Bourbon kings in 1738. This somewhat garbled kingdom was made up of Naples (which included most of the southern Italian mainland) and Sicily, which were united in the Middle Ages, then separated and unofficially reunited under

Spanish domination during the 16th and 17th centuries. With the rule of the Bourbon kings, the Neapolitan golden age began in earnest, as their rule was generally benevolent, as far as Campania was concerned, and their support of the papal authority in Rome was an important factor in the development of the rest of Italy. The rule of Charles III of Bourbon, along with that of his son Ferdinand IV, was important artistically: Both kings not only built many of the architectural showpieces of the city—the Palace of Capodimonte, Teatro San Carlo, and the Palaces of Caserta and Portici, to name just a few— they also sponsored noted musicians, artists, and writers, who were only too willing to submit to court life in such magnificent natural surroundings. But the modern world came knocking in the person of Napoléon, whose forces dethroned the Bourbons in 1799. The glamour of the Empire style came to the city when Napoléon appointed his brother-in-law, Joachim Murat, king of Naples. In 1815 the Bourbons returned to power, Murat was shot, and Ferdinand IV exclaimed that the poor general had been a better upholsterer than an administrator. In 1816, with Napoléon out of the way on St. Helena, Ferdinand officially remerged the two kingdoms, proclaiming himself Ferdinand I of the Kingdom of Two Sicilies. His reactionary and repressive rule earned him a few more colorful titles among his rebellious subjects. Finally, Giuseppe Garibaldi launched his expedition, and in 1860 Naples was united with the rest of Italy.

Clearly, as the historic capital of Campania, Naples has been perpetually and tumultuously in flux. Neapolitans are instinctively the most hospitable of people, and they've often paid a price for being so, having unwittingly extended a warm welcome to wave after wave of invaders. Lombards, Goths, Normans, Swabians, Spanish viceroys and kings, and Napoleonic generals arrived in turn, most of whom proved to be greedy and self-serving. Still, if these foreign rulers bled the populace dry with taxes, they left the impoverished city with a rich architectural inheritance.

Much of that inheritance is on display on the Piazza Gesù Nuovo—a showplace for the city's most beloved churches and a showcase for the city's greatest attraction, the Neapolitan people. On the piazza, watch and rub elbows with them. Listen to—or rather watch—them as they talk. Let their charm, their gaiety, their effervescence, their completely undiluted spontaneity sweep you into their unique but glorious concept of life and living. You'll soon begin to realize there's something about Naples that makes the Neapolitans the happiest people in the world. In an hour or two you'll feel like part of the *famiglia* yourself. Compared to most other great metropolises of the world, Naples has little tourist infrastructure, allowing you to become a native very quickly, as you'll find out if you spend some time on the Piazza Gesù Nuovo. Lost? You'll be escorted (probably by way of mamma's house). Hungry? Hey, *paisan,* bring a slice! Can't think of a phrase? A translation is shouted out over the din, and a single word is never sufficient when 10 will do—as you could have seen one September afternoon when an English couple asked for directions to the Church of Pio Monte della Misericordia. One passerby started explaining, but another man suddenly thought of a still shorter way and butted in. In no time 8 or 10 people were kindly proffering their own versions. The arguing that ensued was not severe. A ripped racing form was the only casualty. The inquiring couple never learned the shortest—or, for that matter, any other—way to Pio Monte. But the sun was hot, the sky was blue, and there are plenty of other beautiful churches in Naples.

—Robert I. C. Fisher

Pleasures and Pastimes

La Cucina Napoletana—And It's Good for You!

If you love food you'll love Naples, the birthplace of several of the world's most popular dishes and culinary delights: pizza, spaghetti *al pomodoro* (with tomatoes), mozzarella cheese, as well as most of the pasta shapes everyone knows, like ziti, vermicelli—what most Italians call spaghetti—fusilli, *bucatini,* and linguine, as well as some of the most *delizioso* coffee and desserts served up anywhere. For the most part, these dishes reflect the schizophrenic split of rich and poor that has always characterized the city. Since most Neapolitans as well have long been both very poor and very creative, *cucina povera* —subsistence nourishment alchemically raised to culinary gold—is at its best here. This species of "poor peoples' food" is best represented by pizza. By the 18th century, fishermen were eating like kings and kings like fishermen: Neapolitan royalty was known for its love of the sturdy and virtuous "common" food. Forks were supposedly invented so that Ferdinand II could indulge in spaghetti at state banquets in a dignified manner, and Ferdinand IV used the porcelain kilns at Capodimonte for cooking pizza, so he didn't have to go out late at night to satisfy his cravings.

Beyond pizza and pasta, a number of other specialties take cheap, abundant ingredients and produce solid and dazzlingly delicious nourishment: the local version of Italian bean stew, *pasta e fagioli,* can suffice for a meal. The profusion of fried foods, and small take-out eateries—the *friggitorie*—serving only those items, grew out of the resilience of the many poor Neapolitans, who couldn't afford cooking facilities, if they had a home at all, and so took whatever items they had down to the local fryer and then either brought them home to eat or ate them standing up. There are more variations on fried dough than you may ever have time to try, but no one should miss the famous pea-studded rice croquettes bound with béchamel, best enjoyed at the pizzeria Da Matteo. *Arancioni,* large rice croquettes with tomato and meat sauce and cheese, make a great snack, and zucchini flowers are a popular appetizer at pizzerias. Neapolitan *ragù,*slowly simmered, renders humble cuts of meat (diced but not ground) into ambrosia; and simple pasta with tomato sauce is always a good bet, given the quality of the tomatoes. A number of dishes bear witness to the importance of communal eating (not to mention efficiently recycled leftovers), including *sartù,* an aristocratic and suitably elaborate rice casserole and, if you're around at Easter, *casatiello,* a golden ring of tender dough filled with everything on hand. Spaghetti *alla puttanesca,* tarted up with olives and capers, is a superquick pasta dish said to have been cooked up, as its name indicates, by ladies of the night who didn't have time to slave over the stove.

In part, Neapolitan cooking derives its quality from the availability of superb local ingredients: the rich volcanic soil surrounding the city, nurtured by abundant sun and benevolent breezes, has from ancient times been famous for the quality of its produce. *Friarielli* are a local type of broccoli, almost all stems and no flower, which are blanched like collard greens and tossed on pizza or sautéed with garlic and red pepper and served, delicious and remineralizing, with grilled sausage (*salsiccia e friarielli*). True mozzarella is the property of Campania; the best is made from 100% river-buffalo milk and has a unique tang and velvety consistency. Most *latte di bufala* is mixed (legally) with cow's milk, which tends to dilute its character, but still earns it the title of mozzarella. A slightly different fresh cheese product is *fior di latte,* made entirely from cow's milk. But be sure to try a good *mozzarella di vera bufala* (real buffalo milk mozzarella) while in Naples—it's a revelation: the cheese must be eaten very fresh (the same day is best) and doesn't like to travel. An absolutely simple dish, though, such as the *insalata caprese* (tomato, mozzarella, and basil salad), becomes a voluptuous Titianesque masterpiece when all the ingredients are right—typical of the best dishes of *cucina napoletana*. To top it all off, critics consider southern Italian cooking among the healthiest in the world—unlike the cholesterol-laden butters used in northern Italian cuisine, most Campanian dishes use olive oils. And don't forget that Campania is really one great wine flask. Among the region's wines, Gragnano, Falerno, and Greco di Tufo are fine whites. Ischia and Ravello also produce good white wine. Campania's best-known reds are Aglianico, Taurasi, and the red version of Falerno. The most famous wines, of course, are the Lacrima Christi whites—named because Christ, looking down on the beautiful Bay of Naples, supposedly wept over the sins of the people.

Lodging: A View with a Room

Naples has the range of accommodations you would expect of any bustling metropolis, from the squalid *alberghetti* (little hotels) around the Piazza Garibaldi railway station to the grand landmarks of luxury on the Lungomare and Posillipo. Since Naples is very much a businessperson's city, the better hotels can be quickly booked up by conventioneers (who are willing to pay top prices and even supplements for amenities like air-conditioning), so reserve well in advance for the finer hotels. Unfortunately, the equivalent of the genteel *pensiones* of yesteryear are few and far between: usually small and intimate, several in Naples do still exist, and they often have a quaint appeal that fortunately does not preclude modern plumbing. To plug the gap in low- to mid-range lodgings and cope with the significant rise in demand for discerning city-based tourism, the uncharacteristic bed-and-breakfast option is increasingly offered.

Whether you are in a five-star hotel or a more modest establishment, you may enjoy one of the greatest pleasures of all: a room with a view. In this case it's not *any* view, but the lay-down-and-die panorama of the Bay of Naples and Vesuvius, so be sure to ask for a bayside room if your hotel can provide one. (And when making reservations, be sure to inquire if breakfast is included in the room rate, if there is a supplement for air-conditioning, and if parking facilities come with an extra fee.) When you get to your bayside room, step out onto the balcony prepared to gasp. Everyone does.

Beyond Baroque: Neapolitan Art and Architecture

Naples is commonly categorized as a Baroque city, and it is true that this 17th- and 18th-century style produced defining monuments for the city, but it is a mistake to define Naples simply as Baroque. The city is so much older than that—almost as old as Rome (the city that actually gave rise to the Baroque style). In any case, the "Baroque" exuberance of Naples goes back to ancient times; the style found fertile ground here underneath the volcano. But this chapter aims to introduce the reader to other facets of the city as well, by including unjustly neglected monuments, for Naples has ancient Greek and Roman ruins, vertical heaven-seeking Medieval churches, first-rate chapels of the Renaissance, elegant 19th-century Empire and Neoclassical palaces, and important Modernist buildings from the 20th century as well, much of which tends to be obscured by all the polychrome-marble flourishes of the Baroque style. In the end, the Naples of today is the sum of all these periods—and something timeless as well.

Passion on the High C's: Opera at Teatro San Carlo

Opera is an art form peculiarly suited to the Neapolitan temperament, so do try to attend a performance of, let's say, *Lucia di Lammermoor,* at the Teatro San Carlo (where it received its premiere in 1835). You may find stylized acting and great singing a bad mixture esthetically, some will be embarrassed by the naked emotion on display and the clichéd sentimentality or incomprehensibility of the plot, and some may ridicule the convention that permits a dying Edgardo to rise and sing a powerful aria and perhaps an encore before lying down again to die. But whatever naysayers may think, opera is the lifeblood of Neapolitans, a reflection of the drama of their existence, a sublimation of their personal mythology; their melodrama, burlesque, pantomime, circus, and celebrity concert all rolled into one. Back when the Teatro San Carlo was built (1737), Naples was the musical capital of Italy, and here many of the greatest operas of the melodious trio of Rossini (1792–1868), Bellini (1801–35), and Donizetti (1797–1848) received their loudest ovations, since they often showcased bel canto singing to bravura effect. The bel canto style—in which libretto and dramatic tension are sacrificed to virtuoso singing—produced a typically Neapolitan being, the prima donna: haughty, tempestuous, temperamental, a despot in all her glory. The greatest singers flocked to the San Carlo since they knew Neapolitans were more prepared to stomach over-the-top emotional excess (on and off the stage) than anyone else in Italy. Today opera in Naples is a medium that grows neither old nor old-fashioned. The season lasts from early December to June, and the audience's dress and jewelry on premiere nights sometimes matches the extravagant red-and-gold decor of the auditorium. Under huge clusters of candelabra, the full house resembles an overflowing basket of flowers—a sight to remember, even before the curtain has gone up.

EXPLORING NAPLES

Naples, a bustling city of some 1.2 million people, presents a particular challenge for visitors because of its hilly geographic terrain and its twisty, often congested streets. Though spread out, Naples invites walking; the bus system, funiculars, and subways are also options for surmounting the problem of weary legs. Sightseeing days should begin no later than 9, as most churches are usually open only from 7:30 AM until noon or 12:30, reopening only after the afternoon siesta from 4 or 4:30 until about 7. In winter, schedule church visits for mornings only, as the artificial afternoon lighting can make even the most spectacular church seem dull and gloomy. Some museums now have extended hours, with a few even open in evenings; however, this usually mean that rooms may be open on a roster basis, and if you are making a special journey to see a particular exhibit, it's worth phoning in advance to check if it is viewable. If you come to Naples by car, park it in a garage as fast as you can, agree on the cost in advance, and then forget it for the duration of your stay (otherwise, theft is a constant risk). Use the funiculars to get up and down the hills, and take the Metropolitana—the city's subway system—to such destinations as Piazza Garibaldi, Chiaia, Mergellina, and Pozzuoli; for Pozzuoli and the Phlegrean Fields, Pompeii, Herculaneum, and the towns of the Amalfi Coast, take the Circumflegrea, Cumana, and Circumvesuviana lines.

The heart of Naples stretches along the Bay of Naples from Piazza Garibaldi in the east to Mergellina in the west, with its back to the Vomero Hill. From Stazione Centrale, on Piazza Garibaldi, Corso Umberto I (known as the "Rettifilo") heads southwest to the monumental city center around the piazzas Bovio, Municipio, and Trieste e Trento; here is the major urban set-piece of the Palazzo Reale, Teatro San Carlo, and Galleria Umberto Primo. To the north are the historic districts of old Naples; to the south is the port. Farther west along the bay are the more fashionable neighborhoods of Santa Lucia and Chiaia, and finally the waterfront district of Mergellina. The residential area of Vomero sits on the steep hills rising above Chiaia and downtown. Just to the east is Naples's picturesque quarter, Spaccanapoli—the heart of the *centro storico* (historic center)—once called the Decumanus Inferior in Roman times and today a street that changes names several times on its way through the heart of old Naples (it comprises Via Benedetto Croce and Via San Biagio dei Librai, among others).

Tying much of this geographic layout together is the "spine" of the city, Via Toledo—Naples's major north–south axis, which begins at Piazza Trieste e Trento and heads up all the way up to Capodimonte. It's basically one straight road with four different names (five if you count the official name of Via Roma, which all the locals know it as anyway). Via Toledo links Piazza Trieste e Trento with Piazza Dante. Going further north you get into Via Pessina for about 100 yards which takes you up to the mega-junction with the Museo Archeologico Nazionale. North of that, you head up to the peak of Capodimonte by traveling along Via Santa Teresa degli Scalzi and then Corso Amedeo di Savoia. To make things a bit more confusing, parts of Via Toledo are pedestrianized—and that means no buses or scooters, thankfully—and is just south of Piazza Carità (where Via Toledo/Roma intersects with Via Diaz) all the way to Piazza Trieste e Trento. Currently Via Diaz is closed to through traffic, which means that southbound buses from Piazza Dante have to turn left in Piazza Carità, pass in front of the main post office, and then join the maelstrom downtown towards Piazza Bovio and Corso Umberto. Bear in mind that mobility is further disrupted at the moment thanks to the various works on the new Metropolitana extension line running through the heart of the city: Piazza Municipio is boarded off, as is Piazza Bovio and Piazza Amore, but to compensate you can now take a state-of-the art subway train from the Museo Archeologico up to Piazza Vanvitelli in Vomero without passing through some of the more congested parts of the city.

Long considered a threatened species, the pedestrian in Naples is gradually being provided with a more friendly eco-niche. True, promenading in Naples sometimes takes a little practice. In a city where a red light is often looked at as merely a suggestion, walking across a busy avenue can be like a game of chess—if you hesitate, you capitulate. Most residents just head out into the unceasing flow of traffic, knowing cars invariably slow down to let them cross (trick for the fainthearted: look for an elderly couple—when they cross, you *know* it will be safe). Essentially, you should cross big streets one or two lanes at a time, and don't ever hesitate in the middle of a lane—keep moving so motorcycles can avoid you. In any event, once you've dealt with the hurtling traffic at Piazza Municipio, nothing in life should faze you.

Numbers in the text correspond to numbers in the margin and on the Naples maps.

Great Itineraries

IF YOU HAVE 1 DAY

Begin with the Naples you have always imagined: Spaccanapoli—the historic quarter where palaces and slums, neon-lighted pizzerias and gilded cathedrals, organ-grinders and Mercedes create an open-air museum. Ground zero here is Piazza Gesù Nuovo, site of the churches of the Gesù Nuovo and Santa Chiara and entryway to the spectacular 5-km-long (3-mi-long) pedestrian ribbon called the Spaccanapoli. Explore the memorable sights of this quarter—the Cappella Sansevero, the crèche shops of Via Gregorio Armeno, the Caravaggio altarpiece at the Pio Monte, and the Chapel of San Gennaro at the Duomo—by first walking east along the Spacca, then returning west one block north along Via Tribunali. After lunch at a Spacca pizzeria or café, head over to Via Toledo, Naples's main thoroughfare, and walk back to the ceremonial center of the city: Piazza del Plebiscito, bookended on one side by the Church of San Francesco di Paola, and on the other by the Bourbons' palace, the Palazzo Reale. Combine sightseeing with shopping by touring the Galleria Umberto I and the shops of nearby Via Chiaia, which leads to the "*salone*" of Naples, chic Piazza dei Martiri. Continue south to the bayside Lungomare and walk over to the Castel dell'Ovo for a sunset dinner—with Vesuvius front and center—at one of the restaurants at the harbor port, the Borgo Marinaro.

IF YOU HAVE 3 DAYS

Having survived your first whirlwind day in Naples, begin your second day at the world-famous Museo Archeologico Nazionale (be there when the doors open in the morning to get a jump on the crowds). Packed with archaeological relics of the classical era, it's a must before venturing out of town to see Pompeii and Herculaneum. After viewing the *Hercules Farnese* and other ancient masterworks, you deserve a taxi or bus to reach Museo di Capodimonte, high above the city center and the greatest of the Bourbon palaces. Amble through its grand ballrooms and take in the great art collection, then promenade in its park to admire the views over the bay and city. Return to the city center and bustling Piazza Municipio to view the collections on view at the brooding Castel Nuovo. For your third day take the Funicolare Centrale opposite Galleria Umberto I up the Vomero Hill to explore the Certosa di San Martino, a Baroque extravaganza of a monastery, and the mighty Castel Sant'Elmo. Then walk through the pretty residential quarter to the Villa Floridiana's decorative-arts museum and sylvan park, which has wonderful views high over the city. Take the Funicolare di Chiaia back down to the Lungomare to visit the aristocratic Villa Pignatelli and the celebrated aquarium. Head over to the west end of the Riviera di Chiaia by foot or bus to Mergellina for dinner and an evening boat tour of the waterfront, or opt for an opera performance at the Teatro San Carlo.

IF YOU HAVE 5 DAYS

On your fourth day, take a vacation from your Neapolitan vacation by heading out of town to the nearby 18th-century Palace of Caserta, planned by the Bourbon king Charles III. Tour the gilded salons, majestic park, and English Garden designed by the Habsburg Queen Maria Carolina along guidelines suggested by Sir William Hamilton and his wife, the celebrated Emma. Or, instead, venture out past Posillipo to the Phlegrean Fields and pay a call on the Cave of the Cumaean Sibyl. On your fifth day devote more time to the museums and galleries mentioned above—along with the many others covered in the pages below—that interest you most. Return to further explore a kindred neighborhood—the elegant Chiaia and Vomero or the picturesque Spaccanapoli—allowing plenty of time for poking into odd corners and courtyards and churches, and for café-sitting to watch the passing Neapolitan parade.

Napoli Nobilissima: The Monumental City Center

Naples's setting on the most beautiful bay in the world has long been a boon for its inhabitants—the expansive harbor has always brought great mercantile riches to the city—and, intermittently, a curse. Throughout history, a who's who of Greek, Roman, Norman, Spanish, and French despots has quarreled over this gateway to Campania. Each set of con-

Golfo di Napoli

Rail Lines
Metro
Funicular

0   300 yards
0   300 meters

Aquarium **37**
Banco di Napoli .. **10**
Borgo Marinaro .. **39**
Cappella
Sansevero **13**
Castel dell'Ovo .. **38**
Castel Nuovo **6**
Castel Sant'Elmo . **33**
Catacombe di San
Gennaro **31**

Certosa di San
Martino **34**
Duomo di San
Gennaro **18**
Galleria Umberto I . **4**
Gesù Nuovo **11**
I Girolamini **22**
La Nunziatella ... **43**
Monte di Pietà .. **15**

Museo Archeologico
Nazionale **28**
Museo di
Capodimonte .. **32**
Museo Civico
Filangieri **16**
Napoli
Sotterranea **25**
Orto Botanico .. **30**
Palazzo Gravina .. **9**

Palazzo Reale ... **2**
Palazzo Serra di
Cassano **41**
Piazza Matteotti .. **7**
Pio Monte della
Misericordia .. **17**
San Domenico
Maggiore **27**
San Francesco
di Paola **1**

San Giovanni a
Carbonara **29**
San Giuseppe
dei Ruffi **19**
San Gregorio
Armeno **26**
San Lorenzo
Maggiore **23**
San Paolo
Maggiore **24**

Sant' Angelo
a Nilo **14**
Sant' Anna dei
Lombardi **8**
Santa Brigida ... **5**
Santa Chiara ... **12**
Santa Maria
degli Angeli a
Pizzofalcone .. **40**

Santa Maria di
Donnaregina
Vecchia **21**
Santa Maria
Egiziaca a
Pizzafalcone ... **42**
Santi Apostoli ... **20**
Teatro San Carlo . **3**
Villa Floridiana .. **35**
Villa Pignatelli .. **36**

querors recognized that the area around the city harbor—today occupied by the Molo Beverello hydrofoil terminal and the 1928 Stazione Marittima—was the veritable welcome mat to the metropolis and consequently needed to be turned into a fitting showcase of regal and royal authority. This had become imperative because of the explosive growth of Naples's population, which, by the mid-16th century, had made it into the second-largest city in Europe after Paris. With the mass migration of the rural population to the city, Naples had grown into a capricious, unplanned, disorderly, and untrammeled capital. Thus, the central aim of the ruling dynasties became the creation of a *Napoli nobilissima*—a "most noble" Naples.

The monuments they created remain a prominent feature of the city center today: One of the most magnificent opera houses in Europe, a palace that nearly rivals Versailles, an impregnable *castello,* a majestic church modeled on Rome's Pantheon, and a 19th-century shopping galleria are landmarks that marked the shifts among the ruling powers, from the French Angevins to the Spanish Habsburgs and Bourbons and, later, the postunification rise of the bourgeoisie and the regime of Mussolini. This historic sector is the much-put-upon Cinderella—as Naples is seen by many of her fans—but all dressed up in her princess-to-be jewels and finery and ready to wow the onlookers at the royal ball. In contrast to the intense intimacy of the Spacca, the official center of Naples unrolls its majesty with great pomp along wide avenues and monumental piazzas.

A Good Walk

In a day filled with monarchist grandeur, it may be fitting to start out with breakfast at **Caffè Gambrinus,** on Piazza Trieste e Trento, the very center of Naples and set between Piazza del Plebiscito and Piazza Municipio. Gilded and mirrored, this 19th-century café was once the rendezvous for Italian dukes, prime ministers, and writers like Oscar Wilde, Guy de Maupassant, and Gabriele d'Annunzio (although, truth to tell, you won't find many natives here). Treat yourself to a *cappuccino* and a pastry as rich and velvety as the surroundings, then head directly outside the door to the grand Piazza del Plebiscito. Neapolitans are too often caught up in the present to appreciate their past, and one sad example of this was the decades-long use of this urban showpiece as a parking lot. Now it makes an imposing setting for **San Francesco di Paola** ①, the domed 19th-century church built by Ferdinand I, and its grand Doric hemicycle. Inside, the Roman-style basilica is Naples at its most Neoclassic—imperial, aloof, funereal, and Olympian. From here head directly across the piazza to the main entrance of Naples's Royal Palace. Note the niches on its facade, filled in 1888 on order of King Umberto I of Italy with a series of rather ungainly statues of the kings of Naples, including, on the far right, his own static and unexpressive father, Victor Emanuel II, who had seized the palace (and the kingdom) from the Bourbons. Of all these figures, Joachim Murat comes out looking the most dignified, even if, as Vittorio Gleisejes writes, he appears "a bit too . . . virile in his revealing uniform."

At the **Palazzo Reale** ②, walk up the grand staircase of its Scalone d'Onore and tour the spectacular 18th- and 19th-century salons of the Museo dell'Appartmento Reale. You can't use the hallway constructed by the Bourbon kings to take them directly to the Royal Box of the adjacent **Teatro San Carlo** ③, so head back down to the piazza and make a right turn to the Piazza Trieste e Trento, where opera lovers will want to take a guided tour of the famous red-and-gold theater (weekends only; if a rehearsal is going on, porters at the theater will allow you to see the auditorium for a tip). Directly across the way is the fastidiously elegant vastness of the **Galleria Umberto I** ④. Walk to the far end of this ancestor of the shopping mall to Via Santa Brigida and tour the Church of **Santa Brigida** ⑤, burial place of renowned artist Luca Giordano. Head back through the Galleria and then gently downhill on the Via San Carlo and the Via Vittorio Emanuele III; you'll come to the usually light-drenched Piazza Municipio, with the delightfully discreet Church of San Giacomo ai Spagnoli. It is camouflaged within the bay side of the Banco di Napoli building and a pile of Greek ruins, forming an island in the middle of a daunting expanse of vehicular chaos. Above this piazza rises the civilized fortress of the **Castel Nuovo** ⑥, with the bay as a backdrop. Outside, study its great sculpted triumphal arch of Alfonso of Aragon; inside, explore the museum and Hall of the Barons. Head across Piazza Municipio to Via Medina until you reach the important 20th-century complex at **Piazza Matteotti** ⑦. Then trip across the centuries by continuing up Via Monteoliveto and its piazza, where you'll find both the quiet Church of **Sant' Anna dei Lombardi** ⑧, which is in fact a fascinating and very digestible museum of Renaissance sculpture (with a great frescoed sacristy), and the **Palazzo Gravina** ⑨.

Make a left leaving Sant'Anna dei Lombardi and head over to Piazza Carità and the Broadway of Naples, Via Toledo (often referred to as Via Roma). On the opposite side of the wide thoroughfare are some of Naples's most fascinating (sometimes dangerous) *quartieri,* including the famous Spanish Quarter, or Quartieri Spagnoli. If you don't opt to make this detour, walk the 15 or so blocks back down Via Toledo to the Piazza Trieste e Trento; along the way, take in the **Banco di Napoli** ⑩, do some window-shopping, and pick up a hot, flaky *sfogliatella* pastry at Pinturchio or some cool chocolates at Gay-Odin. Back around Piazza Trieste e Trento make a stop for a leisurely lunch: Ciro a Santa Brigida and Amici Miei are in the neighborhood, as well as a number of places on nearby Via Santa Lucia, while Pizzeria Brandi is just up Via Chiaia. From here on you can take things easy.

Timing

Not including time spent in the enormous Palazzo Reale and Castel Nuovo museums, walking this route will take approximately three leisurely hours. There's no chance of escaping the crowds—this is the very heart of metropolitan Naples, but it's always best to get up early and get a head start—especially as this allows you to see the spectacular Piazza del Plebiscito *senza gente* (without people). With no backpacks or Ray-Bans to be seen, the square looks little changed from the early 19th century.

Sights to See

⑩ **Banco di Napoli** (Bank of Naples). The oldest credit institution in Italy (founded as the *Monte di Pietà* in 1539), the present building is an imposing marble swath designed by Marcello Piancentini, leader of the Historical Monumentalism school of early 20th-century architecture and "official" architect of the fascist regime. ⊠ *Via Toledo 178.*

★ ⑥ **Castel Nuovo.** Brooding over the modern traffic that swirls around it, this castle is one of the most famous landmarks of the city and is often referred to by Neapolitans as the Maschio Angioino (Angevin Keep, in reference to its Angevin builders). Today it is the current seat of the city government, with its courtyard filling up in June with couples registering their wedding vows, and the moat outside is the site of a morning flower market. The castle's shadows, however, hide some legend-haunted events that played out within the dark, *piperno*-stone walls, along with—rumor once had it—King Ferrante's crocodile, which was said to dispatch live prisoners. The founder of the Angevin dynasty, Charles I d'Anjou, first built this fortress, known from its beginning, in 1279, as the "new castle" (to differentiate it from the Castel dell'Ovo and the Castel Capuano). Under his successor, Robert the Wise, it became a great center of culture, with the castle library attracting such luminaries as Petrarch and Boccaccio. Alfonso d'Aragona took up residence here when he conquered Naples in 1443 and marked his arrival with a fairly complete rebuilding, including the five defensive towers now visible and, especially, the impressive marble **Arco di Trionfo** at the entrance. This highly important work of the first Renaissance (1443–68) consciously takes its inspiration from ancient Roman triumphal arches, recombining the elements, however, in a completely innovative composition of two superimposed arches so as to fit the tall, narrow space; many noted sculptors worked on the arch. The most celebrated was Francesco Laurana, who carved the bas-relief above the lower arch, which shows, appropriately, the triumphal official entrance of Alfonso into Naples on February 26, 1443. This grand depiction effectively overrides any memory of Alfonso's earlier foray through the city's underground sewer system (in the middle of the night of June 12, 1442, he emerged from underground into the home of a Neapolitan matron by the name of La Ceccarella, who, betraying her rightful king, guided the regal-looking intruder and his dashing band of armed men to the gates of the city, which they threw open to allow their troops to advance).

Inside the Arco di Trionfo you'll find the ticket office on the left. Across the imposing courtyard is the Palatine Chapel, one of the few remaining structures of the Angevin Palace, its austere facade graced by a portal with delicate reliefs and a Madonna by Francesco Laurana (1474). Decorated inside by Giotto and friends in the 14th century, the frescoes are now reduced to a few fragments, none of which can be attributed to the master. The chapel now houses paintings from the 14th through the early 16th centuries and graceful sculptures by Laurana and Domenico Gagini. Next to it in the left corner is the **Sala dell'Armeria**, the Armory, where part of the flooring has been conveniently glassed over to reveal the remains of a Roman villa and a medieval necropolis. Above the Armeria, with access up a long ramp of steps, is the current Naples city council chamber, the **Sala dei Baroni,** or Hall of the Barons, built for Alfonso by the Majorcan architect Guglielmo Sagrera in 1446–54. Its simple volume is topped with a late-Gothic Moorish-inspired octagonal star vault whose ribs, in gray *piperno,* provide a harmonious accent to the yellow-tufa walls. The hall gets its name from a famous party held here in 1486, when Ferdinand I of Aragon invited a number of troublesome, powerful lords to dinner and then had them arrested and executed. For souvenirs of the event, he had several of the victims embalmed; their bodies were brought out from time to time to entertain more fortunate guests, who still must have been a bit nervous. The dungeons where the unlucky lords were to await death are below the Palatine Chapel (you would think that their moans would have disturbed mass) and can be viewed today.

The rest of the public space of the castle houses the **Museo Civico,** which is an interesting, low-key collection of painting and sculpture, especially strong in 19th-century landscapes with views of a lost or transformed Naples, but also with some nice 17th-century paintings and the bronze doors that Ferrante commissioned from William the Monk in 1475 to record his victory over John d'Anjou. ✉ *Piazza Municipio,* ☎ *081/7952003.* ▦ *€5.15.* ⊘ *Mon.–Sat. 9–7, Sun. 9–1 (courtyard only).*

❹ **Galleria Umberto I.** In 1885, in reaction to the devastating cholera epidemic of the previous year, authorities hastily implemented a massive urban renewal plan whose "clean-up" of Naples especially entailed the destruction of slum areas between Spaccanapoli and the Palazzo Reale. With facades on Via Toledo—the most animated street in Naples at the time—and across from the Teatro San Carlo, this galleria, built in 1887–90 according to a design by Emanuele Rocca, had a prestigious and important location from the start. As with its larger predecessor, the Galleria Vittorio Emanuele II in Milan, the Galleria Umberto Primo exalts the taste of the postunification commercial elite in a virtuoso display of new technology clothed in traditional style. Here are the iron-ribbed glass barrel vault and 188-ft-high dome by Paolo Boubée, which represented the latest advance in modern form yet is layered over with the reassuring architectural ornament of the 14th century (another era when the bourgeoisie triumphed in Italy). The ground floor was designed to offer weatherproof shopping for the new class of spenders; professional studios, fashion ateliers, and newspaper offices occupied the three upper stories. A small underground theater, the *Salone Margherita*, was constructed near the Via Toledo entrance for chamber-music concerts, but within a few months of opening it evolved into a legendary nightclub and a center of Naples's turn-of-the-20th-century nightlife.

Neapolitans used to come here for a leisurely Campari; today they occasionally visit for a quick espresso, since the grand gallery has a somewhat forlorn air. Still, it makes a soothing passageway by virtue of its sumptuous marble inlay, while the block of light streaming through one of the upper-level loggias into the magnificent vastness of the arcade makes for a great scene. At Christmastime a huge public Nativity crèche is set up, and the space becomes quite festive. ⊠ *Entrances on Via San Carlo, Via Toledo, Via Santa Brigida, Via Verdi.*

❾ Palazzo Gravina. A dignified Renaissance palace in the Tuscan style with a vigorous *bugnato* (diamond-point) facade, the palazzo was begun in 1513 for Ferdinando Orsini, duke of Gravina, by Gabriele d'Angelo, a student of Alberti and Brunelleschi. The monumental doorway was added by Mario Giuffredo in a restoration of 1762–72, and an extra story was added in 1839, which is clearly visible from the beautiful courtyard. Largely burned down in 1848 by Swiss Guards trying to flush out a group of armed patriots, it now houses the modern School of Architecture, so feel free to wander around to observe how old and new coexist. ⊠ *Via Monteoliveto 3.*

★ ❷ Palazzo Reale. One of the showplaces of Naples, the Palazzo Reale, or Royal Palace, was meant to be the apotheosis of Bourbon power in the city. Renovated and redecorated by successive rulers in a style that can only be called overblown imperial, once lorded over by a dim-witted king who liked to shoot his hunting guns at the birds in his tapestries, and filled with salons designed in the most deliciously lavish 18th-century Neapolitan taste, it remains a palatial pile. The Spanish viceroys commissioned it in 1600, ordering Swiss architect Domenico Fontana to build a suitable new residence for Philip III, should he chance to visit Naples (which he didn't); the immense complex was not in fact completed until 1843 (by Gaetano Genovese). The palace saw its greatest moment of splendor in the 18th century, when Charles III of Bourbon became the first permanent resident; during that century Luigi Vanvitelli filled in half the arcades in the lower register of the facade to strengthen it, and Ferdinando Fuga created the State Wing after the accession of Ferdinando IV in 1759. Today this wing comprises the Museo dell'Appartamento Storico, or **Royal Apartments,** where visitors can get a taste of Bourbon glory.

To view these 30 rooms on the first floor, enter the courtyard and ascend the monumental Scalone d'Onore on the left (the vaulted cham-

bers housing the ticket booth are near the Piazza Plebiscito entrance),
keeping to the left side of the stairway. Montesquieu, the French 18th-
century writer, considered this to be the finest staircase in Europe, and
it sets a tone for the glitter and grandeur to come. The first doors on
the right open up into the **Court Theater,** built by Ferdinando Fuga for
Charles III, who in 1763 had created an opera company for private performances of comic opera. It was inaugurated in 1768 in honor of the
royal wedding between Ferdinand I and Maria Carolina of Habsburg
with *Peleo e Teti,* by Giovanni Paisiello, but soon afterward fell into
disuse. Damaged by World War II bombing, it was restored in 1950;
note the resplendent royal box, which abandons the lure of monumentality
for intimate luxury. Following are the suite of rooms around the courtyard that constitute the royal apartments. Through a series of an-
techambers, you eventually reach Room VI, the **Throne Room,** with
wine-red striped-silk walls and gilded stuccos representing the 12
provinces of the Kingdom of the Two Sicilies; the ponderous Empire-
style throne in fact dates from after 1850. Giuseppe Bonito painted the
two portraits of the ambassadors from Turkey and Tripoli in 1741; the
entourage from Tripoli (to the right of the throne) looks like they'd be
much more fun, but of course they were still pirates.

The decoration picks up in the **Room of the Ambassadors** (Room
VIII), where a pair of choice 18th-century Gobelin tapestries grace the
light-green walls together with a lovely Annunciation by Artemisia Gentileschi. The ceiling painting honoring Spanish military victories is by
local artist Belisario Corenzio and his school (1610–20). Room IX, with
pale gold walls and a simple white vault, was the bedroom of Charles's
queen, Maria Amalia of Saxony, and hides a small, brilliantly gold private oratory in the corner, with beautiful paintings by Francesco Liani
of Parma (1760). Above the exit door is a Madonna and Child attributed
to the charming Spanish mannerist Ruviales. This door takes you a bit
toward the courtyard to rejoin the inner rooms along the third side.

The **Great Captain's Room** (Room XI), small and square, has wonderful ceiling frescoes by Battistello Caracciolo (1610–16)—all velvet,
fire, and smoke, they reveal the influence of the recent visit by Caravaggio to Naples—a jolly series by Federico Zuccari depicting 12
proverbs on small wood panels, along with, last but not least, a Titian
portrait (circa 1543) of Pier Luigi Farnese. Room XII, the Flemish Hall,
has a rather brash 19th-century gilded ceiling with 12 paintings representing the coats-of-arms of the kingdom's provinces and a large neo-
Gothic centerpiece depicting the 12th-century Tancred and Constance.
At eye level is a curious 18th-century "musical" clock by Charles Clay
and a spectacularly overdone enamel and gilt-bronze birdcage on a flower
stand, given by Czar Nicholas I to Ferdinand when he visited in 1846;
the table flaunts views of the czar's various palaces. As for paintings,
there is a simpatico portrait of a flutist by Alexis Grimou and a wonderfully hard-edged and cynical depiction of two tax collectors by van
Roymerswaele (1538).

Room XIII was **Joachim Murat's writing room** when he was king of
Naples; he brought with him from France some regal furniture by the
great French *ébeniste* (cabinet-maker) Weisweiler, originally commissioned by Marie Antoinette and completed by commissions of his own
(including the desk and two dignified clocks) in 1812. The next few
rooms combine ponderous 19th-century furnishings and rather better
Baroque paintings: Room XVII, in particular, has a good selection of
paintings by followers of Caravaggio; Room XVIII has an intensely
colored Guercino depiction of Joseph dreaming; and Room XIX is full
of still lifes from the important Neapolitan school. The huge Room

XXII, painted in green and gold with kitschy *faux* tapestries, is known as the **Hercules Hall**, for in a moment of glory it once housed the *Hercules Farnese*. The authentic tapestries are from the Royal Factory of Naples (1783–89), but the things to look at here are the porcelain creations from Sèvres, including the Atlas with his starry globe and the huge green-chrome vase (1812), painted by Louis Béranger.

The **Palatine Chapel**, redone by Gaetano Genovese in the 1830s, is a disappointing affair as chapels go, having been gussied up with too much gold, but it has a stunning Technicolor intarsia altar from the previous chapel (Dionisio Lazzari, 1678). Note the false-perspective panels, which almost propel the altar into the stratosphere of bad taste. Also here on a long-term loan is the famous *Presepio* (Nativity) scene of the Banco di Napoli—it may lack the spectacular setting of the *Presepio Cuciniello* in the Museo di San Martino but has even better sculpture, with pieces by important sculptors such as Giuseppe Sammartino (the shepherdess at the table in the tavern scene on the right), Francesco and Antonio Viva, Francesco Celebrano, and others. There are some pleasant 19th-century landscapes in the next few rooms, as well as Queen Maria Carolina's Ferris wheel–like reading lectern (which enabled her to do a 19th-century reader's version of channel surfing).Speaking of reading, another wing of the complex holds the **Biblioteca Nazionale Vittorio Emanuele III**, the largest library in southern Italy and one of the most important in the country. Begun, as with so many other Bourbon collections, with Farnese bits and pieces, it was enriched with the priceless papyri from Herculaneum found in 1752 and opened to the public in 1804. You can view these and a splendid choice of manuscripts and rare editions in the elegant rooms open to visitors. To actually use the library for research, you need to apply for a card. The library also has a lovely garden, which looks out on the Castel Nuovo. ✉ *Piazza del Plebiscito*, ☎ *081/5808111*. 🎫 *€4.13.* 🕐 *Sun.–Tues. and Thurs.–Fri. 9–7, Sat. 9–9.*

❼ Piazza Matteotti. In 1925 Mussolini issued a famous (now notorious) call for "good Italian architecture," hoping to revive its glories and underline the power of the modern Italian state. He was fortunate in having a flood of talented architects answer the call, but the troublesome political context of the resulting constructions has tended to push a number of magnificent structures into oblivion. The area between Piazza Carità and Piazza Municipio in Naples represents one of the most significant and successful urban transformations of this period, and the pride of this vast program is the Piazza Matteotti, object of an important 1927 competition.

The piazza, which combines a number of important civic buildings in a modern forum, is dominated by the strong parabolic curve of the post office, or **Palazzo delle Poste e Telegrafi**, a surprisingly contemporary building by Bolognese architect Giuseppe Vaccaro. The post office combines elements of the Rationalist Functional style—in which the plan and decoration of the building clearly articulate its functions—with subtle historical references. The lower band of dark gray diorite not only alludes to the gray *piperno* of local Renaissance construction, it also delineates the large public spaces on the ground floor. Inside, the building refreshingly retains its original interior furnishings, and the streamlined decoration of the public rooms buffers the boredom of waiting in endless lines with *Metropolis*-style elegance.

The other jewel of the piazza is the **Palazzo della Provincia,** to the left of the post office, by the young Neapolitan engineer Marcello Canino. This is a good example (along with the Banco di Roma) of the other predominant architectural current in the fascist era: Historical Monumentalism, which sought to translate ancient forms (arches, colon-nades, basilical structures, and so forth) into a modern idiom. The Rational Functionalist school was generally judged too international and rootless a style for an Italy intent on reviving its own specific past glory. Although the **Questura** looks every bit the totalitarian police station that it once was, with a stubbornly horizontal and forbiddingly spartan mass of travertine crying out "Abandon hope, all ye who enter here," it should be said in its defense that at least its form expresses function. ⊠ *Intersection of Via Monteoliveto, Via A. Diaz, and Via Battisti.*

★ ❶ **San Francesco di Paola.** Modeled after Rome's Pantheon, this circular basilica is the centerpiece of the Piazza del Plebiscito and remains one of the most frigidly voluptuous examples of the Stil Empire, or Neoclassic style, in Italy. Commissioned by Ferdinand I in 1817 to fulfill a vow he had made in order to enlist divine aid in being reinstated to the throne of the Kingdom of the Two Sicilies, it rose at one end of the vast parade ground built several years earlier by Joachim Murat. It managed to transform Murat's inconveniently grandiose colonnade—whose architect was clearly inspired by the colonnades of St. Peter's in Rome—into a setting for restored Bourbon glory. The church also usefully fulfilled a prophecy by the 15th-century saint Ferrante d'Aragona, for whom it is named, that one day a large church and square would occupy the crowded site. Pietro Bianchi from Lugano in Switzerland won a competition and built a slightly smaller version of the Pantheon, with a beautiful coffered dome and a splendid set of 34 Corinthian columns in gray Mondragon marble; but the overall lack of color (so different from the warm interior of the Pantheon) combined with the severe geometrical forms produces an almost defiantly cold space. To some, this only proves the ancients did sometimes know their own architecture better. Art historians find the spectacle of the church to be the ultimate in Neoclassic *grandezza*; others think this Roman temple is only fitting to honor Jove, not Christ. In any event, the main altar, done in gold, lapis lazuli, and other precious stones by Anselmo Caggiano (1641), was taken from the destroyed Church of the Santi Apostoli and provides some relief from the oppressive perfection of the setting. ⊠ *Piazza del Plebiscito,* ☏ *081/7645133.* ☉ *Mon.–Sat. 8–1 and 3:30–5:30, Sun. 8–noon.*

❺ **Santa Brigida.** The Lucchesi fathers built this church around 1640 in honor of the Swedish queen and saint who visited her fellow queen, Naples's unsaintly Giovanna I, in 1372 and became one of the first persons to go on record as denouncing the loose morals and irrepressible sensuality of the Neapolitans. The height of the church's dome was limited to prevent its interfering with cannon fire from nearby Castel Nuovo, but Luca Giordano, the pioneer painter of the *trompe l'oeil* Baroque dome, effectively opened it up with a spacious sky serving as the setting for an *Apotheosis of Saint Bridget* (1678), painted (and now in need of restoration) in exchange for his tomb space, marked by a pavement inscription in the left transept. ⊠ *Via Santa Brigida 72,* ☏ *081/5523793.* ☉ *Daily 7:30–12:30 and 5:30–7.*

❽ **Sant' Anna dei Lombardi.** Long favored by the Aragonese kings, this church, simple and rather anonymous from the outside, houses some of the most important ensembles of Renaissance sculpture in southern Italy. Begun with the adjacent convent of the Olivetani and its four cloisters in 1411, it was redone in the Baroque style in the mid-17th century by Gennaro Sacco, although this is no longer so visible, as the bombs of 1943 rather radically altered the decoration and led to a modern restoration favoring the original *quattrocento* (15th-century) lines. The wonderful coffered wooden ceiling, currently under restoration, will add a bit of pomp. Inside the porch is the tomb of Domenico Fontana, one of the major architects of the late 16th century, who died in Naples after beginning the Palazzo Reale. Once inside the entrance door, you enter a simple single-nave church with side chapels. Turn around and you will see, on either side of the entrance wall, two fine Renaissance tombs. The one on the left as you face the door belongs to the Ligorio family (whose descendant Pirro designed the Villa d'Este in Tivoli) and is a work by Giovanni da Nola (1524); the tomb on the right is a masterpiece by Giuseppe Santacroce (1532) for the del Pozzo family. To the left of the Ligorio Altar (the corner chapel on the immediate right as you face the altar) is the Mastrogiudice Chapel, whose altar contains precious reliefs of the *Annunciation* and *Scenes from the Life of Jesus* (1489) by Benedetto da Maiano, a great name in Tuscan sculpture. On the other side of the entrance is the Piccolomini Chapel, with a Crucifixion by Giulio Mazzoni (circa 1550), a refined marble altar (circa 1475), a funerary monument to Maria d'Aragona by another prominent Florentine sculptor, Antonello Rossellino (circa 1475), and on the right, a rather sweet fresco of the Annunciation by an anonymous follower of Piero della Francesca.

The true surprises of the church, however, are off to the right of the altar, in the presbytery and adjoining rooms. The chapel just to the right of the main altar, belonging to the Orefice family, is richly decorated in pre-Baroque (1596–98) polychrome marbles and frescoes by Luis Rodriguez; from here you continue on through the Oratory of the Holy Sepulcher, with the tomb of Antonio D'Alessandro and his wife, to reach the church's showpiece: a potently realistic life-size group of eight terra-cotta figures by Guido Mazzoni (1492), which make up a Pietà; the faces are said to be modeled from actual people at the Aragonese court. Toward the rear of the church is Cappella dell'Assunta, with a fun painting in its corner of a monk by Michelangelo's student Giorgio Vasari, and the lovely Sacrestia Vecchia (Old Sacristy), adorned with one of the most successful decorative ensembles Vasari ever painted (1544) and breathtaking wood-inlay stalls by Fra' Giovanni da Verona and assistants (1506–10) with views of famous buildings (ask the attendant for access to the Old Sacristy). ⊠ *Piazza Monteoliveto 15 (entrance through a black gate to the right of the church).* ⊙ *Tues.–Thurs. and Sat. 8:30–12:30.*

★ ③ **Teatro San Carlo.** La Scala in Milan is more famous, but San Carlo is more beautiful, and Naples is, after all, the most operatic of cities. First built in eight months and 10 days in 1737 by Angelo Carasale for Charles III of Bourbon—and opened on the king's saint's name day—it burned down in 1816 and was rebuilt, with its facade of five rustic arches in gray *piperno* surmounted by an elegant loggia, in only nine months. This time the architect was Antonio Niccolini, working under the impetus of Domenico Barbaja, the Milanese director appointed by Joachim Murat in 1810. Barbaja, San Carlo's most legendary director, started out as a waiter in a tavern and enriched himself through a talent for gambling. He obviously wanted to keep his job under the new regime and therefore made a bet with the king to have the theater open within nine months. More important, he also managed in the same year to convince Gioacchino Rossini to come to Naples as conductor and house composer; Stendhal hailed Ferdinand's wise retaining of Barbaja and his prompt sponsorship of the theater as a "coup d'état" for the deep and immediate bond it created between the ruler and his opera-loving populace. This was further cemented by the many operas composed for the house, including Donizetti's *Lucia di Lammermoor* and Rossini's *La Donna del Lago*.

Nearly 200 boxes are arranged on six levels, and the huge stage (12,000 square ft) permits productions with horses, camels, and elephants and even boasts a removable backdrop that can lift to reveal the Palazzo Reale Gardens. Above the rich red-and-gold auditorium is a breathy ceiling fresco, by Giuseppe Camarano, suitably representing Apollo presenting poets to Athena. At many performances, however, all eyes were on the sumptuous royal box, which seats 15 and is topped by a gigantic gilded crown. Check the local press (*Il Mattino, La Repubblica, Corriere della Sera*) or the *Qui Napoli* for information on performances, or pick up a schedule at the ticket office and get ready for a great evening of opera. Standards are among the highest in Europe at the San Carlo—even the great Enrico Caruso was hissed here. Even if you can't catch a performance, try to take the 30-minute guided tour (€2.58) to see the splendid theater—as Stendhal once wrote: "The first impression one gets is of being suddenly transported to the palace of an oriental emperor. There is nothing in Europe to compare with it, or even give the faintest idea of what it is like." ⊠ *Via San Carlo 101–103,* ☎ *081/7972331 (gate); 081/797–2412 (ticket office),* ℻ *081/400902,* ⓦⒺⒷ *www.teatrosancarlo.it.* ⊙ *Guided tours Sat. and Sun. 2–3:30.*

Spaccanapoli: The Heart and Soul of Naples

If you arrive in Naples just to do the sights, you'll see the city, but you won't get to its essence. To do that, you need to discover Spaccanapoli, the unforgettable neighborhood that is the heart of old Naples. A buzzing hive of daily chaos in a constantly re-created grid of ancient patterns, this densely populated neighborhood presents the city's most familiar face. This is the Naples of peeling facades spackled with enough drying laundry to suggest a parade; of arguments in the streets (or are they arguing? it's sometimes hard to tell) swelling to operatic proportions, often with onlookers adding contributions to supplement the lyrical principals; of small alleyways with freshly laid flowers at the many shrines to the Blessed Virgin. Here, where the cheapest pizzerias in town feed the locals like kings, the full raucous street carnival of Neapolitan popular culture is punctuated with improbable oases of spiritual calm. All the contradictions of Naples—splendor and squalor, palace and slum, triumph and tragedy—meet here and sing a full-throated chorale. The amazing thing is that it seems, somehow, more real in its conscious theatricality. And, paradoxically, it also seems impossible to remain stressed out in the midst of all this ricocheting vitality.

Spaccanapoli (literally, "Split-Naples") is actually the name of the ruler-straight street that divides the neighborhood in half—a fantastic 5-km-long (3-mi-long) pedestrian ribbon that was originally the ancient Roman Decumanus Maximus, or main thoroughfare. Today the street changes names six times along its route, with Via Benedetto Croce and Via S. Biagio dei Librai among the most prominently used. This breathtaking roadway-cum-piazza is a palisade of towering 19th-century tenements (once the highest in Europe, they soared up to eight floors because of the population density and their tufa-rock construction), faded palazzi, and Baroque churches. But the Spacca is not simply picturesque. It also contains some of Naples's most important sights, including a striking conglomeration of churches—Lombard, Gothic, Renaissance, Baroque, Rococo, and Neoclassical. Here are the majolica-adorned cloister of Santa Chiara; the sumptuous Church of the Gesù Nuovo; two organ-set piazzas; the city duomo (where the Festa di San Gennaro is celebrated every September); the Cappella Sansevero; the greatest painting in Naples—Caravaggio's *Seven Acts of Mercy* altarpiece—on view at the Church of Pio Monte; and Via Gregorio Armeno, where shops devoted to *Presepio* (crèche) wares nearly transform every morning into Christmas. This region is best explored by heading up the Spacca to the Duomo, then back along Via dei Tribunali. The Via dei Tribunali is often referred to as part of the city's Decumano Maggiore, but as it is only one block over from the Spacca, the entire region is also commonly grouped under the name Spaccanapoli. Wherever you head, you'll find half of Naples's populace crowded at your elbow, with everyone pursuing life *con gusto*. The beautiful thing is that despite the Punch and Judy appearance of things, almost everyone turns out to be a sweetheart. If the Spacca is the heart of Naples, it pumps for all.

Numbers in the text correspond to numbers in the margin and on the Naples map.

A Good Walk

Begin at Piazza Gesù Nuovo with a visit to the Church of **Gesù Nuovo** ⑪ (1584) to give a shot of Jesuit pomp to your morning cappuccino. As you exit, admire the piazza's extravagant carved-stone spire that honors the Virgin Mary, the Guglia dell'Immacolata, whose saints and cherubs, sculpted by Francesco Pagano and Matteo Bottigliero after a design by Giuseppe Genuino (1743), are considered a high point of 18th-century Neapolitan sculpture. Across the square, immerse yourself in the 14th century at **Santa Chiara** ⑫, a broodingly severe Gothic monument built by Robert of Anjou. In noisy Spaccanapoli, peace breaks out in the cloisters of the district, none more beautiful here than the Chiostro delle Clarisse, transformed in 1742 into a rococo-era showpiece by a colorful majolica-tile overlay on its columns and benches. At this point the piazza debouches into the pedestrian roadway nicknamed the Spaccanapoli. Past a block full of moldering palazzi—note Palazzo Filmarino at the corner of Via S. Sebastiano, the home of Benedetto Croce, the noted aesthete and philosopher, and now site of his library—is the Piazza San Domenico Maggiore, where the Guglia di San Domenico (1737) and the apse of San Domenico Maggiore create one of Naples's most charming urban set-pieces. Residents of the district move into this piazza during spring and summer months, making it a "living room"—the furniture is the umbrellaed tables of Scaturchio, Naples's celebrated *gelateria* (ice-cream parlor). After enjoying a time-out here, head up the right-hand side of the piazza to Via Francesco de Sanctis and the **Cappella Sansevero** ⑬ (1590), the tomb-chapel of the Sangro di San Severo family, which features three showstopping 18th-century sculptures, including Giuseppe Sammartino's *Veiled Christ*.

Backtrack to the Spaccanapoli roadway and take in the pretty 18th-century Church of **Sant' Angelo a Nilo** ⑭ and picturesque Largo Corpo di Napoli, where the statue of the Egyptian river god Nile reclines on a pedestal. Farther down the Spaccanapoli—whose name changes here from Via Benedetto Croce to Via S. Biagio dei Librai—is the tiny Church of San Nicola a Nilo, whose horseshoe-shape steps serve as an open-air antiques store. Just across the street is the **Monte di Pietà** ⑮, whose Cappella della Pietà and spectacularly opulent 17th-century salons can be found just beyond the courtyard (open Saturday and Sunday only). Continue down the Spacca to view the storefront Ospedale delle Bambole—a doll hospital—at No. 81, then make a right turn on Via Duomo to the atmospheric **Museo Civico Filangieri** ⑯. Head back up Via Duomo two blocks to Via Tribunali and make a right to the **Pio Monte della Misericordia** ⑰, whose church contains one of the greatest 17th-century altarpieces in Europe, Caravaggio's *Seven Acts of Mercy*. Head back to the Via Duomo and turn right to the **Duomo di San Gennaro** ⑱, the majestic cathedral built for Charles I of Anjou in the 14th century and home to the Cappella del Tesoro di San Gennaro. If you have more adrenaline to burn for Baroque, turn right from the duomo up the avenue to Via Apostoli to see **San Giuseppe dei Ruffi** ⑲ and **Santi Apostoli** ⑳. Nearby is a monument of Neapolitan Gothic, **Santa Maria di Donnaregina Vecchia** ㉑.

Head back down Via Duomo one block to the Via dei Tribunali—the other great historic thoroughfare of the district. Turn right along the street and discover the first of the street's many imposing churches—the elegant **I Girolamini** ㉒ and the gigantic **San Lorenzo Maggiore** ㉓, whose 18th-century facade hides a Gothic-era nave. The church is at the corner of Via San Gregorio Armeno, probably the most charming street in Naples. Famed for its lavishly rococo Church of **San Gregorio Armeno** ㉖, whose towering campanile arches over the street, this thoroughfare is lined with nearly a dozen *presepi* (crèche) stores. After exploring the shops along the street, head back up to Via dei Tribunali and the impressive 16th-century church of **San Paolo Maggiore** ㉔, diagonally across small Piazza San Gaetano (former site of the Greek and Roman Agora marketplace) from San Lorenzo; on San Paolo's left-hand flank, you'll find one of the entrances to **Napoli Sotterranea** ㉕, the fascinating route through underground Naples. Coming out of San Paolo Maggiore, turn right and head east for about 10 blocks—passing the mammoth **San Domenico Maggiore** ㉗ on your way—to find pretty Piazza Bellini, whose cafés are perfect for a time-out and restorative espresso. You'll learn that, for the price of an aperitif or an ice cream, the cafés of the Spaccanapoli bestow instantaneous club membership on a patron. From the moment you settle into a seat, you belong.

TIMING

Because many churches open at 7:30 AM and close for the afternoon around 1 PM, it's imperative to get an early start to fit in as many sights as possible before the midday break. The famous Cappella Sansevero is open through the day, while the Monte di Pietà is only open on weekends. During the midday break, wander around savoring *couleur locale* and enjoy lunch at any of a number of good inexpensive restaurants in this neighborhood (it's best to plan on paying cash for this lunch). Scaturchio in Piazza San Domenico is the perfect place for after-lunch espresso. Then fit in a bit of shopping by browsing around Piazza Dante, Port'Alba, and the Via Santa Maria di Costantinopoli for used books and antiques, or head over to the Via San Gregorio Armeno to pick out a manger figure to take back home. By 4 many of the churches reopen. Plan on a good two hours to walk this route, plus a quarter to a half hour for each of the principal churches you decide to visit. However, Spaccanapoli is the most memorable part of Naples so take a full day, if you can, to explore its wonders.

Sights to See

★ ⑬   **Cappella Sansevero.** Rightly one of the emblematic monuments of Naples in the popular imagination, this dazzling masterpiece, the funerary chapel of the Sangro di Sansevero princes, combines noble swagger, overwhelming color, and a touch of the macabre—which is to say, it expresses Naples perfectly. The di Sangros were renowned military leaders as far back as the Dark Ages, and they boast no fewer than six saints in their family (who are portrayed in the chapel's painted roundels between the windows). The chapel was begun in 1590 by Giovan Francesco di Sangro, the result of a vow to be fulfilled if he were cured of a dire illness. He lived for another 14 years, which was good for the building campaign, but the present aspect of the chapel is due to his descendant Raimondo di Sangro, prince of Sansevero, who had it completely redone between 1749 and 1770.

Youthful portraits show this fascinating character with a pronounced pointy chin. Confident and sophisticated in his tastes, obviously brilliant, and an important mover in Naples's Enlightenment, this princely intellectual, mad scientist, and inventor was accused of just about everything then considered base: atheism, alchemy, and Freemasonry. The last two are likely: he seems to have been a Grand Master of the Freemasons, and his claim to be able to reproduce the miracle of St. Gennaro's blood got him kicked out of the Fraternity of the Treasure of St. Gennaro. He left a personal touch in the basement, down the stairs to the right, where two glass cases house a pair of "anatomical machines," which are astonishing even if fake. Purporting to be an encyclopedic reconstruction of the blood vessels of an adult male and a pregnant female, they are supposedly based on two of the prince's servants, who fell victim to his curiosity when he injected them while still alive with what is conjectured to be a mercury solution that hardened their arteries.

Prince Raimondo is generally credited with the design of the splendid marble-inlay floor; he hired Francesco Maria Russo to paint the ceiling with a *Glory of Paradise* (1749) and also hired a young team of up-and-coming sculptors, whose contributions remain the focal point for most visits here: the showpiece is smack in the middle of the chapel, Giuseppe Sammartino's *Veiled Christ* (1753). The artist was only 33 years old when he sculpted this famous work, which was originally meant to be placed in the crypt. It was too good to leave down below with *those things;* the audacious virtuosity of the clinging drapery showing the wounds underneath is one of the marvels of Neapolitan sculpture. A taste for the *outré* and extravagant had already been demonstrated by other statues in the chapel, especially Francesco Quierolo's *Disillusion,* to the right of the altar, with its chisel-defying net making a spectacular transition to empty space. This Genovese sculptor also did the female statue representing *Sincerity* on the right and the commemorative *Altar to St. Odorisio* between the two Allegories. Antonio Corradini, who came to Naples from the Veneto region via Rome, is responsible for the allegorical statue to the left of the altar, *Veiled Modesty* (1751), widely considered his masterpiece; he also sculpted the funerary monument and allegorial figure of *Decorum,* on the inside of the front wall to the right of the exit. The main altar and its reliefs are the work of Francesco Celebrano, and the angels on either side are by a sculptor from nearby Sorrento, Paolo Persico. Celebrano also contributed the stunning funerary monument above the front door, with Cecco di Sangro leaping out of his coffin in commemoration of one of his most famous exploits—when, having been left for dead, he suddenly reappeared, fully armed, in the thick of the battle. Celebrano also did the tomb on the left of this monument. This team of sculptors is essentially responsible for the remainder of the sculptural decor as well, with the notable exception of the three 17th-century tombs in the front bays of the side walls. ✉ *Via Francesco di Sanctis 19,* ☎ *081/5518470.* 🎫 *€4.13.* ☉ *Mon. and Wed.–Sat. 10–5, Sun. 10–1:30.*

★ ⑱ **Duomo di San Gennaro.** The shrine to the paterfamilias of Naples, San Gennaro, the city's cathedral is home to the saint's devotional chapel, among the most spectacular—in the show-biz sense of the word—in the city. With a colonnade leading to an apse bursting with light and Baroque splendor, the duomo's nave makes a fitting setting for the famous **Miracle of the Blood,** when the blood of the martyred San Gennaro liquifies (hopefully) in its silver ampule every September 19 before an audience of thousands massed in front of the duomo's altar. *San Genna, fa'o miracolo! Fa ampresso! Nun ce fa suffrì!* yell the congregants during the ritual—"Saint Genna, do the miracle! Hurry up!

THE GLITTER AND THE GOLD: NEAPOLITAN BAROQUE ART AND ARCHITECTURE

TIME, LIKE A RIVER, has dropped its silt over Naples, leaving in each age its characteristic deposit. Today, however, this deposit is not neatly layered, waiting for a distant spade to uncover, as at Pompeii, but one that is capricious, unplanned, and disorderly. Naples is a city of dramatic pairings: Baroque with medieval, plenty with want, grandeur with muddle. Of the numerous artistic styles that comprise this feast, however, none suited the Neapolitan temperament better than the Baroque—the style that came to the fore in the 17th century and continued in the 18th century under the Bourbon kings.

In a city of volcanic passions, the flagrantly emotional, floridly luxurious Baroque—an art that seems perpetually on the point of bursting its bonds—found immediate favor. The departure of the austere Spanish viceroys in the 17th century gave free rein to the city's natural inclination for this extroverted style, allowing artists like Caravaggio and the Spaniard Il Ribera, and architects like Ferdinando Sanfelice and Cosimo Fanzago, to strut their aesthetic stuff.

With untrammeled individualism given full play, the results—most still visible today—were theatrical, dramatic, dynamic, vivid, alive, and sometimes wonderfully showy. Venture into the Gesù Nuovo (mother church of the *Padri Gesuiti*, or Jesuit Fathers) and note the buoyant swirl of stucco, inlaid marble, and gilt work, a florid tangle that mirrors the chaos of the piazza outside its door. Like the city itself, the decorative scheme is diffuse and disjunctive, with little effort to organize everything into an easily understood scheme. Throughout the city, artists loved using illusionistic trompe l'oeil tricks of ingenious device on church cupolas, as in the Cappella di San Gennaro at the Duomo. Here, as in other churches, you'll see reliquaries studded with semiprecious stones and covered with gold, gold, and more gold. Elsewhere, statues were made hyper-real, either thanks to amazing technique—such as the marble figures in the Cappella Sansevero, where fishing nets and veils were carved from pure stone—or by being dressed in silk and velvet garments. Thanks to the Counter-Reformation, the Catholic church was then busy making an overt appeal to the congregant, using emotion and motion to get the message across—no more so than in 17th- and 18th-century Naples, a city which, incidentally, had some 20,000 clerics, more than in Rome itself.

The most representative practitioner of Neapolitan Baroque was Cosimo Fanzago (1591–1678). A Lombard by birth, he arrived in Naples to study sculpture, so even when he decorated a church, he usually covered it head to toe with colored and inlaid marbles, as in his work at the Church of San Martino in the Certosa (charterhouse) that sits atop the Vomero Hill. Two decades earlier, Caravaggio (1571–1610) had arrived in Naples from Rome and this great painter of chiaroscuro took the city by storm. He was on the point of bringing the Baroque style back to earth in Naples—thanks to the unflinching truthfulness and extroverted sensuality in his paintings—but other forces prevailed.

Neapolitan Baroque painters were generally a mediocre bunch. Many, in fact, banded together to form a *"Facione de' Pittori"* headed by the favored painter of the Spanish viceroyalty, Il Ribera. These *Dependentii*, or disciples, formed more than just a "union": they were a full-fledged gang and led to the persecution that plagued most painters who came to Naples for work, such as the noted Domenichino and Guido Reni, both of whom fled the city and the cabal to save their lives (or nearly so: it was widely believed that Domenichino was mysteriously poisoned shortly after leaving the city). Thanks to the disciples of Spagnoletto (Il Ribera's nickname), pride, pomposity, glitter, and gold conquered all.

You'll pay for it if you don't do it!" If St. Januarius (to use his ancient Latin name) doesn't cooperate, however, it's usually the city that winds up paying, or so the locals believe: Eruptions of Vesuvius, cholera outbreaks, and defeats of the Naples's soccer team have all been blamed on the saint if the *miracolo* doesn't occur.

The duomo was first established by Charles II of Anjou, using imported French architects, on the site of a previous structure, the Cattedrale Stefania (AD 570), and next to an even earlier structure, the still-extant Basilica di Santa Restituta (4th century AD). Already restored in 1456 and 1484, it was largely redesigned in 1787 and 1837. The original facade collapsed in the earthquake of 1349, and the present pseudo-Gothic concoction is a modern (1877–1905) fake by Enrico Alvino and Giuseppe Pisanti, which, however, reemploys the doors—still majestic in spite of extensive damage—from the 1407 facade. The central door, by Antonio Baboccio, features a *Madonna and Child* by Tino da Camaino under its arch. Inside, the splendid nave welcomes all, with a gilt wooden ceiling (1621) and golden roundels painted above the pillars by Luca Giordano and his school depicting various saints. From the nave head to the right side of the church to see the chapel devoted to the city's patron saint.

The **Cappella del Tesoro di San Gennaro**, or Chapel of the Treasure of San Gennaro, was built in 1608–37 by the Theatin architect Francesco Grimaldi to fulfill a desperate vow pronounced by city fathers during an outbreak of the plague (January 13, 1527), some 80 years earlier. The chapel honors San Gennaro (250–305), one of the earliest Christian martyrs; as bishop of Benevento, he was executed at Pozzuoli during the rule of Emperor Diocletian. The entrance to the chapel is marked by a heavy gilt-bronze (1668–86) by noted architect Cosimo Fanzago, who also designed the chapel's superb floor, and is flanked by statues of Sts. Peter and Paul by Giuliano Finelli. Inside, the elegant Greek-cross plan is decorated everywhere possible with gold, colored marble, bronze, and paint, but nothing could be too overdone for the home of San Gennaro's most famous DNA sample and the fabulous treasure of jeweled offerings bestowed by numerous sovereigns. The 40-odd *brocatello* columns, with their musty tones of dried roses, were sent from the quarries of Tortosa in Valencia, Spain. Numerous bronze statues of saints keep permanent watch over the chapel. The high altar on the back wall (1689–90), designed by the painter Francesco Solimena, seems to swell as it tries to contain the opulence of the central relief, created in silver (circa 1692) by Giovan Domenico Vinaccia (who inserted into it a portrait of himself holding eyeglasses). Above the altar, against the wall, is a large bronze of St. Gennaro on his bishop's throne by onetime Bernini assistant Giuliano Finelli. Also behind the altar are two silvered niches donated by Charles II of Spain to house the reliquaries containing the blood of the saint (the right-hand one) and his skull. This latter reliquary consists of the famous gilded medieval bust done by three French artists (1305) set on a silver base from 1609, the actual repository of the precious vials of the saint's blood.

Most of the frescoes are by the Bolognese artist Domenichino, but his compatriot Guido Reni was originally engaged to paint the cycle, and thereby hangs a tale. The celebrated painter came to Naples only to find his life made miserable by jealous local artists indignant at seeing such an honor given to an outsider. Ultimately, the commission went to the great Domenichino, who came to Naples only after the viceroy himself guaranteed his protection. He started painting under armed guard in 1630 and had almost completed the ensemble in 1641 when he died

suddenly. Poisoning was suspected, and the committee at this point refused to even consider any Neapolitan painter, so the Roman Giovanni
Lanfranco was called in to bravely (and quickly) finish the dome, and
it was he who painted the dome's frescoed vision of Paradise. Also note
Il Ribera's *San Gennaro in the Furnace* (1647), on the right-hand
wall—perhaps the most beautiful church painting in Naples. Dating
from his early Neapolitan period, it shows the clear but well-digested
influence of Velasquez visible in the figures on the left, and it is im-
bued with a Mediterranean luminosity that is rare in his work. The
chapel, a veritable church-within-a-church, also has its own sacristy
(sometimes closed), which contains a luxurious washbasin by Cosimo
Fanzago. This room leads into a suite of rooms with frescoes by Giacomo Farelli and a splendid altarpiece by Massimo Stanzione; at the
back are kept the 51 statues of the "co-patron" saints, displayed in
the chapel proper in May and September and which accompany the
reliquary of the blood on its annual procession to Santa Chiara.

The main altar sits in the resplendent apse redesigned in 1744 by Paolo
Tosi and framed by two magnificent jasper columns found in a dig in
1705. The paintings in the apse are the work of Stefano Pozzi (ceiling
and left wall) and Corrado Giaquinto (right wall). A staircase on either side of the entrance to the presbytery (high altar area) descends
to the Caraffa Chapel, better known as the **Succorpo di San Gennaro,**
or, more simply, the crypt (1497–1506), a Renaissance masterpiece by
Tommaso Malvito in the form of a rectangular room divided into
three naves by rows of columns. Malvito also carved the imposing statue
of Cardinal Oliviero Caraffa, who commissioned the chapel. A simple antique terra-cotta vase underneath the main altar contains the bones
of San Gennaro.

Coming back up into the nave and continuing in a counterclockwise
direction, you find the Chapel of San Lorenzo, with highly restored
frescoes by Lello da Orvieto (circa 1314–20). This chapel hides an elevator that ascends one of the corner towers to the roof, which offers
an intimate yet panoramic view of the historic quarter. Nearby is the
tomb of Pope Innocent, sculpted in 1315 and redone in the 16th century by Tommaso Malvito. The sarcophagus to the left belongs to Andrea of Hungary, the unfortunate consort of Queen Joan I, who
allegedly had him strangled in Aversa (at least the dogs at the foot of
the deceased show a little sadness). Beyond the tombs of Pope Innocent XII and the late-Renaissance chapel of the Brancaccio family, a
door leads to the Chapel of Santa Restituta.

The **Cappella di Santa Restituta** is in fact the oldest church in Naples,
dating from the 4th century AD and, according to tradition, built by
order of the first Christian emperor, Constantine, on the site of a temple to Apollo. It was dedicated to St. Restituta in the 8th century when
the martyr's relics were transferred to the church. To the left is a ticket
booth for the visit to the baptistery and underground archaeological
area (entrance: €2.58). This allows you to visit a fairly dry exhibit of
ancient fragments; the Baptistery of San Giovanni in Fonte (off to the
right), however, is in itself worth the ticket price—a square room with
an octagonal dome, built by Bishop Soterus in the middle of the 5th
century, it still dazzles with its rare, gorgeous, and important early Christian mosaics. ⊠ *Via Duomo 147,* ☎ *081/449097.* ☉ *Daily 9–noon
and 4:30–6:30.* ▣ *Santa Restituta Chapel: €2.58.*

★ ⑪ **Gesù Nuovo.** *Opulenza* and *magnificenza* are the words that come to
mind when describing this floridly Baroque church, the centerpiece of
the Piazza del Gesù Nuovo. Its formidable diamond-point facade is actually a remnant of the Renaissance palace of the Sanseverino princes

(1470), destroyed to make way, in 1584–1601, for a generically stupendous exercise in the full-throated Jesuit style, albeit one with an unusual Greek-cross plan. The dome has been rebuilt twice (this is an earthquake zone); the present version dates from the early 19th century. The bulk of the interior decoration took more than 40 years and was completed only in the 18th century. You will find the familiar Baroque sculptors (Naccherino, Finelli) and painters. The gracious *Visitation* above the altar in the second chapel on the right is by Massimo Stanzione, who also contributed the fine frescoes in the main nave: they are in the presbytery (behind and around the main altar). In the chapel to the left of this are some interesting frescoes by the young Francesco Solimena, who became a leading Baroque painter, and to the left of that is a wonderful gallery of reliquary portraits, each placed in its own opera box, and around the corner is a small devotional room where statues are draped head to toe with silver body-part votive offerings. ⊠ *Piazza del Gesù Nuovo,* ☎ *081/5518613.* ⊙ *Mon.–Sat. 6:30–12:45 and 4:15–7:30, Sun. 6:30–1:30.*

㉒ **I Girolamini.** The Girolamini is another name for the Oratorians, followers of St. Philip Neri, to whom this splendid church is dedicated. Built in 1592–1619 by the Florentine architect Giovanni Antonio Dosio, the dome and gray-and-white facade were rebuilt after a design by Ferdinando Fuga (circa 1780) in the most elegant Neoclassic style. Hit by Allied bombs in 1943, the intricate carved-wood ceiling is still being restored, and the church is essentially closed off. Yet you can still get a good look at the grandiose fresco (1684) by Luca Giordano on the inside of the entrance wall. The Oratorians also built the Casa dei Padri dell'Oratorio, down the block at Via Duomo 142. Step through its gate to see the two improbably calm and disciplined cloisters, designed by the Florentine architects Giovanni Antonio Dosio, Dionisio di Bartolomeo, and Dionisio Lazzari sometime around 1600. Just off the larger cloister enclosing a prolific forest of lemon and loquat trees is the Girolamini Pinacoteca. With its high-quality, intimate collection of 16th- and 17th-century paintings, the recently opened gallery more than compensates for the closure of the adjacent church. Here, too, is one of the most gloriously decorated 18th-century libraries in Europe, the 60,000-volume Biblioteca dei Girolamini, now used by scholars. In fact, this area was an important nucleus of intellectual life in the Renaissance and Baroque periods, thanks to the presence of the Girolamini Library. Directly across the street as you exit the Girolamini note an inscription by Naples's profusely subtle philosopher, historian, and politician Benedetto Croce (1866–1952) to mark the house in which his illustrious predecessor, Giambattista Vico, lived for nearly 20 years. On the left is the Palazzo Manso, where the Marchese di Villa hosted the noted 16th-century poet Torquato Tasso. ⊠ *Via Duomo 142,* ☎ *081/449139.* ⊙ *Daily 9:30–12:50.*

★ ⑮ **Monte di Pietà.** As Spaccanapoli was home to both Naples's poorest and richest residents, the latter formed several charitable institutions, of which the Monte di Pietà was one of the most prominent. At the beginning of the 16th century, it constructed this palazzo (F. Cavagna, 1605), with a grand courtyard leading to the Cappella della Pietà, with gilt stuccoes and beautiful frescoes by B. Corenzio. Leading off the chapel are a number of salons, including the Sala delle Cantoniere, with inlaid marbles and precious intarsia wood work. Since most Neapolitan residential palace interiors are private or have disappeared, this 17th-century enfilade of salons offers a rare glimpse of Naples at its most sumptuous and should be a must-see for anyone interested in Neapolitan decorative arts. Concerts and theatrical performances are often held in the courtyard during the summer. Today the palazzo is an office for the Banco di Napoli. ⊠ *Via Biagio dei Librai 114,* ☎ *081/5517074.* ⊙ *Sat. 9–7, Sun. 9–2.*

⑯ **Museo Civico Filangieri.** Housed in the Florentine-style Palazzo Cuomo, this is now a unique museum—the residue of a once-important collection created by Prince Gaetano Filangieri, who donated it to the city in 1888. The palazzo was originally built in the Tuscan Renaissance style, only to be demolished when Via Duomo was laid out. It was reconstructed (1879), then World War II scattered the important canvases. Still, it preserves the private air of a connoisseur's house, with weapons, paintings, furniture, medallions, and costumes displayed in 19th-century-style salons. ⊠ *Via Duomo 288,* ☎ *081/203211.* 🖃 *€2.58.* ⊙ *Tues.–Sat. 9–2, Sun. 9–1.*

㉕ **Napoli Sotterranea.** Outside San Paolo Maggiore (on your right as you're coming out) on Piazza San Gaetano along Via dei Tribunali is one of the entrances to *Napoli Sotterranea*—Underground Naples. This is a fascinating tour (be prepared to go up and down a lot of steps and squeeze through some tight spaces) through a portion of Naples's fabled underground city and a good initiation into the complex layering of history in the city center. Most of the tufa mound on which Naples rises is honeycombed with successive layers of tunnels, well shafts, and underground halls whose interconnections permit a passage from Porta Capuana to the Palazzo Reale without ever seeing the light of day. Used by the soldiers of Belisarius in the 6th century AD, and again by the troops of Holy Roman Emperor Otto IV of Brunswick in the Middle Ages, the complicated network remained largely forgotten until the Neapolitan architect and engineer Guglielmo Melisurgo undertook a well-documented exploration beginning in 1880. The surprisingly large caves served a vital military purpose during the popular uprising against the Nazis in 1943. The Germans, cognizant of the location of some of the principal caverns but unable to mount a credible assault given the general chaos in the streets, bombed a number of entrances in a departing act of gratuitous vengeance, trapping the crowds underground, but arriving American soldiers dug out thousands of desperate people. Tours are provided every day at 10, noon, 2, and 4. ⊠ *Piazza San Gaetano,* ☎ *081/296944.* 🖃 *€5.16.*

★ ⑰ **Pio Monte della Misericordia.** One of the defining landmarks of Spaccanapoli, this octagonal church was built around the corner from the duomo (practically in front of its constantly used side door) for a charitable institution founded in 1601 by seven noblemen. The institution's aim was to carry out acts of Christian charity: feeding the hungry, clothing the poor, nursing the sick, sheltering pilgrims, visiting prisoners, ransoming Christian slaves, and burying the indigent dead—acts immortalized in the history of art by the famous altarpiece painted by Caravaggio (1571–1610) depicting the *Seven Acts of Mercy* and now the celebrated focus of the church. In this haunting work the artist has brought the Virgin in palpable glory, unforgettably borne atop the shoulders of two angels, right down into the street—and not a rhetorical place, but a real street of Spaccanapoli (scholars have in fact suggested a couple of plausible identifications) populated by figures in whose spontaneous and passionate movements the people could see themselves given great dignity. Along with other paintings in the church, the sculptures by Andrea Falcone on its porch refer to this commitment. The original church was considered too small and destroyed in 1655 to make way for the new church, designed by Antonio Picchiatti in 1658–78. Pride of place is given to the great Caravaggio above the altar (for a discussion of this work, see the Close-Up box, "Chiaroscuro Plus: Caravaggio's *Seven Acts of Mercy*") but there are other important

Baroque-era paintings on view here; some hang in the church while others are in the adjoining Pinacoteca, or picture gallery.

The extraordinary expressiveness and efficiency of the Caravaggio altarpiece can be judged by comparison with the church's other paintings, commissioned from Neapolitan painters after Caravaggio hit the road again (to Malta) to stay one step ahead of the law. In particular, in the painting to the left of the altar, *St. Peter Rescuing Tabitha* (1612), Fabrizio Santafede is clearly struggling to modify his Technicolor formalist style to suggest the dramatic impact of the altarpiece—but the figures here merely occupy the space of the painting, rather than animate it. Upon seeing Caravaggio's altarpiece, a number of artists changed their style radically, although often giving a personal interpretation to one aspect of Caravaggio's style. The painting to the right of the exit door is a beautiful work by one of the best of the Neapolitan Caravaggesques, Giovan Battista Carraciolo, who was 29 years of age when the slightly older artist came to town. Depicting the *Liberation of St. Peter* (1615), the composition is almost shockingly spartan, nearly all dark brown with contained blocks of white, red, and flesh tones. For more paintings of the Neapolitan Seicento, head up the staircase in the courtyard around the left of the church to the church's small **Pinacoteca**, a museum of 17th- and 18th-century paintings. ✉ *Via Tribunali 253,* ☎ *081/446944.* ⊙ *Mon.–Sat. 9–1; Pinacoteca museum by appointment only at least 24 hours in advance Thurs. and Sat. 9–1.*

NEED A BREAK? When leaving the Pio Monte during the summer months, note that a street vendor named **Ciro** often sets up in the small square directly across from the church and sells a silky homemade lemon slush (*limonata*) given a shy blush by a dose of strawberry juice. Smoothly tart, ice cold, and—well—*real,* it makes for a uniquely satisfying complement to Caravaggio's vision of daily grace.

❷❼ **San Domenico Maggiore.** One of the largest churches of Spaccanapoli, this Dominican house of worship was originally constructed by Charles I of Anjou in 1238. Legend has it that a painting of the crucifixion spoke to St. Thomas Aquinas when he was at prayer here. This early structure, however, was nearly gutted by a fire three centuries later and, in 1850, a neo-Gothic edifice rose in its place, complete with a nave of awe-inspiring dimensions. In the second chapel on the right are remnants of the earlier church—14th-century frescoes by Pietro Cavallini, a Roman predecessor of Giotto. Along the side chapels are also some noted funerary monuments, including those of the Carafa family, whose chapel, to the left of Cosimo Fanzago's 17th-century altar, is one of the most beautiful Renaissance-era set-pieces in Naples. ✉ *Piazza San Domenico Maggiore 8/a,* ☎ *081/5573204.* ⊙ *Mon.–Sat. 8:30–noon and 5–8, Sun. 9–1 and 5–7:30.*

❶❾ **San Giuseppe dei Ruffi.** Half a block from the Duomo, this late-17th-century church, built by Dionisio Lazzari, features one of the most impressively solid and dramatically Baroque facades in Naples. The order must have spent most of its money on it, since they wound up painting the nave walls in faux marble to keep up appearances. This place can be a relaxing stop in the morning, especially if the nuns are singing. ✉ *Piazza San Giuseppe dei Ruffi 2,* ⊙ *Mon.–Sat. 7:30–1 and 4–6; Sun. 7:30–10:30.*

❷❻ **San Gregorio Armeno.** Landmarked by a picturesque campanile that spans Via San Gregorio Armeno, this convent was one of the oldest and most important in Naples. The nuns (often the daughters of

CHIAROSCURO PLUS: CARAVAGGIO'S *SEVEN ACTS OF MERCY*

THE MOST UNFORGETTABLE painting in Naples, Michelangelo Merisi da Caravaggio's *Seven Acts of Mercy* takes pride of place in the Church of Pio Monte della Misericordia, as well as in nearly all of southern Italy, for emotional spectacle and unflinching truthfulness. Painted in 1607, it combines the traditional seven acts of Christian charity in sometimes abbreviated form in a tight, dynamic composition under the close, compassionate gaze of the Virgin (the original title was *Our Lady of Mercy*). She flutters down with the Christ child into a torchlit street scene borne by two of the most memorable angels ever painted.

Illuminated in the artist's landmark chiaroscuro style (featuring pronounced contrasts of light, *chiaro,* and deep shadow, *scuro*), a man is being buried, a nude beggar is being clothed, and—this artist never pulled any punches—a starving prisoner is being suckled by a woman. Caravaggio, as with most geniuses, was a difficult artist and personality. His romantic bad-boy reputation as the original bohemian, complete with angry, nihilistic, rebel-with-a-cause sneer and roistering and hippie-like lifestyle, has dominated interpretations of his revolutionary oeuvre and tend to present him as an antireligious painter. This is perhaps understandable—most of the documents pertaining to his life relate to his problems with the law and make for a good story indeed (he came to Naples after killing a man in a bar brawl in Rome, where his cardinal patrons could no longer protect him).

But in spite of (or perhaps because of) his personal life, Caravaggio painted some of the most moving religious art ever produced in the West, whittling away all the rhetoric to reveal the emotional core of the subject. His genuine love of the popular classes and for the "real" life of the street found expression in his use of ordinary street folk as models, though if his art seems to surge directly from the gut, his famous "objectivity" of observation and reduced palette have clear antecedents in paintings from his home region in northern Italy. The simplicity and warts-and-all depictions of his characters show a deeply original response to the Counter-Reformation writings on religious art by Carlo Borromeo, a future saint, also from Lombardy.

The *Seven Acts of Mercy,* the first altarpiece commissioned for the new church of the charitable institution, has been called "the most important religious painting of the seventeenth century" by the great 20th-century Italian art critics Roberto Longhi and Giuliano Argan, and if that may not be immediately obvious, it's nevertheless easy to imagine the impact this astonishing painting had on artists and connoisseurs in Naples. It is easy to imagine that Caravaggio was a natural Neapolitan of the heart, like the recent soccer player–turned–hero Maradona, and had his maverick virtuosity similarly appreciated. And like Maradona, he came, dazzled them, and left, though in the year he spent in Naples he managed to paint at least three other major works, now in Vienna, London, and the Museo di Capodimonte (the *Flagellation*) as well as a few lost works. Naples affected his style, too: it began to express visual relations purely in terms of dramatic light and shadow, which only further exalted the contrasts of human experience.

Naples's richest families) who lived here must have been disappointed
with Paradise when they arrived—banquets here outrivaled those of
the royal court, hallways were lined with paintings, and the church
groaned with an an orgy of gilt stucco and semiprecious stones. Described as "a room of Paradise on Earth" by Carlo Celano and designed
by Niccolò Taglicozzi Canle, the church has a highly detailed wooden
ceiling, unique papier-mâché choir lofts, a nuns' gallery shielded by 18th-
century jalousies, a shimmering organ, candlelighted shrines, and important Luca Giordano frescoes of scenes of the life of St. Gregory, whose
relics were brought to Naples in the 8th century from Byzantium. Inside, the convent's cloister has a grand view of the Bay of Naples, while
rooms such as the Salottino della Badessa—generally not on view, as
this is still a working convent—are preserved as magnificent 18th-
century interiors. ⊠ *Piazzetta San Gregorio Armeno 1,* ☎ *081/
5520186.* ⊙ *Daily 8:30–noon.*

㉓ San Lorenzo Maggiore. One of the grandest medieval churches of the
Decumano Maggiore, San Lorenzo features a very unmedieval facade
of 18th-century splendor. Due to the effects and threats of earthquakes,
the church was reinforced and reshaped along Baroque lines in the 17th
and 18th centuries, and remaining from this phase is the facade by Ferdinando Sanfelice (1742) based on the sweeping curves of Borromini's
Filomarino altar in the Church of Santi Apostoli. Begun by Robert d'Anjou in 1265 on the site of a previous 6th-century church, the church's
single, barnlike nave reflects the desire of the Franciscans for simple
spaces with enough room to preach to large crowds. Numerous statues and paintings from the 14th century are indicative of San Lorenzo's
importance during this period. In 1334, in fact, Boccaccio met and fell
in love with his fabled Lady Fiammetta here, and in 1343 another great
Italian poet, Petrarch, resided in the monastery next door. During the
20th century late-Baroque accretions were stripped off to reclaim the
original Gothic design. Entering the huge nave and then beginning at
the right, view a number of notable tombs and chapels, including the
tomb of the Admiral Ludovico Aldomorisco in the second chapel, a
fine Renaissance composition by Antonio Baboccio (1421); and the
Cacace Chapel, a Baroque masterpiece with a typically sumptuous
marble-inlay display from the workshop of Cosimo Fanzago. The
transept is announced by a grandiose triumphal arch, while the main
altar (1530) is the sculptor Giovanni da Nola's masterpiece; notice the
fascinating historical views of Naples in the reliefs.

The apse was built by an unknown imported French architect of great
caliber, who gives here a brilliant essay in the pure French Angevin style,
complete with an ambulatory of nine side chapels that is covered by a
magnificent web of cross arches. The most important monument in the
church is found here: the tomb of Catherine of Austria (circa 1323),
by Tino da Camaino, one of the first sculptors to introduce the Gothic
style into Italy. The left transept contains the 14th-century funerary monument of Carlo di Durazzo and yet another Fanzago masterpiece, the
Cappellone di Sant'Antonio—Cappella being too diminutive a word,
especially in this behemoth of a church. Outside the 17th-century
cloister is the entrance to the excavations under San Lorenzo, which
are a good initiation to the Roman and Greek cities beneath the modern one. Near the area of the forum, these digs have revealed streets,
markets, and workshops of another age. ⊠ *Via dei Tribunali 316,* ☎
081/2110860. ▨ *Excavations €2.58.* ⊙ *Daily 8–12 and 5–7; excavations Mon.–Wed. 9–1 and 3–5:30, Sat. 9–5:30 and Sun. 9:30–1:30.*

㉔ San Paolo Maggiore. Like Santi Apostoli, this church was erected for
the Theatin fathers in the late 16th century (1583–1603), the period

of their order's rapid expansion. This was another instance where Francesco Grimaldi, the (ordained) house architect, erected a church on the ruins of an ancient Roman temple, then transformed it into a Christian basilica. Spoils from the temple survive in the present incarnation, especially the two monumental Corinthian columns on the facade holding up a piece of their architrave to form a portal over the entrance door. The cloaked torsos of the ancient gods, which used to lie under the statues of Peter and Paul, have been moved. An earthquake knocked down the original facade in 1688, and World War II coupled with decades of neglect did further damage. As of press time (fall 2001), the church is closed for extensive restoration. ✉ *Piazza San Gaetano,* ☎ *081/454048.*

⑭   **Sant' Angelo a Nilo.** Originally built by Cardinal Brancaccio in the late 1300s, this church was redesigned in the 16th century by Arcangelo Guglielminelli. Inside the graciously beautiful interior is the earliest evidence of the Renaissance in Naples: the cardinal's funerary monument, sculpted by the famous Donatello, assisted by the almost-as-famous Michelozzo, in 1426–27. The front of the sarcophagus bears a bas-relief *Assumption of the Virgin,* testament to Donatello's legendary *"stiacciato"* trompe-l'oeil technique. Beyond the small courtyard is the Palazzo Brancaccio, where the learned prelate opened the first public library in Naples in 1690. ✉ *Piazzetta Nilo, along Via San Biagio dei Librai,* ☎ *081/5516227.* ◷ *Mon.–Sat. 8:30–12 and 5–7, Sun. 8:30–12.*

★ **⑫**   **Santa Chiara.** Across from the Gesù Nuovo and offering a stark and telling contrast to the opulence of that church, Santa Chiara is the leading monument of Angevin Gothic in Naples. The fashionable church for the nobility in the 14th century, and a favorite Angevin church from the start, Santa Chiara was intended to be a great dynastic monument by Robert d'Anjou. His second wife, Sancia di Majorca, added the adjoining convent for the Poor Clares to a monastery of the Franciscan Minors so she could vicariously satisfy a lifelong desire for the cloistered seclusion of a convent; this was the first time the two sexes were combined in a single complex. Built in a Provençal Gothic style between 1310 and 1328 (probably by Guglielmo Primario) and dedicated in 1340, the church had its aspect radically altered, as did so many others, in the Baroque period, when the original wooden roof was replaced with a vault dripping in stuccos. A six-day fire started by Allied bombs on August 4, 1943, put an end to all that, as well as to what might have been left of the important cycle of frescoes by Giotto and his Neapolitan workshop: Giorgio Vasari, writing in the mid-16th century, tells us that the paintings covered the entire church. The interior, a large, luminous rectangular hall, nevertheless offers ample serenity, the 18th-century marble floor by Domenico Antonio Vaccaro has been decently restored, and the tombs, in the back, are worth a look. The most important tomb in the church towers behind the altar. Sculpted by Giovanni and Pacio Bertini of Florence (1343–45), it is, fittingly, the tomb of the founding king: the great Robert d'Anjou, known as the Wise. To the right of the altar is the tomb of Carlo, duke of Calabria, a majestic composition by Tino da Camaino and assistants (1326–33), and answering it on the side wall is Tino's last work, the tomb of Carlo's wife, Marie de Valois.

Around the left side of the church at Via Santa Chiara 49/c is a gate leading to the **Chiostro delle Clarisse,** the most famous cloister in Naples. It's clear here that we are not dealing with any normal convent; the benches and octagonal columns upholding the trellis of vine shading this privileged garden comprise a light-handed masterpiece of painted majolica designed by Domenico Antonio Vaccaro, with a de-

HOW TO USE THIS GUIDE

Great trips begin with great planning, and this guide makes planning easy. It's packed with everything you need—insider advice on hotels and restaurants, cool tools, practical tips, essential maps, and much more.

COOL TOOLS

Fodor's Choice Top picks are marked throughout with a star.

Great Itineraries These tours, planned by Fodor's experts, give you the skinny on what you can see and do in the time you have.

Smart Travel Tips A to Z This special section is packed with important contacts and advice on everything from how to get around to what to pack.

Good Walks You won't miss a thing if you follow the numbered bullets on our maps.

Need a Break? Looking for a quick bite to eat or a spot to rest? These sure bets are along the way.

Off the Beaten Path Some lesser-known sights are worth a detour. We've marked those you should make time for.

POST-IT® FLAGS
Dog-ear no more!

Post-it is a registered trademark of 3M.

ICONS AND SYMBOLS

Watch for these symbols throughout:

★	Our special recommendations
✕	Restaurant
🏨	Lodging establishment
✕🏨	Lodging establishment whose restaurant warrants a special trip
☉	Good for kids
☞	Sends you to another section of the guide for more information
✉	Address
☎	Telephone number
FAX	Fax number
WEB	Web site
💵	Admission price
☉	Opening hours
$-$$$$	Lodging and dining price categories, keyed to strategically sited price charts. Check the index for locations.
①❶	Numbers in white and black circles on the maps, in the margins, and within tours correspond to one another.

ON THE WEB

Continue your planning with these useful tools found at **www.fodors.com**, the Web's best source for travel information.

"Rich with resources." —*New York Times*

"Navigation is a cinch." —*Forbes* "Best of the Web" list

"Put together by people bursting with know-how."
                                        —*Sunday Times* (London)

Create a Miniguide Pinpoint hotels, restaurants, and attractions that have what you want at the price you want to pay.

Rants and Raves Find out what readers say about Fodor's picks—or write your own reviews of hotels and restaurants you've just visited.

Travel Talk Post your questions and get answers from fellow travelers, or share your own experiences.

On-Line Booking Find the best prices on airline tickets, rental cars, cruises, or vacations, and book them on the spot.

About our Books Learn about other Fodor's guides to your destination and many others.

Expert Advice and Trip Ideas From what to tip to how to take great photos, from the national parks to Nepal, Fodors.com has suggestions that'll make your trip a breeze. Log on and get informed and inspired.

Smart Resources Check the weather in your destination or convert your currency. Learn the local language or link to the latest event listings. Or consult hundreds of detailed maps—all in one place.

lightful profusion of landscapes and light yellow and green floral motifs realized by Donato and Giuseppe Massa and their studio (1742). Where the real vines leave off and the painted ones took over was once hard to say, but much of the cloister is now being replanted, so the complete effect is missing. The elegant 14th-century porch around the garden is enlivened by fading frescoes. In the back corner you can enter the Museo dell'Opera, built on the visible remains of an old Roman bath establishment and containing some interesting sculptural fragments from the damaged church (look for Giovanni da Nola's moving wooden *Ecce Homo* of 1519 on the upper floor) and objects illustrating life in the cloister. ⊠ *Via Benedetto Croce,* ☎ *081/5526209.* ⊠ *€3.09.* ☉ *Church daily 7–12:30 and 4:30–6:30; cloister Mon.–Sat. 9:30–1 and 2:30–5:30, Sun. 9:30–1.*

㉑ **Santa Maria di Donnaregina Vecchia.** The towering Gothic funeral monument of Mary of Hungary, wife of Charles II of Anjou (circa 1254–1309), who is said to have commissioned the frescoes in the church at a cost of 33 ounces of gold, is contained within this church. Don't confuse this church with another, nearby in the piazza, of the same name, but Baroque. ⊠ *Vico Donnaregina 25,* ☎ *081/299101.* ☉ *By appointment only.*

⑳ **Santi Apostoli.** This Baroque church in a basic Latin-cross style with a single nave shares the piazza with a contemporary art school in a typically anarchic Neapolitan mix. Built (1610–49) by the ordained architect Francesco Grimaldi for the Theatin fathers above a previous church, itself built on the remains of a temple probably dedicated to Mercury, it is worth a quick peek inside for its coherent, intact Baroque decorative scheme. There are excellent paintings on the inside of the entrance wall and on the ceiling by Giovanni Lanfranco (circa 1644), with a good number painted by his successors Francesco Solimena and Luca Giordano. The terra-cotta and marble floor is a work of the late 17th century by Francesco Viola. For lovers of Baroque architecture, there is an altar in the left transept by the great architect Francesco Borromini. Commissioned by Cardinal Ascanio Filomarino, this is the only work in Naples by this architect, whose freedom from formality so inspired the exuberance of the Baroque in southern Italy, although its massive virile flourish of monochrome gray stone comes as a bit of a shock in the midst of this polychromed city. ⊠ *Largo Santi Apostoli 9,* ☎ *081/299375.* ☉ *Mon.–Sat. 9–12, Sun. 9–1.*

Art and Antiquity: From the Museo Archeologico Nazionale to the Museo di Capodimonte

It is only fitting that the Museo Archeologico Nazionale—the single most important and remarkable museum of Greco-Roman antiquities in the world (in spite of itself, some observers say)—sits in the upper *decumanus,* or neighborhood, of ancient Neapolis, the district colonized by the ancient Greeks and Romans. Repository of many of the greatest surviving art treasures of antiquity—including most of the celebrated finds from Pompeii and Herculaneum—the museum has so many rooms it almost constitutes its own walking tour. As Naples's preeminent treasure trove, it deserves your undivided attention early in the day, but if two hours is your limit for gazing at ancient art, discover other nearby sights off the beaten track but prized by connoisseurs of Naples: the Catacombs of San Gennaro; the Orto Botanico, the city's botanical gardens; and the historic Church of San Giovanni a Carbonara. The final leg of the tour leads to the northern suburbs of the city, whose highest point is crowned by the Museo di Capodimonte, the greatest of the Bourbon palaces, now a regal museum.

A Good Walk

Provided your feet don't call a sit-down strike after touring the enormous complex of the **Museo Archeologico Nazionale** ㉘, walk eastward along Piazza Cavour until it becomes Via Foria. This will first take you past the recently opened metro station of Museo and then into Piazza Cavour, one of the busiest intersections in town. Go past the picturesque Porta San Gennaro on your right, a relic of the old 15th-century city walls, and take a diagonal right turn down Via Carbonara toward the important Church of **San Giovanni a Carbonara** ㉙, set back from the road 100 yards down on the left. If you prefer lush gardens to great architecture, simply hop on one of the many buses going down Via Foria towards Piazza Carlo III, getting off some 10 blocks later when you see the towering trees of the **Orto Botanico** ㉚ on your left behind the formidable protective wall. Backtrack to the Museo Archeologico Nazionale and take Bus No. R4 up Via Santa Teresa Degli Scalzi (an extension of Via Toledo/Via Roma) up the Corso Amedeo di Savoia Duca D'Aosta until you reach the *Tondo* (roundabout) close to the **Catacombe di San Gennaro** ㉛ and below the steps leading up to the **Museo di Capodimonte** ㉜.

TIMING

The Museo Archeologico Nazionale and the Museo di Capodimonte are Naples's two most famous museums and both now enjoy extended opening hours throughout the year. However, especially in the Museo Archeologico, a good portion of the lesser known rooms may be closed at any one time, so if you are particularly keen to see, say, the exhibition on prehistory in Campania or the Egyptian section, a prior phone call will avoid disappointment. If you want the full feast, get an early morning start. This tour could easily take six hours, not including transportation time between the city center and Capodimonte, and a snack perhaps in the moderately priced cafeteria inside the Palace of Capodimonte.

Sights to See

㉛ **Catacombe di San Gennaro.** These catacombs—designed for Christian burial rather than as bolt-holes—go at least as far back as the 2nd century AD. This was where San Gennaro's body was brought from Pozzuoli in the 4th century, after which the catacombs became a key pilgrimage center. The 45-minute guided tour of the two-level site takes you down a series of vestibules with fine frescoed niche tombs. The imposing bulk of the early 20th-century church looms over the site (Madre del Buon Consiglio), apparently inspired by St. Peter's in Rome. ⊠ *Via Capodimonte 16, next to the Madonna del Buon Consiglio church,* ☎ *081/7411071.* ▣ *€2.58.* ☉ *Guided tours daily every 45 mins 9:30–11:45 AM; afternoon tours for groups by appointment only.*

★ ㉘ **Museo Archeologico Nazionale** (National Museum of Archaeology). Those who know and love this legendary museum have a tendency, upon hearing it mentioned, to heave a sigh: it is famous not only for its unrivaled collections but also for its off-limit rooms, missing identification labels, poor lighting, billows of dust that attack the unwary visitor, suffocating heat in summer, and indifferent personnel—a state of affairs seen by some critics as an encapsulation of everything that's wrong with southern Italy in general. Precisely because of this emblematic value, the National Ministry of Culture has decided to lavish attention and funds on the museum in a complete reorganization. This process has been ongoing for some time and looks as if it will continue for a while longer. Ticketing has been privatized, new opening hours introduced (until 7 PM), and vastly improved guiding services are now on offer. Rooms covering recent archaeological discoveries in the Greco-Roman settlements and necropolises in and around Naples have been opened, with helpful informational panels in English. And even if some rooms may be closed (and others only open during peak-season, mid-day hours), this still leaves available the core of the museum, a nucleus which puts most other museums to shame and is still worth a detour. For it includes the legendary Farnese collection of ancient sculpture, together with local sculptural finds, and almost all the good stuff—the best mosaics and paintings—from Pompeii and Herculaneum. The quality of these collections is unexcelled and, as far as the mosaic, painting, and bronze sections are concerned, unique in the world.

History of the Museum. The museum was born in the mind of Charles III, who had inherited the various Farnese collections from his mother. The Farnese family had collected antiquities quite aggressively in Rome during the 16th century, when there were still quite a few important pieces to be found—their excavations of the Baths of Caracalla, in particular, produced a number of marvels, including the Farnese Bull and Farnese Hercules—and these pieces, together with the paintings, made an ideal endowment for a new museum. Charles originally intended to house the collection, together with the Farnese collection of paintings and precious objects, in a new palace at Capodimonte, which would be at once a dynastic monument and an avant-garde intellectual endeavor of the Enlightenment, but the antiquities collection soon outstripped the available space. In 1738, the same year the definitive project for Capodimonte got underway, excavations began at the site explored by Prince d'Elboeuf—Resina, in the Herculaneum area—which yielded a stunning sample of marble and bronze statues. And then, in 1748, a new site opened up that surpassed every archaeologist's dreams: Pompeii. By 1750 a makeshift museum had been set up in the royal palace at Portici to house the rapidly growing finds, and Naples, with its exciting excavations, had become an obligatory stop on travelers' Grand Tour itineraries.

After a time the question of a fitting museum became an international issue, and given the precarious position of Portici (it lies under Vesuvius), a solution was deemed urgent—even if it did not seem so to the king. (When Vesuvius erupted in 1767 and ministers pleaded with him to find a safe, permanent home for the collection, Charles of Bourbon replied that if the worst happened and they were buried anew, they would be the crowning joy of excavators' digs 2,000 years later.) A decision was made in 1777 to utilize a former university, the Palazzo degli Studi, on the hill of Santa Teresa. Ferdinando Fuga was given orders to draw up a plan, but his innovations as usual stirred up controversy, and when he died in 1782, nothing had been built, and the project was passed on to the Roman architect Pompeo Schiantarelli. During this decade the Farnese collection of ancient sculpture finally arrived. This was totally illegal—Cardinal Alexander Farnese's will of 1587 specifically stipulated that the collection was to stay in Rome. But Ferdinand IV, son of and successor to Charles III, politely ignored the strident complaints of the Pope and various other personages, including Goethe, and calmly packed up the loot for transfer.

The museum, named the Royal Library of Naples, finally opened in 1801—perhaps a bit late, given that Ferdinand had just massacred nearly all of his city's intellectual elite in "appreciation" of their Republican ideas. On the whole, however, the museum, if not the Neapolitans themselves, did well from the Napoleonic wars. The French had already packed up the Farnese Hercules for transport to the new Louvre, but the new king of Naples, Joachim Murat, was able to use his considerable military clout within Napoléon's empire to keep the museum's contents in Naples (the rest of Italy was thoroughly and expertly plundered). Murat's wife, Caroline (who rather usefully happened to be Napoléon's sister), herself collected antiquities; so Ferdinand proudly added her collection to the museum in 1816, once he had reestablished himself on the throne with the help of his friends. Just in case anyone had any doubts about who the owner was, or what sort of government had set it up, he renamed it the Royal Bourbon Museum. The building was finally finished in 1822, just in time to house the spectacular mosaics uncovered in the 1830s in the House of the Faun in Pompeii. With the fall of the Bourbons and unification with the emergent Italy, the collection was reorganized as a so-called National Museum. The result of course was immediate mismanagement and a number of scandals, concerning not only the ideological content underlying the display program but also the large number of pieces that simply went missing, including important items from the Boscoreale treasure now in the Louvre. Damage inflicted on the building by the 1980–81 earthquakes was the impetus for the last two decades' campaign of modernization.

Room-by-Room Tour of the Collections. As you enter the building, the ticket booth is immediately on the left, with a sign indicating which rooms are open and which closed (read this before buying your ticket). Ahead of you is the large **Atrium of the Magistrates,** which contains a dignified but discreet introduction to the sculpture collections, including a pair of Dacians from Trajan's Forum in the middle aisle and a number of toga-wearing figures and members of the Balbi family from Herculaneum. If you want to continue with marble sculpture, wend your way back to the door near the ticket barrier, the one framed by two columns of antique Numidian yellow marble, and enter the Room of the Tyrannicides. It makes more sense, however, to start your visit on the top floor of the museum, which contains some of the more demanding works on the eye, and work your way down. Head for the stairs flanked at the base by two large reclining 2nd-century AD river deities. Placed unavoidably halfway up the stairs is a ridiculous statue of Ferdinand IV in the guise of Athena, by Canova (which shows that some people should just never wear drag, especially if they have a regal dignity to maintain). While the text found below has an extensive description of the entire collection, you might wish to invest in an up-to-date printed museum guide, as exhibits are generally poorly labeled.

Go up two flights of stairs to the first floor (that's by Italian accounting; the mezzanine only counts for half a floor—except when it comes to subsidies). To the right is the important collection of bronzes. The first room (CXV) presents a delightful collection of small decorative bronzes (Silenus heads, children's portraits, leopard antefixes) from the grandiose Villa of the Papiri in Herculaneum, while the adjoining room (CXIV) has a permanent exhibition on the papyrus scrolls, from where the villa got its name, with pride of place given to the curious 19-century device invented to unwind them. The scrolls have now almost all been read—with the aid of rather more sophisticated technology—and are now housed in the Biblioteca Nazionale. The big room (CXVI) ahead contains statues from the villa that most museums would sell their souls to get as virtually all metal objects from antiquity, especially bronze statues, were melted down. Here you have a treasury of life-size masterpieces, with a splendid set of heads along the left wall illustrating the ancient themes of illustrious men—Hellenistic princes, philosophers, poets—and generic, ideal figures referring to aspects of civilized life: theatrical figures and athletes (note the head of Thespis with the bronze curls soldered on separately). In front of these sit a pensive *Hermes* from a local workshop and the famous

Drunken Satyr, a pair of deer, the two running athletes (copies after Lysippus) with their original encrusted eyes, and, in the corner next to the left window, a bust of Dionysus with extravagant, meticulously rendered hair. The far wall has a celebrated set of five female *Dancers* (recently reinterpreted as water carriers and identified with the Danaids, who were condemned to draw water endlessly) in the stiff but expressive Severe style. The next room (CXVII), just beyond, contains another fine series of bronze herm heads, an impressive 1st-century BC copy of a lance-throwing *Athena Promachos,* which replicates the monumental statue that once decorated the Acropolis in Athens, and the justifiably renowned portrait head known as the *Seneca,* whose world-weary expression will still move you deeply, even if he is placed too low for the viewer to receive its full impact (bend down low). An equally impressive collection of small bronzes will eventually be displayed in the rooms along the courtyard.

Rooms CXVIII to CXXI shift the focus from Herculaneum to ancient Neapolis and the first Greek settlement overlooking what is now Castel dell'Ovo, Palaeopolis. Exhibits include important finds from public buildings and necropolises during the Greco-Roman period. With helpful information panels (in English), this recently opened section shows what and how much lies buried beneath the modern city center, and gives insight into religious and cultural practices during the various periods.

Back through the bronze galleries and to the right at the staircase, you come into the large **Sala della Meridiana,** designed as the reading room of the library and presently wasted space, gussied up with a series of huge 19th-century mediocrities detailing the family history of the fabulous Farnese. At the far end of the room is a famous statue of the titan *Atlas* from the Farnese collection, which bears the oldest known complete depiction of the constellations of the zodiac. Off the door to the right, a suite of rooms along the front facade of the *palazzo* houses newly renovated displays of findings from pre-Roman Campania, with lots of the usual pottery. On the other side of the Sala della Meridiana, a pair of Trajan-era kneeling Persians in white and purple *pavonazzettó* marble drapery provides a suitable announcement of the celebrated ancient fresco collection beyond.

Room 1 (or CXVI; most rooms are numbered in both Arabic and Roman styles) starts off with some excellent *Fourth-Style painted-stucco friezes from the House of Meleager* in Pompeii that refer to the cults of Dionysus and Hercules, but this is just an antechamber to the cream of the crop, spread around the rooms branching off from Room 2 (CXVIII). Handy English-language displays of information, on the left as you enter, give a good presentation of the so-called Four Styles of Roman painting as seen in Pompeii and Herculaneum, evidence of the "golden age" of Roman wall painting. The room to the right displays what's left of the Third Style *paintings from the villa at Boscoreale,* discovered in 1900; the next room (LXX) contains two versions of the *Three Graces* on the right. The third bay (LXXI) has a display case in the center with some exquisite monochrome paintings on marble, including *Fight with a Centaur,* rendered in a confident, precise line reminiscent of Ingres. The bay with the window shows off the famous paintings from the Basilica of Herculaneum, discovered in 1739, including a panel of an oddly nonchalant Hercules discovering his son Telephus being nursed by a doe in Arcadia. Room LXXII has a wonderful *Perseus Freeing Andromeda* from the House of the Dioscuri in Pompeii, plus the celebrated image of *Theseus and the Minotaur* next to the exit door. The last room (LXXIII) along the front facade houses a number of panels in the refined but cold antiquarian current of the Third Style, a reflection of Augustan classicism. Nearby are the six rooms (LXXIX–LXXXIV) that feature material recovered from the Temple of Isis.

Room LXXXV starts the **Glass Collection,** with one of the museum's showstoppers in the center: the *Blue Vase from Pompeii,* an astonishing example of antique cameo glasswork, with white swirls of vegetation and wildlife surrounding some erotes or cupids against an intense cobalt blue. In an adjacent room is the spectacular 100:1 scale model of Pompeii made in 1879. The main part of the glass and jewelry collection (Room LXXXVI) has some fine mosaic glass bowls which would grace any *triclinium* dining table. Stairs take you back down to the mezzanine, site of the **Mosaic Collection.** And what mosaics they are! The first room, which gives just a taste of things to come, sports a striking spotted leopard and a small panel showing a drunk Silenus trying to ride a donkey. The next room on your right (LVIII) concentrates on *nymphaeum* and fountain mosaics in glass paste while Room LIX features the much-reproduced black-and-white depiction of Death. A stunningly sensitive portrait of a woman in micro-mosaic is found in Room LXIV. The finest works are saved for the last two rooms: the world-renowned *opus vermiculatum* mosaics from the House of the Faun in Pompeii. The star piece here is the gigantic *Alexander and Darius at the Battle of Issus* on the far wall. Considered to be a copy of a famous painting by Philoxenos of Eretria done for King Cassander of Macedonia (end of the 4th century BC), this mosaic copy, which dates to 125–120 BC, would be, even if clumsily rendered, of priceless documentary value for our knowledge of the lost art of Greek painting; as it turns out, the mosaic itself is a masterpiece. Nearby, cat fans will appreciate the small panel with the cat attacking a bird, while the scene of the *Satyr and Nymph* next to the Alexander mosaic presents lust in an astringently frank manner.

Tucked in discreetly by the mosaic area is the **Gabinetto Segreto,** a unique collection of objects covering a gamut of sexually explicit themes from phalluses in imaginative poses to Pan doing indescribable things to a nanny-goat. After many years of closure due either to 19th-century prudery or 20th-century restoration, the Gabinetto can now be viewed (guided tours only, every 30 minutes) by prior request at the main ticket office. The information panels here are helpful, so you might like to browse at your own pace rather than join the hurried guided tour.

Once back on the ground floor, cross the **Atrium of the Magistrates** and go through the yellow columns on the side wall near the ticket takers to the **Room of the Tyrannicides** (Room 1), named for the group in the center, a 2nd-century AD Roman copy of a famous bronze by Kritios and Nesiotes cast in 477 BC. To the right, notice the beautiful fragmentary *head of Apollo from Baiae,* with traces of red paint still in his hair. Through the door to the left of this head, you enter the **Gallery of the Great Masters** (Rooms II–VI), which contains mostly copies of works by Greek masters, but some of these copies are among the finest, or they are the only such examples known, including the *Apollo Citharedos,* between Bays II and III, with his rich, flowing hair, and the *Doriphoros of Polycleites* in Bay II. The window-side of the leftmost bay (Room VI) shows off a pair of gorgeous, if damaged, Greek originals of the 4th or 3rd century BC: Nereids with flowing "wet" drapery carved in succulent honeycomb-color stone. Back into the Room of the Tyrannicides and to your right is the **Gallery of Flora** (or Gallery of the Carracci, Room VIII), with a beautifully intact *Artemis of Ephesus* in basalt and antique yellow marble, her fecundity underlined by her multiple breasts and the numerous animals adorning her raiment. In the middle of the gallery stands a voluptuous *Aphrodite Callipygos* ("of the beautiful buttocks"), originally found in the area of Nero's Domus Aurea in Rome.

The collections of ancient sculpture culminate in the **Gallery of the Farnese Bull** (Rooms XI–XV), whose monumentality is no less than the grandiose sculptures from the Baths of Caracalla deserve. The right end of the gallery is dominated by the awesomely powerful *Farnese Hercules,* a signed ("Glykon of Athens made this") copy of a 4th-century BC bronze by Lysippus. His left arm is a restoration, and the nearby set of legs was made by Guglielmo della Porta in the 16th century to complete the statue when it was first discovered; the originals, found afterward, were long judged inferior to these and were not reintegrated until much later. At the left end, the splendid *Farnese Bull*—the largest sculptural group to come down to us from antiquity—answers the Hercules in magnificence. Yes, it has been highly restored (this is well documented on the wall), but all in all, the restorers did a decent job. The strong composition, with its calm depiction of murder, still inspires awe, and numerous artists, from Michelangelo to Picasso, have been influenced by this sculpture.

Behind the Hercules is a discreet door leading into two small rooms housing the **Farnese Collection of Gems,** mostly ancient cameos. The centerpiece of the collection is the fabled *Farnese Cup,* a true stunner, carved to translucent thinness out of a solid layered block of agate and sardonyx; various color layers are brilliantly used to portray a group of mythological figures on the interior and a Medusa's head on the exterior. Probably a royal commission of the court of the Ptolemies in Egypt from the 2nd or 1st century BC, this masterpiece most likely became Roman imperial property before passing through the court of Frederick II Hohenstaufen in Palermo and ending up in Rome, where Lorenzo the Magnificent bought it in 1471. It takes good eyes to appreciate the rest of the collection because the pieces are small, but the ensemble as a whole is fascinating.

Once back out of the Gallery of the Farnese Bull and into the Gallery of Flora, turn right toward the rear of the building; this second half of the inner gallery contains more masterpieces, including one of the best versions of the emperor Hadrian's favorite, *Antinous,* as well as a pliant *Ganymede* with a threatening eagle farther down on the left. Below the stairs is the **Egyptian Collection.** Regrettably, there are currently few resting places and no refreshments available within the museum itself: The nearest options are in the Galleria across the road and in the pedestrianized area in front of the Accademia delle Belle Arti (Academy of Fine Arts) reachable through the Gallery. ✉ *Piazza Museo,* ☎ *081/440166.* 🖳 *€7.23.* ⊘ *Wed.–Mon. 9–7:30 (center core collection; other collections may only be open during mid-day hours).*

★ ㉜ **Museo di Capodimonte.** The grandiose 18th-century Neoclassic Bourbon royal palace, in the vast Bosco di Capodimonte (Capodimonte Park), which served as the royal hunting preserve and later as the site of the Capodimonte porcelain works, is a spectacular setting for Naples's finest collection of old master paintings and decorative arts. Perched on top of a hill overlooking all of Naples and the bay, the palace was built in 1738 by Charles III of Bourbon as a hunting retreat, then expanded by Antonio Medrano—architect of the Teatro San Carlo—to become the repository of the fabled Farnese art collection he inherited from his mother, Elizabeth Farnese. For this art-loving king, however, collecting was not enough; to compete with his father-in-law, Frederick Augustus, the Elector of Saxony, who had founded the celebrated

Meissen porcelain factory, Charles decided to set up his own royal factory, opposite the Capodimonte Palace (today still an art college), and before long, the "soft-paste" porcelain figurines of Pulcinello, biscuit vendors, and pretty nymphs were the chicest collectibles for Europe's rich. Fittingly, the most unique room in the palace is entirely crafted from porcelain (3,000 pieces of it)—**Queen Maria Amalia's Porcelain Parlor** (1757–59), built for the royal palace at Portici but relocated here.

But Capodimonte's greatest treasure is the excellent collection of paintings, well displayed in the **Galleria Nazionale** on the palace's first and second stories. Before you arrive at this remarkable collection, a magnificent staircase leads to the royal apartments, where you'll find beautiful antique furniture, most of it on the splashy scale so dear to the Bourbons, and a staggering collection of porcelain and majolica from the various royal residences. The walls of the apartments are hung with numerous portraits, providing a close-up of the unmistakable Bourbon features, a challenge to any court painter. The main galleries on the first floor are devoted to work from the 13th to the 18th centuries, including many familiar masterpieces by Dutch and Spanish masters, as well as by the great Italians: Simone Martini's *St. Louis Crowning King Robert* (1317), Masaccio's *Crucifixion* (1426), Giovanni Bellini's *Transfiguration* (1480), Annibale Carracci's *Pietà* (1600), Parmigianino's *Antea* (1531), Gentileschi's *Judith and Holofernes* (1630), Caravaggio's *Flagellation* (1607–10), and a bevy of famous Titians, including the *Danaë* (1545).

On the top floor, a new set of galleries features international contemporary art—including Andy Warhol's *Mount Vesuvius,* painted when the artist visited Naples in 1985—while the second floor holds extensive collections of 14th- to 19th-century Neapolitan painting and decorative arts, including plenty of dramatic renditions of Vesuvius in all its raging glory. When you've had your fill of these, take time to admire the genuine article from the shady parkland outside, designed by Ferdinando Sanfelice and then adapted into the "natural" English style, which affords a sweeping view of the bay. You can get to the museum via Bus No. 24 from Piazza Municipio or Piazza Carità. ☒ *Via Miano 2 (Porta Piccola), Via Capodimonte,* ☏ *848/800288 (information and bookings for special exhibitions).* ▧ *€7.23; €6.19 from 2–5.* ◷ *Tues.–Sun. 8:30–7:30 (ticket office closes at 6:30). Closed Mon.*

㉚ Orto Botanico. Founded in 1807 by Joseph Bonaparte and Prince Joachim Murat as an oasis from hectic Naples, this is one of the largest of all Italian botanical gardens, comprising some 30 acres. Nineteenth-century greenhouses and picturesque paths hold an important collection of tree, shrub, cacti, and floral specimens from all over the world. Next to the Orto Botanico, with a 354-meter (387-yd) facade dwarfing Piazza Carlo III, is one of the largest public buildings in Europe, the Albergo dei Poveri, built in the 18th and 19th centuries to house the city's destitute and homeless; it is now a UNESCO World Heritage Site awaiting an ambitious restoration scheme. ☒ *Via Foria 223,* ☏ *081/449759.* ▧ *Free.* ◷ *By appointment Mon.–Fri. 9–2.*

★ **㉙ San Giovanni a Carbonara.** This sadly neglected church—many guides give it short shrift, if they don't omit it altogether—is a coherent complex of Renaissance architecture and sculpture that can hold its own against any church in Florence or Rome in terms of quality, if not size. Its curious name is the result of its location during medieval times near the city trash dump, where refuse was burned (carbonized); this location is just outside the Capuana Gate of the old city walls. Its history starts in 1339, when the Neapolitan nobleman Gualtiero Galeota gave a few houses and a vegetable garden to a small convent of Augustinian monks who ministered to the poor neighborhood nearby. Four years later, in admiration of the monks' simplicity and piety, he added another two contiguous gardens and built a church to his family's patron saint, John the Baptist. At this point, some monks moved out, judging the new complex too luxurious; however, King Ladislas judged it too small and 50 years later started a new church, enriching the complex enough to serve as a suitable site for his tomb (together with his sister and successor to the throne, Joan II). Redone in the 18th century and badly damaged in 1943, the church has been returned to its original appearance thanks to a conservation scheme.

To enter the church, go up the dramatic staircase in *piperno* stone with a double run of elliptical stairs—modeled after a 1707 design by Ferdinando Sanfelice (similar to other organ-curved stairways in Rome, such as the Spanish Steps). Together with the courtyard on top, this staircase formed the scene of one of the first major battles of the Neapolitan revolt against the Nazis in September–October 1943 (known as the Four Days of Naples). Upon entering the rectangular nave, the first thing you see is the Monument of the Miroballo family, which is actually a chapel on the opposite wall, finished by Tommaso Malvito and his workshop in 1519 for the Marchese Bracigliano; the magnificent statues in the semicircular arch immediately set the tone for this surprising repository of first-class Renaissance sculpture.

To the right—beyond the skeletal main altar which has recently been stripped of its 18th-century Baroque additions—is the suitably royal (59 ft tall), if not megalomaniacal, funerary monument of King Ladislas and Joan II, finished by Marco and Andrea da Firenze in 1428. Four monumental female statues of Virtues hold up the sarcophagi of Ladislas and his sister, as well as statues of the two monarchs seated on thrones, and, finally, an energetic armed Ladislas on horseback being blessed by a bishop (the king died excommunicate, but you can buy anything in Naples). A door underneath this monument leads to the **Ser Caracciolo del Sole Chapel,** with its rare and beautiful original majolica pavement—the oldest (1427) produced in Italy, from a workshop in Campania, it shows the influence of Arab motifs and glazing technique.

Coming back out into the nave and immediately turning right at the altar, you enter another circular chapel, the **Caracciolo di Vico Chapel,** restored by the descendants of the Caracciolo family in 1997. This cohesive, sophisticated ensemble shows how Italian art history, first written by Tuscans with a regional agenda, tends to simplify the evolution of Renaissance art and architecture at the expense of other centers. The dating for the chapel is the object of debate; usually given as 1517, with the sculptural decor complete by 1557, the design (usually attributed to Tommaso Malvito) may go back to 1499 and thus precede the much more famous Tempietto in Rome, by Bramante, which it so resembles. In fact, the chapel's superlative quality has led some scholars to reject the traditional attribution and give it to Bramante himself or one of the Sangallos under the assumption that such a fine work should naturally be by someone quite famous. Coming once again into the nave, see if the next door on the right is open (or ask the custodian): this leads to the small rectangular room of the **Old Sacristy,** commissioned by the Caracciolo di Sant'Erasmo. The walls are decorated with 18 richly colored fresco panels depicting scenes from the Old and New testaments as well as saints and doctors of the Church, painted by Giorgio Vasari, disciple of Michelangelo and godfather of Renaissance art history. (Note that the sacristy was closed for restoration at press time.) Outside the church in the courtyard there is a chapel on the right (the Chapel of the Crucifix), with a *Crucifixion* by Giorgio Vasari, and the tomb of Antonio Seripando (1539). You can be thankful this great church is off the path of tour groups so you can absorb the ordered beauty of the decoration in peace. ⊠ *Via San Giovanni a Carbonara 5,* ☎ *081/295873.* ☉ *Mon.–Sat. 9:30–1.*

Funiculi, Funiculà: The Vomero to the Lungomare

When the French writer and philosopher Montesquieu visited Naples in 1728, he exclaimed: "Nothing is more beautiful than the siting of Naples in the gulf: Naples is like an amphitheater on the sea." This tour starts at the top of that theater—the Vomero Hill—then goes back down to its elegant "orchestra" level: Naples's waterfront area, the Lungomare, which runs from the Riviera di Chiaia to the Castel dell'Ovo, the harbor castle. Neapolitans often say their town's glories are vertical—the white *guglia* obelisks that festoon the historic quarter, the eight-story tenements of Spaccanapoli, and Vomero, the towering hill that overlooks the city center. Even longtime residents love to head up here to gaze in wonder at the entire city from the balcony belvedere of the Museo di San Martino. Before them, a big rich spread of southern Italian amplitude fills the eye: hillsides dripping with wedding-cake hotels, miles of villainously ugly apartment houses, streets short and narrow—leading to an unspeakable as well as unsolvable traffic problem—countless church spires and domes, and far below, the reason it all works, the intensely blue Bay of Naples. To tie together the lower parts and upper reaches of the city, everyone uses the *funivia*—the cable-car system that runs on three separate routes up and down the Vomero. Before you know it, you can be hopping and skipping over the city with these funiculars, whistling, of course, "Funiculì-funiculà," the famous 1880 song composed by Neapolitans Peppino Turco and Luigi Danza to celebrate the opening of the first line.

Thanks to the funiculars, you can readily take in many of Naples's aristocratic pleasures and treasures: the chic Piazza dei Martiri sector; the gilded 19th-century Villa Pignatelli; three museums that crown the Vomero Hill—the Villa Floridiana, the Certosa di San Martino, and the Castel Sant'Elmo; the Lungomare, the most champagne stretch of waterfront in Naples; and finally, the historic Pizzofalcone quarter. In the 19th century Naples's waterfront harbored the picturesque quarter that was called Santa Lucia, a district dear to artists and musicians and known for its fishermen's cottages. The fishermen were swept away when an enormous landfill project extended the land out to what is now Via Nazario Sauro and Via Partenope, the address for some of Naples's finest hotels. Today, the waterfront promenade has lost much of its former color, but it still retains a uniquely Neapolitan charm.

A Good Walk

Begin at the main station of the Funicolare Centrale, on the tiny Piazza Duca d'Aosta, just opposite the Via Toledo entrance to the Galleria Umberto I. After two hillside stops, get off at the end of the line, Stazione Fuga, near the top of the Vomero Hill. To get to the Castel Sant'Elmo/Certosa di San Martino complex, head out from the station, turning right on Via Cimarosa, then left on Via Morghen. At the next street, Via Scarlatti—the main thoroughfare of the neighborhood—turn right and walk up the steps of the hill, cut twice across the snake-like Via Morghen, then follow the path around the left side of the Montesanto funicular until you run into the Via Tito Angelini. This street, lined with some of Naples's best Belle Epoque mansions, leads to the **Castel Sant'Elmo** ㉝ and the adjoining **Certosa di San Martino** ㉞, which commands magnificent vistas over city and sea to Vesuvius. After viewing this enormous complex (its star exhibition is the collection of

Presepe, or Nativity, scenes), backtrack to Via Scarlatti until you make a left on Via Bernini at Piazza Vanvitelli. This piazza, with no shortage of smart bars and trattorias, remains the center for the Vomero district, and is also the site of the city's first pedestrianism project (Via Scarlatti, between Piazza Vanvitelli and Via Luca Giordano), now a fun gathering point for talented street performers. Walk right onto Via Cimarosa for two blocks until you reach the entrance to the **Villa Floridiana** ㉟, today a museum filled with aristocratic knickknacks and surrounded by a once-regal park. After viewing the villa, make a right from the park entrance on Via Cimarosa for two blocks until you reach the Stazione Cimarosa of the Chiaia funicular, which will take you back down to the Lungomare area. From the Amedeo funicular station walk down Via del Parco Margherita, past Piazza Amedeo, making a left onto Via Colonna, and taking the first right onto the steps at the top of Via Bausan. The steps will take you down to the Riviera di Chiaia (*chiaia* means "beach" in the Neapolitan dialect), where a final right turn brings you to the **Villa Pignatelli** ㊱, whose red-velvet salons still seem warm with the spirits of the Rothschilds, Actons, and other aristos who once called this home. From here cross the Riviera to the waterfront park of the Villa Comunale and its **Aquarium** ㊲.

For a late lunch, follow the Riviera past the Piazza della Vittoria onto Via Partenope and the spectacular **Castel dell'Ovo** ㊳. In its shadow is the enchanting **Borgo Marinaro** ㊴—a dollhouse of a fishermen's village, where seafood restaurants offer good food. From here, take a left turn on Via Partenope and then the first right onto Via Dumas, cross Via Chiatamone parallel to Via Partenope and climb the Rampa di Pizzofalcone to your right, a quiet road closed to through traffic. This will take you up to the top of historic hill of **Pizzofalcone,** also known as Monte Echia, site of the very first Greek settlement in the area. Transformed into an elegant residential quarter in the Baroque and Rococo periods, the area is gradually shaking off its neglected, traffic-ridden reputation of recent years and undergoing a long-awaited clean-up. Explore the church of **Santa Maria degli Angeli** ㊵ (if it's after 4:30 PM when churches reopen for evening hours). View Naples's finest 18th-century palace courtyard at the **Palazzo Serra di Cassano** ㊶, then take in **Santa Maria Egiziaca** ㊷. Check out if there is any theatrical performance you wish to attend at the Pizzofalcone's theater, the Politeama. Return to the church of Santa Maria degli Angeli on Via Nicotera to find the elegant Empire-era Ponte di Chiaia, a 17th-century gateway restored in the 1880s. To view the gateway properly, take the elevator down—*never* take the neighboring stairway, as its deserted route makes it a haunt for juvenile delinquents—to the elegant shopping and dining of the Chiaia district. If you're looking for a place for a pizza dinner, not far away is Naples's most historic pizzeria, Brandi, at Salita Sant'Anna di Palazzo 1. Head back along Via Chiaia to the Piazza dei Martiri to join chic Neapolitans on their evening *passeggiata,* shopping the boutiques, bookstores, and antiques shops lining the streets that radiate off the piazza (particularly the designer-dense stretch of Via dei Mille). The Metropolitana Piazza Amedeo station is nearby, while the R3 bus route, Tram 1, and Bus 140 follow the Riviera di Chiaia, which is the main avenue of the Lungomare.

TIMING

As always in Naples, it's best to start out early in the morning to fit most of your sightseeing in before the luncheon break—and the midday heat. Allow at least two hours to look round the San Martino complex and the adjacent Castel Sant'Elmo and a further half-hour for the Villa Floridiana, being careful to time your visit to coincide with the tours. If you run out of steam at the end of the morning, there are a number of relaxed snack and dining options in the Vomero, though without the atmospheric backdrop of the Borgo Marinaro down at sea level.

Numbers in the text correspond to numbers in the margin and on the Naples map.

Sights to See

㊲ Aquarium. Named by the Greeks after the mermaid Parthenope (who slew herself after being rejected by Odysseus, at least in the poet Virgil's version), it is only fitting that Naples should have established one of Europe's first public aquariums in 1874. At the time—when, not so incidentally, the public imagination was being stirred by Jules Verne's Captain Nemo and Hans Christian Andersen's Little Mermaid—technological innovations came into place to funnel seawater directly from the bay into the aquarium tanks, which showcase some 200 species of fish and marine plants (undoubtedly better off here than in the somewhat polluted Bay of Naples, their natural habitat). Officially named the Stazione Zoologica, founded by the German scientist Anton Dohrn, and housed in a Stil Liberty building designed by Adolf von Hildebrandt, the aquarium quickly became the wonder of Naples for children and art-exhausted adults. Today the ground floors contain the aquarium tanks—fishy "living rooms" decorated with rocks and plants of the region and all illuminated by skylights. Upstairs are research facilities and the library, which is decorated with Hans von Marées's magnificent mosaics showing the Lungomare area as it looked when the Aquarium opened, which was then set directly on the water. To see the library you need to make a special request when buying your tickets. ⊠ *Stazione Zoologica, Viale A. Dohrn,* ☎ *081/5833263 for information and library visits,* 𝗪𝗘𝗕 *www.szn.it.* ⊠ *€1.54.* ☉ *Mar.–Oct., Tues.–Sat. 9–6, Sun. 9:30–7:30; Nov.–Feb., Tues.–Sat. 9–5, Sun. 9–2.*

★ ㊴ Borgo Marinaro. If your thoughts of Naples involve the strumming of a mandolin, fishermen singing "Santa Lucia," and idyllic seaside sunsets, the city can be a sad disappointment—that is, until you venture to the Borgo Marinaro, a toy fishermen's village nestled in the shadows of mighty Castel dell'Ovo. After the cholera epidemic of 1884, entire quarters of the city were demolished and the rubble was transported to the Santa Lucia quarter as *colmata,* or landfill. For the most part, picturesque fishermen's houses were replaced by the Lungomare's luxurious hotels, but something of old Naples remains here at this little harbor port, officially called the Porto di Santa Lucia. Adorned with kitschy seafood restaurants, lovely outdoor cafés, and thriving boat shops, it inhabits the small islet called Megaris by the ancients and now connected to the mainland by the mole-pier of the Castel dell'Ovo. From the Santa Lucia shrine (just under the mole), stroll along the Lungomare past the Hotel Excelsior to the **Fontana dell'Immacolatella** (1622), sculpted by Pietro Bernini, father of the famous Gianlorenzo, which frames a great vista of Vesuvius. ⊠ *Via Partenope, at Castel dell'Ovo.*

㊳ Castel dell'Ovo. The oldest castle in Naples, the Castel dell'Ovo sits on the most picturesque point of the bay, standing guard over the city it protects. Occupying the isle of Megaris, it was originally the site of the Roman villa of Lucullus—proof, if you need it, that the ancient Romans knew a premium location when they saw one (for the same reason, some of the city's top hotels share the same site today). By the 12th century, it had become a fortress under the Normans; it was once the prison of Conradin and of Beatrice, daughter of Manfred, last of the Hohenstaufen rulers. Its name refers to the legend that the poet Virgil saw a magical egg rise from the waves here. This must have been one tough egg to crack, as the fortress still looks awe-inspiring and impregnable, although it lost many of its towers and battlements centuries ago. Today, it is also used as a conference center and exhibition gallery, and if you can attend one of the events here, such as the September Antiqua show, do so: The castle's gigantic rooms, rock tunnels, and belvederes over the bay are among Naples's most striking sights. ⊠ *Via Partenope, at the Borgo Marinaro,* ☎ *081/2400055.* ⊒ *Free.* ⊙ *Mon.–Sat. 9–5, Sun. 9–1:30.*

㉝ Castel Sant'Elmo. Long a powerful symbol of foreign and governmental domination, the imposing fortress of the Castel Sant'Elmo broods over the city center from its hilltop perch above the Vomero and seems to be policing you wherever you walk in Naples. Originally built by Charles I of Anjou in 1275 and enlarged by the Angevin kings in the 1330s, it was transformed in the 16th century by Pedro Scrivà under viceroy Don Pedro de Toledo into its present stoutly fortified six-point-star configuration. The castle cells housed many prisoners over the centuries, including the philosopher monk Tommaso Campanella (1568–1639), leaders of the Masaniello rebellion, and even patriots of the short-lived 1799 Neapolitan revolution against the Bourbons. From the ramparts panoramic views of the city extend in all directions. Today the great rooms of the castle often host temporary exhibitions and conferences. ⊠ *Largo San Martino,* ☎ *081/5784030.* ⊒ *€1.29.* ⊙ *Tues.–Sun. 9–2.*

★ **㉞ Certosa di San Martino.** Atop a rocky promontory with a fabulous view of the entire city, and with majestic salons that would please any monarch, the Certosa di San Martino is a monastery that seems more like a palace. In fact, by the 18th century Ferdinand IV was threatening to halt the order's government subsidy, so sumptuous was this *certosa*, or charterhouse, which had been started in 1325 under the royal patronage of Charles of Anjou. With the Carthusians's vast wealth and love of art, it was only a matter of time before dour Angevin Gothic was traded in for varicolor Neapolitan Baroque, thanks to the contributions of many 17th- and 18th-century sculptors and painters. Although the Angevin heritage can be seen in the pointed arches and cross-vaulted ceiling of the Certosa Church across the courtyard just opposite the ticket barrier, the church was overhauled from 1631 onward, partly as a response to Naples's deliverance from Vesuvius the same year. Other pre-1631 survivors are the remarkable wooden inlaid cupboards in the sacristy (1587–1600), at the back left of the church: the top row shows stories from the Scriptures while the bottom row regales us with fine (imaginary) perspectives.

The sacristy leads into the later Cappella del Tesoro, with Luca Giordano's ceiling fresco of Judith holding aloft Holofernes's head and the painting by Il Ribera (the *Pietà* over the altar is one of his masterpieces). The Baroque signature style note was set by Cosimo Fanzago (1591–1678), an architect, sculptor, and decorator who was as devout as he was mad. His polychrome marble work is at its finest here in the church, while he displays a gamut of sculptural skills in the **Chiostro Grande** (Great Cloister), also adding the curious small monks' graveyard, bounded by a marble balustrade topped with marble skulls. Fanzago's ceremonial portals at each corner of the cloister are among the most spectacular of all Baroque creations—aswirl with Mannerist volutes and Michelangelo-esque ornament, they serve as mere frames for six life-size statues of Carthusian saints, who sit atop the doorways, judging all with deathless composure.

Most of the monastery, which was suppressed in 1861, now serves as a museum. For a sound introduction to monastic life and a well-signposted history of the Carthusians and San Martino, see the panoramic renovated galleries of the **Museo dell'Opera** around the Chiostro Grande. Room 24 has a helpful 18th-century scale model of the monastic complex, while Room 26 has 19th-century paintings of monastic life. Dalbono's 13 gouaches of Vesuvius in various angry poses are attractively displayed in Room 28. If you're beginning to think that the 17th century in Naples was all grand masters and opulence, Room 37 and the various paintings depicting the plague might correct that impression. Nearby is the **Sezione Presepiale,** the greatest collection of Nativity crèches in the world. Ranging in size from a nutshell to an entire room, they offer supreme evocations of 18th-century life. Many figures are garbed in exquisite costumes and with portraitlike faces. The most noted is the *Presepe Cuciniello,* with more than 160 shepherds, eight dogs, countless angels, Moors, chickens, cheese wheels, beggars, and dwarfs, all worshiping the holy family against a brilliant blue sky. If visiting around the Christmas period, expect to share the displays with hundreds of Italian schoolchildren unless you manage to arrive at opening time in the morning.

Just by the entrance to the monastery's terraced gardens and plush 19th-century carriages is the **Quarto del Priore,** the prior's apartment, which was the residence of the only monk who had any contact with the outside world. It is an extravaganza filled with frescoes, 18th-century majolica-tiled floors, and paintings, with extensive gardens where scenic pergolati overlook the bay—a domicile that might be called the very vestibule of heaven. ⊠ *Museo Nazionale di San Martino, Largo San Martino,* ☎ *081/5781769.* ▨ *€5.68, including admission to the adjacent Castel Sant'Elmo.* ⊙ *Tues.–Sun. 8:30–7. Some rooms are often closed afternoons (Quarto del Priore), while others are opened up seasonally (Sezione Presepiale).*

㊸ La Nunziatella. In 1736 the Jesuits asked Ferdinando Sanfelice, then at work several blocks away on the magnificent Palazzo Serra di Cassano, to transform a novitiate into a church; the result is one of the jewels of 18th-century Neapolitan architecture, with rich but not overwhelming marble-inlay work and an excellent series of contemporary frescoes by Francesco de Mura. The interior of the church can occasionally be viewed in the morning if you ask the guard or chaplain at the adjoining military college, but usually you need official permission from the Ministry of Defence. ⊠ *Via Generale Parisi,* ☎ *081/7641520.*

★ **㊶ Palazzo Serra di Cassano.** By the late 18th century, Via Monte di Dio had become one of Naples's poshest addresses. Lined with palazzi and villas, it was chosen by Prince Aloisio Serra di Cassano for his family palace, designed by Ferdinando Sanfelice, the most important architect of domestic architecture in Naples. In this city where spectacle and love of show have always been important, the appropriately gigantic double-flight staircase that Sanfelice built in the palace courtyard wouldn't have been out of place in a lavish 1950s MGM musical. The regal staircase was reduced to back-door status when the palazzo's main door on Via Egiziaca was closed by the prince in honor of his son Gennaro, executed as one of the participants in the 1799 revolution. Today the Istituto Italiano per gli Studi Filosofici, an institute devoted to philosophy studies, occupies much of the palazzo; it offers a full calendar of courses and lectures throughout the year. ⊠ *Via Monte di Dio 14–15,* ☎ *081/2452150.* ⊙ *Weekdays 7:30–1 and 3–7, Sat. 7–noon.*

Pizzofalcone. In the 7th century BC, Pizzofalcone (Falcon's Beak) *was* Naples. The ancient Greeks had settled here because, legend says, the body of the siren Parthenope had been found washed ashore on the beach at the foot of the Pizzofalcone Hill, then known as Monte Echia. Over two millennia later, in the 18th century, the hill, mere feet from the bay and the Castel dell'Ovo, became a fashionable address as Naples's rich and titled sought to escape the congestion and heat of the city center. The rocky promontory soon became studded with Baroque palaces and rococo churches. You can walk up to Pizzofalcone by taking Via G. Serra just to the right-hand colonnade of the Church of San Francesco di Paola, on Piazza del Plebiscito, to Pizzofalcone's main piazza, Santa Maria degli Angeli, or take the elevator during daylight hours (never the dark staircase) by the bridge on Via Chiaia. The leading sights are the palazzi along Via Monte di Dio—including Palazzo Serra di Cassano—and the churches of La Nunziatella, Santa Maria degli Angeli, and Santa Maria Egiziaca. Like other parts of Naples, Pizzofalcone harbors both palaces and slums; unlike other parts, it's off the beaten path, so don't stop to answer questions from seemingly innocuous strollers. ⊠ *Piazza Santa Maria degli Angeli, accessed via the elevator at the Ponte di Chiaia on Via Chiaia.*

40 **Santa Maria degli Angeli a Pizzofalcone.** In 1590 the princess of Sulmona, Costanza Doria del Carretto, commissioned this church not far from her palace on Pizzofalcone. In the 17th century the church was given to the Theatine order and enlarged by an architect belonging to the order. The lively vault and dome frescoes are by Giovanni Beinaschi from Turin, better known as a painter of genre scenes, and there are some good paintings by Luca Giordano and Massimo Stanzione tucked away in the smaller side chapels and oratory. ⊠ *Piazza Santa Maria degli Angeli,* ☎ *081/7644974.* ☉ *Daily 7:30–11:30 and 5:30–7.*

42 **Santa Maria Egiziaca a Pizzofalcone.** This church is probably the masterpiece of Cosimo Fanzago, a Lombard architect and sculptor who became one of the leading innovators of Neapolitan Baroque. The octagonal form of the church was to influence the work of many of his contemporaries, although Fanzago was never to finish this church; the project died a natural death in 1665 along with that of its patron, Spanish king Philip IV. The white cupola—contrasting starkly with the rest of the skyscape in this area—was only completed in 1714 and the church first consecrated in 1717. ⊠ *Via Egiziaca 30,* ☎ *081/7645199.* ☉ *Daily 9:30–1.*

35 **Villa Floridiana.** Now a chiefly residential neighborhood, the Vomero Hill was once the patrician address of many of Naples's most extravagant estates. La Floridiana is the sole surviving 19th-century example, built in 1817 on order of Ferdinand I for Lucia Migliaccio, duchess of Floridia—their portraits greet you as you enter. Only nine shocking months after his first wife, the Habsburg Maria Carolina, died, when the court was still in mourning, Ferdinand secretly married Lucia, his longtime mistress. Scandal ensued, but the king and his new wife were too happy to worry, escaping high above the city and court gossip to this elegant little estate. Designed by architect Antonio Niccolini in Neoclassic style, the house is now occupied by the **Museo Nazionale della Ceramica Duca di Martina**, a museum devoted to the decorative arts of the 18th and 19th centuries. Countless display cases are filled with what Edith Wharton described as "all those fragile and elaborate trifles the irony of fate preserves when brick and marble crumble": Sèvres, Limoges, and Meissen porcelains, gold watches, ivory fans, glassware, enamels, majolica vases. Sadly, there are no period rooms left to see. Due to economic measures, escorted visits (not tours per se) are now provided through the myriad rooms. Outside is a park designed in the English style by Degenhardt, who also designed the park at Capodimonte. Nannies and their charges walk along the winding paths between spreading pines and araucarias, while joggers head for the cool of the holm-oak wood on the shady east side. Unfortunately, and despite the army of park attendants and gardeners, the park is not well tended—graffiti defaces the Grecian Tempietto and red plastic fencing prevents access to much of the panoramic viewing platform at the bottom of the park. ✉ *Via Cimarosa 77,* ☎ *081/5788418.* ▨ € *2.60.* ☽ *Museum Mon.–Sat. 9:30, 11, and 12:30 (escorted visits); park 9–1 hr before sunset.*

NEED A
BREAK?

Walking down the fashionable Via Scarlatti in the Vomero, once a traffic-choked artery and now a bustling pedestrian precinct, you'll come upon **Bar Daniele** (✉ Via Scarlatti 104, ☎ 081/5780555), a stalwart Vomero café producing a wide range of cakes and waist-threatening delicacies. If you need something more substantial, look at the *rosticceria* selection at the back.

㊱ Villa Pignatelli. More officially known as the Museo Diego Aragona Pignatelli Cortes, this is one of the few patrician homes of old Naples that is open to the public. When built in 1826 by architect P. Valente for the aristocratic Acton family (Sir Harold Acton, who died in the mid-1990s, was the author of many books on Neapolitan history; Princess Acton, whose family to this day hosts the best New Year's Eve parties in Naples, still occupies the family palazzo, which towers over nearby Via Chiaia), it was one was of the city's premier houses, with a imperially grand Grecian-temple front and a beautiful park. In 1841 the barons Rothschild took over and redid rooms in Second Empire splendor, including the leather-lined smoking salon and the Sala Rosso, a red velvet-and-gold jewel box. Prince Pignatelli Cortes's daughter donated the house to the city in 1952, and he must be spinning in his grave at the shoddy state of the house today, its lighting dimmed, enough dust to cover Pompeii, and rooms used as warehouses. The house may be spruced up for some of the temporary exhibitions held here from time to time, but it usually looks like a set for Violetta's death scene in *La Traviata*. What makes a visit worthwhile is the Banco di Napoli art collection on the *piano nobile*, with fine works by the 19th-century sculptor Vincenzo Gemito and a delightful gallery of 18th- and 19th-century landscapes (Room 6). On the grounds is a carriage house (currently undergoing restoration) that contains the **Museo delle Carrozze** (Carriage Museum), with coaches from the late 1800s to the early 1900s. A stroll in the park here is a pleasant respite from the noisy city streets. ✉ *Riviera di Chiaia 200,* ☎ *081/669675.* ▨ €*2.06.* ☽ *Tues.– Sun. 8:30–7:30.*

OFF THE
BEATEN PATH

PARCO VIRGILIANO AND POSILLIPO – At the far western end of the city lie two of Naples's most tranquil spots—the Parco Virgiliano, named after the great ancient Roman poet Virgil, and the suburb of Posillipo. The park is still beautiful and is, according to legend, the site of the poet's tomb, which is now judged to be an anonymous Roman *columbarium* (funerary monument). It is set not far from both the Crypta Neapolitana, an ancient Roman tunnel now caved in, and the tomb-memorial of Giacomo Leopardi, the noted 19th-century poet. The vista from the bluff overlooking the bay and city is world famous. Gain access to the park from behind the church of Santa Maria di Piedigrotta, close to Piazza Piedigrotta, just outside the Stazione di Mergellina station. The park rises to the left immediately after the railway bridge crossing Via Piedigrotta, just before the road tunnel entrance. Farther to the west along the coast is the seaside suburb of Posillipo, whose name comes from the ancient Greek *Pausilypon* ("respite from pain"). This was once the place for Naples's most idyllic shoreline and villas, but is now sadly overrun with apartment buildings. Still, the beaches and coves here harbor picturesque spots like the hamlet of Marechiaro ("clear sea")—home to two of Naples's best restau-

rants and some of the city's nicest beaches and bathing establishments—
and not far from the Palazzo Donn'Anna, built by Cosimo Fanzago for
the wife of the Spanish viceroy in 1637 and one of the city's most romantic, legend-haunted structures; another fabled abode, the former casino-
villa of Sir William Hamilton, is nearby (both villas are still private). Bus
route No. 140 trundles along Via Posillipo and the sea, climbing steadily
towards the headland at the end of the run. The headland of Posillipo at
the end of Viale Virgilio, called "Parco della Rimembranza" (confusingly
also known as the Parco Virgiliano) will probably become an archaeological park, but until that time, probably in 2003, it is a semi no-go
area. You can get to Posillipo's famed Marechiaro area by bus on a
fairly circuitous route (bus No. 11), although it will be quicker to be left at
the main street (by bus No. 140) and walk down to the water. (Bus No.
11 currently runs every half-hour, but only during the day and weekends—it is the only route which has a timetable posted at every bus stop
and runs rather infrequently at night, so a taxi is often the best option.) ⊠
Parco Virgiliano, Salita della Grotta 20, ☎ *081/669390.* ▨ *Free.* ☉
9–1 hr before sunset.

DINING

Let's be honest: you really want a traditional Neapolitan dinner with
lots of tomato sauce and a great show of Neapolitan love songs to get
you crying into your limoncello. There's no reason to feel guilty, because even the natives love to get into the spirit. But listening to someone warble "Santa Lucia" while feasting on a pizza *Margherita* (with
basil, mozzarella, and tomatoes) from a table overlooking the Bay of
Naples is just one example of the pleasures awaiting diners in Naples.
From *vitello alla Principe di Napoli* (veal garnished with truffles) to
sea bass in *acqua pazza*—that is to say, poached in water "maddened"
with anchovy, bay leaves, *peperoncino,* and olive oil—to Neapolitan
pastries like ricotta-rich *babà al Rhum,* the city expresses its gastronomic self in many ways. The *haute*-hungry should look elsewhere (particularly Ristorante Don Alfonso 1890, just across the bay in Sorrento)
and so should those in search of newer-than-now nouvelle flights of
fantasy, designer plates, and *dernier-cri* fusion dishes. While these can
be found, the cuisine in Naples is by and large earthy, pungent, and
delicioza, as attested to by those signature dishes: *mozzarella in car-
rozza* (mozzarella in a carriage, with the cheese fried between two slices
of bread); *polpo all luciana* (octopus stewed with garlic, peppers, and
tomatoes); *risotto ai frutti de mare* (seafood risotto); and *spaghetti puttanesca* (streetwalker's spaghetti). In Naples it is still the old reliables
that apply, the recipes time-tested by centuries of mammas that still
manage to put meat on your bones and smiles on your faces.

This means pizzerias aplenty. As the birthplace of pizza, Naples prides
itself on its vast selection of pizzerias, the most famous of which—Da
Michele, Brandi, or Trianon—deserve the encomium "incomparable."
Many Neapolitans make lunch their big meal of the day, then have a
pizza for supper or—just watch the jeweled operagoers at the Teatro
San Carlo head over to Ciro a Santa Brigida—a late-night treat.

When it comes to *i secondi*—or main dishes—you can find a first-rate
chicken offering, but the reason visitors to Naples want to eat seafood
is a good one: geography. Naples's position, hugging a rich bay, has
guaranteed that marine creatures feature prominently on local menus.
Marinated seafood salad (*insalata di frutti di mare*) is a classic antipasto,
as well as marinated white anchovies (*alici*). Spaghetti *con le vongole
veraci* (with clams, garlic, and a baby's fistful of chopped flat-leaf Ital-

HEY, IT NEVER TASTED LIKE THIS BACK HOME

THERE'S NO PIZZA LIKE real Neapolitan pizza. If you don't believe it, try one at **Ciro a Santa Brigida** (✉ Via Santa Brigida 71, ☎ 081/5524072). This restaurant is a little more upscale than a typical Neapolitan pizzeria, but its pizza is the real thing, and it's proper to eat it with your napkin stuffed into your shirt to avoid tomato stains. The restaurant's owner, Antonio Pace, president of the True Neapolitan Pizza Association, is behind an unusual initiative to upgrade the quality of pizza worldwide. Mr. Pace and Professor Carlo Mangoni di Santo Stefano, a nutritionist at the University of Naples, have written what they call a Pizza Discipline, a treatise that discusses everything from the history of pizza to the correct ingredients for the perfect Neapolitan pie. Based on the Pizza Discipline, the city of Naples recently registered a logo that pizzerias can hang in their window if, and only if, they serve true Neapolitan pizza. That means using sinfully luscious buffalo-milk mozzarella made in certain areas near Naples, kneading the dough for a full 30 minutes, and letting it rise for four hours. (The "discipline" includes photos of dough taken through a microscope before and after it has risen.)

It may take a while before pizzerias around the globe actually hang the logo in their windows. But the city of Naples wants it to eventually be a sign of quality as distinctive as the DOC (*Denominazione di Origine Controllata*, or denomination of controlled origin) on wine labels. The logo will be blue, with Mt. Vesuvius in the background, a red pizza with mozzarella in the center, and PIZZA NAPOLETANA written across the foreground. Make sure you're the first to spot it!

Some pizza history, as recounted by Professor Mangoni (who scoffs at claims that pizza was invented in the United States):

Pizza marinara, which doesn't have mozzarella at all but is simply a pie with tomatoes, garlic, oregano, and olive oil, first appeared in Naples around 1760. King Ferdinand of Naples liked the pizza, but his wife, a Habsburg princess, wouldn't allow pizza in the palace. The king would often sneak out to one of the world's first pizzerias, making the places famous.

Even earlier, there's a mention of plates of flour with other food on top in Homer's *Iliad*, but Professor Mangoni says this was just a precursor to pizza, not the real thing. Tomato sauce, says Mangoni, dates back to 1733.

Mozzarella came later. The pizza Margherita was invented in 1889, when Naples chef Raffaele Esposito was called on to prepare a meal for the Italian Queen, Margherita. He made a pizza with tomato sauce and mozzarella, and his wife had the idea of adding basil to honor Italy's red, white, and green flag.

According to the Pizza Discipline, the only true pizzas are marinara and Margherita. Anchovies, pepperoni, and so on are heresy. So don't expect to see the logo with Mt. Vesuvius at your local pizza joint anytime soon.

In Antonio Pace's family, pizza goes back a long way. He claims his grandfather's grandfather made pizza in 1856. Pizza fact or fiction aside, at Ciro a Santa Brigida, everything is delicious. Ask for a taste of plain buffalo mozzarella and just savor it in your mouth. If you have a lactose intolerance, there's still hope—Professor Mangoni and his team of scientists are developing lactose-free mozzarella. If they manage to match the taste of real mozzarella, he says, pizzerias will be allowed to use it and still display the Pizza Napoletana logo. Go figure.

ian parsley) is of course a popular and dependable standard, as are myriad variations on linguine or fresh pasta with mixed seafood (mussels, shrimp, clams, and so forth), usually "stained" with fresh cherry tomatoes. As for seafood Neapolitan style, the best—*spigola* (sea bass), *pesce spada* (swordfish), and, if you can find it, the *San Pietro* (sort of a sole for grown-ups) is grilled simply and ennobled with a splash of olive oil and a squeeze of lemon. Fresh calamari, kissed lightly by a grill, can be exquisitely delicate, but the fried version, which can be uniquely satisfying, is, alas, too often done these days with frozen squid. Another good way to have fish is *all'acqua pazza* (literally, in crazy water), poached with anchovy, bay leaves, red pepper, and olive oil, a brew said to have been invented by returning fishermen using seawater to cook up a meal on the beach.

In the end, veterans know that the best restaurants in Naples are the simplest. But no matter where you head, you'll be delighted (or exasperated, depending on how critical you are): after all, you're in Naples, and the mise-en-scène—Vesuvius as a backdrop to your flambéed chicken Vesuvio or a table on a charming alleyway—can't be beat. Note that many restaurants in Naples close up for at least a week around August 15 to celebrate the Ferragosto holidays.

CATEGORY	COST*
$$$$	over €43
$$$	€31–€43
$$	€13–€31
$	under €13

per person for a main course at dinner

City Center

Appropriately, the monumental city center features some of Naples's most famous restaurants.

$$–$$$ ✕ **Brandi.** If you haven't been to Brandi, you haven't been to Naples.
★ Forget that this historic place gave the world pizza Margherita—the classic combo of tomato sauce, mozzarella, and basil, named after King Umberto's queen. This is, hands down, one of the most picturesque restaurants in Italy. Set on a cobblestone alleyway just off chic Via Chiaia, it welcomes you with an enchanting wood-beamed salon festooned with 19th-century memorabilia, saint shrines, gilded mirrors, and bouquets of flowers, beyond which you can see the kitchen and some of Naples's most famous *pizzaioli* (pizza makers) at work. Upstairs are two tiny, rickety, low-ceiling rooms adorned with mirrors and celeb photos. Most Neapolitans stay away, but it's their loss: join Luciano Pavarotti, Chelsea Clinton, and groups of Japanese tourists to a very *delizioso* ambience. In addition to the Margherita, the menu features an array of other pizza choices plus a few meat and fish main courses. ✉ *Salita Sant'Anna di Palazzo 1,* ☎ *081/416928. AE, DC, MC, V. Closed Mon.*

$–$$ ✕ **Amici Miei.** A place favored by meat eaters who can't take another bite of sea bass, this small, dark, and cozy den of comfort is well loved for specials such as tender carpaccio with fresh artichoke hearts and a rice and arugula dish featuring duck breast. Happily, there are also excellent pasta dishes, such as *orecchiette* with chick-peas, or that extravaganza, the *carnevale lasagne,* an especially rich concoction relied on to sustain the taste buds in the build-up before Lent. Everyone ends with the homemade fruit tart. ✉ *Via Monte di Dio 78,* ☎ *081/7646063. AE, DC, MC, V. Reservations essential Fri. and Sat. eves. Closed Mon. and Aug. No dinner Sun.*

$–$$ ✗ **Ciro a Santa Brigida.** Off Via Toledo near the Castel Nuovo, Ciro has been an obligatory entry on any list of Neapolitan cooking (as opposed to cuisine) since 1932 and the days when Toscanini and Pirandello used to eat here. Popular with business travelers, artists, and journalists who prefer food over frills, Ciro is famous for a wide variety of canonical favorites with an emphasis on rustic food, from the very fine pizzas (lunchtimes, too) and their justly famed versions of *pasta e fagioli* to the classic *sartù*—rice loaf first conjured up by Baroque-era nuns—and the splendid *pignatiello e vavella*, or shellfish soup. The menu looks too large for all its items to be good, but the owners must be doing something right, since the place is often packed with Neapolitan regulars. The old waiters are darling wherever you sit, but try to get a table upstairs, which has a more pleasant atmosphere. ✉ *Via Santa Brigida 71,* ☎ *081/5524072,* WEB *www.ciroasantabrigida.it. AE, DC, V. Closed Sun. and last 2 wks in Aug.*

$–$$ ✗ **Dante e Beatrice.** Crowds still head here, but the chefs have gotten lazy in recent years making the glory days of this landmark a thing of the past. ✉ *Piazza Dante 44,* ☎ *081/549–9438. MC, V.*

Spaccanapoli

Rapidly becoming *the* evening location to combine *buona cucina* and both low-brow and high-brow culture, the super-picturesque neighborhood of Spaccanapoli has a large number of fairly inexpensive eateries which begin to fill up after 9 PM. Although several of the classier restaurants are closed at lunchtime, there's still plenty of choice both for lingering meals and quick streetside snacking.

$$–$$$ ✗ **'A Canzuncella.** This is one of those places where you can come for a traditional dinner accompanied by a show of Neapolitan crooners—a performance only an entrenched curmudgeon would fail to enjoy. On Saturday evenings, host and showman Aurelio Fierro lays on a special musical session, with banquet and entertainment for a combined price of €52. Standards of both *cucina* and *servizio* are high—as indeed it has to be for loyal but demanding clients, mainly drawn from the *Napoli bene* (Naples upper crust). ✉ *Piazza Santa Maria La Nova 17/18,* ☎ *081/5519018. Reservations essential Sat. eve. AE, DC, MC, V. Closed lunchtime and Sun. eve.*

$$ ✗ **La Taverna dell'Arte.** On a small side street near the university, this gracious trattoria, warmed with touches of wood, prides itself on its fresh interpretations of Neapolitan classics: excellent salami, mozzarella, and *frittate* (fried vegetables) among the appetizers, cabbage soup fragrant with good beef stock, and meat and fish grilled over wood. Typical Neapolitan desserts—babas and the familiar crunchy almond cookies called *quaresimali*—are served with homemade liqueurs. ✉ *Rampe San Giovanni Maggiore 1/a,* ☎ *081/5527558. MC, V. Reservations essential. No lunch. Closed Sun. and last 2 wks in Aug.*

$$ ✗ **Porta Venosa.** Affable owner-chef Corrado Pezzella has brought his years of experience in restaurants to fruition in one of Naples's most pleasant new establishments. The decor is resolutely contemporary and discreetly hip; the ever-changing menu features fresh variations on Mediterranean specialties (try the range of antipasti *deliziosi* featuring raw artichokes, arugula, and grana cheese, and asparagus rolled in bacon). Downstairs in the cellars of this 18th-century building is a special room which can be booked for gastronomic evenings (minimum 4 people, maximum 8). ✉ *Largo San Giovanni Maggiore 15,* ☎ *081/5526127. AE, DC, MC, V. Closed Sat. lunch and Sun.*

$$ ✗ **Vulcani.** Known as an *associazione culturale* and featuring a variety of evening cultural events, newly opened Vulcani is just down the road from the cloisters of Santa Chiara. Each table is given the name of a volcano—chef Rossella Celi has moved from the slopes of Etna to Vesuvius—and streams of memorable Sicilian platters, such as pasta *alla cavalfiore e prugne* (with cauliflower and plums) and *coniglio con la cioccolata* (rabbit in chocolate sauce), emerge from an unbelievably poky kitchen. Even the highly palatable house red wine, Nero d'Avola, is shipped specially from Trapani in western Sicily. ⊠ *Via Santa Chiara 25b,* ☎ *081/5526224. DC, MC, V. Closed Tues.*

$–$$ ✕ **Anima e Cozze.** Young, noisy, and hip, this new restaurant/bar is a friendly mixing spot at night and a great place for a take-out pizza or lunch roll while you're discovering Spaccanapoli. They have a wide and innovative selection of pizzas and a stimulating selection of salads for vegetarians who are tired of plain tomato and mozzarella. ⊠ *Piazza del Gesù Nuovo 26,* ☎ *081/5518427. DC, MC, V.*

$–$$ ✕ **Lombardi a Santa Chiara.** Located right on Spaccanapoli opposite the Palazzo Croce, home to the philosopher and historian Benedetto Croce, this is one of the city's most famous pizzerias, packed night after night. The young crowd heads down into the more boisterous basement, while the atmosphere upstairs is calmer and more congenial to conversation at standard decibel levels. You can watch the owner himself, Don Luigi, working the pizza dough, manipulating each pizza as if it were a live creation. ⊠ *Via Benedetto Croce 59,* ☎ *081/5520780,* WEB *www.paginegialle.it/lombardilu. AE, DC, MC, V. Closed Sun. and last 2 wks in Aug.*

$ ✕ **La Cantina di Via Sapienza.** There's a strong whiff of 1920s Paris intelligentsia in this hangout of students and young professionals, although the garb is now in Technicolor shades and every dish is spiced up with garlic. Busy and not big enough (expect to share a table—and if they're not shy, why should you be?), but the prices can't be beat, and the daily selection of a good dozen vegetable side plates merits a detour on its own, even if you're not a vegetarian. ⊠ *Via Sapienza 40,* ☎ *081/459078. No credit cards. Closed eves. and Sun.*

$ ✕ **Sorbillo.** The locals still wait in line for their turn to sit down and devour a basic Neapolitan pizza cooked to perfection—after all, the third generation of pizza-makers runs this place. Try the unique Pizza al pesto. Don't expect tablecloths: here you have the joy of eating on traditional white-marble table tops. ⊠ *Via dei Tribunali 32,* ☎ *081/446643. No credit cards. Closed Sun.*

Piazza Garibaldi and Environs

Forget waterfront restaurants and outdoor candlelit terraces. This is an area noted for fine no-nonsense eating, with some of the city's most traditional restaurants offering excellent value for money. If returning to base after dark, stick to well-lit main roads or ask one of the restaurant staff to order a taxi.

$$–$$$ ✕ **Mimì alla Ferrovia.** This Neapolitan version of a grand Parisian
★ brasserie is an institution—clients have included Fellini and that magnificent true-Neapolitan comic genius and fake noble, Totò—but even so, Mimì manages to live up cheerfully to its history, proudly serving fine versions of everything from pasta e fagioli to fresh fettuccine with lobster, or the sea bass *al presidente,* baked in a pastry crust and enjoyed by any number of Italian presidents on their visits to Naples. Not so much a place to see and be seen as a common ground where both the famous and the unknown can mingle, feast, and be of good cheer, Mimì is dressed in sober beige and green hues and accented with updated art deco features, pale-yellow tablecloths, and retro bentwood chairs—all of which pleasantly tone down the bustle. ⊠ *Via A. D'Aragona 19/21,* ☎ *081/289004,* WEB *www.mimiallaferrovia.com. AE, DC, MC, V. Closed Sun. and last 2 wks in Aug.*

70

Naples Dining and Lodging

KEY

┈┈┈┈ Funicular

1 Hotels

▦▦▦▦ Metro

──── Rail Lines

(1) Restaurants

0   300 yards

0   300 meters

$$ ✕ **La Fila.** To the north of the Stazione Centrale at Piazza Garibaldi, this family-run establishment was considerably brightened up in a 1997 remodeling. If the hostess insists on you having something, trust her, because the simplest dishes, so often done indifferently elsewhere, are here exquisite voyages of discovery: baked pasta with meatballs, pizza with pungent sausage kissed awake by the wood-fired oven, or the ubiquitous potato croquette, here made with respect, real mashed potatoes, and smoked provolone. ⊠ *Via Nazionale 6/c,* ☎ *081/206717. Reservations essential. No credit cards. Closed Mon.*

$–$$ ✕ **Triunfo.** A strikingly clean place near the Stazione Centrale, in a neighborhood that has seen better times, this restaurant sticks out for the quality of its pizza and draws a devoted clientele. The selection of cold antipasti, with lots of simply prepared vegetables, is a welcome change from the usual fried offerings, and the house pizza, with prosciutto and artichokes, makes a wonderful summer dinner. ⊠ *Vicolo II Duchesca 10,* ☎ *081/268948. V. Closed Mon.*

$ ✕ **Da Michele.** You have to love a place that has, for more than 130
★   years, offered only two types of pizza—marinara and Margherita— and a small selection of drinks, and still manages to line them up. The prices have something to do with it, but the pizza itself suffers no rivals, and even those waiting in line are good humored; the boisterous, joyous atmosphere wafts out with the smell of yeast and wood smoke onto the street. ⊠ *Via C. Sersale 1/3,* ☎ *081/5539204. No credit cards. Closed Sun. and last 2 wks in Aug.*

$ ✕ **Trianon.** Across the street from its archrival Da Michele, this is a classic pizzeria with a simple yet upscale Art Nouveau ambience expressed in soothing tile and marble. The classics (Margherita, marinara) are done in an exemplary manner, but you can also feast on pizza with sausage and broccoli greens, while the signature pizza Trianon comes with eight different toppings. ⊠ *Via P. Coletta 46,* ☎ *081/ 5539426. No credit cards. No lunch Sun.*

Santa Lucia and Chiaia

While Santa Lucia is a classic choice for both chic and touristy fish restaurants with that just-how-you-imagined-Naples sea view, the upscale area of Chiaia is a favorite with both locals and discerning expatriates and is likely to offer better value for money.

$$$–$$$$ ✕ **Caruso.** When you get the urge to dress up, head to the panoramic rooftop restaurant of the Hotel Vesuvio—a very chic locale that is not as expensive as you might think. The food wisely declines to compete with the view of the bay but instead accompanies it suavely. Seafood predominates, from the marinated *frutti di mare* and fish-stuffed ravioli to the classic grilled sea bass, but if you're tired of shrimp and such, try the delicate lemon risotto or the *bucatini alla Caruso* (tubular spaghetti with fresh tomatoes, sweet peppers, and sautéed zucchini). ⊠ *Hotel Vesuvio, Via Partenope 45,* ☎ *081/7640044,* 〼 *www.vesuvio.it. AE, DC, MC, V.*

$$$–$$$$ ✕ **La Cantinella.** A cool, curvy decor with bamboo armchairs and wrought-iron lamps, La Cantinella is a well-known address for sophisticated seafood dishes and a relaxed but luxurious atmosphere. A wide selection of appetizers, with all the Neapolitan specialties, including a very well done insalata di frutti di mare and a house appetizer with salmon in a zucchini crust on an eggplant ragout, leads into rigatoni with swordfish, onions, capers, and cherry tomatoes or pasta with tiny shrimp, clams, and green pepper. The abundant scampi *al gratin* are justly famous, but this is also a good place to try the less expensive *orata* (bream) *all'acqua pazza.* There is an extensive, reasonable, and well-organized wine list. ⊠ *Via Cuma 42,* ☎ *081/7648684,* 〼 *www. lacantinella.it. AE, DC, MC, V. Closed Sun. May–Oct.*

$$$ ✕ **Casanova Grill.** Soft lights and a trendy art-deco look set the tone at Hotel Excelsior's restaurant. The seasonal specialties and antipasti arranged on the buffet will whet your appetite for such traditional Neapolitan dishes as the simple *spaghetti al pomodoro* and the classic *carne* (meat) *alla pizzaiola.* ✉ *Hotel Excelsior, Via Partenope 48,* ☎ *081/7640111. AE, DC, MC, V.*

$$–$$$ ✕ **La Bersagliera.** On the port at Santa Lucia, in the shadow of the looming medieval Castel dell'Ovo, this spot is touristy but fun, with an irresistible combination of spaghetti and mandolins. Dalí and De Chirico, Sophia and Marcello all came here in the grand old days to enjoy uncomplicated time-tested classics, such as spaghetti with mixed seafood and eggplant *alla parmigiana.* But as any Neapolitan will tell you, simple grilled fish always tastes better when seasoned with sea air. ✉ *Borgo Marinaro 10,* ☎ *081/7646016,* WEB *www.labersagliera.it. AE, DC, MC, V. Closed Tues. and 2 wks in Aug.*

$–$$ ✕ **La Stanza del Gusto.** Set opposite the Teatro Sannazzaro on Via Chi-
★ aia, this welcome new entry amply lives up to its name (the "room of taste"). Located on an unbelievably quiet and leafy *vicoletto* (alley) near some of the city's busiest streets, the discreet ambience within reinforces the sense of escape from the hectic world outside. This is the place to try those stalwarts of Neapolitan cuisine, *soffritto*—a sauce made from liver, kidneys, lung, and other unmentionables—and *arancini* (rice-balls), here transformed almost beyond palatal recognition with prawns and local greens. ✉ *Vicoletto Sant'Arpino 21,* ☎ *081/401578. DC, MC, V. Reservations essential. Closed Sun., Mon., and Aug.*

$$ ✕ **'A Taverna é Zi Carmela.** Not far from the Villa Comunale gardens, this is a reasonable, family-run alternative in the pricey Santa Lucia area. Don't pay attention to the haphazard decor; the pizza is excellent, from the ubiquitous basics to such original specialties as the brashly-named *incazzata,* a calzone stuffed with spicy pasta *all'arrabbiata* (for those who can't decide if they want pizza or pasta). If you do want pasta, try the hearty gnocchi with beans, or the superb house spaghetti with fresh tomato and a perfectly cooked medley of fresh seafood. ✉ *Via Niccolò Tommaseo 11/12,* ☎ *081/7643581. No credit cards.*

$$ ✕ **Vadinchenia.** Serving up all the trimmings of a first-class restaurant
★ at surprisingly modest prices, husband-and-wife team Saverio and Silvana steer their guests through an innovative menu against a backdrop of refreshingly minimalist decor. Adventurous palates will enjoy bold combinations like *paccheri alle alici e pecorino* (pasta with sardines and sheep's cheese), while recidivist carnivores will delight in the filletto al vino *e sale grosso* with rock salt. ✉ *Via Pontano 21,* ☎ *081/ 660265 AE, DC, MC, V. Reservations essential. No lunch. Closed Sun. and Aug.*

$–$$ ✕ **I Re di Napoli.** With its inviting blue-and-green custom-tile interior and tables set along the seafront drive, this chic pizzeria is an essential hangout for Naples's gilded youth and really gets going toward midnight on weekends. The various stuffed pizzas named after kings are classics with a modern twist: try the *Boccone di Re Ferdinando,* filled with *speck* (lean cured pork), *provola* cheese, and artichokes. ✉ *Via Partenope 29/30,* ☎ *081/7647775. AE, MC, V.*

$–$$ ✕ **Marino.** This famous pizzeria offers up its delights in a cool white-and-blue room. Try the house specialty, the Anastasia, with cherry tomatoes and lots of premium mozzarella. Recent extensions to the sidewalk and partial pedestrianization of Via Santa Lucia make this a pleasant outdoor venue in summer. ✉ *Via Santa Lucia 118/120,* ☎ *081/ 7640280. AE, V. Closed Mon. and Aug.*

$ ✕ **Da Antonio.** Once you have actually found this welcoming trattoria, settle back and enjoy the informal setting of an archetypal family eatery. The locals usually plunge straight away into the self-service buffet, an impressive array of vegetables and pies cooked *alla napoletana*. There *is* a menu, but—as is often the case in Naples—you're better off listening to the day's specials, here rendered by waiter-cum-owner Michele. The pasta dishes may be consumed as a *tris* or threesome, an attractive option if you think you could miss out on something interesting—though remember to hold something back for the homemade cakes at the end of the meal. ⊠ *Vico II Alabardieri 30, near the Cinema Arlecchino, two minutes away from Piazza dei Martiri,* ☎ *081/ 407147. No credit cards. Closed Sun.*

Mergellina and Posillipo

These bayside suburbs feature some of the most popular restaurants in Naples. Several of these spots are found at the end of bayside cul-de-sacs, so unless you have your own wheels, taxis will be the most convenient option.

$$$–$$$$ ✕ **Dora.** Though in an unflattering location up a narrow *vicolo* (alley) off the Riviera di Chiaia, this restaurant has achieved cult status for its seafood platters. It is remarkable what Giovanni, the owner-chef, can produce from his tiny *cucina*: Try to create some space for the richly garnished pasta dish *mezzanello,* with its full complement of seafood, and perhaps follow it up with a *pezzogna* (blue-spotted bream). Like most of the restaurants near the seafront, Dora has its own guitarist, Roberto, who is often robustly accompanied by the kitchen staff. ⊠ *Via Ferdinando Palasciano 30,* ☎ *081/680519. Reservations essential. DC, MC, V. Sun. and 2 weeks around mid-Aug.*

$$$–$$$$ ✕ **La Sacrestia.** A bit faded from its glory days as the "temple of Neapolitan gastronomy," Naples's most famous restaurant was founded in 1972 by Arnaldo Ponsiglione, a passionate scholar of historical Neapolitan recipes; his son Marco continues this tradition while amplifying it with contemporary improvisations. La Sacrestia has a terrace that is appropriately perched on the heights above Mergellina, a superb location. For starters try the risotto with baby squid or the pasta with shrimp, artichokes, and olives, or, if you're feeling regal, the *bucatini alla Principe di Napoli* (pasta ennobled by an abundance of un-Neapolitan truffles). Wonderful grilled fish and fritto misto follow, as well as a changing selection of innovative seafood dishes. ⊠ *Via Orazio 116,* ☎ *081/664186. AE, DC, MC, V. Closed Aug. No dinner Sun., no lunch Mon.*

$$–$$$ ✕ **'A Fenestella.** One of the most beloved of Neapolitan restaurants,
★   this is picturesquely perched over a beach in Posillipo near the end of a long winding side road (taxi is the preferred mode of transportation). In the 19th century, a legend had grown up surrounding this house's seaside window, or fenestella—any Juliet would promise herself simply by showing herself in the window to the Romeo sailing in the boat below, or so the story goes, and the famous Neapolitan folk song that was inspired by it. Today, the restaurant is blatantly traditional with a comfortable decor and the usual suspects on the menu (for stylish food and people, head just across the road to Da Cicciotto). Still, sitting at a window table overlooking the sea here remains a quintessential Neapolitan memory for many old-timers. ⊠ *Calata del Ponticella a Marechiaro 23,* ☎ *081/7690020,* WEB *www.afenestella.it. AE, MC, V. Closed Wed. lunch; Sun. eve. in summer.*

$$–$$$ ✕ **Da Cicciotto.** Want to dine among Naples's rich and fashionable? Most
★   of them prefer to dine at the city's *circoli*, or private clubs, rather than at restaurants—but there's a fair chance you'll find a Neapolitan count or a world-famous decorator enjoying this jewel, one of Naples's best-kept secrets. With a tiny stone terrace overlooking a pleasant anchorage (and the famous Fenestella restaurant), centered around an antique

column, and with seats and canopy exquisitely upholstered in blue-and-white matching-but-mixing fabrics, this is the dreamy setting for *cucina vera*—real Neapolitan food. To appreciate that outdoor setting, come here for lunch, not dinner. If you're a regular you don't even bother with a menu but just start digging into the sublime antipasti and go with the owner's suggestions. ⊠ *Calata del Ponticella a Marechiaro 32,* ☎ *081/5751165. AE, DC, MC, V. Closed Mon. in winter.*

$$–$$$ ✕ **La Cantina di Triunfo.** Founded by Carmine Triunfo in 1890 as a wine shop with food, this warm and inviting establishment has stayed in the family ever since, with great-grandson Antonio now looking after the wines and mother Tina at the helm in the *cucina*. The specialty here is well-prepared *cucina povera* ("poor peoples' food"), from the antipasto of hot peppers, salami, and cheese to the famous *vermicelli alle vongole fujute* (pasta with "escaped" clams, flavored with a dose of seawater) and the "meatballs" made of bread, but more aristocratic specialties take their place on the menu as well: sartù—the famous rice-based dish—or the fabulous shrimp au gratin in lemon leaves. ⊠ *Riviera di Chiaia 64,* ☎ *081/668101. Reservations essential. DC, V. Closed lunch, Sun., and Aug.*

Vomero

The Vomero now offers a range of economical dining options to complement the lively new cultural events happening on the hill, such as the Rassegna Cinematografica film fest at San Martino and the street happenings on Piazza Vanvitelli.

$$ ✕ **Trattoria Vanvitelli.** From an inconspicuous entrance on the main piazza, the restaurant opens out onto a large covered courtyard set between early 20th-century palazzi. Pizzas here have the traditional high *cornicione* rim, and are richly filled, though this might also be the place to try *calzone di Don Pinuccio,* a pizza filled with sausage and the local green beet, *friarielli.* For a pasta dish, opt for *paccheri alla siciliana* (pasta with eggplant and cheese). Service is usually brisk and efficient, except on weekends when the restaurant becomes a victim of its own popularity. ⊠ *Piazza Vanvitelli 9/c,* ☎ *081/5563015. DC, MC, V.*

$–$$ ✕ **Acunzo.** If you see a long line of hungry-looking patrons near the top station of the Chiaia Funicular, you know you are close to Pizzeria Acunzo. To avoid anxious waits, many like to get in here as soon as it opens for the busier evening session at 7:30 PM. When ordering, few variations on the pizzas are permitted, but then, owner Michele and his wife Caterina have been running the establishment since 1964 and have an amply tried and tested product. The house specialty, *pizza Acunzo,* comes replete with a daunting list of ingredients, but ends up being *fenomenale.* ⊠ *Via Cimarosa 60–62,* ☎ *081/5785362. Sun. AE, MC, V.*

$ ✕ **Euridice Genio Vinicolo.** This *enoteca* (wine bar) is a welcome addition to the Naples dining—and drinking—scene. To the left of the shop counter is a staircase winding down into the vast cellars of a solidly built early 20th-century palazzo. Try some of Campania's best wines served with *tagliere* (wooden platters) sporting selections of cold meats and cheeses. The highlight is the competively priced Rubrato, a smooth red Aglianico from one of the region's up-and-coming wineries. This locale is also the focal point for wine appreciation courses, besides selling a fine range of wine accessories. ⊠ *Via Scarlatti 30,* ☎ *081/5560398. AE, DC, MC, V. Closed Mon. No lunch.*

Caffès and Coffee

Naples is ground zero for coffee lovers, and a snappy, definitive antidote to the hysterical pretensions of Seattle. Espresso was invented here and is still considered by the Neapolitans to be an essential and priceless part of their cultural patrimony (the word *espresso,* by the way, should probably be understood here in its meaning "pressed out," rather than the more common interpretation of "quick"). For many cognoscenti, Naples has the best coffee in the world. Almost any bar you walk into, no matter how dingy or how close to the train station, is likely to serve up an espresso that would make any Malibu hotspot wilt in envy. Even Italian bars do not specialize in alcoholic beverages per se and are generally tied to, as English pubs once were with brewers, a coffee roaster/distributor. The sponsoring brand is indicated with a sign on the outside, so you can choose your bar by looking for the sign of your favorite brand. Brands tend to be highly regional; the most widely advertised Neapolitan brand is Kimbo, but Moreno and Salimbene are considered far superior by the cognoscenti. Some small, family-run caffès still roast their own.

You won't find any double low-fat mochas with extra vanilla here; in Naples you take your coffee like a grown-up. Individuals do have a choice of certain permitted variations: *corretto,* with a shot of grappa or the local moonshine thrown in; *al vetro,* in a glass; *macchiato,* "stained" with a burst of steamed milk; and, of course, cappuccino. On the whole, cóffee is a Neapolitan sacred ritual with precise rules. Cappuccino, for instance, is essentially a breakfast beverage, accepted in the afternoon with a pastry but looked strangely at after a meal (they claim it's bad for the liver). Many Italians like to order a glass of water (*bicchiere d'acqua*) with their coffee as a chaser. As for flavored coffees, Neapolitans, like all Italians, stubbornly believe that you only add flavorings to coffee to hide imperfections in the original grind. Coffee is perhaps the one feature of life in which Neapolitans don't gild the lily. Why fix what works?

For a true Neapolitan coffee, go to **Scaturchio** (✉ Piazza San Domenico Maggiore 19, ☎ 081/5516944), which constitutes a complete and essential Neapolitan experience in itself. This is a stand-up affair, as is the small **Caffè del Professore** (✉ Piazza Trieste e Trento 46, ☎ 081/403041), which offers a superb espresso, as well as a house specialty, the *caffè nocciolato,* which is sweetened with a coffee-and-walnut syrup. If you want to sit down and milk the experience, the most famous coffeehouse in town is the **Caffè Gambrinus** (✉ Via Chiaia 1/2, ☎ 081/417582), catercorner to the Palazzo Reale across the Piazza Trieste e Trento. Founded in 1850, this 19th-century jewel functioned as a brilliant intellectual salon in its heyday but has unfortunately fallen into a Sunset Boulevard–type existence, relying on past glamour, at the mercy of tourists and their pitiless cameras, and with often indifferent service. **La Caffetteria** (✉ Piazza dei Martiri 30, ☎ 081/7644243) is a classic address in the chic Chiaia district, and it has a second space in Vomero (✉ Piazza Vanvitelli 10/B, ☎ 081/5782592). Both addresses sell their famous coffee-flavored chocolates in the shape of tiny coffeepots. The **Gran Bar Riviera** (✉ Riviera di Chiaia 181–183, ☎ 081/665026) also has good profiteroles and fresh tiramisu, and is an excellent late-night stopover for clubbers. If you're in Santa Lucia, **Megaride** (✉ Via Borgo Marinaro 1, ☎ 081/7645300), on the port under the shadow of the Castel dell'Ovo, provides a romantic outdoor setting for a coffee or aperitif. Piazza Bellini, in the Spaccanapoli area, contains a gaggle of good and hip cafés, and almost any of the pastry shops mentioned below will have an excellent brew.

Pastry and Gelati Shops

On the whole, Neapolitan pastry tends to suffer from the excesses that mar most southern Italian desserts: Falstaffian enthusiasm rather than precision in technique, ricotta clogging up everything, embarrassingly sentimental glops of glaze, and over-effusive dousings of perfumed syrups: one local specialty, the Babà al rhum, often succumbs to this latter vice. But the Neapolitan tradition of pastry is an old and venerable one, and the most classic local invention in matters of *pasticceria* (pastry making), the *sfogliatella,* is a true Baroque masterpiece, with puff pastry cut on a bias and wrapped around a nugget of cinnamon-sugar ricotta to form a simple but intricate shell. These are best eaten hot, and they are easy to find in Naples this way. The classic address is **Pintauro** (⊠ Via Toledo 275, ☎ 081/417339). If you need a hot-out-of-the-oven morsel as soon as you get off the train, **Attanasio** (⊠ Vico Ferrovia 2, ☎ 081/285675), directly off Piazza Garibaldi, is justifiably famous. Better hotels often serve them warm with breakfast. *Torta caprese,* a simple, rich chocolate cake with ground almonds, is another Neapolitan favorite, as are eclairs of all flavors and forms.

Scaturchio (⊠ Piazza San Domenico Maggiore 19, ☎ 081/5516944) is the essential Neapolitan pastry shop. Although the coffee is top-of-the-line and the ice cream and pastries quite good—including the specialty, the *ministeriale,* a pert chocolate cake whipped with rum-cream filling—it's the atmosphere that counts here (though not the luxe—it's a rather unprepossessing sort of place). In the heart of Spaccanapoli, it's where nuns, punks, businessmen, and housewives commune on the good things they all have in common. Up in Vomero, **Daniele** (⊠ Via Scarlatti 104, ☎ 081/5587554) features refined renditions of traditional specialties and a stellar orange mousse. The largest number of good pastry shops are in the upscale Chiaia neighborhood. **Moccia** (⊠ Via San Pasquale a Chiaia 21, ☎ 081/411348) is often said to be the finest pasticceria in the city, and they have great babas and an out-of-this-world pound cake injected with just the right dose of intense lemon curd. Connoisseurs will say the most refined and tasty pastry in town can be found at **Gran Caffè Cimmino** (⊠ Via G. Filangieri 12/13, ☎ 081/418303). Stop here on your afternoon shopping marathon (or late at night) for the wonderful coffee accompanied by crisp, light cannoli; airy lemon eclairs; *choux* paste in the form of a mushroom laced with chocolate whipped cream; and delightful wild strawberry tartlets, precise and Lolita-innocent, with only a dewy spray of ruby glaze as a discreet enticement to perdition.

All these addresses will have exemplary ice cream as well, but you may prefer a more informal setting. **Scimmia** (⊠ Piazza Carità 4), in the center of town, scoops out a luscious variety of ice cream flavors. Young Neapolitans often go down to Mergellina to have a cone at one of the outdoor chalets in the garden along the port; **Chalet Ciro** (⊠ Via F. Caracciolo, 1 block west of Mergellina hydrofoil pier, ☎ 081/669928) is the best; they also whip up astonishing milk shakes and smoothies using a wide selection of fruit that looks as if it grew in fruit paradise. Just off Via Gramsci, a five-minute walk west of the Villa Comunale and the American Consulate, is the highly rated gelateria **Remy** (⊠ Via F. Galiani 29/A, ☎ 081/667304). If you're going to abandon your low-cholesterol diet, this is definitely the place to do it, preferably with a selection of their *semi-freddi* (a cross between an ice-cream and a mousse). A number of ambulant vendors around town sell absolutely first-rate lemon ice, or granita, for derisory prices; this can be a godsend in summer.

Chocolate lovers will be relieved to know that **Gay Odin** (⊠ Via Toledo 214, ☎ 081/400063, WEB www.gay-odin.it), Naples's most famous *cioccolateria,* has eight stores distributed around town—all recognizable by their inviting dark-wood Art Nouveau decor; try the signature chocolate forest cake (*foresta*) or their unusual "naked" chocolates (*nudi*), a suave mixture of chestnuts and walnuts. A small alleyway leading off the side of the Gesù Nuovo toward Via Toledo hides a little-known jewel that is worth the detour: **Gallucci** (✉ Via Cisterna dell'Olio 6, ☎ 081/5513148), founded in 1890, specializes in fruit-filled chocolates (the cherry and grape are memorable) and also produces a delightfully original local cult item, chestnuts filled with marsala.

Food Shopping

The makings of delicious sandwiches can be had at any neighborhood *salumerie*, which specialize in cured meats and cheese. You'll find the cheapest and freshest fruits and vegetables in the open-air markets. Cubbyhole mom-and-pop groceries offer basic food stuff and sometimes produce. For exotic (including American) ingredients, **Tropical Fruit** (✉ Via Montesanto 6, ☎ 081/5801006) is the only international specialty-foods store in town, offering a limited supply of organic products, an excellent assortment of dried fruits, and a generally reliable source of peanut butter.

LODGING

Since Naples is not known for peace and quiet, it's good news that it features a bevy of hotels that deliver exactly that—most accommodations are cool and tranquil sanctums, with the emphasis on cool (as one of Europe's hottest and busiest cities, its hotels feature some of the strongest air-conditioning around). Unfortunately, rare is the hotel that fills every measure on our yardstick—character, national aura, centrality to interesting locations. Yet there are grand hotels that still conjure up the days of steamship travel and whose window views allow you to indulge in reveries of Vesuvius, several options that set out to be ideal business hotels (with faxes, copiers, and modems at the ready), and even a pensione that occupies the former palace of the Princes di Sangro. When booking, inquire if there is an additional fee for air-conditioning, parking facilities, and breakfast.

CATEGORY	COST*
$$$$	over €200
$$$	€120–€200
$$	€60–€120
$	under €60

*All prices are for a double room at high season, excluding tax and service.

Lungomare and Santa Lucia

This prominent stretch of seacoast, with an unsurpassed view of the Bay of Naples, naturally attracts the greatest concentration of luxury hotels in the city, although more reasonable lodging is available on the side streets.

$$$$ ✕⌨ **Hotel Santa Lucia.** There may be luxury hotels in Naples as fetch-
★   ing as this one (the Grand Hotel Parker springs to mind), but none enjoys this dreamy location: directly opposite the Borgo Marinaro, the tiny fishermen's marina on the bay. Open your window here to find the port immortalized in the song "Santa Lucia," bobbing with hundreds of boats, lined with charming seafood restaurants, and with a backdrop of the medieval Castel dell'Ovo directly below your balcony. Even if your room doesn't have this view, the hotel's luxurious, quietly understated polish will win you over. In 1997 a renovation spruced up the decor, now aglow with antiques, chandeliers, and full-length portraits of Neapolitan aristocrats. The brocaded and very comfortable guest rooms are traditional in style (some readers carp some are too small for the price),

with bathrooms paved in terra-cotta and often equipped with whirl-pool bath. Just off the lobby, the restaurant Megaris is one of the best hotel-based restaurants in town. ⊠ *Via Partenope 46, 80121,* ☎ *081/ 7640666,* FAX *081/7648580,* WEB *www.santalucia.it. 107 rooms with bath. Restaurant, bar, air-conditioning, meeting room. AE, DC, MC, V.*

$$$$ 🖫 **Excelsior.** A swarm of maharajahs, emperors, and Hollywood legends has stayed at this hotel, a grand-tradition outpost since 1909. The exterior—with the hotel's name magnificently picked out in Pompeian red—is awash in elegant detail, while the interior is a symphony of soaring columns, gilded French doors, and Venetian chandeliers. Guest suites feature the best views of Vesuvius in Naples. Today the hotel caters to corporate chiefs, its ballrooms host company meetings, the breakfast is delicious, but there's not a maharajah or Hollywood legend in sight. ⊠ *Via Partenope 48, 80121,* ☎ *081/7640111,* FAX *081/7649743,* WEB *www.excelsior.it. 109 rooms with bath, 12 suites. 2 restaurants, bar, air-conditioning, meeting room, parking. AE, DC, MC, V.*

$$$$ 🖫 **Vesuvio.** Caruso died here, Queen Sophia of Sweden stayed here (just after a cholera epidemic, as a gesture of good will), Oscar Wilde and his lover Lord Alfred Douglas escaped here—but you'd never guess that this is the oldest of Naples's great seafront hotels from its exterior, now defaced with one of the ugliest modern facades in existence. As if to make up for the sickly gray and Miami Beach–pink, however, the interior soothes your eye with a very pleasant interior. Guests can get pampered here—a spa is in the works and there are a myriad of special services on request; atop the hotel is the famous Caruso restaurant, with a Cinerama vista of the bay as a garnish to some excellent dining. Guest rooms can be lullingly luxurious—traditional in style, with antique accents (framed prints, marble lamps) and vibrantly colored walls, plus cove moldings, parquet floors, gleaming bathrooms; many have grand views of the bay. But the best thing about these rooms may be that they are the one place from which you can't see the hotel exterior. ⊠ *Via Partenope 45, 80121,* ☎ *081/7640044,* FAX *081/7644483,* WEB *www.vesuvio.it. 146 rooms with bath, 17 suites. Restaurant, bar, air-conditioning, exercise room, meeting room, parking. AE, DC, MC, V.*

$$$–$$$$ 🖫 **Miramare.** Like a relic of a more gracious age, this turn-of-the-20th-
★ century town house in the Liberty (or Art Nouveau) style sits above the frantic traffic of Via Nazario Sauro like a dowager at a disco party. Once the American consulate, it still offers the air of a private home, an air much fostered by manager Enzo Rosolino, a household name in Italy thanks to his nephew, gold medallist at the Sydney Olympic Games. He often presides over guests in the main parlor, seeing to their comfort with a courteous attention to detail, as shown by the electric teapots and the selection of videocassettes available in the rooms. Guest rooms, with an airy Deco feel to them, are handsome, quiet, and exquisitely air-conditioned. The hotel looks directly onto the bay (and that traffic, although dulled by double-paned windows; for real peace and quiet opt for a room at the back of the hotel) and you can enjoy a breakfast atop the roof garden. A 10-minute walk takes you to the Piazza del Plebiscito and the center of Naples. The hotel offers good deals at weekends, over Christmas, and during August, and generous discounts are negotiated with affiliated restaurants, including La Cantinella. ⊠ *Via N. Sauro 24, 80132,* ☎ *081/7647589,* FAX *081/7640775,* WEB *www.hotelmiramare.com. 31 rooms with bath. Breakfast room, air-conditioning, 2 meeting rooms, parking. AE, DC, MC, V.*

$$$ 🖫 **Parteno.** Welcoming owners Alex Ponzi and mother Adele have in-
★ stalled an exclusive and elegant bed-and-breakfast right on the seafront near the Villa Comunale, 5 minutes from Castel dell'Ovo and 15 from the hydrofoils to the islands. The spacious and serene rooms are taste-fully decorated with period etchings and gouache views of Naples, and

all possess a small balcony, with some looking onto the bay; most rooms face a sidestreet, happily removed from the swirling traffic on the bay-side avenue. For those suffering from Internet addiction disorder, Alex has arranged a 24-hour connection in each room—computers can be borrowed—together with a fax and a refrigerator for downloading Neapolitan goodies as well as Web pages. Breakfast is à la carte, and can be ordered either by e-mail or just *a voce*. ⊠ *Via Partenope 1, 80121,* ☎ FAX *081/2452095,* WEB *www.parteno.it. 6 rooms with bath. Air-conditioning. AE, DC, MC, V.*

Piazza Garibaldi and Environs

This is by no means the nicest or most interesting part of town to stay in, but it's convenient to the train station, and there's almost always a room somewhere.

$$$ 🔝 **Mexico.** A warm and inviting art deco lobby with multicolor inlaid marble floors provides an apt welcome to this hotel. Upstairs, guest rooms are cozy and air-conditioned, with wooden floors and ice-green fabric-covered walls. Clean and comfortable, the Mexico also features friendly personnel. The interior contrasts starkly with life in this fairly depressed quarter of Naples, where the *motorino* (motor scooter) lords over all. But then it is a mere five-minute walk to that mother of all churches, San Giovanni a Carbonara. ⊠ *Via C. Rosaroll 13/15, 80139,* ☎ *081/266330,* FAX *081/266554,* WEB *www.webshop.it/hotelmexico. 40 rooms with bath. Bar, air-conditioning, parking. AE, MC, V.*

$$$ 🔝 **Suite Esedra.** Hidden on a tiny piazza off frantic Corso Umberto—one of the main traffic trunks leading away from Piazza Garibaldi—this is a hotel that's convenient to transportation as well as to the romantic neighborhood of Spaccanapoli. The hotel's decor, based on an astrological theme, takes itself lightly enough to work. Each guest room expresses a different planet or sign of the zodiac, all in the coolest faux-Memphis style, with plenty of sleek woods and Philippe Starck–esque touches. However, the hotel is in a densely packed district (reach out your window and you can practically touch the building across the way), so the building has sliver dimensions with guest rooms on the pe-tite side, except for two suites which have their own private terrace with whirlpool. Still, the lobby, library, and dining room are all suavely dec-orated. ⊠ *Via A. Cantani 12, 80133,* ☎ *081/5537087,* FAX *081/287451,* WEB *www.sea-hotels.com. 17 rooms with bath. Bar, air-conditioning, ex-ercise room. AE, MC, V.*

$$$ 🔝 **Terminus.** Immediately to your left as you come out of the train sta-tion onto hectic Piazza Garibaldi, this hotel is a cool pastel oasis of calm—sleek, clean, and stylish, with up-to-date, comfortable rooms and a panoramic breakfast buffet from the vantage point of the seventh floor restaurant. A real plus is the excellent staff. ⊠ *Piazza Garibaldi 91, 80142,* ☎ *081/7793111,* FAX *081/206689,* WEB *www.starhotels.it. 168 rooms with bath. 2 restaurants, bar, air-conditioning, exercise room, meeting rooms, parking. AE, DC, MC, V.*

$ 🔝 **Hotel Eden.** Just off Piazza Garibaldi to the right as you exit the Stazione Centrale, this is the best inexpensive lodging near the station. Brothers Nicòla and Enzo furnish salt-of-the-earth advice and func-tional rooms. No breakfast is provided, though a drinks dispenser near the lobby will keep you topped up with *acqua minerale* at all hours. The front rooms are right on the busy four-lane Corso Novara, so for less sleep-disturbed nights ask for one of the quieter rooms at the back. ⊠ *Corso Novara 9, 80142,* ☎ *081/285344,* FAX *081/285690. 44 rooms with bath. No credit cards.*

$ 🔝 **Hotel Ginevra.** This inexpensive, family-run pensione is around the corner from the Eden, but up two flights of stairs flanked by walls cry-ing out for a fresh coat of paint (there's no elevator). Despite such initial impressions of tattiness, the interior of the hotel is clean and smoothly run. If you're bothered by night-time traffic, ask for a room overlooking the unglamorous but quietish courtyard at the back. ✉ *Via Genova 116, 80142,* ☎ *081/5541757,* FAX *081/283210,* WEB *www.mds.it/ginevra. 15 rooms, 6 with bath. AE, MC, V.*

$ ⊞ **Pensione Mancini.** On the other side of Piazza Garibaldi from the main station, this new pensione-cum-hostel is a safe and comfortable outpost in the middle of the daily carnival of Neapolitan street life. With several double rooms—but also dormitory-type accommodation available for those on a tight budget—this is a good base if backpacking on your own and in need of company for evening forays into downtown Napoli. Human dynamo Lello on reception doubles up as night porter, besides running a sorting office for other reputable low-price hotels in the area when the Mancini is full. Book well in advance to ensure a place here. ✉ *Via Mancini 33, 80142,* ☎ *081/5536731,* FAX *081/5546675,* WEB *www.mds.it/mancini. 6 rooms, 3 with bath. Bar. No credit cards.*

Spaccanapoli and Piazza Municipio

Spaccanapoli is a good choice if you're traveling on a budget and want to enjoy the flavor of Naples's most historic quarter; the area around Piazza Municipio, although close by, sports a collection of upscale large-capacity business hotels.

$$$$ ⊞ **Grand Hotel Oriente.** This is an excellent businessperson's hotel with
★   all the conveniences and in a great location. A three-minute walk away is the pedestrianized Via Toledo, leading down to Piazza Plebiscito and the Royal Palace. Just outside the hotel is a new metro station (to be opened in 2002/3) linking up with the National Archaeological Museum and the Vomero. Despite the severe marble facade, the interior is welcoming: after a long, hard day it's a boon to return here and find comfortable, soundproof guest rooms. ✉ *Via Diaz 44, 80134,* ☎ *081/ 5512133,* FAX *081/5514915,* WEB *www.oriente.it. 130 rooms with bath, 2 suites. Bar, breakfast room, air-conditioning. AE, DC, MC, V.*

$$$ ⊞ **Executive.** Near Santa Maria la Nova and a 10-minute walk from
★   both the port and Spaccanapoli, this restored convent still grants a privileged solace from the busy world. The airy, well-insulated rooms come complete with a phone in the bathroom. The bar area is an exquisitely decorated nook. ✉ *Via del Cerriglio 10, 80134, Via del Cerriglio is the fist road on your right as you go up Via G. Sanfelice from Piazza Bovio (Borsa),* ☎ *081/5520611,* FAX *081/5528163,* WEB *www. sea-hotels.com. 19 rooms with bath. Bar, air-conditioning, sauna, exercise room. AE, DC, MC, V.*

$$$ ⊞ **Mediterraneo.** A large, modern, efficient business hotel, this place is within walking distance of both the Teatro San Carlo and Spaccanapoli. Reasonably priced and personable for its category, it also features a beautiful roof garden. ✉ *Via Nuova Ponte di Tappia 25, 80133,* ☎ *081/5512240,* FAX *081/5525868,* WEB *www.italyhotel.com/napoli. 256 rooms with bath. Restaurant, bar, air-conditioning. DC, MC, V.*

$$$ ⊞ **Mercure Napoli Angioino.** Right off Piazza Municipio and close to the Teatro San Carlo, this popular place has a sober yet luminous lobby and quiet, tastefully appointed guest rooms, some of which are reserved for nonsmokers. This is a good choice if you are taking a boat from the nearby Molo Beverello. ✉ *Via De Pretis 123, 80133,* ☎ *081/ 5529500,* FAX *081/5529509,* WEB *www.mercure.com. 85 rooms with bath. Breakfast room, air-conditioning, no-smoking rooms, meeting room. AE, DC, MC, V.*

$$ ⊞ **Albergo Sansevero.** This is a superbly located option—as handy to
★   the main thoroughfare of Via Toledo as it is to the historic enchantments of Spaccanapoli. Ten blocks away from its sister establishment,

the Soggiorno Sansevero, this albergo, or small hotel, is just off caffè-set Piazza Bellini, the prettiest of the Spacca's squares, and its address is one of the city's great 19th-century boulevards. As with many of the city's alberghi, there is no elevator here (and quite a number of steps). If unable to find accommodation here or at the Soggiorno, ask for space at their other stylish hotel, Sansevero Degas. ⊠ *Via S. Maria di Constantinopoli 101, 80131,* ☎ *081/210907,* 𝖥𝖠𝖷 *081/211698,* 𝖶𝖤𝖡 *www.albergosansevero.it. 11 rooms, 9 with bath. AE, DC, MC, V.*

$$ 🖾 **Europeo.** Right around the corner from Piazza San Domenico Maggiore, this is an excellent choice if you are looking for a clean, firm bed at budget prices in the middle of the university quarter. The international student atmosphere extends to dorm rooms available downstairs. No breakfast is offered, but you're right around the corner from Scaturchio. ⊠ *Via Mezzocannone 109/c, 80131 (look for the Cinema Astra; the entrance gate is to the right),* ☎ 𝖥𝖠𝖷 *081/5517254. 17 rooms, 7 with bath. AE, MC, V.*

$$ 🖾 **Soggiorno Sansevero.** If you want to soak up the atmosphere of old
★   Naples, this is ground zero. Within the very heart of Spaccanapoli, this pensione occupies a floor in the former palace of the princes di Sangro di San Severo, who built the famous family chapel directly behind this building. Although the palazzo overlooks the opera-set-like Piazza San Domenico, the tiny Soggiorno is on the palazzo's quiet inner courtyard. Rooms are simply furnished—linoleum floors, modern beds, great-grandmama's boudoir bureau—and may even come with ghosts: Carlo Gesualdo, inventor of the madrigal song, murdered his wife and her lover on the palace's staircase October 16, 1590. As with the other hotels in this local group, the staff is very friendly and helpful. ⊠ *Piazza San Domenico 9 (Palazzo Sansevero), 80131,* ☎ *081/5555949,* 𝖥𝖠𝖷 *081/211698,* 𝖶𝖤𝖡 *www.albergosansevero.it. 6 rooms, 4 with bath. AE, DC, MC, V.*

Chiaia–Vomero–Posillipo

Chiaia is the ritziest residential neighborhood of Naples, studded with 19th-century mansions and an elegant shopping district bordering the Villa Comunale gardens by the water. Above Chiaia rises the Vomero hill, offering great vistas of the bay. The bayside atmosphere continues at Mergellina, a transportation hub set at the far western end of the Riviera di Chiaia, and beyond at the suburban coastal district of Posillipo.

$$$$ ✕🖾 **Grand Hotel Parker's.** This landmark hotel, which first opened
★   its doors in 1870, continues to serve up a supremely elegant dose of old-style atmosphere. It now welcomes a good number of visiting V.I.P.s, ranging from rock stars to Russian leaders, who probably enjoy the hotel decor—a homage to the Neoclassical style, brought to Naples by Napoléon and his general Joachim Murat. Gilt-trimmed Empire bureaus, 19th-century paintings, shimmering chandeliers, fluted pilasters, and ornate ceilings all create a splendidly glittering environment, newly renovated in 1997. Set midway up the Vomero Hill (and convenient to funicular lines), the hotel's perch offers fine views of the bay and distant Capri, but if your room doesn't have one of these vistas, drink it all in from the excellent rooftop-garden restaurant. Off the lobby is the soigné bar, a favored spot for refined relaxation. ⊠ *Corso Vittorio Emanuele 135, 80121,* ☎ *081/7612474,* 𝖥𝖠𝖷 *081/663527,* 𝖶𝖤𝖡 *www.bcedit.it/parkershotel.html. 83 rooms with bath. Restaurant, bar, air-conditioning, meeting room, parking. AE, DC, MC, V.*

$$$ 🖾 **Britannique.** As one reader put it, "this is an elegant but far from pretentious place, full of history with a charm that can only be born of time." Adjacent to Grand Hotel Parker's, this reserved and traditional hotel has light, well-appointed, very spacious rooms with even better views across the bay and city, thanks to the small private garden across the street (reserved for guests) which prevents any obstruction—so if you want to immortalize the Bay of Naples in watercolor, do it here. Guest rooms are very comfortably furnished and also double-glazed– a wise precaution on the Corso, one of Naples's busiest night-time streets. ⊠ *Corso Vittorio Emanuele 133, 80121,* ☎ *081/7614145* FAX *081/660457,* WEB *www.hotelbritannique.it. 86 rooms with bath. Restaurant, bar, air-conditioning, meeting room, parking. AE, DC, MC, V.*

$$$ ⚃ **Delle Terme.** In the same complex as the Agnano Spa—complete with mud wallows and saunas—in the Campi Flegrei, this recently remodeled hotel in a park is an ideal spot if you are traveling by car (it's easy to get to, and you don't have to drive into Naples) and want a relaxing and convenient base for a few days. Access is provided to Naples via municipal bus which takes you to the Metro stop at Campi Flegrei. The spa gives discounts on their various services to hotel guests. ⊠ *Via Agnano Astroni 24, 80125,* ☎ *081/5701733,* FAX *081/7626441,* WEB *www.hotelterme.it. 62 rooms with bath. Restaurant, bar, air-conditioning, parking. AE, DC, MC, V.*

$$$ ⚃ **Paradiso.** This impressive hotel on the hillside of Posillipo is famous for the views of the Bay of Naples from its rooms, roof-garden restaurant, and garden terrace. From your own flower-bedecked balcony you can also take in the immediate neighborhood, less enchantingly filled with apartment buildings. While located at the western edge of the city, the nearby funicular takes you efficiently to the harbor port and transportation hub of Mergellina, at the end of the Riviera di Chiaia. ⊠ *Via Catullo 11, 80122,* ☎ *081/2475111,* FAX *081/7613449,* WEB *www.bestwestern.it/paradisohotel. 74 rooms with bath. Restaurant, bar, air-conditioning, parking. AE, DC, MC, V.*

$$$ ⚃ **Pinto Storey.** A fascinating old pensione, overflowing with warmth and charm, this is located on the third floor of an elegant late-19th-century building off the chic Piazza Amedeo. Guest rooms are simple and airy. In all events, this is extremely popular, so book way in advance. ⊠ *Via G. Martucci 72, 80125,* ☎ *081/681260,* FAX *081/667536,* WEB *www.pintostorey.it. 25 rooms with bath. Air-conditioning. AE, DC, MC, V.*

$$$ ⚃ **Splendid.** A five-minute walk from the top of the Mergellina funicular, with views sweeping across western Naples towards Pozzuoli and the islands of Ischia and Procida, this 1970s hotel is a functional yet pleasant hilltop alternative in the well-heeled suburb of Posillipo. ⊠ *Via A. Manzoni 96, 80123,* ☎ *081/645462,* FAX *081/7146431,* WEB *www. hotelsplendid.it. 50 rooms with bath. Bar, air-conditioning, parking. AE, DC, MC, V.*

$$$ ⚃ **Villa Capodimonte.** Far from the hurly-burly of the city, set in its own pleasingly manicured park near the majestic Museo di Capodimonte, this recently opened "villa" combines gracious Neapolitan hospitality with thoroughly modern comfort. The spacious rooms have panoramic views over the city, and there is a tennis court for those who can't do without. ⊠ *Via Moiariello 66, 80131,* ☎ *081/459000,* FAX *081/299344,* WEB *www.villacapodimonte.it. 60 rooms with bath. Restaurant, air-conditioning, tennis court, convention center, parking. AE, DC, MC, V.*

$$ ⚃ **Ausonia.** The spic-and-span rooms of this hotel are decorated in a nautical motif and it retains a homey feel. In the courtyard of a building on the waterfront at Mergellina, this is quite handy if you are taking a boat from the Mergellina pier. ⊠ *Via Caracciolo 11, 80122,* ☎ *081/682278,* FAX *081/664536. 20 rooms with bath. AE, MC, V.*

$$ ⚃ **Le Fontane al Mare.** Come here for semi-luxury accommodations at a relatively low price. Most of the elegant rooms have balconies overlooking the sea (although only five rooms have private bath), and

you're a short walk from the Villa Comunale, the pleasant park on the
bay. ⊠ *Via Niccolò Tommaseo 14, 80121,* ☎ *081/7643811,* ℻ *081/
7643470. 20 rooms, 5 with bath. AE, DC, MC, V.*

$$ 🖭 **Ruggiero.** In the same building as the Pinto Storey, this bright,
cheerful pensione has clean rooms at reasonable prices with convenient
access to the Metropolitana, the funicular to Vomero, and the Villa Co-
munale gardens. ⊠ *Via G. Martucci 72, 80121,* ☎ ℻ *081/7612460.
18 rooms, 17 with bath. DC, MC, V.*

NIGHTLIFE AND THE ARTS

The Arts

A vast array of opera, music, dance, and film is offered in Naples. Sched-
ules of events are published in daily newspapers, particularly *Il Mat-
tino, La Repubblica,* and *Corriere della Sera,* and the excellent monthly
periodical *Qui Napoli* (available in an English-language version and
usually gratis at hotels and visitor centers). Highly recommended for
information about cultural events is the recently launched monthly pub-
lication *Le Pagine dell'Ozio.* Information and ticket sales are pro-
vided by the following ticket agencies: **Box Office** (⊠ Galleria Umberto
I 15–16, ☎ 081/5519188, WEB www.boxoffice.it); **Concerteria** (⊠ Via
Schipa 21, ☎ 081/7611221); **Botteghino** (⊠ Via Pitloo 3, ☎ 081/
5564684); **MC Teatro e Musica** (⊠ Via Giulio Palermo 124, ☎ 081/
5462264, WEB www.prevenditenapoli.it).

Concert Halls and Theaters

In addition to the world-famous Teatro San Carlo, Naples has several
other leading concert halls and theaters. Each theater generally plans
its entire season—which usually runs October through May—in ad-
vance with a printed schedule. **Auditorium RAI-TV** (⊠ Via Marconi, ☎
081/7251111) is a modern facility within the television studio com-
plex at Fuorigrotta. The **Augusteo** (⊠ Piazza Augusteo, ☎ 081/414243,
WEB www.teatroaugusteo.it) is a large, centrally located theater off Via
Toledo that usually presents commercial Italian theater and concerts.
Galleria Toledo (⊠ Via Montecalvario 36, ☎ 081/425824, WEB www.
galleriatoledo.it) attracts the hip set with avant-garde theater presen-
tations. **Teatro Bellini** (⊠ Via Conte di Ruvo 14, ☎ 081/5499688) is
a gilded Belle Epoque theater that presents plays and concerts of a more
academic flavor. **Teatro Cilea** (⊠ Vomero, ☎ 081/643705) is a mod-
ern facility on the grounds of the Domenico Martuscelli Institute for
the Blind. **Teatro delle Palme** (⊠ Via Vetriera 12, ☎ 081/418134), a
rather ugly postwar plywood auditorium, usually hosts concerts pre-
sented by the Associazione Alessandro Scarlatti. **Teatro Mercadante** (⊠
Piazza Municipio, ☎ 081/5513396) is a Belle Epoque theater that hosts
the Corto-Circuito (Short Circuit) Video Festival from time to time.
Taking the thousands of miles into consideration, the **Teatro Politeama**
(⊠ Via Monte di Dio 80, ☎ 081/7645001) could almost be consid-
ered another off-Broadway playhouse, considering its challenging bill
of fare. For a satisfying Neapolitan "soul" experience, catch a local
singer like Lina Sastri or Lara Sansone warbling at the **Teatro Sannazzaro**
(⊠ Via Chiaia 157, ☎ 081/403827); traditional Neapolitan plays by
Edoardo di Filippo are also often presented here. Finally, the **Pala-
partenope** (⊠ Via Barbagallo, ☎ 081/5706806) is an enormous hangar
at Fuorigrotta where most pop concerts are performed.

Film

Neapolitans take their cinema seriously: the city has many cinema and
video stores and rental outlets, and several cinemas even run their own
"cineforums" one day a week to cater for more discerning cinema-goers.

From the end of June to mid–September, open-air cinemas come into their own, and provide film aficionados with a chance to catch up on movies they missed during the year. The city's love fest with the movies reaches its high point every year with the Napoli Cinefest Film Festival, usually presented every June at the **Cinema Modernissimo** multiplex (⊠ Via Cisterna dell'Olio 59, ☎ 081/5511247). Most cinemas are in and around the city center. **Ambasciatori** (⊠ Via Crispi 33, ☎ 081/7613128). **Arlecchino** (⊠ Via Alabardieri 10, ☎ 081/416731). **Delle Palme** (⊠ Via Vetriera 12, ☎ 081/418134). Within a short walk of the Castel dell'Ovo and the waterfront hotels is **Santa Lucia** (⊠ Via Santa Lucia 59, ☎ 081/7648837). For the most panoramic cinema foyer in town and a good selection of films, try the **America Hall** (⊠ Via Tito Angelini 21, ☎ 081/578–8982) in San Martino. As elsewhere in Italy, your favorite movie star will be speaking fluent Italian on the big screen—the dubbers still have a stranglehold on the industry—unless you choose the only (usually Tuesdays) English language cinema in town, **Abadir** (⊠ Via Paisiello 35, ☎ 081/5789447). Consult *Il Mattino, La Repubblica,* or *Corriere della Sera* for updated film programs.

Opera and Classical Music

The historic **Teatro San Carlo** (⊠ Via San Carlo 101–103, ☎ 081/7972331, WEB www.teatrosancarlo.it) is the luxury liner of all the opera houses in southern Italy. Today the concert hall still gleams with its mid-19th-century gilded furnishings and thick red-velvet drapes. For the opera season (December through June), many seats are presold by subscription but there are usually some seats available if you go along to the box office some days before the performance (unless, say, Pavarotti is performing, when tickets might get sold out as soon as they are available). How far in advance can you book? This depends on the opera and time of year. For some opera performances tickets could only be bought five days before the performance, but at other times it might be weeks in advance. Unlike many leading opera companies in the United States, the San Carlo does not operate on a revolving repertory schedule: Each opera or ballet presentation is usually scheduled for a mini-run, generally in a 10-day period.

Prices vary due to both location and date. The front rows of the stalls, known as *poltronissime*, might be as much as €180 for a performance on the first night of an opera, while up in the sixth tier, the Balconata VI, you would pay a fifth of that price, or much less if you went on a later night. Prices are always highest at first nights with the best opera *diva*, then fall off as top performers are sometimes substituted after a few nights. If you get a box seat, keep in mind that there are as many as six people sharing a box, so it is worth getting there early to get a front seat. Some people tip the *maschere* (ushers) and this is especially appreciated if they have fixed you up with a better seat than the one you were allocated originally (maybe a season ticket holder didn't show up). Ballet and concert performances are up to 50% less expensive than opera presentations. One way of getting into the San Carlo for much less would be to go on a guided tour (Saturdays and Sundays only, 2 to 3:30 PM). At €2.70 a shot, you soak up some of its magnificence and it might be preferable to paying 50 times as much and sitting through five hours of the Ring cycle. For complete information, contact the **box office** (☎ 081/7972331 or 081/7972412), which is open Tuesday to Saturday, 10–1 PM and 4:30–6:30, and Sunday 10–1 PM only.

The **Conservatorio San Pietro a Maiella** (⊠ Via San Pietro a Maiella 15, ☎ 081/459255) is home to the **Associazione Alessandro Scarlatti** (⊠ Piazza dei Martiri 58, ☎ 081/406011, WEB www.napoli.com/assoscarlatti) and is one of Italy's most noted music conservatories.

Naples features a full calendar of classical and chamber music concerts; check the newspaper listings and street posters for information about concerts frequently held in the historic churches of the city. Popular venues for small-scale performances are the **Goethe Institute** (⊠ Riviera di Chiaia 202, ☎ 081/411923) and the **Anglican Church** (⊠ Via San Pasquale a Chiaia 15, ☎ 081/411842).

A classical music festival known as **International Music Weeks** takes place throughout May in Naples. Concerts are held at the Teatro San Carlo, the Teatro Mercadante, and in the Neoclassic Villa Pignatelli. For information contact the Teatro San Carlo box office.

Nightlife

As soon as the sun goes down, nightlife ignites everywhere in Naples with more pubs and piano bars than you can shake a pizza at. There is something for everyone—from 19th-century-style *caffè-concerts* at the **Caffè Gambrinus** (⊠ Via Chiaia 1/2, ☎ 081/417582) in Piazza Trieste e Trento until 1 AM to the cutting-edge hangouts favored by the crowd now called Tendenza by the Neapolitan press. In many of the cafés and discos of Mergellina, Piazza Vittoria, Piazza dei Martiri, Via Partenope, and the Borgo Marinaro, baby Sophia Lorens and Frank Sinatras swarm the streets and alleys, while a bohemian crowd lingers on in Piazza Bellini until 3 AM. Even at this late hour many streets and piazzas in the historic Spaccanapoli quarter are alive with youth. The chic and stylish postyuppie crowd sticks to Piazza dei Martiri, Via dei Mille, and Piazza Amedeo, frequenting old-guard watering holes. But unlike those places, many nightspots open and close with alarming frequency, so be sure to call ahead when planning a club tour of Naples. For the scoop about the latest club and nightlife happenings, consult the monthly publication *Le Pagine dell'Ozio*.

Most disco clubs issue a €10 drink card at the door that must be returned when you leave, stamped to show you've consumed at least one drink. After the first or second drink, other drinks usually run less (about €5). Discos host nights devoted to various themes and trends—techno/house, gay, retro-1970s—organized by talented Neapolitan art directors and DJs. The youth set goes crowd-hopping in the Centro Storico, particularly Spaccanapoli, from Wednesday to Sunday nights from 10:30 PM to 4 AM, with some places becoming so crowded that the street scene outside becomes a key part of the experience. Hordes of postpunk and grunge night owls begin by regrouping in the main squares of Spaccanapoli, such as Piazza San Domenico Maggiore and Piazza Gesù Nuovo, to plan their strategies for the evening, usually around the **Lazzerella Bar** (⊠ Calata Trinità Maggiore), the adjacent SKA Social Center, and a nearby hotspot: the **Velvet Garage** (⊠ Via Cisterna dell'Olio 11, ☎ 0347/8107328, WEB www.clicnet.it/velvet). The next stop on the loop is **Notting Hill** (⊠ Piazza Dante 88/A, ☎ 081/5642830, WEB www.nottinghill.net), a steamy disco that features theme nights. **Tongue** (⊠ Via Manzoni 207, ☎ 081/7690800) appeals especially to gays and techno-heads.

In Spaccanapoli, the bar crowd heads to Piazza Bellini, where the arty and literary take up residence at the **Caffè Intramoenia** (⊠ Piazza Bellini 70, ☎ 081/290720). A popular place to discuss life, death, and Dante is the **Caffè 1799** (the date of the Neapolitan Revolution) (⊠ Piazza Bellini). Some choose to make the scene at the **Art Cafe** (⊠ Piazza San Domenico Maggiore). The **Hayli Club** (⊠ Via San Giovanni Maggiore Pignatelli 45, ☎ 081/5520340) has its own special coterie. Near the Piazzetta Nilo, crowds descend on **Kukuwaya** (⊠ Via Giovanni Paladino 16, ☎ 081/5521760), the **Blu Colbalto** (⊠ Via Giovanni

Paladino 3), and the **Vineria del Centro** (⊠ Via Giovanni Paladino 8) for a taste of artistic anything. A bit off the beaten track, **Ferdinand-strasse** (⊠ Piazza Porta Nova 8, ☎ 081/207390) began life as a gay disco bar but now attracts a wide array of figures from the art world.

A dressier crowd hangs out in the Chiaia zone. The center for Naples's *jeunnesse dorée* is Piazza dei Martiri, where the elegant **La Caffetteria** (⊠ Piazza dei Martiri 25/26, ☎ 081/7644243) draws night owls. Near the Piazza dei Martiri is **Vinarium** (⊠ Via Cappella Vecchia 7, ☎ 081/7644247), a refined wine bar. The Piazza dei Martiri area also has a number of hip discos, including **My Way** (⊠ Via Cappella Vecchia 30/c, ☎ 081/2451887) and the fashionable **Beloved** (⊠ Via dei Mille), a hotbed of 1970s looks and sounds. Along elegant Via dei Mille are a number of old-guard nightclubs, such as **La Mela** (⊠ Via dei Mille 40, ☎ 081/413881) and **Chez Moi** (⊠ Parco Margherita 13, ☎ 081/407526), particularly simpatico for Neapolitan aristocrats. Along the Via Partenope, traffic jams occur outside the new nightspot **Pinterré** (⊠ Via Partenope)—but who knows what the scene is like? It's just too packed to enter, and the decor is "curated" to change with the seasons. A savvy group heads to **Gabbiano** (⊠ Via Partenope 26, ☎ 081/7645717), where live music is usually on tap. A cool option is the **Otto Jazz Club** (⊠ Salita Cariati 23, ☎ 081/5524373). A hot disco is **Up-stroke** (⊠ Via Coroglio, ☎ 081/5708992). In a district just beyond Vomero, **Madison Street** (⊠ Via Sgambati 47, ☎ 081/5466566) remains a vast, fun, and tacky disco that allows all persuasions to trip the night fantastic.

During the sweltering summer months, the disco crowd moves west-ward to above-ground dance floors in the Campi Flegrei, the volcanic region to the west of the city. The shorefront **Arenile di Bagnoli** (⊠ Via Nuova Bagnoli 10, ☎ 081/2303050 is both a megadisco, concert venue, and open-air cinema, set incongruously in the industrial land-scape of the old Italsider plant, Bagnoli's decommissioned iron-and-steel works, and now attracting Neapolitans of all ages, inclinations, and social milieus.

OUTDOOR ACTIVITIES AND SPORTS

For complete news and information about sporting events, check the local newspaper *Il Mattino* and *La Repubblica* and *Corriere della Sera*, and the free English-language monthly guide *Qui Napoli*. Many sport-ing facilities in Naples, such as those for golf and horseback riding, are run as private clubs, so they are not listed here. The major sports area of Naples is the Fuorigrotta area, to the west of the city center, site of the Stadio San Paolo (soccer stadium). Here, too, is **Edenlandia,** the largest amusement park in Campania. ⊠ *Viale Kennedy,* ☎ *081/2398040,* WEB *www.edenlandia.it.* ▣ €2.50, €8.50 all rides except the towers, 3-D movie dimension, and flight simulator. ◔ Oct.–Mar., weekends only 10:30 AM–midnight; Apr.–Jun. and Sept., weekdays 2 PM–8 PM, weekends 10:30 AM–midnight; Jul.–Aug. daily 5 PM–midnight.

Participant Sports

Beaches, Spas, and Water Sports

Beaches are few and far between in Naples proper, although out of des-peration Neapolitans like to take to the Lungomare rocks that line the waterfront from the Castel dell'Ovo to the little port of Mergellina (swim-ming here is officially banned, although the young and reckless disre-gard the law). For true swimming pleasure, head to the Posillipo coast that lies just west of the Mergellina harbor. Here are three ancient fishing ports: **Giuseppone a Mare,** at the end of Via Ferdinando Russo; **Marechiaro,** at the end of Discesa Marechiaro; and **La Gajola** (local dialect for "The Cage"), at the end of Discesa Gajola. These are quite picturesque spots immortalized in Neapolitan songs, landscape paintings, and poetry. The more policed and costly facilities in the Posillipo zone are: the **Elena** (⊠ Via Posillipo 14, ☎ 081/5755058, WEB www. bagnoelena.it); **Gabbiano** (⊠ Via Marechiaro 115, ☎ 081/5755650); **Le Rocce Verdi** (⊠ Via Posillipo 68, ☎ 081/5756716); **Marechiaro** (⊠ Calata Ponticello a Marechiaro 33, ☎ 081/7691215); and **Villa Imperiale** (⊠ Via Marechiaro 90, ☎ 081/5754344). Of course, for the best paradisiacal beaches head to Ischia and the Amalfi Coast.

With millennia of volcanic activity in the region, the Bay of Naples area is home to many spas. Two ancient Roman period structures, or *sudatoria,* are still active today as spa facilities near Naples: The **Stufe di Nerone** (⊠ Via Stufe di Nerone 37, Bacoli, ☎ 081/8688006) offers thermally heated spring pools and natural steam caves where you can enjoy lava mud baths and massages using eucalyptus leaves; it also has a new children's pool. At the **Stufe di San Germano** (⊠ Via Agnano Astroni 24, ☎ 081/5702122), you can enjoy regional spa treatments.

Fitness Facilities
Parco Virgiliano has a beautiful outdoor running and gymnastics area. The locals are friendly and courteous to out-of-town *salutisti* (health-conscious travelers) and usually just let you join in. Most major facilities are in Neapolitan suburbs. **Magic World** (☎ 081/8048389), at Licola, is a new large-scale outdoor fitness and swimming facility. **Piscina Folgore** (⊠ Via Giochi dei Mediterraneo 75, ☎ 081/7624014) is a public swimming and fitness center in Fuorigrotta. Closer to the center of town is the **Athenae Palestra** (⊠ Via dei Mille 16, ☎ 081/407334) and the **Hotel Vesuvio Fitness Center** (⊠ Via Partenope 45, ☎ 081/7640044).

Tennis
At the Villa Comunale near the American Consulate (⊠ Piazza della Repubblica) is the **Tennis Club Napoli** (⊠ Viale Dohrn, ☎ 081/7614656). This club is private, but inquire about special privileges and passes. For a unique experience within the park of the Mostra D'Oltremare in Fuorigrotta, try one of the clay courts at the **Tennis Club Mostra** (⊠ Mostra D'Oltremare, ☎ 081/2390444). If you have no partner, Gino, the court manager and general dispenser of bonhomie, can arrange for both partner and racket hire once you have become a club faithful.

Spectator Sports

Soccer
Considering the position of importance and the popularity of *calcio,* or soccer, for the Neapolitan people, the San Paolo Stadium is probably a shrine only a fraction less important than the duomo. This shrine's last "saint" was Diego Maradona, who, in 1987, led the town team (their name, incidentally, is just Napoli) to first place in Italy's national championships. Matches are played at the **Stadio San Paolo** (☎ 081/2395623, WEB www.calcionapoli.it), in a suburb to the west of Mergellina (beware: *very* raucous crowds on their way to a game can clog up public transportation throughout the city). Tickets range from about €18 (at the highest tier of the giant stadium) to €270 (for the new Top Club facility). Despite several years of fluctuating fortunes, the team still attracts large crowds by any yardstick, and tickets for major matches may be hard to come by. The stadium is across the piazza from the Ferrovia Cumana train station at Mostra and can also be reached via the Metropolitana stop at Piazzale Tecchio. Other than the box office, tickets are available through **Azzurro Service** (⊠ Via F.

Galeota 17, ☎ 081/5934001) near the stadium and **Concerteria** (✉ Via Schipa 23, ☎ 081/7641221).

SHOPPING

Naples is a fascinating and largely underrated city for shopping. From the delightful *Presepi* (Nativity scenes) shops that transform Via San Gregorio Armeno into a perpetual Christmas morning to its noted leather-goods emporia, the city's rich history of skilled workmanship means it abounds in unique souvenirs and gifts, including some of the world's best ties (**Marinella**), crèche figures (**Ferrigno**), masks (**Nel Regno della Pulcinella**), shoes (**Mario Valentino**), and intarsia tabletops (**Domenico Russo**). At the other end of the price scale are world-famous, dirt-cheap bootleg cassettes and CDs of Italian and Neapolitan music for you to check out. A sense of adventure is once again the key, especially in the open markets, which are worth a visit just as a social experience—bargaining here is an art (watch your wallets and leave the expensive extra camera lenses at the hotel).

Shops are generally open from around 9:30 in the morning to 1:30, when they close for lunch, reopening around 4:30 and staying open until 7:30 or 8. Most stores are closed Sunday, but certain higher-volume addresses have procured a license allowing them to open on Sunday morning. Sales run twice a year, from mid-January to mid-March for the fall/winter collections and from mid-July to early September for the spring/summer collections, with half-price discounts common.

Department Stores and Shopping Malls

La Rinascente (✉ Via Toledo 343, ☎ 081/411511, WEB www.rinascente.it) is a good, basic department store with a wide variety of clothes, cosmetics, household items, and so forth. **Coin** in the Vomero (✉ Via Scarlatti 100, ☎ 081/5780111, WEB www.coin.it) is a packed department store, boasting a tasteful array of kitchenware in **Coincasa** on the top floor. **Standa** (✉ Via Solimene 143, ☎ 081/5780480), in the Vomero, is part of the same Coin group but a less expensive chain, with a supermarket attached. **Upim** has a wide variety of inexpensive goods available, with stores in the Vomero (✉ Via Alvino 18, ☎ 081/5562817), Chiaia/Piazza Amedeo (✉ Via dei Mille 59, ☎ 081/417520), and Piazza Matteotti (✉ Via Diaz 2, ☎ 081/5523354).

There are two elegant shopping centers in the Vomero—**Galleria Scarlatti,** on Via Scarlatti, and **Galleria Vanvitelli,** off Piazza Vanvitelli—as well as the more famous (though increasingly lackluster) **Galleria Umberto I,** across from the Teatro San Carlo, if you want to browse indoors and under cover.

Markets

Shopping in an outdoor market is an essential Neapolitan experience; do prepare yourself against pickpockets (now you've been warned, so relax and don't wear your tiara). Food markets are all over town, offering a Technicolor feast for the eyes as well as free street theater. The **Mercato di Porta Nolana** (✉ Via Carmignano, open Monday–Saturday 8–6 and Sunday 8–2, is just south of Piazza Garibaldi, with a great display of seafood. The **Mercato di Sant'Antonio** (✉ Via Sant'Antonio Abate) is open daily 9–8 and north of the Porta Capuana. The **Mercatino della Pignasecca** (several blocks to the west of Piazza Carità, off Via Toledo) is open Monday–Saturday 8–2. The **Mercatino di Antignano,** in Vomero (✉ Piazza degli Artisti), is open daily 8–1. The **Mercatino della Torretta** (✉ Viale Gramsci), which is open Monday–Saturday 8–1, has everything from fresh fish and vegetables at thrillingly low prices to clothes and appliances. Specialty markets also abound.

Photographers will want to explore the flower market, which opens at dawn every day in the moat of the Castel Nuovo. On the last two weekends of each month there is an **antiques market** in the Villa Comunale, where junk from grandmother's attic nuzzles up to some surprisingly fine furniture and objects; it's open daily 8–4.

Clothes merit a special mention. Neapolitans are the world masters of the used-clothing trade and also specialize in—well, let's call them unofficial brand-name knockoffs, sometimes of excellent quality. If you trust your eye, you can have a field day: excellent shoes often made by the same factories that turn out top brands, quality leather purses, secondhand cashmere at the price of discount-store cotton. Of course, quite often you have to wade through a lot of dismal stock of no interest in order to get to the good stuff, but that's part of the fun. The best stomping ground is the **Mercato di Ponte Casanova** (⊠ Porta Capuana), which is open Monday–Saturday 8–sunset and which must have the world's greatest collection of jeans and a surprising number of untagged name-brand items at half price. The above-mentioned markets of **Antignano** in Vomero and **Torretta** on Viale Gramsci in Mergellina also have a good selection of clothing.

Shopping Districts

Most of the luxury shops in Naples are along a crescent that descends the Via Toledo to Piazza Trieste e Trento and then continues along Via Chiaia to Via Filangieri and on to Piazza Amedeo, as well as continuing south toward Piazza dei Martiri and the Riviera di Chiaia. Within this area, the Via Chiaia itself probably has the greatest concentration and variety of shops (and café-pastry shop Cimmino, on the corner of Via Filangieri and Via Chiaia, makes for an excellent rest stop along this route). The area around Piazza Vanvitelli, and Via Scarlatti in particular, in the Vomero also has a nice selection of shops outside the tourist zone, with the **Galleria Scarlatti** on Via Scarlatti and **Galleria Vanvitelli** in Piazza Vanvitelli; this area can be conveniently reached by funicular from Piazza Amedeo or the Cumana station. Used-book dealers tend to collect in the area between Piazza Dante, Via Port'Alba, and Via Santa Maria Constantinopoli toward Piazza Bellini. The shops specializing in *Presepi* (Nativity scenes) are in Spaccanapoli, on the Via San Gregorio Armeno.

Specialty Stores

ART GALLERIES

Back in the late-1970s, the late Lucio Amelio operated the finest contemporary art gallery in Naples and succeeded in luring international superstars like Andy Warhol and Joseph Beuys to the city (Warhol wound up lingering on past his summer holidays and contributed paintings of Vesuvius to the "Terrae Motus" show, held to benefit the city after the earthquake of 1980). Lia Rumma, together with her late husband Marcello Rumma and art critic Achille Bonito Oliva, helped create the Arte Povera and Transavantguardia movements, while the standard-bearers of the Neapolitan aesthetic—Francesco Clemente in painting; Philip-Lorca di Corcia in photography—maintain worldwide reputations. They and other leading contemporary artists frequently exhibit in the city's leading art galleries: **Galleria Lucio Amelio** (⊠ Piazza dei Martiri 58, ☎ 081/ 422023) is the place to head for blue-chip masters like Cy Twombley and Joseph Beuys. **Galleria Beppe Morra** (⊠ Via Calabritto 20, ☎ 081/ 7643337) has several palazzo outposts which highlight the most avant-garde of Neapolitan artists, including the **Fondazione Morra** (⊠ Via Vergina 19) and the **Studio E-M Arts** (⊠ Via Calabritto 20). **Galleria Lia Rumma** (⊠ Via Vannella Gaetani 14, ☎ 081/7643619) has a status-heavy array of artists, including Cindy Sherman, Anselm Kiefer, and Vanessa Beecroft, along with upcoming Neapolitan sculptors. **Galleria Trisorio** (⊠ Riviera di Chiaia 215, ☎ 081/414306) has cutting-edge exhibits by such masters as Mimmo Jodice and Luigi Ghirri.

BOOKS AND PRINTS

Naples is a paradise for bibliophiles. It helps if you read Italian, of course, but you can find a reasonable selection of delightful surprises in French- or English-language publications as well. The best area to hunt is between Piazza Bellini and Piazza Dante, along the streets of Via Santa Maria di Constantinopoli, Via San Sebastiano, and Via Port'Alba. **Libreria Guida** (✉ Via Port'Alba 20/23, ☎ 081/446377) has a wide selection of current publications in English and is a good place to mingle with the locals. For lunchtime or weekend browsing when many of the other bookshops are closed, try the well-stocked, customer-friendly **La Feltrinelli** (✉ Piazza dei Martiri, ☎ 081/2405411, ⓦⓔⓑ www.feltrinelli.it), with its extensive range of CDs and videos, and—unique for Naples— an inviting coffee bar on the lower ground floor. Rare-book enthusiasts will want to check out **Casella** (✉ Via Carlo Poerio 92, ☎ 081/ 7642627, ⓦⓔⓑ www.abebooks.com/home/libreria_casella), just above the Riviera di Chiaia, a famous source that also specializes in authors' autographs. **Colonnese** (✉ Via San Pietro a Maiella 32/33, ☎ 081/ 459858), near Via Port'Alba, has a wide assortment of antique postcards and magical objets d'art. If you're an art history student and pictures are what matter, browse the booksellers near Piazza Bellini and take Via Port'Alba to Piazza Dante, where **Alpha** (✉ Via Sant'Anna dei Lombardi 10, ☎ 081/5525013) has a great selection of cut-rate art books. For antique prints and engravings, the best shop in town is **Bowinkel** (✉ Piazza dei Martiri 24, ☎ 081/7644344), in the Chiaia area; it also has antique postcards, watercolors, photographs, and fans. **Arethusa** (✉ Riviera di Chiaia 202/b, ☎ 081/411551) specializes in collectible posters and has an excellent selection of both rare and inexpensive editions.

CLOTHING AND ACCESSORIES

Neapolitans are famous for their attention to style, and Naples abounds in clothing stores for every pocketbook. National chains are present, of course. A good selection of affordable clothes can be found at **G. B. Pedrini** (✉ Via Toledo 330, ☎ 081/404949). **Benetton** (✉ Via Chiaia 203/204, ☎ 081/405385) represents easy Italian chic to most of the world. **Camomilla** (✉ Via Scarlatti 185, ☎ 081/5782004) has a nice array of casual-stylish designs. Up the price scale, **Emporio Armani** (✉ Piazza dei Mille 64, ☎ 081/425816) is in the Via dei Mille/Via Filangieri area of the Chiaia district, as are the luxe outfitters **Versace** (✉ Via Calabritto 7, ☎ 081/7644210) and **Prada** (✉ Via Calabritto 9, ☎ 081/7641323).

A number of smaller, local, or more exclusive shops are also worthy of notice. **Amina Rubinacci** (✉ Via dei Mille 16, ☎ 081/415486) is the queen of knitwear, featuring her famous "ostrich" pullover and a wide range of colors in sweaters. The various outlets of **Maxi Ho** (✉ Via N. Nisco 23/27, ☎ 081/427530 and ✉ Piazza dei Martiri 53, ☎ 081/ 7647067) have the latest in men's and women's fashion trends. **Eddy Monetti** (✉ Via dei Mille 45 a/b/c, ☎ 081/407064 for men's shop; ✉ Piazza Santa Caterina a Chiaia 7–9 for women) offers classic, elegant sportswear.

Women can find provocative clothes by the local designer and erstwhile pal-of-Andy-Warhol Ernesto Esposito at **Staffelli** (✉ Via Carlo Poerio 12, ☎ 081/7646922), off the Piazza dei Martiri above Riviera di Chiaia. **Barbaro** (✉ Galleria Umberto I 3/7, ☎ 081/414940) has a stylish choice of name designers. For chic, up-to-date fashions at accessible prices try **Livio de Simone** (✉ Via D. Morelli 15, ☎ 081/7643827), whose choice of hand-painted fabrics in vibrant colors reflects the city so well.

Naples is a surprisingly good city for male fashion and tends to completely spoil its male clotheshorses (many would use the word *peacocks*). **Pour les Amis** (⊠ Piazza dei Martiri 28, ☎ 081/7643103) is a good example of what is meant by spoiling; the careful and refined selection of clothing and accessories is complemented by impeccable service. Another excellent address is the hip but easygoing **Giorgio** (⊠ Via Calabritto 29, ☎ 081/7644122). Finely tailored shirts with hand-sewn buttonholes can be found at **Luigi Borelli** (⊠ Largo Sant'Orsola a Chiaia 3b, ☎ 081/410070). If you feel like indulging in a custom-made suit, try **Blasi** (⊠ Via dei Mille 29/31/35, ☎ 081/415283), which also has some soigné ready-to-wear items. Superb ready-to-wear items are on tap at **Sartoria dal Cuore** (⊠ Piazza Vittoria 6, ☎ 081/2451056). You'll find high-class souvenirs that are more immediate and more accessible at **Marinella** (⊠ Riviera di Chiaia 287, ☎ 081/2451182), where Maurizio Marinella, grandson of the founder, Eugenio, cuts made-to-measure ties for the world's royalty and other sensitive necks—these are widely considered by globe-trotting VIPs to be the finest ties in the world, and most important, they are never considered vulgar. The selection of fabrics is so vast it's impossible *not* to find the perfect tie. **Argenio** (⊠ Via Filangieri 15, ☎ 081/418035) is another famous and exclusive address for men's accessories, and former supplier of scarves, cuff links, buttons, tiepins, and so forth to the royal Bourbons of the House of the Two Sicilies.

Mario Valentino (⊠ Via Calabritto 10, ☎ 081/7644262) offers fine handmade shoes in his fashionable shoe store. **Spatarella** (⊠ Via Calabritto 1, ☎ 081/7643794) is a top source for shoes by local craftsmen, as well as for high-quality belts, purses, and luggage. For gloves, head to **Pistola** (⊠ Via Santa Caterina a Chiaia 12, ☎ 081/422058), famous for more than 100 years for the expertise of its craftsmen, and which, in addition to the classic models, offer a surprising selection of chic, high-tech sports gloves.

CRAFTS AND GIFTS

The classic handicraft of Naples is the *Presepe*—or Nativity crèche scene—with elaborate sets and terra-cotta figurines and elements of still life. The tradition goes back to the medieval period, but its acknowledged golden age arrived in the 18th century. Famous sculptors of the day churned out stunningly lifelike figurines, which were then custom-dressed by the chicest tailors to the aristocracy, providing a delightfully picturesque, if idealized, view of Neapolitan street life. The most stunning masterpieces from this period are the Presepe Cucinello, in the Museo di San Martino; one that belongs to the Banco di Roma displayed in the Palazzo Reale; and the Royal Nativity Scene in Capodimonte. The tradition is alive and flourishing; although the sets and figurines retain their 18th-century aspect, the craftsmen keep their creativity up to date with famous renditions of current political figures and other celebrities: porn star and member of parliament Ilona Staller, better known as La Cicciolina, was a big hit a few years back (not as the Virgin Mary—there's a limit to everything, even in Naples), as was exiled political leader Bettino Craxi, represented, with typical Neapolitan humor, in Arab dress (he was hiding out in Tunisia at the time) as one of the wise men. In 1998 Clinton and Lewinsky made an appearance, while local-born TV cult figure (from *Grande Fratello,* Italy's enormously popular version of "Big Brother") stole the limelight in 2000. The scenes are appropriately completed with a profusion of domestic animals and food of all sorts, meticulously rendered. A number of the smaller articles make great Christmas tree ornaments, if you don't feel up to adopting an entire Bethlehem-on-the-bay Nativity scene. Shops cluster along the Via San Gregorio Armeno in Spaccanapoli, and they're all worth a glance, but the undisputed master is **Giuseppe Ferrigno** (✉ Via San Gregorio Armeno 10, ☎ 081/5523148), who still faithfully uses 18th-century techniques. If you're seriously bitten by the Presepe collecting bug, you can find rare antique Nativity figures at **Marisa Catello** (✉ Via Santa Maria Costantinopoli 124, ☎ 081/444169). **Salvatore Iermano** (✉ Via Domenico Morelli 30, ☎ 081/7643913) is a popular maker. **Gramendola** (✉ Via San Gregorio Armeno 51, ☎ 081/5514899) offers the noted creations of Matteo Prencipe.

The **Ospedale delle Bambole** (✉ Via San Biagio dei Librai 81, ☎ 081/203067)—a tiny storefront operation—is a world-famous "hospital" for dolls, a wonderful photo-op, and a great place to take kids. **Nel Regno di Pulcinella** (✉ Vico San Domenico Maggiore 9, ☎ 081/5514171), another great address for kids and adults alike, specializes in handmade Neapolitan masks.

Music lovers can get a prestigious mandolin at **Liuteria Calace** (✉ Vico San Domenico Maggiore 9, ☎ 081/5515983, WEB www.calace.it) or a greater range of instruments along Via Costantinopoli, close to the Naples *Conservatorio*. You'll get a spontaneous and more accessible musical experience at any of the *bancarelle,* or ambulant sellers, specializing in bootleg cassettes and CDs; you'll find them in most outdoor markets, or along Corso Umberto I, or walking around the city center with boomboxes blasting the latest songs. Bear in mind that both purchaser and vendor risk hefty fines if caught in mid-transaction, and that your bootleg product is unlikely to have any lyrics and may well be substandard.

Elegant office supplies—notebooks, pens, and stationery—can be had at **P & C** (✉ Largo Vasto a Chiaia 86, ☎ 081/418724), a treasure trove for writing enthusiasts. Many adore the gifts at **Gli Artigiani del Libro** (✉ Calata Trinità Maggiore 4, ☎ 081/5511280). **Bottega della Carta** in Chiaia (✉ Via Cavallerizza a Chiaia 22, ☎ 081/421903) has a stylish array of goodies. **Bruno Acampora Profumi** (✉ Via G. Filangieri 70, ☎ 081/414162) is a famous local perfume maker selling prized fragrances in signature minimalist aluminum flasks.

HOUSEHOLD DECORATION AND ANTIQUES

For household linens, **La Cage** (✉ Largo Duca della Ferrantina 10, ☎ 081/403811) has the most exclusive selection in Naples. The national chain **Frette** (✉ Via dei Mille 2, ☎ 081/418728) is justifiably famous throughout Italy for the quality of its sheets, towels, and bedspreads.

Galleria Elena (✉ Viale Gramsci 15/c, ☎ 081/667822) crafts luxury floors in wood, marble inlay, mosaic, and terra-cotta and has a splendid collection of high-quality reproductions of Renaissance majolica tiles. Another good address for hand-painted ceramic tiles is **Capri Due,** in the Vomero (✉ Via Scarlatti 61–65, ☎ 081/5789400). **Domenico Russo e Figli** (✉ Via Bisignano 51, ☎ 081/7648387) continues the centuries-old Neapolitan tradition of marble-inlay work, creating precious tables and console tops. The Muscariello brothers produce museum-quality replica furniture (they copied the ancient furniture from Herculaneum for the Getty Museum) at **Il Cirmolo** (✉ Via Santa Maria di Costantinopoli 32, ☎ 081/451140). **Salvatore Molino** (✉ Via Alabardieri 21/22, ☎ 081/426505) painstakingly handcrafts furniture, using time-tested techniques. Fine bronze reproductions can be found in the area of Capodimonte at the **Patrizio di Pietro** foundry (✉ Corso Amedeo di Savoia 248, ☎ 081/7410217).

If you're interested in original antiques, several prestigious dealers are clustered along Via Domenico Morelli south of Piazza dei Martiri. **Arte**

Antica (⊠ Via Domenico Morelli 45, ☎ 081/7646897) has a fine display of porcelain objects. **Maurizio Brandi** (⊠ Via Domenico Morelli 11, ☎ 081/7643906) is known for its 17th and 18th century Neapolitan antiques. **D'Amodio** (⊠ Via Domenico Morelli 6/bis, ☎ 081/7643872) is the place for historic majolica. **Florida** (⊠ Via Domenico Morelli 13, ☎ 081/7643440) is famous for its painting on glass and silver Rococo and Neoclassic candelabra. Fine collectible 20th-century furniture and objects (basically Art Nouveau and Art Deco) can be seen in Chiaia at **Nabis** (⊠ Via Cavallerizza a Chiaia 52, ☎ 081/422493). For current designs, go by **Agorà** in Posillipo (⊠ Via Orazio 138/a, ☎ 081/651056); **Novelli** in Piazza Amedeo (⊠ Piazza Amedeo 21/22, ☎ 081/413233); or **San Patrignano Casa d'Arte** (⊠ Via Santa Lucia 133, ☎ 081/7640878), which shows high-quality, limited-edition, handcrafted furnishings and objects and is worth a visit even if you have no intention of buying.

JEWELRY

The best selection of goldsmiths' and jewelers' shops is, fairly incongruously, located in what has become one of the poorest areas of town on and around Via degli Orefici (Street of the Goldsmiths) between Corso Umberto and Via Marina. The nearest you get to a gold supermarket in Naples is **Presta** (⊠ Via Scialoia 2–10, ☎ 081/5545282), which has unbelievably competitive prices. In the center of Spaccanapoli is **Gioielleria Caso** (⊠ Piazza San Domenico Maggiore 16, ☎ 081/5516733), which has antique jewelry and silver and great coral works. **Brinkmann** (⊠ Piazza Municipio 21, ☎ 081/5520555) creates pieces using rare coins, including an exquisite collection of watches. **Ventrella** (⊠ Via Carlo Poerio 11, ☎ 081/7643173) is a posh salon showing original designs by the most exclusive contemporary workshop.

Naples has also long been famous for its coral and cameos, and although the raw material now comes most often from the Far East, it is Neapolitan technique and inspiration that transform the shells and coral into works of art. A number of touristy shops along the Sorrento coast sell cameos of varying quality and price, but if you want to see how beautiful they can get, go to Torre del Greco and visit **Bianca Lombardi** (⊠ Via Tironi 10, ☎ 081/8816344) or **Giovanni Apa** (⊠ Via de Nicola 1, ☎ 081/8811155). **Gioielleria Caso** has the best selection in Naples.

SIDE TRIPS

Caserta is the Italian answer to Versailles, although if you proceed to Benevento, you'll view an almost perfectly preserved Roman arch. Benevento was badly damaged by World War II bombings, but among the modern structures there are some medieval and even older relics still standing in the old town. If you go by car, make a brief detour to the medieval hamlet of Casertavecchia (Old Caserta) on the hillside, where there is a very old cathedral and one or two good restaurants.

Caserta

★ *25 km (16 mi) northeast of Naples.*

The royal palace known as the **Reggia di Caserta** is exemplary of mid-18th-century Bourbon royal living. Architect Luigi Vanvitelli devoted 20 years to its construction under Bourbon ruler Charles III, whose son, Ferdinand IV, moved in when it was completed in 1774. Both king and architect were inspired by Versailles, and the rectangular palace was conceived on a massive scale, with four interconnecting courtyards, 1,200 rooms, and a vast park. Though not as well maintained as its

French counterpart, the main staircase puts the one at Versailles to shame, and the **royal apartments** are sumptuous. It was here, in what Eisenhower called "a castle near Naples," that the Allied High Command had its headquarters in World War II, and here German forces in Italy surrendered in April 1945. The horses and buggies in the grounds have virtually all been replaced by shuttle buses (departures about every 15 min.) which ferry visitors from the palace up the mile-long stretch of lawns interspersed with fountains, to the *Grande Cascata*, where life-size sculptures of Diana and her maidens stand, and close to the entrance of the *Giardino Inglese*, a delightfully landscaped English garden created for Queen Maria Carolina in the late 18th century through the auspices of Sir William Hamilton, husband to the famous Emma. ⊠ *Piazza Carlo III,* ☎ *0823/447147.* 🎫 *Royal apartments €4.20; park €2.10; Giardino Inglese €1.10; shuttle bus €.20.* ☉ *Royal apartments Tues.–Sun. 8:30–7:30; park Tues.–Sun. 8:30–1 hr before sunset; Giardino Inglese 8:30–1 hr before park closure, guided visits (Italian only) every 30 min.*

Benevento

35 km (22 mi) east of Caserta; 60 km (37 mi) northeast of Naples.

Benevento owes its importance to its establishment as the capital of the Lombards, a northern tribe that invaded and settled what is now Lombardy before being ousted by Charlemagne in the 8th century. Tough and resourceful, the Lombards moved south and set up a new duchy in Benevento, later moving its seat south to Salerno, where they saw the potential of the natural harbor. Under papal rule in the 13th century, Benevento built a fine cathedral and endowed it with bronze doors that were a pinnacle of Romanesque art. The cathedral, doors, and a large part of the town were blasted by World War II bombs. The **duomo** has been rebuilt, with the remaining panels of the original bronze doors in the chapter library. Fortunately, the majestic 2nd-century AD **Arco di Traiano** survived unscathed. The arch honors Roman emperor Trajan, who sorted out Rome's finances, added parts of the Middle East to the empire, and extended the Appian Way through Benevento to the Adriatic. The ruins of the **Teatro Romano,** which had a seating capacity of 20,000, are still in good enough shape to host a summer pop concert season. ⊠ *Take Via Carlo from the duomo.* 🎫 *€2.06.* ☉ *Daily 9–1 hr before sunset.*

NAPLES A TO Z

AIR TRAVEL TO AND FROM NAPLES

CARRIERS
Alitalia, Lufthansa, and British Airways all fly from Naples, although few if any fly here from their originating country.
➤ AIRLINES AND CONTACTS: **Alitalia** (reservations on national flights ☎ 848/865641; international ☎ 848/865642, WEB www.alitalia.it). **British Airways** (reservations ☎ 848/812266, WEB www.britishairways.com). **Lufthansa** (☎ 06/65684004, WEB www.lufthansa.it).

AIRPORTS AND TRANSFERS
Capodichino Airport, 8 km (5 mi) north of Naples, has many domestic and European connections but hosts few international flights.
➤ AIRPORT INFORMATION: **Capodichino Airport** (☎ 081/7896259).

AIRPORT TRANSFER
Bus 14 runs from Piazza Garibaldi to the airport (hourly, 25 minutes) between 5:15 AM and 10:05 PM. A shuttle bus also runs from 6 AM to

midnight between the airport and Piazza Municipio (hourly, 30 minutes, €1.70), stopping in Piazza Garibaldi along the way. If you take a taxi from Piazza Garibaldi, expect to pay between €13–€17 for the 15-minute trip.

➤ TAXIS AND SHUTTLES: **Shuttle bus** (☎ 081/5311706).

BOAT AND FERRY TRAVEL

If you're heading to the Aeolian Islands, other parts of Sicily, or Sardinia, Naples may be a convenient departure point. A major long-distance carrier is Tirennia, which departs from Stazione Marittima, near Piazza Municipio. Tirennia's main competitor is Linee Lauro, which departs from Molo Belvedere below Castel Nuovo.

Boats leave once weekly for Tunis (18 hours southwest, €90), and more frequently for Sardinia (14 hours west, €28–€55), Palermo (11 hours southwest, €35–€50), and the Aeolian Islands (8–14 hours, €35–€40), among other places.

For trips around the Bay of Naples, the main port is Molo Beverello, below Castel Nuovo. Many carriers send boats to the islands all day until 7 or 8, though in the off-season service is less frequent. Carriers include Linee Lauro, Caremar, and Navigazione Libera del Golfo. Hydrofoils (but not ferries) also leave from the port at Mergellina, a short walk below the Mergellina train station; these are run by SNAV and Alilauro. Major destinations from both ports include Capri (hydrofoils: 40 minutes south, €11; ferries: 1 hour 20 minutes, €8), Procida (hydrofoils: 30 minutes southwest, €11; ferries: 1 hour, €8), and Ischia (hydrofoils: 40 minutes southwest, €11; ferries: 1 hour 20 minutes, €8). Several hydrofoils also ply to Sorrento (25 minutes southeast, €11).

FARES AND SCHEDULES

Departure times and additional info on some routes, including the local ferry and hydrofoil lines listed below, can be found in *Qui Napoli* or in the newspapers *Il Mattino, La Repubblica,* and *Corriere della Sera.* ➤ BOAT AND FERRY INFORMATION: **Alilauro** (☎ 081/7614909, WEB www.alilauro.it). **Caremar** (☎ 081/5513882, WEB www.caremar.it). **Linee Lauro** (☎ 081/5513352, WEB www.lineelauro.it). **Navigazione Libera del Golfo** (☎ 081/5527209, WEB www.navlib.it). SNAV (☎ 081/7612348, WEB www.snavali.com). **Tirennia** (☎ 8408/99000 or 081/7201111, WEB www.tirrenia.it).

BUS TRAVEL TO AND FROM NAPLES

Medium- and long-distance buses out of Naples are handled by several companies. The main operator is SITA, whose buses leave from either Piazza Garibaldi or Via G. Pisanelli near Piazza Municipio, but a host of other coach companies operate on long-haul routes southeastwards into Puglia. For detailed information check the local paper *Il Mattino* with its comprehensive list of operators and destinations.

FARES AND SCHEDULES

➤ BUS INFORMATION: **SITA** (☎ 081/5522176, WEB www.sita-on-line.it).

BUS TRAVEL WITHIN NAPLES

Bus routes in Naples change frequently, the signs posted at bus stops aren't too helpful, and there's no bus map available. That said, they have recently reorganized the system around a small network of frequent routes that shuttle you efficiently among a few major junctions. These are the R1, which runs between Piazza Medaglie d'Oro in Vomero and Piazza Bovio (at the end of Corso Umberto near Piazza Municipio) by way of

Via Toledo and Via Diaz; the R2, which runs between Piazza Garibaldi and Piazza Municipio; the R3, which runs between Piazza Municipio and Piazza Trieste e Trento and Mergellina; and the R4, which runs from Piazza Bovio and the Ospedale Cardarelli above Vomero by way of the Museo Archeologico Nazionale. Other useful buses include the 24, which takes you from downtown (Piazza Castello by way of Via Monteoliveto) to Capodimonte; the C25, which connects Piazza Bovio, Piazza Municipio, Via Santa Lucia, and Piazza Amedeo; the 105, which will get you to the duomo from Piazza Bovio by way of Corso Umberto; the 140, which takes you from Via Santa Lucia to Posillipo by way of Piazza Sannazzaro; and the 152, which runs between Fuorigrotta and Piazza Garibaldi, passing through Mergellina. The E1 is handy in the city center; it makes a loop from Piazza del Gesù Nuovo around the Museo Archeologico Nazionale and the duomo and back by way of Via Monteoliveto. Since transfers are free, a few mistakes won't deplete your bank account. For further information call ANM.

FARES AND SCHEDULES
➤ Bus Information: **ANM** (✉ Via G. B. Marino 1, ☎ 081/7631111, WEB www.anm.it).

CAR RENTAL
Be careful if you rent a car outside Campania; there is always extra insurance for this region, and most companies refuse to let you take a Mercedes or BMW into Campania and make you sign a retainer accepting all responsibility for the car if you do take it there. Car thieves here are some of the fastest and most organized in the world; the car is usually dismantled and in Eastern Europe the next day (there's a big market with the new Eastern European mafiosi for relatively inexpensive trophy cars). Some excellent deals can sometimes be arranged through local hotels on the spot, especially for the faint-hearted who may prefer a driver. Some rental agencies in Naples are listed below; Maggiore has offices at the airport and central train station, as well.
➤ Major Agencies: **Avis** (✉ Stazione Centrale, ☎ 081/5537171; ✉ Aeroporto di Capodichino, ☎ 081/7805790, WEB www.avis.com). **Europcar** (✉ Aeroporto di Capodichino, ☎ 081/7805643, or 800/014410 toll-free, WEB www.europcar.it). **Hertz** (✉ Aeroporto di Capodichino, ☎ 081/7802971 or 800/868016 toll-free, WEB www.hertz.it; ✉ Piazza Garibaldi 93, ☎ 081/206228). **Maggiore** (✉ Via Cervantes 92, ☎ 081/5521900 or 848/867067, WEB www.maggiore.it).

CAR TRAVEL
Naples is located on the major north-south Autostrada del Sole, more commonly known as the A1 to Rome and Milan and the A3 to Salerno. The A30 acts as an express highway through Campania, cutting out the busy A3 between Naples and Salerno where traffic jams are endemic; the A16 winds southeast in the direction of Bari. As they near Naples, the autostradas meet the Tangenziale di Napoli (€0.65 toll), a busy six-lane highway which borders the city's northern sector. The Tangenziale is the main access route from the airport to the city center, and continues on to Pozzuoli and the Phlegrean Fields region to the west of the city center. From Naples, the A3 for Salerno is best reached via the Tangenziale (follow the green signs for the motorways) unless you are close to Santa Lucia and the port area, in which case follow the traffic eastward along the waterfront and the port until you reach the autostrada sliproad at the end of Via Marina.

GASOLINE
Gas and service stations can be found—somewhat surprisingly—in several monumental city-center locations: Piazza Municipio (Q8); Piazza

Mergellina (AGIP); Via Manzoni (Esso); Via Ugo Foscolo (API); Via Falcone (IP); and Corso Europa (AGIP) are likely to be open at night.

PARKING

For those who decide to tempt fate, it is advisable to leave your car only in designated parking areas. The *parcometro,* the Italian version of metered parking in which you put coins into a machine for a stamped ticket that you leave on the dashboard, has been introduced in Naples, but the safest option is to park your car in a garage. Most of the hotels in the Santa Lucia district have (expensive) garages, but the following are some of the more centrally located and reasonably priced options. In Santa Lucia, try the Garage Chiatamone or Garage dei Fiori. In the historic center—Garage Santa Chiara. In the Molo Beverello zone by the harbor, try Garage Turistico, and near the Mergellina train and Metropolitana stations Garage Mergellina and Garage Sannazzaro are good bets.

➤ GARAGES: **Garage Chiatamone** (✉ Via Chiatamone 26, ☎ 081/ 7642863). **Garage dei Fiori** (✉ Via Colonna 21, ☎ 081/414190). **Garage Mergellina** (✉ Via Mergellina 112, ☎ 081/7613470). **Garage Sannazzaro** (✉ Piazza Sannazzaro 142, ☎ 081/681437). **Garage Santa Chiara** (✉ Pallonetto Santa Chiara 30, ☎ 081/5516303). **Garage Turistico** (✉ Via dei Gaspari 14, ☎ 081/5525442).

TRAFFIC

Traveling by car through Naples calls to mind the many circles described in Dante's *Inferno.* Congestion and stunt driving are par for the course, as is the rush-hour gridlock that sets in on weekdays. Weekends aren't much better: Suburbanites like to pile into their cars, enter Naples from Via Marina and do a traffic loop to Mergellina and the Via Caracciolo waterfront. This nightlife traffic-jam phenomenon takes hours and seems to now be a favorite pastime. At peak hours, even buses (which usually have their own separate traffic lanes) get blocked. Clearly, walking, funicular, railway, or the metro are better alternatives.

CONSULATES

➤ UNITED KINGDOM: (✉ Via Dei Mille 40, ☎ 081/4238911, WEB www.ukinitalia.it; ⊙ weekdays 9–12:30 and 2–4).
➤ UNITED STATES: (✉ Piazza della Repubblica 2, at west end of Villa Comunale, ☎ 081/5838111, WEB www.usembassy.it; ⊙ weekdays 8–1).

EMERGENCIES

The main police station has an *ufficio stranieri* (foreigners' office) that usually has an English speaker on staff. For an English-speaking dentist or for a general physician, call one of the numbers listed below. You can also consult the English Yellow Pages, available in major hotels. Naples has some excellent general hospitals, which are also listed below. In case of a medical emergency after 8 PM call the Medical Emergency number below and ask for an English-speaking nurse.

If you need a late-night pharmacy, try the one in Via Carducci above the Villa Comunale, as well as in the hallway of Stazione Centrale. If these are closed, they will post the addresses of those that are open (the others take turns staying open late); you can also call 192 or buy a copy of the newspapers *Il Mattino, La Repubblica,* or *Corriere della Sera* for a daily list of pharmacies that are open nights and weekends in your neighborhood.

➤ DOCTORS AND DENTISTS: **Dentist** (☎ 081/664436). **Doctor** (☎ 081/ 5567253, WEB www.englishyellowpages.net).
➤ EMERGENCY SERVICES: **Ambulance** (☎ 081/7528282). **Fire** (☎ 115). **General emergencies** (☎ 113). **Police** (☎ 112). **Police Station** (✉ Via

Medina 75, ☎ 081/7941111; foreigners' office ⊠ Via Ferraris 131, ☎ 081/6064111).
➤ HOSPITALS: **Ospedale Cardarelli** (⊠ Via Cardarelli 9, ☎ 081/7471111). **Ospedale dei Pellegrini** (⊠ Via Portamedina 41, ☎ 081/2543333). **Ospedale San Paolo** (⊠ Via Terracina 219, ☎ 081/7686274). **Universitaria Policlinico Federico II** (⊠ Via S. Pansini, ☎ 081/7461111).
➤ HOT LINES: **Medical Emergency** (☎ 081/7613466).
➤ LATE-NIGHT PHARMACIES: **Pharmacy** (⊠ Via Carducci 21–23, ☎ 081/417283).

ENGLISH-LANGUAGE MEDIA
BOOKS
For romance, philosophy, or a handy thesaurus, head to Universal Books, inside a palazzo off Corso Umberto near Piazza Bovio, open weekdays 9–1 and 4–7, and on Saturdays 9–12.
➤ BOOKSTORES: **Universal Books** (⊠ Corso Umberto 22, ☎ 081/2520069).

NEWSPAPERS AND MAGAZINES
See English-Language Media in Smart Travel Tips *in* Chapter 5.

FUNICOLARE AND TRAM TRAVEL
If you're heading up to the Vomero Hill, funicolari (cable cars) make the trek; contact ANM for more information. The Funicolare Centrale from its Via Toledo station links the city center with the Piazza Fuga station atop the Vomero Hill. The Funicolare di Chiaia links Via del Parco Margherita to the Via Domenico Cimarosa station on the Vomero Hill. The Funicolare di Montesanto travels from Piazza Montesanto to the station at Via Morghen. In addition, the Funicolare di Mergellina links the waterfront at Via Mergellina with Via Manzoni. The basic funicular fare is €0.80, valid for 90 minutes and only one funicular ride. The Chiaia and Centrale funiculars usually run from 7 AM to 1 AM with departures every 10–15 minutes, while the others close at 10 PM. The city's tram system runs northwest–southeast; Tram 1 will take you from Piazza Garibaldi to Mergellina along the waterfront and on to Campi Flegrei.
➤ CONTACTS: **ANM** (☎ 081/7631111, WEB www.anm.it).

MAIL AND SHIPPING
The main post office has *fermo posta* (held mail) and a *sportello filatelico* (philatelic counter) for stamp collectors. The postal code is 80100. Branch offices are usually open weekdays 8:15–1:30 and Saturday 8:15–12:10.
➤ POST OFFICES: **Post office** (⊠ Piazza Matteotti, off Via Diaz, ☎ 081/5511456; ☉ weekdays 8:15–7:20 and Sat. 8:15–1:30).

MONEY MATTERS
ATMS
With cash available virtually on tap from any number of ATMs throughout the city, the traditional exchange offices near the port area have felt the squeeze. The only charge on the ATM card will be whatever your bank charges for using a bank not your own, and the exchange rate is whatever you'd get charging something on a credit card. The only disadvantage is you won't know the exact rate until you get home and look at your bank statement to see precisely how many dollars were deducted from your account.

CURRENCY EXCHANGE

If you want convenience and aren't changing a big wad, use the Ufficio Cambio near the ticket office inside Stazione Centrale(☞ Train
Travel); it's open daily 7:30 AM–7:30 PM. Most banks are geared to
changing cash and travelers' checks, although the queuing and red tape
can be frustrating. Also, banks in Naples are equipped with metal detectors, so you have to leave all your worldly goods outside in lockers
before entry.

SAFETY

After a decade-long offensive against crime, Naples is now as safe as
any other modern metropolis. Employment is up, poverty is down, and
armies of *polizia* now patrol the city's main thoroughfares. Provided
you stay clear of the remaining pockets of crime (most of these neighborhoods, like the Sanità, Forcella district, and the Spanish Quarter,
are well off the beaten tourist path), you can enjoy a safe stay. That
noted, some advice is in order. In the city's picturesque quarters, streets
aren't just streets—they are literally "living rooms," so act as you
would as a guest in someone else's house: Don't gawk at residents as
you stroll through Spaccanapoli or the Pignasecca market. Have fun
taking photographs—most Neapolitans are extremely proud of their
neighborhoods—but don't make a production number out of it. In the
poorer sectors, don't wave a 20-carat diamond around, nor an expensive
Nikon, or, for that matter, your guide book. It's best to blend in with
the natives, so you might even camouflage yourself by storing your camera and pocketbook in a shopping bag from one of the city stores.

The main hazard in Naples is *lo scippo,* or bag-snatching, usually per-
petrated by two youths riding a souped-up motor scooter. As a general rule, give all scooters a wide berth, and use a small daybag rather
than a handbag, which can be an inviting target. For safe, undisturbed
shopping, opt for the pedestrianized areas like Via Toledo and Via Scarlatti, where scooter fiends are less likely to strike. Wear a concealed
money belt or remain aware of the stray pickpocket on the jammed
buses and subways. As they are fond of saying in Naples, if you think
something bad is going to happen to you, it will: So, smile and enjoy
yourself.

SUBWAY TRAVEL

Naples's main urban Metro line, Metropolitana Napoli, runs through
the city from Gianturco, east of Stazione Centrale, through the lower
level of Stazione Centrale, and takes you as far west as Pozzuoli. Useful stops include Piazza Cavour (just up the street from the Museo Archeologico Nazionale), Montesanto (near the Cumana railway station and
Montesanto funicular line), Piazza Amedeo (in the tony Chiaia district
and near the Chiaia funicular line), and the Stazione Mergellina (near
the Mergellina funicular line and hydrofoils for the islands).

A state-of-the-art line extending to the suburbs and hospital district
north of Naples is also operational: the Metropolitana Collinare. Unlike its creaking and squeaking downtown counterpart, this line does
not share its track with freight trains and high-speed passenger trains,
so published schedules are rigorously followed. The main Naples nexus
for this line is Piazza Vanvitelli, atop the Vomero Hill. In 2001 the line
was extended to connect with the main center-city line at Piazza Cavour,
just south of the Museo Archeologico Nazionale. Eventually, the new
line will dart south to Piazza Dante and Via Diaz, bend round to Piazza Municipio, and then head east via Piazza Bovio to Piazza Garibaldi,
with a target completion date of 2005.

FARES AND SCHEDULES

Subway tickets cost €0.80; the main line usually runs from 6:40 AM to 10:54 PM, with departures every 15 minutes.

➤ SUBWAY INFORMATION: **Metropolitana Napoli** (☎ 081/7484111).

TAXIS

Maligned and mistrusted for decades, Neapolitan taxi drivers are now beginning to shake off their somewhat tarnished image. However, tricks-of-the-trade are still used (taking you from the airport to your seafront location in Naples via the Tangenziale exit of Agnano is an old favorite and failing to switch on the meter are two favorites). Never take an "unofficial taxi" (the people who accost you at the airport and train station, offering you a taxi: real taxi drivers wait at a taxi stand). Do make sure that the meter has been turned on. It will start at €2.6, although the minimum fare is €4.5. Regular supplements are charged for the following services: €1.6 for Sundays and holidays, €2.1 for nighttime service (10 PM to 7 AM), €0.60 for each bag, €2.6 for service to or from the airport, and €0.80 for a radio call. Expect to pay from €6–€15 for most trips in town during the day, and €15–€20 to or from the airport. If taking a taxi to a location outside the city boundaries, you will have to pay double the fare on the meter, in addition to any supplements like autostrada tolls.

Taxis in Naples rarely cruise, but if empty they will stop if you flag them down. Taxis wait at stands or can be paged by telephone. Radio taxi numbers are listed below. When you phone, you should wait until you're given the taxi's ID (always the name of a city combined with a number). Obviously it's cheaper and occasionally quicker to reach a nearby taxi stand. The principal ones are: in the center, Piazza Garibaldi and Piazza Carità; near the seafront, Via Partenope, Piazza Vittoria, Piazza Amedeo, and Piazza Mergellina; and on the hills, Piazza Medaglie d'Oro and Piazza Vanvitelli in the Vomero.

➤ TAXI COMPANIES: **Radio taxi** (☎ 081/5707070, 081/5525252, 081/5560202, 081/5564444, or 081/5515151).

TELEPHONES

PHONE CARDS

For making long-distance calls, pick up a prepaid *scheda telefonica* (telephone card), sold at most newspaper kiosks and tobacconists and usable in any payphone.

TOURS

EXCURSION TOURS

You can book tours to Pompeii, Vesuvio, and the islands with CIT and through Bopa, conveniently open on Sundays, too.

➤ FEES AND SCHEDULES: **Bopa** (✉ Stazione Centrale, ☎ 081/267125). **CIT** (✉ Piazza Municipio 70, ☎ 081/5525426).

SPECIAL-INTEREST TOURS

If you're a spelunker at heart, call the Libera Associazione degli Escursionisti Sottosuolo for adventurous tours of Naples's underground; tours take place on the weekends, and meet at 10 AM at the Piazza Trieste e Trento in front of Bar Gambrinus. Other exciting tours of Naples's underground are offered weekends at 10 AM by Napoli Sotterranea.

For personalized tours specializing in art history contact Fine Arts cultural association.

➤ FEES AND SCHEDULES: **Fine Arts cultural association** (✉ Vico San Marcellino 8, ☎ 081/291634). **Libera Associazione degli Escursionisti Sottosuolo** (✉ Via Santa Teresa degli Spagnoli 24, ☎ 081/400256,

WEB www.lanapolisotterranea.it). **Napoli Sotterranea** (meet in Piazza San Gaetano to the left of San Paolo Maggiore, ☎ 081/449821).

Agencies in town offering guided tours with official guides include Carrani Tours, Milleviaggi, and Tourcar.
➤ CONTACTS: **Carrani Tours** (in Rome, ☎ 06/4880510 or 06/4742501). **Milleviaggi** (✉ Riviera di Chiaia 252, ☎ 081/7622064). **Tourcar** (✉ Piazza Matteotti 1, ☎ 081/5520429, WEB www.tourcar.it).

TRAIN TRAVEL

Stazione Centrale overflows onto Piazza Garibaldi, northeast of old Naples and the port. Services in this hectic station include a pharmacy, a travel agency, money exchange office, 24-hour luggage check (€2.7 every 12 hours), post office, and visitor information office. A Wasteels branch office sells BIJ train tickets Monday–Saturday 9–7:30. If you're staying in Mergellina, many trains stop first at Stazione Mergellina, also near a hydrofoil port. If you arrive at night, consider taking a taxi to your hotel, especially as local rail transport around the stations grinds to a halt between 10 and 11 PM.

Naples has two sets of commuter rail lines, each with its own tickets. The Ferrovia Circumvesuviana leaves for points east from the Stazione Circumvesuviana, on Corso Garibaldi; all trains also stop on the lower level of Stazione Centrale. Destinations include Ercolano (Herculaneum), Pompei (Pompeii), and Sorrento. SEPSA manages two railway lines that leave from the Stazione Cumana, near Montesanto Metro station. Both end at Torregaveta, at the west end of the Gulf of Naples; the Cumana line goes along the coast and stops at Pozzuoli and Lake Lucrino, among other places.

FARES AND SCHEDULES

Trains from the Stazione Centrale leave at least hourly for Rome (2½ hours northwest, €14–€23) and several times daily for Milan (7 hours northwest, €35–€55) and Reggio di Calabria (4½ hours southeast, €22–€35).
➤ TRAIN INFORMATION: **Ferrovia Circumvesuviana** (☎ 081/7722244, WEB www.vesuviana.it). **SEPSA** (☎ 081/7354111, WEB www.sepsa.it). **Stazione Centrale** (✉ Piazza Garibaldi, ☎ 848/888088, WEB www. fs-on-line.it). **Stazione Mergellina** (✉ Corso Vittorio Emanuele 4, ☎ 848/888088, WEB www.fs-on-line.it). **Wasteels branch office** (☎ 081/ 201071).

TRANSPORTATION AROUND NAPLES

A major saving grace in the city's transit system is the Giranapoli (€0.80), a 90-minute ticket that works for the Metropolitana (subway), the Cumana network, tram, *funicolari* (funiculars), and AMN city buses, as long as you are within the city limits. You can purchase tickets at most tobacco shops (look for the TABACCHI sign) or newsstands. If you buy a day pass (€2.4), remember to stamp it the first time you use it.

TRAVEL AGENCIES

Every Tour travel agency, open weekdays 9–1:30 and 3:30–7, and Saturdays 9–1, provides the entire range of American Express services. Dedicated to helping students, Eurostudy Travel, open weekdays 9:30–1:30 and 3–6, is across from the central university building; the ticket office is also open Saturday 9:30–12:30.
➤ LOCAL AGENTS: **Every Tour** (✉ Piazza Municipio 5–6, ☎ 081/ 5518564). **Eurostudy Travel** (✉ Via Mezzocannone 119, ☎ 081/ 5520947; ticket office, ✉ Via Mezzocannone 87; WEB www. vacanzegiovani).

VISITOR INFORMATION

The numerous tourist offices in Naples aren't always open when they claim to be, but most are generally open from Monday to Saturday 8:30–8 and Sunday 8:30–2 except where noted. There's an EPT office in Stazione Centrale, where the people are quite friendly and helpful; the main administrative center (with an atmosphere of Baroque mothballs) is in Piazza dei Martiri, and is open weekdays 8:30–2. There is also a branch at Stazione Mergellina. An AACST office specializes in information on old Naples but generally just gives out brochures. A second office, which is closed on Sundays, is handily inside the Palazzo Reale.

➤ TOURIST INFORMATION: **AACST**(✉ Piazza Gesù Nuovo, ☎ 01/5523328; ✉ Palazzo Reale, ☎ 081/2525726). **EPT** (✉ Stazione Centrale, ☎ 081/268779; ✉ Piazza dei Martiri 58, ☎ 081/405311; ✉ Stazione Mergellina, ☎ 081/7612102; WEB www.ept.napoli.it).

2 AROUND THE BAY: FROM POMPEII TO THE PHLEGREAN FIELDS

From steaming volcanic craters to peaceful archaeological sites, the area around the Bay of Naples has lost none of the fascination that first attracted the ancient Greeks and Romans. Here, within sight of Mount Vesuvius, are Pompeii, Herculaneum, Cumae, and Baiae—towns that now look like abandoned Cecil B. DeMille movie sets. When you've gorged yourself on Roman antiquities, sample the sumptuousness of the Royal Palace of Portici. Blessed with centuries-old traditions of fine gastronomy and hospitality, Campania Felix—Campania, the Happy Land, as the Romans called it—remains a lush landscape where the dividing line between myth and reality is tenuously drawn.

By Mark
Walters

Updated by
Mark Walters

F YOU'RE HEADING TO NAPLES, YOU CAN EITHER GET THERE by train, bus, or car, or you can "arrive" aboard a boat. If you're lucky enough to travel by water, a peacock's tail of splendor unfolds as you enter the vast Golfo di Napoli, or Bay of Naples. Enshrined in 1,001 travel posters, this nerve-tingling vista offers a turquoise-rimmed crescent of isles, hills, azure sky and sea, ancient cities, and modern villas, all arrayed around the bay to the east and west of Naples. But on each side of the city the earth fumes and grumbles, reminding us that all this beauty was born of cataclysm. Along the coast to the west are the Campi Flegrei, or the Phlegrean Fields of the ancients, where the crater of the Solfatara spews satisfyingly Dante-esque gases and where hills like Monte Nuovo have a habit of emerging overnight. Nearby are the dark, deep waters of Lago d'Averno, the lake that was allegedly the ancient doorway to Hell, or Hades, as it was then called. To the southeast is slumbering Vesuvius, the mother of all mounts, looking down from its 4,000-ft height at the coastal strip stretching from modern and ancient Pompeii all the way to Naples. With potential death and destruction so close at hand, it is small wonder that southern Italians—and in particular the inhabitants of Campania around Naples—plunge so enthusiastically into living life to its fullest, obeying to the letter Horace's precept—*carpe diem,* "seize the day."

Even with the most famous volcano in the world looming over the scene like a perpetual and living tombstone, visitors should feel perfectly safe. The observatory on Vesuvius's slopes keeps its scientific finger on the subterranean pulse and will warn when signs of misbehavior become evident, so no one need worry about becoming an unwilling exhibit in some future Pompeii. You can simply concentrate on the memorable sights that fringe the spectacularly blue bay. The whole region is fraught with legend and immortal names. Sixteen kilometers (10 mi) to the west of Naples lies an area where the emperors Claudius and Nero schemed and plotted in their villas (and worked on their suntans, no doubt), Virgil composed his poetry, and the Apostle Paul landed to spread the Gospel. Here are ancient sites, such as the Greeks' first colony in mainland Italy, the city of Cumae, home of the famed Cumaean Sybil; the luxury-loving Baiae, whose hot springs and dissolute living made it ancient Rome's most fashionable pleasure dome; and the Amphitheater of Pozzuoli, whose subterranean galleries are far better preserved than even Rome's Colosseum. Here are the Campi Flegrei—inspiration for Dante's *Inferno*—and the sulfur-ridden Solfatara, the "Little Vesuvius." Leapfrogging over Naples and spread out east along the bay are the glittering Bourbon palaces of Portici, the ancient palace at Oplontis, and, under the shadow of Vesuvius, Herculaneum and Pompeii—two of the largest archaeological sites in Europe. Nowhere else in Italy is there such a spectacular mingling of natural beauty with the remains of antiquity.

Rich archaeological and literary evidence shows that there has been a continuous human presence in the area for millennia. Used as outposts probably by the Minoans and Mycenaeans in the second millennium BC, the area was first colonized by Greeks from Euboea in the 8th century BC, who settled on the island of Pithekoussai (modern day Ischia) and later on the mainland at Cumae. So much we learn from a very valuable literary source, the Greek geographer Strabo (64 BC–after AD 21), who must have traveled extensively in the area. The early Greeks traded widely with the Etruscans and local Italic peoples, eventually extending their sphere of influence to Neapolis and southward and northward along the shores of the Tyrrhenian Sea.

Greek civilization flourished for hundreds of years along this seaboard, but there was nothing in the way of centralized government until centuries later when the Romans surged southward and began to set up colonies of their own for added protection, especially after foreign incursions led by such flamboyant figures as Pyrrhus and Hannibal in the 3rd century BC.

From the 1st century BC onward, Campania became synonymous with sybaritic wealth. It was here that the wealthy Romans built their palatial residences, tapping the naturally hot springs for their fabled baths and harnessing the rich volcanic soils in the area to produce wines lauded by Latin poets. Here emperors indulged in vices that would have been unseemly in the capital, and there was the usual complement of public baths and theaters to keep the plebeians happy.

The merrymaking to the east of Naples was truncated in AD 79 by a jolt from Vesuvius, believed by few at the time to harbor any danger for those living at its base. We are fortunate to have Pliny the Younger's memorable description of his uncle being overwhelmed by fumes and dying of asphyxiation in Stabiae, now Castellammare di Stabia. Although written some years after the event, Pliny's letter to Tacitus is a unique and moving account of the disaster. But as so often happens in history, other people's cataclysms are an archaeologist's dream: Pompeii, Herculaneum, and outlying lesser-known settlements such as Oplontis were spared the ravages of the centuries and have been remarkably preserved for posterity.

Following the fall of the Roman Empire and the period of general decay that prevailed during Byzantine times, more than 1,000 years were to pass before the area's classical greatness was once again appreciated, this time by young, well-heeled 18th- and 19th-century travelers from northern Europe, for whom a visit to Vesuvius and the various ancient sites was the culmination of their Grand Tour.

Many would say that the region is now experiencing a second Renaissance. Increasingly, conventional modes of tourist development are being scaled back in favor of a more global appreciation of the landscape. The designation of Vesuvius as a national park in 1996 and, together with the villas on its lower slopes, as a UNESCO World Heritage Site in 1998, points the way toward a resource-rich future, guaranteeing travelers an enthralling mix of archaeology, history, folklore, gastronomy, and nature for years to come.

Pleasures and Pastimes

Dining

If *Betae garo cum olivis capparibusque* and *Cassata oplontis* seem a somewhat unusual listing on a menu, fitting perhaps for an antiquarian Vatican dinner party, further surprises will be in store when dining out in the modern town of Pompeii. At the Principe restaurant, Roman banquets are re-created with ingredients that would have been used 2,000 years ago. You might even be able to taste one of the dishes mentioned above (the first is beet with fish sauce, olives, and capers). Fortunately, the ancients committed much of their culinary expertise to writing, thanks mainly to authors like Cato, Cicero, and the renowned gourmet of Augustan times, Apicius.

To the west of Naples, Cumae is thought to have been the setting for part of Petronius's *Satyricon,* a picaresque novel probably written in the 1st century AD, containing the memorable scene of a dinner hosted by the nouveau-riche Trimalchio. In the same area of the Campi Flegrei, the tradition of abundance, if not excess, continues in a host of local restaurants and trattorias. This is where many local Neapolitans migrate on weekends to buy their *frutti di mare* (seafood) or dine in Lucullan style at one of the many waterside restaurants in the area, at half the price they would spend at restaurants nearer home.

The wines, too, are unlikely to disappoint: the white-grape variety Falanghina, from the Campi Flegrei, has justifiably built up a reputation as a fine accompaniment to fish-centered meals, while the slopes of Vesuvius produce Lacrima Christi (red, white, and rosé). If available, try the range of wines produced at competitive prices by local bottlers Cantina Grotta del Sole or De Falco.

CATEGORY	COST*
$$$$	over €21
$$$	€14–€21
$$	€7–€14
$	under €7

per person for a main course at dinner

Hiking

For challenging hikes off the beaten track, parts of Vesuvius have been mapped out with trails for public access. What looks like a barren wasteland from down below turns out to be a profusion of well-adapted plant and animal life, which is at its best in spring and early summer. Deserted paths cut across ancient lava fields and pyroclastic material, through lunarlike terrain and then suddenly into Mediterranean scrub and woodland. As an alternative, on torrid summer days, take an eight-minute cable-car ride from Castellammare di Stabia up to Monte Faito, which rises impressively to almost 4,000 ft on the southeastern sweep of the Bay of Naples. A short walk takes you into shady beech woods reminiscent of Italy's Apennine backbone, while more ambitious trails marked by the Club Alpino Italiano lead across imposing landscapes to the Amalfi Coast.

Lodging

To avoid what might seem like glorified Pompeian *lupanaria*—those favored abodes of ancient ladies of the night—the choice of hotel merits special attention throughout the area. Most hotels will give excellent value for money compared with locations in the city of Naples and will be a good deal quieter as well. However, where hotels are close to main roads—and that means motor scooters at night—ask for quiet rooms at the back, especially in the busy towns of Pompeii and Pozzuoli. As throughout Italy, high season is usually at Christmas, Easter, and during the summer, when temperatures, prices, and visitor numbers reach a crescendo. At Pompeii avoid visiting during religious festivities if at all possible, as local hotels are likely to be booked up with pilgrims months in advance. As a general rule, to ensure you get the right room at the right time, book well ahead of your expected arrival.

CATEGORY	COST*
$$$$	over €155
$$$	€103–€155
$$	€51–€103
$	under €51

*All prices are for a double room at high season, excluding tax and se

Nature

If you're suffering from a surfeit of archaeology or feel
compensate for overindulging in the local *cucina*, a vis
extinct volcanic craters near Naples could produce di
troni crater, now a preserve run by the World Wid

offers breathtakingly beautiful walks amid Mediterranean woodland only 16 km (10 mi) from the very heart of Naples. Picnic sites have been thoughtfully laid out in various shady spots within the crater perimeter. At the base, there is the added interest of small brackish lakes overlooked by an observation hide, so there's a good chance of seeing a variety of bird species. Like so many places here, the crater is steeped in history: used by the Romans for its natural thermal baths, this whole area became the hunting domain of the Aragonese in the 15th century and then of the Bourbon kings in the 18th and 19th centuries.

A smaller crater near the coast to the west of Pozzuoli offering shorter and less shady walks is Monte Nuovo, whose cone formed in just eight days of explosive activity in 1538. Innovatively run by the town council of Pozzuoli together with a local school, the cone still exhibits some residual volcanic activity in the form of fumaroles. This is the place to hone your botanical skills, with many of the main species of the Mediterranean maquis having been planted and clearly labeled close to the site offices.

Exploring Pompeii, Herculaneum, and Mt. Vesuvius

The lower slopes of Vesuvius, which is the most densely inhabited volcanic region in the world, are crisscrossed by major roads and several railway lines, providing easy access to most of the archaeological sites. Start with Pompeii, work your way clockwise around the volcano to Oplontis and Herculaneum, and then shoot off at a tangent to the Museo Archeologico Nazionale in Naples to study the many artistic treasures excavated from these towns. To make a chronological departure from classical times, while in Ercolano do a short detour to visit the sumptuous Royal Palace of Portici and a Vesuvian villa such as the attractively restored Villa Campolieto, both built during Bourbon rule in the 18th century. The best form of transportation is the Circumvesuviana light railway, its stations never being more than a 10-minute walk from the major sites.

Numbers in the text correspond to numbers in the margin and on the East of Naples, Pompeii, and West of Naples maps.

Great Itineraries

With limited time at your disposal, priority should be given to the sites of **Herculaneum** ② and **Pompeii** ⑥–㉖, although a single day will merely whet the appetite. A practical minimum for really absorbing the splendors of this area and getting a healthy balance of archaeology, history, museums, and cuisine is about three days. To take in the entire span from the Campi Flegrei to Pompeii, including some of the undeservedly less-visited sites such as Stabiae in **Castellammare di Stabia** ㉗ and **Baia** ㉝, you would be advised to make a weeklong trip with at least two base camps, one on either side of Naples.

IF YOU HAVE 3 DAYS

Begin at **Pompeii** ⑥–㉖, allowing at least half a day for the archaeological site, which will be just enough to take in the main civic buildings, a representative sampling of villas, and the hotspots of ancient Roman entertainment, such as the Amphitheater. Given the part it played in AD 79, **Vesuvius** ③ also merits a visit, though temperatures at the peak in winter months can be pretty frigid. Then head for **Herculaneum** ②, for its less-visited but more evocative ruins. In between, you should slot in the villa of **Oplontis** ⑤, located in the town of Torre Annunziata, now included in the three-day archaeological pass.

IF YOU HAVE 5 DAYS
More time in the area will enable you to head west of Naples into the Campi Flegrei, where a little exploring will pay immediate dividends. To experience the volcanic nature of this otherworldly terrain, walk across the crater of the **Solfatara** ㉘ and then soak up the archaeological sites of **Pozzuoli** ㉙ and **Baia** ㉝. Reserve half a day for the site of **Cumae** ㉞ and appreciate the sweeping views of Italy's Tyrrhenian coastline from its impressive acropolis.

IF YOU HAVE 7 DAYS
With a little more time to unwind and appreciate the diversity of this remarkable landscape, try to fit in a visit to one of the extinct craters—now nature reserves—of **Monte Nuovo** ㉜ or the **Astroni** ㉚, west of Naples. With time left over, sample the opulence of a Vesuvian villa on the so-called Miglio d'Oro, or Golden Mile, built by the aristocracy in Bourbon times close to the Royal Palace of **Portici** ①.

WHEN TO TOUR POMPEII, HERCULANEUM, AND MT. VESUVIUS
This part of the Mediterranean is at its best in spring and fall. Winter months occasionally reserve chill surprises for visitors, with roads on the upper slopes of Vesuvius becoming dangerously icy at times. In April and May watch out for the hordes of (nonpaying) schoolchildren at archaeological sites and, as a general rule—to avoid the crowds—visit sites first thing in the morning or in the late afternoon before closing time (usually an hour before sunset). Pompeii rewards its overheated summer visitors with open-air theatrical performances on the site during the evenings, while other sites such as Cumae and Oplontis have rival attractions. For nature lovers, this part of the Mediterranean, especially the verdant Campi Flegrei, becomes a floral feast at springtime, while the north-facing slopes of Vesuvius are still awash with color as late as June and July.

UNDER THE SHADOW OF VESUVIUS: PORTICI TO HERCULANEUM

Though barely more than a third as high as Mt. Etna, its Sicilian counterpart, Vesuvius with its relatively modest 4,189 ft has achieved unparalleled status in the collective consciousness of the Italians and the world. "Vesuvius is nature committing suicide," Madame de Staël reported back to Parisians during the Age of Enlightenment. For centuries this still-active volcano had offered a spectacle to visitors who flocked to the Bay of Naples to marvel at its small-scale eruptions, ever-present plumes of smoke, and thundering fumaroles. In the mid-18th century, in fact, the entire court of Naples set up shop in Portici, at the foot of the mountain, building summer villas that served as ringside seats to the volcano's pyrotechnics. Artists painted the mountain in eruption, streams of lava rendered in lurid hues of blood. Romantic poets climbed the peak under the full moon to create odes extolling its sublime and terrible power. Duchesses (fashionably attired with earrings and cameos made of lava stone) would hire chair porters to bear them up to the rim, where, down below, rainbow mounds of sulfurous ash, vents hissing steam, lunarlike boulders—everything it seems but little *i* dashing about with long Luciferian pitchforks—presented a hellish
All the while, inhabitants living around the cone would stu*
vius for signs of impending destruction. "*Napoli fa i peccati*
li paga," the residents of nearby Torre del Greco used to mut*
sins and the Torre suffers." When reports of depraved *
culated about Neapolitans across the bay, chastisemen*
expected.

In the 18th century, the Roman towns of Pompeii and Herculaneum—buried by the devastation wrought by the famous AD 79 eruption—were first excavated and became the most celebrated archaeological sites in Europe. Today, thousands of visitors arrive every day, most with one eye monitoring *Il Vesuvio*, just a few miles away. There have been many major and minor eruptions of the volcano in the past 2,000 years, the most recent in 1944. The fact remains that there have been around 30 eruptions since AD 79 with only two in the 20th century. This might be construed as good news, but many vulcanologists think it is ominous when a living volcano is so silent, and they now maintain a constant watch.

Portici

❶ *7 km (5½ mi) southeast from Naples; 1 km (½ mi) northwest from Ercolano.*

Portici, whose Reggia, or Royal Palace, offers a peek into the gilded lives of the 18th-century rich and famous, is set rather incongruously within the urban sprawl of the *Comuni Vesuviani*. A little more than 250 years ago, the area was chosen by the first Bourbon King of the Two Sicilies, Charles III, as the site for a royal palace that would be sufficiently close to Naples for him to be able to return to the capital at a moment's notice, yet far enough away for the king and his entourage to indulge in hunting, one of the main Bourbon pursuits. No matter that courtiers were worried by the proximity of Vesuvius; Charles refused to show concern at any imminent danger, proclaiming, "God, the immaculate Virgin, and San Gennaro will protect us." The royal presence in the area triggered a boom in real estate, with more than 120 ducal villas being built in the subsequent half century on a stretch of land that came to be known as the "Miglio d'Oro" (Golden Mile). Here life became one long *fête champêtre*, with costume balls, picnics, concerts, and entertainment, some of which enchanted the likes of Goethe and Lord Byron. Today, progress is being made by the *Ente per le Ville Vesuviane* (Vesuvian Villa Agency) to purchase and restore the villas to their former glory.

The showpiece is Portici's *Reggia* (palace), or **Palazzo Reale.** Straddling the Via Nazionale delle Calabrie (Statate 18), the main road that led south of Naples in past centuries, now renamed Via Università, this royal palace was designed by the architect Canevari, complete with a layout of 75 acres of woodland, and executed by another architect, Ferdinando Fuga, 1738–42. It stands impressively at the foothills of Vesuvius and enjoys sweeping views across the Bay of Naples from both the south-facing inner courtyard and its upper floors. Although the agriculture department of Naples University still occupies most of the palace, the cultural heritage ministry has taken over a few of the rooms on the *piano nobile* and currently uses them for temporary exhibitions, thereby restoring to the public one of the main landmarks of Bourbon history and architecture.

The palace is conveniently located on a trolley-bus route (No. 255) between Ercolano and Portici, a 10-minute walk northwest up Corso Resina from the Herculaneum archaeological site. The bus stop is unmistakable, in the middle of the courtyard right between the northern and southern wings. Head for the university porters' lodge on the seaward side (a parking lot just beyond) and mount the monumental staircase leading up to the piano nobile. At the risk of developing a crick in your neck, admire the well-preserved 18th-century trompe l'oeil frescoes decorating the walls and the ceiling and generally enjoy these now-hallowed halls of academia. Horatio Nelson would have walked up the same staircase on his way to a royal banquet held in his honor by

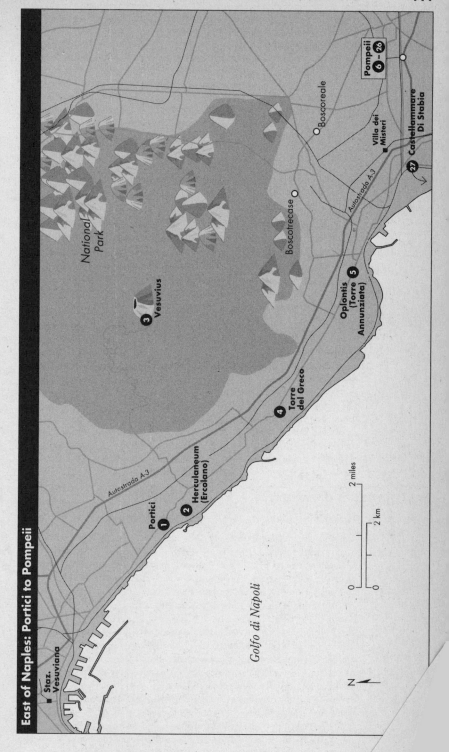

East of Naples: Portici to Pompeii

King Ferdinand IV and Queen Carolina in 1798, where he sat opposite and first met Sir William Hamilton and his wife, Emma. At the
time the palace was used as a repository for many of the early finds
from Herculaneum, now in the Museo Archeologico in Naples, and it
was noted particularly for the decorative 18th-century panels from the
finest salon—called the porcelain, or china, room—which were subsequently moved to the Royal Palace of Capodimonte, where they can
still be admired today. ⊠ *Via Università 100,* ☎ *081/7751251.* ☒ *Free.*
⊘ *Sept.–July, weekdays 8:30–7.*

Opposite the entrance to the Royal Palace of Portici lies the **Orto
Botanico** (Botanical Garden), founded in 1872. It is housed within the
palace grounds and abuts the magnificent Holmoak Wood, the hunting preserve of the Bourbon kings. The original collection was severely
damaged in World War II, when the botanical institute was requisi-
tioned and the garden used as a vehicle parking area by Allied forces.
Since then the collection has recovered and expanded, with new ac-
quisitions especially from Madagascar and Central and South America, a delightfully shady palmery, an impressive variety of cycads, and
some unusually large specimens of the exotic Asian tree *Ginkgo biloba.*
If assistance or guidance is at hand, ask to see the rare southern African
desert plant *Welwitschia mirabilis,* and the native but endangered
primrose *Primula palinuri.* In addition to normal opening hours, guided
visits can also be arranged by appointment with the curator. ⊠ *Via
Università,* ☎ *081/7754850.* ☒ *Free.* ⊘ *Sept.–July, weekdays 8–1.*

Dining

$ ✕ **A' Cantinella do Cunvento.** A short walk down Via Università from
the Royal Palace of Portici brings you to this unpretentious ristorante-
pizzeria, known to the locals as Da Peppino after its owner-manager
Giuseppe. Although crowded with staff from the nearby college at
lunchtime, there is nothing donnish about the down-to-earth service
or prices. The competitive all-in-one price—an incredibly good value—
includes first course (pasta or rice), main course (octopus salad is a specialty), and fruit. ⊠ *Via Università 64, Portici,* ☎ *081/7755301. No
credit cards. Sometimes closed weekends.*

Herculaneum (Ercolano)

★ ➋ *12 km (8 mi) southeast of Naples; 40 km (25 mi) northwest of Salerno.*

A visit to the archaeological site of Herculaneum neatly counterbalances
the hustle of its larger neighbor, Pompeii. And although close to the heart
of the busy town of Ercolano—indeed, in places right under it—the ancient site seems worlds apart, and you have the sensation of being cat-
apulted back into the past, for here there is ample supply of ancient allure
and splendor (unlike Pompeii, whose site is much more ruined). Like
Pompeii, Herculaneum was buried by Vesuvius's eruption in AD 79. Unlike Pompeii, it was submerged in a mass of volcanic mud that sealed
and preserved wood and other materials (at Pompeii, most organic matter rotted away over time). Much smaller than its famous neighbor, Herculaneum was wealthier, more select, and more of what has been found
has been left in place. Several villas have inlaid marble floors that evoke
the same admiration as the mosaics in Naples's Museo Archeologico.
Elsewhere it is possible to gauge how the less privileged lived: more remains of the upper stories than in Pompeii, so you can view the original stairs to the cramped, poorly lighted rooms that gave onto the
central courtyard. Here there is more of a sense of a living community
than Pompeii is able to convey. Like all the other sites in the Vesuvian
area, Herculaneum is served efficiently by the Circumvesuviana railway,
which provides fast, frequent, and economical connections; from

Naples's Stazione Centrale or Stazione Vesuviana, take the Circumvesuviana train to the Ercolano stop (5 per hour, 20 minutes east, €1.03). The ruins are a five-minute walk down Via Novembre toward the Bay of Naples. Archaeology buffs will want to bring a flashlight to better see into the dark corners of the excavated houses.

Lying more than 60 ft below the town of Ercolano, the **Scavi di Ercolano** (Excavations of Herculaneum) are set among the acres of greenhouses that make this area one of Europe's chief flower-growing areas. It was named, like several other Greek colonies around the Mediterranean, after its legendary founder Heracles (Hercules), but details surrounding its foundation date by its Greek settlers has yet to be revealed. Certainly the grid layout of the town plan suggests affinities with nearby Neapolis (now Naples), so it could have been an offshoot of its neighbor on the Bay of Naples. Like many Greek sites in southern Italy, in about the 4th century BC it fell under Samnite influence and finally became a *municipium* under Roman dominion in 89 BC. At the time of its destruction in AD 79, it had about 5,000 inhabitants (as compared to Pompeii's 20,000), many of whom were fishermen, craftsmen, and artists, while a lucky few patricians owned villas overlooking the sea. In contrast with Pompeii, most of the damage here was done by volcanic mud. This semiliquid mass seeped into the crevices and niches of every building, covering household objects and enveloping textiles and wood—sealing all in a compact, airtight tomb.

Casual excavation—and haphazard looting—began at the beginning of the 18th century under the prince of Elbeuf, who purchased the land after a farmer had made several chance finds in marble. The excavation technique at the time consisted of digging vertical shafts and horizontal galleries, and whenever possible, gunpowder was used to speed up the work—techniques that make those of the much-maligned Heinrich Schliemann, discover of Troy, sound positively scrupulous. It was precisely through this network of underground tunnels that 18th-century visitors from northern Europe on their Grand Tour—such as Horace Walpole and Thomas Gray—were to experience the buried city. Systematic digs were not initiated until the 1920s, by which time many of the sugarplums buried within the cake had already been damaged or removed. Today less than half of Herculaneum has been excavated; with present-day Ercolano and the unlovely Resina quarter (famous among bargain hunters as the area's largest secondhand clothing market) perched on top of the site, progress is understandably limited. On entry, in addition to getting a good overview of the site, you get an idea of the amount of volcanic matter that had to be removed during excavations as you walk down the ramp to the lower entrance on the seaward side, with the neatly laid-out streets and well-preserved edifices to your right.

Although Herculaneum had only one-fourth the population of Pompeii and has only been partially excavated, what has been found is generally better preserved. In some cases you can even see the original wooden beams, staircases, and furniture. Lending a touch of verdant life, some of the peristyle gardens have been replanted. Today much excitement is focused on one excavation in an inaccessible corner of the site, the **Villa dei Papiri,** built by Julius Caesar's father-in-law. The building takes its name from the 1,800 carbonized papyrus scrolls dug up here in the 18th century, leading scholars to believe it may have been a study center or library. Now Italian archaeologists and geologists have uncovered part of the villa itself and hope to unearth more of the library—given the right funds and political support. Little of the villa can be seen above ground, though visitors to the J. Paul Getty Museum in California can see a modern version of the villa, modeled according to drawings made by the Swiss antiquarian Carl Weber in the 18th century and now the spectacular repository for the Getty's important collection of classical antiquities.

Walk through the ticket office down the slope to the southern end of the site toward the large modern structure of the Antiquarium (yet to be opened). This is a good point at which to view the grid system of roads, with the three *cardines* (from northeast to southwest) being intersected by two *decumani* from left to right. The blocks, as in Pompeii, are referred to as *insulae,* each containing four or five main villas and sometimes a row of shops. In general, and unsurprisingly, the best mosaics, wall paintings, and any organic remains such as wooden furniture are found in those parts that were excavated in the 20th century. The 19th-century open-air excavators—though systematic—took few precautions to preserve the upper stories (just note the ruinous state of Insula II, in the southwest corner) and, in addition, the artwork has been exposed to the air for an extra century.

Entry to the site is currently gained via an underground passage which cuts down through 60 feet of volcanic deposits and emerges by the southern (lower) end of the site. The path then crosses a marshy area which was the original sea level and the site of a small port. This means that thanks to various eruptions (especially AD 79 and AD 1631), the topography of the land has changed beyond all recognition. It is now hard to believe that Herculaneum lay *"inter duos fluvios infra Vesuvium"* (between two rivers below Vesuvius). Visitors are nowadays channeled up to the town past the **Terme Suburbane** (Suburban Baths, usually open mornings only). The plinths were the bases for marble statues dedicated to the town benefactor, Marcus Nonius Balbus, long since carted off to the Archaeological Museum in Naples. Much of the volcanic mud here has been left in situ, so you get a good idea not only of a Roman baths complex, but especially of the problems that the archaeologists faced when excavating it. ⊠ *Il Quartiere Suburbano.*

In antiquity, the **Casa dei Cervi** was one of the first houses that visitors to the town would have passed as they entered the city from the seaward side. Like most top-notch town residences, however, the entranceway is plain and leads into a long narrow corridor called the *fauces,* or *vestibulum,* which then opens onto an atrium. The showpiece in this particular house is the garden area surrounded by a cryptoportico and terminating in a partially reconstructed gazebo. Of course, prior to the eruption, the house would have had a fine view over the Bay of Naples. ⊠ *Insula IV.*

As you walk around Herculaneum, you'll notice the narrow entrances of the houses and the wider entrances for shops, inns, and other buildings where large numbers of people required access. A case in point is at the corner of Cardo V and the Decumanus Inferior where you'll see two access points and counters with large amphoras for keeping dishes warm. This was one of the town's **Thermopolia,** the fast-food outlets of the ancient world. Some of its customers may well have come from the building next door on the seaward side, the **Lupanare** (brothel), complete with its waiting room at the back right, where potential clients could have pored over sketches to decide exactly what type of service they required from the *meretrices* in the warren of cubicles within. ⊠ *Insula IV.*

Of course, no town would have been complete without its sports facilities and Herculaneum was no exception. Just opposite the *thermopolium* on Cardo V is the entrance to the large **Palaestra** where a variety of ball games and wrestling matches would have been staged.

Here, when you look at the peristyle columns and realize that only three of a total of over 20 have been excavated, you appreciate how much of the ancient town still lies buried under solidified volcanic mud. ⊠ *Insula Orientalis II.*

On Cardo IV parallel to Cardo V, close to the Forum Baths, is the **Casa del Nettuno ed Anfitrite** (The House of Neptune and Amphitrite). It takes its name from the mosaic that still sports its bright blue coloring and adorns the wall of the small secluded nymphaeum, or shrine, at the back of the house. According to legend, in the time-honored fashion of the Olympians, Neptune (or Poseidon) saw Amphitrite dancing with the Nereids on the island of Naxos, carried her off, and married her. The adjacent wall, in similar mosaic style though less well preserved, has a hunting scene with a stag being pursued by a dog. Annexed to the same house is a remarkably preserved wineshop, where amphorae still rest on carbonized wooden shelves.

Aside from its fine mosaics, this house has a good example of an atrium (courtyard) with an *impluvium* in the middle in which to collect rainwater, channeled to an underground cistern (just lift the metal lid to have a look). At the back of the atrium there would have been a *tablinum,* a main reception room where the *patronus* (host) would receive his *clientes* (guests). In some houses there would have been a screen to provide more privacy for the master of the house. Where there was space, a colonnaded garden (peristyle) was considered desirable, complete with fountains and a *triclinium* (open-air dining room). *Cubicula* (bedrooms) were sometimes on either side of the entrance, although this is by no means the rule in Herculaneum. Also try to spot the service area (kitchen), with the servants' quarters often immediately above. ⊠ *Insula V.*

Stories of Roman licentiousness are belied by the **Terme del Foro** (Forum Baths), where there were separate sections for men and women. Here you see most of the architectural ingredients of *thermae* (baths). But besides the mandatory trio in the men's section (a round *frigidarium,* a cool swimming pool; a *tepidarium,* a semi-heated pool; and a *calidarium,* or heated pool), there is also an *apodyterium,* or changing room, with partitioned shelves for depositing togas and a low podium to use as seating space while in line to use the facilities. For more attractive mosaics—particularly a spectacular rendition of Neptune—go around into the women's baths (with seemingly no frigidarium). The heating system in the tepidarium was also different (no hot air piped through or under, only braziers). Note the steam vents ingeniously built into the bath's benches and the small overhead cubbies in which bathers stored their togas. ⊠ *Insula VI.*

An outstanding example of carbonized remains is in the **Casa del Tramezzo di Legno** (House of the Wooden Partition), as it has been prosaically labeled by archaeologists. Following renovation work in the mid-1st century AD, the house was designed to have a frontage on three sides of Insula III and included a number of storerooms, shops, and second-floor habitations. This suggests that the owner was a wealthy *mercator,* a member of the up-and-coming merchant class that was starting to edge the patricians out of their privileged positions. The fauces in this house lead into an airy atrium, with a lovely garden. Look closely at the impluvium, and you'll see the original impluvium flooring below, which was later replaced with marble, perhaps under a change of owners. Next to the impluvium is an elegant marble table, or *cartibulum,* while behind is the tablinum partially screened off by a bronze-studded wooden partition (the central part of which is missing) that would also have had hooks for hanging *lucernae* (lamps). ⊠ *Insula III, 11–12.*

If you're looking for decorations, these are especially delicate in the **Casa del Atrio a Mosaico** (House of the Mosaic Atrium), with a geometrically patterned flooring in the vestibulum leading into a black-and-white checkerboard pattern in the atrium, with the tablinum in the background. The tablinum is unusually elaborate, with its three aisles separated by two rows of pillars topped by Corinthian capitals, conforming to the design described by the great Roman architect Vitruvius as *"oecus aegyptius,"* or Egyptian-style room. Like many other houses in both Herculaneum and Pompeii, this may be kept locked, and you could be restricted to a peek through the entrance. This villa enjoyed a sweeping view of the sea, a vantage point utilized by the many rooms that had windows. ⊠ *Insula IV, 1–2.*

One of the more spectacular sights at Herculaneum is also a well-guarded secret: the **underground theater** dating to about the 1st century BC, in the northwest corner of the site but only accessible by prior arrangement with site guides or local travel operators. Access is gained from a small square building painted in Pompeian red at Corso Resina 23, about 5 minutes' walk farther along the road to Portici, opposite the Church of Santa Caterina. If you're visiting in summer months, you can get some extra atmosphere by seeing the evening show, performed in Italian, that's set in the various houses down in the archaeological site. Ask at the ticket office or local Azienda di Soggiorno (Information Bureau) for information. ⊠ *Corso Resina 6, Ercolano,* ☎ *081/ 7390963.* 🎟 *€8.26 for 4 sites (one day) or the "Biglietto Cumulativo" for €13.42 for 5 sites (Pompeii, Herculaneum, Boscoreale, Oplontis, and Stabiae) valid for 3 days.* ⊙ *Daily 9–1 hr before sunset (ticket office closes 2 hrs before sunset).*

Leaving the archaeological site of Herculaneum and heading southeast along Corso Resina with Vesuvius on your left and the Bay of Naples on your right, after about 980 ft you'll pass the entrance to **Villa Campolieto,** one of the most attractive villas, which—like most historic buildings still standing in the area—has survived centuries of volcanic eruptions, earthquakes, and post-Bourbon neglect. Go in through the well-tended gardens past the information kiosk (leaflets are available in English) and turn left into the main building. If you're motorized, ask at the kiosk to use the parking facilities at the far end of the gardens.

The construction of Villa Campolieto was commissioned by Prince Luzio of Sangro and entrusted to no less than four architects during its troubled conception from 1755 to 1775, with the final touches added by the architect Luigi Vanvitelli, better known for his work on the Royal Palace of Caserta, and his son Carlo. After entering through the gardens—this was in fact the original main entrance, as the large doorway on the Via Nazionale delle Calabrie (now Corso Resina) would have been reserved for carriages—proceed up the Vanvitellian staircase (similar to the one at the palace at Caserta) to the piano nobile, currently used for art exhibitions and as lecture halls. Note the classical scenes in most of the frescoes on this floor, with fine illusionist work by Jacopo Cestaro, including depictions of Minerva and Mercury set in a Vanvitelli-style colonnade. Cestaro was also responsible for the beautifully restored frescoed ceilings in both front rooms facing Vesuvius. At ground-floor level, the main peculiarity is the elliptical rotunda, which provides a picturesque setting for outdoor concerts and theatrical performances during the Vesuvian Villas Festival in July. Note the natural gray shading of the steps and lower facade, characteristic of many buildings erected in the Bourbon era, from the local volcanic *piperno* stone. This villa is the headquarters for the Ente per le Ville Vesuviane association. ⊠ *Corso Resina 283, Ercolano,* ☎ *081/7322134.* 🎟 *Free.* ⊙ *Tues.–Sun. 10–1.*

Dining

$–$$ ✕ **Trattoria da Calcagno.** Catering to locals and foreigners alike—always a good sign in areas with large tourist flows—this eatery is a five-minute walk up from the excavations of Herculaneum just off Via 4 Novembre. Dishes and wines vary according to season: *pasta e fagioli* (pasta with beans) is a winter favorite while richly garnished spaghetti with clams is a summer stalwart, all washed down by lively Vesuvian wines. ✉ *Corso Italia 17, Ercolano,* ☎ *081/7390405. No credit cards. Closed Sun.*

Shopping

Donadio Manifattura Coralli (✉ Via del Corallo, just by the Ercolano exit of the Napoli-Salerno *autostrada*, Ercolano, ☎ 081/7752900, WEB www.donadio.net) is first and foremost a cameo factory; it also sells directly to the public. Local artisans can be observed making the cameos, an age-old tradition in which shells are meticulously carved to produce mythological scenes in relief, exploiting the natural layering and contrasting colors of the raw material.

Vesuvius

❸ *16 km (10 mi) east of Naples; 8 km (5 mi) northeast of Herculaneum; 40 km (25 mi) northwest of Salerno.*

Today Vesuvius may have lost its plume of smoke, but it has lost none of its fascination. Although the destructive powers of Vesuvius are undoubtedly diminished, the threat of an eruption is ever present for the local population that lives crowded at its base. While the administrators in the 13 *comuni* surrounding the volcano are well versed in risk-management procedures, because its slopes are more densely populated than any other volcano in the world, the practicalities of evacuating over half a million people are daunting. In bygone ages the task of protecting the local inhabitants fell to the martyred patron saint of Naples, San Gennaro, or St. Januarius, whose statue was often borne aloft through the streets of Naples in attempts to placate the volcano's wrath. Nowadays, volcanic activity is attentively monitored by the Osservatorio Vesuviano, founded under Bourbon king Ferdinand II in the mid-19th century and the facility where the seismic scale was invented. The original observatory, conspicuous with its Pompeian red facade, has survived unscathed on the volcano's upper slopes and now serves as a conference center and small museum, the **Museo dell'Osservatorio Vesuviano** housing a mineralogical display, characteristic landscape gouaches, early seismographs, and information panels. Access during the week is restricted to scientific groups, associations, and schools, but the museum is open weekends to the general public. ✉ *Via Osservatorio, Ercolano,* ☎ *081/7777149 or 081/7777150,* WEB *www.parks.it.* ✆ *Free.* ☉ *Sat.–Sun. 10–2.*

Seen from the other side of the Bay of Naples, Vesuvius appears to have two peaks: on the northern side is the steep face of Monte Somma, possibly part of the original crater wall in AD 79; to the south is the present-day cone of Vesuvius, which has actually formed within the ancient crater. The AD 79 cone would have been considerably higher, perhaps peaking at more than 2,150 ft. The upper slopes bear the visible scars left by relatively recent eruptions, the most striking being the lava flow from 1944 lying to the left (north side) of the main approach road from Ercolano on the way up. On earlier lava flows, such as that of 1872, the grayish lichen named after the volcano, *Stereocaulon vesuvianum,* has had more time to break up the volcanic rocks and prepare the way for pioneer plants like red valerian and the characteristic leggy Mt. Etna broom, which transform the upper slopes into a blaze of dark pink and yellow in late spring.

Under its new status as a national park and having been designated a World Biosphere Reserve by UNESCO, Vesuvius currently enjoys substantially greater protection from urban encroachment and other land uses that have ravaged the towns lying at its base. The **park office** (☎ 081/7717549) has mapped out a series of trails open to the public; a popular one includes the Valle del Gigante (Giant's Valley) and the Valle dell'Inferno (Hell's Valley). To reach this, head downhill from the summit parking lot on the north side and look for the footpath descending on the other side of the guardrail at the first bend. Those seeking a barren lunar landscape will be disappointed: the flora here is remarkably diverse, boasting 23 species of orchids set amid an interesting combination of montane vegetation and Mediterranean maquis. Birders should watch out for peregrine falcons soaring over Monte Somma and for ravens at lower altitude, in addition to various warbler species that have found their eco-niches on the upper slopes of Vesuvius.

For public transport users, the Vesuvius bus run by **Transporti Vesuviani** (☎ 081/5592582) does about five trips a day up Vesuvius (one-way from Pompei: €2.54, from Ercolano: €1.52). It starts from Piazza Anfiteatro in modern Pompei, stops at Piazza Esedra near the *autostrada* toll booths, does another pickup at the Ercolano station, snakes its way up the mountain to the foot of the long-defunct *seggiovia* (chairlift) and the aborted *funicolare* (cable car) of the 1980s (2,943 ft), and then after a brief stop heads farther uphill to Quota 1000, the car park near the top (let the driver know if you want to visit the Museo half-way up). This is the end of the road for all but service vehicles up to the crater and the best place to reward yourself with a drink after the ascent; take a seat outside the café, weather permitting (unlike much of Italy, it's the same price whether you're sitting or standing). For those driving up, the road is sometimes confusingly signposted, but as a general rule look for the brown Parco Nazionale del Vesuvio signs from the Herculaneum (Ercolano) or Torre del Greco autostrada exits and keep heading upward for about 20 minutes. (Incidentally, for taxi rides up Vesuvius from Torre del Greco or Pompeii expect to pay about €76 round-trip.) The road is not much better than in the days of Lord and Lady Hamilton, but it is certainly dirtier. When you get to the parking lot at the top, for extra security opt for paying the €2.54 parking charge. The parking lot and bus terminal at Quota 1000 lie roughly 30 minutes' walk (about a 400-ft climb) from the nearest viewing point down into the crater. You will be handed a sturdy walking stick on leaving the parking lot (a small tip is appreciated on your return). The path is kept in good repair, but bring nonskid shoes (not sandals) and come prepared for strong winds. You have to pay a fee near the crater of €5.09 (open from 9 AM to two hours before sunset), which covers the cost of a compulsory but somewhat elusive guiding service. Once you've seen the fumaroles and gazed down as much as 600 ft into the wondrous depths of the crater, take in the broad sweep around the Bay of Naples—though you'll probably find the city of Naples more photogenic from lower down the slopes, near the observatory. As you walk up the volcano path, you cannot look too long or unwarily at the splendid views without worrying about your feet—there are some spots where a little chain fence is all that prevents you from taking a steep fall. Near the top is the ticket seller's booth and postcard stands. In the old days, postcards at this lofty outpost cost twice as much as the ones found at the car park at the foot of the mountain—but today that charming scheme has been abandoned.

Torre del Greco

❹ *16 km (10 mi) southeast of Naples; 11 km (7 mi) northwest of Pompeii.*

Being in an area of high volcanic risk, Torre del Greco has borne the brunt of Vesuvian eruptions over the centuries. The demolition work of the historic center begun by Vesuvius was almost completed by the postwar building boom; with more than 100,000 inhabitants, Torre del Greco is now close behind its neighbor Portici as one of the most densely populated towns in the world. However, some architectural jewels have survived—including the 18th-century Vesuvian villa Palazzo Vallelonga, on Via Vittorio Emanuele—and the Museo dei Coralli on Piazza Palomba will show you why the Torresi (the townspeople) are still considered the world's best fashioners of coral and cameos. This is also a good base camp for exploring the Vesuvian area, with well-paved, clearly signposted roads north of the Torre del Greco autostrada exit.

Dining and Lodging

$$-$$$ ✕ **La Mammola.** A secluded restaurant on the grounds of the Hotel Marad, La Mammola has departed in an interesting way from the standard platters found around the Bay of Naples. It has succeeded in achieving a touch of stylishness without succumbing to pretension. Ask for a sample of its seafood *primi piatti* (first courses), including the dark gnocchi dish *gnocchetti neri con vongole e asparagi* (with clams and asparagus). Wash it down with some fine Pietrotorcia wine from Ischia, a blend of two ancient grape varieties, Biancolella and Forastera, that Tiberius and Nero might have enjoyed. ⊠ *Via San Sebastiano 24,* ☎ *081/8825664. Reservations essential Sat. eve. AE, DC, MC, V. Closed Mon., no dinner Sun.*

$$$ 🏨 **Hotel Marad.** Dominated by huge spreading umbrella pines and conveniently close to the Torre del Greco exit of the Naples–Salerno A3 autostrada, the Marad bristles with efficiency and is an obvious base for exploring the area around Vesuvius and Herculaneum. Booking in advance makes good sense, as the hotel doubles as a conference center. Lying at the lower end of the price range, it offers four-star facilities at three-star prices, and a choice of two excellent restaurants. Travelers without cars will appreciate the pickup service from the nearest Circumvesuviana station. ⊠ *Via San Sebastiano 24, 80059,* ☎ *081/8492168,* 𝔽𝔸𝕏 *081/8828794,* 𝕎𝔼𝔹 *www.marad.it. 74 rooms with bath. 2 restaurants, air-conditioning, pool, meeting rooms, parking. AE, MC, V.*

Oplontis (Torre Annunziata)

❺ *20 km (12 mi) southeast of Naples; 5 km (3 mi) west of Pompeii.*

Surrounded by the fairly drab urban landscape of Torre Annunziata, thrown up in the 1960s, Oplontis justifies its reputation as one of the more mysterious archaeological sites to be unearthed in the 20th century. The villa complex has been imaginatively ascribed—from a mere inscription on an amphora—to Nero's second wife, Poppaea Sabina, whose family was well known among the landed gentry of neighboring Pompeii. As Roman villas go, Poppaea's Villa, or Villa A, as it is called more prosaically by archaeologists, is way off the top end of the scale. What has so far been excavated covers more than 7,000 square meters (75,000 square ft), and because the site is bound by a road to the west and a canal to the south, we are unlikely ever to gauge its full extent. Complete with porticoes, a large peristyle, *piscina* (pool), baths, and extensive gardens, besides the standard atria, triclinia, and a warren of cubicula, the villa has been thought by some to have been a training school for young philosophers and orators. Certainly, for those overwhelmed by the throngs at

Pompeii, a modern-day visit to the site of Oplontis offers a chance for contemplation and intellectual refreshment.

Access is easiest from the Circumvesuviana station of Torre Annunziata (about 200 yards away). Outside the station turn left and then right downhill, and the site is just after the crossroads down on the left. If coming by car, take the Torre Annunziata turnoff from the Naples–Salerno autostrada, turn right, and then look for signs on the left for Oplontis at the first major crossroads. Try to negotiate a parking space in the site car park, especially if your car is laden with luggage. The main entrance to the site is from the north—you basically go into the villa through the gardens, with the atrium on the southern side lying under about 16 ft of pumice and pyroclastic material from Vesuvius. This is a good time to have a close look at the stratigraphy of the volcanic deposits: note the thin layers of the lighter surge flow deposit near the base of the profile. Although pumice fallout presented few problems for local inhabitants during the eruption, it was the high-temperature surge cloud which proved lethal to those who stayed behind.

Oplontis offers the full gamut of Roman wall paintings, with its occupants showing a particular penchant for the illusionist motifs of the so-called Second Pompeian Style. There are some good examples in the west wing of the villa, especially in the triclinium (Room 14—look for the room numbers above the doors) giving onto the small portico (Room 13), which abuts the west end of the site and the road above. Although the stucco work in the thermae, or baths, is less impressive than in Pompeii and Herculaneum, the calidarium (Room 8) has a delightful miniature landscape scene surmounted by a peacock in a niche at its eastern end, above a more visible fresco of Hercules in the Garden of the Hesperides. Nearby, in the tepidarium (Room 18) there is an interesting glimpse into the structural design of Roman baths; here the floor is raised by *suspensurae,* small brick supporting pilasters, enabling warm air to pass beneath.

Such initial opulence sets the scene for the rest of the site. Although there are exceptions to the rule—for example, from their relatively small size and less elaborate frescoes, the cubicula, or bedrooms, are perhaps conspicuous by their simplicity—a visit to the eastern wing confirms the earlier impression. The warren of rooms gives way to much larger spaces, featuring long corridors, peristyles fit for large gaggles of stoics, and a large piscina, or swimming pool, with its complement of porticoes and terraces, at the eastern end. Note that Oplontis is now back in use as a theater venue, with recent productions featuring ancient plays by Plautus (in Italian); tickets can be bought at the Proloco in Torre Annunziata (close to the Oplontis site). ⊠ *Via Sepolcri 1, Torre Annunziata,* ☎ *081/8621755.* ▨ *€5.15, €8.26 for 4 archaeological sites (1 day), or the "Biglietto Cumulativo" for €13.42 for 5 sites (Pompeii, Herculaneum, Boscoreale, Oplontis, and Stabiae) valid for 3 days.* ☉ *Daily 9–1 hr before sunset.*

POMPEII: CITY OF VESUVIUS

Mention Pompeii and most travelers will think of ancient Roman villas, prancing bronze fauns, writhing plaster casts of Vesuvius's victims, and the fabled days of the Caesars. Mention Pompeii to many southern Italians, however, and they will immediately think of Pompeii, home to the Santuario della Madonna, the 19th-century basilica in the center of the town of Pompeii, with the archaeological ruins taking second place. Although millions of culture seekers worldwide head for ancient Pompeii every year, the same number of Italian pilgrims converge on Pompeii's basilica as a token of faith—joining processions, making *ex-voto* offerings, or just honoring a vow. Wealthy Neapolitans come to make their donations to assist the Church carry out its good deeds. New-car owners come to get their vehicles blessed—and given driving standards in these parts of the world, insurance coverage from on high is probably a sensible move.

Caught between the hammer and anvil of cultural and religious tourism, the modern town of Pompeii has shaken off its rather complacent approach and is now endeavoring to polish up its act. In attempts to ease congestion and improve quality at street level, parts of the town have been pedestrianized and parking restrictions tightened. Departing from the rather sleazy reputation of previous years, several hotels have filled the sizable niche in the market for quality deals at affordable prices. As for recommendable restaurants, if you deviate from the archaeological site and make for the center of town, you will be spoiled for choice. Unlike many archaeological sites in the Mediterranean region, those around Naples are almost all well served by public transport. Pompeii has all of three railway stations, and it's a short hop from here to the impressive villa of Oplontis, in Torre Annunziata.

Pompeii

★ *24 km (15 mi) southeast of Naples; 11 km (7 mi) southeast of Herculaneum.*

Tomb of a civilization, petrified memorial to Vesuvius's eruption on the morn of August 23, AD 79, the **Scavi di Pompei** is probably the most famous system of excavations anywhere. It is certainly the most accessible and one of the largest. Two hours are the absolute minimum for a visit, and buying the guidebook is a necessity unless you don't mind getting lost three or four times during your independent tour. That may not be such a bad thing. Today Pompeii is choked with both the dust of 25 centuries *and* over a million tourists every year; only by escaping the hordes and lingering along its silent streets can you truly fall under the site's spell. On a quiet backstreet, all you need is a little imagination to sense the shadows palpably filling the dark corners, to hear the ancient pipe's falsetto and the tinny clash of cymbals, to envision a rain of rose petals gently covering a Roman senator's dinner guests. Come in the late afternoon when the site is nearly deserted, and you will understand that the true pleasure of Pompeii is not in the seeing but in the feeling.

Ancient Pompeii was much larger than Herculaneum; a busy commercial center with a population of 10,000–20,000, it covered about 160 acres on the seaward end of the fertile Sarno Plain. In 80 BC the general Sulla turned Pompeii into a Roman colony, a place where wealthy patricians could escape the turmoil of city life. The town was laid out in a grid pattern, with two main intersecting streets. The wealthiest took whole blocks for themselves; those less well endowed built a house and rented out the front rooms, those facing the street, to shopkeepers. The facades of these houses were relatively plain and seldom hinted at the care and attention lavished on the private rooms within. An arriving visitor entered through a narrow corridor giving onto an open atrium, in the rear of which was a reception room. Behind this was another open area, called the peristyle, with rows of columns and perhaps a garden with a fountain. Only close friends ever saw this private part of the house, which was surrounded by the family's bedrooms and a dining area.

Pompeian houses were designed around an inner garden so that families could turn their backs on the outside world. Today we install picture windows that break down visual barriers between ourselves and

BURIED PLEASURE: UNLOCKING THE VILLA OF THE MYSTERIES

A FUNNY THING HAPPENS on the way to the forum as you walk through Pompeii. Covered with dust and decay as it is, the city seems to come alive. Perhaps it is the familiar signs of life observed along the ancient streets: the beer shops with tumblers' rings still fresh in the counter, the stanchion where horses were tethered outside the taverna, the tracks of chariot wheels cut in the pavement. Coming upon the *thermopolium* (drinking bar), you imagine natives calling out, "One for the road." The *macellum* (marketplace) would be crowded with *palanchini* (litters); and at the dentist booth, iron implements stood at the ready for reluctant customers. But a glance up at Vesuvius, still brooding over the scene like an enormous headstone, reminds you that these folks—whether imagined in your head or actually wearing a mantle of lava dust—have not taken a breath for centuries.

In its day, Pompeii was celebrated as the Côte d'Azur, the seaside Brighton, the Fire Island of the ancient Roman empire. Evidence of a Sybaritic bent is everywhere. In the town's grandest villas as well as rowdiest *lupanaria* (brothels), murals still reveal a worship of hedonism. Images of satyrs, bacchantes, hermaphrodites, and acrobatic couples indulge in hanky-panky. Even entryways are adorned with the Roman guardian against the Evil Eye—a painted Phallus. People came here to do the things Greeks had a word for, and there is no more astounding, magnificently memorable evidence than the world famous frescoes on view at the Villa dei Misteri, or Villa of the Mysteries, a palatial abode build at the far northwestern fringe of Pompeii. Unearthed in 1909, this villa had over 60 rooms painted with frescoes, but the finest are the series that represent the Dionysian rites of initiation, found in the *triclinium,* or banquet room.

Painted in the most glowing Pompeian reds and oranges, the panels relate the saga of Ariadne, a young bride, and her initiation into the sacred mysteries of the cult of Dionysus. A god imported to Italy from Greece, Dionysus and then given the Latin name of Bacchus. The Villa of the Mysteries frescoes were painted circa 50 BC, most art historians believe, and represent the peak of the Second Style of Pompeian wall painting. The triclinium frescoes are thought to have been painted by a local artist although the theme may well have been copied from an earlier cycle of paintings from the Hellenistic period.

Tour groups permitting (though detached from the rest of Pompeii, this room gets its fair share of through-traffic), try to stand by the protective chain and study the paintings from left to right. In all there are ten scenes, beginning with the reading of the ritual by a child (Dionysus, perhaps) assisted by a seated matron, followed by a servant pouring libations to carry out some type of sacrificial ceremony. The third picture (on the left-hand wall) depicts a Silenus with his musical accompaniment, somehow connected with the fourth, a frightened woman. The slightly damaged frescoes on the front wall depict Dionysus (recognized by his staff, or *thyrsus*) slumped over an enthroned Ariadne, flanked by a Silenus and satyrs on the left and, on the right, a kneeling woman (perhaps a bacchante) unveiling a phallus with a winged figure wielding a *flagellum* standing over her. The south wall (on the right) depicts a woman being flogged while a naked bacchante does a twirl—but is the woman being flogged or does she simply want to veil her eyes from the phallus? The last two scenes show a seated woman, possibly preparing for a bridal ceremony, while the last portrays a mantled woman, perhaps the spouse and priestess of the god. Unlike with Greek vase painting, for example, we are not assisted in interpretation by inscriptions with the names of the main characters, so some of the above construct—now the verdict of most archaeologists—is debatable. Today, all visitors here must ponder love among the ruins as they wander through the silent villa and contemplate the mysteries of its celebrated frescoes.

Pompeii

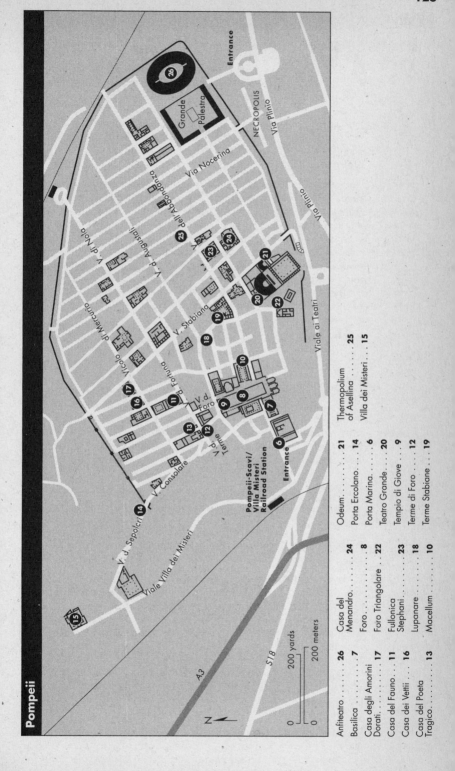

our neighbors; the people in these Roman towns had few windows, preferring to get their light from the central courtyard—the light within. How pleasant it must have been to come home from the Forum or from the baths to your own secluded holding, with no visual reminders of a life outside your own preserve. Not that public life was so intolerable. There were wineshops on almost every corner, and frequent shows were given at the Amphitheater. The public fountains and toilets were connected to huge cisterns by lead pipes beneath the sidewalks. Since garbage and rainwater collected in the streets of Pompeii, the sidewalks were raised, and huge stepping stones were placed at crossings so pedestrians could keep their feet dry. Herculaneum had even better drainage, with an underground sewer system that led to the sea.

The ratio of freemen to slaves was about three to two. A small, prosperous family had two or three slaves, although many had far more. Since manual labor was considered degrading, the slaves did all the housework and the cooking, including the cutting of meat, which family members ate with spoons or with their fingers. Everyone doted on grapes, and figs were also popular. Venison, chicken, and pork were the main dishes. People ate the fruit of the quince tree (a good source of vitamin C) to guard against scurvy. Bread was made from wheat and barley (rye and oats were unknown) and washed down with wine made from grapes grown on the slopes of Vesuvius.

The government was considered a democracy, but women, gladiators, and Jews were denied the vote. They did, however, express their opinions on election day, as you'll see from campaign graffiti still visible on public walls. Some 15,000 instances of graffiti were found in Pompeii and Herculaneum. Many were political announcements—one person recommending another for office, for example, and spelling out his qualifications. Some were bills announcing upcoming events—a play at the theater, a fight among gladiators at the Amphitheater. Others were public notices—that wine was on sale, that an apartment would be available on the Ides of March. A good many messages were personal and lend a human dimension to the disaster. Here are a few:

At the baths: "What is the use of having a Venus if she's made of marble?"

At a hotel: "I've wet my bed. My sin I bare. But why? you ask. No pot was anywhere."

At the entrance to the front lavatory at a private house: "May I always and everywhere be as potent with women as I was here."

6 Enter through **Porta Marina**, so called because it was on the seaward side prior to the eruption in AD 79 (the sea would have been accessible from here via a narrow canal). The layout here is less gridlike than in other parts of town because you're in the oldest section of Pompeii, originally a smallish Oscan or pre-Roman settlement. In Roman times the road up to Porta Marina itself would have been steep and difficult for larger conveyances to negotiate—fortunately there were seven other gates to choose from—although this was by far the quickest way of getting to the hub of civic life, the Forum. In this case there were two passages, the one on the left for pedestrians and the one on the right for animals and light vehicles.

7 Beyond the Porta Marina and past the Temple of Venus is the **Basilica**, the law court and the stock exchange of the town. These oblong buildings ending in a semicircular projection (apse) were the model for early Christian churches, which had a nave (central aisle) and two side aisles separated by rows of columns. Standing in the Basilica, you can recognize the continuity between Roman and Christian styles of architecture, though here, instead of a sacral area being placed at the end, there was the tribunal.

8 The Basilica opens onto the **Foro** (Forum), with which it shares some elements of its design: a large rectangular area with a colonnade surmounted by a loggia, running along three sides. This served as the political, commercial, and religious center of city life, with the main temples, law courts, and commercial and government buildings grouped around it. It was here that elections were held and speeches and official announcements made. In AD 79 the Forum would have been adorned with statues of the great and the good, many of them probably equestrian, as testified by some larger bases left on the south side. One of the bases is wider and more massive than the others, indicating that it may have been the *suggestum,* or orator's rostrum.

9 At the far (northern) end of the Forum is the **Tempio di Giove** (Temple of Jupiter), sacred to the Capitoline triad of Jupiter, Juno, and Minerva, with the brewing cone of Vesuvius behind. Little more than the base of this 2nd-century BC temple has been preserved. Like many buildings in Pompeii, it was severely damaged in an earthquake in AD 62 and was still in a ruined state at the time of the eruption in AD 79.

10 On the eastern side of the Forum fronted by an elegant three-column portico is the **Macellum,** the covered meat and fish market dating back to Augustan times. Like the ancient Greek *agora* in Athens, the Forum was a busy shopping area, complete with public officials to apply proper standards of weights and measures.

11 The renowned **Casa del Fauno** (House of the Faun) gets its name from the small bronze statue in the middle of its spacious impluvium. The original—like so many of the best works of art unearthed in Pompeii—is housed in the Museo Archeologico Nazionale in Naples. This is both one of the earliest and most sumptuous private dwellings in Pompeii. The front part of the house is arranged around two atria, behind which is the peristyle with a portico of 28 Ionic columns. On its discovery in 1830, particular attention was focused on the fine mosaic all done in tiny tesserae depicting the Battle of Issus fought between Alexander the Great and the Persian emperor Darius III in 330 BC, found in the *exedra* (discussion room) fronted by stuccoed columns immediately behind the first peristyle—again, on display in the Museo Archeologico Nazionale in Naples. The exedra was flanked by two *triclinia* (dining rooms) giving onto a megaperistyle at the back.

12 The **Terme di Foro** (Forum Baths), on Via delle Terme, are smaller than the Terme Stabiane but have more delicate decoration. The tepidarium and calidarium in the men's section are extremely well preserved and provide a useful insight into heating systems. The tepidarium was warmed by a brazier while beneath the calidarium were brick pillars, or *suspensurae,* which together with hollow walls, ensured the passage of hot air. Note the inscription in bronze letters around the great *labrum* (fountain) recording the names of the officials who installed the labrum, as well as its cost (5,420 sesterces) in the years AD 3–4.

13 The **Casa del Poeta Tragico** (House of the Tragic Poet), opposite the Forum Baths, is a typical middle-class house from the last days of Pompeii. On the floor is a mosaic of a chained dog and the inscription CAVE CANEM ("Beware of the dog"). The house owes its name and fame to a mosaic found in the tablinum representing a *choregos,* or theatrical sponsor, along with, on the walls of the atrium and peristyle, a superb series of pictures, now in the Naples museum, of mythological subjects like the Sacrifice of Iphigenia.

⑭ The beautiful **Porta Ercolano** (Herculaneum Gate) was a main gate that led to Herculaneum and Neapolis. The gate has three archways—the central one for wheeled conveyances and the two side openings for pedestrians. It is thought to have been constructed without a defensive strategy in mind. This would imply a fairly late construction date, when the colonization of southern Italy was well consolidated and the native Italic peoples were no longer restless.

One of the most evocative roads in Pompeii, the Via dei Sepolcri, leads out from the Porta Ercolano and is lined with tombs—a favorite spot for painters and photographers of the early 20th century. This road ★ **⑮** leads to the celebrated **Villa dei Misteri** (Villa of the Mysteries), lying 200 meters (220 yds) outside Pompeii's walls and therefore in theory not part of the ancient town. It contains what some consider the greatest surviving group of paintings from the ancient world, telling the story of a young bride (Ariadne) being initiated into the mysteries of the cult of Dionysus. Bacchus, to give Dionysus his Latin name, was the god of wine, fertility, theater, and other forms of racier entertainment. So he was naturally popular in a town so devoted to the pleasures of the flesh. But he also represented the triumph of the irrational—of all those mysterious forces that no official state religion could fully suppress. The cult of Dionysus, like the cult of the Cumaean Sibyl, gave people a sense of control over fate, and in its focus on the Other World helped pave the way for Christianity.

★ **⑯** The **Casa dei Vettii** (House of the Vettii) is the best example of a house owned by wealthy *mercatores* (merchants). Faithfully restored, it contains vivid murals—a magnificent *pinacoteca* (picture gallery) within the very heart of Pompeii. The scenes here—except for those in the two wings off the atrium—were all painted after the earthquake of AD 62. Within this visual feast, cast an admiring glance at the delicate frieze around the wall of the triclinium (on the right of the peristyle garden as you enter from the atrium), depicting cupids engaged in various activities, such as selling oils and perfumes, working as goldsmiths and metalworkers, acting as wine merchants, or performing in chariot races. This is definitely the place to refresh your memory of Greek mythology. In another *oecus* (room) facing onto the peristyle (in the right-hand corner) are other masterpieces of the Fourth Style of Pompeian painting, including one scene of Daedalus showing Pasiphaë, Minos's wife, as a wooden cow, a disguise which would enable her to consummate her divine-inflicted passion for a bull. Opposite this scene is the omnipresent Dionysus surprising Ariadne while asleep, and on the end wall is Ixion bound to a wheel by Hephaestus with Hera standing by disdainfully—a torture devised by Zeus to punish Ixion for having dared to seek the love of Hera, Zeus's wife. Given Zeus's amply testified philandering, Ixion could have been forgiven for thinking the coast was clear.

Another room close to the exit (such is the throng of visitors here that a one-way traffic system has been introduced) depicts the baby Hercules strangling snakes sent by Hera, while the opposite wall shows the punishment inflicted on Dirce—she was bound to the horns of a bull and dragged to death—in return for enslaving and maltreating Antiope, daughter of a Boeotian river-god. On the far wall is Pentheus, King of Thebes, prior to dismemberment by a group of Maenads for having opposed the introduction of the cult of Dionysus. Not everyone's choice of sitting-room decor perhaps: but then the Vettii brothers were unlikely to be considered arbiters of fine taste amongst the area's old-style patricians. Another of the main attractions in the Casa dei Vettii is the small cubicle beyond the kitchen area (to the right of the atrium) with its faded erotic frescoes now protected by perspex screens.

⑰ The **Casa degli Amorini Dorati** (House of the Gilded Cupids) is an elegant, well-preserved home with original marble decorations in the garden. The house may well have belonged to the Poppaei family, better known for their family connections with Nero, who married the notorious Poppaea the second time around. Its pictorial decorations express elegant and refined theatrical tastes dating to Nero's time (AD 54–AD 69). The house is named after the cupids engraved in gold leaf that adorn one of the *cubicula* (bedrooms). Stroll around the peristyle in the garden, which would have been adorned with sculptures, marble tables, and a pool.

⑱ On the walls of the well-preserved **lupanare** (brothel) are scenes of erotic pastimes in which clients could engage. Several of the rooms were on the upper floor, served by an independent staircase, suggesting separate facilities for customers who wanted to keep a lower profile. At ground level, small painted panels above the entrances illustrated the specialty offered by each *meretrix* (courtesan).

⑲ The **Terme Stabiane** (Stabian Baths) were heated by underground furnaces whose warmth circulated among the stone pillars supporting the floor, rose through flues in the walls, and escaped through chimneys. The water temperature could be set for cold, lukewarm, or hot. Bathers took a lukewarm bath to prepare themselves for the hot room. A tepid bath came next and then a plunge into cold water to tone up the skin. A vigorous massage with oil was followed by rest, reading, horseplay, and conversation. The Stabian Baths are the most complete in Pompeii and among the oldest baths from Roman times. This was the basic pattern used for the grand imperial baths of antiquity, such as the Baths of Caracalla in Rome, although the latter were built to a massive scale. Like the Forum Baths, these had a palaestra, or porticoed area (note the fine stucco work on the palaestra walls), where athletes could train, play a *sphaeristerium* (ball game), and then remove dirt and oils from their bodies with a strigil before cooling off in the the frigidarium. Most of the Stabian Baths complex is roped off, and access is currently limited to the men's entrance hall, *apodyterium* (changing room) and palaestra from the entrance on Via dell'Abbondanza. To compensate, there are two cases with plaster casts of bodies in their original agony throes, found nearby during excavations in the 19th century. It was Giuseppe Fiorelli, appointed Professor of Archaeology after Italy's unification in 1860, who invented the ingenious method of pumping liquid plaster into cavities left by the decayed bodies within the hardened deposits of volcanic ash and pumice.

⑳ Not far from the Stabian Baths was the theater area on the southern side of town. The **Teatro Grande** (large theater), originally dating from the 2nd century BC but subsequently restored, had a seating capacity of about 5,000. It was designed to fit in to the natural slope of the hill, so that spectacles would be performed against a backdrop of the *Mons Lactarius* (Lattari Mountains). Little remains of the original *cavea* (seating area) except for some of the lower tiers, some of the *media cavea* halfway up, and the framework of the *summa cavea* (top gallery). Behind the theater lie the gladiators' barracks, though this porticoed area is thought to have served as a space for the audience to unwind between plays. Of course, with the advent of racier entertainment down in the Amphitheater, this large theater lost much of its pull.

㉑ Adjacent to the Teatro Grande is the **Odeum,** also called Teatrum Tectum (Covered Theater). Built between 80 BC–75 BC and with a seating capacity of 1,000, the Odeum is a gem of theatrical architecture and was far less heavily restored in antiquity than its predecessor next door. The semicircular cavea was truncated and transformed into an almost square-shape design to facilitate the building of a roof. With theatrical performances often held on hot summer days, ancient Pompeians would have welcomed the shade provided.

㉒ Some of the oldest structures in Pompeii are to be found in the **Foro Triangolare** (Triangular Forum), west of the theater complex. In the middle of the Forum are the remains—just a few column capitals in Doric style—of a temple dating as far back as the 6th century BC, originally dedicated to Hercules, the founder of the city. This is one of the quietest areas of the archaeological site, and the ample shade afforded by trees here makes it a good spot to pause and muse on what you've seen.

The main street running most of the way from the Forum to the Amphitheater was the bustling **Via dell'Abbondanza** (incidentally, the name is not authentic and was made up by archaeologists). Shops were by no means restricted to the Forum area, and many were located along the Via dell'Abbondanza. Shops can easily be distinguished from private houses by their much broader fronts (6–10 ft wide) with wooden shutters for nighttime security. Private houses had narrower—almost poky—entrances, thereby reducing exposure at street level to an absolute minimum. As you go along Via dell'Abbondanza away from the Forum, two blocks beyond the Stabian Baths you'll notice on the left the current digs at the Casa dei Casti Amanti (House of the Chaste Lovers), screened off behind unsightly corrugated iron fencing. A team of plasterers and painters were at work here when Vesuvius erupted, redecorating one of the rooms and patching up the cracks in the bread oven near the entrance—caused by earth tremors a matter of days before. Thanks to modern archaeological techniques and the assistance of many scientific disciplines, the site has provided a mine of information and is expected to be opened shortly to public viewing.

㉓ Togas, the required Roman attire, were washed at **Fullonica Stephani.** The cloth was dunked into a tub full of water and chalk, then stomped upon like so many grapes. Once clean, the material was stretched across a wicker cage and exposed to sulfur fumes. The fuller (cleaner) carded it with a long brush, then placed it under a press. The harder the pressing, the whiter and brighter it became. When excavated in 1911, the entrance to the fuller's premises was still shuttered and locked. Behind was a body clutching a bagful of sesterces. Could these have been the last takings of the *fullonica?* Or had a passerby, carrying his worldly wealth, stopped inside and sought refuge behind the door from the hail of lapilli outside?

㉔ Many paintings and mosaics were executed at the **Casa del Menandro** (House of Menander), a patrician's villa. The Greek comic poet Menander is depicted in a rectangular niche on the far wall in the peristyle, although you need go no farther than the atrium to see three scenes from the Trojan war in a small exedra to the left: the death of Laocoön and his sons (right); Cassandra trying to dissuade the Trojans from making the fatal mistake of bringing the wooden horse into Troy; and (left) one of the Greek heroes with Helen. This impressive residence also had a small complex of private baths, just next to the kitchen to the right of the peristyle. The siting of the baths next to the kitchen quarters was common practice in many of the larger villas, enabling heat from cooking to be exploited for warming the caldarium. At the time of writing the Casa del Menandro, like many of the houses in the site, was closed to the public.

㉕ The **Thermopolium of Asellina** (Asellina's Inn), on the Via dell'Abbondanza, is the most complete example of an inn to be discovered in Pompeii. On the ground floor was the characteristic *thermopolium,* a counter with built-in earthenware containers holding snacks and hot drinks—perhaps that famed delicacy *garum,* made from marinated fish innards (or anchovies, if you were lucky)—while the upstairs part had guest rooms. At street level, customers ate standing up or on the move, as there were few taverns that offered a choice of either sitting or standing.

★ ❻ The **Anfiteatro** (Amphitheater) was the ultimate in entertainment for local Pompeians and offered a gamut of experiences, but essentially this was for gladiators rather than wild animals. Unlike the amphitheater at Pozzuoli, there are no underground *cellae* for the penning of animals and, besides, *venationes* (combats with wild animals) only really became popular from well into the 1st century AD onward. With the large palaestra close by and the gladiatorial barracks near the theater area, there were extensive facilities to train gladiators in many types of combat. Teams worked for impresarios, who hired them out to wealthy citizens, many of whom were running for office and hoping that the gory entertainment would buy them some votes. Most gladiators were slaves or prisoners, but a few were those from the far-flung reaches of the empire who enjoyed fighting. When a gladiator found himself at another's mercy, he extended a pleading hand to the president of the games. If the president turned his thumb up, the gladiator lived; if he turned his thumb down, the gladiator's throat was cut. The arena got pretty bloody after a night's entertainment and was sprinkled with red powder to camouflage the carnage. The victorious gladiator got money, or a ribbon symbolizing his exemption from further fights. If he was a slave, he was often set free. If the people of Pompeii had trading cards, they would have collected portraits of gladiators; everyone had his favorite. Says one piece of graffiti: "Petronius Octavus fought thirty-four fights and then died, but Severus, a freedman, was victor in fifty-five fights and still lived; Nasica celebrates sixty victories."

By Roman standards, Pompeii's Amphitheater was quite small (seating capacity: 20,000). Built in about 80 BC, it was oval and divided into three seating areas, like a theater. There were two main entrances—at the north and south ends—and a narrow passage on the west, called the *Porta Libitinensis,* through which the dead were most probably dragged out. A wall painting found in a house near the theater (now in the Naples Museum) depicts the riot in the Amphitheater in AD 59 when several citizens from the nearby town of Nucera were killed. After Nucerian appeals to Nero, shows in the Amphitheater were suspended for 10 years.

Just behind the Amphitheater is the second entrance to Pompeii (at Villa dei Misteri there is only an exit), with the main town square and its 19th-century basilica a short walk to the east. By the Amphitheater is a poorly signposted **Percorso Extramurario** (Outside the Walls Promenade), a walkway which links the Amphitheater, three of the old city gates, and the Porta Ercolano Necropolis at the northern and eastern sides of the site (within the site fence); the route takes about 30–40 minutes in all. Speaking of time, to get the most out of Pompeii, allow at least three or four hours. You should have a pocketful of small change (euro coins) for tipping the guards who are on duty at villas where access is restricted. They may unlock doors for you, insist on explaining the attractions, show you some soft Pompeian pornography if you ask for it, and expect a tip for their services. If hiring a guide, make sure the guide is registered for an English tour and standing inside the gate; agree beforehand on the length of the tour and the price, and prepare yourself for soundbites of substandard English mixed with dollops of hearsay. Alternatively, stock up with one of the official publications at the bookshop by the ticket office. For refreshments, the only restaurant inside the site is both overpriced and busy, so it makes sense to pre-purchase any water and snacks you might need. For information on reaching the other sites (Boscoreale, Oplontis, and Stabiae) included in the multi-site Pompeii ticket—it would be overly ambitious to attempt more than three on one day—ask about transport and access at the helpful information kiosk at Porta Marina. If you intend to visit both Pompeii and Herculaneum within the space of three days, then you should buy the *Biglietto Cumulativo* (three-day pass), which also includes the above three sites.

The archaeological site of Pompeii has its own stop (Pompei–Villa dei Misteri) on the Circumvesuviana line to Sorrento, close to the main entrance at the Porta Marina, which is the best place from which to start a tour. If—like many potential visitors every year—you get the wrong train from Naples (stopping at the other station "Pompei"), all is not lost. This station is just a seven-minute walk from the amphitheater, the second entrance to the site. ✉ *Pompei Scavi, Via Villa dei Misteri 2*, ☎ *081/5365154.* 🎫 *€8.26 for 4 sites (1 day) or the "Biglietto Cumulativo" for €13.42 for 5 sites (Pompeii, Herculaneum, Boscoreale, Oplontis, and Stabiae) valid for 3 days.* ◷ *Oct.–Feb., daily 8:30–5 (ticket office closes at 3:30); Mar.–Sept. daily 8:30–7:30 (ticket office closes at 6).*

Dining and Lodging

$$$–$$$$
★
✗ **Il Principe.** This is the closest you'll get to experiencing the tastes of ancient Pompeii, though the wines (fortunately) will be quantum leaps better. Also the food is so artistically presented that it seems boorish to pick up a knife and fork. Try the *pasta vermiculata garo*, otherwise known as spaghetti with *garum pompeianum*, a fish-based sauce consumed widely in Roman times. Don't forget to round off the meal with the *cassata Oplontis*, inspired by a famous still-life fresco found in a *triclinium* (dining-room) at the site of Oplontis. On several evenings between September and March the restaurant offers theme menus devoted to ancient Roman cooking. The decor is luxe, with echoes of Stil Liberty (Art Nouveau) in its style. ✉ *Piazza B. Longo 8*, ☎ *081/8505566*, 📠 *081/8633342*, 🌐 *www.ilprincipe.com. AE, DC, V. Closed Sun. dinner, Mon. (except lunch in summer), and 3 wks in Aug.*

$$–$$$
★
✗ **Ristorante President.** The Gramaglia father-and-son team are well versed in top-level catering and make sure that customers sigh with satisfaction after every course. For something different, try the *astice ubriacata* (drunken lobster) accompanied by some imaginative side dishes, like *sfoglie di zucca in agrodolce* (sweet-and-sour pumpkin strips). Beautiful presentation, impeccable service, and excellent value for money all add up to a stellar meal. ✉ *Piazza Schettini 12*, ☎ *081/8507245*, 📠 *081/8638147. AE, DC, MC, V. Closed Mon.*

$–$$
✗ **Ristorante Pizzeria Carlo Alberto.** This is a small, efficiently run restaurant with an impressive repertory comfortably out of the reach of large tour groups. If you're a vegetarian, try *pizza con mozzarella, rucola, e mais* (pizza with mozzarella, arugola, and corn) or just have a plain *focaccetta* instead of bread to accompany your meal. Those who make it through to the *dolce* (desserts) should sample the delicate *Grappa del Vesuvio*, made from Lacrima Christi grape varieties. ✉ *Via Carlo Alberto 15*, ☎ *081/8633231. Reservations essential weekends. DC, MC, V.*

$$$
🏨 **Hotel Amleto.** *Appassionati* and connoisseurs of historical styles of furnishings will find this hotel a real treat. Enjoy the Pompeian-type mosaic in the reception room and the mesmerizing House-of-the-Vettii–type scene in the breakfast room before retiring to your quarters, either 19th-century Neapolitan in style or Venetian in taste. Convenient to say the least, this spot is near the archaeological site and close to Pompeii's cathedral. ✉ *Via B. Longo 10, 80045*, ☎ *081/8631004*, 📠 *081/8635585*, 🌐 *www.hotelamleto.it. 26 rooms with bath. Air-conditioning, solarium, meeting room, parking. AE, D, MC, V.*

$$ 🏨 **Hotel Forum.** Handily close to the ancient site, though set back enough from the road to be fairly quiet, the Forum is an excellent base for a short stay. Linger over breakfast downstairs with a well-kept garden as a backdrop. ✉ *Via Roma 99, 80045,* ☎ *081/8501170,* FAX *081/8506132,* WEB *www.hotelforum.it. 25 rooms with bath. Air-conditioning, meeting room, parking. AE, DC, MC, V.*

$$ 🏨 **Villa Laura.** This is an unusual hotel (with a mini-museum of antiques in the reception area), attentively run under the guidance of its owner, *Signora* Antonella. Ask for one of the more spacious, quieter rooms at the back overlooking the garden. ✉ *Via de la Salle 13, 80045,* ☎ *081/8631024 or 081/8631036,* FAX *081/8504893,* WEB *www.villalaura.com. 25 rooms with bath. Air-conditioning, parking. AE, DC, MC, V.*

Nightlife and the Arts

Pompeii's long-running late-summer festival of the performing arts, known as the Panatenee Pompeiane, was canceled in 2000. Occasionally, there may be still be a popular music concert in the Amphitheater, usually organized by the Sovrintendenza. Inquire at the information office in Porto Marina (not at the tourist office) about any possible summer evening events, or just scan the weekly newspapers for listings. Note that the nearby ancient site of Oplontis is now the venue for summer plays.

Castellammare di Stabia

㉗ *26 km (16 mi) southeast of Naples; 37 km (23 mi) northwest of Salerno; 19 km (12 mi) northeast of Sorrento.*

Castellammare di Stabia is better known in classical circles as just Stabiae, the site where Pliny the Elder in 79 AD carried out an ill-fated attempt to rescue a friend by the name of Pomponianus. Stabiae formed the easternmost settlement along the Bay of Naples, the last of an almost continuous coastal strip of villas and towns comprising Pompeii, Oplontis, Herculaneum, Neapolis across to Puteoli, Baiae, and Cape Misenum on the western side. Post-war urban development has been somewhat unkind to the town of Castellammare, a fashionable spa resort in its heyday and now better known for its shipyards, pasta factories, and canning industry. Nowhere is this more obvious than when you visit the two grandiose Roman villas of ancient Stabiae perched atop the hill of Varano, overlooking what used to be the ancient shoreline, and then gaze down over a sea of apartment blocks.

Admission to Stabiae is now included in the Pompeii entry fee together with Oplontis and the Antiquarium of Boscoreale, though you would be hard-pushed to do more than two of the four sites in the day allotted, especially if dependent on public transport. From the Naples direction, take the Sorrento line of the Circumvesuviana and get off at Via Nocera. Turn left outside the station and take a bus (Linea Azzurra, one run every 20 minutes) opposite the Farmacia Gava on Via Cosenza. By car, take the Castellammare di Stabia exit from the A3 autostrada and follow signs to Sorrento (not Castellammare). Take the first exit (Gragnano) from the Sorrento road at the end of the first tunnel; the Passeggiata Archeologica starts at the junction (opposite) where the exit road meets the main Gragnano–Castellammare road.

With such relatively complex access routes, it comes as little surprise that these sites are often virtually deserted. The older complex, **Villa Arianna** (Villa Ariadne), dates back to the first century BC, and has all the trappings of quality real estate: its own baths, including a *laconicum* or steam-room, two dining rooms (summer and winter), its own palaestra (only part of which has been unearthed), and fine wall paintings, some of which were considerably left in place by Bourbon excavators in the 18th centuries. If you are astounded by the opulence of Villa Arianna, there is more to come: **Villa San Marco,** about 1 km (½ mi) away to the northeast, outstrips it in size and architectural quality, although the decoration is better down the road. With its *natatio* (swimming-pool) fringed by plane trees, and innovative architecture designed to fit the lie of the land, this was clearly the place to retreat from Horace's *profanum vulgus* (secular crowd) down in the plains of Pompeii. ⊠ *Via Passeggiata Archeologica, Castellammare di Stabia,* ☎ *081/8714541.* ☑ *€3, €8.26 for 4 archaeological sites (one day), or the "Biglietto Cumulativo" for €13.42 for 5 sites (Pompeii, Herculaneum, Boscoreale, Oplontis, and Stabiae) valid for three days.* ☉ *Daily 9–1 hr before sunset.*

Lodging

$$$ 🏨 **Grand Hotel La Medusa.** Within walking distance of the archaeological sites of Stabiae and strategically located for forays down into the plains, this recently renovated hotel is set in luxuriant grounds well away from the urban hustle of Castellammare. The rooms, service, and facilities are everything you'd expect from a well-run four-star hotel. ⊠ *Via Passeggiata Archeologica 5, 80053,* ☎ *081/8723383,* 𝔽𝔸𝕏 *081/ 8717009,* 𝕎𝔼𝔹 *www.lamedusahotel.com. 54 rooms with bath. Restaurant, air-conditioning, pool, tennis court, meeting rooms, parking. AE, D, MC, V.*

OFF THE
BEATEN PATH
For quick relief from a surfeit of Mediterranean heat at sea-level, take the **Funivia di Monte Faito** (cable car) run by the local railway departing from the main Castellammare di Stabia Circumvesuviana station roughly every 20 minutes. In only 8 minutes, you will be whisked up over 3,000 ft with some nerve-tingling vistas over the *Golfo di Napoli.* Once at the upper station (by a *piazzetta,* refreshments available) continue walking upwards on Trail No. 36 mapped out with distinctive red and white markers by CAI, the Italian Alpine Club, which will take you into the heart of the beechwoods. This is the start for some challenging hikes across the Monti Lattari chain to the Costiera Amalfitana (about 5 hours), which should not be attempted without a good walking map (i.e., with contour lines) and ample supplies of food and drink. For those who have finally succumbed to Roman-style *otium* (leisure), settle for a shady stroll along the same track through the woods in the company of bird species more associated with northern European climes, such as the nuthatch, robin, and various tits or chickadees. At ground level admire the spring-flowering cyclamen and look for orchids come May and June in the clearings. You can either rejoin the road below and take it back to the funivia or aim for the church of San Michele at 4,000 ft (estimated 2 hours' walk along Trail No. 36, 550 ft above the funivia station) and then retrace your steps or take the road down. ⊠ *Monte Faito Funivia, Stazione Circumvesuviana, Castellammare di Stabia,* ☎ *081/ 8793097,* 𝕎𝔼𝔹 *www.vesuviana.it.* ☑ *€4.64 one-way, €6.71 return.* ☉ *Apr.–Oct., with departures roughly every 30 min from 9:15 AM to 4:30 PM, and from 7:30 AM to 7:15 PM mid-June through end of Aug.*

WEST OF NAPLES:
THE PHLEGREAN FIELDS

Extinct volcanoes, steaming fumaroles, natural spasms, and immortal names, all steeped in millennia of history, are the basic ingredients of the Campi Flegrei, or Phlegrean Fields (from the ancient Greek word *phlegraios,* or burning). Pompeii and Herculaneum, to the east of Naples, may be the most celebrated archaeological sites in Campania, but back in the days of the Caesars they were simple middle-class towns compared to the patrician settlements to the west of Naples. Here, at Baiae, famed figures like Cicero, Julius Caesar, Nero, and Hadrian built sumptuous leisure villas (*villae otiorum*) and ports for their gigantic pleasure barges; here St. Paul arrived at Pozzuoli on board an Alexandrian ship; here the powerful came to consult the oracles of the Cumaean Sibyl; and here Virgil visited Lago d'Averno—the legendary entrance to the underworld—to immortalize it in his *Aeneid.* Although several villas have now sunk beneath the sea, there are many archaeological sights still extant: the Flavian Amphitheater, which, if not as imposing above ground as the Colosseum at Rome, is far better preserved in the galleries and cages below the arena in which wild beasts, gladiators, and stage props were kept in readiness; the ruins of the Sibyl's Cave in Cumae; and the ancient baths of Baia. To such archaeological riches, add a pinch of local hospitality and an essence of gastronomy, and you'll soon see why the area holds so much fascination for the present-day traveler.

The Solfatara

㉘ *8 km (5 mi) west of Naples; 2 km (1 mi) east of Pozzuoli.*

Here at the sunken volcanic crater Solfatara you can experience firsthand the otherworldly terrain of the Campi Flegrei. The only eruption of this semiextinct volcano was in 1198, though according to one legend, every crater in the area is one of the mouths of a 100-headed dragon named Typhon that Zeus hurled into the crater of Epomeo on the island of Ischia. According to another, the sulfurous springs of the Solfatara are poisonous discharges from wounds the Titans received in their war with Zeus. Both legends, of course, are attempts to dramatize man's struggle to overcome the mysterious and dangerous forces of nature. Appropriately, it was given the name of *Forum Vulcani* by the ancient Romans, who thought it the residence of the god Vulcan. The Solfatara has been a powerful magnet for travelers over the past 300 years. No self-respecting 18th-century aristocrat taking the Grand Tour would have returned to northern Europe without visiting the site, which has always been much more accessible from the center of Naples than the better-known Vesuvius on the other side of the city.

The Solfatara lies on two bus routes out of Naples (152, M1), with stops just outside the main entrance, and is a 15-minute walk uphill (1 km [½ mi]) from the Metropolitana station of Pozzuoli. By car take the *tangenziale* (bypass) from Naples toward Pozzuoli, getting off at the Agnano, Exit 11, about 4 km (2½ mi) away from the crater. Then follow signs to Pozzuoli and look for the VULCANO SOLFATARA sign when beginning the descent into Pozzuoli. Enter the Solfatara through the arch of the turn-of-the-20th-century, long defunct baths complex (parking facilities and ticket office inside). You approach the volcanically active area down an avenue of holm oak trees, with the attractive Solfatara campsite making full use of all available shade on either side. Complete with year-round bar and **seasonal restaurant** (☎ 081/5268144 or 081/5262341), open April–October, providing honest fare to campers and other visitors, this must be one of the best-appointed volcanic craters in the world. After you have cleared the refreshment area, emerge from the vegetation into a light clay expanse that in bright sunlight makes you reach instinctively for your sunglasses. Helpful information panels both on the surrounding vegetation and the volcanic action at the core of the crater will steer you past the century-old brick *stufe* (ovens)

West of Naples: Campi Flegri (The Phlegrean Fields)

Naples

Staz. Centrale

Staz. Vesuviana

Staz. Cumana

Castel Dell'ovo

Mergellina

Gulf of Naples

Marechiaro

Fuorigrotta

S. Paolo

Posillipo

Mostra D'Oltremart

Agnano Terme

CAMPI FLEGREI

Astroni

30

Lago Grapae

28 Solfatara

29

Pozzuoli

Monte Nuovo

32

Gulf of Pozzuoli

Amphitheater

31

Lago d'Averno

Lago Lucrino

Baia

33

Lago Miseno

Sibyl's Cave

Cumae

34

Lago del Frusard

Capo Miseno

N

0   2 km
0   2 miles

resembling a Roman *sudatorium* (sauna), where you could until recently (it's now been bricked up) be parboiled in a matter of seconds. The sulfur fumes were supposed to cure those afflicted with diseases of the respiratory tract, the skin, and the joints. While musing on advances in modern medicine, move on to the fenced-off area of the fumaroles, known as the *Bocca Grande,* where steam whooshes out at about 160°C. Continuing the circuit, note the *fangaia,* or mud baths, which produce highly prized mineral-rich mud for medicinal purposes. The dark veining on the mud surface consists of bacteria that are superresistant to high acidity and temperature. The walk continues past a 19th-century well that was sunk to tap mineral water from an underlying aquifer 30 ft below and which was in active use until the 1920s. ⊠ *Via Solfatara 161, Pozzuoli,* ☎ *081/5262341,* WEB *www.solfatara.it.* ⊠ €4.13. ☉ *Daily 8:30–1 hr before sunset.*

Dining and Lodging

$–$$ ✕ **Taverna Viola.** Lying just a three-minute walk down the road from the Solfatara, this rustic-style restaurant/pizzeria has a pleasing view over the Bay of Pozzuoli and the added attraction of serving pizzas at lunchtime. This is the place to deviate from a pizza margherita and have one *con prosciutto e rughetta* (with ham and a peppery, leafy green) or even branch out into a fish-based dish, depending on the season and weather conditions at sea. ⊠ *Via Solfatara 76, Pozzuoli,* ☎ *081/ 5269953. MC, V.*

$$ ⌂ **Hotel Solfatara.** A clean, functional hotel built in 1983 and recently refurbished, this is handily located just outside the Solfatara entrance. For extra peace and quiet, ask for a room at the back (no view). ⊠ *Via Solfatara 163, 80078,* ☎ *081/5267017,* FAX *081/5263365,* WEB *www.hotelsolfatara.it. 34 rooms with bath. Restaurant, air-conditioning, parking. AE, DC, MC, V.*

$ ⌂ **Camping Vulcano Solfatara.** With its gamut of bungalows, caravans, and tents for hire, this campsite set in Mediterranean woodland within the Solfatara crater offers tranquillity, unique ambience, and good facilities at very reasonable prices. Reservations are essential for bungalows. ⊠ *Via Solfatara 161, 80078,* ☎ *081/5267413,* FAX *081/5263482. Restaurant, pool, shop, parking. AE, DC, MC, V. Closed end Oct.– end Mar.*

Pozzuoli

㉙ *8 km (5 mi) west of Naples.*

Legendary spirits populate Pozzuoli. St. Paul stepped ashore at the harbor here in AD 61 en route to Rome: his own ship had been wrecked off Malta, and he was brought here on the *Castor and Pollux,* a grain ship from Alexandria that was carrying corn from Egypt to Italy. Not far away from the harbor esplanade, San Gennaro, patron saint of Naples, earned his holy martyrdom by being thrown to the lions at an imperial gala staged in the town's enormous amphitheater, constructed by the Flavian emperors (the wild beasts were said to have torn the rags from Gennaro's body but to have left him unharmed—at which point he was taken to the public square and finished off). More recently, that latter-day goddess Sophia Loren was born in a house still standing on a back-street; later she set off to Naples and celluloid fame. Today Pozzuoli is a well-connected busy town with about 70,000 inhabitants who live chiefly on its fisheries, shipping, and tourism. Built on geologically unstable land, the area near the port was partially evacuated in the early 1980s due to a phenomenon known locally as bradyseism, or the rise and fall of the land surface. Since then it has been gradually recolonized and partially gentrified: many of the buildings in the Centro Storico have been given a face-lift, the main park (Villa Avellino) has become a mecca for open-air summer festivals, and the town's reputation as a center for gastronomy has been firmly established. Pozzuoli has also capitalized on its strategic position close to two of the islands in the Bay of Naples, Procida and Ischia. One of its main selling points is its main arena—apart from Rome, Puteoli (to use the ancient Latin name of the town) was the only place in the empire to boast two amphitheaters—offering glimpses into the life of *panem et circenses* (bread and circuses) in classical times, when Puteoli was one of the busiest ports in the Mediterranean and easily eclipsed Neapolis (today's Naples).

★ The **Anfiteatro Flavio** (seating capacity, 40,000) is a short walk from the Pozzuoli Metropolitana railway station and about 15 minutes' walk down from the Solfatara. Despite the wear and tear of the millennia and the loss of some of the masonry to lime making in the Middle Ages, the site is one of the marvels of Roman architecture in the Campi Flegrei area. The foundation date is open to question. Like many sites in antiquity, the period from conception to final execution could stretch over decades. It was probably built under Vespasian (AD 70–AD 79), given various inscriptions reading COLONIA FLAVIA AUGUSTA PUTEOLANA PECUNIA SUA (by the Flavian colony of Puteoli with its own money), although some maintain that work may have started under Nero (AD 54–AD 69) and merely completed later. As you approach the site, note the external part in *opus reticulatum* (masonry arranged in a pattern) and brick, which is typical of the Flavian emperors, while the pillars of the external portico are all in brick, which would suggest a 2nd-century addition. Although we now get a fairly good idea of the horizontal ground plan in ancient times, comparison with the Colosseum in Rome shows that much of the superstructure has been lost: the outside part consisted of three stories surmounted by an *atticus* (decorative attic) while the *cavea* or sitting area would have had a portico above the top row of seats decorated with a number of statues and supported by columns (now found in the underground part). At ground level there was an *ambulacrum* (walkway) along which spectators would have passed to reach the *vomitoria* (exits) or outlets inside.

Judging from the complex underground network of *carceres,* or cells, which definitely merit a visit, entertainment consisted mainly of *venationes,* or fights, often involving exotic animals like lions and tigers brought from far-flung corners of the Roman Empire through the port of Puteoli. The *fossa,* or large ditch in the middle of the arena, may well have contained the stage setting, which could be raised when necessary to provide a scenic backdrop. According to tradition, several early Christians—including the Naples protector St. Januarius, or San Gennaro—were condemned to be savaged by wild beasts in Puteoli under the Fourth Edict, passed in AD 305, but the sentence was later commuted to a less spectacular *decapitatio* carried out farther up the hill on Via Solfatara at a site now commemorated by the Church of St. Januarius.

Down near the port, a three-minute walk from the Cumana railway stop of Pozzuoli in Piazza Serapide, are the evocative remains of the ancient **macellum,** or food market, a porticoed courtyard with a *sacellum* (shrine) at its northern end. Known commonly—but erroneously—as the Temple of Serapis and proven to have been below sea level (see the perforations in the columns made by mollusks) for much of its history, this is almost all that remains of the ancient harbor district of Puteoli. The macellum is closed to the public but easily visible and photographed from Via Roma on the waterfront. ✉ *Anfiteatro Grande, Via Terraciano 75,* ☎ *081/5266007.* ▨ *€2.* ☾ *Daily 9–1 hr before sunset.*

Dining

$–$$ ✕ **Antica Trattoria da Ciuffello.** With fish browning invitingly on the barbecue outside and a welcoming roomy feel to the interior, this *caratteristica* trattoria is conveniently—and appropriately—located very close to the ancient macellum, the food market. Sample its much vaunted *zuppa di pesce* (fish soup), which is a *primo* and *secondo* course rolled into one. ✉ *Via Dicearchia 11 bis,* ☎ *081/5269397. DC, V. Closed Mon. in winter.*

$–$$ ✕ **Ristorante Don Antonio.** Despite its unflattering location up a *vicolo* (alley) one block from the Pozzuoli waterfront, this restaurant has achieved cult status in Neapolitan circles for its fresh seafood and unbeatable prices. Unlike other hostelries, which will happily serve well into the afternoon siesta or late at night, Don Antonio rolls down the shutters as soon as the day's catch has been consumed. ✉ *Via Magazzini 20 (off Piazza San Paolo),* ☎ *081/5267941. Reservations not accepted. No credit cards. Closed Mon.*

Astroni

③⓪ *7 km (4 mi) west of Naples; 3 km (2 mi) northeast of Pozzuoli.*

The extinct volcanic crater of the Astroni is one of the natural marvels of the Campi Flegrei. Its peaceful shady avenues running through attractive Mediterranean woodland have made it a popular retreat for families and nature lovers alike. It also has something of a historical pedigree: the Romans came for the sulfur-rich waters, although their *thermae* (baths) have yet to be physically located. The Aragonese dynasty in the 15th century made the crater a royal hunting reserve, which was further consolidated by the Bourbons under Charles III in the mid-18th century. Most structures in the crater, as well as the high wall around the perimeter, date to the latter period. Saved from further decline and neglect only in the 1980s, it was converted into a wildlife refuge managed by the World Wide Fund for Nature (WWF) and now serves as a center for environmental education in the Naples area. Access to the reserve is gained through the ancient Bourbon gatehouse at the top of the crater on the southern side. Maps and suggested itineraries are displayed at the ticket office. The best walks, combining splashes of history amid scenic trails, lead downhill to the base of the crater. On the road down (only service vehicles are allowed along its 2-km [1-mi] stretch) take in the sweeping views of thick woodland and the lakes at the base of the crater, a landscape reminiscent of those painted by the 18th-century court artist Hackert—and certainly not what you'd expect to find within a 10-minute drive of the city of Naples. The Astroni Reserve can be best reached by car; from Naples take the tangenziale Exit 11 at Agnano and turn right toward Pianura; you'll see the entrance on your left after about 2 km (1 mi) (free parking outside). As an alternative, you can take Bus C2, which starts from outside the Campi Flegrei Metropolitana station and ask the driver or fellow passengers for the nearest stop to Astroni (about a 15-minute walk). Special guided tours are available on Sunday. ✉ *Riserva degli Astroni Oasi WWF, Agnano,* ☎ *081/5883720,* WEB *www.astroni.it.* 🎫 *€5 (free for WWF members).* ☉ *Daily 9:30–4:30 (last admission at 2).*

Lago d'Averno

③① *11 km (7 mi) west of Naples; 3 km (2 mi) north of Baia.*

When the great poet Virgil wrote *"Facilis descensus Averno"*—"The way to hell is easy"—it was because he knew what he was talking about. Regarded by the ancients as the doorway to Hades, the fabled Lago d'Averno (Lake Avernus) was well known by the time the great poet settled here to write *The Aeneid*. Today the scene has changed a fair amount: in summer, the whole area pulsates to the sound of down-market disco music booming from lakeside clubs and you would be more likely to come across members of the 21st-century underworld than meet the shades of the dead that Virgil so evocatively describes. As with Lago Lucrino (Lake Lucrino) less than 1 km (½ mi) to the south, a tarmac road skirts much of the lake, opening out at times into litter-strewn lay-bys. However, some of the spell is restored by the backdrop: forested hills rise on three sides and the menacing cone of Monte Nuovo looms on the fourth. The water is indeed "black," the smell of sulfur sometimes hangs over the landscape, and blocked-off passages lead into long-abandoned caves into which Virgil might well have ventured. On the approach road from Lago Lucrino, look for remnants of the Roman channel dug in the 1st century BC, which transformed Avernus into a protected inner harbor and linked it to the Lucrine lake and the sea beyond. An even greater feat of engineering was the tunnel (now blocked off) from the northwestern side of Avernus leading to the center of Cumae. Also not far away is the Mare Morto of ancient Romans, who identified it as the Stygian Lake of the Dead, where Charon plied his trade and ferried souls across into the underworld. Nearby is the spring that was thought to flow directly from the River Styx, and it was there that Aeneas descended into Hades with the guidance of the Cumaean Sibyl, as famously recounted in *The Aeneid* of Virgil. To reach the Lake Avernus, take the Cumana railway to Lucrino (a 10-minute walk away); by car, drive westward from Pozzuoli, hugging the coast where possible, and turn right (inland) at Lucrino, about 4 km (2½ mi) away.

Dining

$$$-$$$$ ✕ **La Ninfea.** In antiquity, the site of some of the most celebrated oyster beds and fish farms, Lake Lucrino is now the setting for this stylish restaurant, which treats cooking as one of the fine arts. On your way in, admire the aquarium brimming with crustaceans of all shapes and sizes, and if overwhelmed by the choice of seafood consult the waiter or even Antonio, the experienced sommelier. For a *primo piatto* with a difference pamper yourself with the *tagliolini alla Sofia* with its garnish of lobster, cream, and cheese. ⊠ *Piazza Italia, Lucrino,* ☎ *081/8661326. AE, DC, MC, V.*

$$ ✕ **La Cucina di Ruggiero.** Starting from a bizarre but *simpatico* welcome announced through a booming megaphone, this restaurant is likely to be very different from anything you've previously experienced. Besides running this homely restaurant on the western shore of Lake Lucrino, Ruggiero is also a writer and poet—though his clients would insist that the real artist is his wife, Maria, whose culinary repertory and imagination are boundless. No written menus here and no choice—for a global figure of between €20–€30 you eat what has been prepared that day: a family meal with a difference. ⊠ *Via Intorno al Lago Lucrino, Lucrino,* ☎ *081/8687473. Reservations essential. No credit cards. Closed Mon.–Tues. No lunch Wed.–Thurs.; no dinner Sun.*

Monte Nuovo

32 *10 km (6 mi) west of Naples; 3 km (2 mi) west of Pozzuoli.*

Monte Nuovo is the youngest volcano in the Campi Flegrei and the only one to have formed in historical times. Overlooking the Bay of Pozzuoli and lying between the town of Arco Felice and Lake Lucrino, at its highest point on the eastern side the volcanic cone rises more than 400 ft above sea level. The center consists of a funnel-shape crater with a maximum diameter of 1,300 ft. When Monte Nuovo erupted in 1538, it destroyed the ancient site of Tripergole on its lower western slopes, filled in much of Lake Lucrino and some of Lake Avernus, thus burying a considerable amount of archaeological evidence. The access road to Monte Nuovo (Via Virgilio) branches off Via Milliscola, linking Pozzuoli and Lucrino at roughly the midpoint between the Cumana stations of Arco Felice and Lucrino (about a 15-minute walk). The area is jointly run by the municipality of Pozzuoli and a local scientific school whose pupils first adopted the site in 1996. Much of the lower part has been landscaped and restored for educational purposes. A series of trails start from the visitor center (ask here about evening concerts) taking between one and two hours, with the possibility of descending into the heart of the crater. ⊠ *Oasi Naturalistica di Monte Nuovo, Via Virgilio, Arco Felice, Pozzuoli,* ☎ FAX *081/8041462.* ☜ *Free.* ☉ *Weekdays 9–1 hr before sunset, weekends 9–1* PM. *Guided tours Sun. 11* AM *weather permitting.*

Baia

❸ *12 km (7 mi) west of Naples; 4 km (2½ mi) west of Pozzuoli.*

Now largely under the sea, ancient Baiae was once the most opulent and fashionable resort area of the Roman Empire, the place where Sulla, Pompey, Cicero, Julius Caesar, Tiberius, and Nero built their holiday villas. Petronius's *Satyricon* is a satire on the corruption, intrigue, and wonderful licentiousness of Roman life at Baiae. (Petronius was hired to arrange parties and entertainment for Nero, so he was in a position to know.) It was here that Cleopatra was staying when Julius Caesar was murdered on the Ides of March (March 15) in 44 BC; here that Emperor Claudius built a great villa for his third wife, Messalina (who is reputed to have spent her nights indulging herself at local brothels); and near here that Agrippina (Claudius's fourth wife and ultimate murderer) is believed to have been killed by henchmen sent by her son Nero in AD 59. Unfortunately, the Romans did not pursue the custom of writing—"Here lived Crassus" would help—so it is difficult to assign these historical events to specific locations. Consequently, conjecture is the order of the day: Julius Caesar's villa is now thought to be at the top of the hill behind the archaeological site and not near the foot of the Aragonese castle, though we cannot be absolutely certain. We do know, however, that the Romans found this area staggeringly beautiful. A visit to the site can only confirm what Horace wrote in one of his Epistles: *Nullus in orbe sinus Baiis praelucet amoenis* ("No bay on Earth outshines pleasing Baiae").

★ Access to the **Parco Archeologico e Monumentale di Baia** (Archaeological Park) is relatively straightforward on the Cumana railway (trains leave every 15–20 minutes from Montesanto in Naples, travel time 30 minutes, nearest stop Lucrino) followed by a shuttle bus for the last 3 km (2 mi). Where the bus stops in the square outside the Baia station, cross the disused railway line on a footbridge, noting the impressive dome of the so-called Temple of Diana, part of the ancient baths complex sundered from the rest of the archaeological site by the railway, obviously built well before the days of impact assessment. Continue upward for about five minutes until you reach the entrance to the site (limited parking facilities also available). Unlike Pompeii, Oplontis, and Herculaneum, where visitors are left stranded with very little site information—it's good for sales of guidebooks and guiding services—at the Baia ticket office you should receive a small map to the site while information panels in readable English are at strategic intervals. In antiquity this whole area was the Palatium Baianum (the Palace of Baiae), dedicated to *otium*—the ancient form of dolce far niente—and the residence of emperors from Augustus to as late as Septimius Severus in the 3rd century AD. The first terrace, the aptly named Villa dell'Ambulatio, is one of the best levels from which to appreciate the topography of the site: the whole hillside down to the level of the modern road near the waterfront has been modeled into flat terraces, each sporting different architectural features. While up on this terrace, look for the exquisite stuccoed artistry with its depictions of dolphins, swans, and cupids in the *balneum* (bathroom) (Room 13) and admire the elaborate theatrical motifs in the floor mosaic in Room 14. Below the balneum and inviting further exploration is a nymphaeum, or miniature theater, which can be reached from the western side. The suggested itinerary around the site is somewhat confusing, especially as part of the site is roped off. This regrettably includes the Temple of Mercury, on the lowest level, which has held so much fascination for travelers from the 18th century onward. It has been variously interpreted as a frigidarium and as a *natatio* (swimming pool) and is the oldest example of a large dome (50 BC–27 BC), predating the cupola of the Pantheon in Rome. If possible, have a peek inside the temple and test the impressive echo within.

If visiting during weekends and you have some surplus energy after touring the main archaeological site, continue up Via Fusaro away from Baia and branch left at the next roundabout. After about 150 yards along Via Bellavista look for a large gate on the left with a panda symbol. This marks the entrance to the newly created archaeological heritage park run by dedicated WWF volunteers. A short walk through small vegetable plots and vineyards will take you up to the summit and what is now believed to be Julius Caesar's villa, complete with the remains of a World War II gun emplacement and a commanding view both east and west. The park now hosts traditional concerts and poetry readings throughout much of the year (entrance is free but donations are welcome) and provides a focal point for local *contadini* (farmers) to sell their produce. For the schedule of events, ask at the archaeological site **ticket office** or at the Museo Archeologico dei Campi Flegrei (☎ 081/5233797). ✉ *Parco Archeologico e Monumentale di Baia, Via Fusaro 75, Baia,* ☎ *081/8687592.* 🖼 €2.06. ☉ *Tues.–Sun. 9–1 hr before sunset.*

Housed in the Castle of Baia commanding a fine 360° view—eastward across the Bay of Pozzuoli and westward across the open Tyrrhenian—
★ is the recently established **Museo Archeologico dei Campi Flegrei.** Regular bus service leaves the old Baia station (in the direction of Bacoli; buy a ticket for the return journey, too, at the kiosk outside the old railway station) and stops about 2 km (1 mi) away, just opposite the ramp ascending to this impressively located castle. Though its foundation dates to the late 15th century, when Naples was ruled by the House of Aragon and an invasion by Charles VIII of France looked imminent, the castle was radically transformed under the Spanish viceroy Don Pedro de Toledo after the nearby eruption of Monte Nuovo in 1538. Indeed, its bastions bear a striking resemblance to the imposing Castel Sant'Elmo in Naples, built in the same period. This is an ideal spot for museumphobes: spacious, uncluttered rooms display tastefully contextualized finds; there is a virtual absence of large tour groups; if required there's access to bastion terraces; and a viewing time of approximately one hour at the most is all that need be allotted. The south side of the castle is also the venue for outdoor classical music recitals and other performances (on summer evenings; ask at the ticket office about forthcoming events).

Of the three main exhibitions, the first on the suggested itinerary consists of plaster casts from the Roman period found at the Baia archaeological site. This gives valuable insights into the techniques used by the

Romans to make copies from Greek originals in bronze from the Classical and Hellenistic periods. Displayed in the cases are plaster molds and casts from a local sculptor's workshop active around the 1st century BC, which were then used to produce marble copies of well-known works, such as that of the Athenian Tyrannicides, which would have stood in the Agora of Athens. Thanks to the Romans' love of Greek art and their fondness for marble copies of the bronze originals, we have been able to reconstruct much of the history of ancient Greek sculpture.

Pride of place in the museum goes to the sacellum, or small sanctuary, transported from nearby Misenum and tastefully displayed inside the Aragonese tower, *Torre Tenaglia*. Standing about 20 ft high, the sacellum has been reconstructed, with two of its original six columns (the rest in steel) and a marble architrave with its dedicatory inscription to the husband-and-wife team of *Augustales* (imperial cult devotees), who commissioned restoration of the sanctuary in the 2nd century AD, this surmounted by a pediment depicting the beneficent couple. Behind the facade are the naked statues of Vespasian (left) and Titus (right) in a flattering heroic pose, at least from the neck downward. To the right outside the sanctuary is a bronze equestrian statue (1st century AD) originally depicting Domitian. After his death and the subsequent *damnatio memoriae* (the imperial decree issued by emperors who wanted to disgrace predecessors by destroying all sculpted likenesses of them) the statue was extensively—but all too visibly—remodeled to represent his successor, Nerva. Such changes in favor and falls from grace were common in the 1st century AD, and there are cases where faces were resculpted so many times that the statues ultimately became unrecognizable.

Moving on to the upper floor of the tower, you come to the other *capolavoro,* or showpiece, of the museum, the reconstruction of Emperor Claudius's nymphaeum. Discovered in 1959 but only systematically excavated in the early 1980s, it now lies together with much of the ancient site of Baiae under 20 ft of water in the Bay of Pozzuoli. The sculptural elements salvaged from the seabed include a recognizable scene of a headless Odysseus plying Polyphemus (statue never found) with wine, aided by a companion with a wineskin. The other statues filling the niches along the two longer walls of the nymphaeum include Claudius's mother, Antonia, and a rather poignant sculpture of perhaps one of his daughters who died young. She is depicted holding a butterfly about to take wing, thought to be symbolic of the spirit of life departing. In contrast, there are two statues of the youthful Dionysus (one crowned, the other with panther), making any thematic connections between the statues rather hard to draw. The function of the nymphaeum is suggested by the marble supports for *klinai* (couches) set on the floor near the entrance: this must have been a showy triclinium, with its full complement of statues and fountains designed to ease the weight of imperial cares and provide due source for reflection and inspiration. ⊠ *Via Castello 39, Bacoli,* ☎ *081/5233797.* 🖭 €2. ☉ *Tues.–Sat. 9–1 hr before sunset, Sun. 9–2.*

Boat Excursions

From the small modern-day port of Baia you can board a boat with glass panels on the lower deck and view part of the *città sommersa,* the underwater city of ancient Baiae. The guided tour—usually only in Italian, but can be arranged in English by prior appointment—takes about 1¼ hours and is best undertaken in calm conditions when you can get good glimpses of Roman columns, roads, villa walls, and mosaics. The fare (€8 per person) also includes a brief talk illustrating the significant changes in the coastline over the last two millennia and the main underwater sights. Sailings are scheduled mid-March–mid-November, Saturday at noon and 4 PM, Sun. at 10:30 AM, noon, and 4 PM. Night sailings are also offered mid-June–mid-September, Saturday and Sunday at 9 PM and 10:30 PM. For further information and bookings, contact **Associazione Aliseo** (⊠ Piazza della Repubblica 42, Baia, ☎ 081/5265780).

Dining and Lodging

$–$$ ✕⬚ **Azienda Agrituristica Il Casolare.** Il Casolare offers the rare chance of dining and lodging within a 10,000-year-old volcanic crater (thankfully extinct). This place is particularly known for its restaurant, perched on the inner slopes of the volcano, offering a view of the patchwork of farmed plots on the crater floor. Specializing in *cucina contadina napoletana,* the owner Tobia serves whatever is in season. No agonizing over menus here (the all-inclusive set price is about €20–€25): expect about a cornucopia of different antipasti (including possibly goat's ricotta, and *poppacelle,* or peppers done in vinegar) and some novel vegetarian dishes like pasta *e cicerchia* (vetchling). The four rooms, or *mini-appartmenti,* are small but tastefully furnished, a perfect base for exploring the surrounding area. Transfers can be arranged from the nearby railway station of Lucrino. There is also convenient parking, situated up an unbelievably narrow lane (Via Selvatico) almost opposite the entrance to Baia Castle. If you're coming to dine, a flashlight is provided evenings for descending to the restaurant in the crater. ⊠ *Via Selvatico, Contrada Coste dei Fondi di Baia, 80070,* ☎ *081/5235193. Reservations essential. 4 rooms with bath. Restaurant, parking. No credit cards. Closed Mon. No dinner Sun.*

Cumae

③④   *16 km (10 mi) west of Naples; 5 km (3 mi) north of Baia.*

Being perhaps the oldest Greek colony on mainland Italy, Cumae overshadowed the Phlegrean Fields and Neapolis in the 7th and 6th centuries BC, since it was home to the **Antro della Sibilla,** the fabled Cave of the Cumaean Sibyl—one of the three greatest oracles of antiquity—who is said to have presided over the destinies of men. In about the 6th century BC the Greeks hollowed the cave from the rock beneath the ridge leading up to the present ruins of Cumae's acropolis. Today you can walk—just as Virgil's Aeneas did—through a dark, massive 350-ft-long stone tunnel that opens into the vaulted Chamber of the Prophetic Voice, where the Sibyl delivered her oracles. Standing here in one of the most venerated sites of ancient times, the sense of the *numen*—of communication with invisible powers—is overwhelming. "This is the most romantic classical site in Italy," wrote H. V. Morton. "I would rather come here than to Pompeii."

Cumae was founded in the third quarter of the 8th century BC by Greek colonists. The name has legendary origins: myth has it that Euboean mariners found a woman who had miscarried a baby on the beach here, and the fetus was washed out to sea by great breakers on the shore. Thinking this an omen from the gods of fertility, the mariners built an altar here and called their new settlement *kuema* (or "fetus" in Greek). Centuries later Virgil wrote his epic of *The Aeneid,* the story of the Trojan prince Aeneas's wanderings, partly to give Rome the historical legitimacy that Homer had given the Greeks. On his journey, Aeneas had to descend to the underworld to speak to his father, and to find his way in, he needed the guidance of the Cumaean Sibyl. Virgil did not dream up the Sibyl's Cave or the entrance to Hades—he must have actually stood both in her chamber and along the rim of Lake Avernus, as you yourself will stand. When he described the Sibyl's Cave in Book VI of *The Aeneid* as having "*centum ostia*"—a hundred mouths—and depicted the entrance to the underworld on Lake Avernus so vividly, "*spelunca alta . . . tuta lacu nigro nemorum tenebris"*—"a deep cave . . . protected by a lake of black water and the glooming forest"—it was because he was familiar with this awesome landscape. In Book VI of *The Aeneid*, Virgil describes how Aeneas, arriving at Cumae, sought Apollo's throne (remains of the Temple of Apollo can still be seen) and "the deep hidden abode of the dread Sibyl/An enormous cave . . ." On either side of the entrance to the cave today are inscribed one of Virgil's most powerful verses: "On one side of the Eubean rock/Is cut a huge cavern. To it lead/A hundred broad ways, a hundred mouths/From which there tumble out as many voices,/The Sibyl's answers. As they all arrived/Upon the threshold of the cave the virgin/Cried out: 'The time to question fate is now!/The god is here, the god!' As she spoke/Before the temple doors her countenance/Changed suddenly, her color changed, her hair/Fell loose about her shoulders and she panted/Violently, her wild heart grew great within her,/She seemed taller, her voice was not a mortal's/Because the god's power had breathed upon her."

In general, Sibyl was the title given to inspired prophetesses, usually of Apollo. As the god of light who pierced through all darkness, Apollo was also the god of divination, and there were oracles throughout the ancient world interpreting his will. Although Cumae never achieved the status of Delphi, it was the most important oracular center in Magna Graecia, and the Sibyl would have been consulted on a whole range of matters. Foreign governments consulted the Sibyl before mounting campaigns. Wealthy aristocrats came to consult with their deceased relatives. Businessmen came to get their dreams interpreted or to seek favorable omens before entering into financial agreements or setting off on journeys. Farmers came to remove curses on their cows. Love potions were a profitable source of revenue; women from Baiae lined up for potions to slip into the wine of handsome charioteers who drove up and down the street in their gold-plated four-horsepower chariots. Still, it was the Sibyl's prophecies that ensured the crowds here, prophecies written on palm leaves and later collected into the corpus of the Sibyline books. However, with the coming of the Olympian gods, the earlier gods of the soil were discredited or given new roles and names. Ancient rites, such as those surrounding the Cumaean Sibyl, were now carried out in secret and known as the Mysteries. The Romans—like the later Soviets—tried in vain to replace these Mysteries by deifying the state in the person of its rulers. Yet even the Caesars appealed to forces of the Other World. And until the 4th century AD, the Sibyl was consulted by the Christian bishop of Rome, one reason why Michelangelo portrayed the Cumaean Sibyl—one of his most magisterial creations—on the Sistine Chapel ceiling.

However little of ancient Cumae now stands above ground—and the Temple of Apollo has suffered woefully over the millennia—the underground passages are virtually intact, though not entirely visitable. There are detailed information panels to guide you through the site, with extra information on flora and fauna supplied by the locally respected World Wide Fund for Nature. As you walk through, you'll soon appreciate what a good choice it was to colonize this site: it was surrounded by fertile land, offered opportunities for development on various levels, had relatively easy access to the sea (though no natural harbor), and an acropolis at the top providing an excellent vantage in all directions. Allow at least two hours for this visit to soak up the ambience, study the ruins, and reach the top level overlooking the Acherusia Palus—now Lago Fusaro—to the south and part of the Silva Gallinaria, the thick holm oak ground cover to the north, once an immense forest stretching almost all the way to Rome. Unlike in Greek and Roman times, when access to Cumae was through a network of underground passages, an overground bus service leaves the old Baia station at regular intervals. If driving, leave the Naples Tangenziale (bypass) at the Cuma exit and then continue to follow signs for about 3 km (2 mi). There is a free parking lot. ⊠ *Via Acropoli 39, Cumae,* ☎ *081/8543060.* ▨ €2. ☉ *Daily 9–1 hr before sunset.*

AROUND THE BAY A TO Z

BUS TRAVEL
In general, in this area it's best to travel on rails than on wheels, as local roads can be frustratingly slow. However, for the trip up Vesuvius the bus run by Transporti Vesuviani (€2.58 from Piazza Anfiteatro in Pompei, €1.54 from Ercolano Circumvesuviana station) will take you up to the car park and the starting point of the path up to the top of the cone.
➤ Bus Information: **Transporti Vesuviani** (☎ 081/5592582).

CAR TRAVEL
Pompeii is a very short distance off the A3 autostrada (toll from Naples or Nocera: €1), though this major highway with only two lanes in each direction can get very congested with ill-disciplined drivers.

A car could be useful for exploring the Campi Flegrei region on the west side of Naples, especially for sites like Cumae and Lake Avernus where public transport is either infrequent or nonexistent, as well as the Astroni and Monte Nuovo craters. From Naples travel toward Pozzuoli on the Tangenziale—the Naples bypass (toll: €.6)—exiting at the appropriate junction.

PARKING
Most archaeological sites are fairly accessible by car and usually have reasonably safe parking facilities. Take customary precautions when parking and leaving your vehicle: use a *parcheggio custodito* (attended parking lot) and avoid on-street unattended parking when possible.

ROAD CONDITIONS
Off the main highways, signposting is sometimes poor, with road signs suffering intense competition from advertising placards, so navigating becomes an invaluable skill. The westbound Tangenziale (Napoli–Pozzuoli) should be avoided Saturday evenings and Sundays in summer (crowds heading out of Naples for nightlife or beaches). Road surfaces are usually fair, though conditions near the top of Vesuvius can become icy in winter.

EMERGENCIES
➤ Pompeii: **Ambulance** (☎ 081/8637816). **First Aid** (⊠ Via Colle San Bartolomeo 50, Pompeii, ☎ 081/5359111). **Police** (☎ 081/8506172).
➤ Ercolano (Herculaneum: **Ambulance** (☎ 081/7775600). **Hospital** (⊠ Ospedale Maresca, Via Montedoro, Torre del Greco, ☎ 081/8824033). **Police** (⊠ Ercolano [Herculaneum], ☎ 081/7321858).
➤ Pozzuoli: **Ambulance** (☎ 081/5266954). **Hospital** (⊠ Ospedale S. Maria delle Grazie, Via Domiziana, Pozzuoli, ☎ 081/8552111). **Police** (☎ 081/8041100).

CURRENCY EXCHANGE
In Pompeii, aside from the Banco di Napoli, there are several exchange bureaux around and off the main square, Piazza Longo, near Porta Marina, and an ATM conveniently located by the main ticket office at Porta Marina. Exchange services in Pozzuoli and Ercolano are listed below.
➤ Exchange Services: **Banco di Napoli** (⊠ Piazza B. Longo 37 Pompeii, ☎ 081/8631001; ⊠ Via N. Terracciano 18, Pozzuoli, ☎ 081/

5256111). Exchange Bureau, **Alesi Travel International** (⊠ 1 Traversa
IV Novembre 12, Ercolano, ☎ 081/7397587).

TRAVELER'S CHECKS

TAXIS

➤ TAXI COMPANIES: **Ercolano** (⊠ Stazione Circumvesuviana, ☎ 081/
7393666). **Pompeii** (⊠ Piazza Santuario, ☎ 081/8632686; ⊠ Piazza
Esedra, ☎ 081/5367852). **Pozzuoli** (⊠ Piazza della Repubblica, ☎ 081/
5265800).

TRAIN TRAVEL

The main station in Naples (Stazione Centrale, at Piazza Garibaldi) is
also the main interchange node for public transport both east and west
of Naples. A branch of the aptly named Circumvesuviana railway
serves the main archaeological sites at the foot of Vesuvius. Trains leave
from the Corso Garibaldi station in Naples, then make a stop at the
main terminal at Piazza Garibaldi just 10 blocks away to link up with
the Naples *metropolitana,* and then head southeast for Sorrento (about
two trains per hour; €1.13 to Ercolano, €1.65 to Torre Annunziata
and Pompei Scavi-Villa Dei Misteri). Confusingly, the station called
"Pompei" lies on a different line which will leave you not at the main
entrance to the archaeological site but just behind the cathedral, close
to the amphitheater.

For the Phlegrean Fields to the west of Naples, take the Cumana line
run by SEPSA, with trains every 15–20 minutes, from the terminus at
Piazza Montesanto near Montesanto Metropolitana station. Alternatively, take the Metropolitana all the way to Pozzuoli from one of the
railway stations in Naples, either Piazza Garibaldi or the more welcoming station of Mergellina, with one departure every 10–15 minutes. This will drop you near the amphitheater and the Solfatara crater.

When not affected by wildcat strikes or landslides, the railway network
either side of Naples is cheap and reliable, though with the many stops
along the way you're unlikely to experience nerve-tingling velocity. As
in any mass transit system through a fairly depressed area, not all your
fellow-passengers will be well versed in train etiquette so brace yourself for clandestine smoking, etc., especially on the Circumvesuviana.
➤ TRAIN INFORMATION: **Circumvesuviana railway** (☎ 081/7722444).
Mergellina (☎ 081/5543188). **SEPSA** (☎ 081/5513328).

TRAVEL AGENCIES

➤ LOCAL AGENTS: **Alesi Travel International** (⊠ 1 Traversa IV Novembre 12, Ercolano [Herculaneum], ☎ 081/7397587, FAX 081/7772872,
WEB www.alesitravel.com). **Amorini Viaggi** (⊠ Via Lepanto 235, Pompeii, ☎ 081/8502614, FAX 081/8561689). **Campi Elisi Viaggi e Turismo**
(⊠ Via Solfatara 13, Pozzuoli, ☎ 081/5266466, FAX 081/5266845).

VISITOR INFORMATION

Azienda Autonoma di Cura Soggiorno e Turismo offices in Pompeii
and Pozzuoli are open 9–2, closed Sunday. Ufficio Informazione in Herculaneum is open 9–5 daily. Ufficio Turistico in Ercolano (Herculaneum)
is open 9–2, closed Sunday.
➤ TOURIST INFORMATION: **Azienda Autonoma di Cura Soggiorno e
Turismo** (⊠ Via Sacra 1, Pompeii, ☎ 081/8508451, ☎ toll-free 800/
013350, FAX 081/8632401, www.uniplan.it/pompei/azienda; ⊠ Piazza
Matteotti 1/a, Pozzuoli, ☎ 081/5266639, FAX 081/5265068, WEB
www.campnet.it/aziendaturismo/pozzuoli). **Ufficio Informazione** (⊠
Piazza Porta Marina 12, Ercolano [Herculaneum], ☎ 081/5365154,
WEB www.pompeiisites.org). **Ufficio Turistico** (⊠ Via IV Novembre 82,
Ercolano [Herculaneum], ☎ 081/7881243).

3 CAPRI, ISCHIA, AND PROCIDA

Emperors, kings, and artists have all made the Bay of Naples's sea-wreathed isles their abodes for more than 2,000 years. And well they might, for the islands of Capri, Ischia, and Procida are compact realms of undiluted beauty. Bathed in 24-karat sunshine, Capri has been a chic resort ever since the Caesars made it their private playpen; Ischia is famous for its volcanic spas where there's nothing between you and the rest of the world except for a layer of fango mud; while the magical waterfront of Procida has been immortalized in the Oscar-winning film *Il Postino*. The locals dare you to find lovelier islands, even in your own imagination.

By Mark
Walters

Updated by
Mark Walters

THE ISLANDS OFF NAPLES ARE SO DIFFERENT FROM EACH OTHER that you wonder how they can possibly be in the same bay—indeed, some would insist they are not, that they lie just beyond its outer fringes. The contrast goes beyond mere geology and vegetation. They all occupy different niches in the traveler's mind, with Capri pandering to the whims of the international great-and-good, Ischia servicing the needs of its predominantly German and Italian clientele, and Procida—the closest to the mainland—being more dependent on the weekend and summer influx of Neapolitans. Chosen by the Greeks, the great connoisseurs and aesthetes of antiquity, as their first base in Italy, the islands of Capri, Ischia, and Procida combine a broad gamut of experiences.

Islandophiles, of course, have always had a special love for Capri (pronounced with the accent on the first syllable). Erstwhile pleasure dome to Roman emperors, and still Italy's most glamorous seaside getaway, this craggy, whale-shape island tips one of the two points of the crescent of the Bay of Naples (Ischia tips the other). The island's beauty is an epic one: cliffs that are the very embodiment of time, bougainvillea-shaded pathways overlooking the sea, trees seemingly hewn out of rock by the Greeks. It's little wonder that tales tell of visiting tourists snapping up villas while their unsuspecting wives were out doing, so they thought, last-minute souvenir shopping, or of American industrialists who, determined to stay forever, simply sent a wire home to sell everything. Capri has always been a stage that lesser mortals could share with the beautiful people, often an eclectic potpourri of duchesses who have left their dukes home, fading French film actresses, pretenders to obscure thrones, waspish couturiers, and sleek supermodels. Today Capri's siren song continues to seduce thousands of visitors. The summer scene calls to mind the stampeding of bulls through the narrow streets of Pamplona: meaning, if you can visit in the spring or fall, do so. Yet even the crowds are not enough to destroy Capri's very special charm. The town itself is a Moorish stage-set of shiny white houses, tiny squares, and narrow medieval alleyways hung with flowers, while its hillsides are spectacular settings for luxurious seaside villas. The mood is modish but somehow unspoiled. The upper crust bakes in the sun in private villas; the secret is that you also should disappear while the day-trippers take over—offering yourself to the sun at your hotel pool or exploring the hidden corners of the island. Even in the height of summer, you can enjoy a degree of privacy on one of the many paved paths that wind around the island hundreds of feet above the sea.

In terms of settlements, conquests, and dominion, the history of the islands is a microcosm of that of the mainland. For eastern Mediterranean traders in the second and first millennia BC, Capri and Ischia were both close enough to the mainland to provide easy access to trade routes and impervious enough to afford natural protection against invaders. Ischia, or Pithekoussai, as it used to be called—a word probably derived from the Greek for a large earthenware jar (*pithos*) rather than the less plausible word, *pithekos*, meaning monkey—is renowned in classical circles as being the first colony founded by the Greeks on Italian soil, as early as the 8th century BC. Capri, probably colonized a century or so later, is amply described in the early years of the Roman Empire by authors such as Suetonius and Tacitus, as this was the island where Tiberius spent the last 10 years of his life.

After the breakup of the Roman Empire, the islands, like many parts of the Mediterranean, suffered a succession of incursions. Saracens, Normans, and Turks all laid siege to the islands at some stage, interspersed with periods of relative stability under the Swabians, the Angevins, the

Aragonese, and the Spanish. After a short interregnum under the French at the beginning of the 19th century, a period of relative peace and prosperity ensued.

Over the next century, from the opening of its first hotel in 1826, Capri saw an influx of visitors that reads like a Who's Who of literature and politics, especially in the early decades of the 20th century. Ischia and Procida established themselves as holiday resorts much later, with development taking place from the 1950s onward. Recent years have seen a diversification in the type of experiences offered on the three islands. From being entirely dependent on its thermal springs, Ischia is now the archaeological front-runner in the bay, with the opening of a new museum in Lacco Ameno. Procida is starting to capitalize on its chief natural asset, the unspoiled island of Vivara, as well as the pastel colors of its fishing harbor, the set for the widely acclaimed film *Il Postino*. On Capri, for those seeking peace and quiet away from its main thoroughfares, a number of walks have been mapped out past some of the major geological landmarks and through delightfully species-rich Mediterranean maquis.

Pleasures and Pastimes

Dining

Though relatively close together, the three islands enjoy different culinary traditions. Capri has lent its name to two dishes that are also widely consumed on the mainland: *insalata caprese,* a dish with a color scheme like the Italian flag—made with alternating slices of mozzarella and tomato and served with a sprig of basil; and *torta caprese,* a plain cake combining chocolate and finely chopped almonds and topped with a sprinkling of powdered sugar. Unlike Capri and Procida, where seafood tends to predominate, the Ischitani exploit their naturally fertile volcanic soils to good effect: wine flows—notably from Biancolella and Forestera grape varieties—and is a pleasing accompaniment to the renowned dish from Ischia, *coniglio all'ischitana,* rabbit in a rich tomato-based sauce together with aromatic herbs like basil, rosemary, thyme, and marjoram. The sauce is also used as an accompaniment to *bucatini,* spaghetti-shape pasta with a hole running from one end to the other. Note that restaurant listings for both Capri Town and Anacapri—the two major settlements of Capri—are united in one section.

CATEGORY	COST*
$$$$	over €18
$$$	€13–€18
$$	€6–€13
$	under €6

*per person for a main course at dinner.

Lodging

Although island prices are generally higher than those on the mainland, it is definitely worth paying the difference for an overnight stay. On Capri, once the day-trippers have left center stage and headed down to the Marina Grande for the ferry home, the streets regain some of their charm and tranquility. Again, although Ischia can be sampled piecemeal on day excursions from Naples, given the size of the island, you'd be well advised to arrange a stopover. Bear in mind that there is considerable competition for hotel rooms, especially at moderate prices. Weekends on the islands are popular with the Italians from the mainland, as are the months of July and especially August. On Capri hotels seem to fill almost as quickly as your wallet empties, so book well in advance to be assured of getting first-pick accommodations. Note that hotel listings for Capri Town and for Anacapri are united in one section.

CATEGORY	COST*
$$$$	over €200
$$$	€120–€200
$$	€60–120
$	under €60

All prices are for a double room at high season, excluding tax and service.

Exploring Capri, Ischia, and Procida

Lying equidistant from Naples (about 25 km [16 mi]), Ischia and Capri stand like guards at the main entrance to the Bay of Naples, with Ischia to the west and Capri to the south, while Procida is like a small stepping-stone halfway between Ischia and Capo Miseno (Cape Misenum), on the mainland. The islands can be reached easily from various points in and near Naples, with the port of Pozzuoli offering the closest access to Procida and Ischia, and the port of Sorrento lying almost opposite Capri.

All the islands are well served by road networks, with buses plying the main roads and a funicular on Capri to reach the main town from the Marina Grande, as well as a chairlift to the top of Monte Solaro (1,932 ft) from Anacapri. Note that on a few of Capri's major roads only cars, taxis, and buses are permitted—elsewhere on the island foot power is the preferred mode of transportation. Life on Capri gravitates around the two centers of Capri Town (on the saddle between Monte Tiberio and Monte Solaro) and Anacapri, higher up (984 ft). Ischia's larger population is distributed into six main urban areas and countless smaller villages and farmsteads dotted around the slopes of Monte Epomeo, the highest point on the island (2,582 ft). Both Ischia and Capri contrast strikingly with Procida, much of which is built-up apart from the less developed southwestern end and the island of Vivara, linked by a pedestrian causeway to Chiaiolella.

Great Itineraries

If archaeology and history are at the top of your list of priorities, choosing between Ischia and Capri can be difficult. Moving around Capri to the main sites is generally easier—and can be done in a day if pushed—while Ischia calls for more chilling out at your destination, especially in summer months. If time is limited, Procida can be tacked on to your stay as a day trip from Ischia or from the mainland.

IF YOU HAVE 1 DAY

With no chance of overnighting, take an early ferry from the mainland to Capri so that you get to the main sites before the human tsunami hits the island. Take a quick tour of glamorous Capri—**La Piazzetta** ②, the idyllic Via Tragara, and the famed **I Faraglioni** ⑨ and **Punta Tragara** ⑩. Return by route of the romantic **Certosa di San Giacomo** ⑪, then, if you're up for an hour's hike, head up to the **Villa Jovis** ⑤ to gaze in wonder at Tiberius's Leap and the sea views. After lunch, take a breathless bus ride up to Anacapri to visit the mountaintop gardens of Axel Munthe's **Villa San Michele** ⑭. From Anacapri catch the bus to the **Grotta Azzurra** ⑳—the matrix-blue light at this grotto scintillates even in late afternoon and by then the crowds are gone.

IF YOU HAVE 4 DAYS

After the day outlined above, overnight on Capri—even more magical when the day-trippers have departed—and enjoy more of its sights on your second day. Begin with a morning jaunt around the Giro dell'Arco Naturale to view the **Grotta di Matermania** ⑦ and the **Villa Malaparte** ⑧. For more scenic splendor, head back up to Anacapri and the chairlift up **Monte Solaro** ⑮, then explore the churches of **Santa Maria** a **Cetrella** ⑯ and **San Michele** ⑲. If you just want to be busy doing nothing, opt instead to laze the afternoon away at the bathing lido at **Marina Piccola** ⑬. On day three head to Ischia. Visit **Ischia Ponte** ㉒ and the "doorman" to the island—the magnificent Castello Aragonese—then visit the museum of Greek and Roman antiquities at **Lacco Ameno** ㉕ and **Forio** ㉖, where you'll find the island's most picturesque church, the Santuario del Soccorso, and the famous gardens of La Mortella. On your final day you'll want to save time for a welcome dip into Ischia's soothing waters, either at Citara Beach, or at one of the noted spas: if you want the gamut of natural saunas with access to a dreamy beach, head to Poseidon in Forio; for more stylish surrounds and landscaped Mediterranean gardens, check out Negombo in Lacco Ameno. Or take the ferry and explore nearby Procida.

IF YOU HAVE 7 DAYS

A week should be enough to sample a gamut of pleasures ranging from natural saunas to trails winding through thick Mediterranean maquis, with plenty of time left over for experiencing the local brands of dolce vita in the evenings. On Capri go for a round-the-island boat trip and spend a lazy day on Procida combining a walk on Vivara with a lingering lunch at a quayside restaurant at the quiet marina of Chiaiolella.

WHEN TO TOUR CAPRI, ISCHIA, AND PROCIDA

Lying at a latitude of just more than 40° north, the islands in the Bay of Naples enjoy a typical Mediterranean climate, with hot dry summers, which means the area can be pretty torrid in July and August. Spring is excellent for wildflowers and birds, although it also attracts large numbers of vacationers, especially from northern Europe. If you're looking for a quiet break, the holiday season calms down considerably from the end of September, while sea temperatures are still pleasantly warm by Mediterranean standards even to the end of October. At any time of year outside the summer, conditions can be stomach churning in the Bay of Naples and on exceptionally rough days ferry services to the mainland may be canceled.

In winter *la caccia* (hunting) is a common pursuit, especially on Ischia, so it's best to schedule country walks for nonhunting days (usually Tuesday and Friday, check locally). Watch out for Pasquetta (Easter Monday), when the ferries to the islands are crammed with Neapolitans hell-bent on their annual country picnic. This is definitely a no-go day for travel or country walks.

CAPRI: A SIREN LANDSCAPE

D. H. Lawrence once called Capri "a gossipy, villa-stricken, two-humped chunk of limestone, a microcosm that does heaven much credit, but mankind none at all." He was referring to its once rather farouche reputation as well as its unique natural beauty. Fantastic grottoes, soaring conical peaks, caverns great and small, plus villas of the emperors and thousands of legends combine with Suetonius's ancient Roman tales of "exquisite tortures" to give the isle an air of whispered and mysterious evil, and an intoxicating quality as heady as its rare and delicious wines. Emperor Augustus was the first to tout the island's pleasures by nicknaming it Apragopolis—the city of sweet idleness—and Capri has drawn escapists of every ilk since. Ancient Greek and Roman goddesses are no longer worshiped here, having been supplanted by the likes of Jacqueline Onassis, Elizabeth Taylor, and Brigitte Bardot, who made the island into a papparazzo's paradise in the 1960s. Today, the island's allure for glitterati is as strong as ever—in 2001,

Vanity Fair wrote up the isle as a favored getaway for the ilk of Julia Roberts and Whitney Houston.

Of all the peoples who have left their mark on the island during its millennia of history, the Romans and the sybaritic wealth they displayed here have had the greatest effect in modeling the island's psyche. Capri became the very center of power in the ancient Roman Empire when Tiberius scattered 12 villas around the island and decided to spend the rest of his life here, refusing to return to Rome even when, 10 years on, he was near death. Far from being a dirty old man who was only interested in orgies, this poor, misunderstood gentleman used Capri as a base to set up many of the governmental edicts that literally created the ancient Roman Empire. All his hard work and happy play—he indulged his secret passion for astronomy here—were overlooked by ancient scandalmongers, prime among them Suetonius, who wrote: "In Capri they still show the place at the cliff top where Tiberius used to watch his victims being thrown into the sea after prolonged and exquisite tortures. A party of mariners were stationed below, and when the bodies came hurtling down, they whacked at them with oars and boat-hooks, to make sure they were completely dead." Thankfully, present-day Capri is less fraught with danger for visiting dignitaries and travelers from afar. The main risks now are overexposure to the Mediterranean sun and overindulgence in pleasures of the palate.

Capri Town and Environs

From the main harbor, Marina Grande, you can take a bus or funicular to reach the hub of the island, Capri Town. This white-on-white fantasy of Capriote architecture, window boxes filled with blooms, and stylish boutiques rests on a saddle between rugged limestone cliffs to the east and west, where huge herds of *capre* (goats) once roamed, hence the name of the island. Beyond Capri Town lies some of the island's most spectacular sights, including I Faraglioni and the Villa Jovis. As you disembark at the marina quay, note that unlike the other islands in the Bay of Naples, Capri is not of volcanic origin but was formed by marine deposits laid more than 100 million years ago and then uplifted during plate tectonic activity in the Pleistocene era (as recently as 1–2 million years ago); Monte Tiberio, to the left of the Marina Grande, and Monte Solaro, to the west, powerfully attest to this.

A Good Walk

Once you get off the ferry and have picked up a decent map of Capri (€.80 at the information office on the main jetty), take a funicular ride up from the harbor area of **Marina Grande** ① to Capri Town (only one stop, €1.3 one-way; if for any reason it's not working, there's a bus and taxi service). For energetic foot soldiers, there's a former mule track starting from a small square on the quayside called Largo Fontana that will get you up in about 15 minutes, emerging just below the clock tower in Capri Town. The top funicular station brings you out onto Piazza Umberto I, better known locally as **La Piazzetta** ②. On peak days in the summer this area gets so crowded it's rumored the local police only give you 20 minutes to sip your Campari before moving you on. Admire the majolica decoration of the clock tower dial and inspect the 17th-century church of **Santo Stefano** ③, just off the upper side of the square in Piazzetta Cerio. On the same tiny square is the **Museo Caprense Ignazio Cerio** ④, a small four-room display of archaeological and fossil finds, and useful as a back-up site on a rainy day. Then forge your way across the main Piazzetta to Via Le Botteghe; if you are thinking about a picnic lunch, you can stock up on provisions here (try Sfizi di Pane, a baker at Via Le Botteghe 4 for a slice of frittata *di*

Capri

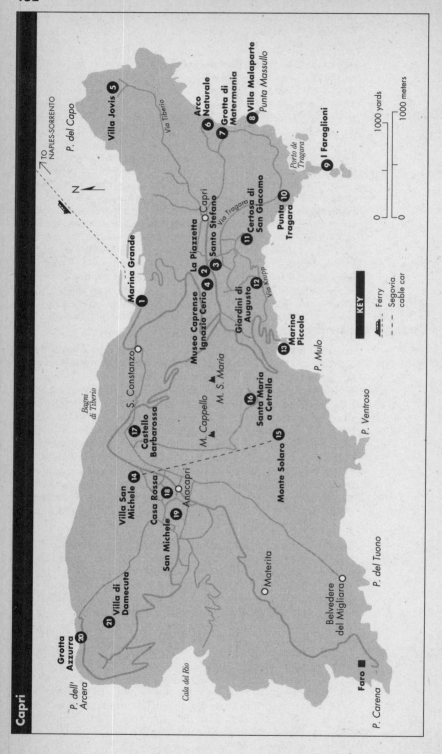

P. del Capo

TO
NAPLES-SORRENTO

N

Via Tiberio

Villa Jovis 5

Via Tiberio

Arco
Naturale 6
Grotta di
Matermania 7
Villa Malaparte 8
Punta Massullo

Marina Grande 1

La Piazzetta
Capri
2
Santo Stefano
4 3

Via Tragara

Certosa di
San Giacomo
11

Punta
Tragara 10

Porto de
Tragara

I Faraglioni 9

Museo Caprense
Ignazio Cerio
Giardini di
Augusto

12
Via Krupp

Marina
Piccola 13

P. Mulo

S. Constanzo

Bagni
di Tiberio

M. Cappello

M. S. Maria

Santa Maria
a Cetrella 16

Monte Solaro 15

Castello
Barbarossa 17

Villa San
Michele 14

Casa Rossa 18

Anacapri

San Michele 19

Materita

Belvedere
del Migliaria

P. Ventroso

P. del Tuono

Villa di
Damecuta 21

Grotta
Azzurra 20

P. dell'
Arcera

Cala del Rio

Faro

P. Carena

KEY

Ferry

Segovia
cable car

1000 yards

1000 meters

0

0

maccaroni or a more orthodox *panino,* or roll, and fixings). Look on the right for the discreet supermarket, to complete the meal or just to stock up with liquid refreshments at accessible prices.

The farther you get away from La Piazzetta, the quieter this pedestrianized road becomes. Via Le Botteghe becomes Via Fuorlovado and then Via Croce, developing gradually into an avenue fringed by bougainvillea and spreading oleander trees. This is an area where real estate now changes hands for at least €5,500 a square meter (more than $500 per square ft). After about 10 minutes the road to the Arco Naturale branches off to the right. Archaeology buffs will instead want to continue straight on up Monte Tiberio for about 45 minutes to reach Tiberius's famous mountaintop **Villa Jovis** ⑤—on the way you'll pass the entrance to the Villa Lysis, one of Capri's most legendary private homes, built by the poet Baron Fersen and now the property of a very lucky Chilean millionaire. The café at the crossroads is one of the last watering holes before heading out to the Arco Naturale. Then follow the ceramic signs for Arco Naturale along Via Matermania until the path forks after about 15 minutes (Arco Naturale, to the left; Grotta di Matermania, to the right). Peer at the **Arco Naturale** ⑥ (Natural Arch), keeping in mind that the path is a cul-de-sac, so every step you go down has to be retraced. Then, knee joints permitting, take the hundreds of steps—and we mean hundreds (don't worry, you won't have to backtrack)—down to the **Grotta di Matermania** ⑦, an impressive natural cave where the ancient Romans worshiped the goddess Cybele every dawn.

The path continues southward through fine Mediterranean maquis vegetation (most of the evergreen trees are holm oak) high above the shoreline, affording fine views of Punta Massullo where **Villa Malaparte** ⑧—possibly the most important creation of 20th-century Italian architecture—perches over the sea. Two hundred yards farther on is a panoramic point from which you can gaze at **I Faraglioni** ⑨, Capri's three, striking offshore rocks, which now loom into sight. As you continue westward, look first for the most romantic house on Capri, the Villa Solitaria—once home to novelist Compton MacKenzie, it is set on a bluff high over the sapphire sea and was built in the early 1900s by architect Edwin Cerio—then look for the towering rock pinnacle Pizzo Lungo (High Point), which the ancients thought was the petrified form of Polyphemus, the giant who was blinded by Odysseus's men. The end of the Giro dell'Arco Naturale (Natural Arch Circuit) is reached at another panoramic point, the **Punta Tragara** ⑩, which marks your arrival back in Capri Town. From here take Via Tragara—lined with elegant hotels and villas, it is the most beautiful street on Capri (some say in the world)—until it joins with Via Camerelle. Look for a left turn down Via Cerio to the **Certosa di San Giacomo** ⑪ (Charterhouse of St. James) to enjoy Capri's grandest architectural set-piece. About five minutes' walk away up Via Matteotti are the **Giardini di Augusto** ⑫ (Gardens of Augustus), which give an excellent view over the southern side of the island towards the Faraglioni. Here, however, the road stops. The impressive Via Krupp has been blocked off, making access to Marina Piccola impossible from this point. So retrace your steps until you get to Via Serena—you'll recognize it from the vast oleander bushes on either side of the walkway which form a picturesque arch, which is a mere five-minute walk from the Piazzetta. Once back at base, reward yourself with a granita or a fruit-based cocktail (perhaps fresh peaches or strawberries with spumante) at the Gran Caffè, the very first bar to grace the square 40 years ago. As standard drinks like caffè espresso and cappuccino are outrageously expensive, you might as well splurge on something really memorable.

Allowing time for a refreshment stop, a little shopping, and a fair amount of camera lens focusing, the walk will take between three and five hours, with an extra half-hour factored in if you opt for the museum. Those who aren't up for a lot of hiking should choose either the trek to the Villa Jovis or the Giro dell'Arco Naturale; the latter is a cliffside path that includes hundreds of steps (going downhill mostly), so be prepared. Most of the sites and shops are open throughout the day, but as there's more than a fair amount of up-and-down, you'd be well advised to avoid the stickiest hours—weather-wise—from noon to 3 PM during the peak summer season.

Sights to See

6 **Arco Naturale.** One of Capri's most famous natural wonders, this geologic arch is all that remains of a large limestone cave which has suffered the erosive effects of wind and rain over the millennia. The cave was probably hollowed out by wave action, then broken apart 1 to 2 million years ago as it was lifted up to its present position hundreds of feet above sea level. Frequently depicted by 19th-century engravers, it became a favorite pictorial landmark for travelers in the era of Romanticism. ⊠ *Via Arco Naturale, at the end of Via Matermania.*

★ **11** **Certosa di San Giacomo** (Charterhouse of St. James). Nestled between the Castiglione and Tuoro hills, this grand, palatial complex was a Carthusian monastery for centuries dedicated to St. James. It was founded between 1371 and 1374 by Count Giacomo Arcucci, who was given the lands and the means to create the monastery by Queen Giovanna I of Naples; both the count and queen died during the upheaval of the Angevin monarchy. After the monastery was sacked by the pirate Dragut in the 16th century, it was heavily restored and rebuilt—thanks partly to the heavy taxes exacted from the populace. The friars within were often detested by the *Capresi,* since they refused to open their gates to minister to them when the plague broke out through the centuries.

You enter the complex via a grandly imposing entryway, which leads to the **Biblioteca Comunale Popolare Luigi Bladier** (public library) and the spacious **Church of San Giacomo** (built in 1690). After admiring the church's Baroque frescoes, follow the signpost down toward the *Parco,* which leads down an avenue flanked by pittosporum and magnolia toward the monastery gardens and some welcome benches. Beyond a covered road lies the **Chiostro Grande** (Large Cloister)—originally the site of the monks' cells and now the temporary home of a local high school. Nearby is the much prettier 15th-century **Chiostro Piccolo** (Small Cloister), now the venue for summertime open-air concerts. Before leaving be sure to visit the **Museo Diefenbach,** a collection of large canvases by the German painter K. W. Diefenbach, who visited Capri in 1900 and stayed until his death in 1913. Not even a protracted stay on such an uplifting island was able to cure Diefenbach of his chronic depression, and his tormented soul emerges clearly in his stunningly powerful paintings filled with apocalyptic storms and saintly apparitions. From La Piazzetta take Via Vittorio Emanuele and then Via F. Serena to reach this beautiful monastic complex. ⊠ *Via Certosa, Capri Town,* ☎ *081/8376218.* ⊠ *Free.* ⊙ *Tues.–Sun. 9–2, park 9–1 hr before sunset.*

12 **Giardini di Augusto** (Gardens of Augustus). You'll see some spectacular views of the southern side of Capri from the southernmost terrace of this well-kept park lying on both sides of Via Matteotti. The pretty gardens are only that (a tacky fountain doesn't help). In one corner of the gardens is a monument to Lenin, who visited Gorky and his Capri-based school for revolutionaries between 1907 and 1913. Above the gardens is the Villa Krupp, now a hotel of the same name. This was the home of the German industrialist Friedrich Alfred Krupp, who commissioned the zigzagging Via Krupp, now closed to the public, designed by Emilio Mayer and built in 1902. An amateur marine biologist, Krupp fell in love with Capri after coming to Naples to visit its aquarium. Although heir to a munitions fortune, Krupp was the most peaceful of men and bestowed monies on many island charities. For his troubles, he was hounded by malicious gossip that he held orgies at his villa and in the island grottoes, and he committed suicide in 1902. More than one critic has observed that Via Krupp shows that roads can be works of art as well as functional structures. Currently undergoing a massive renovation, it usually connects Giardini di Augusto and the Punta del Cannone with the Marina Piccola. ⊠ *Via Matteotti, Capri Town.*

❼ **Grotta di Matermania.** Set in the bowels of Monte Tuoro, this legend-haunted cave was dedicated to Cybele, the Magna Mater, or Great Mother of the gods, hence the somewhat corrupted name of the cave. A goddess with definite eastern origins, Cybele did not form part of the Greek or Roman pantheon: her worship was introduced to Italy in 204 BC at the command of the Sibylline oracle, supposedly for the purpose of driving Hannibal out of Italy. At dawn the cave is touched by the rays of the sun, leading scholars to believe it may also have been a shrine where the Mithraic mysteries were celebrated. Hypnotic rituals, ritual sacrifice of bulls, and other orgiastic practices made this cave a place of myth, so it was not surprising when later authors reported (erroneously) that Emperor Tiberius used it for orgies. Nevertheless, the cave was adapted by the Romans into a luxurious nymphaeum (small shrine), but little remains of the original structure aside from the walls, which would have been covered by tesserae, polychrome stucco, and marine shells. If you want to see the few ancient remains, you have to step within the now-unprepossessing cavern. ⊠ *Giro del'Arco Naturale.*

★ ❾ **I Faraglioni.** Few landscapes set more artists dreaming than that of the famous Faraglioni—three enigmatic, pale-ochre limestone colossi that loom out of the sea just off the Punta Tragara on the southern coast of Capri. Soaring almost 350 ft out of the water, the Faraglioni have become for most Italians an immediately recognizable symbol of Capri and have been poetically compared to Gothic cathedrals or modern skyscrapers. The first rock is called Faraglione di Terra, since it is attached to the land; at its base is the famous restaurant and bathing lido Da Luigi, where the luncheon menus come with beach mattresses. The second is called di Mezzo or Stella, and little boats can often be seen going through its picturesque tunnel, which was caused by sea erosion. The rock farthest out to sea is Scopolo and is inhabited by a wall lizard species with a striking blue belly, thought by some to be endemic to this particular area, while mainstream biologists just consider it a local variant; legend has it that they were originally brought as pets from Greece to delight ancient Roman courtiers.

The "three sons of Capri" can be best seen from the famous lookout **❿** point at **Punta Tragara** at the end of gorgeous Via Tragara. At this point, a path—marked by a plaque honoring the poet Pablo Neruda, who loved this particular walk—leads down hundreds of steps to the water and the feet of I Faraglioni, and perhaps lunch at one of the two lidos at the rock base: Da Luigi, a household name in the Bay of Naples, or La Fontelina, an exclusive sun-drenched retreat nearby. After lunch, habitués then hire a little boat to ferry them back to nearby Marina Piccola and the bus back to town. Another place to drink in the view of I Faraglioni, which is most romantic at sunset, is the Punta Del Cannone, a hilltop belvedere reached beyond the Certosa di San Giacomo and the Giardini di Augusto. ⊠ *End of Via Tragara, Capri Town.*

② La Piazzetta. The English writer and Capriophile Norman Douglas called this square, officially known as Piazza Umberto I, "the small theater of the world." The rendezvous point for international crowds, this *"salone"* became famous as the late-night place to spot heavenly bodies— of the Hollywood variety, that is: Frank Sinatra, Rita Hayworth, Julie Christie, and Julia Roberts are just a few of the celebs that made La Piazzetta the place where the rich and famous come to watch other rich and famous folk. Today, at the height of summer, it's rumored that the *polizia* give you 20 minutes on the square before moving you on. If, in fact, *le tout Capri* bothers to make an appearance any longer, they show up at 8 in the evening to enjoy an aperitif and some peppery *tarallucchi* breadsticks, only to return for a late-night limoncello.

In any event, the square is never less than picturesque and has been a natural crossroads and meeting point on the island since Roman times. The religious complex of Santo Stefano was built around the square in the 17th century, but the clock tower and Municipio, or town hall (once the archbishop's palace) are the only remnants of its cathedral. Capri's Big Ben—the characteristic bell tower, or Torre de'Orologio— is perched over the ancient gateway. Just above the gateway on the lower side is a Latin inscription erected by an American man of letters, Thomas Spencer Jerome, at the beginning of the 20th century; Jerome wished to restore "honor and dignity" to the much-maligned Emperor Tiberius. ⊠ *At intersection of vias Botteghe, Longano, and Vittorio Emanuele, Capri Town.*

① Marina Grande. Besides being the main gateway to Capri and the main disembarkation point for the mainland, Marina Grande is usually the starting point for round-island tours and trips to the Blue Grotto. Originally a conglomeration of fishermen's houses built on ancient Roman foundations, it is now an extended hodgepodge of various architectural styles, with buildings that almost exclusively service the tourist industry. Warehouses and storerooms in which fishermen once kept their boats and tackle have now become shops, restaurants, and bars, most either tacky or overpriced. The marina has faded in the glare of neon since the days when it was Sophia Loren's home in the 1958 film *It Started in Naples.* To the west lies the historic Church of San Costanzo, Palazzo a Mare (the former palace of emperor Augustus), and the chic Baths of Tiberius beach.

⑬ Marina Piccola. Just a 10-minute ride from the main bus terminus in Capri (Piazzetta d'Ungheria), Marina Piccola is a delightfully picturesque inlet that provides the Capresi and other sun worshipers with their best access to reasonable beaches and safe swimming. The entire cove is romantically lined with *stabilimenti*—elegant bathing lidos where the cabanas are often air-conditioned and the bodies can be Modigliani-sleek. The most famous of these lidos (a fee must be paid if you wish to use their facilities), found closest to I Faraglioni, is La Canzone del Mare, once presided over by the noted British music-hall singer Gracie Fields and for decades favored by the smart set, including Noël Coward and Emilio Pucci (who set up his first boutique here). La Canzone del Mare's seaside restaurant offers a dreamy view of I Faraglioni and a (pricey) luncheon here can be an iconic Capri moment. Jutting out into the bay is the **Scoglio delle Sirene**, or Sirens' Rock—a small natural promontory— which the ancients believed to be the haunt of the Sirens, whose song seduced Odysseus in Homer's *Odyssey.* This rock separates the two small beaches: Pennaulo, to the east, and Marina di Mulo, site of the original Roman harbor, to the west. ⊠ *Via Marina Piccola.*

❹ Museo Caprense Ignazio Cerio. Reopened in spring 2001 after extensive renovations, the museum conserves interesting Pleistocene fossil finds of pygmy elephant, rhino, and hippopotamus (Room 1) which all grazed here 200,000–300,000 years ago when the climate and terrain were very different. Although most of the important archaeological finds—such as the statues found in the Blue Grotto—have been shipped off to Naples, Room 4 displays the leftovers, a fairly scantily labeled collection of vases, mosaics, and stucco work from the Greek and Roman periods. ✉ *Piazzetta Cerio 8a, Capri Town,* ☎ *081/ 8376681,* ℻ *081/8370858.* ⌨ *€2.7, guided tours by appointment €16.* ⊙ *Tues.–Wed. and Fri.–Sat. 10–1, Thurs. 3–7. Closed Sun.–Mon.*

❸ Santo Stefano. Towering over La Piazzetta, with a dome that is more sculpted than constructed and with *cupolettas* that seem molded from frozen zabaglione, Capri's mother church is a prime example of *l'architettura baroccheggiante*—the term historians use to describe Capri's fanciful form of Baroque architecture. Often using vaults and molded buttresses (since there was little wood to support ceilings on such a scrubby island), Capri's architects became sculptors when they adapted Moorish and Grecian styles into their own "homemade" architecture. Sometimes known unglamorously as the ex-cathedral, the church was built in 1685 by Marziale Desiderio of Amalfi on the site of a Benedictine convent (founded in the 6th century), whose sole relic is the clock tower campanile across the Piazzetta. As in so many churches in southern Italy, there has been a good deal of recycling of ancient building materials: the flooring of the high altar was laid with polychrome marble from Villa Jovis, while the marble in the Cappella del Sacramento was removed from the Roman villa of Tragara. Inside the sacristy are exhibited some of the church treasures, including a silver statue of San Costanzo, the patron saint of Capri, whose holy day is celebrated every May 14. Opposite the church on the tiny Piazzetta I. Cerio are the Palazzo Cerio, with its Museo Caprense Ignazio Cerio; the Palazzo Farace, which houses the Biblioteca Caprense I. Cerio (I. Cerio Library); and the Palazzo Vanalesti, the executive offices of the Capri tourist board. Ignazio Cerio's son, Edwin, is the author of many eloquent books about Capri and was also the architect of some of the island's most celebrated early 20th-century villas. ✉ *Piazza Umberto I, Capri Town.*

★ ❺ Villa Jovis. Named in honor of the ancient Roman god Jupiter, or Jove, the villa of the emperor Tiberius is riveted to the towering Rocca di Capri like an eagle's nest overlooking the strait separating Capri from Punta Campanella, the tip of the Sorrentine peninsula. Lying near the easternmost point of the island, the villa is reached by a well-signposted 50-minute walk that climbs gradually from the Piazzetta in Capri Town and offers several opportunities along the way to slake your thirst and draw breath if necessary (if possible, resist temptation until you get to the welcoming Bar Jovis, about five minutes' walk from the site on Via Tiberio). Although criticized by locals for the state of neglect in which it is kept, Villa Jovis is nonetheless a powerful reminder of the importance of the island in Roman times. What makes the site even more compelling are the accounts of the latter years of Tiberius's reign from Capri, between AD 27 and AD 37, written by authors and near-contemporaries Suetonius and Tacitus. They had it that this villa was famous for its sybaritic living, thus sounding a leitmotif that extends down to the luxurious hotels of today.

There are remarkably few discrepancies between the two historiographers. Both point to Tiberius's mounting paranoia in Rome, while Tacitus outlines his reason for choosing Capreae (*Annals,* Book IV). "Presumably what attracted him was the isolation of Capreae. Harborless, it has few roadsteads even for small vessels; sentries can control all landings. In winter the climate is mild, since hills on the mainland keep off gales. In summer the island is delightful, since it faces west and has open sea all round. The bay it overlooks was exceptionally lovely, until Vesuvius's eruption transformed the landscape." Capri in Roman times was the site of 12 spacious villas, but Villa Jovis is both the best preserved and must have been the largest, occupying nearly 23,000 square ft. It was believed by ancient tattletales that Tiberius, fearful of assassination, slept in different villas every night, even putting wax effigies of himself in all of them to confuse evildoers. Although Tacitus spits with characteristic venom in his account, Suetonius leaves little to the imagination: Tiberius's character is systematically vilified and pilloried, while the atrocities committed at Villa Jovis are described in gory detail in *The Twelve Caesars*.

The entrance to the site lies just beyond the *pharos* (lighthouse) built under Tiberius and used until the 17th century to warn ships of the narrows between Capri and the mainland. Pick up a site map at the ticket office, which gives a useful breakdown of the various areas of the villa to be visited. This is also the area with the **Salto di Tiberio** (Tiberius's Leap), the place where ancient gossips believed Tiberius had enemies, discarded lovers, and even unfortunate cooks hurled over the precipice into the sea some 1,000 ft below. After taking stock of this now-harmless viewing platform with the information panels, take the upper path past the baths complex around the palace residential quarters to the heavily restored Chapel of Santa Maria del Soccorso with its large bronze statue of the Madonna. This walk round the perimeter of the site gives an idea of the overall layout of the palatial residence, which in places rose to five stories in height. From here descend some steps and then a ramp to the *ambulatio* (walkway) or belvedere, which offers additional spectacular views and plenty of shade, as well as a *triclinium* (dining room) halfway along. The center of the site is a complex devoted to cisterns. Unlike in Pompeii, there was no aqueduct up here to provide fresh running water, so the cisterns next to the bath complex were of prime importance. ⊠ *Via A. Maiuri,* ☎ *081/8370381.* ☜ *€2.10.* ☉ *Daily 9–1 hr before sunset.*

❽ Villa Malaparte. Nicknamed the *Casa Come Me* (House Like Myself) and perched out on the rocky Punta Massullo, this villa is considered by some historians to be a great monument of 20th-century architecture. Built low to be part of the ageless landscape, the red-hued villa was designed in Rationalist style by the Roman architect Adalberto Libera in the late 1930s for its owner Curzio Malaparte (author of the novel *La Pelle,* which recounts various World War II experiences in Naples). Unfortunately, the aesthetic concerns of this house are inextricably entailed with political ones: Curzio Malaparte was a full-blown Fascist and the only reason why this house was allowed to be built along this otherwise unsullied stretch of coast was by special fiat from none other than Mussolini. Malaparte was unhappy with the design and made a number of alterations during the construction phase, including the famous trapezoidal staircase that seems to grow out of the roof. The villa is private, but if you want to see it up close, it was featured as a suitably striking backdrop for Brigitte Bardot in Jean-Luc Godard's underrated film *Contempt* (1963). ⊠ *Giro dell'Arco Naturale.*

From Anacapri to the Blue Grotto

A tortuous road up from Capri Town (465 ft) leads 3 km (2 mi) up a dramatic escarpment to sky-swimming Anacapri (930 ft), the island's only other town and leading settlement on the island's peaks, poetically referred to as the Monte Sirene (Siren Heights). Crowds are thick-

est around the square that is the starting point of the chairlift to the
top of Monte Solaro and close to Villa San Michele, the main magnet
up here for tour groups. To get here, take the bus from the terminus
in Via Roma (Capri Town) or go directly from the port of Marina Grande
(€1.30). Allow plenty of time for getting back down again, as space
on the local buses can come at a premium. The very athletically in-
clined could try the 900 steps of the Scala Fenizia, or Phoenician Stairway (more likely to have been built by the Greeks than the Phoenicians),
leading all the way down to Marina Grande (about 20 minutes' walk
away; for access to this elusive path, continue walking past Villa San
Michele away from Piazza Vittoria). Long in a state of disrepair, this
ancient pathway has only recently been restored and reopened. As a
fitting finale, take the convenient bus down the hill from Anacapri to
the water's edge and the fabled Blue Grotto.

A Good Walk

From Anacapri's main square of Piazza Vittoria, take Via Capodimonte
to **Villa San Michele** ⑭, about a 10-minute walk on the right, past a
formidable array of garish boutiques, bars, and liqueur factories, all
vying to ensnare unwitting passersby. As with many sites on the island,
it's best to get to the villa shortly after it opens, or in the early evening
when the day-trippers have moved through. After browsing through
its rooms and strolling through the gardens and the eco-museum, retrace your steps to Piazza Vittoria and make for the lower station of
the *Seggiovia* (chairlift) to **Monte Solaro** ⑮. You will soon be whisked
out of town over whitewashed houses and carpets of spring-flowering
broom and rockrose to the viewing platform at the top of Solaro. From
here a path leads northward downhill toward the sublimely picturesque
Church of **Santa Maria a Cetrella** ⑯ through some of the most beautiful wooded countryside on Capri. During both spring and autumn
look out for migrating birds. A splash of yellow combined with an un-
dulating flight could be the golden oriole; the multicolor bee-eater also
migrates via Capri in May and September. On the way back down from
Cetrella follow the signs to Anacapri along Via Monte Solaro (downhill), passing close to the ruins of the **Castello Barbarossa** ⑰ and then
emerging right by Villa San Michele. If you have time and energy left
over, make for Via Orlandi, a useful street for stocking up on provisions. Pass the impressive **Casa Rossa** (Red House) ⑱, on your right,
and then take the next right turn (Via San Nicola) to Piazza San Nicola
and the Church of **San Michele** ⑲. If possible, savor its magnificent majolica tile floor depicting the Garden of Eden from the organ loft, then
head back to the Piazza Vittoria. By mid- to late afternoon, the crowds
will have vanished from the **Grotta Azzurra** ⑳ (Blue Grotto), at the sea
below Anacapri. Catch the convenient bus that links the town with the
grotto and enjoy this fabled sight around 4 PM or 5 PM, when connoisseurs
swear that the light is best. History buffs and vista lovers will want to
top out their day with a trek to the nearby **Villa di Damecuta** ㉑,
thought to have been one of Emperor Tiberius's secret retreats.

TIMING
The walk takes approximately three hours in all, allowing at least one
hour for the visit to Villa San Michele and its gardens, and a further
two hours' leisurely ambling on the round-trip. If armed with a packed
lunch, you're most likely to find a picnic site near Cetrella—in attempts
to discourage low-spending day-trippers from the mainland, consumption of picnics is made fairly difficult on Capri.

Sights to See

⑱ **Casa Rossa** (Red House). Capri is famous for its turn-of-the-20th-
century villas built by artists, millionaires, and poets who became will-

ing prisoners of Capri during the Gilded Age. Elihu Vedder, Charles Coleman, Lord Algernon, and the Misses Wolcott-Perry were some of the people who constructed lavish Aesthetic Movement houses. This particular villa, near the center of Anacapri, was built between 1876 and 1898 with walls hued in distinctive Pompeian red around a 14th-century Aragonese tower by the American colonel J. C. MacKowen from Louisiana. A historian and archaeologist, MacKowen wrote a guide to Capri and brought to light marble fragments and statues inside the Blue Grotto, thus showing its importance as a nymphaeum in Roman times. The house is closed to the public. ⊠ *Via G. Orlandi, Anacapri.*

⑰ Castello Barbarossa. The foundation of this ruined castle, almost cling-ing to the side of the cliff above Villa San Michele, dates to the late 10th century, when Capri was ruled by the ancient maritime republic of Amalfi. Named after the admiral of the Turkish fleet, Khair-Eddin, or Barbarossa (Redbeard), who stormed and took the castle in 1535, much of the original layout was changed over the centuries. The cas-tle is part of the Swedish-run Axel Munthe Foundation, which orga-nizes weekly guided visits on Thursday afternoons from May to October (telephone the Foundation to reserve a place and for precise time of visit) besides carrying out ornithological research in the surrounding area. ⊠ *Axel Munthe Foundation, Anacapri,* ☎ *081/8371401.*

★ ⑳ Grotta Azzurra (Blue Grotto). Only when the spectacular Grotta Az-zurra was "discovered" in 1826 by the Polish poet August Kopisch and his Swiss friend, the artist Ernest Fries, did Capri become a tourist heaven. The watery cave's breathlessly blue beauty quickly became a symbol of the era of Romanticism—a monument in man's return to nature and revolt from Reason. The pair's discovery triggered widespread inter-est and began the flow of Grand Tour visitors to the island. In fact, however, the grotto had been an island landmark since time im-memorial. In the Roman era, as testified by the extensive remains pri-marily below sea level and several large statues, it had been the elegant, mosaic-decorated nymphaeum of the adjoining Roman villa of Gradola. Historians can't quite agree if it was simply a lovely little pavilion where rich patricians would cool themselves for midday picnics or if it was truly a religious site where sacred mysteries were practiced.

The Grotta Azzurra can be reached from Marina Grande or from the small embarkation point below Anacapri on the northwest side of the island, reached by bus from Anacapri. If you're pressed for time, skip this sometimes frustrating and disappointing excursion. You board one boat to get to the grotto, and you have to transfer to another smaller one in order to get inside (the opening is only just over 3 ft high). If there's a backup of boats waiting to get in, you'll be given precious lit-tle time to enjoy the gorgeous color of the water and its silvery reflec-tions. Instead, tour Anacapri first, then head to the Piazza Vittoria for the bus that connects the town with the seaside grotto. Be prepared to dicker with the boatmen at the grotto entrance. Swimmers are "free." Yes, adventuresome types (who know that this type of activity is offi-cially banned here) can enjoy the intoxicating experience of a grotto swim, but only after-hours. Note that the Blue Grotto is just one of Capri's many seaside caves: there is also a Grotta Bianca (White Cave), Grotta Verde (Green Cave), Grotta Rossa (Red Cave), and numerous other caves, many of which can be explored if you hire a boat for a classic *giro*, or tour, of the island. And what about the best time to see the fabled blue color? It's often been quoted that the optimum time is from 10 AM to 1 PM—however, those hours were said to be prime by native Capresi, who, in truth, actually preferred to siesta their early afternoons away. The best time to come—especially as unknowing

MY BLUE HEAVEN: THE LURE OF THE GROTTA AZZURRA

CERTAINLY ONLY A COMPLETELY soulless being could fail in his mind's eye to people Capri with nymphs, dryads, and centaurs, its grottoes and caverns with mermaids and dancing fauns, while in the imagined palatial villas strewn about the island Greeks and Romans mingle with pirates, Saracens, Norman princes, and Renaissance courtiers in a vast and gay time-forgetting revel. But nowhere is Capri's hold on the imagination greater than at its Blue Grotto, or Grotta Azzurra.

Famously, it was once thought to be the haunt of Emperor Tiberius. Legend had it that the old gent stayed incognito at the nearby Villa di Dame Occulte (the modern Capri landmark Damecuta is said to derive from the name) and gained access to the wondrous grotto by a secret passage, which many thought to be the *cloaca maxima* (sewer) of Anacapri. After the mists of legend swept in, the Grotta Azzurra was only "rediscovered" on August 18, 1826 by the two painters August Kopisch and Ernst Fries, with their Capri host Don Giuseppe Pagano. Then, believe it or not, it was forgotten again. Only when, two years later, the young German poet Wilhelm Waiblinger came to Capri and wrote an ode about the blue cave, which became an overnight sensation back in Germany and which inspired Hans Christian Andersen to use the Grotta Azzurra as a setting in his 1835 novel, *The Improvisor*, was the Blue Grotto's modern fame assured.

As one of the most famous tourist attractions in the world, it can be overrun with tour boats during peak midday hours. Perhaps this is why, after hours, Capri's prowling young and daring often steal into the watery cavern, its midnight-blue waters and opaline walls—once so dear to Emperor Tiberius's heart—the irresistible lure. Legend claims a ship with a cargo of Tyrian purple dye (a color the exclusive province of Roman emperors) sank below the grotto and has forever colored its waters a wine-dark blue. Of course, making Emperor Tiberius's reputed retreat your own is frowned upon and officially banned by the authorities. Since local convention (and Fodor's) never considers such unofficial dunking, hail instead a magic carpet over to your hotel pool to indulge your own craving for lavish soaking.

If thrill-seekers cannot avoid the grotto's lure, they attempt to swim into the cave early in the morning or after 5:30 in the evening when the boats have left. Needless to say, they do this only if the sea is perfectly calm—fatalities have occurred in rougher weather—and always with companions at hand. Swimming in the Blue Grotto can be an ethereal experience, and is now enjoyed by many who arrive and leave their clothes at the bar just above the entrance (no doubt it would be politic to have an *aperitivo* there after the swim).

Swimmers enter the cave by holding onto the chain that threads the entrance—but all swimmers attempting entry should keep in mind that the only resting place inside is on a ledge on the back wall and the distance to it a good 100 ft. This area was once the site of an ancient Roman nymphaeum, and marble statues that were found here are now on view at Capri's Certosa di San Giacomo museum. With a face mask, snorkel, and flippers, experienced snorkelers like to swim into the cave in the usual way, then about-face and dive under for 10 or so ft, then swimming toward and under the huge undersea arch to finally pop up in the sea outside. The distance is about 65 ft, so this should only be attempted by professional snorkelers with companions. Old-timers tell you to watch out for the small purple jellyfish that deliver a rather annoying sting. If you decide to be venturesome here, always take extra precautions and be ever alert for your own safety.

crowds have long since departed—is around 4 PM or 5 PM. ⊠ *Grotta Azzurra.* 🖃 *€13 or €11 (depending on boat company) from Marina Grande, €9 by rowboat from Grotta Azzurra near Anacapri.* ⊙ *9–1 hr before sunset, closed if sea is even minimally rough.*

⑮ Monte Solaro. An impressive limestone formation and the highest point on Capri (1,932 ft), Monte Solaro affords gasp-inducing views toward both bays of Naples and Salerno. A 12-minute chairlift ride will take you right to the top (refreshments available at bar), which is a starting point for a number of scenic trails on the western side of the island. Picnickers should note that even in the summer it can get windy at this height, and there are few trees to provide shade or refuge. ⊠ *Piazza Vittoria, Anacapri,* ☎ *081/8371428.* 🖃 *€3.7 one-way, €4.8 round-trip.* ⊙ *Daily Mar.–Oct. 9:30–sunset, Nov.–Feb. 10:30–3.*

⑲ San Michele. The octagonal Baroque church of San Michele on Piazza San Nicola, finished in 1719, is best known for its exquisite majolica pavement (1761), designed by Solimena and executed by the Abruzzese *mastro-riggiolaro* (master tiler) Leonardo Chiaiese. A walkway skirts the rich ceramic carpet depicting Adam and a duly contrite Eve being expelled from the Garden of Eden, but you can get a breathtaking overview from the organ loft, reached by a winding staircase near the ticket booth (a privileged perch you have to pay for if access is allowed— the loft was closed for restoration at press time (summer 2001). Outside the church is the Via Finestrale, which leads to Anacapri's noted **Le Boffe quarter.** This section of town, slightly lower on the hillside, is centered around the Piazza Ficacciate and the Church of Santa Sofia and owes its name to the distinctive domestic architecture prevalent here, which uses vaults and sculpted groins instead of cross beams. The word *boffe,* as it turns out, comes from the Neapolitan dialect for "swollen." ⊠ *Piazza Nicola, Anacapri,* ☎ *081/8372396.* 🖃 *€1.1.* ⊙ *Nov.–Mar., daily 9:30–4; Apr.–June, daily 9:30–5; July–Oct. daily 9:30–7.*

⑯ Santa Maria a Cetrella. Scenically perched on the slopes of Monte Solaro, this small sanctuary in late-Gothic style—with its older parts dating to the late 14th century—offers a truly picturesque frame for a panorama that takes in much of the island. It also marks the top of the second access route (Il Passetiello) used in ancient times, which linked Capri Town with Anacapri. This is the pathway that the Carthusian monks of San Giacomo would have used to reach their properties in the upper part of the island. The church was substantially rebuilt by Franciscan monks in the early 17th century, when a sacristy was added. To reach Santa Maria, you can climb a path leading off Viale Axel Munthe (an hour-long walk); an alternative is to descend a path leading from the Monte Solaro chairlift. ⊠ *Monte Solaro.*

㉑ Villa di Damecuta. Sited strategically on a ridge with views sweeping across the Bay of Naples toward Procida and Ischia, the main access to this Roman villa would have been from the landing stage right by the Blue Grotto at Gradola. This was probably one of the villas mentioned by Tacitus in his *Annals* as having been built by Tiberius: "Here on Capreae, in twelve spacious, separately named villas, Tiberius settled." Like Villa Jovis to the east, Villa di Damecuta was extensively plundered over the centuries prior to its proper excavation in 1937. Below the medieval tower (Torre Damecuta) there are two rooms (*domus* and *cubiculum*) that are thought to have been Tiberius's secret summer refuge. Affinities with Villa Jovis may be seen in the *ambulatio* (walkway), complete with seats and stunning backdrop. To reach Villa Damecuta, get the bus from Anacapri to Grotto Azzurra and ask the driver to let you off at the right stop. Alternatively, you can walk from the center of Anacapri down the bus route (about 30 minutes, but no sidewalks) or try your luck in the network of virtually traffic-free little alleyways running parallel to the main road. ⊠ *Via A. Maiuri.* ⬚ *Free.* ⊙ *Daily 9–1 hr before sunset.*

★ ⑭ **Villa San Michele.** Henry James called this villa and garden "the most fantastic beauty, poetry, and inutility that one had ever seen clustered together," and this encomium can't be topped. At the ancient entrance-way to Anacapri just at the top of the Scala Fenicia and occupying the site of an ancient Roman villa, Villa San Michele was built (beginning in 1896) in accordance with its owner's instructions, Axel Munthe (1857–1949). Physician to the Swedish royal family, Munthe practiced both in Paris and in Rome, thereby building up a substantial fortune, much of which he plowed into real estate in Anacapri. He was also known as a philanthropist because of his lifelong dedication to the sick and destitute. Munthe's *The Story of San Michele* is an evocative—if not entirely reliable—autobiography.

Those 19th-century artists Alma-Tadema and Lord Leighton—specialists in painting scenes *all'antica*—would have set up their easels in a minute at the villa, since it is set around Roman-style courtyards, marble walkways, and atriums. Rooms display the doctor's varied collections, which range from bric-a-brac to classical antiquities (once thought so important J. Pierpont Morgan arrived to spend millions on them, but the good doctor knew that most were fakes so refused all offers). Medieval choir stalls, Renaissance lecterns, and gilded statues of saints comprise the esthetic setting, with some rooms preserving the doctor's personal memorabilia, enabling the visiting public to find out more about this enigmatic patron of the arts and humanist. The villa is connected by a spectacular pergola path overlooking the entire Bay of Naples. This leads to the famous Sphinx Parapet, where an ancient Egyptian sphinx sits and looks out over to Sorrento (you cannot see its face—on purpose). It is said that if you touch the sphinx's hindquarters with your left hand while making a wish, it will come true. The parapet is connected to the little Chapel of San Michele, which once stood on the grounds of one of Tiberius's villas. When Munthe bought the property, its missing bells were said to ring as a sign that Tiberius was seeking forgiveness for having sentenced a certain carpenter from Galilee to death.

Besides hosting summer concerts, the Axel Munthe Foundation has a recently established eco-museum that fittingly reflects Munthe's fondness for animals, where you can learn about various bird species—accompanied by their songs—found on Capri. Not only did Munthe aid people, he bought up the hillside as a sanctuary for birds, which prevented the Caprese from capturing quail by terrible means (lured by songbirds that had been blinded to make them sing better). Today, thanks to the good Dr. Munthe, this little realm is still an Eden. ⊠ *Viale Axel Munthe, Anacapri,* ☎ *081/8371401,* � *www.caprionline.com/axelmunthe.* ⬚ €4.10. ⊙ *Nov.–Feb. daily 10:30–3:30; Mar. daily 9:30–4:30; Apr. daily 9:30–5; May–Sept. daily 9–6; Oct. daily 9:30–5.*

Dining and Lodging

Most restaurants and hotels are either in Capri Town—on the lower haunch of the island—or in Anacapri, atop its dizzying Siren Heights. Each review lists the locale of the restaurant or hotel. As you can imagine, even basic accommodations come at a premium on Capri and all the zeros on the hotel bills are likely to make you feel dizzy. Many hotels charge extra for breakfast, so you might just wish to enjoy a coffee and *cornetto* at a town café, while some add a hefty surcharge for air-conditioning. Note that while many hotels close for the winter months, some of these reopen to celebrate the Christmas and New Year holidays.

Since cars are generally not permitted on Capri, most hotels will arrange porterage from the Marina Grande port if you tell them when you're arriving (on what boat/hydrofoil, etc.). Sometimes this is a complimentary service. **Porterage services** can be obtained for a fee down at the port (☎ 081/8370896).

$$$–$$$$ ✕ **I Faraglioni.** With natural shade provided by a 100-year-old wisteria plant, this is a popular, fairly stylish restaurant which is both centrally located and yet almost immersed in Mediterranean greenery. Meals here usually kick off with *uovo alla Monachina,* an egg-shape dish stuffed with mystery ingredients. For a first course, try the *straccetti con gamberi e pomodorini* (fresh green pasta with shrimps and small tomatoes). ✉ *Via Camerelle 75, Capri Town,* ☎ *081/8370320. Dinner reservations essential. AE, DC, MC, V. Closed Nov.–Mar.*

$$$–$$$$ ✕ **La Canzone del Mare.** This is the legendary bathing lido of the Marina Piccola, erstwhile haunt of Gracie Fields, Emilio Pucci, Noël Coward, and any number of 1950s and '60s glitterati. The VIPs may have departed for the Bagni di Tiberio beach but the setting is as magical as ever: Enjoy luncheon (no dinner served) in the thatched-roof pavilion looking out over the sea and I Faraglioni in the distance—this is Capri as picture-perfect as it comes. You need to pay a fee to actually use this bathing *stabilimenti,* but why not make a day of it—after all, the menu comes with a beach mattress. ✉ *Via Marina Piccola 93, Capri Town,* ☎ *081/8370104,* WEB *www.emmeti.it. AE, DC, MC, V. Closed Nov.–Mar. No dinner.*

$$$–$$$$ ✕ **La Capannina.** Isn't that Whitney Houston at the table by the door?
★ Known as one of Capri's most celebrity-haunted restaurants, La Capannina is only a few steps from the busy social hub of the Piazzetta. It has a discreet covered veranda—opened up in the summer—for dining by candlelight in a garden setting, with most of the regulars avoiding the stuffy indoor rooms. The specialties, aside from an authentic Capri wine with the house label, are homemade *ravioli capresi* and *linguine con lo scorfano* (flat spaghetti with scorpion fish). ✉ *Via Le Botteghe 14, Capri Town,* ☎ *081/8370732. Reservations essential evenings. AE, DC, MC, V. Closed mid-Jan.–mid-Mar. and Wed. in Mar. and Nov.*

$$$–$$$$ ✕ **La Fontelina.** Lying just below Punta Tragara at the base of Capri's
★ impressive offshore rocks known as the Faraglioni, this is the place to enjoy a delightfully comatose day on the island. Given its position right on the water's edge, seafood is almost de rigueur. For a slightly different starter, try the *polpette di melanzane* (egg-plant fritters), and then dip into the vegetable buffet. Highly recommendable is the house sangria, a blissful mix of white wine and fresh fruit. If overwhelmed by large-size portions of pasta, order half portions (and pay half). This also functions as a lido, with steps and ladders affording access into fathoms-deep blue water. Access by boat from Marina Piccola or on foot from Punta Tragara (10 minutes). Only lunch is served. Just across the way is its archrival lido-restaurant, Da Luigi, with a more evocative setting but now a bit too famous for its own good. ✉ *I Faraglioni, at end of Via Tragara, Capri Town,* ☎ *081/8370845. AE. Closed mid-Oct.–Easter and for dinner.*

$$$ ✕ **Il Cucciolo.** Nestling in thick maquis high above the Blue Grotto and a five-minute walk from the Roman site of Villa Damecuta, this must be one of the most romantic locations in the Mediterranean. The cucina is refreshingly inventive: ask for their specialty *fagottini all'ortica,* pasta stuffed with cheese and stinging-nettles. There is evening chauffeur service to and from Anacapri. ✉ *Via La Fabbrica 52, Anacapri,* ☎ *081/8371917. Reservations essential eves. AE, DC, MC, V. Closed Nov.–mid-Mar. No lunch mid-June–mid-Sept.*

$$-$$$ ✕ **Al Grottino.** This small and friendly family-run restaurant, which is handy to the Piazzetta, has arched ceilings and lots of atmosphere; autographed photos of celebrity customers cover the walls. House specialties are gnocchi with tomato sauce and mozzarella and linguine *ai gamberetti* (with shrimp and tomato sauce). ⊠ *Via Longano 27, Capri Town,* ☎ *081/ 8370584. Reservations essential. AE, MC, V. Closed Nov. 3–Mar. 20.*

$$-$$$ ✕ **Da Tonino.** It is well worth making the short detour off the beaten track to the Arco Naturale to be pampered by creative chef Tonino. With the emphasis more on land-based dishes, try the *terrina di coniglio* (rabbit terrine) or ask for the pigeon dish with pesto, rosemary, and pine nuts, accompanied by wine from an unbelievably well-stocked cellar. ⊠ *Via Dentecala 12–14, Capri Town,* ☎ *081/8376718. AE, DC, MC, V. Closed Jan. 10–Mar. 15.*

$$-$$$ ✕ **La Rondinella.** This is an airy ristorante-pizzeria looking onto the main pedestrianized street of Anacapri. In summer, make sure you reserve a table out on the popular terrace. If you have difficulty choosing from the extensive menu, ask for advice or opt for one of their favorite pasta dishes, *linguine macchiavelle,* with capers, olives, and cherry tomatoes. ⊠ *Via Orlandi 295, Anacapri,* ☎ *081/8371223. AE, DC, MC, V. Closed Jan. 10–Feb. and Thurs. Oct.–May.*

$$-$$$ ✕ **Le Grottelle.** Enjoying one of Capri's most unique settings, this ex-
★ tremely informal trattoria is built up against the limestone rocks not far from the Arco Naturale—a cave at the back doubles up as the kitchen and wine cellar. Whether you stumble over this place, or make it your pointed destination after a island hike, Le Grottelle will prove memorable, thanks to that ambience and seaview. The food? Oh, that . . . the menu is chiefly seafood, with *linguine con gamberetti e rucola* (pasta with shrimp and arugula) one of the more highly prized specialties. ⊠ *Via Arco Naturale 13,* ☎ *081/8375719. Reservations essential eves. AE. Closed mid-Nov.–Mar.*

$$-$$$ ✕ **Ristorante Pizzeria Aurora.** Though often frequented by celebri-
★ ties—photographs of famous guests adorn the walls inside—this restaurant offers courtesy and *simpatia* irrespective of your persona. If you want to eat out and be seen, reserve one of the tables outside on one of Capri's most chic thoroughfares; otherwise go for extra privacy and ambience within. The cognoscenti start off by sharing a Pizza all'Acqua, a thin pizza with mozzarella and a sprinkling of *peperoncino* (chili). If tiring of pasta, try the *sformatino alla Franco* (a rice pie in a prawn sauce) but hold something back for the homemade sweets at the end. ⊠ *Via Fuorlovado 18–20, Capri Town,* ☎ *081/8370181. Reservations essential eves. AE, DC, MC, V. Closed Jan.–Feb.*

$$ ✕ **Da Gelsomina.** Set amidst its own terraced vineyards with inspiring views across to the island of Ischia and beyond, this is much more than just a well-reputed restaurant. It has an immaculately kept swimming pool and is located close to the island's finer walks—an excellent base for a whole day or longer. There is also a five-room pensione, with free transfer service by request from Anacapri center. ⊠ *Via Migliera 72, Anacapri,* ☎ *081/8371499. AE, DC, MC, V. Closed Jan.–mid-Feb. and Tues. in winter.*

$-$$ ✕ **La Giara.** Only about two minutes' walk from the bustling Piazza Vittoria in Anacapri, this pizzeria-ristorante has a wide range of palatable *piatti* served briskly and courteously. For a change from seafood, try their *pennette aum aum,* pasta pleasingly garnished with eggplant, mozzarella, cherry tomatoes, and basil. ⊠ *Via Orlandi 67, Anacapri,* ☎ *081/8373860. AE, DC, MC, V. Closed Dec.–Jan. and Wed.*

$-$$ ✕ **Mamma Giovanna.** This ristorante-pizzeria sits just below Piazza Diaz in the heart of the old town of Anacapri, facing the 16th-century church of Santa Sofia. The no-frills ambience belies the quality of the cucina: besides *pizze* (served midday and evenings), Mamma Giovanna specializes in *primi piatti*, such as *maccheroncelle al cartoccio* (pasta cooked in the oven with seafood). ✉ *Via Boffe 3/5, Anacapri,* ☎ *081/8372057. Reservations essential eves. No credit cards. Closed Jan.–Feb. and Wed. Oct.–Apr.*

$$$$ ⊡ **La Scalinatella.** If you're bronzed and beautiful, or just bronzed, or
★   even just beautiful, this is your kind of hotel. A white Moorish mansion out of the Arabian Nights, it conjures up Capri in finest Hollywood fashion. The name means "little stairway," and that's how this charmingly small hotel is built, on terraces following the slope of the hills, with winding paths and bougainvillea arbors. Inside, the decor is *Architectural Digest*–opulent, with Venetian blackamoor statues, Empire-era consoles, and Valentino fabrics. Guest rooms have overstuffed sofas, bright colors, large terraces, and his-and-her bathrooms (with whirlpool baths). Outside, one of Capri's bluest pools is the fetching setting for delicious luncheons. ✉ *Via Tragara 8, Capri Town 80073,* ☎ *081/8370633,* ℻ *081/8378291. 52 rooms with bath. Restaurant, bar, air-conditioning, pool, tennis court. No credit cards. Closed Nov.–mid-Mar.*

$$$$ ⊡ **Punta Tragara.** Pity the billionaire who thinks his ship has sailed in
★   and has never stayed here. When you factor in everything, this place is easily the finest hotel on Capri. Clinging to the Punta Tragara, it has a hold-your-breath perch directly over the rocks of I Faraglioni. Originally a villa enjoyed by Churchill and Eisenhower, its exterior was renovated by Le Corbusier in traditional Capri style, then opened as a hotel in the 1970s by Countess Manfredi. Baronial fireplaces, gilded antiques, and travertine marble set the style in the main salons, while guest rooms— no two are alike—are sumptuously cozy-casual. The garden area is out of a dream, with two drop-dead beautiful saltwater pools. One is adorned with exotic trees and cacti, bordered with flagpoles flying yachting colors. The other is a jet-powered, aquamarine jewel set a Versace pareu away from the idyllic, arbor-covered restaurant, La Bussola—all in all, one of the most Edenic corners in all Italy. To top it off, the entire staff seems to have been sent to the finest finishing schools. If you really want to taste the good life, stay here. ✉ *Via Tragara 57, Capri Town 80073,* ☎ *081/8370844,* ℻ *081/8377790,* ⊞ *www.hoteltragara.com. 48 rooms with bath. Restaurant, bar, air-conditioning, 2 pools. AE, DC, MC, V.*

$$$$ ⊡ **Quisisana.** This was one of Capri's first and most celebrated hotels and, today, still packs them in. This seems to be the operative phrase, for this place seems nearly as elephantine as a Las Vegas hotel (rather a sacrilege on tiny Capri, don't you think?). The mile-long lobby leads to the pool area—gorgeous, yes, but the size of a set for an Esther Williams MGM movie. The Quisisana remains a favorite with some because of its shiny and luxe restaurants, see-and-be-seen bars, professional service, array of facilities, and location (just down the street from the crowded Piazzetta, this is *too* convenient). Spacious guest rooms have arcaded balconies—the only problem is that there are floors and floors of them. Still, the Quisisana still draws them in: the hotel's new Krug Bar is Capri's latest hangout for the rich and famous. ✉ *Via Camerelle 2, Capri Town 80073,* ☎ *081/8370788,* ℻ *081/8376080,* ⊞ *www.quisi.com. 150 rooms with bath. Restaurant, bar, air-conditioning, pool, sauna, tennis court. AE, DC, MC, V. Closed Nov.–mid-Mar.*

$$$$ ⊡ **Villa Brunella.** This quiet family-run gem nestles in a garden setting just below the lane leading to the Faraglioni. Comfortable and tastefully furnished, the hotel also has spectacular views, a swimming pool, and a terrace restaurant known for good food. ✉ *Via Tragara 24, Capri Town 80073,* ☎ *081/8370122,* ℻ *081/8370430. 18 rooms with bath. Restaurant, bar, air-conditioning, pool. AE, DC, MC, V. Closed Nov.–Mar.*

$$$–$$$$ ⊡ **Caesar Augustus.** In 2001, this landmark hotel was splashed across
★   the pages of *Vanity Fair* as a new glitterati mecca. In fact, this hotel has long been considered a Caprese paradise thanks to its breathtaking perch

atop an Anacapri cliff and the grandeur of its villa and gardens. As for accommodations, think chic, charming, and casual: the chairs are plump, the beds enormous, the bouquets fragrant. You won't give a second's thought to decor, however, once you catch sight of the fabled stone terrace and its Cinerama view of the Bay of Naples or the new pool—a jaw-dropping extravaganza nearly levitating 1,000 feet over the sea and now easily one of the most glamorous spots on earth. Blissfully distant from Capri Town's crowds, the hotel has a private van to shuttle pampered guests back and forth, but chances are they'll rarely want to leave this dreamy domain. ⊠ *Via G. Orlandi 4, Anacapri 80071,* ☎ *081/8373395; reservations 081/8371421,* FAX *081/8371444,* WEB *www. caesar-augustus.com. 56 rooms with bath. Bar, coffee shop, lounge, air-conditioning, pool. AE, DC, MC, V. Closed Nov.–mid-Apr.*

$$$–$$$$ 🏨 **La Palma.** Though the oldest on Capri (1822), this attentively run hotel has certainly not rested on its laurels. When you arrive at its front door you're immediately given a blast of island glamour, with gleaming lobby, palm trees, and majolica-tiled rooms providing a delightful contrast to the hustle at street level outside (this is just down the street from La Piazzetta). Room prices dip substantially outside peak season, making it more affordable to enjoy enjoy this aura of style and tranquility in the town center. ⊠ *Via V. Emanuele 39, Capri Town 80073,* ☎ *081/8370133,* FAX *081/8376966. 72 rooms with bath. Restaurant, bar, air-conditioning, meeting room. AE, DC, MC, V. Closed Jan.–Easter.*

$$$ 🏨 **Biancamaria.** This tastefully refurbished hotel with its pleasing facade and whitewashed spreading arches lies in a traffic-free zone close to the heart of Anacapri. The front rooms have large terraces looking toward Monte Solaro, while those at the back are quieter and more private. ⊠ *Via G. Orlandi 54, Anacapri 80073,* ☎ *081/8371000,* FAX *081/ 8372060,* WEB *www.villasarah.it. 25 rooms with bath. Air-conditioning. AE, MC, V. Closed Nov.–Mar.*

$$$ 🏨 **Villa Sarah.** This whitewashed Mediterranean building has a homey look and bright, simply furnished rooms. It's close enough to the Piazzetta (a 10-minute walk) to give easy access to the goings-on there, yet far enough away to ensure restful nights. There are a garden and a small bar. ⊠ *Via Tiberio 3/a, Capri Town 80073,* ☎ *081/8377817,* FAX *081/8377215. 20 rooms with bath. Bar, air-conditioning in some rooms. AE, DC, MC, V. Closed Nov.–Mar.*

$$–$$$ 🏨 **Aida.** A 10-minute walk from the town center in a tiny lane that borders the Gardens of Augustus, the Aida offers a tranquil haven from Capri's bustle and hard sell. The staff is sociable, and the rooms, which look onto a small garden, are spacious, comfortably furnished, and immaculately clean. ⊠ *Via Birago 18, Capri Town 80073,* ☎ *081/ 8370366. 7 rooms with bath. MC, V. Closed Nov.–Mar.*

$$–$$$ 🏨 **Gatto Bianco.** A literary atmosphere pervades this spacious but discreet hotel located only two minutes' walk from the Piazzetta. This was where Jacqueline Kennedy sought refuge when hounded by paparazzi. It now provides old-world charm and character with a distinct local flavor. ⊠ *Via Vittorio Emanuele 32, Capri Town 80073,* ☎ *081/ 8370203,* FAX *081/8378060. 44 rooms with bath. Air-conditioning. AE, DC, MC, V. Closed Nov.–mid-Mar.*

$$–$$$ 🏨 **San Michele.** You'll find this large white villa-hotel next to Axel Munthe's home. Surrounded by luxuriant gardens, the San Michele offers solid comfort and good value, along with spectacular views. It's modern, with some Neapolitan period pieces adding atmosphere. Most rooms have a terrace or balcony overlooking either the sea or island landscapes. ⊠ *Via G. Orlandi 5, Anacapri 80071,* ☎ *081/8371427,* FAX *081/8371420,* WEB *www.sanmichele-capri.com. 59 rooms with bath. Restaurant, pool. AE, DC, MC, V. Closed Nov.–Mar.*

$$-$$$ 🔟 **Villa Krupp.** Occupying a beautiful house overlooking the idyllic Gardens of Augustus, this historic hostelry was built by the tortured German munitions millionaire and was once the home of Maxim Gorky, whose guests included Lenin. Rooms are plain but spacious, and some have south-facing terraces with awesome views—the Punta Cantone viewpoint, Certosa di San Giacomo, and I Faraglioni are all just a few minutes away. ✉ *Viale Matteotti 12, Capri Town 80073,* ☎ *081/8370362,* 𝔽𝔸𝕏 *081/8376489. 12 rooms with bath. MC, V. Closed Nov.–Feb.*

$$ 🔟 **Villa Eva.** Named after its dynamic owner-manageress, this is a popular international stopover for young *Wandervögel* (travelers) who have a more laid-back approach to traveling. Accommodation is in small, low-impact villas set in luxuriant gardens. When not tending the grounds, Vincenzo, Eva's husband, will take you down to the nearby Blue Grotto for a late-afternoon swimming expedition. ✉ *Via La Fabbrica 8, Anacapri 80073,* ☎ *081/8371549,* 𝔽𝔸𝕏 *081/8372040,* 𝕎𝔼𝔹 *www. caprionline.com/villaeva. 24 rooms with bath. AE, DC, MC, V. Closed mid-Nov.–mid-Feb.*

$$-$$ 🔟 **Villa Helios.** The charming Villa Helios is set in a 19th-century, lilac-hued, Moorish-inspired villa, surrounded by extensive orchards and located on a quiet Capri lane. Don't come here for luxe—floors are linoleum-covered and some rooms share baths. Do come here for peace—a lovely chapel occupies part of the first floor. For a small fee (€2.1) all guests become members of the Centro Italiano Turismo Sociale, a Christian organization operating Italy-wide. Profits from the operation are thoughtfully channeled by the villa's owners (Franciscan nuns) into a local hospice. ✉ *Via Croce 4, Capri Town 80073,* ☎ *081/8370240,* 𝔽𝔸𝕏 *06/2332–01945,* 𝕎𝔼𝔹 *www.villahelios.it. 25 rooms, 20 with bath. MC, V. Closed mid-Oct.–Apr.*

Nightlife and the Arts

As would be expected, Capri offers a fair spread of evening entertainment, especially on weekends and during the busier months of July and August, when many upper-crust Italians from the mainland occupy their holiday homes on the island. For music that is fairly gentle on the ears, try one of the traditional *taverne,* which are peculiar to Capri Town. There are also a number of discos and piano bars from which to choose. Christmas on Capri is a special time, when most of the island visitors are Italians. On New Years' Eve, the Piazzetta is definitely the place to be seen, with dancing and music culminating in a magnificent fireworks display. On New Year's Day there are marching bands, pageants, and all the revelry you would expect on this exuberant island.

Discos

For 360° music almost any night of the year, **Underground** is the clubbing spot for cognoscenti of various ages. Unlike most other discos in Italy, no admission fee is charged, though you are expected to knock back the odd drink (about €7 each). On Tuesdays in July and August, make a point of going down to Antonio Beach near the Faro, where Underground arranges open-air discos by the water's edge (✉ Via Orlandi 259, Anacapri, ☎ 081/8372523) beginning at 10:30 PM.

Taverne

Anema e Core (✉ Via Sella Orta 39/e, Capri Town, ☎ 081/8376461) means "soul and heart" in Caprese dialect. This popular place is tucked down a quiet side street two minutes' walk from the Piazzetta. Admission (€25) includes an eclectic range of lightish live music (after 11 PM) and a drink from the bar. No food is served so come well sated. There's no dancing here officially, though some guests—including celebrities—occasionally take to the tables. The spot is closed Mondays and is usually open 9 PM to 3 AM. Reservations are essential on weekends. Tucked well away from the hub of the Piazzetta is **Guarracino** (✉ Via Castello 7, Capri Town, ☎ 081/8370514).

The Arts

Culturally speaking, Capri has a fairly long hibernation. Recitals and other low-key cultural events are held in winter in the Centro Caprense Ignazio Cerio, though from June through September the island comes alive with various events, including an outdoor concert season. It is a magical experience to see works performed at the Villa San Michele or in the Certosa di San Giacomo. In general, for information about cultural events and art exhibitions, ask at the local tourist information office or scan the posters in shop windows.

Music and Concerts

Concerts are held regularly at the Certosa di San Giacomo in the attractive Chiostro Piccolo from June through September (usually Wednesday and weekends), while the Axel Munthe Foundation lays on co-sponsored free concerts on the grounds of Villa San Michele on weekends. This means that if you're interested, you'll also have to arrange an overnight stay on the island.

Outdoor Activities and Sports

Although there are several tennis courts on the island, most are restricted access, so the vast majority of people looking to burn up excess energy do so at sea level or below. For naturalists, bird-watching is particularly good in spring and autumn as Capri lies on a migration pathway, while botany lovers will be thrilled by the various walks, especially from April to June.

Scuba Diving

For those who want something more adventurous than a little snorkeling off Marina Piccola, scuba diving can be arranged from Marina Grande, and you can hire your own Zodiac (no license required) to take you round the coast to one of the many lesser-known grottoes on the island. As a general rule, avoid weekends, as island sea traffic makes navigation trying. When scuba diving, always use safety buoys to signal your presence underwater. The main outfitter is **Whales** (✉ Via Colombo 17, Marina Grande, Capri, ☎ 081/8375833), which charges about €35 per hour to hire a six-seat *gommone* (Zodiac). For the inexperienced, **Sercomar** (✉ Via C. Colombo 64, Marina Grande, ☎ 081/8378781, 🖥 www.caprisub.com) organizes diving courses mainly around the Marina Piccola area, leading to certification.

Swimming

Capri is not noted for its fine beaches. The habitués cram onto **Marina Piccola,** generally considered to have the best beach on the island. It's certainly the most historic: Homer believed this to be the legendary spot where the Sirens nearly snared Odysseus. Social go-getters seem to prefer the less picturesque Bagni di Tiberio beach near Marina Grande. At Marina Piccola, expect to pay about €12 per person for the use of showers, lockers, and a sun chair/sun bed. It is definitely worth investing in snorkeling gear, as the sea is rich in marine life, and visibility is often excellent.

Tennis

Almost right in the town center but pleasingly secluded are three clay courts at **Tennis Capri** (✉ Via Camerelle 41, Capri Town, ☎ 081/8370261, 🖥 € 17 per hour per court, € 28 per lesson, racquets for hire). Access is off Via Sella Orta.

Shopping

Although Capri is hardly likely to be a bargain hunter's paradise, shopping here is almost an experience in its own right. In the main town near the Piazzetta, the shop windows are usually immaculately dressed, while the shops themselves are generally designed to be low impact and pleasing on the eye. Large neon signs are definitely out. Frustratingly though, goods are often displayed without price tags, which means you have to shop Italian-style: Decide whether you like an article first and then inquire as to its price, rather than vice versa.

Bookstores

An antiquarian's delight and one of the most elegant bookstores in Italy, **La Conchiglia** not only offers the largest selection of books on Capri and the Bay of Naples islands but publishes many sumptuous tomes through their own imprint. In addition to books, an attractive array of prints, gouaches, and old editions of English books on Capri and the south of Italy is offered at their art gallery–cum–store (⊠ Via Camerelle 18, Capri Town, ☎ 081/8378199, WEB www.laconchigliacapri.com), although a greater variety of titles is offered at their other location (⊠ Via Le Botteghe 12, Capri Town, ☎ 081/8376577). There is also a branch in Anacapri (⊠ Via Orlandi 205, Anacapri, ☎ 081/8372646).

Jewelry

The extra security of being on a virtually crime-free island means that you can actually wear the expensive items you might want to buy. Some tax-free "bargains" might be possible from **Cartier** (⊠ Via Vittorio Emanuele 47, Capri Town, ☎ 081/8370618), though their range of goods is unlikely to vary worldwide. Alternatively, try **Alberto and Lina** (⊠ Via Vittorio Emanuele 18, Capri Town, ☎ 081/8370643, WEB www.capridream.com/linacapri) for perhaps a distinctive locally crafted brooch or some cuff links displaying ancient Roman coins.

Perfume

If you're looking for something that is easily portable to take back from Capri, then eau de toilette, some potpourri, or perfumed soap might be just the thing. **Carthusia** has been making perfumes since 1948, but—as they will proudly tell you—the tradition of perfumery on the island stretches back hundreds of years to the days of Queen Giovanna of Anjou. The factory close to the Certosa di San Giacomo is open for visits and a limited range of purchases, although there are no official guided tours of the premises. *Factory:* ⊠ *Via Matteotti, Capri Town,* ☎ *081/8370368; showrooms:* ⊠ *Via Camerelle 10, Capri Town,* ☎ *081/8370529;* ⊠ *Via Capodimonte 26, Anacapri,* ☎ *081/8373668,* WEB *www.carthusia.com.*

Resortwear

Capri's main shopping streets—the Via Vittorio Emanuele and Via Camerelle—are crammed with world-famous names (Fendi, Gucci, Benetton, Ferragamo, Hermès). But if you are overwhelmed by the choice and are looking for something stylish but Capri-distinctive—in an astonishing range of colors—then try the resortwear sold at one of the many stores run by Roberto Russo. His larger boutiques are: **Capri Uomo** (⊠ Piazzetta Quisisana, Capri Town, ☎ 081/8388200, WEB www.russocapri.com) and **Capri Donna** (⊠ Via Vittorio Emanuele 5, Capri Town, ☎ 081/8388200). Browse round **Rubinacci** (⊠ Via Camerelle 9, Capri Town, ☎ 081/8377295) for something smart yet casual in cotton, linen, or cashmere. Sandals are a Capri speciality. With a family business stretching back 82 years, **Giuseppe Faiella** (⊠ Via Vittorio Emanuele 49, Capri Town) is justifiably proud of his made-to-measure footwear. Expect to pay €35–€50 for a carefully handcrafted pair.

ISCHIA: THE SEASIDE CURE

Although Capri leaves you breathless with its charm and beauty, Ischia takes its time to cast its spell. In fact, an overnight stay is definitely not long enough for the island to get into your blood. Here you have to look harder for the signs of antiquity, the traffic is reminiscent of Naples—albeit on a good day—and the island displays all the hallmarks of rapid, uncontrolled urbanization. Ischia does have its jewels, though. There are the wine-growing villages beneath the lush volcanic slopes of Monte Epomeo, and unlike Capri, it enjoys a life of its own that survives when the tourists head home. Ischia has some lovely hotel-resorts high in the mountains, offering therapeutic programs and rooms with dramatic views. Should you want to plunk down in the sun for a few days and tune out the world, then go down to sea level: against the towering backdrop of Monte Epomeo and with one of island's inviting beaches—or natural hot baths—close at hand, you might wonder what Emperor Augustus could have been thinking when he surrendered Ischia to the Neapolitans in return for Capri. Still, many find Ischia's physical charms pale in comparison to Capri's splendor.

Unlike Capri, Ischia is volcanic in origin. From its hidden reservoir of seething molten matter come the thermal springs said to cure whatever ails you. Today the island's main industry, tourism, revolves around the 100 or so thermal baths, some of which are attached to hotels while others just operate as day centers. In the height of summer, the island's population of 60,000 swells more than sixfold, with considerable strain placed on local water resources and public transport facilities and with decibel counts rising notably. However, most of the *confusione* is concentrated within the island's six towns and along its main roads, and it is relatively easy to find quiet spots even close to the beaten path.

Ischia Ponte to Lacco Ameno

With easy access to the coastline, the area from Ischia Ponte to Lacco Ameno is almost a continuum of *stabilimenti balneari* (private bathing establishments) during the summer months, set against the scenic backdrop of Monte Epomeo and its verdant slopes. Most port traffic to the island—mainly ferries and hydrofoils from the mainland—is channeled into Ischia Porto and Casamicciola, both towns also being burgeoning resorts and busy spa centers. The Castello Aragonese in Ischia Ponte, which is in fact a vast medieval complex rather than just a castle, is probably the island's main historic sight, while Lacco Ameno with its immense archaeological heritage and more upmarket ambience is a good base for exploring the north of the island. Buses between the main towns are both frequent and cheap, though somewhat overcrowded.

Ischia Ponte

㉒ *2 km (1 mi) southeast of Ischia Porto.*

★ Marked by the spectacular **Castello Aragonese,** the harbor at Ischia Ponte is Ischia's main gateway. From afar you can make out the brooding, towering castle, which sits atop an islet just off the main shore at Ischia Ponte (or Ischia Bridge), so-called because of the causeway built in the mid-15th century to connect it with the rest of Ischia. The little island was settled as early as the 5th century BC, when the tyrant Hiero of Syracuse came to the aid of Cumae in its power struggle against the Etruscans. This was his reward: an almost unassailable natural offshore island more than 300 ft high, on which he erected high watchtowers to monitor movements across the Bay of Naples. The island changed

Ischia

P. Cornacchia
Bay of San Montano
Montevergine
(25) Lacco Ameno
Casamicciola (24)
Observatory
Ischia Porto (23)
Ischia
Ischia Ponte (22)
Forio (26)
Monterone
Gurgitello
Castello Aragonese
M. Epomeo
Cuotto
Fontana
Sant' Antuono
Ciglio
Piedimonte
Molara
Buonopane
M. di Vezzi
P. dell 'Imperatore
Panza
(29) Barano D'Ischia
(27) Serrara Fontana
Testaccio
P. S. Pancrazio
(28) Sant' Angelo
P. S. Angelo
0 — 2 miles
0 — 3 km

hands in the succession of centuries, with Greeks from Neapolis, Romans, Visigoths, Vandals, Ostrogoths, Saracens, Normans, Swabians, and Angevins, all staking successful claims to the island and modifying the fortifications and settlements. This was where the population of Ischia sought refuge in 1301, when Epomeo's last eruption buried the town of Geronda on the other side of the causeway. The new influx of inhabitants led to a flurry of building activity, most notably the construction of the **Cattedrale dell'Assunta,** built above a preexisting chapel that then became its crypt. In the following century the Angevin castle was rebuilt by Alfonso of Aragon (1438), who gave it much of its present form. However, its turbulent history continued well into the 19th century, when it was seriously damaged by the English in their attempts to dislodge the French during the Napoleonic Wars (1809). Parts of the citadel were then used to house political (anti-Bourbon) prisoners until the Risorgimento and Italy's unification in 1861.

Two hours should be enough to give you a feel of the citadel, stroll along its ramparts, and visit its key religious sites. Don't miss the frescoed 14th-century crypt beneath the cathedral (Giotto school), while the ruined cathedral itself, with its noticeable 18th-century additions—such as the Baroque stucco work—is quite atmospheric. Access to the citadel is via an elevator from the base, and the various walks at the top are clearly signposted. While taking in the whole site, enjoy the stunning views from the various vantage points. ⊠ *Castello Aragonese, Ischia Ponte,* ☎ *081/992834.* ☎ *€7.7.* ☉ *Summer, daily 9–7; spring and autumn, daily 9–5. Closed mid-Nov.–Dec. 26 and Jan. 7–Mar. 1.*

Dining and Lodging

With signs like BIER VOM FASS and SPAGHETTI-EIS HIER, you could be forgiven if you thought you were actually in northern Europe rather than on the Mediterranean. Fortunately, the Germans who flock to Ischia tend to be fairly discerning customers when it comes to dining and lodging, and standards in both departments tend to be high when measured against respective prices. In general, when choosing a hotel on Ischia, make sure it does not look onto the busy Strada Nazionale, the main road linking the six towns on the island. When choosing wines, the draught house wines—especially whites—are usually quite palatable and significantly cheaper than the bottled variety. Note that restaurant and hotel reviews for Ischia are listed under each town.

$$–$$$ ✕ **Ristorante Cocò Gelo.** This inviting restaurant sits on the causeway linking the Aragonese castle to the rest of Ischia and is renowned for its fresh fish, which is highly prized by the Ischitani. For specialties try the linguine *ai calamaretti* (with squid), while a good starter in winter months is the vegetable-based *zuppa di fagioli e scarola* (bean and escarole soup). ⊠ *Via Aragonese 1,* ☎ *081/981823. AE, DC, MC, V. Closed Jan.–Feb. and Wed. Oct.–Mar.*

$–$$ ⊞ **Pensione Il Monastero.** Uniquely located within the Castello Aragonese ★ at Ischia Ponte and with fairly rustic rooms that peer down into the Mediterranean hundreds of feet below, this is the ultimate in ambience combined with the peace and quiet of a traffic-free area. Half-board is compulsory at all times. This is a highly popular hotel, so book way in advance. ⊠ *Castello Aragonese 3, 80077,* ☎ FAX *081/992435,* WEB *www.castelloaragonese.it. 21 rooms, 20 with bath. MC, V. Closed Oct. 20–end Mar.*

Nightlife and the Arts

There is a rich tradition in Ischian local festivals, with the feast of Sant 'Anna (July 26) holding pride of place with its skillful choreography and floating procession in the marina at Ischia Ponte below the Aragonese Castle. For year-round frolicking, Ischia Ponte has a well-known discotheque, actually within the Aragonese Castle, which in its heyday (1960s and 1970s) used to attract world celebrities (now it's a magnet for the teenage scooter brigade): **Castillo D'Aragona** (⊠ Castello Aragonese 39/e, Ischia Ponte, ☎ 338/1829107).

Ischia Porto

㉓ *4 km (3 mi) east of Casamicciola.*

Ischia Porto is the largest town on the island and the usual point of debarkation. It's no workaday port, however, but a pretty resort with plenty of hotels and low flat-roofed houses on terraced hillsides above the water. Its narrow streets often become flights of steps that scale the hill, and its villas and gardens are framed by umbrella pines. The port area was originally a landlocked volcanic crater through which the Bourbon king Ferdinand II had a channel cut to create an opening seaward and then converted it into a sheltered port (1854). As you walk into the town along the waterfront, note the grandiose facade of the ancient municipal baths, where Ferdinand II used to take the waters, now used for town council offices and occasional art exhibitions. While exploring Ischia Porto, be sure to stop by **Ciccio,** near the ferry piers (⊠ Via Jasolino), for the best gelati on Ischia.

Dining and Lodging

$$–$$$ ✕ **Da Gennaro.** This small family restaurant on the seafront at Ischia Porto serves excellent fish in a convivial atmosphere. Specialties include spaghetti with clams and linguine *all'aragosta* (with lobster). ⊠ *Via Porto 66,* ☎ *081/992917. AE, DC, MC, V. Closed Nov.–mid-Mar.*

$$$ ⊞ **Villa Rosa.** A highlight at this gracious family-run hotel, in a villa with bright and airy rooms, is the thermally heated pool in the garden. In high season half-board is required, and you must reserve well

in advance. Prices fall into the lower end of this category. It's in the heart of Ischia Porto and only a short walk from the beach. ⊠ *Via Giacinto Gigante 3, 80077,* ☎ *081/991316,* FAX *081/992425,* WEB *www. lavillarosa.it. 37 rooms with bath. Restaurant, air-conditioning in some rooms, pool. AE, DC, MC, V. Closed Nov.–Mar.*

$$ ⊡ **Del Postiglione.** This attractive pink Mediterranean-style edifice is smaller than it appears, with only 15 guest rooms. Its aura of understated luxury is created by marble floors, tropical plants adorning the outside, and generous balconies overlooking one of Ischia Porto's quiet back streets, a couple of minutes from the seafront. Half-board only is accepted in August. ⊠ *Via Giacinto Gigante 19, 80077,* ☎ *081/ 991579,* FAX *081/985956,* WEB *www.hotelpostiglione.it. 15 rooms with bath. Restaurant, bar, baby-sitting. V.*

Nightlife and the Arts

In Ischia Porto, nightlife is concentrated around what the locals know as the Rive Droite, the eastern side of the port. In some private gardens, occasional concerts and cultural events are offered during the summer months. On the eastern side of the harbor in Ischia Porto is a cluster of restaurants and *enoteche* (wine bars) sometimes offering evening entertainment along the street known as the Rive Droite. Nightlife on Ischia is geared to start late in the evening, and you should be prepared to stay the course until the early hours. **Valentino Club** (⊠ Corso Vittorio Colonna 97, Ischia Porto, ☎ 081/982569), in the center of Ischia Porto, is the focal point for anyone but the gel-and-scooter set, with clientele in its early twenties and above. Admission varies between €16 and €22, depending on what's on offer.

In season (from April to the end of October) the town hall premises of Ischia Porto (and sometimes also that of Lacco Ameno) may be used to display paintings and sculptures, primarily by local artists. For information on forthcoming cultural events throughout the island, check at the Azienda Autonoma di Cura, Soggiorno e Turismo (information office) in Ischia Porto or inquire at a local *agenzia di viaggi* (travel agency).

Outdoor Activities and Sports

Tennis has the most facilities of any sport on Ischia, with an average of three to four clubs in each town, in addition to those attached to private hotels. Playing at a well-established club with good clay courts is likely to set you back about €12 per hour per court. The **Tennis Club Pineta** (⊠ Corso Vittorio Colonna 84/G, Ischia Porto, ☎ 081/993300) is a centrally located club that welcomes temporary members.

Shopping

For leather goods and clothing boutiques, most islanders head straight for Via Roma in Ischia Porto, just a two-minute walk from the harbor. A number of shops sell competitively priced leather articles such as bags and belts, while there is also a fair array of clothing boutiques. But don't expect any of the big names found on Capri. The best shops in Ischia are to be found along the pedestrianized streets of Ischia Porto and Forio (along with Ischia Ponte and, to a lesser extent, Sant'Angelo)—though the island as a whole is not renowned as a shoppers' paradise.

Casamicciola

㉔ *2 km (1 mi) east of Lacco Ameno.*

Known properly as the spa town of Casamicciola Terme, the town revolves around the busy Piazza Marina with its statue of the Italian king Vittorio Emanuele II and its marble plaque to Henry Ibsen, who was inspired by the beauty of the area to write *Peer Gynt* here. The town has retained some charming examples of 19th-century architecture. About 2 km (1 mi) from the center is a small **geophysical observatory** from the 19th century, set up to monitor the seismic activity on the island. The *osservatorio* has various antique monitoring devices and a cranky seismic tank designed by the scientist Giulio Grablovitz. ✉ *Osservatorio Geofisico, Località Sentinella,* ☎ *081/996163.* ☉ *By appointment only.*

| NEED A BREAK? | While out and about, make for **Gelateria Calise** (✉ Piazza Marina), just opposite the landing stage, for some divine gelati and ices. |

Lacco Ameno

㉕ *6 km (4 mi) west of Ischia Porto; 3 km (2 mi) north of Forio.*

The smallest of the six *comuni* on the island, Lacco Ameno is a mecca for some of Italy's rich and famous. Italian magnate Gianni Agnelli anchors every summer close to the Fungo, a most distinctive mushroom-shape rock in volcanic tufa sculpted by wave action in the small marina, now one of the most notable natural landmarks in the Bay of Naples. Luchino Visconti, the noted realist film director and opera designer, had his Villa La Colombaria nearby in Baia San Montano, now used by the local council to promote the film industry on the island. The Bay of San Montano, a brilliant blue-sapphire buckle along the coast, is now the setting for the Giardini Negombo, the most stylish of the thermal complexes on the island. Lacco Ameno was colonized by the Greeks as early as the 8th century BC, and the landscape here has remained epic: it was used as the backdrop for the barge scene in Elizabeth Taylor's *Cleopatra*. The main road along the seafront (Corso Rizzoli) has thankfully been pedestrianized and is now virtually a large promenade flanked by low-key shops, cafés, and restaurants.

★ Lacco Ameno's archaeological importance—it lies just below the very first Greek settlement on the island at Monte Vico (380 ft) to the west—is amply reflected by the finds displayed in the new **Museo Archeologico di Pithecusae** and the ancient site beneath the Church of Santa Restituta. The museum occupies much of the Villa Arbusto, built by Carlo d'Aquaviva in 1785 on top of a Bronze Age settlement, and houses a large range of Greek pottery unearthed at the ancient necropolis site near the Baia di San Montano, much of it dating to the earliest years of the Greek colony (late 8th century BC), including Nestor's Cup, a kotyle vase in geometric style. Villa Arbusto combines musical *serate*, or evening soirées, in summer months with visits to the new antiquities museum. ✉ *Villa Arbusto, Lacco Ameno,* ☎ *081/900356,* 🌐 *www.pithecusae.it.* 💳 *€5.2.* ☉ *Tues.–Sun. 9:30–1 and 3–7. Closed Mon.*

From the nearby Church of Santa Restituta, almost completely rebuilt following a catastrophic earthquake in 1883, you can gain access to the underground excavations at the **Museo e Scavi Santa Restituta,** which are a memorable lesson in stratigraphy. Discovered in 1950 when the old majolica pavement above was removed, the underground site shows the building activities of several different periods (archaic Greek, Hellenistic, Roman, and early Christian), faithful reconstructions of an ancient loom and a miller's workshop, and the various finds discovered in situ. Although the structures are poorly labeled and it takes an expert eye to discern which buildings belong to which periods, this gives you a good idea of historical continuity on the island. ✉ *Piazza Santa Restituta, Lacco Ameno,* ☎ *081/980538.* 💳 *€2.58.* ☉ *Mar.–May and Sept.–Oct., Mon.–Sat. 9–noon and 3–6, Sun. 9–noon; June–Aug., Mon.–Sat. 9:30–12:30 and 5–7, Sun. 9:30–noon.*

Lodging

$$$$ ⊞ **Grande Albergo Mezzatorre.** Far from the madding, sunburnt
★ crowds that swamp Ischia, this luxurious forgetaway perches in splendid isolation on the extreme promontory of Punta Cornacchia. Standing on the terraces of this renovated castello, set over the blue Bay of
San Montano, with yachts parading below you, it's not hard to understand why film director Luchino Visconti chose to live just up the
hill. This hotel has nearly everything to tempt its privileged guests to
just stay put and *relax*: storybook cove, glamorous pool area, full
health and beauty treatments—although the vast Negombo spa is just
down the road—serious chef, and hundreds of pine trees for true peace
and quiet. The ancient fortress has been sleekly renovated—perhaps
too much so from the look of its umber-red exterior. Inside, all is
white-on-white with antiques and ancestral portraits as accents. The
official address is Forio but this is much closer to Lacco Ameno, where
you should get off if you're using the bus. ⊠ *Via Mezzatorre 13, Lo-
calità San Montano, Forio d'Ischia, 80075,* ☎ *081/986111,* FAX *081/
986015,* WEB *www.mezzatorre.it. 58 rooms with bath. Restaurant, air-
conditioning, pool, hair salon, sauna, spa, tennis court, parking. AE,
DC, V. Closed Nov.–mid-Apr.*

$$$$ ⊞ **Regina Isabella.** Built in the early 1960s (not the most elegant of
eras) and tucked away in an exclusive corner of the beach in Lacco
Ameno, Ischia's largest luxury hotel has full resort facilities and pam-
pers guests with spa treatments as well. The rooms are ample and decorated in warm Mediterranean colors, and most have terraces or
balconies. Don't miss the fun of socializing with chic vacationers in
the elegant bar or restaurant or at poolside. When filming *Cleopatra*
on Ischia, Elizabeth Taylor and Richard Burton camped out here. ⊠
Piazza Santa Restituta, 80076, ☎ *081/994322,* FAX *081/990190,* WEB
*www.reginaisabella.it. 90 rooms with bath, 20 suites. Restaurant, bar,
air-conditioning, 2 pools (1 indoors), spa, tennis court, beach. AE, DC,
MC, V. Closed mid-Oct.–mid-Apr.*

$$–$$$ ⊞ **Hotel Della Baia.** A small tastefully furnished hotel on a pedestri-
anized road, this is near the magical bay of San Montano and just opposite the elegant Negombo Gardens, with their luxuriant thermal pools.
Half-board terms include free entry to Negombo, except in August.
⊠ *Baia di San Montano, 80076,* ☎ *081/995453,* FAX *081/986342. 20
rooms with bath. Bar, air-conditioning. AE, DC, MC, V. Closed mid-
Oct.–mid-Apr.*

Nightlife and the Arts

The main theatrical venue on Ischia is the **Teatro-Arena** in the Giardini Negombo spa complex (⊠ Baia di San Montano, ☎ 081/986152,
WEB www.negombo.it). This outdoor theater has hosted some pretty big
music and rock stars, including Tina Turner and Mireille Mathieu. To
find out the schedule of upcoming summer performances—usually on
tap from June through September—log onto the Web site. For reservations, use phone number above or go to arena box office (tickets not
available elsewhere).

Outdoor Activities and Sports

If you visit one of Ischia's many *terme*, or spa baths, you will not only
be following a well-established tradition stretching back more than
2,000 years but also sampling one of the major contemporary delights
of the island. You should allow at least half a day for this experience, as
it is a pity to rush through. If you do decide to restrict yourself to half
a day, then go in the afternoon, when the hefty entrance fee is lowered.
The larger establishments have a plethora of pools offering natural hydromassage at different temperatures and in different settings, with a complement of bars and restaurants to enable customers to stay on the

premises right through the day. Most terme are equipped with beauty centers, offering an unbelievably broad range of services, from mud-pack treatments and manicures to tattoo removal and bioenergetic massage.

For the ultimate Ischian spa escape, try the tastefully landscaped park of **Giardini Negombo.** Designed around a beach of the finest sand, by the scenic bay of San Montano, it was created decades ago by Duke Luigi Camerini, a passionate botanist (who named his resort in honor of its resemblance to a bay in Sri Lanka). There are 12 saltwater or thermal pools here, plus facilities for hydromassage, a beauty center with sauna and Turkish bath, sports facilities for diving, windsurfing, volleyball, yoga, a bar, restaurant, and, according to the brochure, "a boutique for irresponsible purchases." All this is set in gardens with 500 species of Mediterranean plants and several panoramic views. Everything here—modern stone waterfalls, elegant poolside tables with thatched-leaf umbrellas, sensitive landscaping—is in the finest taste. At night, the outdoor arena hosts big-name concerts. ⊠ *Baia di San Montano, Lacco Ameno,* ☎ *081/986152,* WEB *www.negombo.it.* ☜ *€21 all day, €16 after 12:30 PM, €11.2 after 3:30 PM.* ☉ *Apr.–Oct., daily 8:30–7.*

In terms of water sports, virtually every beach offers windsurfing, waterskiing, and sailing facilities in season. For a rowboat, go to the outfitters along the oceanfront at Lacco Ameno such as **Isolaverde Viaggi** (⊠ Piazzetta Pontile 1/3, Lacco Ameno, ☎ 081/980455). Expect to pay €6–€9 per hour for nonmotorized boat rental.

From Forio to Barano

Although the northern side of the island has the lion's share of history and archaeology, the south and west sides offer the best beaches. Vacationers flock to the water's edge at Citara and Maronti, where you can seek out the underwater geothermal vents and enjoy your own thermal bath free of charge. On the south side is the unspoiled village of Sant'Angelo, a restful antidote to the hectic towns elsewhere on the island. Higher up on the slopes of Epomeo is Serrara Fontana, the starting point for an excursion up to the highest point on Ischia.

Forio

㉖ *9 km (6 mi) west of Ischia Porto.*

Lying close to the main wine-producing area of the island, Forio is a busy seaside resort with beaches barely a minute's walk from its town center. At first glance, it seems to provide sad evidence of suburban sprawl, and its natural setting of flat coastline is not the most alluring. However, the island's most picturesque church is here: the 14th-century whitewashed Church of Santa Maria della Neve, down at the

★ harbor, better known as the **Santuario del Soccorso.** This is a good spot for a sunset evening stroll and for getting a clearer overview of the rest of the town, from the Torrione, one of 12 towers built under Aragonese rule in the 15th century to protect Forio's inhabitants from the ever-present threat of pirate raids.

Two km (1 mi) north of Forio is one of the most stunningly beautiful

★ gardens in Mediterranean Italy, **La Mortella.** The garden was a labor of love designed in 1956 by the famous landscape architect Russell Page for Sir William Walton and his Argentine-born wife, Susana. It was created within a wide, bowl-shape rocky valley, originally not much more than a quarry, overlooking the Bay of San Francesco and with spreading views toward Monte Epomeo and Forio. This is where Lady Walton, now a talented gardener in her own right, first planted the flowering trees of her childhood, such as jacaranda and the rare bromeliad. Native wild plants were encouraged in the upper reaches of the gardens, with dainty vetches and orchids as well as myrtle, from which the garden got its name, La Mortella. Besides some soothing strolls among the well-labeled flower beds and landscaped rock gardens, try to spend some time in the museum dedicated to the life and works of the late English composer, William Walton. The gardens have excellent facilities, including a shop selling Sir William's music and Lady Walton's lively biography of her husband, *Behind the Facade,* as well as light, homemade refreshments. Needless to say, there is a concert series scheduled in the gardens during summertime. ⊠ *Via Calise 35, Forio,* ☎ *081/986220,* WEB *www.ischia.it/mortella.* 🎫 *€6.* ◔ *Tues., Thurs., and weekends 9–7.*

Dining and Lodging

$$ ✕ **Bar-Ristorante Bagno Teresa.** This is an unpretentious restaurant on Citara Beach (no dress code) that offers a range of fresh seafood at reasonable prices served with lively local wine. This is the place to come if you want to stay light for the afternoon swim—there's no need to order a full Mediterranean splurge. ⊠ *Baia di Citara,* ☎ *081/907647. No credit cards. Closed Nov.–Mar.*

$$$ ⊞ **La Bagattella.** *The* place to stay in Forio, this high-style oasis has a
★ white wedding-cake, arabesque ambience, with flower-covered balconies, sleek illuminated pool, exotic plants, and palm trees. The lobby is handsomely accented with wood antique furniture, while most guest rooms are modern and as spacious as apartments. A new wing has the less desirable accommodations, but everyone staying here can enjoy the truly orchidaceous atmosphere. ⊠ *Via Tommaso Cigliano 8, 80075,* ☎ *081/986072,* FAX *081/989637,* WEB *www.labagattella.it. 56 rooms with bath. Bar, air-conditioning, pool. AE, MC, V. Closed Nov.–Mar.*

$$ ⊞ **Hotel Semiramis.** A quiet family-run hotel, this is within a minute's walk of Citara Beach and the crowded Giardini Poseidon spa. The rooms are decorated tastefully in thematic styles, with the best and most expensive in the panoramic new wing on the upper terrace. To cap it all, there is a child-friendly, secluded swimming pool tapping water from geothermal aquifers 30 ft down. ⊠ *Spiaggia di Citara, 80075,* ☎ *081/ 907511,* FAX *081/907511. 33 rooms with bath. Bar, pool. No credit cards. Closed Nov.–Mar.*

$$ ⊞ **La Pergola.** This is one of the very few opportunities to stay on a working farm on Ischia. La Pergola is a whitewashed villa perched attractively on the slopes of Monte Epomeo and surrounded by vineyards and olive and fruit trees, with sweeping views westward over Citara Beach. Its dynamic young owners also operate a thriving restaurant serving local specialties including the fabled rabbit dish *coniglio all'ischitana.* The owners offer cooking courses on occasion and have a small farm shop with homemade jams, liqueurs, and olive oil. ⊠ *Via San Giuseppe 8, 80075,* ☎ *081/909483,* FAX *081/909483,* WEB *www.terranostra.campania.it/ cciaana/lapergol.html. 7 rooms with bath. No credit cards.*

Nightlife and the Arts

For much of the summer the William Walton Foundation arranges a busy schedule of concerts during the late afternoon within the magical gardens of La Mortella, admission to which is included in the price of the ticket. For tickets, contact La Mortella by phone or get information on its Web site.

Outdoor Activities and Sports

The largest spa on the island, with the added boon of a natural sauna hollowed out of the rocks, is the **Giardini Poseidon Terme.** Here you can sit like a Roman senator on a stone chair recessed in the rock and let the hot water cascade over you. With countless thermally regulated pools, promenades, and steam pools, plus lots of toga-clad kitschy statues of the Caesars, Poseidon exerts a special pull on Germans, many of them grandparents shepherding grandchildren. On certain days, the place is overrun with people—so be prepared for crowds and wailing babies. ✉ *Citara Beach, Forio,* ☎ *081/907122,* WEB *www.giardiniposeidon.it.* ✇ *€24 all day, €18 after 1 PM, €5.2 for visitors (no bathing) between 6 PM and 7 PM.* ☉ *Apr.–Oct., daily 8:30–7.*

Unlike on Capri, aficionados of water sports are unlikely to leave Ischia dissatisfied. On a calm day a canoe will carry you into that secluded bay you've spotted from afar, perhaps with its sea cave that's worth exploring. A good place to start—considered by locals to be one of the best beaches on the island—is Citara, near the Giardini Poseidon, on the edge of the township of Forio. Canoe and boat rental from many beaches on Ischia is run by **Dario Mazzara Marine Service** (✉ Via F. Di Lustro 10, Forio, ☎ 081/5071328).

Shopping

With all the beauty farms on Ischia, ladies may enjoy visiting the main cosmetics factory on the island, **Ischia Thermae** (✉ Via Schioppa 17, ☎ 081/997745, WEB www.omnitel.it/shopcenter/ischiathermae), which occupies an 18th-century palazzo in the town center of Forio. Besides poring over some of the formidably named articles in their retail outlet (such as Thermal Mud Purifying Mask Exfoliator), guided tours of the factory are offered twice a week (Wednesday and Friday at 5) with the bonus of a free sample of their products.

Serrara Fontana

㉗ *8 km (5 mi) southeast of Forio.*

The name of this town reflects the merging of two small hill communities, Serrara and Fontana, into one larger *comune*. Apart from being a primarily agricultural community, Fontana is also known as the departure point (take Bus CS or CD from Ischia Porto, get off in the Piazzetta) for the hike up **Monte Epomeo** (mules can be rented near the parish Church of Santa Maria della Sacca). Don't be put off by signs saying *Strada militare* or *Vietato l'ingresso* (entry forbidden) at the start of the walk. Carry on up this standard route until you get to the barrier, where a path to the left will take you up to the top. You should allow about two hours for this hike. Though it is rather underwhelming in terms of wildlife—sadly, hunting has decimated the numbers of larger birds and small mammals—the 360° view at the very summit of Monte Epomeo, more than 2,500 ft above sea level, makes you feel that the two-hour round-trip was well worthwhile.

Sant'Angelo

㉘ *2 km (1 mi) south of Serrara Fontana.*

A sleepy fishing village out of season, Sant'Angelo, with its promontory of La Roia, has preserved its character remarkably well over the years. The area has been spared much of the *speculazione edilizia* (speculative building, often without planning permission) that has hit the rest of the island, and the steep winding paths by the sea are closed to traffic. Well connected by public transport (Bus CS from Forio or Ischia Porto, Bus CD from Ischia Porto only), this is a perfect site for an early evening *passeggiata*: you can peek into local pottery shops or tasteful boutiques, and then nestle into a café near the quayside for an aperitivo.

Dining

$–$$ ✕ **Pizzeria dal Pescatore.** A pizzeria with pleasing decor, this spot enjoys a fine view from the terrace overlooking the promontory of La Roia at Sant'Angelo. Some imaginative pizzas are served here—try the *a fiori di zucchini* (zucchini pizza) or just trust in the chef's special. ⊠ *Piazza Ottorino Troia 7,* ☎ *081/999206. AE, DC, MC, V. Closed Nov.–Mar.*

Barano D'Ischia

🕗 *6 km (4 mi) east of Serrara Fontana; 6 km (4 mi) south of Ischia Porto.*

Perched on a ridge 650 ft up, Barano combines the two industries of agriculture and tourism. Life here revolves around the main Piazza San Rocco with its two churches, San Sebastiano (the town's patron saint) and San Rocco (17th century). Like many churches on the island, San Sebastiano has undergone profound changes since its original foundation as an Augustine monastery in the 17th century. The pale yellow-and-white campanile was an 18th-century addition, contemporary with the paintings by Di Spigna within. Barano is also the staging post for the south-facing Beach of Maronti, which is well worth a visit outside the busy months of July and August.

PROCIDA: ISLAND OF CONTRASTS

Lying barely 3 km (2 mi) from the mainland and 10 km (6 mi) from the nearest port of Pozzuoli, Procida is an island of enormous contrasts. It is the most densely populated island in Europe—almost 11,000 people crammed into less than 3½ square km (2 square mi)—and yet there are oases like Marina Corricella and Vivara, which seem to have been bypassed by modern civilization. The inhabitants of the island—the Procidani—have an almost symbiotic relationship with the Mediterranean: many join the merchant navy while others either fish or ferry vacationers around local waters. And yet land traffic here is more intense than on any other island in the Bay of Naples.

In scenic terms this is the place to admire what the Italians call "Spontaneous," or folkloric Mediterranean, architecture: Look for the tall archways on the ground floor, which signals places where boats could be stowed in winter, the outside staircases providing access to upper floors without cramping interior living space, and the delicate pastel colors of the facades contrasting with deeper, bolder blues at sea. Picturesquely scenic, it is no surprise that Procida has strong artistic traditions and is widely considered the painters' island par excellence. If on the island at Easter, make sure you see the striking Good Friday procession through the island's major streets.

Terra Murata and Abbazia di San Michele

Boats pull into the main port, **Marina Grande Sancio Cattolico,** which is fetchingly adorned with pastel-hue houses and the church of Santa Maria della Pietà (1760). Hike up to the Piazza San Martiri on your way up to the **Castello** (now a prison). Magnificent views can be seen from the piazza in front of the castle, including the enchanting fishermen's village of the Marina della Corricella. Continue along Via San Michele to the highest point on the island, the town of Terra Murata—a fascinating cluster of ancient buildings, including churches, palazzi, fortifications, ancient walls, and gateways, mostly in yellow-gray tufa stone. A Benedictine abbey was founded here in the 7th century, safely tucked away from mainland marauders, and the area became the focal point for the inhabitants of the island. Perched precariously at the top of a cliff facing the small bay of Corricella is the 16th-century **ex-convent of Santa Margherita Nuova,** which is currently undergoing restoration. The easily distinguishable **Palazzo Reale** built at the same time—confusingly, sometimes called Il Castello—was used as a prison until 1986. Rumor has it that its inmates were a little miffed at having to abandon the perks of being on the sun-drenched island of Procida.

Within Terra Murata is the **Abbazia di San Michele.** San Michele (St. Michael) is the island's patron saint and a key figure in its history and traditions. Legend has it that in 1535, when the sultan of Algeria's admiral laid siege to the island, San Michele appeared above the pirate force and put them to flight (the 17th-century painting depicting the scene is in the choir of the abbey's 17th-century church, while one of the invaders' anchors can also be viewed). On the wall close to the richly coffered ceiling of the church is another depiction of San Michele, this time by the grandmaster Luca Giordano (1699). As you walk around the church, note the holes in marble flagstones on the floor, which were in effect trapdoors through which bodies could be lowered to the underground cemetery below. There are also a remarkable number of statues, several of which are still borne through the streets of Procida during its Easter processions. ⊠ *Terra Murata,* ☎ *081/8967612,* WEB *www. abbaziasanmichele.it.* ☞ *Free, but donations welcome. Guided tours (€1.70 per person) to the church and museum available on request at the bookstore at entrance to abbey.* ☉ *Apr.–Oct, Mon.–Sat. 9:45–12:45 and 3–6; Nov.–Mar., Mon.–Sat. 3–5.*

Corricella

★   Perched under the citadel of the Terra Murata, the **Marina di Corricella** is Procida's most iconic sight. Singled out for the waterfront scenes in *Il Postino* (*The Postman,* the 1995 Oscar-winner for Best Foreign Film), this fishermen's cove is one of the most eye-popping villages in Campania—a rainbow-hue, horizontal version of Positano, comprising hundreds of traditional Mediterranean-style stone houses threaded by numerous scalatinelli. The inhabitants of Corricella have been relatively immune to life in the limelight, and apart from the opening of an extra restaurant and bar, there have been few changes in this sleepy fishermen's village. This is the type of place where even those of us with failing grades in art classes feel like reaching for a paintbrush to record the delicate pinks and yellows of the waterfront buildings.

Dining and Lodging

With such a strong seafaring tradition on Procida, you'd be wise to stick primarily to seafood, especially in summer. And if you have space left over at the end of the meal, try the local variety of *torta di limone,* made from the island's wondrously large lemons.

$$–$$$ ✕ **La Gorgonia.** This atmospheric restaurant sits right on the waterfront down at Corricella. The specialty here is a combination of seafood and locally grown vegetables, such as pasta *con fagioli e cozze* (with beans and mussels). ⊠ *Marina Corricella,* ☎ *081/8101060. AE, DC, MC, V. Closed Nov.–Feb. and weekdays Mar.–May and Oct.*

$$ 🏠 **Casa Gentile.** This is a very quiet hotel with spacious rooms overlooking Corricella, designed to blend in tastefully with the local Mediterranean architecture. If interested in fishing, ask the owner, Vincenzo, if you can join him on his nighttime travels around the Bay of Naples. The hotel offers a water-taxi service to and from port. ⊠ *Marina Corricella 88, Procida,* ☎ *081/8967799,* FAX *081/8969011. 11 rooms with bath. AE, D, MC, V. Closed Nov.–mid-Mar.*

Vivara

On the western coast of Procida, beyond the pretty beaches of Spiaccia Giraccio, Ciraciello, and the Lido is the small port and beach of the **Marina di Chiaioletta,** studded with a few hotels and basically known as a port-of-call for all sorts of water activities, ranging from boating to scuba-diving; The shortest way to get to Chiaioletta is from the main port of Marina Grande Sancio Cattolico. Opposite Chiaioletta is Vivara, a crescent-shape island and terminal segment of a volcanic cone, today a living museum of natural history with unsullied Mediterranean maquis vegetation. It has miraculously survived the designs of property speculators over the past 30 years and is now awaiting a proper management plan from the Regione Campania. Apart from a few historic buildings on the island, including a Napoleonic fort near the entrance gateway, the main cultural interest lies in its rich archaeological finds dating to prehistoric times, especially the Bronze Age, as testified to by a wealth of Mycenaean pottery fragments. The island is at its best in springtime, with most of its plants in flower and lots of birds on the move. The path winds up from the causeway to a cluster of abandoned settlements at the highest point of the island (357 ft). On the way admire the dense *maquis* on either side with characteristic plant species like tree heather, the strawberry tree, and rockrose, the latter of which sports delicate pink flowers in spring. Although you'll hear birds—especially the blackcap—don't expect to see any of these skulking warblers except perhaps around the clearing at the center of the island. At migration time look out for two of the Mediterranean's more exotic-looking summer visitors, the hoopoe, a bird that looks more in keeping with the African savanna, and the bee-eater, a splash of unusually vivid colors. For information about access and guided tours on Vivara, contact the **Azienda Autonoma di Cura, Soggiorno e Turismo** (✉ Via Roma, Procida, ☎ 081/8101968) before trekking out to the island.

Dining and Lodging

$$ ✕🅃 **Crescenzo Hotel-Ristorante.** A short walk from Vivara, this is a three-story whitewashed hotel overlooking the small yachting marina of Chiaiolella. Half-board only in August, though with specialties like spaghetti *ai ricci di mare* (with sea urchins) you should consider half-board at other times of the year as well. Even if not a guest, enjoy a seafood delight or two here. ✉ *Marina di Chiaiolella*, ☎ *081/8967255*, ⅢⅫ *081/8101260. 10 rooms with bath. Restaurant, bar, free parking. AE, DC, MC, V.*

Nightlife and Sports

Nightlife

Procida's nightlife revolves around Via Roma in the port town of Marina Grande Sancio Cattolico, though there are a number of late-closing bars and restaurants around the Marina di Chiaiolella, too. The **Birreria Pub Sotto Sopra** (✉ Via Roma 11, Procida, ☎ 081/8101013) serves good draft lager almost around the clock in a fairly congenial quasi-nautical setting.

The Arts

Procida was the setting for Elsa Morante's novel *L'Isola di Arturo,* which has lent its name to the literary competition held every September on Procida. Art exhibitions are occasionally held down at the port in several of the palazzi along Via Roma, while the Abbazia di San Michele in Terra Murata lays on special exhibitions connected with religious and literary themes. Ask about forthcoming events at the Azienda Autonoma di Cura, Soggiorno e Turismo (information office) in Marina Grande Sancio Cattolico.

Outdoor Activities and Sports

With its famous nautical school and centuries-old seafaring traditions, Procida is an ideal base for chartering yachts of various sizes or just exploring the seabed with one of the diving schools on the island.

SAILING

One of the market leaders in Italy is **Sail Italia** (✉ Via Roma 10, Sancio Cattolico Marina Grande, ☎ 081/8969264 or 081/8969962, WEB www.sailitalia.it). Except for the even-pricier month of August, chartering a 10-berth 40-ft yacht for a week—enough time to visit the other islands in the bay as well as the gorgeous island of Ponza, farther afield—will set you back about €4,000 inclusive of skipper and final clean. If reckoned on a daily per-person basis, this is an interesting alternative to hotel stays on the various islands.

SCUBA DIVING

The **Procida Diving Center** (✉ Lido di Procida, Marina Chiaiolella, ☎ 081/8968385) organizes courses and provides equipment for divers of all levels. You may be taken into shallower waters, like Secca delle Formiche, near Vivara, or shown the coral formation off one of the headlands on the island. The cost for a session averages about €27 per person, and the season runs roughly from May to October.

CAPRI, ISCHIA, AND PROCIDA A TO Z

Capri

BOAT AND FERRY TRAVEL

Capri is well connected with the mainland in all seasons, though there tend to be more sailings between April and October. However, you can't return to Naples after about 8 PM, so if you want to see an evening concert, you'll have to arrange for hotel accommodations. Ferries, hydrofoils, Seacats, and similar vessels leave from Molo Beverello (below Piazza Municipio) in Naples and from Sorrento's Marina Piccola, while *aliscafi* (hydrofoils) also sail from the small marina of Mergellina, a short distance west of the Villa Comunale in Naples. For locals in Naples there are restrictions on taking cars onto the island, while non-Italians can move relatively freely. Bear in mind that much of Capri town is pedestrianized, and a car on the island may well be more of a hindrance than a help.

Caremar offers five hydrofoil departures from Molo Beverello (€11, with a travel time of 40 minutes) and six ferry departures per day (€5.5 high season, with a travel time of 1 hour, 15 minutes). Four ferries leave daily from Sorrento (€6, travel time 30 minutes).

Linee Marittime Partenopee offers one to three hydrofoil departures every hour from Sorrento (€8, travel time 20 minutes), seven ferries per day from Sorrento (€6.5, 50 minutes), and one hydrofoil per day from Ischia (in the morning, €12, one hour).

From Naples, Navigazione Libera Del Golfo has roughly one hydrofoil departure per hour (€11, travel time 40 minutes). From Easter to October, the company also offers one jetfoil from Positano and Amalfi (approximately €12.5, travel time 50 minutes), and one ferry from Positano and Amalfi (€10, travel time 1 hour, 20 minutes).

SNAV offers one hydrofoil every hour from Mergellina (€ 11, travel time 40 minutes).

FARES AND SCHEDULES

Departure schedules are listed every day in several daily papers (*Corriere della Sera, Il Mattino, La Repubblica*). If you are planning to move on from Capri to Ischia or the Amalfi Coast, there is regular service from May to October, when demand is higher. As for ferry costs, there is little to be gained—sometimes nothing—from buying a round-trip ticket, which will just tie you down to a return schedule of only one shipping line.

➤ BOAT AND FERRY INFORMATION: **Caremar** (☎ 081/5513882 or 081/8370700, WEB www.caremar.it). **Linee Marittime Partenopee** (☎ 081/8781430 or 081/8071812). **Navigazione Libera Del Golfo** (☎ 081/5527209 hydrofoils from Naples, 089/875092 ferry and hydrofoils from Positano). **SNAV** (☎ 081/7612348).

EMERGENCIES
➤ CAPRI: **Police** (☎ 081/8370000). **First Aid** (☎ 081/8381205). **Hospital** (⊠ Ospedale Capilupi, ☎ 081/8381111).
➤ ANACAPRI: **Police** (☎ 081/8371011). **First Aid** (☎ 081/8381205). **Hospital** (⊠ Ospedale Capilupi, ☎ 081/8381111).

CURRENCY EXCHANGE
➤ EXCHANGE SERVICES: **Banca di Roma** (⊠ Piazza Umberto I, Capri Town, ☎ 081/8375942). **Banco di Napoli** (⊠ Via Orlandi 150, Anacapri, ☎ 081/8371202). **Cambio** (⊠ Via Roma 33, Capri Town, ☎ 081/8370785). **La Piazzetta 2** (⊠ Piazza Vittoria 2b, Anacapri, ☎ 081/8373146).

TAXIS
➤ TAXI COMPANIES: **Taxis** (☎ 081/8371175 in Anacapri; 081/8370543 in Capri Town).

TOURS
Gruppo Motoscafisti offers excursions to Blue Grotto from Marina Grande (€ 13, with Sunday supplement) and round island tour, or *giro* (€11), taking in other grottoes and getting good close-ups of the Faraglioni. For just the Faraglioni expect to pay €8 with Sunday supplement. Laser Capri leads excursions to Blue Grotto from Marina Grande (€12.5, with Sunday supplement) and round island tour (€8.5). Cooperativa Battellieri Capresi manages the rowboats covering the short distance into the Blue Grotto.
➤ FEES AND SCHEDULES: **Cooperativa Battellieri Capresi** (⊠ Via C. Colombo 23, Marina Grande, Capri, ☎ 081/8370973). **Gruppo Motoscafisti** (⊠ Molo del Porto, Marina Grande, Capri, ☎ 081/8375646). **Laser Capri** (⊠ Via Ruocco 45, Marina Grande, Capri, ☎ 081/8375208, WEB www.lasercapri.com).

TRANSPORTATION AROUND CAPRI
Most of Capri's sights are reasonably accessible by either boat or bus, except for Villa Jovis and Cetrella, which involve some walking (about 40 minutes). The bus service is relatively cheap and frequent, while taxis are likely to cost 10–20 times as much as public transport. Don't be tempted into buying a *biglietto giornaliero* (day pass) for the bus and funicular (€7) unless you are thinking of covering almost every corner of the island—you would need to make 6 separate trips to make it pay, and locals deem it a bit of rip-off.

Access to the Blue Grotto is usually from Marina Grande in a 20-seater boat, decanting into smaller rowboats near the grotto. Some prefer to take the bus to Anacapri and then change onto another line that passes close to the grotto on the northwest side of the island. This operation involves taking just one boat and will reduce your overall cost by about €2. However, don't set your heart on an excursion to the Blue Grotto, as visits cannot be made when the sea is even minimally choppy. An alternative is the Giro dell'Isola (round island tour), which is a better value for money compared with the Blue Grotto excursion. However, some giros do not include a stop at the Blue Grotto, which is fiercely and territorially the private province of its own boat operators; you can be sure that giro tours that do pay a call on the Blue Grotto will require extra payment for this stop.

Off the major bus routes, many roads are pedestrianized. The trails close to Villa Jovis and the Arco Naturale are all well paved and well maintained, while those on the steeper parts of Monte Solaro are the only ones where walking shoes are advisable. If you go down the Scala Fenicia footpath from Anacapri, take your time. Although not dangerous, some stretches are quite steep and should be undertaken with caution.

TRAVEL AGENCIES
Grotta Azzurra can arrange ticketing for flights, trains, etc. on the mainland and provide incoming services such as hotel reservations, customized tours of the island, and mainland tours to Herculaneum, Pompeii, and the Amalfi Coast, as well as scooter rentals.
➤ LOCAL AGENTS: **Grotta Azzurra** (✉ Via C. Colombo 64, Capri, ☎ 081/8370410, FAX 081/8377528).

VISITOR INFORMATION
Azienda Autonoma di Cura, Soggiorno e Turismo offices in Capri, Capri Town, and Anacapri are open 8:30–8:30 in high season, and 9–1 and 3–7 (approximately) in winter.
➤ TOURIST INFORMATION: **Azienda Autonoma di Cura, Soggiorno e Turismo** (✉ Banchina del Porto, Marina Grande, Capri, ☎ 081/8370634; ✉ Piazza Umberto I, Capri Town, ☎ 081/8370686; ✉ Via G. Orlandi, 19/A, Anacapri, ☎ 081/8371524; WEB www.capritourism.com).

Ischia

BIKE TRAVEL
About 100 yards from Ischia Porto's ferry terminal, Del Franco, opposite Hotel Jolly, has a fair range of sturdy bicycles costing €11 per day.
➤ BIKE RENTALS: **Del Franco** (✉ Via Alfredo De Luca 121 Ischia Porto, ☎ 081/991334).

BOAT AND FERRY TRAVEL
Like the other islands in the Bay of Naples, Ischia is well connected with the mainland in all seasons. However, the last sailings leave for Naples and Pozzuoli at about 8 in the evening, and you should allow plenty of time for getting to the port and locating the relevant ticket office. Unlike Capri and Procida, Ischia has three separate ports—Ischia Porto, Casamicciola, and Forio (hydrofoils only)—so you should choose your ferry or hydrofoil according to your destination. The closest mainland port to Ischia is that of Pozzuoli, where you have the added bonus—besides paying lower fares—of walking through the colorful fish market on your way to the jetty. Many of the sailings go via Procida, giving you an attractive glimpse of its waterfront but also extending travel time by 10–15 minutes. As on Capri, local Italians are subject to restrictions on taking cars over to the island, while non-Italians can move relatively freely.

Alilauro has roughly one hydrofoil per hour traveling from Mergellina, Naples to Ischia Porto (€12 high season, €11 low season, travel time 40 minutes). Five hydrofoils depart per day May through September to Forio (€13 high season, €12 low season travel time, 50 minutes).

Caremar offers six hydrofoil departures from Molo Beverello, Naples to Ischia Porto (€11, travel time 50 minutes), and six ferry departures per day (€5, travel time 1 hour, 10 minutes). Ferry departures are also available from Pozzuoli (€6, travel time 1 hour).

Linee Lauro sends roughly one hydrofoil every two hours from Molo Beverello, Naples to Ischia Porto (€12, travel time 40 minutes), and eight ferry departures per day to Ischia Porto (€6, travel time 1¼ hours).

SNAV offers a hydrofoil every hour from Mergellina, Naples, to the marina of Casamicciola (€11, travel time 50 minutes).

Traghetti Pozzuoli has a ferry departing every hour from Pozzuoli, sometimes docking at Casamicciola (€6, travel time 1 hour).

Departure schedules are listed every day in several daily papers (*Corriere della Sera, Il Mattino, La Repubblica*). Buy a single ticket rather than a round-trip, which would tie you to the same shipping line on your return journey.
➤ BOAT AND FERRY INFORMATION: **Alilauro** (☎ 081/7611004, WEB www.alilauro.it). **Caremar** (☎ 081/5513882, WEB www.caremar.it). **Linee Lauro** (☎ 081/5522838). **SNAV** (☎ 081/7612348). **Traghetti Pozzuoli** (☎ 081/527736, WEB www.traghettipozzuoli.it).

BUS TRAVEL
The main bus terminus is in Ischia Porto at the start of Via Cosca from where buses run by the company SEPSA radiate out around the island. There are also convenient *fermate* (stops) at the two main beaches of Citara and Maronti, with timetables displayed at the terminus. At €1 per ticket, the service may be considered good value though conditions can get very hot and crowded at peak beach-visiting times.
➤ BUS INFORMATION: **SEPSA** (☎ 081/991808).

CAR RENTAL
➤ LOCAL AGENCIES: **Del Franco** (⊠ Via Alfredo De Luca 121, opposite Hotel Jolly, Ischia Porto, ☎ 081/991334).

CAR TRAVEL
Given the much larger size of Ischia compared to the other islands Capri and Procida (where cars are virtually redundant), having your own transport on Ischia could be handy, especially if you have to schlep large quantities of diving equipment, say, around the island. However, in most towns there are now strict parking restrictions, and *vigili urbani* (traffic police) are constantly on the lookout for aberrant motorists. The police are also clamping down on seat belt violations, so if you do drive, be sure to wear your belt even on the shortest journey.
➤ CONTACTS: **Police** (⊠ Ischia Porto, ☎ 081/991336). **First Aid** (⊠ Ischia Porto, ☎ 081/994044). **Hospital** (⊠ Ospedale Rizzoli, Lacco Ameno, ☎ 081/994044).

In general look for exchange bureaus or signs saying WECHSEL (German for "exchange"). Commission rates may be marginally higher than in the local banks, but red tape is virtually nonexistent, and service is likely to be considerably faster.
➤ EXCHANGE SERVICES: **Alilauro Biglietteria** (⊠ Hydrofoil ticket office, Ischia Porto, ☎ 081/7611004). **Viaggi e Turismo Di Leva** (⊠ Piazza Medaglia d'Oro 11, Forio, ☎ 081/997711).

TAXIS
Taxis—and microtaxis—are to be found near the major ferry and hydrofoil terminals, and there are taxi ranks close to all the town centers on the island. The fleet of microtaxis is gradually being upgraded from roaring two-stroke *api*, little more than scooters with a cabin attached but regrettably no earplugs provided, into gently purring state-of-the-art minibuses (carrying 6 passengers), where intelligible conversation can now be attempted. By law all taxis and microtaxis have to use their

meters, so make sure the meter is activated as soon as your journey begins. If the taxi doesn't have a meter, beware: some drivers seem to be pirates in disguise, so work out a flat fee before you set out. If you just go along for the ride, you could wind up being very unpleasantly surprised when you're charged $15 for a two-minute trip.

TRANSPORTATION AROUND ISCHIA
Ischia has an excellent, competitively priced bus network, with all the major sites and beaches within easy reach of one of its 10 lines. Runs continue on some routes until well after 10 PM, making evening sorties feasible even if you haven't got your own transport. Ischia also has taxis and microtaxis, which are basically three-wheelers with a cabin at the back. A number of car and scooter rental facilities are available, although Ischia already has more than its fair share of motorized two-wheelers on the roads and many have undergone engine tampering to improve performance (and boost noise levels). If you use a bicycle on the island, be prepared for lots of ups and downs, and where possible take to the minor roads. Boat and Zodiac rentals are possible at most of the major beaches, and ferrying service is sometimes arranged to reach out-of-the-way beaches.

TRAVEL AGENCIES
Most travel agencies supply the following services: hotel booking, car rentals, guided tours, flight and ferry bookings, and day excursions to the mainland and other islands.
➤ LOCAL AGENT REFERRALS: **Isolaverde Viaggi** (✉ Piazzetta Pontile 1, Lacco Ameno, ☎ 081/980455, FAX 081/995329, WEB www.isolaverde-viaggi.it). **Viaggi Romano** (✉ Via Porto 5–9, Ischia Porto, ☎ 081/991215, FAX 081/991167, WEB www.ischiadirecttours.it).

VISITOR INFORMATION
Azienda Autonoma di Cura, Soggiorno e Turismo in Ischia Porto is open 9 AM–1:30 PM; April through October it is also open 3–7:30 PM.
➤ TOURIST INFORMATION: **Azienda Autonoma di Cura, Soggiorno e Turismo** (✉ Ufficio Informazioni, Banchina Porto Salvo, Ischia Porto, ☎ 081/5074231, FAX 081/5074230, WEB www.ischiaonline.it/tourism).

Procida

BIKE TRAVEL
Signor Basilea Luoni of Associazione Azione Verde has a cycle shop opposite the Scuola Media, which is about a 30-minute walk from the ferry terminal. The shop can arrange for bike delivery to the port.
➤ BIKE RENTALS: **Associazione Azione Verde** (✉ Piazza Sant'Antonio da Padova, Marina Grande Sancio Cattolico, ☎ 081/8967395).

BOAT AND FERRY TRAVEL
Procida's ferry timetable caters to the many daily commuters who live on the island and work in Naples or Pozzuoli. The most frequent—and cheapest—connections are from the Port of Pozzuoli. After stopping at Procida's main port, Marina Grande Sancio Cattolico, many ferries and hydrofoils continue on to Ischia, for which Procida is considered a halfway house.

Caremar has six hydrofoil departing from Molo Beverello, Naples (€8, travel time 40 minutes), and seven ferry departures per day from Molo Beverello, Naples (€5, travel time 1 hour, 10 minutes). There are three ferry departures per day from Pozzuoli (€2.7, travel time 40 minutes).

SNAV hydrofoils leave every two hours from Mergellina, Naples (€8, travel time 35 minutes).

The Procida Lines 2000 ferry leaves roughly every hour from Pozzuoli (€2.3 Monday–Saturday, €2.8 Sunday, travel time 40 minutes).

FARES AND SCHEDULES

As with the other islands, buy a single ticket rather than a round-trip (there is virtually no saving on a round-trip ticket, which is usually twice the single fare, and it ties you down to one operator on your return). ➤ BOAT AND FERRY INFORMATION: **Caremar** (☎ 081/5513882, WEB www.caremar.it). **Procida Lines 2000** (☎ 081/8960328). **SNAV** (☎ 081/7612348).

BUS TRAVEL

The bus terminus in Procida is at the disembarkation point in Via Roma. Provided there is no traffic gridlock along the island's narrow streets, the buses run by the company SEPSA will get you to most destinations within about 10 minutes for €.80. Chiaiolella is the most frequently served destination (about every 15 minutes) and timetables are displayed—and tickets bought—at a newsstand close to the landing stage. In summer the bus service runs until about 4 in the morning. ➤ BUS INFORMATION: **SEPSA** (☎ 081/8101241).

EMERGENCIES

➤ CONTACTS: **Police** (☎ 081/8967160). **First Aid** (☎ 081/8969058). **Hospital** (☎ 081/8101213).

CURRENCY EXCHANGE

➤ EXCHANGE SERVICES: **Credem** (✉ Via Roma 102, Procida).

TAXIS

For about €12, microtaxis with a capacity of about five passengers will take you from the port to Chiaiolella. This can be a welcome service in summer, when buses get overcrowded and steamy. For the round island tour, expect to pay upwards of €30. However, this includes frequent stops along the way plus a shotgun-quick visit to the Abbazia. Although by law all microtaxis have to use their meters, it may be worth your while to agree on a fixed price beforehand. Taxis can be hired at Marina Grande. On the southern coast, taxis can be hired at Marina Chiaiolella. ➤ CONTACTS: **Marina Chiaiolella** (☎ 081/8968785). **Marina Grande** (☎ 081/8968785).

TRANSPORTATION AROUND PROCIDA

There are four main bus lines that will take you to practically every corner of the island as well as a fleet of microtaxis operating round island tours and plying the route between the port and the Marina di Chiaiolella, on the southwest of the island. To get to Vivara, a road climbs westward out of Chiaiolella, and motorized access is barred shortly before reaching the causeway linking the two islands. Though Procida has fewer hills than either Ischia or Capri, cycling is really only feasible when the roads are closed to motorized traffic (evenings in summer). Most islanders get around on mopeds and scooters, which means the streets between the port and the center of the island are both noisy and loaded with pollutants, making casual strolling and window-shopping stressful. Beaches can be reached by sea or land, with local fishermen improvising as water-taxi drivers.

TRAVEL AGENCIES

Graziella Travel provides listings of guided tours in the area. ➤ LOCAL AGENT REFERRALS: **Graziella Travel** (✉ Via Roma 117, Procida, ☎ 081/8969594, FAX 081/8969190, WEB www.isoladiprocida.it).

VISITOR INFORMATION

Azienda Autonoma di Cura, Soggiorno e Turismo is open April to October, daily 9:30–1 and 4–7:30, and November–Easter, daily 9:30–1.

➤ TOURIST INFORMATION: **Azienda Autonoma di Cura, Soggiorno e Turismo** (✉ Stazione Marittima Ferry ticket office, Via Roma, Procida, ☎ 081/8101968, WEB www.procidaweb.it).

4 SORRENTO AND THE AMALFI COAST

One of the most gigglingly gorgeous places on earth, this corner of Campania tantalizes, almost beyond bearing, the visitor who can stay but a day or two. Poets and millionaires have long journeyed here to see and sense its legendary sights: Sorrento—Italy at its Belle Epoque best; perfect Positano—a claim that is more than alliteration; Amalfi—a shimmering medieval city; and romantic mountain-high Ravello. Connecting these towns is the Amalfi Drive, a cliff-hugging stretch of road that tests one's faith in civil engineering. This roller-coastal route offers views that are drop-dead breathtaking (literally, it sometimes seems).

By Lea Lane

Updated by
Mark Walters

THANK ODYSSEUS FOR LETTING THE SIRENS LURE HIM to their lair near Sorrento's coastal waters. Here, as the *Odyssey* tells us, the first traveler of record resisted the seductive song of the *Sirene*—two formidable monsters with the heads of women and the bodies of birds. The wily navigator outwitted them by having himself tied to the ship's mast and sealing his crew's ears with wax. The myth became further embroidered by later mariners' tales: The number of the Sirens increased to three, the monsters became physically attractive—barring the rather fishy tail—and attempts were made to identify the ancient location. The current consensus is that the three Sirens spitefully chose to live out eternity as rocky outcrops, right here on the islands called Li Galli, in the waters off Positano on the Amalfi Coast. Even today, it is difficult to resist the allure of this part of southern Italy, a palmy and balmy land stretching south from the Bay of Naples and the Sorrento Peninsula to the Amalfi Coast and the Bay of Salerno, rimmed by the true-bluest waters of the Mediterranean. Like Homer, you'll be able to spin your own tale of lemon-scented breezes, emerald grottoes, sun-kissed vistas, sea-fresh food, and an embracing, generous people. Like a 21st-century Odysseus, to leave these blessed shores willingly you may have to hang on to the ferry rail, close your eyes, and turn your Discman up to full blast.

The Sorrento Peninsula was put on the map by the ancient Romans. The emperors—who knew a good thing when they saw it—claimed the region for their own, crowning the golden, waterside cliffs of what was then called "Surrentum" (or Land of Sirens) with their palatial villas. Where they staked out their vacation spots, resorts now stand, the broken columns and capitals and marble busts of the Caesars now scattered among orange trees and terraces, attesting to their power—and its decline. Sorrento goes as far back as the Etruscans, the bon viveurs of the early ancient world, and for much of its existence has remained focused, in fact, on pleasure. It became a major stop on the elite's Grand Tour itinerary beginning in the late 18th century, thanks to reports from Goethe, Lord Byron, Shelley, and Richard Wagner. By the mid-19th century, grand hotels and wedding-cake villas had sprung up to welcome princes, khans, and tycoons.

Gently faded, like a stereopticon image, and set with sherbet-hued villas, Sorrento still exudes a special pull—from its bustling piazza named for the famous 16th-century poet Tasso, a native son, to the belvederes framing the slowly setting sun. For anyone suffering *"nostalgia di Napoli"*—a longing for tarantellas, strumming mandolins, and dolce far niente—this is the ideal place, since Naples itself has become so urbanized. As a hub for must-see sites—Pompeii, Naples, Capri, and the Amalfi Coast to the south—Sorrento is unequaled. Because of its convenient location the city can become overrun with visitors during the summer months, so it's fortunate that the rest of the Sorrento Peninsula, with plains and limestone outcroppings, watchtowers and Roman ruins, groves and beaches, monasteries and villages, winding paths leading to isolated coves and panoramic views of the bays of both Naples and Salerno, remains relatively undiscovered. The peninsula's tip was, eons ago, connected to Capri when sea levels fell during the glaciations, and it seems you can practically jump there. Separating grande dame Sorrento from the relatively arriviste Amalfi Coast, this hilly, forested peninsula provides the famed rivals breathing space, along with incredible restaurants and an uncrowded charm all its own.

Heading south, the Amalfi Coast—the Costiera Amalfitana—from Positano to Vietri sul Mare, is arguably the most divinely sensual 48-km

(30-mi) stretch of water, land, and habitation on earth. Legends abound, but the Greeks were early colonizers at Paestum to the south, and Romans fled their own sacked empire in the 4th century to settle the steep coastal ridge now called the Lattari mountains (because of the milk, or *latte*, produced there). Coveted by Lombards, Saracens, and other hopefuls held literally at bay (some of the time), the medieval Maritime Republic of Amalfi dominated the seas and coast until the Normans began their conquest of southern Italy in the 11th century. By the end of the 13th, Naples, the capital of the Angevin kingdom, became the dominant ruler of the region until Italy unified in the mid-19th century.

By the late 19th century, with the creation of the two-lane Amalfi Drive, tourism blossomed, and what a road show. One of the most exciting drives in the world, it seems to be pasted onto the faces of dizzying precipices and far-flung headlands. All along the drive, wind and water erosion has carved limestone mountains into spires and crags that seem to defy gravity, cliffs plummet headlong into the sea, and crushed rock washes up along turquoise inlets. Ravines and valleys, formed by torrential flows from the highlands, are folded into the limestone coast, softening the scene with meadows and chestnut woods. Thanks to this feat of engineering that is the Amalfi Drive, the world soon discovered what has come to be called the "Divina Costiera." The justly famed jewels along this coastal necklace are Positano, Amalfi, and Ravello, but today's traveler will find the satellite baguettes—including Conca dei Marini, Atrani, Scala, and Cetara—just as sparkling. The top towns along the Amalfi Drive may fill up in high season with tour buses, but in the countryside, not much seems to have changed since the Middle Ages: mountains are still terraced and farmed for citrus, olives, wine, and dairy; and the sea is dotted with the gentle reds, whites, and blues of fishermen's boats. Vertiginously high villages, dominated by the spires of duomos, are crammed with houses on, into, above, and below hillsides to the bay; crossed by mule paths; and navigated by flights of steps called *scalinatelle*, often leading to outlooks and belvederes that take your breath away—in more ways than one. Songs have been composed about these serpentine stone steps, and they may come to haunt your dreams as well; some *costieri* (natives of the coast) like to count them one by one to get to sleep.

Semi-tough realities lurk behind the scenic splendor of the Divina Costiera, most notably the extremes of driving, the endless steps, and nonexistent parking. Furthermore, it rains in the spring, the hills can burn dry in the summer, and museums are few. Until you adjust, people seem to talk in maximum decibels. So what. For a precious little time, you are in a land of unmarred beauty.

Pleasures and Pastimes

Beaches

The area's beaches are typically disappointing, as they usually consist of small patches of coarse gray sand, or just a few rocks below the precipices. It's the water that compels: infinite shades of aquamarine, lapis, and amethyst, shimmering in sunshine, glowing silver in moonlight, and becoming transparent in coves. The best regional beaches are on the Sorrento Peninsula, to the west and south, many of them reachable only by footpath or boat. The longest and widest beaches on the Amalfi Coast are in Maiori and Minori, but there are many small beaches and coves from which to choose. As space is at a premium, few organized beachside activities are available—the best bet is at Positano, where you should opt for beautiful Fornillo, the more secluded (but very popular) beach to the west of Spiaggia Grande. For exercise, folks descend (and later ascend) the scalinatelle to rocky coves, where adults dip and sunbathe and children play hide and seek. Most of the beaches shelve quite steeply—the terrain below sea level is as craggy and steep as the land above. This is a boon for good swimmers, but caution needs to be taken, especially with kids.

Boating

People take to boats here with the ease others use buses and subways. Ferries and hydrofoils are regularly scheduled during high season. The waters are calm and beckoning, and boating for pleasure frees you from the tension of coastal driving, so try to arrange to spend at least one day on the water. Bright red-and-blue fishing boats are for hire by the day or for a few hours at the major harbors of Sorrento, Positano, and Amalfi, and by almost any beach wherever you see fishermen. Boats can take you around the Sorrento area and peninsula to the Emerald Grotto, to Capri and offshore islets, to major towns, and otherwise inaccessible cove beaches. They will drop you off and pick you up, or stay with you, depending on your budget. Look for established sites on major beaches and come a day or so ahead to reserve and bargain, especially if you're with a group. Pricing could be around €15 an hour, more or less, depending on the market, the season, and your talent at haggling. If in doubt, ask for suggestions about local boatmen at your hotel or at the town tourist board. And don't expect fishermen to speak much English; you'll have to speak with your hands, as many Italians do.

Dining: La Cucina Costiera

Locals say they have "one foot in the fishing boat, one in the vineyard"— and a fortunate stance it is, as you can count on eating simple, fresh, seasonal food, and lots of it, with *tutti i sapori della campagna verace* (all the true flavors of the countryside). From the gulfs come *pesce alla griglia* (grilled fish), *calamari* (squid), *aragosta* (lobster), and *gamberone* (shrimp). Wood oven–baked thin-crust pizzas start with *salsa alla margherita*—tomato sauce, basil, and cheese—and marinara—with tomato, garlic, and oregano—and go from there to infinity.

Food seems more sensuous amid all this beauty. Sun-dried tomatoes and chili peppers hang in bright red cascades on balconies and shopfronts ("VIAGRA NATURALE" boasts a hand-lettered sign in Amalfi). After spring and autumn rains, peasants still search the ravines for snails, to serve up with hot sauce. Oranges are as big as grapefruits, and lemons as big as oranges are cultivated on seemingly endless net-covered pergolas. From linguine with lemon at trattorias to lemon soufflés at fancy restaurants, the yellow citrus is everywhere, and all parts are used, as in *passolini* (raisins or figs baked in lemon leaves, bound by thin red thread). Not only are lemons a main component of meals and drinks, but they are used as a remedy for everything from flu to bunions.

Ingredients grown in terraced plots include plump olives pressed into oil or eaten whole, tiny spring *carciofi* (artichokes), and sweet figs. *Sponzini,* or *pomodori del pendelo,* the tomatoes carried from Egypt long ago by fishermen, grow in the mountains and muddy fields of Furore and Conca dei Marini. Eggplant, asparagus, and mushrooms thrive in the Tramonte uplands, while tomatoes come from Campora. Soft *fiore di latte* (cow's-milk cheeses)—try *treccia,* the braided variety sold in Sorrento—are from the high hill pastures of Agerola, while the world's best buffalo mozzarella comes from Paestum. Unusual fruits worth seeking out are carobs, and *ponceri*—citrus the size of a melon, often used in pastries.

Pasta is often served with seafood, but regional dishes include *crespelle al formaggio*—layers of crepes with béchamel cheese sauce, and fettuccine-like *scialatielli,* sometimes a house specialty, served with varied sauces. Clams and pasta baked in a paper bag—*"al cartoccio"*—is popular in Amalfi. In Positano, try traditional squid with potatoes, stuffed peppers, and slow-simmering ragù (tomato sauce with meat, garlic, and parsley). Around Cetara, salted anchovies, eggplants, and peppers in oil are the base of the famed sauce called *"garum,"* handed down from the Romans. A lighter version is *colatura di alici,* an anchovy sauce developed by Cistercian monks near Amalfi, served on spaghetti as a traditional Christmas Eve treat. Holidays and celebrations especially inspire the sweet tooth, with *zeppole, mustacciuoli,* and *struffoli* pastries at Christmas and New Year's, and eggy fruit tarts and almond cakes at Easter time. On their saint day, different villages serve different specialties. Residents in Conca dei Marini devour *"Santarosa sfogliatella"*—cakes in the shape of a nun's hood, made from milk, sugar, dried cherries, and dough mixed with San Nicola wine.

Wine here is light, drinkable, and inexpensive, and often consumed mere months after crushing; don't be surprised if it's the color of beer, and served from a jug (*"sfuso"*–loose wine). Practically all of it comes from Campania, often from the town or village in which it's poured, perhaps even from the restaurant's own centuries-old vines. Little of it transports well. Furore, Gragnano, and Ravello produce good bottled wines, both rosso and bianco, with Furore's Cuomo perhaps the finest white. In Sorrento look for rosolio, a liqueur traditionally served to Neapolitan nobles, created by the court of the French king Louis XIV. But the most renowned local digestif is limoncello, capturing in a bottle the color, fragrance, and taste of those tart-sweet lemons. Drink it cold in a tiny, frosty glass or after a shot of hot espresso—a golden memory quenched with each sip.

Although a few restaurants are world renowned, most are family affairs, with *papà* out front, the kids serving, and mamma, aunts, and even old *nonna* in the kitchen. Smile a bit, compliment the cuisine, and you're apt to meet them all.

CATEGORY	COST*
$$$$	over €21
$$$	€14–€21
$$	€7–€14
$	under €7

per person for a main course at dinner.

Festivals

Holy week tableaux and processions in Sorrento and its neighboring towns, Christmas trees fashioned from bougainvillea in Positano, crèches under water at the Emerald Grotto, ancient regattas and pageants in Amalfi, music festivals overlooking the gardens and coastline in Ravello—here, festivals and holidays celebrate the sea, the mild nights, and the beauteous, historic surroundings as well. And each town has its own Saint's Day, with huge quantities of special foods and revelry long into the night. Check out individual listings for further information on these celebrations, and other seasonal cultural festivities. And if possible, consider them when booking.

Lodging

The ghosts of a trysting Garbo in Ravello or ailing Caruso in Sorrento haunt the hotel corridors. Because of logistics, major chains are absent for the most part, and, consequently, the lodging scene offers a true sense of place. Sorrento's 18th- and 19th-century cliffside villas and palazzos, with their big gardens and grand staircases, huge baths and tile floors, have been transformed into spacious hotels, as have

Amalfi's former convents with their peaceful cloisters. *Agriturismo* (country living) sets up farmhouse stays in rural and upland areas; check with local tourist boards.

Great vistas, and balconies from which to ponder them, are available at most lodgings along these coasts. Air-conditioning, phones, and cable TVs are usual at all but the most basic establishments, and a light breakfast is usually included in the price. Few business or fitness centers are available—who needs them here?—even at luxury establishments. Reserve ahead, as hotel rooms are scarce in high season and may be closed altogether in low. **When booking, keep in mind that some hotels offer or require half or even full board and minimum stays in July and August, and around holidays.**

When arranging your booking, find out whether parking is included in the room fee if you're traveling by car. Many guests have nasty shocks in Positano and Amalfi when they find they have to shell out up to €20 per day for parking a car that they're unlikely to use during their stay. Porterage is run by cooperatives, not by hotels, in central Positano and Amalfi, and is another extra charge to be factored in.

Most lodgings in this part of Campania have been owned by the same families for generations, and whether the owner is plain mamma-and-papà or an heir to a ducal line, personality is evident. Along with local management may come quirks, even in the fanciest establishments—floors that dip a bit, faucets off-center, wake-up calls when you're already brushing your teeth. But you just may get your hand kissed or an invitation to chat, or get to know a glossy family dog named Lorenzo, or a cat named Luca, and isn't that sort of thing more memorable in the long run?

CATEGORY	COST*
$$$$	over €220
$$$	€130–€220
$$	€70–€130
$	under €70

All prices are for a double room at high season, excluding tax and service.

Shopping

In the 19th century, travelers to Sorrento loved shopping for regional trifles—local crafts, embroideries, ceramics, inlaid wooden furniture (intarsia), music boxes, dolls in tarantella costumes—and, today, these rather kitschy gifts still enchant the hordes of shoppers along Sorrento's Via San Cesareo. The most esteemed products in the Amalfi Coast area are ceramics from Vietri sul Mare, but some towns also produce local pottery. Amalfi still produces some fine handmade paper, an industry since the Middle Ages. Ravello offers coral jewelry and wines; and Positano is world famous for its handmade, blazingly colorful resortwear. Lemon-based goods of all sorts are available, and foodstuffs include honey, citrus and olive products, and pasta. Bargaining is acceptable sometimes, and as everywhere, prices are best where the locals trade. Shops stay open late, 'til 9 or so, but close from about 3 to 5.

Vistas

Dolce far niente—literally "the sweetness of doing nothing"—seems the major leisure activity around here, and balustrade bend, belvedere gaze, and bench butt are by-products of gazing. The Sorrento area and the Amalfi Coast are studded with belvederes ("beautiful sights") and rest stops built on the roadside for you to pull off safely, especially important if you're the driver and miss what your passengers are oohing and ahhing about. Sorrento's cliffside bay vistas are wider and more serene than the Amalfi Coast's mountain-meets-sea drama. Positano and Ravello have the most dramatic in-town vistas, although great ones peek out and pop up just about everywhere. The Lattari mountains behind the coast are exceptional for wider panoramas. When booking hotels, ask to be on the water side, throw open the shutters, and, at least once, worship the sun: rising on the Amalfi Coast, setting in Sorrento, or doing both on the peninsula.

Walking and Hiking

Throughout this entire region, walking *is* hiking, so be prepared. Positano, where streets usually take the form of staircases, is a resort where you may leave more fit than when you arrived. These towns are picturesque for a reason, and you've probably never seen so many flights of steps—those bothersome scalinatelle: thousands of them, down to the beaches, up to churches, across the hills. Getting around will take a healthy set of lungs, strong calves, time-outs for rest, comfortable shoes, and a big bottle of Ferrarelle water—slow and steady is the way to go. As for intentional hiking, mule paths and footpaths were the only land-means to get around before the car, and most remain in place for hikers' delight. The Sorrento Peninsula has several downhill paths from hubs such as Sant'Agata sui due Golfi, and you can even hike the highlands from Positano to Agerola and thence to Amalfi and Ravello. Check out Julian Tippett's excellent walking book, *Landscapes of Sorrento and the Amalfi Coast* (Sunflower Press), often found at bookstores and newsstands in the area. Even if you're not in shape, you can still participate: take transportation uphill, and let gravity help get you down.

Exploring Sorrento, the Sorrento Peninsula, and the Amalfi Coast

From Sorrento on the north coast of the Sorrento Peninsula to Vietri at the eastern edge of the Amalfi Coast, from the Bay of Naples to the Bay of Salerno, this small ledge of land is a poem of compressed beauty, with two main "verses" and a bridge. Sorrento, on the Bay of Naples, is set solidly on a steep cliff, and neighboring towns slope over the gulf, with deep valleys breaking the terraced watershed behind. The rural, sometimes mountainous peninsula is rimmed by both bays, and two narrow, winding roads, Statale (or State Highways) 145 and 163, feed into the Amalfi Drive at the peninsula's southern edge, which faces the Bay of Salerno, near Positano. If you think a road is just for getting from here to there, the twisty Amalfi Drive is not for you. The natives joke that to journey it from end to end by car in the English manner takes three hours; in the Italian style, a half hour. The going is tense until Minori—as John Steinbeck once observed, the Amalfi Drive "is carefully designed to be a little narrower than two cars side by side"—then tapers off; expect the ride of your life.

Numbers in the text correspond with numbers in the margin and on the Sorrento, Sorrento Peninsula, Amalfi Coast, and Amalfi maps.

Great Itineraries

The coastal sections—steep, winding, and ultrascenic—can only be traversed by boat or by two-lane roads. When driving round-trip, many choose to go only in one direction on the coastal roads, going the other way via the highway at Salerno or by train from Salerno or by boat from Amalfi or Positano. If a once-over of the region's most fascinating sights is enough, three days will allow you to see Sorrento, Amalfi, and Ravello—the musts. A practical minimum for an overview of the splendors to be found on the Sorrento Peninsula, and in Positano, Paestum, and smaller villages along the coast, is five days. To take in the entire span from Sorrento to Paestum, you can put together a glorious 10-day trip.

If staying in one place is a priority, and you aren't going exploring, start by picking a favorite base. If you want to comb the coasts, it's best to plan at least two overnight destinations. **Sorrento** ①–⑨ could be one hub, especially if you're interested in covering the tip of the Sorrento Peninsula. You can get to the Amalfi Coast by private or public transport, and by boat, ferry, and hydrofoil, and also to Naples and environs, and the islands of Capri or Ischia. And the train from Sorrento will deposit you right in front of Pompeii. You'll need a day to enjoy the Sorrento area, plus another leisurely day exploring the Sorrento peninsula, enjoying the best beaches in the area or a rural hike. For the third day, whizzing past the Sorrento Peninsula, it's a rise-early, full-day excursion along the Amalfi Drive with a drive through **Positano** ⑮, a stop at the Emerald Grotto in **Conca dei Marini** ⑳, and brief stops in **Amalfi** ㉑–㉛, at least for the Duomo, and in **Ravello** ㉝ for the villas and a panoramic view; if you want to linger, you can return from Salerno to Sorrento at night via the highway and Sorrento coast. If you prefer more time along the coast rather than the peninsula, or if you want to visit **Paestum** ㊵, spend one of your nights in Amalfi; in so doing, you'll also be able to enjoy nearby adorable **Atrani** ㉜. If you don't mind staying overnight in three different places, a day each in Sorrento and Amalfi and a third day in Ravello or Positano would maximize this brief regional experience. If you're traveling by water, keep in mind that Sorrento, Positano, Amalfi, and Salerno have the most frequent connections. And although these itineraries start in Sorrento, you could travel east to west on the coastal roads just as easily—but remember if you want to stay late and return to Sorrento, you don't want to take rural, scenic roads at night.

With the three-day itinerary as a base, add the extra two days wherever you feel you want to spend more time relaxing or sightseeing. You might stay two days each in **Sorrento** ①–⑨ or **Amalfi** ㉑–㉛, and spend the fifth either in **Positano** ⑮, with its shops and resort atmosphere, or calmer **Ravello** ㉝, with its gardens, villas, and panoramic views. After reading this chapter you'll have a better idea.

With a 10-day tour, you'll have the luxury of staying on at your favorite places, and still being able to see just about everything of note in the region. After enjoying **Sorrento** ①–⑨ and environs, work your way slowly south across the Sorrento Peninsula, then along the Amalfi Coast, and include a separate day trip to **Paestum** ㊵ for a rousing finale. You can take the highway or train back from **Salerno** ㊴ to Naples, Rome, or wherever, on the tenth day. A possible itinerary would be three days in Sorrento and environs; one day at a small rural town by a beach, such as Marina della Lobra below **Massa Lubrense** ⑬ or **Marina del Cantone** ⑭ or, by the sea, sublimely exquisite **Conca dei Marini** ⑳; one day in **Positano** ⑮; two in **Amalfi** ㉑–㉛; and two in **Ravello** ㉝. If visiting from May to October, some travelers will want to fit in a long day exploring coves, islets, and grottoes—either by land or through a blissful sea cruise.

When to Tour Sorrento and the Amalfi Coast

Sheltered by the Lattari mountains arcing east to west across the peninsula and inland from the Amalfi Coast, and exposed to cool breezes from two bays, the region of the Sorrento Peninsula and the Amalfi Coast enjoys a climate that is among the mildest in Italy; the temperature rarely falls below 50°F (10°C) in winter, or climbs above 90°F (31°C) in summer. Winter is least crowded but is sometimes overcast, and many hotels close from November to March. Easter time can also be rainy—locals call it *passione de Pasqua* ("tears of passion"), and assume it will rain on Good Friday. On Italian public holidays (Easter Monday, April 25th, and May 1st) and Sundays, the roads heave with lemming-like Neapolitan motorists, so if you plan on taking a long walk in the country, schedule it for these busier days. Although April and May are sublime, Italian students are then on break and can overrun major sites. Summer is filled with festivities and offers the best weather for sunning and swimming, bringing dense crowds and higher prices, especially during the middle two weeks of August, when Italians vacation en masse.

SORRENTO AND THE SORRENTO PENINSULA

Like the familiar song "Come Back to Sorrento," with its long-held closing notes like a mournful cry (listen to the Pavarotti version and you may shed a tear yourself), Sorrento's beauty is tinged with melancholy. Its streets seem like 19th-century sepia photographs, vestiges of the Roman Empire's ruins are strewn about, and banks of votive offerings of hopeful Sorrentines flicker in the crypt of the basilica of Sant'Antonino. Vesuvius looms in the distance. And with the sun's heart-stopping descent into the Bay of Naples, the isle of Capri fades into the purple twilight, as if disappearing forever. But touched with sadness or not, Sorrento is a temptress above all. Around the 6th century BC, Greeks appear to have settled in the area, and the town was given the name Surrentum—"city of the Sirens." A brief period of Etruscan occupation followed, then Oscans and Romans came; later rulers included Goths and Byzantines, followed by sacking Lombards, Saracens, and Amalfitans. Next were the Normans, in the early part of the 12th century, and the beneficent Aragonese. Decimated in 1558 by the Turks, the city later rebuilt its walls, and in the early 1700s began a comeback which peaked in the following century when Sorrento became a prescribed stop for "Grand Tour" travelers, who sopped up its culture and history and savored its mild winters. Among the literati who played and wrote here were Byron, Keats, Scott, Dickens, Goethe, and Ibsen. According to a letter from his traveling companion in 1876, the philosopher Nietzsche, not known for effervescence, "laughed with joy" at the thought of going to Sorrento, and French novelist Stendhal called it "the most beautiful place on earth."

The tourist industry that began centuries ago is still dominant, although the lords and ladies of bygone days have been replaced with (mainly English) tour groups. Sorrento has become a jumping-off point for visitors to Pompeii, Capri, and Amalfi, but you will probably come to love it for itself. The Sorrentine people are fair-minded and hardworking, bubbling with life and warmth. The tufa cliff on which the town rests is like a great golden pedestal spread over the bay, absorbing the sunlight in deepening shades through the mild days, and orange and lemon trees waft a luscious perfume in spring. In the evening, people fill cafés to nibble, sip, and talk nonstop; then, arms linked, they stroll and browse through the maze of shop-lined lanes. The central piazza is named after the poet Torquato Tasso, born here in 1544. What greater delight than a cozy, burnished town that commemorates a poetic native son—and serves great pasta, too? Chances are, you will *torna a Surriento* ("come back to Sorrento"), as the famous song's lyrics predict. Or, at least, hope to.

The Sorrento Peninsula is bounded on the east by Monte Faito, to the west by Punta della Campanella, to the south by the Monti Lattari (Lattari mountains), and to the north by the Bay of Naples. Filled with forests, vineyards, and olive groves, its largely rural landscape belies its role as a center of hedonism, starting when Roman emperor Augustus designated Sorrento a "place of delights," and it has been one ever since. To reach the relaxing, rural western and southern sections of the peninsula, follow Statale 145 or 163 for a one- or two-day excursion. Or hire a boat to take you around the coast to some of the isolated beaches, set among ruins and watchtowers reachable only by footpath or boat.

Sorrento

48 km (30 mi) south of Naples; 50 km (31 mi) west of Salerno.

A city of under 20,000, Sorrento's population swells with tourists in season, all of whom are here to luxuriate in Italy's prettiest Belle Epoque resort. Winding along a cliff above a small beach and two harbors, the town is split in two by a narrow ravine formed by a former mountain stream. To the east, dozens of hotels line busy Via Correale along the cliff—many "grand" according to their names, and some, indeed, still are. Farther east (and usually out of sight of most tourist itineraries) is modern Sorrento, engulfed in a wave of "concretitis" (Fodor's has received more than one letter despairing of this "ugly" Sorrento, and if you make the wrong turn, you can easily think the city is only made up of apartment blocks and other modern detritus). To the west, however, is the historic sector, which still enchants all— a relatively flat area, with winding, stone-paved lanes bordered by balconied buildings, some joined by medieval stone arches. This part of town is a delightful place to walk, especially in the mild evenings, when people are out and about, and everything is open. Craftspeople are often at work in their stalls and shops and are happy to let you watch; in fact, that's the point.

Most visitors arrive at the Stazione, the end of the line for the Circumvesuviana Railway; a 10-minute walk to the left along Corso Italia will bring you to the Piazza Tasso and the center of the historic quarter. At the station (which also functions as the main bus terminal), note the bust of Ernesto De Curtis, composer of *Torna a Surriento,* that music-box anthem you'll find yourself humming or whistling long after you return home.

A Good Walk

Begin at Sorrento's historic center, **Piazza Tasso** ①, watched over by the statues of the eponymous poet and the city's patron saint, St. Anthony Abbot. Avoid congested Corso Italia and head instead to the southeast corner of the piazza to Via Pietà to take a look at the noted Palazzo Veniero (No. 14) and the **Palazzo Correale** ② (No. 24), whose 18th-century majolica courtyard, now a flower shop, overflows with charm. Follow this street until you reach the Largo Arcivescovado, site of the **Duomo dei SS Filippo e Giacomo** ③. After viewing this grand cathedral, head for its wedding-cake campanile, making a right off Corso Italia down Via Giuliani to enter Sorrento's most picturesque quarter. Here, on Via S. Cesareo, is the beautifully frescoed **Sedile Dominova** ④, the ancient, open-air site of civic discourse. At night, its little square, called the Largo Dominova, is illuminated and makes a fetching backdrop for diners at Caffè 2000. Return to Piazza Tasso along Via S. Cesareo, lit with 19th-century lanterns and one of Sorrento's most picturesque streets. When you arrive at the edge of Piazza Tasso, turn left toward the bay, a block or so along Via De Maio, to pretty Piazza S. Antonino, the site of stately palm trees and the 11th-century **Basilica di Sant'Antonino** ⑤. Across the piazza is the Municipio (town hall), the former monastery of Santa Maria delle Grazie, with cloister and

Sorrento

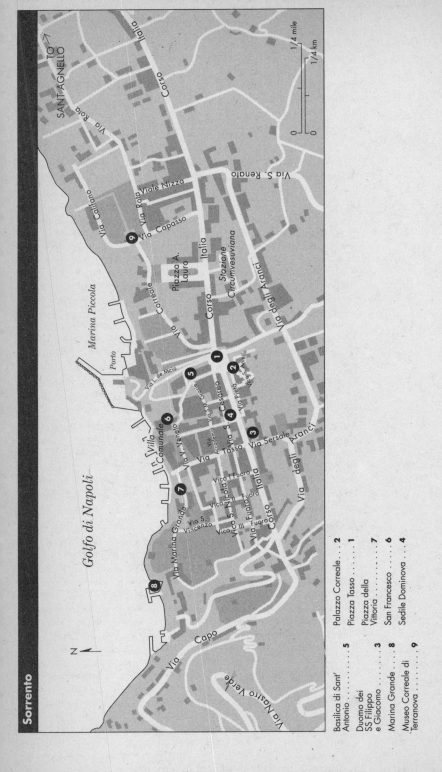

SANT'AGNELLO →

Golfo di Napoli

Marina Piccola

Porto

Via Rota

Corso

Italia

Viale Nizza

Via Rota

Via Capasso

Via Califano

Via Correale

Via del

Piazza A. Lauro

Italia

Corso

Stazione Circumvesuviana

Via S. Renato

Via degli Aranci

Via L. de Mcio

Via V.S.M.Grande

Via Cesareo

Via S. Angelo

Via Pietà

Via S. Cesareo

Comunale

Villa

Via V. Veneto

Via Accademia

Via Tasso S.

Via Sersale

Via degli Aranci

Vico I Fuoro

Vico II Fuoro

Vico S. Nicola

Vico III Fuoro

Via Fuoro

Via Fuoro

Corso Italia

Via S. Vincenzo

Via Marina Grande

Capo

Via

Via Nastro Verde

N

1/4 mile

1/4 km

Basilica di Sant' Antonio **5**

Duomo dei SS Filippo e Giacomo **3**

Marina Grande **8**

Museo Correale di Terranova **9**

Palazzo Correale ... **2**

Piazza Tasso **1**

Piazza della Vittoria **7**

San Francesco **6**

Sedile Dominova ... **4**

church. From there, take Via Santa Maria delle Grazie and Via Don-norso to the church of **San Francesco** ⑥, and its legendary 14th-century "Paradise" cloister. Relax in the adjoining Villa Comunale gardens and enjoy their Cinerama-wide view of the Bay of Naples. Keep going west along Via Veneto to the **Piazza della Vittoria** ⑦. Here the rear facade of the Hotel Tramontano bears a faded "Casa di Tasso" sign, marking the birthplace of the revered poet. Cross the piazza to the aristocratic Hotel Bellevue Syrene, perhaps to enjoy a drink on the hotel's garden belvedere out front. At the back of the hotel is the Villa Pompeiana, a re-creation of a Pompeian villa built for Lord Astor (whose own magisterial house, beautifully restored by new owners, is just along the cliff) and now the restaurant of the hotel. Its spectacular terrace offers a café for luncheon snacks, although you may wish to time yourself instead for luncheon at the albergo Lorelei et Londres (☞ below). Continue past the hotel to exit the walls near the Porta Greca (Greek Gate), and take the stairway down to the fishing port of **Marina Grande** ⑧, where seafood restaurants have good deals. Catch a bus on the Via del Mare (they run very frequently) back up to the old town, or just hike back along Via Marina Grande and the Strettoia San Vincenzo. Once back at Piazza Tasso, walk east along the Via Correale, lined by villas-turned-hotels, to the **Museo Correale di Terranova** ⑨, where its collection of ancient artifacts is set within a pretty garden. End the walk by heading towards the bay to Via Califano and its albergo Lorelei et Londres, a relentlessly picturesque 19th-century pensione; its magical terrace café, which seems to levitate over the Bay of Naples, is the perfect spot for an idyllic luncheon, sundowner drink, or dinner.

TIMING
This complete walk is most enjoyable if you leave sufficient time for discovery and rests; if you wish to include everything, allow at least half a day. If you're not planning to tour the Museo Correale (which is open only until 2 in the afternoon), you may want to throw a sweater over your shoulders the way the Italians do and start your walk—but call it a promenade—in late afternoon; even if you don't visit the Museo Correale, we suggest a walk in that direction, as a visit to the terrace café of the albergo Lorelei et Londres should be an unmissable part of your Sorrento sojourn.

Sights to See

❺ **Basilica di Sant'Antonino.** Gracing Piazza Sant'Antonino and one of the largest churches in Sorrento, the Basilica di Sant'Antonino honors the city's patron saint, St. Anthony Abbot. The church and the portal on the right side date from the 10th century. Its nave and side aisles are divided by recycled ancient columns, and the interior is done in the Baroque style, with fine paintings, including one on the nave ceiling painted by Giovan Battista Lama in 1734. Directly opposite across the piazza is the turn-of-the-20th-century *Municipio* (town hall). ⊠ *Piazza Sant'Antonino.*

❸ **Duomo dei SS Filippo e Giacomo.** Ancient, but rebuilt from the 15th-century right up to 1924, the town's cathedral follows a Latin cross design, its nave and two side aisles divided by thick piers with round arches. A Renaissance-style door and artworks, including the archbishop's 16th-century marble throne and ceiling paintings attributed to the 18th-century Neapolitan school, are easily viewable. Outstanding 19th- and 20th-century marquetry ornaments a magnificent choir loft, entrance panels, and representations of the stations of the cross. Look for the unusual 10th-century marble slab used as a gravestone, with a lioness on the front and a depiction of the deceased on the back. The delightfully florid three-story campanile, topped by a clock and a belfry, has an open, arcaded base and recycled Roman columns. ⊠ *Largo Arcivescovado, at the corner of Corso Italia and Via. R.R. Giuliani.*

Espresso and sweet, raisin-stuffed lemon leaves make a fine afternoon delight at **Piemme** (⊠ Corso Italia 161, ☎ 081/8072927).

❽ Marina Grande. Close to the historic quarter (but not that close—many locals prefer to use the town bus to shuttle up and down the steep hill), the port, or "borgo," of the Marina Grande is Sorrento's fishing harbor. There is a small beach area with its *stabilimento* (beach concession), complete with colorful changing cabins and bright umbrellas, and a few good seafood restaurants within easy reach. It's especially picturesque in early morning, when water-weary fishermen head in, their primary-color boats brimming with the day's catch. Don't confuse this harbor with Marina Piccola, at the base of the cliff, below Piazza Tasso and the Hotel Excelsior Vittoria; that is the area where ferries and hydrofoils dock. ⊠ *Via del Mare.*

❾ Museo Correale di Terranova. Set in an 18th-century villa and lovely garden on land given to the patrician Correale family by Queen Joan of Aragon in 1428, this museum has an excellent private collection amassed by the count of Terranova and his brother. The building itself is fairly charmless, with few period rooms, but the garden offers an allée of palm trees, citrus groves, floral nurseries, and an esplanade with a panoramic view of the Sorrento coast. The collection itself is one of the finest devoted to Neapolitan paintings, decorative arts, and porcelains, so for connoisseurs of the Seicento (Italian 17th century), this museum is a must. Magnificent 18th-century inlaid tables by Giuseppe Gargiulo, Capodimente porcelains, and rococo portrait miniatures remind us of the age when pleasure and delight was all. Also on view are regional Greek and Roman archaeological finds, medieval marble work, glasswork, old master paintings, 17th-century majolicas—even Tasso's death mask. ⊠ *Via Correale 50,* ☎ *081/8781846.* 💶 €5.16. ☼ *Wed.–Mon. 9–2.*

★ ❷ Palazzo Correale. Just off the southeast corner of Piazza Tasso, this palazzo was originally built in the 14th century in Catalan style but transformed into a rococo-era showstopper, thanks to its exquisite **Esedra Maiolicata** (Majolica Courtyard, 1772), one of the many examples of majolica and faienceware, an artisanal highlight of Campanian craftsmen (other notable examples are the Chiostro delle Clarisse in Naples's Santa Chiara and the grand terrace of Positano's Hotel San Pietro). In 1610 the palazzo became the Ritiro di Santa Maria della Pietà and, today, remains private, but all can view the courtyard just beyond the vestryway. Its back wall—a trompe l'oeil architectural fantasia, entirely rendered in majolica tile—is now a suitably romantic setting for the Ruoppo florist shop. Buy a rose here and bear it through the streets of old Sorrento, an emblem of your pleasure in the moment. Leaving the palazzo, note the unusual arched windows on the palace facade, a grace note also seen a few doors away at **Palazzo Veniero** (No. 14), a 13th-century structure with a Byzantine-Arab influence. ⊠ *Via Pietà 24.*

❶ Piazza Tasso. This was once the site of Porta Catello, the summit of the old walls that once surrounded the city. Today, it remains a symbolic portal to the old town, overflowing with apricot-awninged cafés, *Stil Liberty* (Italian Art Nouveau) buildings, the people who are attracted here day and night, and horse-drawn carriages clip-clopping by. In the center of it all is Torquato Tasso himself, standing atop a high base and rendered in marble by sculptor Giovanni Carli in 1870. The great poet was born in Sorrento in 1544, and died in Rome in 1595, just before he was to be crowned Poet Laureate. Writing during a period when Italy was still recovering from devastating Ottoman incursions along its coasts—Sorrento itself was sacked and pillaged in 1558—Tasso is best known for his epic poem, *Jerusalem Delivered,* dealing with the conquest of Jerusalem during the First Crusade over 400 years before. At the northern edge of the piazza, where it debouches into Corso Italia, is the Church of Maria del Carmine, with a rococo wedding-cake facade of gleaming white and yellow stucco. Step inside to note its wall of 18th-century tabernacles, all set, like a jeweler's display, in gilded cases, and the fine ceiling painting of the Virgin Mary. ⊠ *Center of town, along Corso Italia and above the Marina Piccola, at the western edge of the historic district.*

❼ Piazza della Vittoria. Tree-shaded Piazza Vittoria is book-ended by two fabled hotels, the Bellevue Syrene and the Imperial Tramontano, one wing of which was home to famed 16th-century writer Torquato Tasso. Set by the bayside balcony, the facade of the **Casa di Tasso** is all the more exquisite for its simplicity and seems little changed from his day. The poet's house originally belonged to the Rossi family, into which Tasso's mother married, and was set with beautiful gardens (not surprisingly, Tasso's most famous set-piece—the meeting of Rinaldo and the Saracen girl Armida—takes place within a sylvan setting). The piazza itself is supposedly the site where a temple to Venus once stood, and the scattered Roman ruins make it a real possibility. ⊠ *Via Veneto and Via Marina Grande.*

★ ❺ San Francesco. Near the Villa Comunale gardens and sharing its vista over the Bay of Naples, this church is celebrated for its 14th-century cloister. Filled with greenery and flowers, the Arab-inspired cloister has interlaced pointed arches of tufa rock, alternating with octagonal columns topped by elegant capitals, supporting smaller arches, and makes a suitably evocative setting for concerts and theatrical presentations during the summer. The church portal is particularly impressive, with the original 16th-century door featuring intarsiated (inlaid) work. Note the exterior bronze work by sculptor A. Nena. The interior has 17th-century decoration including an altarpiece depicting St. Francis receiving the Stigmata by a student of Francesco Solimena. The convent is now an art school, where students' works are often exhibited. ⊠ *Piazza Gargiulo off Via S. Maria delle Grazie.*

★ ❹ Sedile Dominova. Showpiece of the Largo Dominova—the little square that is the heart of the historic quarter—this is a picturesque open loggia with expansive arches, balustrades, and a green-and-yellow-tile cupola, originally constructed in the 15th century. The open-air structure is frescoed with Baroque-era trompe l'oeil columns and the family coats of arms which once belonged to the *sedile* (seat), the town council where nobles met to discuss civic problems as early as the Angevin period, in the 15th century. The sediles resolved regional differences and members were granted privileges by powerful Naples during the days of the Spanish occupation. Today, Sorrentines still like to congregate around the umbrella-topped tables near the tiny square; in the evening, under the still vibrant and now softly illuminated frescoes, men sitting in the forecourt may still be discussing civic problems while playing cards. ⊠ *Largo Dominova, at the corner of Via S. Cesareo and Via R. R. Giuliani.*

★ Villa Comunale. The largest public park in Sorrento, this offers benches, flowers, palms, and people-watching, plus a seamless vista of the Bay of Naples and Vesuvius. From here steps lead down to Sorrento's quieter and more picturesque harbor, the Marina Grande. ⊠ *Adjoining the Church of San Francesco.*

CAPO DI SORRENTO AND THE BAGNI DELLA REGINA GIOVANNA – Just 2 km (1 mi) west of Sorrento, Statale 145 passes a cluster of buildings known as Capo Sorrento. Look for the rather faded plaque on the facade of a stately villa on the right. This is the 14-room house where Maxim Gorky lived (when he wasn't on Capri) while claiming in letters to his comrades back home in the Soviet Union that he was isolated in an apartment and suffering all kinds of cultural hardship. Take the next right toward the sea, then park and walk a few minutes through citrus and olive groves to get to Punta del Capo, the craggy tip of the cape, with the most interesting ancient ruins in the area. They were identified by the Latin poet Publius Papinius Statius as the ancient Roman villa of historian Pollius Felix, patron of the great authors Virgil and Horace. Next to the ruins are the Bagni della Regina Giovanna, where the infamous 14th-century Queen Joan of Anjou is reputed to have bathed. A cleft in the rocks allows the sea to channel through an archway into a clear, natural pool, with the water turning iridescent blue, green, and violet as the sunlight changes angles. The easiest way to see all this is to rent a boat at Sorrento, and later you can go on to the fishermen's haven of Marina di Puolo by sailing westward for lunch at a modest restaurant with fresh catch.

Dining and Lodging

$$$–$$$$ ✕ **Ristorante Caruso.** A classic international and operatic theme is carried out from "preludio" appetizers, such as Malossol caviar, to the "rapsodia delicatesse" desserts, including crêpes suzette. Sorrentine favorites are tweaked creatively as well, including ravioli with broccoli sauce and squid with almonds. The staff is warm and helpful, the singer on the sound system is the long-departed "fourth tenor" himself, and the operatic memorabilia with posters and old photos of Caruso is viewed in a flattering pink-blush light. This elegant restaurant deserves its longtime reputation and popularity. ⊠ *Via S. Antonino 12,* ☎ *081/8073156. AE, DC, MC, V.*

$$–$$$ ✕ **"La Favorita"—O' Parrucchiano.** This restaurant is set in a sprawling,
★ multi-level, high-ceilinged greenhouse and orchard, with tables and chairs amid enough tropical greenery to fill a Victorian conservatory—the effect is enchantingly 19th century. Opened in 1890 by an ex-priest (O' Parrucchiano means "the priest's place" in the local dialect), La Favorita continues to serve classic Sorrentine cuisine. Though the white-bean soup, cheese baked in lemon leaves, ravioli caprese, lemon tart, and profiteroles are all excellent, they can't compete with the unique decor. ⊠ *Corso Italia 71–73,* ☎ *081/8781321,* WEB *www.manniellohotels.it. AE, DC, MC, V. Closed Wed. mid-Nov.–mid-Mar.*

$$–$$$ ✕ **Aurora-'O Canonico.** This 100-year-old institution in the heart of Sorrento is the place for wood-oven pizza with a choice of 50 toppings, homemade gnocchi, and fresh seafood. The outdoor café, informal trattoria, and more formal ristorante sit side by side, and all are excellent. Try the *scarzette del Cardinale* (Cardinal's hat)—a special pastry here—and choose from a list of over 600 wines. ⊠ *Piazza Tasso 7/10,* ☎ *081/ 8783277,* WEB *www.ristorantecanonico.com. AE, DC, MC, V. Closed Mon.*

$$–$$$ ✕ **Delfino.** Right on the sea, you can eat in the sunshine or in a glassed-in nautical-motif dining area. Cod, anchovies, and octopus are fresh and flavorful, and this informal, economical venue also has a snack bar for light meals. You can even swim off the pier—but please: wait for half an hour after eating! ⊠ *Via Marina Grande 216,* ☎ *081/ 8782038. No credit cards.*

$$–$$$ ✕ **La Lanterna.** On the site of ancient Roman thermal baths (you can still see ruins under a glass section in the floor), this is a historic venue as well as a beloved eatery. Outdoor dining under the lanterns, or indoor under the beamed ceiling and stucco arcades, you'll enjoy *cucina*

tipica, locale e nazionale, including old favorites such as *scaloppina a marsala.* ⊠ *Via S. Cesareo 23/25,* ☎ *081/8781355. AE, DC, MC, V. Closed Wed.*

$$–$$$ ✗ **Zi 'ntonio.** The sixth generation of Uncle Tony's family now runs this rustic restaurant serving huge portions of sensational food. Choose antipasti from a spread of more than 25 dishes, then try specialties including St. Peter's fish with artichokes, lobster and lemon risotto, and savory Parma ham served with mozzarella (*delizioso!*—from the same distributor since the 1950s). Local wines are well priced. Up a chestnut-wood staircase, it's fun to eat aloft in the balcony, but all of the three floors and several rooms are evocative and filled with tiles, flags, murals, plates, and hearty diners. ⊠ *Via Luigi de Maio 11,* ☎ *081/8781623. AE, DC, MC, V. Closed Tues.*

$ ✗ **Giardiniello.** The garden is the seating of choice at this big, inexpensive, simply decorated enterprise with a congenial owner out front and mamma in the kitchen, typical of Sorrento trattorias catering to tourists as well as locals. Pizza is best for lunch; if you stick to pastas, however, you won't be disappointed. ⊠ *Via Accademia 7,* ☎ *081/ 8784616. AE, DC, MC, V.*

$$$$ 🏨 **Bellevue Syrene.** In the late 19th century, Empress Eugénie of France
★ came here for a week and wound up staying three months. You'll understand why if you're lucky enough to become a guest at this soigné retreat, magisterially placed on a bluff high over the Bay of Naples (wait until you see the view of Sorrento from the glass-enclosed lobby). One of Italy's most legendary hotels, this connoisseur's favorite is a gentle fantasia of Venetian chandeliers, Louis-Phillipe rugs, and Belle Epoque murals (some initially painted in order to make the King of Bavaria feel more at home back in the 1860s). All this luxe makes quite a contrast when you step outside and see bathers, a beach, and all of the Bay of Naples at your feet. Guest rooms are sanctums of cozy calm, and if your room doesn't have a bayside balcony, drink in the views from the grand terrace of the hotel's Villa Pompeiana restaurant (originally built in 1905 as part of Lord Astor's villa). No less an authority than Heinrich Schliemann, discoverer of Troy, who stayed here in 1868, declared the hotel's vistas of Vesuvius the grandest in the land. ⊠ *Piazza della Vittoria 5, 80067,* ☎ *081/8781024,* 𝔽𝔸𝕏 *081/8783963,* 𝕎𝔼𝔹 *www.bellevue.it. 73 rooms with bath. 2 restaurants, bar, air-conditioning, gym, beach, dock, meeting room, parking. AE, DC, MC, V.*

$$$$ 🏨 **Excelsior Vittoria.** Overlooking the Bay of Naples, this Belle Epoque
★ dream offers gilded salons worthy of a Proust heroine, gardens and orange groves, and an impossibly romantic terrace where musicians lull guests with equal doses of Cole Porter and Puccini. The complex of two mansions and two 19th-century chalets has been run by the same family for centuries; they have traded witticisms with Alexandre Dumas and Oscar Wilde, welcomed crowned heads, and comforted a dying Caruso in his final days. The public salons are virtual museums with potted palms, Victorian loveseats, and stil Liberty ornaments; like the Hotel Bellevue Syrene, this hotel offers a magical experience of staying in a veritable palace in a casual resort town. Guest rooms are usually spacious and airy, with tile floors, minimal furnishings, and balconies and terraces overlooking bay or gardens. If you—like Princess Margaret, Luciano Pavarotti, and Sophia Loren—want the full treatment, opt for the historic suites. Dine in the open-air seaside restaurant or in the magnificently grand dining hall where waiters in starched white jackets don't look a bit foolish (unhappily, critics have been waiting for years for the standards of the kitchen to improve). Outside is a lulling, better-than-Edenic park, lined with arbored promenades, shaded by orange trees, studded with statues, and home to a giant pool. Step directly outside the protected gates and you are in the heart of Sorrento. ⊠ *Piazza Tasso*

34, 80067, ☎ *081/8071044 or 800/325–8451,* FAX *081/8771206,* WEB *www. exvitt.it. 106 rooms with bath. 2 restaurants, bar, air-conditioning, pool, meeting facilities, parking. AE, DC, MC, V.*

$$$$ ⊤ **Imperial Hotel Tramontano.** What a past! Emperor Augustus's son had his villa here, millennia before this hotel was built in the 18th century near the public gardens. Italian poet Torquato Tasso was born on the site, and it still has a private 15th-century chapel from that era. In its glory days the property hosted Shelley, Byron, and Goethe, and royalty of many lands; today it sees mostly tour groups. The dining room overlooks the water, the pool nestles in a lush garden, and the view of Vesuvius remains as it was in ancient times. Rooms are large, with antiques and small balconies. The high-tech elevator gives audio instructions like the ones in department stores, and the lobby, with atrium ceiling, is a bit tacky and too pink. But how can you not fall for a place upon whose terrace *Torna a Surriento* was both written and sung for the first time? ✉ *Via V. Veneto 1, 80067,* ☎ *081/8782588 or 081/8781940,* FAX *081/8072344,* WEB *www.tramontano.com. 116 rooms with bath. 2 restaurants, bar, café, air-conditioning, pool, beach access, parking. AE, MC, V. Closed Jan.–Feb.*

$$$$ ⊤ **Royal.** Lush, landscaped gardens surround this hotel, which features a pool with sun lounges practically leaning over the bay. An elevator descends to sea level and a private beach. Inside the hotel it's quiet and cool with a spacious lobby, lounge, and indoor or alfresco dining. Ask for a quiet room with a balcony and superb view of the pool, gardens, and bay. ✉ *Via Correale 42, 80067,* ☎ *081/8073434,* FAX *081/8772905,* WEB *www.manniellohotels.it. 96 rooms with bath. 2 restaurants, 3 bars, air-conditioning, pool, beach, meeting facilities, parking. AE, DC, MC, V. Closed Nov.–Easter.*

$$$–$$$$ ⊤ **Ambasciatori.** This salmon-color stucco hotel on a cliff over the sea is gracious inside, with marble floors, antiques, period wall sconces, Oriental rugs, large windows—and a black cat. Rooms have bold mosaic tile floors and standard furnishings, but many open onto balconies or terraces with sea views. Gardens surround the pool and a spacious terrace-on-the-sea beckons guests to lounge or enjoy the occasional dances and buffet dinners organized by the Manniello family, longtime hotel owners. ✉ *Via A. Califano 18, 80067,* ☎ *081/8782025,* FAX *081/8071021,* WEB *www.manniellohotels.it. 103 rooms with bath. Restaurant, bar, 2 snack bars, air-conditioning, pool, beach, dock, meeting facilities. AE, DC, MC, V.*

$$$ ⊤ **Europa Palace.** Broad terraces overlook the Gulf of Naples and an elevator floats guests to a dock for sunning and "helio-therapeutic" bathing. High ceilings, marble floors, a grand piano, and dozens of identical pink Venetian glass chandeliers and sconces make for idiosyncratic decor. Rooms lack spark but do have romantic views from balcony or terrace. Spacious baths have old-fashioned fixtures and, like many villa reconversions, could use some updating. ✉ *Via Correale 34/36, 80067,* ☎ *081/8781501,* FAX *081/8781855. 80 rooms with bath. 2 restaurants, bar, beach, meeting rooms, parking. AE, DC, MC, V.*

$$ ⊤ **Astoria.** You may wake to pealing church bells at this clean, inexpensive little hotel on a quiet side street in the heart of the old town. The unstylish terrazzo-tile, wood-trim lobby is filled with chairs, old photos, and potted palms and looks as if it hasn't been redecorated for decades. Rooms are basic, with art nouveau touches, and you can breakfast on the terrace. Most of your fellow guests will be Brits. ✉ *Via S. Maria delle Grazie 24, 80067,* ☎ *081/8074030,* FAX *081/8771124. 34 rooms with bath. MC, V. Closed Dec.–Feb.*

$$ ⊤ **Del Corso.** This centrally located, colorful pensione is clean and basic, but with baths for all, and quirky touches such as psychedelic-patterned tablecloths and bedspreads. Fresh flowers, an occasional antique, the wooden bar in the lounge, courtyard entrances for some rooms, and rooftop breakfast room nudge up the comfort zone. Lodgings are on the second floor (an elevator is provided from the street). Front-facing rooms are noisy and only some rooms have air-conditioning. ✉ *Corso Italia 134, 80067,* ☎ *081/8071016,* ℻ *081/8073157,* 🕸 *www.hoteldelcorso.com. 20 rooms with bath. Bar, air-conditioning. AE, DC, MC, V. Closed Nov.–Feb.*

\$\$ 🏨 **Lorelei et Londres.** Dream: sunlight on lemon trees, blazing bougainvil-
★ lea, a tiny, inexpensive inn with all the warm charm of the 19th century, suspended over the Bay of Naples. Reality: the Lorelei et Londres. This amazing relic was once favored by *Room-with-a-View* ladies from England and still looks like E. M. Forster's Miss Lavish might pull up at any moment. Out front is a magnificently beautiful terrace café, aflut-ter with red awnings and tablecloths. The welcoming lobby always seems to be filled with guests' laughter, so it seems that few guests mind that the rooms upstairs are tatterdemalion, with simple beds and creaking cupboards. Ask for sea-view rooms away from the noisy road. For luxe and modernity, go elsewhere; come here to take a trip back to the 19th century. ✉ *Via Califano 2, 80067,* ☎ *081/8073187,* ℻ *081/5329001. 27 rooms with bath. MC, V. Closed mid-Nov.–mid-Mar.*

\$\$ 🏨 **Villa di Sorrento.** The best and the worst thing about this self-proclaimed "homely environment," built in 1854, is its central location—an easy walk to most attractions, but right off a noisy street, so request a room over-looking the quiet rear garden. Tile-floored rooms are meticulously clean, with Danish-modern furnishings. The lobby has wood trim, old photos, and old-fashioned touches such as embroidered antimacassars on its many, many chairs. Most rooms have either balconies or terraces, with views of the azure sea and red-clay rooftops. ✉ *Viale Caruso 6, 80067,* ☎ *081/ 8781068 or 081/8785767,* ℻ *081/8072679,* 🕸 *www.belmare-travel.com. 21 rooms with bath. Bar, dining room. AE, DC, MC, V.*

CAMPING

If you wish to enjoy the great outdoors both day and night, consider **Santa Fortunata–Campogaio** (Via Capo 41, ☎ 089/8073579, ℻ 081/ 8073590, 🕸 www.santafortunata.it), near Capo di Sorrento.

Nightlife and the Arts

At night, most weary sightseers will content themselves with dinner, then an evening passeggiata through the old quarter, topped off by cof-fee and dessert at a café. For a particularly festive *notte,* head to the Largo Dominova on Via S. Cesareo—floodlit with the 17th-century Sedile Dominova—and an inexpensive meal or nightcap at the **Caffè 2000,** with serenading musicians crooning Neapolitan favorites. Music spots and bars cluster in the side streets near Piazza Tasso, among them Tiffany, Filov and Trudy. Ask at your hotel about clubs that might in-terest you and to get the latest news. The main watering hole for Sor-rento visitors is the **Circolo dei Forestieri** (✉ Via Luigi de Maio 35, ☎ 081/8074033; closed early December–late February), traditionally packed with Americans, Brits, and Australians. Crowds begin to de-scend on this large villa (also home to the Sorrento tourist office) for an aperitif or beer at sunset, others arrive for casual dinner, while mer-rymakers hold out for the late-night band and karaoke.

The Tarantella Show (✉ Fauno Notte Club and La Mela Club, ☎ 081/ 8781021 or 081/8784463) presents tarantella dances with masks, cos-tumes, and tambourines, plus 17th-century mandolin serenades and 16th-century Neapolitan *pulcinella* (pantomime); a *passariello* (jester) is on hand.

Festas (religious festivals) include an atmospheric procession in the thick of Thursday night before Easter, with locals donning white hoods which are eerily reminiscent of the Ku Klux Klan, followed by a less awesome "black" procession on the Friday evening. Christmas has its usual accompaniment of crèches, while further celebrations are held on February 14—not St. Valentine's day, but St. Anthony's day; he's the patron saint of Sorrento.

Estate Musicale Sorrentina (⊠ cloister of the Chiesa di San Francesco) is the main cultural event of the year, offering a bevy of concerts and theatrical entertainments from the first week of July to the first week of September. Tickets usually run around €10; check with your hotel or the Sorrento tourist office for schedules and information. Throughout the year, free municipal concerts—usually jazz or classical music—are held in several other venues. Just a three-minute bus ride away in the adjacent township of Sant'Agnello, the **Concerti di Cocumella** hosts weekend chamber-music concerts between May and September at the gorgeous 17th-century Church of Santa Maria, now part of the luxurious Hotel Cocumella (⊠ Via Cocumella 7, Sant'Agnello, ☎ 081/8782933).

Shopping

The main shopping street is Via San Cesareo—along this pedestrian thoroughfare, lined with dozens of shops selling local and Italian crafts, the air is pungent with the perfume of fruit and vegetable stands. Corso Italia has more modern boutique offerings. Wood inlay (intarsia) is the most sought-after item, but you'll be surprised by the high quality of embroidery and metalwork. Keep your eye out for stalls that feature tiny crèche figures—tiny Punchinellos, hunchback dwarfs, and Magi figures.

Apreda (⊠ Via Tasso 6, ☎ 081/8782351) produces delicious *treccia* cheese, the local equivalent of mozzarella made from cow's milk. **A. Stinga** (⊠ Piazza F. S. Gargiulo 11–13, ☎ 081/8784286) is a branch of the famed family business known for marquetry and inlaid wood. Goods range from trays to furniture. **Bottega d'Arte di A.** (⊠ Via Luigi de Maio 18/20, ☎ 081/8781162) offers a top selection of old glass, tiles, and jewelry—antique and new. **Di Maio** (⊠ Via degli Archi 16) is the most celebrated name in town for inlaid wood furnishings. The store is famous for its trays, boxes, and furniture adorned with designs inspired by ancient Sorrento mosaic work. **L'Artigianato** (⊠ Via S. Cesareo 45, ☎ 081/8771583) sells attractive handicrafts in wood, ceramic, wrought iron, and other natural materials. **Rosbenia** (⊠ Piazza Lauro 34, ☎ 081/8772341) is renowned for traditional hand-embroidered linen and lace. **La Bottega del Gioiello** (⊠ Corso Italia 179, ☎ 081/8785419) employs master goldsmiths producing jewelry, including cameos and coral. **Libreria Tasso** (⊠ Via San Cesareo, ☎ 081/8071639) has a browseworthy stock of English books and maps. **Limonoro** (⊠ Via S. Cesareo 51, ☎ 081/8072782) produces the lovely local lemon liqueur, limoncello. You can observe the production process in the back of this tiny white shop, and watch the owners paint designs on the pretty bottles. **Olga** (⊠ Via Cesareo 18 on the Decumano Maggiore) sells handmade embroidered articles for children. **Stinga Tarsia** (⊠ Via L. De Maio 16, ☎ 081/8781165) has been crafting and selling fine quality marquetry and inlaid wood, coral, and cameos since 1890.

It is worth making the trek out to the **The Wine Store** (⊠ Via Capo 12, ☎ 081/8074731, start of main road leading westward out of town), which has an excellent range of competitively priced local wines and a well-versed shop manager for advice.

When you pack your MCI Calling Card, it's like packing your loved ones along too.

Your MCI Calling Card is the easy way to stay in touch when you travel. Use it to call to and from over 125 countries. Plus, every time you call, you can earn frequent flier miles. So wherever your travels take you, call home with your MCI Calling Card. It's even easy to get one. Just visit **www.mci.com/worldphone**.

EASY TO CALL WORLDWIDE

1. Just enter the WorldPhone® access number of the country you're calling from.

2. Enter or give the operator your MCI Calling Card number.

3. Enter or give the number you're calling.

Austria ◆	0800-200-235
Belgium ◆	0800-10012
Czech Republic ◆	00-42-000112
Denmark ◆	8001-0022
Estonia ★	0800-800-1122
Finland ◆	08001-102-80
France ◆	0-800-99-0019
Germany ◆	0800-888-8000
Greece ◆	00-800-1211

Hungary ◆	06▼-800-01411
Ireland	1-800-55-1001
Italy ◆	172-1022
Luxembourg	8002-0112
Netherlands ◆	0800-022-91-22
Norway ◆	800-19912
Poland ÷	00-800-111-21-22
Portugal ÷	800-800-123
Romania ÷	01-800-1800
Russia ◆ ÷	747-3322
Spain	900-99-0014
Sweden ◆	020-795-922
Switzerland ◆	0800-89-0222
Ukraine ÷	8▼10-013
United Kingdom	0800-89-0222
Vatican City	172-1022

◆ Public phones may require deposit of coin or phone card for dial tone. ★ Not available from public pay phones.
▼ Wait for second dial tone. ÷ Limited availability.

EARN FREQUENT FLIER MILES

SEE THE WORLD
IN FULL COLOR

Fodor's Exploring Guides bring all the great sights vividly to life with hundreds of photographs, fascinating historical background, and colorful anecdotes. Detailed maps and practical information keep you headed in the right direction.

Pair a **Fodor's** Exploring Guide with your trusted Gold Guide for a complete planning package.

THE SORRENTO PENINSULA: SANT'AGNELLO TO MARINA DEL CANTONE

Grand monasteries, the finest beach along the Gulf of Positano, an Edenic botanical park, and southern Italy's finest restaurant are just a few of the discoveries that await the traveler willing to leave Sorrento's Belle Epoque splendor behind and take to the scenic hills and coasts of the Sorrento Peninsula. As it turns out, many people do just that—the towns here get crowded with weekenders from Naples and Rome, and the two-lane state roads 145 and 163 are often congested. The sights here, however, are worth the bother. If you don't have a car, both blue-color SITA line and municipal orange-color buses run regularly throughout the peninsula, most routes stopping in Sorrento itself. Bus stops are frequent along the peninsula roads but it's always best to be armed with a local timetable to avoid long waits at stops. The destinations here are mapped out in two directions: Northeast of Sorrento, the route leads to Sant'Agnello di Sorrento and Meta; south of Sorrento, the road heads through Sant'Agata sue Due Golfi, Massa Lubrense, Punta Campanella, and Marina di Cantone.

Sant'Agnello

⑩ *2 km (1 mi) south of Meta; 2 km (1 mi) north of Sorrento.*

Back in the 18th and 19th century, the tiny hamlet of Sant'Agnello was an address of choice. To escape Sorrento's crowds, Bourbon princes and exiled Russian millionaires vacationed here, some building sumptuous villas, others staying at the Hotel Cocumella, the oldest hotel on the Sorrento Peninsula. Today, some modern motels blemish its main street, but Sant'Agnello still possesses a faintly ducal air. The 15th- to 16th-century parish church, Chiesa Parrocchiale di Sant'Agnello, is as lyrical as its name: swirls of lemon-yellow and white, decorated with marble-gloss plasterwork. Nearby is a spectacular belvedere, the Terrazza Punta San Francesco, complete with café, which offers a hold-your-breath view of the Bay of Naples. Sant'Agnello's two most famous estates sit side by side. In the early 19th century, the Cocumella monastery was transformed into a hotel, welcoming the rich and famous. Today, only lucky guests can enjoy its gardens, but everyone can attend the chamber music concerts presented by the hotel in its 16th-century Church of Santa Maria. Next door is the **Parco dei Principi**, a botanical park originally laid out in 1792 by the Count of Siracusa, a cousin to the Bourbons. Traversed by a diminutive Bridge of Love, this was a favorite spot for Désireé, Napoleon's first amour, who came here often. Shaded by horticultural rarities, this park leads to the count's Villa di Poggio Siracusa, a rococo iced-birthday cake of a house perched over the bay. Green-thumbers and other circumspect visitors can stroll through the park, now part of the Hotel Parco dei Principi.

Dining and Lodging

$$$$
★ ✕⊞ **Cocumella.** Cognoscenti adore this hotel, one of the most aristocratic in Italy. With a guest list littered with names like Goethe and the Duke of Wellington, set in a cliff-top garden overlooking the Bay of Naples, the Cocumella occupies a Baroque monastery, complete with frescoed ceilings, antique reliquaries, and a marble cloister. The lobby is Italian Victorian, and 19th-century grace notes continue in grand suites offering stone fireplaces, Empire bureaus, and marble-clad bathrooms, but even smaller rooms have great charm. The del Papa family have gilded this lily with a vast pool, a beauty-farm and exercise room, one

Sc. Rovigliano

0   2   4 miles

0   2   4 km

N

Castellammare
di Stabia

Terme d. Scário

Vico Equense

Golfo di Napoli

Marina di Equa

▲ M. Faito
1131

Alimuri

Moiano

Piano di Sorr.

⑪ **Meta**

Sorrento

Marina di Puolo

⑩

Positano ○

Sant'Agnello

Il Deserto

Massa Lubrense

Marina d. Lobra ○ ⑬

⑫ **Sant'Agata
sui Due Golfi**

*Golfo di
Salerno*

Annunziata ○

Metrano ○

Bocca Piccola

Términi ○ ⑭ **Marina del
Cantone**

🐚 *Li Galli*

↙ *Capri*

*Punta
Campanella*

of the most cornucopic breakfasts around, the superb Scintilla restaurant, a 90-ft-long 19th-century yacht for daily excursions on the bay, and even present summer-night chamber-music recitals in the monastery's former church. Ah, the sweet life! ⊠ *Via Cocumella 7, 84067,* ☎ *081/ 8782933,* 🗚 *081/8783712,* 🕸 *www.slh.com/cocumella. 56 rooms with bath. Restaurant, pool, hair salon, sauna, tennis court, gym, private beach, boating. AE, DC, MC, V. Closed Nov.–Mar.*

$$$–$$$$ 🏨 **Parco dei Principi.** This hotel offers the best of both worlds—a stun-
★ ningly romantic park, complete with gilded 19th-century villa, plus a hotel that is 1960s-modern. Up to a decade ago, the latter might have been considered a debit, but now that Sixties Moderne has entered the history books, this building is newly chic. In fact, when opened, this striking white-on-white structure raised the bar for Sixties design, thanks to Gio Ponti, Italy's coolest designer of the era. Inside, all is white walls, blue-glass accents, and bathing-suit friendly; outside is the fabled Parco dei Principi, the lush giardino laid out by the Duke of Siracusa, cousin to the Neapolitan Bourbons, in the early 19th century. Paths lined with rare Washingtonia palm trees and African marigolds still lead to the duke's romantic rococo villa, set on a terrace over the bay—today, a splendiferous setting for the hotel's pool area. Long a tour-group favorite, this hotel is usually jammed and is joyously festive as a result. ⊠ *Via Rota 1, 80067,* ☎ *081/8784644,* 🗚 *081/8783786. 96 rooms with bath. Restaurant, pool, beach. AE, DC, MC, V. Closed Nov.–Mar.*

Meta

⑪ *4 km (2½ mi) northeast of Sorrento; 3 km (2 mi) northeast of Sant 'Agnello.*

Set on a steep slope hovering above the gulf on Statale 145, this charming town is lined with orange trees and its ancient buildings spill right down to the sea. Off the coastal road is the church of the Madonna del Lauro, thought to be the site of an ancient temple built to worship the goddess Minerva. Outstanding are its 16th-century wooden door, and its chapel, with frescoes and wood carvings from the 18th century.

Dining and Lodging

$$–$$$ ✕🖬 **Giosue' a Mare.** Locals crowd this modern *albergo* (small hotel) and ristorante on the bay, and for good reason: it's the best food around these parts. Fish and seafood are pristine (try the cold combo), but you can have popular standbys such as veal marsala, too. If you care to stay on, compact rooms have balconies overlooking the water, tile floors, showers, and crisp blue-and-white decor. ⊠ *Via Caruso 2, 80062,* ☎ *081/8786685,* ⅎⅩ *081/5323450. 27 rooms with bath. Restaurant, air-conditioning, parking. AE, DC, MC, V.*

Sant'Agata sui Due Golfi

⓬ *7 km (4½ mi) south of Sorrento; 10 km (6 mi) east of Positano.*

Because of its panoramic vistas, Sant'Agata was an end-of-the-line pilgrimage site for beauty-lovers through the centuries, especially before the Amalfi Drive opened up the coast to the southeast. As its name suggests, this village 1,300 ft above sea level looks out over both the bays of Naples and Salerno (Sant'Agata refers to a Sicilian saint, honored here with a 16th-century chapel). However, now that the town has become slightly built up, you have to head to various locales on the town outskirts to actually take in the vistas. The most famous vantage point, however, has always been on the far north side of the hill, where an ancient Greek sanctuary was once dedicated to the Sirens of fable and legend. That choice location became **Il Deserto**, a monastery built by the Carmel fathers in the Middle Ages. Now crumbling, its famed belvedere—with panoramic views of the blue waters all around, and of Vesuvius, Capri, and the peninsula—was a top sight for Grand Tour–era travelers. To gain entry, ring the buzzer at the gate for the attendant, who will supply you with a key to the belvedere tower (the monastery often closes for religious retreats, so you must call ahead to check that it is open). To get to the Deserto from the center of Sant'Agata, with your back to the hotel, take the road to the left of the Hotel delle Palme, pass the church of Santa Maria delle Grazie, and keep walking uphill on Via Deserto. ⊠ *Via Deserto,* ☎ *081/8780199.* 🖃 *Free, but donation requested.* ☉ *Daily 3 PM–6 PM.*

Today's travelers head to Sant'Agata less for the sublime beauties of Il Deserto than for its lodging options and to dine at Don Alfonso 1890, the finest restaurant in Campania. Just across the way from Don Alfonso on the town square is the beautiful 16th-century Renaissance church of **Santa Maria delle Grazie.** The shadowy, evocative interior features an exceptional 17th-century altar brought from the Girolamini church in Naples in the 19th century. Attributed to Florentine artists, it is inlaid with lapis, malachite, mother-of-pearl, and colored marble.

Dining and Lodging

$$$$ ✕🖬 **Don Alfonso 1890.** The greatest restaurant in Campania, this is ★ the domain of Alfonso Iaccarino, who counts Prince Rainier of Monaco as one of his many fans. *Haute*-hungry pilgrims head here to feast on culinary rarities, often centuries-old recipes given a unique Iaccarinian spin. Lobster, for instance, is breaded with traditional Sorrentine "porri" flour, then drizzled with sweet-and-sour sauce influenced by the Arabian traders who came to Naples. The braciola of lamb with pine nuts and raisins is a recipe that dates back to the Renaissance period, while the cannoli stuffed with foie gras pays homage to the

Neapolitan Bourbon court. Nearly everything is home-grown, with olive oils *de nostra produzione* created on the family farm, vegetables so lovingly grown they have "bodyguards" not farmers, and even hand-churned butter, which finds its way into sublime desserts such as the *pizzo di cioccolato* (white sugar "mozzarella" on a chocolate "pizza") or the *soufflé di Nirvana*. Don Alfonso has one of the finest wine cellars in Europe, set deep in an Oscan cave—don't be surprised if the sommelier tells you his earliest bottle is a Roman amphora dating from 30 BC. For those who want to make a late night of it, Alfonso and his enchanting wife, Livia, also run an inn above the restaurant, with five apartments furnished in traditional style. ✉ *Corso Sant'Agata 13, 80064,* ☎ FAX *081/8780026. 5 apartments with bath. Restaurant, parking. AE, DC, MC, V. Closed Mon. and Tues. Oct. 1–May 31; Mon. June 1–Sept. 31; and Jan. 10–Feb. 25.*

$$ 🏨 **Sant'Agata.** If you wish to stay in this charming rural town, this comfortable hotel provides clean and pleasant lodging and a good bed to fall into after a meal at Don Alfonso 1890 or a walk to the Il Deserto belvedere. ✉ *Via dei Campi 8/A, 80064,* ☎ *081/8080363,* FAX *081/5330749,* WEB *www.hotelsantagata.com. 33 rooms with bath. Air-conditioning, parking. AE, MC, V. Closed Dec.–Feb.*

Massa Lubrense

⑬ *6 km (4 mi) southwest of Sorrento; 7 km (4½ mi) northeast of Punta Campanella.*

Near the far western tip of the peninsula, off Statale 145, the township of Massa Lubrense—settled in the 10th century and now with a population of about 12,000—sprawls its way through farming and fishing hamlets. Its name derives from the early–Middle Ages *massa* (rural dwellings) and the Latin *delubrum* (a temple, probably dedicated to Minerva). Faithful to the Angevins, it was made a duchy, and later destroyed in 1451 by Ferrante of Aragon. When the Jesuits founded a college here in the 17th century, the town grew into a cultural center. Today, Massa Lubrense is a relaxation destination, close to, but so far from, Sorrento's bustle.

Landmarking the central village, the cathedral of **Santa Maria delle Grazie,** located on the central square, Largo del Vescovado, was renovated in the late 18th century, and features a majolica pavement; in the apse is a painting of the Madonna by Andrea da Salerno. The 16th-century **Sanctuary of Santa Maria della Lobra,** on Via Marina, in the fishing village of Marina della Lobra, is on a site where pagans once worshiped. The church organ is supported by two ancient columns, perhaps from the original temple. Note also the majolica floor, the coffered ceiling, and the 18th-century wooden crucifix. The adjacent cloister was constructed in the 17th century when the complex was a Franciscan convent.

Dining and Lodging

$$–$$$ ✕ **Antico Francischiello da Peppino.** Overlooking olive groves seeming to run into the sea, this fourth-generation establishment has been welcoming hungry travelers for over 100 years. Two huge, beamed rooms with sprays of fernery, antique mirrored sideboards, hundreds of mounted plates, brick archways, old chandeliers, fresh flowers, and tangerine-hued tablecloths is quite a sight. *Tagliolini con zafferano, zucchine e gamberi* (pasta with saffron, zucchini, and prawns), ravioli with clams and arugula, and other bountiful country cuisine is *tutto buono.* ✉ *Via Partenope 27, halfway between Sorrento and Massa Lubrense,* ☎ *081/5339780. Reservations essential Sat. dinner and Sun. lunch. AE, DC, MC, V. Closed Wed. in winter.*

$$ 🏠 **Villa Pina.** This comfortable country inn across the road from the restaurant is managed by the same family who presides over the Antico Francischiello restaurant. Stick to the newer rooms with long decks and tile floors perched over the restaurant, and content yourself with serene views of the bay of Naples and Capri from the balconies. ✉ *Via Partenope 40, Massa Lubrense 80061,* ☎ *081/5339780,* FAX *081/ 8071813,* WEB *www.francischiello.com. 25 rooms with bath. Air-conditioning. AE, DC, MC, V.*

Marina del Cantone

⑭ *5 km (3 mi) southwest of S. Agata sui due Golfi; 5 km (3 mi) southeast of Massa Lubrense.*

The largest (pebble) beach on the Sorrento Peninsula attracts weekend sunworshipers and foodies determined on great country dining at the seaside restaurants here. To get to the beach, usually dotted with dozens of festive umbrellas, a slender road winds down to the sea through rolling vineyards and the small town of Nerano, ending at the Gulf of Positano near the Montalto watchtower. To escape the jam, hire a boat to visit the islets of Li Galli—Gallo Lungo, Castelluccia, and La Rotonda—which sit on the horizon to the east of the beach. They are also called Isole Sirenuse (Isles of the Sirens), after the mythical girl-group who lured unwitting sailors onto the rocks. What goes around comes around: Legend says the sirens' feet became flippers, because the Three Graces were envious of how they danced the tarantella; and, as the folkloric tale concludes, the mermaids' dancing days were really finito when they petrified into the isles themselves.

Dining and Lodging

$$–$$$ ✕ **Lo Scoglio.** Dramatically set on a pier by the beach, you can hear, smell—even *taste*—the waves from here on a rough day. For those wanting to indulge in raw mollusks, this is a no-risk restaurant thanks to owner Peppino, who selects his seafood with an expert eye—all accompanied by home-grown vegetables. Even if you only stop by for a gelato in such informal surroundings, you'll enjoy yourself immensely (especially if you're a water baby, or are accompanied by one). ✉ *Marina del Cantone, on the pier,* ☎ *081/8981026. AE, V.*

$$–$$$ ✕ **Maria Grazia.** A great story lies behind this area favorite. Signora Maria was running this little waterfront trattoria between the world wars when an aristocrat came round unexpectedly to eat with the marina fishermen; she cooked up the best she had on hand—spaghetti with stuffed zucchini blossoms. Through him, the dish and the restaurant became famous. You can still enjoy it, even without a noble title, in season. ✉ *Spiaggia di Marina,* ☎ *081/8081011. AE, DC, MC, V. Closed Wed., except in summer; closed weekdays Nov.–Feb.*

$$$$ ✕🏠 **Quattro Passi.** "A hop, skip, and a jump" is how the name of this hotel and Italian-nouvelle restaurant translates colloquially—appropriately so, since it is located just a five-minute drive above Marina del Cantone, in the groves of the peninsula hillsides. Here, the focus is on relaxation and fine food but the comfortable environs also make it a pleasure to fall into bed. The staff can even pick up and deliver diners to and from some Positano hotels. Some of the young chefs are Japanese, and their delicate touches are evident in the dollop of ham and cheese Napoléon, or a petit shrimp potpie. Dine indoors in modern white decor, on the big terrace in a lemon grove, or have a homemade limoncello in the brick-arched cantina stocked from fine vineyards north of Salerno. Guest rooms are simple, and casually elegant, with tile floors, quilts, antiques, and some two-person whirlpool tubs. This is one of the few places with absolutely no sea view, but to make up

for it, you can help harvest olives in October. This place is in Nerano, midway between Termini and Marina di Cantone. ✉ *Via A. Vespucci 13, Nerano, 80061,* ☎ *081/8082800,* FAX *081/8081271,* WEB *www. ristorantequattropassi.it. 10 rooms with bath. Restaurant, bar, air-conditioning, parking. AE, DC, MC, V. Closed Nov.–mid-Dec.*

$$$–$$$$ ✕🖫 **Taverna del Capitano.** The fascinating cuisine here is based on old
★   recipes from the various cultures—Norman and Moorish among them—that loomed large in the history of the region. The captain's son, Chef Alfonso Caputo, is a wizard at conjuring up not-available-anywhere-else combinations: for example, chicory and prawn soup, and tagliatelle with anchovies, sardines, and fennel. You can rely on the knowledge-able maitre d' for an absorbing commentary on the various dishes and advice on the right wine from a siege-ready cellar. For dessert, opt for candied eggplant filled with ricotta and topped with chocolate sauce. Above the restaurant area is a select 10-room hotel run by the same family, with the best rooms overlooking the waterfront. Lodging prices include full beach facilities. ✉ *Piazza delle Sirene 10/11,* ☎ *081/8081028,* ☎ FAX *081/8981892,* WEB *www.tavernadelcapitano.it. AE, DC, MC, V. Closed Jan.–Feb. and Mon., except in summer.*

POSITANO AND THE AMALFI COAST

Europe's unsurpassingly beautiful coastline is ". . . the only delectable part of Italy, which the inhabitants there dwelling do call the coast of Malfie, full of towns, gardens, springs and wealthy men." Thus raves Boccaccio in his 14th-century *Decameron,* writing about the Costiera Amalfitana—the Amalfi Coast. Rugged, craggy, and extending around the Bay of Salerno from Positano on the west to Vietri sul Mare on the east, this is where the Amalfi Republic held sway in the Middle Ages, when Amalfi was one of the richest towns in Italy. Today, the coast's scenic sorcery makes this a top destination, drawing visitors who gaze longingly at the surroundings almost as much as they do at each other—after all, this is a prime honeymoon location.

Statale 163—the Amalfi Drive, as we call it—was hewn from the lip of the Lattari mountains and completed in 1852, varying from 50 to 400 feet above the bay. You can thank Ferdinand, the Bourbon king of the Two Sicilies, for commissioning it, and Luigi Giordano for de-signing this seemingly improbable engineering feat. A thousand or so gorgeous vistas appear along these almost 40 km (29 mi) stretching from just outside Sorrento to Vietri, coursing over deep ravines and bays of turquoise-to-sapphire water, spreading past tunnels and time-less villages. This is the only coastal road in the region, and the slen-der two lanes hovering over the sheer drops sometimes seem impossible to maneuver by auto, let alone by buses and trucks.

Many arrive from Sorrento, just to the north, connecting to the coast through Sant'Agata sui Due Golfi on the Statale 145—the Strada del Nas-tro Azzurro (Blue Ribbon Road), whose nickname aptly describes its width, and the color at your alternating right and left. This inland region pre-sents rolling hills of olive, lemon, and orange groves and is dotted with rural hamlets. The white-knuckle part, or, as some call it, the Via Smer-aldo (Emerald Road), begins as the road connects back to Statale 163, threading through coastal ridges at Colli di S. Pietro, and continuing to wend its way around the Vallone di Positano. From ravine to ravine, Posi-tano beckons, appearing and disappearing like a flirtatious coquette. Just east of Positano, at Punta San Pietro, Statale 163 again winds sharply around valleys, deep ravines, and precipices, affording more stunning ridge views. Just past Praiano, the Furore gorge is crossed by viaduct. From here on to Amalfi, the ridges soften just a bit.

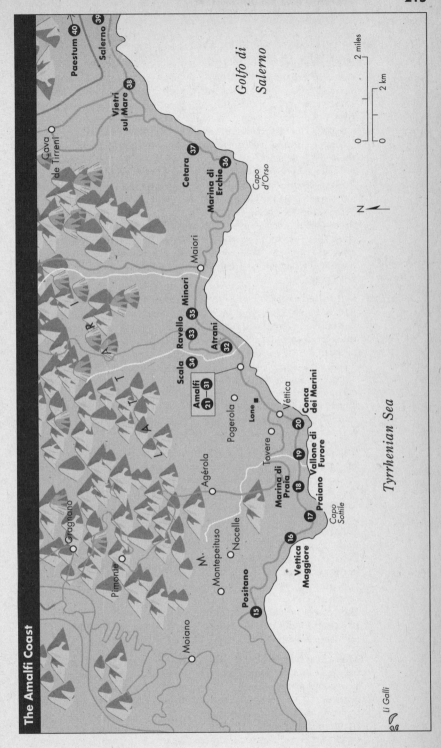

The Amalfi Coast

Golfo di
Salerno

Tyrrhenian Sea

2 miles

2 km

N

Paestum 40
Salerno 39
Vietri
sul Mare 38
Cava
de' Tirreni
Cetara 37
Marina di
Erchie 36
Capo
d'Orso
Maiori
Minori
Ravello 33
Scala 34
Atrani 32
Ravello 35
Amalfi
21 — 31
Pogerola
Véttica
Conca
dei Marini 20
Lone
Tovere 19
Vallone di
Furore
Agérola
Marina di
Praia 18
Praiano 17
Nocelle
Capo
Sottile
Montepeituso
M.
Vettica
Maggiore 16
Positano
Pimonte
Grognano
15
Moiano
Li Galli

Positano

 56 km (35 mi) southeast of Naples; 16 km (10 mi) east of Sorrento.

Positano clings to the Monti Comune and Sant'Angelo and has been called by artist Paul Klee "the only place in the world conceived on a vertical rather than a horizontal axis." Its arcaded, cubist buildings, set in tiers up the mountainside, reflect the sky in dawn-color walls: rose, peach, purple, some tinted the ivory of sunrise's scudding clouds. The colors on these Saracen-inspired dwellings may have originally served to help returning fishermen spot their own digs in an instant. Today, these visual delights have helped make this the most photographed fishing village in the world. The four thousand or so fisherfolk and other Positanesi are joined daily by hordes arriving from Capri, Sorrento, and Amalfi, eager to celebrate the fact that Positano is, impossibly, there. When John Steinbeck lived here in 1953, he wrote that it was difficult to consider tourism an industry because "there are not enough [tourists]." Alas, there are more than enough now. What Steinbeck wrote, however, still applies: "Positano bites deep. It is a dream place that isn't quite real when you are there and becomes beckoningly real after you have gone."

It may have started with bread. Roman Emperor Tiberius, son of poison-happy Livia, sent his three-oar boat to a mill in Positano, understandably afraid that his neighbors on Capri would poison him. The (now modernized) mill still grinds healthful flour, but Positano is now more than just a grocery stop. Its name could be a corruption of the Greek "Poseidon", or derived from a man named Posides, who owned villas here during the time of Claudius; or even from Roman freedmen, called the Posdii. The most popular theory is that the name "Positano" comes from Pestano (or Pesitano), a 9th-century town by a Benedictine abbey near Montepertuso, built by refugees of Paestum to the south, whose homes had been ransacked by the Saracens.

Pisa sacked the area in 1268, but when an elaborate defensive system of watchtowers was in place, Positano once again prospered, briefly rivaling Amalfi. As a fiefdom of Neapolitan families until the end of the 17th century, Positano produced silk and, later, canvas goods, but decline began again in the late 18th century. With the coming of the steamship in the mid-19th century, some three-fourths of the town's 8,000 citizens emigrated to America—mostly to New York—and it eventually regressed into a backwater fishing village. That is, until artists and intellectuals, and then travelers, rediscovered its prodigious charms in the 20th century, especially after World War II; Picasso, Stravinsky, Diaghilev, Olivier, Steinbeck, Klee—even Lenin—were just an inkling of this town's talented fans. Lemons, grapes, olives, fish, resort gear, and, of course, tourism keep it going, but despite its shimmery sophistication and overwrought popularity, Positano's chief export remains its most precious commodity: beauty.

Most car travelers leave their wheels either in one of the few free parking spaces on the upper Sorrento-Amalfi main road or in one of the scarce and pricey garages a few minutes' walk from the beach if their hotel doesn't provide parking. The best bet for day-trippers is to get to Positano early enough so that space is still available. Even those arriving in Positano by SITA bus should get a morning start, as traffic on the Via Smeraldo grows combustible by noon. The bus has two main stops in Positano: Transita, or Upper Town—near the large church of Santa Maria delle Grazie—and Sponda, or Lower Town, to the east of the main beach. Those who can't wait to start the Positano triathalon should get out at the first stop and start walking down. Most, however, opt to begin their walking tour from the Sponda bus stop. From here, it's a step to Via Cristoforo Colombo, which winds down through the heart of town toward the main beach.

Make sure you have some comfortable walking shoes—no heels, please!—and that your back and legs are strong enough to negotiate those picturesque, but daunting and ladderlike scalinatelle. If not, ride the municipal bus, which frequently plies along the one-and-only-one-way Via Pasitea, hairpinning from Positano's central Piazza dei Mulini to the mountains and back, making a loop through the town every half hour. Continuing down from the Sponda bus stop toward the beach, you pass Le Sirenuse, the hotel John Steinbeck stayed at when he wrote his famous essay for *Harper's Bazaar* in 1953. Its stepped terraces offer vistas over the town, so you might splurge on lunch or a drink here on the pool terrace, a favorite gathering place for Modigliani-sleek jet-setters. Continue to Piazza dei Mulini, and make a left turn onto the pedestrianized boutique-flanked Via dei Mulini. If you want to catch your breath after a bus ride to Positano, take a quick time out for an espresso, a slice of Positanese (a chocolate cake as delectable as its namesake), or a fresh-fruit iced "granita" in the lemon-tree garden at Bar-Pasticceria La Zagara at Via dei Mulini 8. Past a bevy of resort boutiques, head to 23 Via dei Mulini to peer into the prettiest garden in Positano—the 18th-century courtyard of the **Palazzo Murat,** named for Joachim Murat, who sensibly chose the palazzo as his summer residence. This was where Murat, designated by his brother-in-law Napoleon as King of Naples in 1808, came to forget the demands of power and lead the simple life. Since Murat was one of Europe's leading stylesetters, the Neapolitan Baroque style suited him grandly, and he is unlikely to have filed complaints about the views from the palazzo (now a hotel).

Just beyond the Palazzo Murat is the Chiesa Madre, or parish church of **Santa Maria Assunta,** its green and yellow majolica dome, topped by a perky cupola, visible from just about anywhere in town. Built on the site of the former Benedictine abbey of St. Vito, the 13th-century Romanesque structure was almost completely rebuilt in the 18th century. The last piece of the ancient mosaic floor can be seen under glass near the apse. Note the carved wooden Christ, a masterpiece of devotional religious art, with its bathetic face and bloodied knees, on view to the left of the choir stalls. At the altar is a Byzantine 13th-century wooden painting of Madonna with Child, known as The Black Virgin, carried to the main beach every August 15 to celebrate the Feast of the Assumption. Legend claims that the painting was once stolen by Saracen pirates, who, fleeing in a raging storm, heard a voice from on high, *Posa, Posa*—"Put it down, put it down." When they placed the statue on the beach near the church, the storm calmed down, as did the Saracens. Positano was saved, and the town's name was established (yet again). Embedded over the doorway of the church's bell tower, set across the tiny piazza, is a medieval bas-relief of fishes, a fox, and a Pistrice, the mythical half-dragon, half-dog sea monster. This is one of the sole relics of the medieval abbey of St. Vito. ⊠ *Piazza Flavio Gioia, just above the main beach.*

The walkway from the Piazza Flavio Gioia leads down to the **Spaggia Grande,** or main beach, bordered by an esplanade and some of Positano's best restaurants. Head over to the stone pier to the far right of the beach as you face the water. Here, a staircase leads to the **Via Positanesi d'America,** a lovely seaside walkway. Halfway up the path you'll find the Torre Trasìta, the most distinctive of Positano's three coastline defense towers, which define the edges of Positano in various states of repair. The Trasìta—now a residence occasionally available for summer rental—was one of the defense towers used to warn of pirate raids. Just beyond the tower is O'Guarracino, a stunningly idyllic, arbor-covered restaurant. Continuing along the Via Positanesi d'America, you pass tiny inlets and emerald coves until the large Spaggia di Fornillo beach comes into view.

Set 3 km (2 mi) directly above Positano, the tiny village of **Montepertuso** (Pierced Mountain) is where Emperor Frederick II of Sicily bred and trained hawks; some feathery descendants—mainly kestrels and peregrine falcons—still nest on seemingly precarious ledges around the area. The dramatic hole in the arched rock—the *arco naturale*—below Monte Sant'Angelo a Tre Pizzi, is one of only three in the world where both the sun's and the moon's rays can penetrate (April–July); the other two are in India. Try to see it in the morning, when the sun shines through. Legend says the hole was created when the devil challenged the Madonna that whoever pierced the rock would own the village. In 10 attempts, the devil could only scratch the limestone, but when the Madonna touched the rock, it crumbled, the sky appeared, and she walked right through, sinking the devil into the hole. On July 2, a holy performance, games, and fireworks commemorate the Virgin's success. Another popular village festival is the Sagra del Fagiolo, held on the last Saturday in August, which celebrates the humble bean. The tiny town is set with numerous stalls full of beans and other fare, with waiters in traditional folkloric garb (but no beanies). An easy way to ride up to the Montepertuso heights is by taking the municipal Positano bus, which leaves from Piazza dei Mulini (one-way €.80).

From Montepertuso you can hike up to the so-called lost village of **Nocelle,** pasted to the mountainside some 1,400 ft above Positano. Cloud-riding Nocelle is a carless universe: only two stone pathways and myriad scalinatelle thread the hamlet, where a tiny piazza and picturesque church look out on a panorama. To the east of the village, the **Sentiero degli Dei,** or Pathway of the Gods hiking trail, begins, climbing 600 ft up the mountain range, crossing the Lattari mountains east to Agerola. This well-trod, steep, and scattered path was once the mountaintop route connecting settlements until the Amalfi Drive was built through the rock below; it is a true challenge, but rewards with uninterrupted views the gods seem to have personally blessed.

Beaches
The Marina is the main boating area, with taupe-color, semisandy Spiaggia Grande, the largest and widest beach of the 10 or so in the area. Fishermen—once the dominant workforce—now function as a cooperative group, supplying local kitchens; they can be seen cleaning their colorful, flipped-over boats and mending their torn nets throughout the day, seemingly oblivious to the surrounding throngs. To the west of town is the less crowded Spiaggia di Fornillo; to the east a string of small, pretty beaches, separated by coves—La Porta, Fiumicello, Arienzo, San Pietro, and Laurito—most of which are accessible only by boat.

Boat Excursions
From Marina Grande you can board a scheduled day boat or hire a private one, including yachts that sleep six or more—with or without a captain—for as long as you'd like, to visit Capri, the Emerald Grotto in Conca dei Marini, or coves and inlets with small beaches. Close by, in the large cave at La Porta (650 ft east of the town center), tools, utensils, and hunting weapons from the Paleolithic and Mesolithic ages have been discovered, the oldest known remains on the coast. The favorite boating destinations, however, are the rocky Li Galli islets (6 km

[4 mi] southwest), seen from any point in Positano (as they are from the beaches of the peninsula), whose name derives from their resemblance to pecking birds. Originally the site of an ancient Roman anchorage, the islands then became medieval fiefdoms of Emperor Frederick II and King Robert of Anjou. The isles remain tempting enough to lure purchasers in search of an exclusive paradise: Russian choreographer Leonide Massine in 1925, and, in 1988, dancer Rudolf Nureyev, who discovered the islands in 1984 when he came to accept the Positano Prize for the Art of Dancing, given each year in honor of Massine. The islands are still private. **L'Uomo e il Mare** (✉ Spiaggia Grande pier, ☎ 089/811613 or 089/875211, ☎ FAX 089/875475, WEB www.sirene.it/gennaroesalvatore) is an outfit run by Gennaro Capraro and his friendly English wife, Valeria, offering boating excursions to Li Galli and many other coastal destinations. Offering both short transfers (especially to beaches and night spots) and all-day affairs, including luncheon stopovers, he usually fills up an excursion party with nine people (€77 per person, including lunch), so it's best to reserve in advance. Boating excursions can also be arranged through **Noleggio Barche Lucibello** (✉ Spiaggia Grande pier, ☎ 089/875032, FAX 089/875326, WEB www.lucibello.it), which also rents motorboats and rowboats by the hour.

Dining and Lodging

$$$–$$$$ ✗ **Donna Rosa.** This minimalist little hideaway in one-street Montepertuso, the hamlet high over Positano, is truly original. Everybody gets into the act: mamma does the creative cooking, to order, papà "makes noise," and the daughters rule out front—Rosa is the namesake nonna. Pasta has arugula *in* it, mixed with clams, mussels, porcini mushrooms, and artichokes. A dessert sampler may include orange-studded mandarin ice cream and sponge cake soaked in limoncello. Fine wine is available by the glass, live music can be anything from jazz to Australian gospel (with a daughter singing sweetly), and free car service is provided. There is a terrace, but the better view is the kitchen. ✉ *Via Montepertuso, Montepertuso,* ☎ *089/811806. Reservations essential for dinner. AE, DC, MC, V. Closed Mon.*

$$–$$$ ✗ **Chez Black.** Nicknamed after owner Salvatore Russo's eternal tan, this nautical-looking institution has been dishing out hearty Italian fare and pouring wines since just after World War II. Sip a *grotta dello smeraldo*—gin, lemon, and crème de menthe—perhaps accompanied by *foglia di limone* (grilled mozzarella in lemon leaves). Try the renowned pizza, or signature spaghetti and crayfish, or maybe grilled *scorfano* (sea scorpion). Red-checked tablecloths, a natural stone lobster tank, a jukebox, and fishermen who haul their catch right into the kitchen make up the scene, which grows festive at dinnertime. ✉ *Via del Brigantino,* ☎ *089/875036. AE, DC, MC, V. Closed Nov.–Mar.*

$$–$$$ ✗ **O' Capurale.** Positano is about easy-come elegance, and this dining
★ spot sums it all up. Graced with a coved ceiling awash with colorful Fauvist-style frescoes, the dining room is filled with happy, stylish diners, literally unwinding before your eyes, thanks to the delicious, serious food (veal cutlet in white wine and cheese crepes *al formaggio* are two favorites) and a lovely setting. Walk downstairs to wind up on a back street that has a charmingly framed view of the beach at tables set for alfresco dining. One luncheon here and you'll forget about all those ugly headlines back home. ✉ *Via Regina Giovanna 12,* ☎ *089/ 875374. AE, DC, MC, V. Closed Nov.–mid-Feb.*

$$–$$$ ✗ **O' Guarracino.** Enjoying a setting to make you fall in love, or rekin-
★ dle it (be careful who you sit with), this arbor-covered, perched-on-a-cleft aerie is about the most idyllic place to enjoy your lemon pasta and glass of vino as you watch the yachts come and go. Set a few steps

above Positano's prettiest seaside path, your view takes in the cliffs, the sea, and Torre Trasìta. Thick, twining vines, little tables covered in cloths that match the tint of the bay, and fine fish specialties are among the big pluses. The super-charming arbor-section of the restaurant is home to a pizzeria oven (adorned with an icon of Saint Pizza). ⊠ *Via Positanesi d'America, between Spiaggia Grande and Spiaggia Fornillo,* ☎ *089/875794. AE, DC, MC, V. Nov.–Mar. (open Dec. 24–Jan. 7).*

$$–$$$ ✕ **Saraceno D'Oro.** Though open also at lunchtime, this is most definitely an evening venue (the outside tables are on the other side of the busy Via Pasitea). Living up to its name, the ambience inside is distinctly Moorish without being pretentious. This is one of the few restaurants actually patronized by the local *Positanesi: Antipasti Misti* are a favorite starter, while bass with leeks, veal with provolone, and local wines are all delicious. ⊠ *Via Pasitea 254,* ☎ *089/ 812050. Reservations essential at dinner. MC, V. Closed Nov.–Feb. (open Dec. 24–Jan. 7).*

$$ ✕ **Da Adolfo.** Several coves away from the Spiaggia Grande, on a little beach where pirates once built and launched their boats, this laid-back trattoria is a favorite Positano landmark. The pirates are long gone, but their descendants now ferry you free to the private cove, round-trip from Positano (look for the boat named for the restaurant; you can also make a steep descent from the main coastal road off the hamlet of Laurito). Sit under a straw canopy on a wooden terrace to enjoy *totani con patate* (squid and potatoes with garlic and oil), then sip white wine with peaches until sundown. Some diners even swim here—so bathing suits are just fine. ⊠ *Spiaggia di Laurito,* ☎ *089/875022. No credit cards. Closed Oct.–May.*

$$ ✕ **La Cambusa.** Two stone lions guard this "pantry" right off the Marina Grande, a safe haven for tasty local cuisine for 25-plus years. Linguine with mussels and fresh fish with new potatoes and tomato sauce are among the favorites. Owners Luigi and Baldo are well known around town for maintaining high standards even during the hectic summer season. The outdoor dining terrace holds pride of place directly above the entrance to the Spiaggia Grande. ⊠ *Piazza Amerigo Vespucci 4,* ☎ *089/875432. AE, DC, MC, V. Closed Wed. except in summer.*

$ ✕ **Il Grottino Azzurro.** High on a hill above Positano, by a church on a pretty piazza, this family-run trattoria serves delicious fresh pasta and fish to locals as well as savvy tourists. Mamma will be happy to help you choose. The bus stops right near here on its regular runs, and if you want to burn off the meal, walk; it's downhill, all the way back to town. ⊠ *Via Chiesa Nuova,* ☎ *089/875466. AE, DC, MC, V. Closed Wed.*

$$$$ ✕⊞ **Le Sirenuse.** As legendary as its namesake sirens, this exquisite,
★   in-town 18th-century palazzo vies with the Hotel San Pietro for best in show, but less flamboyantly. Venetian and Neapolitan museum-quality antiques and artwork, spacious vine-entwined terraces, a private yacht for free boating excursions, refined service, and the coast's most beautiful pool terrace—*the* place to have lunch in Positano—are only parts of the whole. A world-class operation results from the noble Sersale family's constant attentions, Swiss training, and lots and lots of cash. Rooms, each one special and many with whirlpool tubs, are accented with great art and artifacts, such as antique bedsteads or refectory tables. At night the La Sponda restaurant offers some of the best (certainly some of the priciest) food in Italy. Later, repair to the aristocratic reading room or serpentine bar, where contented patrons swap experiences and toast their good luck at being here—and *here.* ⊠ *Via Cristoforo Colombo 30, 84017,* ☎ *089/875066,* ℻ *089/ 811798,* WEB *www.sirenuse.it. 61 rooms with bath. Restaurant, 2 bars, air-conditioning, pool, spa, parking (fee). AE, DC, MC, V.*

$$$$ ✕▥ **Palazzo Murat.** The location is perfect—in the heart of town, near
★ the beachside promenade, and within the shadow of Santa Maria Assunta. You enter through a bougainvillea-draped patio and garden that is one of the most drop-dead gorgeous settings in all Campania—part-orchard, part-patio, the lower section of which offers a delightful setting for dining alfresco (the restaurant—Il Palazzo—has a superb chef) and the occasional summer concert. The old wing is Positano's very grandest palazzo, with soaring limestone walls, shell sconces, and wrought-iron balconies; it was built in the early 18th century and used as a summer residence by Joachim Murat, king of Naples. The new wing, also overlooking the garden, is a modern, Mediterranean-style building with arches and terraces—it's cool, lovely, with scattered nautical motifs and tile accents, and very, very pleasant in ambience. Rooms 5, 24, and 32 have the best views of the Bay of Positano. ✉ *Via dei Mulini 23, 84017,* ☎ *089/875177,* ᶠᴬˣ *089/811419,* ᵂᴱᴮ *www.palazzomurat.it. 32 rooms with bath. Restaurant, bar, air-conditioning (new wing). AE, DC, MC, V. Closed Jan.–Mar.*

$$$$ ✕▥ **San Pietro.** Extraordinary is the word for this luxurious oasis, fa-
★ vored by the likes of Julia Roberts and Princess Caroline of Monaco, both of whom prefer this place since it's several leagues out of town (a shuttle bus whisks you back and forth), far from the crowds and any paparazzi. The place itself is more than camera-ready: Set on a cliff high over the sea, with seven levels of gardened terraces, the San Pietro has a frilly, pretty decor that mixes modern (the hotel was built in the early 1970s) with magnificent (great antiques, elegant Vietri tilework). Who can resist idling away hours on the famous majolica benches of the grand terrace? Before you spreads a God's view of Positano and its bay, magnificently framed by gigantic urns of flowers. Most of the elegantly furnished rooms come with terraces (most look out to the sea, not toward Positano) and plate-glass views; room decors mix chic and charming in best country-style manner. The pool on an upper level is not large, so most guests opt to take the elevator fit for James Bond through hundreds of feet of mountainside to the private beach and beach bar, where Mozzarella and Pomodoro, the bilingual macaws, greet you. The proprietors organize boating excursions and parties, while the restaurant's menu is both ambitious and stylish. Don't you dare leave without trying the hotel's incredibly delicious signature drink, called Elephant's Milk. ✉ *Via Laurito 82, 84017,* ☎ *089/875455,* ᶠᴬˣ *089/811449,* ᵂᴱᴮ *www.ilsanpietro.it. 60 rooms with bath. Restaurant, 2 bars, pool, tennis court, beach, dock. AE, DC, MC, V. Closed Nov.–Mar.*

$$$–$$$$ ✕▥ **Buca di Bacco.** The *Buca* in this hotel and restaurant's name is for tavern and the *Bacco* for the Greek god of wine. Originally an early 19th-century mansion that became a nightspot, its cellar boîte attracted artists and intellectuals at the turn of the last century and still maintains its party roots. Upstairs, white-on-white guest rooms have balconies and tile floors, while suites feature glass walls with sliding doors to field-stone terraces or gardens. The restaurant acts as a town hub. Specialties include the Buca's signature *arancini* rice croquettes, along with *zuppa di cozze* (mussel soup), fresh *spigola* (bass), and figs and oranges in caramel, which can be enjoyed in the upstairs loggia dining room, with its fetching geranium-bordered view of the beach. (The street-level bar-rosticceria confusingly has the same name but is under different management.) ✉ *Via Rampa Teglia 4, 84017,* ☎ *089/875699,* ᶠᴬˣ *089/875731,* ᵂᴱᴮ *www.bucadibacco.it. 47 rooms with bath. Restaurant, air-conditioning. AE, DC, MC, V. Closed Nov.–Mar.*

$$$$ ▥ **L'Ancora.** Close to everything—set back a little from the main road and just a few minutes up from the main beach—this sunny Mediterranean-style hillside hostelry commands expansive views of the deep blue, and of local color, too. The lobby has a sprinkle of an-

tiques, while the recently upgraded guest rooms are bright with local artwork and boldly patterned mosaic tiling. All rooms have balconies or terraces and sea views. ✉ *Via Cristoforo Colombo 36, 84017,* ☎ *089/875318,* FAX *089/811784. 14 rooms with bath, 2 suites. Air-conditioning, free parking. AE, DC, MC, V.*

$$$$ 🏨 **Le Agavi.** Most Positano hotels are set near the sea or on the lower hillsides of town, but Le Agavi is just steps from the sky-high Belvedere di Positano and offers views of the entire town below. Organically constructed from local stone in a succession of greenery-draped terraces (including agave, a kind of cactus), this hotel seems to be built right into the mountainside. A tiny funicular connects the levels that waterfall down (note that rooms close to the rails can be disturbed by mechanical noises). Spacious lobbies and public rooms are eclectic: modern design, wooden floors, Empire and Italianate furnishings, Oriental rugs and accessories, and important antiques. Guest-room balconies jut out over truly dizzying heights—people with vertigo beware! For swimming you can choose between the lavish pool area, which seems to float over all Positano, or take an elevator to the private beach—a treat in a town where most share the sand body-to-body. ✉ *Via G. Marconi 127, 84017,* ☎ *089/875733,* FAX *089/875965,* WEB *www.agavi.com. 55 rooms, 15 suites with bath. 2 restaurants, bar, air-conditioning, pool, beach, business services, meeting room, parking. AE, DC, MC, V. Closed Nov.–Mar.*

$$$$ 🏨 **Covo dei Saraceni.** In Positano sea and town interact, and you see this best from the Covo dei Saraceni, perched on the main beach at the foot of Monte Comune, just steps from the main pier. Modern, charming, and increasingly luxe, this large hotel has a rooftop pool and bar set over the sea. Crisp and cool, the lobby is built around a curved staircase (with a bit too much glitzy marble for some tastes). The Bougainvillea restaurant features a pizza oven, its glass-walled dining area overhung with namesake vines. Guest-room decor is simple but stylized, with wrought-iron balconies; newer rooms and suites are ultra-deluxe and spacious, with whirlpools, larger terraces, and fanciful furnishings. The major plus here is a blissful location—you'd need to stay on a yacht to get any nearer the bay. ✉ *Via Regina Giovanna 5, 84017,* ☎ *089/875400,* FAX *089/875878,* WEB *www.summithotels.com. 61 rooms with bath. 2 restaurants, bar, snack bar, air-conditioning, pool, health club. AE, DC, MC, V. Closed Nov.–mid-Mar.*

$$$$ 🏨 **Poseidon.** One of the most popular and well-liked hotels in Positano, this was built 50 years ago by the Aonzos, the same family running it today. Set in a citrus grove high up the hillside, it offers views over central Positano from its rooftop terrace with pool, sitting room with fireplace, and bar and restaurant. Public rooms have potted palms and ferns, Oriental rugs, marble or terra-cotta floors, a baby grand, and Asian and Mediterranean accents. Enjoy tea in a quiet corner or order a low-calorie specialty in the café. Most guest rooms have sea-view terraces. ✉ *Via Pasitea 148, 84017,* ☎ *089/811111,* FAX *089/875833,* WEB *www.starnet.it/poseidon. 40 rooms with bath. Restaurant, bar, air-conditioning, pool, hair salon, gym, parking (fee). AE, DC, MC, V. Closed Jan. 6–Mar.*

$$$ 🏨 **Casa Albertina.** Clinging to the cliff, this little house is well loved for its Italianate charm, its homey restaurant, and its owners, the Cinque family, with Mamma Annamaria ruling in the kitchen (the hotel requires half-board and the lodging price includes the evening meal). Rooms have high ceilings, bright fabrics, tile flooring, and sunny terraces or balconies overlooking the sea and coastline. Car or motorboat excursions to surrounding towns and attractions can be arranged. Cars can't drive to the doorway, but porters will ferry your luggage. Note: it's 300 steps down to the main beach. ✉ *Via della Tavolozza*

3, 84017, ☎ *089/875143,* FAX *089/811540,* WEB *www.casalbertina.it.
21 rooms with bath. Restaurant, air-conditioning, parking (fee). AE,
DC, MC, V.*

$$$ 🏨 **Miramare.** Prime views, central location, and comfortable elegance
are pleasing elements of this albergo converted from a 100-year-old
mansion. Outdoor and indoor terraces are draped with bougainvillea,
and antiques and comfy seating abound. Charming rooms, some with
fireplace, are upgraded constantly and offer glazed tiles, balconies or
terraces, and windows overlooking the sea. Room 201 is a new suite,
and Room 210 has a huge window wall opening to the terrace. ✉ *Via
Trara Genoino 27, 84017,* ☎ *089/875002,* FAX *089/875219,* WEB
*www.starnet.it/miramare. 15 rooms with bath. Bar, air-conditioning,
parking (fee). AE, DC, MC, V. Closed Nov.–Mar.*

$$$ 🏨 **Villa Franca.** Bay blue, lemon yellow, and cool white are the palette
here, making for a stress-dissolving retreat, set halfway up the town
from the beach. Tile and mosaic floors, decorative urns, and graceful
archways open to sea air and views, and conversation-seating done in
bold fabrics marks the public rooms and piano bar. Similarly furnished, guest rooms all have terraces over the town, while the smallish pool enjoys a delightful view. ✉ *Viale Pasitea 318, 84017,* ☎ *089/
875655,* FAX *089/875735,* WEB *www.villafrancahotel.it. 28 rooms with
bath. Restaurant, bar, pool, Turkish bath, health club, parking. AE,
DC, MC, V. Nov.–Mar.*

$$–$$$ 🏨 **Conca d'Oro.** The name says gold, and the look sure shines at this
bright, white-stucco hillside lodging. Chintz and hand-painted antique
furnishings compete with boldly patterned tile flooring on the terrace.
Guest rooms have ceiling fans and balconies, and there are a broad,
casual dining veranda and a private stretch of beach. All, of course,
overlook the sea and coastline, though some way away from the hub
of the main town center. One of few hotels in Positano to stay open
throughout the year, prices dip considerably in winter months (the lodging price includes the evening meal). ✉ *Via Boscariello 16, 84017,* ☎
089/811494, FAX *089/812009,* WEB *www.albergoconcadoro.it. 38 rooms
with bath. Restaurant, parking. MC, V.*

$$ 🏨 **Casa Cosenza.** This 200-year-old lemon-yellow upscale pensione is
a distant cousin to the more luxe accommodations in town. Still, it's
set halfway up the hills, meaning you get a great view and can still eas-
ily walk to the beach. Breakfast is on a terrace overlooking town and
sea, and rooms are clean and comfortable, many with coved ceilings.
✉ *Via Trara Genoino 18, 84017,* ☎ FAX *089/875063. 7 rooms, 2
apartments with bath. Air-conditioning. No credit cards.*

$$ 🏨 **La Fenice.** Paradise found. This tiny and unpretentious hotel on the
★ outskirts of town beckons with bougainvillea-laden vistas, castaway
cottages, and a turquoise pool, all perched over a private beach, just
across a cove from Franco Zefferelli's famous villa. Once past the gate,
you climb a steep stairway to the main house—but tread slowly: the
paths and stairways here enchantingly frame (sometimes literally with
vines) vistas over land and sea. Thanks to the wonderful family of the
owner, Constantino Mandara, you'll feel right at home in just a few
minutes—that's because this *is* his home. Guest rooms, accented with
coved ceilings, whitewashed walls, and native folk art, are simple
havens of tranquility. Several accommodations are in a house perched
above the road (a bit noisy if trucks rumble by on the road below, but
this happens rarely at night), although the best are the adorable little
cottages set close to the sea. All are linked by *very* steep walkways—
covered with arbors and zigzagging their way across the hill, they tie
together these little acres of heaven. ✉ *Via G. Marconi 4, 84017,* ☎
089/875513, FAX *089/811309. 10 rooms with bath. Pool. No credit cards.*

$ ⊡ **La Ginestra.** Set at about 2,000 feet over Positano in the dizzy heights of the Lattari mountains, the farming cooperative La Ginestra dominates the coastline from a converted 18th-century manor house. The peasants' quarters have been upgraded into a thriving restaurant while the guest rooms above are decorated in simple country style. Though up-and-running only since 1997, this has become a popular retreat for ecologically sensitive townies and rooms need booking well in advance. Positano is accessed via a network of footpaths—remember it's a good hour's slog up from the bottom. This is the perfect base for those wanting to combine the simplicity and organic cuisine of the Italian countryside with a good measure of hiking across the Amalfi Coast. Usually only half-board terms are offered. If arriving by train, get off the Circumvesuviana train at Vico Equense and take the local orange bus uphill to Santa Maria del Castello. ⊠ *Via Tessa, Santa Maria Del Castello, Vico Equense 80069,* ☎ FAX *081/8023211. 8 rooms with bath. MC, V.*

Nightlife and the Arts

The night scene here is liveliest near the waterfront, where the restaurants lined up along the border of the Spiaggia Grande turn into one big open-air party on summer nights. For the latest and most complete information on all the nightspots, concerts, and special events along the Amalfi Coast, from Positano to Salerno, be sure to consult the monthly periodical, *Memo,* available at most regional newsstands. It's a day-by-day, event-filled cornucopia of information.

Music on the Rocks (☎ 089/875036) is a popular disco set in a seaside cave off the beach, favored by the likes of Sharon Stone and Luciano Pavarotti. **La Zagara** (⊠ Via dei Mulini 8, ☎ 089/875964), a noted pastry shop by day, offers music at night. **Easy Pub** (⊠ Via Rampa Teglia 8, ☎ 089/811461) is for grown-ups who are still crazy after all these years.

CHAMBER MUSIC

The **International Chamber Music Courses and Festival** (⊠ Via G. Marconi 45, ☎ FAX 089/812045, WEB www.Positanonline.it/music_ Courses) offers two-week master classes, lectures, and concerts open to the public throughout July. Summer concerts are staged in the atmospheric setting of the Hotel Sirenuse in Positano and the Hotel Cocumella in Sorrento.

CULINARY LESSONS

On a centrally located roof-garden with sweeping views of the coastline, **Diana Folonari** (of the famous wine family) holds weeklong seminars on Italian country cooking, offered in English from May to June and September to October, with wine tastings (⊠ Viale Pasitea 246, 84017, ☎ FAX 089/875784, WEB www.starnet.it/cooking_school). Bring a notebook, pencils, and your own apron.

FESTIVALS

Yearlong, the Positano calendar is filled with festivities and religious *festas.* Summertime plays host to the Moda Mare fashion show, in early June, when concerts are set up on the beach and in Nocelle—the sky-high village that looks down on Positano. The first week in September sees the Premio Leonide Massine dance awards—officially known as the Positano Prize for the Art of Dancing—and the Vittorio de Sica Film Festival, while the last week brings the Festa del Pesce (Fish Festival); acrobats and musicians take to the streets of Montepertuso for Artisti in Strada. The star event of the year and the town's main religious festa is the **Feast of the Assumption,** held every August 15, commemorated by mock battles with the Saracens and evening fireworks on the main beach.

During Christmas, Natale wreaths are fashioned from bougainvillea, and orchestra and choir concerts pop up all over town; the Nuovo Anno (New Year) is greeted with a big town dance and fireworks on the main beach, with other folklore and caffè-concerti musical events. In neighboring Montepertuso a living crèche is enacted. Just outside Positano, heading east, is the tiny chapel of San Pietro, named in honor of St. Peter's landing here in AD 40 (and now marking the entrance to the luxurious Hotel San Pietro). Each year on New Year's Eve, the 120 villagers of San Pietro—give or take a few—greet the dawn telling stories, singing, and eating around a bonfire in the piazza in front of the town church. Visitors are always welcome; bring a blanket.

Outdoor Activities and Sports

High-flying aficionados can join an organized group of hang gliders soaring on the thermals along with the hillside swifts and gulls; check for information at the tourist board by the Chiesa Madre. Hikers often pass through Positano on their way to the region's most famed mountainside trail, the Sentiero degli Dei (Pathway of the Gods), which can be picked up outside nearby Nocelle. For less professional hikers, Ponte dei Libri (a bridge several miles west) spans a pretty valley with soaring rock pinnacles and is a moderate walk. More serious climbers can hike up to Santa Maria del Castello (just over 2,000 ft) from where paths radiate out eastward and westward along the Lattari mountains. Plant-lovers will find hillside walks particularly rewarding in May, when the mountains turn into a flowering rock-garden with fine displays of orchids. As a general rule, allow plenty of time for what look like short distances on paper, take lots of water, and stick to the paths mapped out in red and white stripes by the CAI (Italian Alpine Club). Julian Tippet's hiking guide, *Landscapes of Sorrento and the Amalfi Coast* (available at stores on the coast) is a wonderful book—invest in it.

Sooner or later, everyone takes to the water in Positano. Divers can check out **Centro Sub Costiera Amalfitana** (⊠ Via Fornillo, on the beach beneath the Pupetto and Vittoria hotels, ☎ 089/812148, FAX 089/812884) for dive classes and guided excursions, including night and archaeological dives—there's also a branch in Praiano, at Via Capriglione 21. Day or night trips can be organized with local fishermen, who can even cook your catch and serve it on board. Ask at your hotel or check at the beach. Waterskiing facilities are offered on the main beach, where boats and skis can be rented.

Shopping

Resort wear put Positano on the fashion map in a big way in the early 1960s; it has now taken off in more contemporary directions. Goods range from haute to kitsch, often tight tops and loose pareus in vibrant hues, with prices generally higher than in other coast towns. The fabric industry here began long ago with silk, canvas, and hand embroidery, then made headlines back in 1959 when Positano introduced Italy to the bikini (following the reasoning that less is more, boutiques now sell even more highly abbreviated ones). The most concentrated shopping area, and the least difficult to maneuver, is the souklike area near the cathedral by the beach, where the crowded pedestrian pathway literally runs through boutiques. Lining steep alleyways covered with bougainvillea, small shops display items such as local foodstuffs, wood, lace, pottery, wines and limoncello, and ceramics; you'll even find artisans who can hand-stitch a pair of stylish sandals for you while you wait.

Ceramiche Assunta (⊠ Via C. Colombo 97, ☎ 089/875008, WEB www.ceramicassunta.it) has a collection of the colorful and fanciful traditional ceramics of Vietri, east along the coast. **Cose Antiche** (⊠ Piazza dei Mulini, ☎ 089/811811) offers antiques from minor to big deal. **Costanzo**

Avitabile (⊠ Piazza A. Vespucci 1/3/5, ☎ 089/875366) creates custom sandals in barely a few minutes. **La Tartana** (⊠ Via Rampa Teglia, ☎ 089/875645) is a stylish boutique that tailors and sells handmade suits. **Maria Lampo** (⊠ Via Pasitea 12, ☎ 089/875021) has been creating swimsuits and beachwear in traditional fabrics for almost 50 years.

Vettica Maggiore

🔟 *3 km (2 mi) southeast of Punta San Pietro; 2 km (1 mi) northwest of Praiano.*

From afar, Vettica Maggiore looks like a landscape painting. Up close, it turns out to be just your standard-issue village-along-a-road, but what makes it worth stopping for is the vast piazza, almost levitating over the water. This is a fine place to stretch your legs and view distant Positano, the coast, and the sea. Paved with an intricate, colorful pattern in majolica, the piazza is a fitting setting for the church of San Gennaro, rebuilt in the 16th century, with its notably ornate facade and a gleaming majolica-tiled dome (at night, often trimmed with festive lights). Paintings from the 16th and 17th centuries include *Martyrdom of S. Bartholomew,* by Giovanni Bernardo Lama, decorating the side chapel. Elsewhere, in this most westerly village in the township of Praiano, you'll find a pretty but hard-to-reach cliff-side beach if you follow the "Spiaggia" signs from the church; it's at the end of an olive grove, hidden at the bottom of the hillside, next to a tiny anchorage.

Dining and Lodging

$$–$$$ ✕ **La Brace.** On the second floor of a simple storefront, on the inland side of the drive, you enter a little ristorante that looks disappointingly simple. Its fine reputation, however, is validated as soon as you see the fresh, homemade antipasti and when you dig into the hearty Amalfitan cuisine. The friendly owner recommends the seafood (at remarkably accessible prices), and if you sit next to the big windows, you can see the jagged coastline and serene sea from whence it comes. ⊠ *Via G. Capriglione 146, Vettica Maggiore,* ☎ *089/874226. AE, DC, MC, V. Closed Nov. and Wed. Oct.–Mar.*

$$ ✕ **La Taverna del Leone.** A crowd ranging from Ferrari owners to local fishermen is drawn to this rustic, convivial trattoria because of the pizza—reputedly the best around (evenings only). You can choose from a variety of antipasti and creative pizza toppings, or go for a big meal topped off with a cold beer or glass of local wine, in a lusty roadhouse setting where folks mingle happily and noisily. And if you want to stay over rather than face the drive, a few simple rooms with private baths are here as well. ⊠ *Via Laurito 43, Positano, Amalfi Drive, between Positano and Vettica Maggiore,* ☎ *089/875474. AE, DC, MC, V. Closed Tues. and Jan. 7–Feb.*

$$$$ 🏨 **Tritone.** From afar on the Amalfi Drive, this looks like a shimmer-
★ ing white palace perched on the cliffs. Upon arriving, you'll see no other hotel has such a dizzying roost above the sea. Flagstone terraces and gardens set amid soaring rock pinnacles take full advantage of the location, while the seaside bathing area, accessed by an elevator excavated through 1,000 ft of rock, is jaw-dropping and complete with private beach, rocky tunnels, buffet, and bar. Not jaw-dropping, however, are the public and guest rooms, all very standard-issue and staidly traditional in style. Still, they are all cossettingly restful and come with grand views of the sea and nearby Vettica Maggiore. A small rock chapel in a grotto is on the property should you care to give thanks for the region's natural wonders. ⊠ *Via Campo 5, Vettica Maggiore, 84010, about 1 mi outside Vettica Maggiore on the road to Positano,* ☎ *089/874333,* FAX *089/813024,* WEB *www.tritone.it. 58 rooms with bath. Restaurant,*

2 bars, air-conditioning, 2 pools, beach, meeting room, parking. AE, DC, MC, V. Closed Nov.–Mar.

$$$ ★ ▦ **Tramonto d'Oro.** In the middle of Vettica Maggiore and picturesquely sited close to the town's glorious church of San Gennaro, this hotel is a much-loved option on the coast. Modern, clean, and sleek, the guest rooms are casual-traditional in style. The real plus here is the Esposito family—they also run Conca dei Marini's Terrazze hotel—who have presided over the Tramonto d'Oro for over 50 years with true warmth and charm. The restaurant has a vast glass wall which frames a picture-perfect view over the church and piazza, while the roof has a pleasant pool. Guests are expected to take half-board in July and August. ✉ *Via G. Capriglione 119, Vettica Maggiore 84010,* ☎ *089/874955,* FAX *089/874670,* WEB *www.tramontodoro.it. 40 rooms with bath. Restaurant, air-conditioning, pool, solarium, sauna. AE, DC, MC, V.*

$$ ▦ **Le Fioriere.** Blue-tile rooms are casually furnished, and low-key ambience is in keeping with the slow pace of the village. If requested, breakfast is served on your awning-covered balcony over the blue sea. This basic hotel offers easy access to the beach and to public transportation for trips along the coast. ✉ *Via G. Capriglione 138, Vettica Maggiore 84010,* ☎ *089/874203,* FAX *089/874343,* WEB *www.lefioriere.it. 14 rooms with bath. Bar, air-conditioning, free parking. AE, DC, MC, V.*

Praiano

⑰ *2 km (1 mi) southeast of Vettica Maggiore; 1 km (½ mi) northwest of Marina di Praia.*

Just past Capo Sottile, the fishing village of Praiano juts to the sea at the base of the Monti Lattari. Praiano has less wealth and sophistication than its neighbors and more olive and lemon trees than tourists. The town's name comes from Plagianum, as the people who first inhabited the site were called. Back in the 13th century, King Charles I of Anjou founded a university here, the doges of Amalfi established a summer residence, and, for a while, Praiano was renowned for its silk industry. But the decline of Amalfi's 12th-century maritime republic hit hard; the charming parish Church of San Luca, at the top of the village, is a reminder of those headier times. A medieval lookout tower on the rocks still keeps guard over the coast, and hidden coves are for boating, bathing, and sunning off the rocks. During the summer boats leave the beach here for Capri each morning, and you can glimpse the island's Faraglioni rocks from here. If you look closely, you may be the first person in years to spot the giant *a mama de cernie* (mother of wreckfishes), the local equivalent of the Loch Ness monster.

Lodging

$$ ▦ **Open Gate.** This is a real deal, with much the same view as million-dollar-plus villas nearby. True, you're right on the main road, but the tile-floor guest rooms are white and clean, the private balconies are spacious, and the informal, vine-covered restaurant serves up tasty fare. The obliging staff will drive you to the nearest beach at Marina di Praia while the Grotto dello Smeraldo is only 2 km (1½ mi) away. ✉ *Via Roma 38, 84010,* ☎ *089/874148,* WEB *www.hotelopengate.it. 12 rooms with bath. Restaurant, bar, parking. AE, DC, MC, V.*

$ ▦ **Margherita.** Basic rooms have crucifixes over the beds, French doors to terraces over a side road lined with olive groves, and partial sea views. Tile flooring, velour seating, '70s-type lighting fixtures, and potted rubber trees make up the modest surroundings. Breakfasts are minimal, as is heat. But the price is right, and Margherita and her daughter are helpful. ✉ *Via Umberto I, 84010,* ☎ *089/874628,* FAX *089/*

874628, WEB *www.wel.it/Hmargherita. 28 rooms with bath. Restaurant, bar, air-conditioning, parking. AE, DC, MC, V.*

Marina di Praia

⑱ *1 km (½ mi) southeast of Praiano; 2 km (1 mi) west of Vallone di Furore.*

"Whoever wants to live a healthy life spends the morning in Vettica and the evening in Praiano," goes a local adage. The larger township of Praiano may not fulfill that advice, but its scenic satellite, Marina di Praia, indeed does, since it is home to a landmark eatery and famous disco. Nestling by the sea at the bottom of a dramatic chasm, this is the only anchorage along this rocky stretch where you can hire a boat and dock it and where ferries depart for points and islands along the coast. The super-picturesque hamlet comprises some parking spaces, a small sand beach tucked within cliffs, a few excellent seafood restaurants, a hotel, and a tiny church. Reached along a pretty path through the cliff rocks edging the sea is the L'Africana disco.

Dining and Lodging

$ ✕ **Alfonso a Mare.** Just steps from the Marina del Praia cove, this landmark restaurant is set in a rustic flagstone structure, once a dry haul for boats, partly open to the sea breezes on one side with an open kitchen on the other. Inside are country-style wooden tables, netting, and ceiling baskets, while outside, colorful boats, peasant dwellings, and the chasm's sheer rock walls catch the eye. In nearby Praiano, Alfonso also runs a hotel, where small rooms have tile floors, windows opening to terraces overlooking the gulf, and a few antique touches. ⊠ *Via Marina di Praia 84010,* ☎ *089/874091,* FAX *089/874161. No credit cards.*

$$$ ▦ **Onda Verde.** Built on a rock dramatically jutting over the tiny cove of Marina dei Praia, this fine hotel overlooks a Saracen tower and coastal ridges. Terraces overhang the sea, and common rooms and dining room feature panoramic glass walls, marble flooring, and rattan and plastic furnishings. Rooms are sparse, but some have terraces, and air-conditioning is available for a charge. This is also one of the few nonsmoking hotels on the Amalfi Coast. You can climb down a winding path to the beach, where daily boat excursions leave for Positano, Capri, and Ischia. Both a plus and a minus is the minutes-away walk to L'Africana disco. If you like to party, you can climb right into bed without having to drive; if you don't, be sure to ask for a quiet room. ⊠ *Via Terra Mare 3, 84010,* ☎ *089/874143,* FAX *089/8131049,* WEB *www.ondaverde.it. 20 rooms with bath. Bar, air-conditioning, dock. AE, DC, MC, V. Closed Nov. 5–mid-Mar. (open Dec. 27–Jan. 7).*

Nightlife

Off a mile-long footpath from the Marina del Praia—or accessed via an elevator from Statale 163—**L'Africana** (⊠ Via Torre a Mare, ☎ 089/ 874042) is a classic from the 1960s, a golden oldie on the coast. Even Jackie O danced on the glass-aquarium floor. With open-to-the-sea atmosphere, an indoor boat that's a buffet of antipasti, animal prints, and wildish shows with partial nudity, you can eat lightly, drink heavily, and dance away till the Gulf of Salerno sunrise. Longtime owner Luca Milano has been around the block quite a few times, lives on a cliff beneath the premises, and may even show you his parrot. If coming from Positano, you can also access transport with one of the boats down at the Spiaggia Grande.

Vallone di Furore

⑲ *8 km (5 mi) southeast of Positano; 2 km (1 mi) west of Conca dei Marini.*

The ghost hamlet of Marina di Furore—perhaps ten houses?—beckons as you pass over it on a towering viaduct. This tchotchke of a fishermen's village seems sculpted out of rock walls; once mills, these houses were abandoned when the tiny harbor here closed. After the hamlet was discovered by vacationers, the municipality moved in, restoring and painting it in pastels in 1998. The hamlet is now the site of an eco-museum and short botanical trails have been laid out (down the steps, upstream from the viaduct). The Lilliputian settlement is at the base of a high-walled fissure in the limestone mountains—sometimes hyped as a fjord. The name is from the "furor" of stormy water that once rushed down the Torrente Schiato here, now a mere trickle—with a substantial effluent load from Agerola upstream and uncleared rock slides creating a less-than-gorgeous gorge. From the beach, scalinatelle—each set with 3,000 steps (but who's counting?)—were built to portage goods from the harbor to the town of Furore above it. The hard walk up takes a couple of hours as you climb from sea to sky. To see any of this by car, you have to pay to park in the layby on the Amalfi side of the gorge, just before the gas station. Unless you're in fantastic shape, it's better to boat to the beach and just rubberneck.

Furore, the town high above the Vallone di Furore gorge, can be reached by car via a sharp turn uphill off Statale 163 several miles east of the gorge in Vettica Minore; look for the sign to Agerola. Beyond Furore, the landscape differs from that of the rock-ribbed coast below, containing meadows, terraced fields, dry stone walls (*macere*), chestnut forests, and wild Dolomitic mountains dotted with pine and cypress trees. The local pitched-roof houses seem almost Alpine. The region is noted for dairy products, especially cheeses. You can hike all the way here from Positano, and among the villages you will pass is San Lazzaro; check out its belvedere, whose view stretches from Capri to the Monti del Cilento.

Furore is best known for its delicate, lightly tinted wine, Gran Furore Divina Costiera. Furore used to trade wine and foodstuffs for fish and foreign goods and still makes a profit being a larder for regional restaurants, as the garlands of bright red peppers and tomatoes hanging from many roof beams attest. Today Furore is becoming unexpectedly artsy; The mayor recently commissioned works from artists and sculptors, so murals of agricultural scenes, modern sculptures, and house gates patterned in fuchsia and lime enliven the scene. More ancient art can be seen at the Church of Sant'Elia Profeta, which has what some consider the most important Renaissance painting on the coast, a 15th-century triptych by Angelo Antonello.

Lodging

$–$$ 🏨 **Le Rocce.** Set in the agricultural zone high above the coast, this odd, stone-and-stucco edifice commands the crest of a sheer rock face overlooking the Bay of Salerno and the coastal towns. The lobby looks like an old Italian airport (and the view below seems appropriate), but some redeeming features are the wraparound windows in the restaurant, pleasant rooms with balconies, a rock grotto honoring the Virgin Mary, a nightclub in a cave, and the gentle price tag. ✉ *Via Belvedere 73, Agerola 80051,* ☎ *081/8791182,* ☎ FAX *081/8791893,* WEB *www.costieramalfitana.com/lerocce. 33 rooms with bath. Restaurant, bar, air-conditioning, nightclub, free parking. AE, DC, MC, V.*

Conca dei Marini

★ *2 km (1 mi) east of Vallone di Furore; 4 km (2½ mi) southwest of Amalfi.*

In Lee Radziwill's 2001 book of memories, *Happy Times,* she declares that when she thinks of paradise, she thinks of Conca dei Marini. If you make an overnight here, we're sure you'll agree. Long a favorite of the off-duty famous and rich, the town hides many of its charms, as any sublime forgetaway should. Set on the most dramatic promontory of the coast, Conca dei Marini (the name means "seafarers' basin") was originally a province of ancient Rome called Cossa and later became an important naval base of the Amalfi Republic. Much later, it became a retreat for high-profile types, including John Steinbeck, Gianni Agnelli, and Carlo Ponti, who erected a white Xanadu here by the sea (the villa was built for his first wife, not Sophia). You can see why: The green of terraced gardens competes with (and loses to) the blue sea, while the town's distinctive houses flanking the ridges have thick, white walls, with cupolas, balconies, and external staircases, testimony to former Arabic, Moorish, and Greek settlements. Below, on Capo di Conca, a promontory once used as a cemetery, a 16th-century coastal tower dramatically overlooks the sea. Coral is still harvested in the waters off the coast here, while boats fish for sardines and squid through the night, their prow lanterns twinkling as if some stars above had slipped into the sea.

On the outskirts of town, the **Grotta dello Smeraldo** (Emerald Grotto) is a much-touted stop for day-trippers. The rather tacky sign on the road and the squadron of tour buses may put you off, but it's definitely worth a stop. Steps and an elevator bring you almost to sea level, but more delightful is to arrive by boat, which you can hire at just about any port up and down the coast. The karstic cave was originally part of the shore, but the lowest end sank into the sea when the peninsula subsided (the coast remains active, so it may eventually sink even lower—or rise). Intense greenish light filters into the water from an arch below sea level and is reflected off the walls of the cave, quite living up to emerald expectations. You wait to board a large rowboat with about 20 fellow passengers, and then you set off with a guide, gondolier fashion, through the smallish cavern filled with huge stalactites and stalagmites. Don't let the boatman's constant spiel detract from the half-hour experience—this is one of those tours that points out stalactites that look like Lincoln (for Americans), Napoléon (for the French), and Garibaldi (for the Italians); just tune out and enjoy the sparkles, shapes, and Harry Winston–esque color. A tourist from Amalfi raved in a hotel log in 1858 that the cave ". . . can compete with Vesuvius," but it was forgotten about for years afterwards until the grotto was rediscovered by a local fisherman in the 1930s. The light is best from noon to 3 PM, which is fortunately when hordes of potential visitors will be tucking into their pasta elsewhere. At Christmas there's a special celebration conducted around the underwater crèche. ✉ *Beyond Punta Acquafetente by boat, or off Amalfi Drive,* ☎ *089/ 871107 (tourist board of Amalfi).* ▣ *€5.5.* ☉ *Apr.–Oct., daily 9–4; Nov.–Mar., daily 10–3.*

The main Conca dei Marini SITA bus stop is directly in front of the Hotel Belvedere. From here head west along the highway to the Saracen Tower (a private bathing beach sits within its shadow, but you might ask to dine at its café) and farther on for the Emerald Grotto. To the east, you can walk along the highway for views of Conca's harbor and lagoon. A staircase to the left of the Hotel Belvedere will take you down to the harbor—but unfortunately a major 1997 landslide closed off the quay and the little Chapel of Santa Maria della Neve to visitors. Walk as far as you can, however—who knows, by the time you're in Conca, the harbor may have opened for visitors again. Hopefully so, for this dollhouse-size harbor is one of the most idyllic patches along the entire coast.

For Conca *in excelsis,* however, head up the mountainside to the northern reaches of the town (the road leads upward opposite the Hotel Belvedere, and then you can opt to take the gently climbing roads or the steeper staircase ever upward). Your reward as you climb up the hillside roads and steep scalinatelle is three stunningly sited churches. The first is neo-Byzantine **San Pancrazio,** set in a lovely palm-tree garden. From here head up to the Scalinatella San Pancrazio to the tiny town piazza. To the east along the cliff-side road is the sky-swimming church and **Convento di Santa Rosa** (now a private home). In the 18th century the nuns of the convent created one of the great local dishes, *sfogliata Santa Rosa* (sweet cheese and ricotta pastry shaped like a nun's hood). The mother superior distributed this delicacy free to the locals back then. Today, on every Saint's Day in August, the pastries are baked, and savored, by local families and revelers in town. The convent church is now used as a regular venue for chamber music concerts laid on by the Ravello Concert Society. Heading back to the piazza from the convent, take Via Due Maggio and Via Roma to **Sant' Antonio di Padova**—an elegant white church spectacularly cantilevered hundreds of feet over the coastline on a stone parapet. The church itself is only open for Sunday-morning services, but you might ask locals if someone can open the church with a key for a quick visit ("Dov'è la persona che ci può far visitare la chiesa.") For those who want to see churches in coastal villages, this may be the only way to gain entry.

Lodging

$$$
★
Belvedere. To understand this place, you must look on it not as a hotel but as a home. This is the sort of place where guests ask for the room their great-grandparents favored. Happily, everyone, not just regulars, are treated like family here and you'll find it difficult to say goodbye to the remarkably friendly and helpful staff. Set in one of the grande dame villas of Conca dei Marini, featuring salons top-heavy with overstuffed sofas and a ravishing pool area resting by water's edge, the Belvedere is handily located for exploring Conca dei Marini, as it is set equidistant from the town's lagoon and Saracen tower. ✉ *Via Smeraldo 19, Conca dei Marini 84010,* ☎ *089/831282,* FAX *089/ 831439,* WEB *www.belvederehotel.it. 36 rooms with bath. Restaurant, bar, air-conditioning, pool, parking. AE, DC, MC, V. Closed Nov.–Mar.*

$$
Le Terrazze. As opposed to the yesteryear glow of the Hotel Belvedere, this place, set just a few feet down the road, is a spankingly modern alternative. The *Wallpaper* crowd might love this place for its sleek, retro-chic '60s style; you half expect to see Monica Vitti and Alain Delon haunting the shadowy corridors, waiting for their cue from director Michelangelo Antonioni. Everything, however, is as it should be, which, considering the gentle price, is very pleasant indeed. Most rooms have their own balconies, which allow you to look down across the bay at the grand villa built by Carlo Ponti, and—best of all—you are just a few staircases away from Conca's adorable harbor. Guest rooms are accented with local Vietri majolica tiles and all are delightfully clean and airy. For those who wish *tranquillità,* this is a fine option. ✉ *Via Smeraldo 11, 84010,* ☎ *089/831290,* FAX *089/831296,* WEB *www.hotelleterrazze.it. 27 rooms with bath. Bar, air-conditioning. AE, DC, MC, V. Closed Nov.–Mar.*

AMALFI: FIRST OF THE SEA REPUBLICS

★ *18 km (11 mi) southeast of Positano; 32 km (20 mi) west of Salerno.*

On Amalfi's main waterfront, an honorary statue bears this inscription: "The judgment day, when Amalfitans go to Heaven, will be a day like any other." Visitors to this charming city, set in a verdant valley of the Lattari mountains, will soon understand what it means. At first glance, it's hard to imagine that a millennium ago this resort destination, with cream-color and pastel-hue buildings tightly packing a gorge on the Bay of Salerno, was in the 11th and 12th centuries the seat of the Amalfi Maritime Republic, one of the world's great naval powers, and a sturdy rival of Genoa and Pisa for control of the Mediterranean. The harbor, which once launched the greatest fleet in Italy, now bobs with ferries and blue-and-white fishing boats. The main street, lined with leather shops and *pasticcerie,* has replaced a raging mountain torrent, and ter- raced hills where *banditi* (bandits) once roamed now flaunt the green and gold of lemon groves. Bearing testimony to its great trade with Tunis, Tripoli, and Algiers, Amalfi remains honeycombed with Arab-Sicilian cloisters and covered passages that suggest Asian caravansaries. In a way Amalfi has become great again, showing off its medieval glory days with sea pageants, convents-turned-hotels, ancient paper mills, covered streets, and its mosquelike cathedral. "The sun—the moon—the stars and—Amalfi," Amalfitans used to say. Standing on the terrace of the town's Cappuccini Convento (Capuchin Convent), you'll have to agree.

Amalfi's origin is clouded. One legend says that a general of Constantine's army, named Amalfo, settled here in 320; another tale has it that Roman noblemen from the village of Melphi (in Latin, "a Melphi"), fleeing after the fall of the empire, were first in these parts, ship- wrecked in the 4th century on their way to Constantinople. Myth be- comes fact by the 6th century, when Amalfi is inscribed in the archives as a Byzantine diocese, and the historical pageant really begins. Its ge- ographic position was good defense, and the distance from Con- stantinople made its increasing autonomy possible. Continuously hammered by the Lombards and others, in 839 it rose against and fi- nally sacked nearby Salerno, to which its inhabitants had been deported. In the 10th century, Amalfi constructed many churches and monasteries and was ruled by judges, later called doges—self-appointed dukes who amassed vast wealth and power.

From the 9th century until 1101, Amalfi remained linked to Byzan- tium but also was increasingly independent and prosperous, perhaps the major trading port in southern Italy. Its influence loomed large, thanks to its creation of the Tavola Amalfitana, a code of maritime laws taken up by most medieval-era kingdoms. It created its own gold and silver coins—or *tari,* engraved with the cross of Amalfi—and ruled a vast ter- ritory. With trade extending as far as Alexandria and Constantinople— where a large colony of Amalfitan merchants resided—it became Italy's first maritime republic, ahead of rivals Pisa, Venice, and Genoa; the population swelled to about 100,000, many of them seafarers and traders. As William of Apulia wrote in the 11th century, ". . . No other is richer in silver, cloth and gold. A great many navigators live in this city . . . famous almost throughout the world as those who travel to where there is something worth buying."

But the days of wine and doges were about to end. In the 11th century Robert Guiscard of Normandy—in the duplicitous spirit of politicos to this day—first aided, then sacked the town, and the Normans from Sicily returned, after a short Amalfitan revolt, in the 12th century. Then, when the Republic of Pisa twice conquered it, Amalfi fell into decline, hastened by a horrific storm in 1343, then by an indirect blow from Christopher Columbus's discoveries, which opened the world beyond to competing trade routes. By the 18th century, the town had sunk into gloom, looking to its lemons and handmade paper for survival. After the state road was built by Ferdinand, the Bourbon king of Naples, in the 19th century, Amalfi evolved into a tourist destination, drawing Grand Tour–era travelers like Richard Wagner, Henry Wadsworth Longfellow, and Henrik Ibsen, all of whom helped spread Amalfi's fame.

Exploring Amalfi

Amalfi's compact tourist center is split between the bustling *lungomare* (waterfront), with its public and private transportation hubs, and the piazza in front of the Duomo. Parking is a big problem, as the small lot in the center of town fills up fast. Traveling here via ferry and bus or staying in a hotel with a parking garage are good ideas. Once you explore the main sights near the waterfront, take off and explore the souklike center, then escape to the outskirts and the terraced hills of the Valle dei Mulini, site of Amalfi's ancient paper mills. At a little waterfall a block or so north of the Museo della Carta, look to the left for a set of scalinatelle and climb the 20-plus steps; follow a footpath to the right, where there's a bench at the edge of a lemon grove. If you buy a fresh lemon along the way—its leaves will be intact and its taste sweeter than you're accustomed to—and down it with a pinch of salt, you'll be passing time as the locals have since the age of the republic.

A Good Walk

Start on the festive waterfront, near the **Porta della Marina** ㉑, where a ceramic panel honors Amalfi's merchant seamen. Past the traffic-filled harborside **Piazza Flavio Gioia** ㉒, which is centered around the Flavio Gioia Monument—named for the Amalfitan inventor of the maritime compass—head east up the waterfront esplanade, lined with palm trees and Victorian streetlights, to the Palazzo dei Municipio (town hall) and its **Museo Civico** ㉓, devoted to civic history (a sculpted overview is on the museum's southern wall). Some may wish to continue along the waterfront up the gentle hill to the Torre di Amalfi, one of the 16th-century defensive towers along the coast, now part of the **Luna Convento** ㉔, a former Franciscan monastery–turned–hotel, where you can relax in its famous 13th-century cloister. From the museum (three minutes) or from the Luna Convento (10 minutes), look for the campanile of the Duomo di Sant'Andrea and head for the piazza in front. This is the very heart of the city, adorned with cafés and the Fontana del Popolo, graced (only in Italy, folks) by both a statue of St. Andrew and a marble female nymph whose breasts spout water. Take·a deep breath and head up the monumental staircase to the **Duomo di Sant' Andrea** ㉕, with its museum, crypt, and noted Paradise Cloister. Head up to the hilltop **Cappuccini Convento** ㉖, reached from the small Piazza dei Dogi off Piazza Duomo by climbing Via Annunziatella—one of Amalfi's most evocative, covered passageways (or head out along the waterfront on busy Via M. Camera to the hotel's cliffside elevator). The view from this 13th-century monastery will be worth the blisters. After exploring the cloister and the hotel's frozen-in-time salons, lunch on its terrace, with all Amalfi at your feet.

Head back to Piazza Duomo and go through the medieval arch facing the piazza to the Piazza dei Dogi, also called the blacksmith area, where the Doges' Palazzo stood. The **Arsenale della Repubblica** ㉗ is just south. North, you'll cross covered passageways and little lanes such as Vico dei Pastai, and Via Herculano Marini, leading to the Contrada Campo. From here you can descend to the Via Capuano which cuts

Amalfi

Golfo di Salerno

N

0   440 yds

0   400 m

through the center of Amalfi along the riverbed of the mountain torrent. With the sound of water gurgling below the road, head up Via Lorenzo di Amalfi toward Via delle Cartiere (Paper Street), a 15- or 20-minute, slightly uphill stroll. Here is the beginning of the **Valle dei Mulini** ㉘, where the mostly converted mills and waterfalls and the Museo della Carta are evidence of Amalfi's paper industry, still hanging on from the Middle Ages. You can picnic here if you've shopped for take-out *panini* (sandwiches) along the Via Lorenzo d'Amalfi on the way. Back down the same road, and close to the Porta dell'Ospedale, is the marble entrance to the well-known and nearly straight **Ruga Nova Mercatorum** ㉙, also known as Via dei Mercanti, an old covered street. From here, Salita dei Curiali wends among houses with gardens, and ends at a charming square with the churches of the **Santa Maria Maggiore** ㉚ and the **Maria Santissima Addolorata** ㉛. Look for the nearby campanile of the duomo, and it's back to the piazza there, with a cathedral visit if you haven't paid your respects yet.

TIMING

You'll need at least a half day, perhaps more, depending on how long you spend in the duomo and museums, whether or not you take the optional meanderings—leading to hidden piazzas, the Valle dei Mulini, or lunch at the Cappuccini Convento. Most properties close up by 1 PM, so it's best to start early. Small churches are often open only during mass; ask at your hotel. If you leave right after breakfast and keep a blistering pace, you could finish in time for a late lunch, followed by a long beach siesta.

Sights to See

㉗ **Arsenale della Repubblica.** From the middle of the 11th century, Amalfi's center of shipbuilding, custom houses, and warehouses was the Arsenale, today the only (partially) preserved medieval shipyard in southern Italy. Ships and galleys up to 80 ft, equipped with up to 120 oars, were built at this largest arsenal of any maritime republic. The boat now used for the historical regatta (held every four years, next in Amalfi in June 2005) and other ship models are kept in the two large halls accented with Gothic arches. Ten of the original 22 stone piers remain, the others destroyed by storms and changes in the sea level on this ever-active coast. ⊠ *South of Piazza dei Dogi, on corner of Via Camera, by the waterfront.* ☉ *Mon.–Sat. 10–1.*

★ ㉖ **Cappuccini Convento.** A noted stop for Grand Tour–era travelers, this medieval monastery enjoys a magnificent hilltop perch. Long famous for its gardens, its ½-km-long (¼-mi-long) terrace over Amalfi's harbor, and its Arab-Sicilian cloister, the monastery was originally founded by Cistercian monks in the 13th century as the Convento di S. Pietro della Canonica. Then abandoned, the complex was taken over by the Capuchins in 1583, only to be transformed into a hotel in the mid-19th century when the king of Naples suppressed the religious orders. Immortalized in postcards and paintings, the view of Amalfi's waterfront from the hotel terrace became one of the first travel icons of the 19th century. Henry Wadsworth Longfellow composed a poem to celebrate its beauty and Richard Wagner forsook his guest room to camp out under the stars. Stroll through the monastery and the centuries unwind: the 13th-century cloister has the intertwined Arabic columns of the Amalfi cathedral's great Paradise Cloister, the little church is a rococo confection, while spirit-warm hallways and salons are little changed from the 19th century. Use the elevator from Via Camera if you don't want to tackle the hillside Via Annunziatella climb. ⊠ *Hotel Cappuccini Convento, Via Annunziatella 46,* ☎ *089/871877.*

★ ㉕ **Duomo di Sant' Andrea.** Complicated, grand, delicate, and dominating, the 9th-century Amalfi cathedral has been remodeled over the years with Romanesque, Byzantine, Gothic, and Baroque elements, but retains a predominantly Arab-Norman style. Cross and crescent seem to be wed here: the campanile looks like a minaret wearing a Scheherazadian turban, the facade conjures up a striped burnoose, and its Paradise Cloister is an Arab-Sicilian spectacular.

The power of Amalfi is evident in the approach to the cathedral, set atop 62 broad steps that lead to a mosaic facade, redone in the 19th century, and framed by bands, arches, and patterned squares. The imposing bronze doors, the first in Italy, were cast in Constantinople before 1066 and signed by Simeon of Syria; they were commissioned by the leader of the large Amalfitan colony there. Silver incrustations on the doors, now difficult to see, are images of Christ, Mary, and saints.

Visitors are now channeled first into the adjoining **Chiostro del Paradiso** (Paradise Cloister), built around 1266 for Bishop Augustariccio as a burial ground of Amalfi's elite and one of the architectural treasures of southern Italy. Its flower-and-palm-filled quadrangle has a series of exceptionally delicate, intertwining arches on slender double columns in a combination of Byzantine and Arabian styles. Note the geometric patterns of colored mosaics in the walls, comprising parts of former pillars and pulpits of the earlier church. The striking 12th-century bell tower in front of the complex has a Romanesque base and an elaborate yellow-and-green-tile top with arches in the local style, a round center surrounded by four smaller cupolas. Spiced with Saracen colors and the intricate tile work of High Barbary, Amalfi's jaunty duomo seems to bring a touch of old Istanbul to town.

The chapel at the back of the cloister leads into the earlier (9th-century) basilica. The structure, called the Basilica of the Crucifix, is in

Romanesque style, with a nave, two aisles, and a high, deep apse. Of special note is a 14th-century crucifixion scene by a student of Giotto. This section has now been transformed into a museum, housing sarcophagi, sculpture, Neapolitan goldsmiths' artwork, and other treasures from the cathedral complex.

Steps from the basilica lead down into the crypt of St. Andrew. The cathedral above was built in the 13th century to house the saint's bones, which came from Constantinople and supposedly exuded a miraculous liquid believers call the "manna of St. Andrew." Amalfi's cathedral had always lured pious devotees—from Francis of Assisi to Pope Urban IV—but after the 14th-century manna manifestation the pilgrim trade really picked up. The saint's remains (sans head, which is in the Vatican) are kept under the 13th-century high altar in this exceptionally beautiful crypt adorned with marble statues sculpted by Pietro Bernini, father of the famed Gianlorenzo Bernini.

Following the one-way traffic up to the cathedral itself, you finally get to admire the elaborate polychrome marbles, and painted, coffered ceilings from its 18th-century restoration; art historians shake their head over this renovation, as the original decoration of the apse must have been one of the wonders of the Middle Ages. However, the original basilica plan has been preserved. The first chapel on the left of the entrance has a red porphyry baptismal font, supposedly crafted from the ruins of ancient Paestum. Other treasures include a mother-of-pearl cross given by the people of Jerusalem in 1930, in gratitude for Amalfi's help in establishing a 2,000-bed hospital there in 1112, which later became the first military and religious order, the Knights of St. John. ✉ *Piazza Duomo,* ☎ *089/871324.* ▯ *€2.* ☉ *Daily Mar.–June and Oct. 9–7; July–Sept. 9–9; Nov.–Feb. 10–1 and 2:30–5:30.*

㉔ **Luna Convento.** Legendarily founded by none other than St. Francis of Assisi, the Luna Convento was built in the 13th century and retains it famous cloister, with distinctive Arab-Sicilian arcaded columns and a crypt with frescoes. Transformed into the earliest hotel on the Amalfi Coast in the early 19th century, the hotel was where Henrik Ibsen wrote a large chunk of *A Doll's House.* ✉ *Via Pantaleone Comite 19,* ☎ *089/871002.*

㉛ **Maria Santissima Addolorata.** This church is adjacent to the confraternity founded in 1777 to organize Amalfi's Good Friday celebrations. The entrance gate bears a late-Gothic bas-relief of the Crucifixion, once belonging to nobility from the nearby village of Scala and identified by its coat of arms at the foot of the cross. The interior is Neoclassical, with a harmonious scale and coffered ceiling; note the 16th-century marble Madonna and Child in the sacristy. ✉ *Largo Santa Maria Maggiore.*

㉓ **Museo Civico.** The Municipal Museum of Amalfi contains artifacts from Amalfi's medieval period, including paintings, ancient coins, banners, and jeweled costumes. The highlight is the original 66-chapter draft of the code of the *Tavole Amalfitana,* the sea laws and customs of the ancient republic used throughout the Italian Mediterranean from the 13th to the 16th centuries. The Tavole established everything from prices for boat hires to procedures to be followed in case of shipwreck. Long one of the treasures of the Imperial Library of Vienna, the draft was returned to Amalfi after more than 500 years. Note the ceramic panel on the south outside wall of the museum, between Corso delle Repubbliche Marinare and Piazza del Municipio, created by Diodoro Cossa in the 1970s. The scenes provide an overview of local history: Roman refugees establishing themselves in nearby Scala in the 4th century; the founding of Amalfi by these same Romans; Amalfi's commercial and diplomatic role in the Mediterranean; the arrival of St. Andrew's body; the invention of the maritime compass, among other historic events. ⊠ *Piazza Municipio, entrance off Corso Roma,* ☎ *089/871066.* ⊠ *Free.* ☉ *Mon.–Sat. 8:30–1.*

㉒ **Piazza Flavio Gioia.** A statue, set in a circular greensward in front of the harbor, honors the Amalfitan credited with inventing the maritime compass in 1302. Many say it was the Chinese who invented the compass, passing the idea along to the Arabs, who traded with Amalfi; Gioia may have adapted it for sea use (some even believe there was no such person as Gioia). ⊠ *On the waterfront.*

㉑ **Porta della Marina.** This gateway "door" to the harbor bears a ceramic panel, created by Renato Rossi in the 1950s, commemorating the trade routes of the republic during the Middle Ages. For one example, ships loaded up with timber from Italy, traded it in North Africa, then used the gold obtained from those sales to buy gems, spices, and silks in Asia to trade in Italy. ⊠ *Across from Piazza Flavio Gioia, next to arsenal.*

㉙ **Ruga Nova Mercatorum.** Also known as Via dei Mercanti, evocative Ruga Nova was the main thoroughfare of medieval Amalfi, and it remains the most fascinating "street" in town. Claustrophobes, beware: it is completely covered, like a tunnel, but is especially wonderful when the light from alleys and windows plays on its white walls. Stretching from the Porta dell'Ospedale to the Salita dei Curiali, it ends at a medieval-era *contrada*, or neighborhood, filled with gardens and churches. ⊠ *Contrada S. Simone, just north of Maria Santissima Addolorata.*

㉚ **Santa Maria Maggiore.** Constructed by Duke Mansone I in 986, as inscribed on a capital at the entrance, the church has a Byzantine layout, although a 16th-century overhaul inverted the entrance and high altar, and the decoration is now mostly Baroque; the remains of San Felice and an 18th-century crèche scene are worth noting. The campanile dates from the 12th century. ⊠ *Largo Santa Maria Maggiore, near cathedral.*

㉘ **Valle dei Mulini.** The Valley of the Mills, uphill from town, was for centuries Amalfi's center for papermaking, an ancient trade learned from the Arabs (who learned it from the Chinese). Beginning in the 12th century, former macaroni mills in the town were converted to the production of paper made from cotton and linen, being among the first in Europe to do so. In 1211 Frederick II of Sicily prohibited this lighter, more readable paper for use in the preparation of official documents, favoring traditional sheepskin parchment, but by 1811 more than a dozen mills here, with more along the coast, were humming. Natural waterpower ensured that the handmade paper was cost-effective, but catastrophic flooding in 1954 closed most of the mills for good, and many of them have now been converted into private housing. The **Museo della Carta** (Museum of Paper) opened in 1971 in a 15th-century mill; paper samples, tools of the trade, old machinery, and the audiovisual presentation are all enlightening. A 20-minute stroll from the Piazza Duomo will take you to the valley via the main thoroughfare of Via Genoa, turning onto Via Capuano, at the edge of town. ⊠ *Museo della Carta,* ☎ *089/872610.* ⊠ €1.50. ☉ *Tues.–Sun. 9–1 and 3–7.*

OFF THE BEATEN PATH | **VIA MAESTRA DEI VILLAGGI –** West to Pogerola, with its two small churches and tower overlooking an expanse of the coast, you will have to climb about 1,000 steps through a valley—more or less; you can also take a bus or car along the upland road. A trek by foot along a path called Via Maestra dei Villaggi, which cuts inland just past the west end of the Amalfi road tunnel, will bring you to Vettica, Lone, Pastena, and Tovere, a series of villages William Wadsworth Longfellow—who didn't just stay in New England writing about Hiawatha—described as "heaven beyond the sea."

Dining and Lodging

$$$–$$$$ ✕ **Da Gemma.** Cognoscenti have sung the praises of this understated landmark since 1872. Tile floors, green tablecloths, and a terrace set above the main street are soothing elements. The kitchen glistens, the menu is printed on local handmade paper, and Amalfi foodies appreciate favorites that include *cianfotta*, a creation featuring eggplant, potatoes, onions, and peppers; and *paccheri del marinaio*, or macaroni with monkfish and squid. ⊠ *Via Fra Gerardo Sasso 9,* ☎ *089/871345. Reservations essential. AE, DC, MC, V. Closed Jan. 15–Feb. 15 and Wed. Sept.–June.*

$$$–$$$$ ✕ **Eolo.** This is both one of the newest restaurants on the Amalfi Coast
★ and one of the most sophisticated. The decor is suavely tranquil—white coved ceilings, Romanesque columns, mounted starfish—although the kitchen is anything but: masterminded by a member of the Gargano family (who also own the Hotel Santa Caterina), it tosses out gastronomic delights like lobster risotto, sea bass with lemon salt and fennel leaves, zucchini flan, and a fine dessert of eggplant and chocolate. Many dishes are fetchingly adorned with blossoms and other visual allures, but nothing compares to the view of Amalfi's harbor from one of the tables in Eolo's picture-window alcove. If you don't land one of these, don't fret—the entire room is pretty enough as it is. ⊠ *Via Pantaleone Comite 3,* ☎ *089/874241. Reservations essential. AE, MC, V. Closed Jan.–Feb. and Wed.*

$$$–$$$$ ✕ **La Caravella.** Cobalt blue napery, antiques, tall candles, lace tablecloths, floral curtains, marble floors, and Andrea Bocelli's golden voice on the sound system have helped to make this the most romantic restaurant in Amalfi, at least since 1959. The tasting menu is imaginative, but if you have to choose, just utter the lilting phrase *"Bocconcini di pesce con fagioli"* for a masterful dish of fish gouillons with cherry tomatoes and beans. ⊠ *Via Matteo Camera 12, near Arsenale,* ☎ *089/871029. AE, MC, V. Closed Nov. and Tues.*

$$–$$$ ✕ **Al Pesce d'Oro.** The big-hearted brothers who oversee the place, their kids who serve you, and mamma and the other family-folk who keep the kitchen hopping at this comfortable roadside restaurant just west of town will win your heart. None of them speak much English—it's a local fave, so they don't have to—but you'll have fun getting by, and you'll have a terrific meal, featuring—what else?—*pesce*, fresh as the sea. Try the fusilli with mussels and clams. ⊠ *Via Giovanni Agustariccio,* ☎ *089/831231. AE, DC, MC, V.*

$$–$$$ ✕ **Lo Smeraldino.** Open since 1949, this airy, popular fish restaurant on Amalfi's almost-emerald waterfront dishes out reasonably priced seafood and *cucina tipica Amalfitana*, such as the tasty penne with tomatoes, cream, eggplant, peppers, basil, and cheese. You can see the boats bringing in the day's catch, along with Amalfi itself, and at night there's pizza on the terrace amid the twinkling lights of hills, sea, and sky. ⊠ *Piazzale dei Protontini 1,* ☎ *089/871070. AE, DC, MC, V.*

$$–$$$ ✕ **Trattoria da Ciccia-Cielo-Mare-Terra.** Big windows overlook the sky, sea, and land, and there is ample free parking, so this modern seafood restaurant is a good place to stop if you're driving. Young owner Francesco Cavaliere will give you a warm welcome. Spaghetti *al cartoccio*, baked in a paper bag with clams, olives, capers, and tomatoes, is an Amalfi tradition. Finish up with a lemon profiterole, a nice adaptation for the ubiquitous citrus. ⊠ *Via Giovanni Agustariccio, across from Al Pesce d'Oro,* ☎ *089/831265. AE, DC, MC, V. Closed Nov. and Feb.*

$$ ✕ **Il Teatro.** Once a children's theater, this informal, high-ceiling, white-stucco restaurant in the medieval quarter is 50 steps above the main drag and most charming. A house pasta specialty is *scialatielli al teatro* and the pizzas are terrific. ✉ *Via E. Marini 19,* ☎ *089/872473. AE, MC, V. Closed Wed. and Jan.–mid-Feb.*

$–$$ ✕ **Il Tari.** Locals highly recommend this cozy little ristorante named after the ancient coin of the Amalfi Republic and located a few minutes' walk north of the Duomo. Appealing touches include local art, red tablecloths, old photos, and tile floors—not to mention wood-oven-baked thin-crust pizza with fresh sauces, and pasta specialties including tagliatelle *alla Tari.* ✉ *Via P. Capuano,* ☎ *089/871832. AE, MC, V. Closed Nov.*

$$$$ ⌂ **Il Saraceno.** Gothic, Arabic, Oriental—and Las Vegas—influences
★ combine to form this gorgeous extravaganza set on a chunk of cliff 3 km (2 mi) from Amalfi (its official address, but the hotel is really just outside Conca dei Marini). The evocatively exotic decor, which refers to Saracen pirates who roamed this coast centuries ago, begins in the lobby adorned with museum-quality 19th-century Orientalist oil paintings and antiques. Below, night-illuminated garden terraces descend the entire hillside to the enormous private beach, which features a saltwater pool. Dining options include a Romanesque cellar with candelabra and fireplace, and a formal restaurant called Castello, an alfresco terrace under a vine-covered lattice. Mosaic floors, elaborate antique lighting fixtures, a medieval warrior in full armor, and gilded murals are accents, and guest rooms have crown-molded ceilings, rich colors, antiques, and terraces with floor-to-ceiling window panoramas. The hotel also maintains a private Romanesque stone chapel. Whew. ✉ *Via Augustariccio 33, Conca dei Marini (on the road to Amalfi), 84011,* ☎ *089/831148,* FAX *089/831595,* WEB *www.saraceno.it. 56 rooms with bath. 2 restaurants, 2 bars, air-conditioning, pool, beach, meeting facilities, free parking. AE, DC, MC, V. Closed Nov.–Mar.*

$$$$ ⌂ **Luna Convento.** Founded as a convent in 1222, allegedly by no less a personage than St. Francis of Assisi, the hotel has been owned by the Barbaro family since 1822 and visited by Otto van Bismarck, Mussolini, Ingrid Bergman, and Tennessee Williams, among other noted figures. The restaurant and bar are in the 15th-century Saracen Tower, perched on a rock over the sea, providing a view that spans from Capo dei Conca to Capo d'Orso. Coved ceilings, graceful arches, and marble columns mark the architecture, along with Flemish religious artwork, church and convent artifacts, antique furnishings, and mosaic flooring, all of which mix with modern comforts. The heart of the hotel is the famed southern Romanesque cloisters and the beautiful Baroque chapel. Below the tower is a rocky beach and waterside pool. Ask for a room in the renovated wing. The food, alas, does not measure up. Half-board is sometimes required here; inquire when booking. ✉ *Via P. Comite 33, 84011* ☎ *089/871002,* FAX *089/871333,* WEB *www.lunahotel.it. 45 rooms. Restaurant, bar, pool. AE, DC, MC, V.*

$$$$ ⌂ **Santa Caterina.** When Elizabeth Taylor and Richard Burton wanted
★ to escape, they headed here, and who can blame them? Owned by the Gargano family for generations, this quietly elegant, supremely comfortable, and very beloved hotel has long been one of the treasures of the coast. No wonder guests have been coming here since grandmother's grandmother's day. Just outside Amalfi proper (giving it a grand vista of the town), the Santa Caterina takes full advantage of its hillside location. There are vast, terraced gardens and orchards overlooking the sea, and down by the water is a luscious seawater-pool area, complete with an idyllic thatched-roof, open-air café. The lobby is charmingly coved, while decor is unobtrusively traditional, with Belle Epoque accents. The luckiest guests are allowed to book the hotel's extraor-

dinary, 19th-century hunting-box châlet, set at water's edge at the far
end of the hotel's romantic orchards. ⊠ *Strada Amalfitana 9, 84011,*
☎ *089/871012,* FAX *089/871351,* WEB *www.hotelsantacaterina.it. 54
rooms with bath. Restaurant, bar, pool. AE, DC, MC, V.*

$$$ 🏨 **Aurora.** Regarded for its location near the beach of Spiaggia delle
Sirene and the fishing harbor, this well-run little hotel is a good deal
for sand potatoes who prefer absorbing rays to hiking the highlands.
Amid a greenery-filled setting with three levels of arched windows, guest
rooms are clean, with water views, and although just a flat and easy
10-minute walk to the town duomo, crowds rarely venture to this nook.
⊠ *Lungomare, on the harbor between Scalo d'Oriente and Lungomare
dei Cavalieri, 84001,* ☎ *089/871209,* FAX *089/872980. 29 rooms with
bath. Restaurant, breakfast room. AE, MC, V. Closed Nov.–Mar.*

$$$ 🏨 **Cappuccini Convento.** The most richly atmospheric of any hotel on
★ the Amalfi Coast—if not in all of Italy—this legendary place (correction,
time machine) can be a magical experience. Founded as a convent in the
14th century, transformed into a hostelry in the early 19th, its ambience
is staggeringly frozen-in-amber and little changed from the days when
it welcomed Longfellow, Wagner, kings, queens, dukes, and duchesses.
Set on a sky-touching cliff above the sea, its bougainvillea-draped terrace frames a view of Amalfi's harbor so perfect it became the iconic image
of the region in the 19th century—Wagner decamped from his room to
sleep under the stars on the fabled loggia, today set with tables for food-
with-a-view meals. With its umbilical cord to the past, this hotel has sublimely forgotten about the present and future—so don't come here
looking for what any other hotel can give you: enormous buffets of four-
star food, high-tech facilities, pools. Guest "activities?" You'll find people writing novels, painting watercolors. No, come here to escape to the
sepia-toned past, creaking beds, dusty corridors, and all. The public areas
are threaded with intriguing passages lined with Victorian lecterns and
Savonarola chairs; other decor treasures include a famous Arab-Sicilian
cloister (now a reception center) and a rococo-era chapel. Most guest
rooms are converted friar's cells and suites—some as bare as two beds,
a bureau, and a chandelier—but they also come with unforgettable
views overlooking the blue, blue sea and, more important, six centuries
of peace and quiet. Critics have complained that the management here
has not "kept up the hotel." Thank heavens. ⊠ *Via Annunziatella 46,
84011,* ☎ *089/871877,* FAX *089/871886,* WEB *www.hotelcappuccini.it. 54
rooms with bath. Restaurant, bar, parking. AE, MC, V.*

$$$ 🏨 **Miramalfi.** High above the main coastal drive, this white-stucco hotel
overlooks deep blue water and coastal ridges. The hotel's elevators, or
a steep hike, deposit you at the pool, with a rock ledge for sunbathing
carved from the cliff. Lobbies are sleekly decorated, and the dining room
serves up wraparound panoramas along with a nightly buffet; guests
may also dine on the sea-air terrace. Rooms have vibrant tile flooring,
brightly painted furnishings, floral fabrics, wicker, and lots of windows.
All have private sea-view balconies, and some have whirlpools. ⊠ *Via
Quasimodo 3, 84011,* ☎ *089/871588,* FAX *089/871287,* WEB *www.
miramalfi.it. 48 rooms with bath. Restaurant, bar, air-conditioning, pool,
beach, parking. AE, DC, MC, V. Closed Nov.*

$$ 🏨 **La Bussola.** Originally a mill and pasta factory, this clean, well-run,
moderate-price hotel is on a relatively quiet street across from the har-
bor. The chrome-and-wood American bar, velour seating, psychedelic
tile flooring, and wall sculptures combine to create an ingenuously funky
setting—the Austin Powers of decor. A big terrace features wooden shutters, wrought-iron grilles, and azure-blue tiles echoing the hue of the
sea visible over the railing. The smallish guest rooms have soft lighting, warm wood furnishings, and small balconies. This is a great value
for the money. ⊠ *Lungomare dei Cavalieri 16, 84011,* ☎ *089/871533,*

FAX *089/871369,* WEB *www.labussola.it. 62 rooms with bath. Restaurant, bar, parking. AE, DC, MC, V.*

$$ 📺 **Piccolo Paradiso.** A location in the Amalfi harbor area just across from the Arsenale already makes this upscale B&B a special choice. A small elevator deposits you in the cozy house, sunny yellow with green shutters, with a casually furnished sea-air and sun-bright terrace. The atmosphere is more pleasing and elegant than that of a typical pensione. A common area has tile flooring, and rooms are smallish but comfortable, with wicker seating and wrought-iron headboards, even some private terraces. Open only a few years, everything sparkles, and you'll get to know your fellow international guests in this little paradise. ✉ *Via M. Camera 5, 84011,* ☎ *089/873001. 6 rooms with bath. No credit cards.*

$–$$ 📺 **Sole.** This three-story, white-stucco pensione near the municipal museum and an easy stroll from the harbor has a café and flower boxes on the balconies. The lobby is clean and airy, with a graceful staircase, archways, and wrought-iron lighting fixtures, and there's an old mahogany bar. Some simply furnished rooms have balconies or terraces. Though the place is pretty basic, choose a double room, and you will have adequate accommodations, and with half- or full-board, extra-special value. ✉ *Largo della Zecca 2, 84011,* ☎ *089/871147 or 089/ 871559,* FAX *089/871926,* WEB *www.starnet.it/hsole. 13 rooms with bath. Restaurant, bar, parking. AE, DC, MC, V.*

Festivals

Amalfi's festivals best reflect the splendor of its past. The **St. Andrew Race** every June 27, dedicated to Amalfi's protector of seamen, is a joyous religious celebration commemorating the defeat of Barbarossa and the Moslem fleet in 1544. A procession of white-robed men carry a silver-gilt replica of the saint to the harbor, and fishermen at the beach run it back to the cathedral and—in one dramatic dash—straight up its 62 steps. Later, the statue gleams silver in the sunshine of the piazza, as fishermen hang tiny wooden and gilt fish amulets from the saint's left wrist as tokens of gratitude. In the evening, guitar music drifts from many boats, and candlelight flickers.

Even more of a pageant is the **Regatta Storica delle Antiche Repubbliche Marinare** (Historical Regatta; ☎ 089/871107), the mock battles in which four boats, each with eight oarsmen, represent the medieval maritime republics of Amalfi, Pisa, Genoa, and Venice. The prize, held by the winner for a year, is a scale-model gold-and-silver replica of an antique sailing ship. Each of the former republics is represented by 80 participants; Amalfi's musical contingent is adorned in jewel-encrusted costumes on loan from the town museum—doges, dogaressas, merchants, and commoners from the prosperous past come colorfully to life, with the day's festivities culminating in a show of fireworks. Held yearly on the first Sunday in June, with the four cities alternating as the urban stage sets, the pageant is scheduled to be in Amalfi in 2005.

Amalfitans love to celebrate holidays. The Good Friday candlelight procession, Easter Sunday, and Christmas pageants with crèche competitions (with cribs mounted in the city fountains) are all excuses for lavish family occasions, with special foods and church ceremonies.

Nightlife

Amalfi doesn't have many clubs for music or dancing. Check out **Torre Saracena** (✉ across from Luna Convento Hotel, on the water, ☎ 089/ 871064)—a historic watchtower recycled to offer music and dancing.

Shopping

A must-must-must for lovers of art, vintage prints, and fine books is down by the waterfront: **Andrea de Luca** (✉ Largo Cesareo Console

8, ☎ 089/872976), a publisher of fine books and postcards, whose shop sells desk accessories, objets d'art, and art tomes. The **Cartiera Amatruda,** in the Amatruda Mill (✉ Via Fiume 100, beyond the museum, ☎ 089/871315), is run by descendants of an Amalfi paper-making dynasty dating from at least 1500; it is probably the oldest crafts paper shop in Italy and still produces and sells fine parchment-color handmade paper. The shop is a short uphill walk north of Largo Marini on Via delle Cartiere. If pining for English language newspapers, wanting a book on Amalfi's history, or just looking for a suitable poolside novel, try the **Libreria-Edicola Internazionale** (✉ Via Repubbliche Marinare 17, ☎ 089/871180) near the tourist office. Leather goods are popular items in small shops along the main streets; one good option is **Bazar Florio** (✉ Via P. Capuano 5/7, ☎ 089/871980), with a fair and friendly owner. It features handbags, wallets, and backpacks. **D'Antuono** (✉ Piazza Duomo 10, ☎ 089/ 872368, WEB www.cartadiamalfi.it) sells art books, old prints, and fine paper goods. **Mostacciuto** (✉ Piazza Duomo 22, ☎ 089/871552) is run by a well-known and respected coral craftsman.

Atrani

★ ③② *1 km (½ mi) east of Amalfi; 5 km (3 mi) southwest of Ravello.*

Ask hotel owners and longtime residents of the Costiera Amalfitana where their favorite spot is along the coast, and they often respond "Atrani." Most actually whisper, as if it were some secret treasure—and in some respects, it is: set atop a crag between cliffs overlooking the sea, and just a 10-minute walk from the western outskirts of Amalfi—take the seaside stairs off the drive, past the Luna Convento—this stage-set of a medieval town is centered around a small piazza. When closely linked to the republic, the town was the residential choice of Amalfi aristocracy. Now home to 1,000 or so residents, Atrani is largely overlooked by tourists, who drive right by it over the riverbed of the Torrente Dragone. But its special charms are most evident from the sea, as it appears like an amphitheater ready for a royal pageant.

Adorable Piazza Umberto I, entirely enclosed by four-storied houses, is the setting for the basics of Italian life: general store, stationery store, coffee shop, bar, fruit stand, restaurant, barber, and, of course, police station (the constable struts about as though in command of the pigeons strutting alongside him). The uncrowded square is filled with simple scenes: children giggle at hide-and-seek, *duenas* gossip, and men debate and take sips from the venerable fountain as if the world had little changed from the days of the doges. An arcade to one side offers a glimpse of beach, fishing boats, a mule or two, and the sea beyond. At Christmas the whole town congregates here at dawn to drink cappuccino and share traditional cakes.

Atrani's closely packed, dollhouse-scaled backstreets are filled with pastel and white houses and shops, fragrant gardens, arcaded lanes, and spiraling scalinatelle. But the hamlet's stellar attractions are the Baroque-style churches which dominate the skyline, and around which parish houses cluster in true medieval style.

The bell of the 10th-century Church of **San Salvatore de Bireto** tolled to announce the crowning of a new doge. The coronation ceremony was restricted to those wearing a *bireto,* the cloth cap that would be ceremoniously placed on the new doge's head, and someday worn at his burial in the same church. The church was remodeled in 1810; the dome is beautifully tiled, and the paneled bronze doors cast in the 11th century came from Constantinople, as did the doors in the Amalfi

Duomo. Within is a carved 12th-century marble plaque showing two peacocks, the left hand one standing over a human head between two sirens, the other on a hare being attacked by two birds; peacocks were considered immortal, but the symbolism of the two in this setting is open to interpretation.

The Church of **Santa Maria Maddalena,** set on a piazza, was built in 1274 and given a neo-Baroque facade in 1852. The dome is covered in majolica tile, and the bell tower has an octagonal belfry similar to the campanile of the Carmine church in Naples. Among the treasures here are an altar in richly colored marbles and 16th-century paintings attributed to Amalfi Coast artists: *St. Magdalen between St. Sebastian and St. Andrew* by Giovannangelo D'Amato of Maiori, and *The Incredulity of St. Thomas* by Andrea da Salerno.

Feisty little Atrani, which produces colorful ceramics along with its charm, gained its independence from Amalfi in 1578, with whom it maintains a friendly rivalry; locals say the town holds its processions on its narrow inner streets to discourage Amalfitans from participating.

Dining and Lodging

$$-$$$ ✕ **A. Paranza.** At the back of the piazza, on the main walkway, this fine old restaurant, graced by a mural of fishermen, is the best to be found in Atrani. Everything glistens, from the tile floors to the fresh seafood. Dine on the special tasting menu—depending on the day's catch—or you can always count on spaghetti *ai frutti di mare.* ⊠ *Via Dragone 1/2,* ☎ *089/871840. AE, DC, MC, V. Closed Dec. 8–26 and Tues. Oct.–May.*

$$ ✕ **Le Arcate.** A cave is not where you'd normally expect to find good food, but this one changes the rules. The simple, dark, old restaurant tucked under the road also has a large terrace overlooking the beach. Folks dig its *Scialatielli Masaniello*—fresh pasta named after the local boy who made good—as well as its pizza and grilled fish. It's been here for 50 years, a drop in the gulf around these parts. ⊠ *Via G. Di Benedetto 4, under arcades of roadway connecting Amalfi and Atrani,* ☎ *089/871367. AE, DC, MC, V. Closed Jan. and Mon. in winter.*

$$ ▦ **A' Scalinatella.** Filippo, the Donald Trump of Atrani, runs just about the only game in the village, with hostel beds, private rooms, and apartments (some with kitchens and washing machines) spread all over the place. These are only modest digs, but if you want to wake up in Atrani, you'll deal with it. A family restaurant on the piazza offers good, inexpensive food, for guests only, and there's a special low-price menu for students. ⊠ *Piazza Umberto I 5, 84010,* ☎ *089/871492,* ℻ *089/871930,* WEB *www.amalficoast.it/hotel/scalinatella. 30 rooms, some with bath. No credit cards.*

RAVELLO TO PAESTUM

Perched atop a ridge of Monte Cerreto "closer to the sky than the sea," according to French philosopher André Gide, Ravello gazes down on the Bay of Salerno and the humbler towns surrounding it, including Atrani. This cloud-riding perch is just one reason why some travelers give it the laurel as the Amalfi Coast's—some say Italy's—most beautiful town (in fact, the town has long been nicknamed *La bellissima*). Hearty souls trek between Atrani and Ravello by a path that climbs through the Valle del Dragone, or Dragon's Valley, a name inspired by the morning mists here. Most Ravello-bound travelers, however, take the municipal bus from Amalfi's Piazza Flavio Gioia, which corkscrews its way up 1,000 ft along a road in the southern Monti Lattari. Cars follow the same route and really come in handy when driving farther south along Statale 163 to the towns rimming the Bay of Salerno, which have their off-the-beaten-track appeal. If you're based in Naples and have singled out Ravello for a day's sampling of the Amalfi Coast, by far the quickest route is via the mountain pass called the Valico di Chiunzi, easily reached via the A3 Naples–Salerno *autostrada* from the exit at Angri.

Many travelers end their southward journey along the Amalfi Coast in Ravello. They might have a point (what can top that mountaintop paradise?), but other travelers savvy enough keep heading southward, for ahead lie less crowded seaport villages, the bustling city of Salerno, and fabled Paestum, site of three of the greatest ancient Greek temples in the world.

After dropping down to sea level from Ravello or going eastward from Amalfi, the coast road, Statale 163, descends into Minori, known for its good beach and ancient Roman heritage. The road climbs up the cape by Torre Mezzacapo, then drops back down to sea level near the 15th-century Church of San Francesco. Statale 163 then goes though the town of Maiori, with its much broader river valley producing another good beach, and passes Capo di Baia Verde, near the misleadingly named 17th-century Torre Normanna. The coast here becomes dramatic again, giving grand views of the sea as you climb past the promontory topped by Torre di Badia. Capo Tummolo and then Vallone di San Nicola, with the little village of Marina di Erchie, are ahead of you. The drive then descends to the fishing village of Cetara, set along a narrow inlet, then continues along the coast, passing Torre de Fuenti and Vallone di Albori, and then faces the sea near Torre della Marina di Albori. At the junction of Raito, a lush little village, you cross the bridge over the Vallone Bonea to the town of Vietri, at which point traffic-light reality returns. Follow Statale 163 to the city of Salerno. The Autostrada A3 south connects to E45, which leads to Battipaglia and the turn-off for the ancient temples of Paestum. Alternatively, hug the coast, driving along Salerno's *lungomare,* and continue along the fairly degraded coastline until you reach Paestum, 40 km (25 mi) from Salerno.

Ravello

★ ③ *6½ km (4 mi) northeast of Amalfi; 29 km (18 mi) west of Salerno.*

Positano may focus on pleasure, and Amalfi on history, but cool, serene Ravello revels in refinement. Thrust over Statale 163 and the Bay of Salerno on a mountain buttress, below forests of chestnut and ash, above terraced lemon groves and vineyards, it early on beckoned the affluent with its island-in-the-sky views and secluded defensive positioning. Gardens out of the *Arabian Nights,* pastel palazzos, tucked-away piazzas with medieval fountains, architecture ranging from Romano-Byzantine to Norman-Saracen, and those sweeping blue-water, blue-sky vistas have inspired a panoply of large personalities, including Wagner and Boccaccio, princes and popes, aesthetes and hedonists, and a stream of famous authors from Virginia Woolf to Tennessee Williams. Author and part-time resident Gore Vidal, not an easy critic, has called the town's Villa Cimbrone panorama "the most beautiful view in the world."

Though its origins are lost in obscurity, it may have been settled by Romans fleeing the sack of their dying empire. The town itself was founded in the 9th century, under Amalfi's rule, until residents prosperous from cotton tussled with the superpower republic and elected their own doge in the 11th century; Amalfitans dubbed them *rebelli* (rebels). In the 12th century, with the aid of the Norman king Roger, they even succeeded in resisting Pisa's army for a couple of years, though the powerful Pisans returned to wreak destruction along the coast. Even so, Ravello's skilled seafaring trade with merchants and Moors from Sicily and points east led to a burgeoning wealth, which peaked in the 13th century, when there were 13 churches, four cloisters, and dozens of sumptuous villas. Neapolitan princes built palaces; life was privileged.

But as is inevitable with all supernovas, Ravello's bright light diminished, first through Pisa's maritime rise in the 14th century, then through rivalry between its warring families in the 15th century. When the plague cast its shadow in the 17th century, the population plummeted from upwards of 30,000 to maybe a couple of thousand souls, where it remains today. When Ravello was incorporated into the diocese of Amalfi in 1804, a kind of stillness settled in. Despite the decline of its power and populace, Ravello's cultural heritage and special loveliness continued to blossom. Gardens flowered and music flowed in the ruined villas, and artists, sophisticates, and their lovers filled the crumbling palazzos. Grieg, Wagner, D. H. Lawrence, Chanel, Garbo and her companion, conductor Leopold Stokowski, and then, slowly, tourists, followed in their footsteps. Today, at the Villa Rufolo, the noted Fèstival Musicale di Ravello is held in its shaded gardens. Here, special Wagnerian concerts are often held to pay homage to the great composer, who was inspired by these gardens to compose scenes of *Parsifal*.

With the exception of the Villa Rufolo concerts, however, the hush lingers, especially in off-season, when there seem to be more cats than cars. Empty, narrow streets morph into whitewashed staircases rising into a haze of azure, which could be from the sea, the sky, or a union of both. About the only places that don't seem to be in pianissimo slow motion are Piazza Duomo, in front of the cathedral, during the evening passeggiata, or cafés at *pranzo* (luncheon) or *cena* (dinner) time. Languor becomes Ravello's mood, a bit out of sync with the world below, and it makes this town a lovely place to catch your breath. Ravello, the slightly aloof star high above the coast, remains there for the reaching and is worth the stretch. Note that the town likes to celebrate religious festas throughout the year—one of the nicest celebrations is the blossom-strewn celebration of Pentecost (usually the first week of June), when Piazza Duomo is ornamented with sidewalk pictures created with flower petals.

Although cars need to park in the municipal parking lot, most arriving buses deposit their passengers near the hillside tunnel that leads to Piazza Duomo. On the square you'll find the tourist office, just to the left of the 11th-century duomo stairs, and the Bric-a-Brac shop, a great resource for books on Ravello. Here, pride of place is taken by the **Duomo,** or town cathedral, dedicated to patron San Pantaleone and founded in 1086 by Orso Papiro, the first bishop of Ravello. Rebuilt in the 12th and 17th centuries, it retains traces of medieval frescoes in the transept, an original mullioned window, a marble portal, and a three-story 13th-century bell tower playfully interwoven with mullioned windows and arches. The 12th-century bronze door (1179) features 54 embossed panels depicting Christ's life, and saints, prophets, plants, and animals, all narrating biblical lore. It was crafted by Barisano da Trani, who also fashioned the doors of the cathedrals of Trani and Monreale. The nave's three aisles are divided by ancient columns, and treasures include sarcophagi from Roman times and paintings by southern Renaissance artist Andrea da Salerno. Most impressive are the two medieval *ambos,* or pulpits: The earlier one, used for reading the Epistles, is inset with a mosaic scene of Jonah and the whale, symbolizing death and redemption. The more famous one, used for reading the Gospels, was commissioned by Nicola Rufolo in 1272 and created by Niccolò di Bartolomeo da Foggia. It seems almost Tuscan in style, with exquisite Cosmatesque mosaic work and bas-reliefs and six twisting columns sitting on lion pedestals. An eagle grandly tops the colonnette fronting the inlaid marble lectern.

A chapel is dedicated to the left of the apse to San Pantaleone, a physician, who was beheaded in the 3rd century in Nicomedia. Every July 27 devout believers gather in hope of witnessing a miracle (similar to that of San Gennaro in Naples), in which the saint's blood, collected in a vial and set out on an inlaid marble altar, appears to liquefy and come to the boil (it hasn't happened in recent years) In the crypt is the **Museo del Duomo,** which displays treasures from around the 13th century, during the reign of Frederick II of Sicily, in an elegant setting. You'll find gold and silver work, sculpture, and a classic Campanian marble bust of a half-smiling woman from the Rufolo dynasty, whose name was Sichelgaita (try saying that one with a mouthful of *scialatielli*). ✉ *Museo del Duomo, Piazza del Duomo,* ☎ *089/858311.* ⌨ *€1.10.* ☉ *Church daily 9–1 and 3–7; museum Apr.–Oct. daily 9:30–1 and 3– 7 (open weekends only Nov.–Mar.).*

Hard by the duomo on the main piazza is the three-aisle 13th-century **Santa Maria a Gradillo** with its lovely dome. This was the place where the town noblemen gathered to discuss civic issues; its atrium collapsed in the 18th century. The small Sicilian-Saracenic bell tower has two light mullion windows. Next door is the private **Museo del Corallo** (Coral Museum), which shows the venerable tradition of Italian workmanship in coral, harvested in bygone centuries from the gulfs of Salerno and Naples and crafted into jewelry, cameos, and figurines. Look in particular for a carved Christ from the 17th century and a tobacco box covered in cameos. ✉ *Piazza Duomo.* ☉ *Mon.–Sat. 10–noon and 3–5.*

★   Opposite the duomo is the **Villa Rufolo,** which—if the master story-teller Boccaccio is to be believed—was built in the 13th century by Landolfo Rufolo, whose immense fortune stemmed from trade with the Moors and the Saracens. Now the setting for the Fèstival Musicale di Ravello, its Romanesque walls contain a scene that seems from the earliest days of the Crusades. Norman and Arab architecture mingle in profusion in a welter of color-filled gardens so lush that composer Richard Wagner used them as inspiration for Klingsor's Garden, the home of the Flower Maidens, in his opera *Parsifal.* Beyond the Arab-Sicilian cloister and the Norman tower are two flower-bedded terraces that offer the prime vista of the Bay of Salerno, set off by the cupolas of the 13th-century Church of Santissima Annunziata and a dramatic umbrella pine tree. In 1851 the villa was acquired by Sir Francis Nevile Reid, a Scotsman, who hired Michele Ruggiero, head of the excavations at Pompeii, to restore the villa to its full splendor and replant the gardens with rare cycads, cordylines, and palms. Highlights of the villa are its Moorish cloister—an Arabic-Sicilian delight with interlacing lancet arcs and polychromatic palmette decoration—and the 14th-century Torre Maggiore, the so-called Klingsor's Tower, renamed in honor of Richard Wagner's landmark 1880 visit and today a dramatic spot for chamber-music recitals (note that when weather is rainy, concerts are moved into a nearby charmless room). Beyond lie two spectacular terrace gardens, with the lower one, the "Wagner Terrace," often the site for orchestral concerts. ✉ *Piazza Duomo, 84010,* ☎ *089/857866.* ⌨ *€3.2.* ☉ *Daily 9–sunset (closes earlier on concert days).*

For a closer look at the **Santissima Annunziata** (now a center hosting conferences of the Center for Research for Villas and their Urban Environments, based at the Villa Rufolo), exit the villa and take a sharp right to reach the Via dell'Annunziata stair path, which plummets you down the hillside past the church to the scenic Via della Repubblica. Head back up the road—which offers a panoramic vista of the blue bay—to the town square and take Via Richard Wagner, behind the tourist office, to Via San Giovanni a Toro, the address of Ravello's grandest palazzi (now hotels). **Villa Episcopio,** a 12th-century bishop's residence, was formerly called Villa di Sangro. Amid the gardens and ruins, Italy's King Vittorio Emanuele III abdicated in favor of his son, and Jackie Kennedy enjoyed breaks from her public obligations. Vineyards here have been cultivating grapes since 1860, and varieties of Ravello rosso and bianco, as refined as their namesake, can be purchased in town.

Farther along the Via San Giovanni del Toro, gourmands and art lovers will want to stop at the **Hotel Caruso Belvedere,** set in a historic palazzo which has the most ravishing room on the entire Amalfi Coast: an Empire-era *grande salone,* with frescoed ceiling, walls adorned with dozens of 19th-century Neapolitan paintings, and grand antiques. Picnickers can opt instead to enjoy the wonderful view of the adjacent Belvedere Principessa di Piemonte. Across the tiny piazza is the 11th-century Church of **San Giovanni del Toro.** Its evocative interior has three high apses and a crypt with 14th-century frescoes of Christ and the apostles. A 12th-century ambo (pulpit) by Alfano da Termoli startles the eye with its blue Persian majolica and four columns topped with elaborate capitals. The chapel of the Coppola family in the left aisle has an exceptional 14th-century relief of St. Catherine of Alexandria. The small church's three porticos adorned with lunettes show an Arabian influence and the tripart back facade is exquisite. ⊠ *Piazza San Giovanni del Toro.*

★ To the west of the main square, a hilly 10-minute walk along Via San Francesco brings you to the **Villa Cimbrone,** whose gardens and Belvedere of Infinity perch 1,500 ft above the sea. The ultimate aerie, this medieval-style fantasy was created in 1905 by England's Lord Grimthorpe and made world famous when Greta Garbo found sanctuary here from the world press when she holidayed in Ravello with Leopold Stokowski in 1937. The Gothic *castello-palazzo* is set in idyllic gardens, which are divided by the grand Alleé of Immensity, leading in turn to the literal highpoint of any trip to the Amalfi Coast—the legendary **Belvedere of Infinity.** This grand stone parapet, adorned with amusing stone busts, overlooks the entire Bay of Salerno. Be sure to explore all the pathways of the garden to find its mock-Gothic crypt, its Temple of Bacchus tempietto (under which Lord Grimthorpe is buried), its tea pavilion done in the style of Florence's Pazzi Chapel, and its Grotto of Venus. Many feel this is the most beautiful garden in all Italy; be sure to visit here and decide for yourself. The villa itself is now a hotel. ⊠ *Via S. Chiara 26,* ☎ *089/857459.* 🎟 €*4.2.* ☉ *Daily 9–half hr before sunset.*

Nearly every street in Ravello has a historic church or villa. Two notable religious sites are the church and convent of **San Francesco,** founded in 1222 by St. Francis of Assisi, with a small Gothic cloister; the church was rebuilt in the 18th century (on Via S. Francesco). Majolica flooring in the 13th-century **Monastero di Santa Chiara** (on Via S. Chiara) is one special element; another is the *matronaeum,* or women's gallery, the only one left on the Amalfi Coast (not known for segregating the sexes, or anything else). Buy some gelati on the piazza by the duomo and walk east to the **Piazza Fontana Moresco,** below the Hotel Parsifal and above the gates of the walled perimeter, to check out the two stone lions on the fanciful 1,000-year-old fountain, still spewing water.

Dining and Lodging

$$$ ✕ **Palazzo della Marra.** The young chef-owners of this restaurant attempt to turn Campania classics into something more—and they usually succeed. Past a fireplace that flickers in season, vaulted ceiling, and museum-size paintings and down wide stairs, you descend into a white, modernized 13th-century setting. The daily *menu turistica* may offer such dishes as *scarola ripiena* (stuffed endive), *risotto con zucca rossa e capesante dorate alla salvia* (red-pumpkin risotto with seafood in sage), and *lombo di agnello al rosmarino con spinaci all'uvetta* (lamb cutlets with spinach and raisins). Tasting menus—to suit various appetites and wallet-sizes—are even more creative, with unexpected combinations. To match the food, the owners provide a wine list featuring the best of the region. ✉ *Via della Marra 7,* ☎ *089/858302. AE, DC, MC, V. Closed 3 wks in Nov. and 6 wks Jan.–Feb. and Tues. in winter.*

$$ ✕ **Cumpa' Cosimo.** Lustier-looking than most Ravello spots, Cumpa' Cosimo is run devotedly by Netta Bottone, whose family has owned this *cantina* for 70 of its 300-plus years. She herself has been cooking under the arched ceiling for more than 30 of them. You can't miss here with any of the dishes featuring classic Ravellian cuisine. A favorite (share it—it's huge) is a *misto* of fettuccine, fusilli, tortellini, and whatever other homemade pasta inspires her, served with a fresh, fragrant pesto. Meats are generally excellent—after all, they are supplied by the butcher shop next door, run by Netta's father. Local wines ease it down gently, and homemade gelato is a luscious ending. ✉ *Via Roma 46,* ☎ *089/857156. Reservations essential. AE, DC, V. Sometimes closed Mon. in winter.*

$$ ✕ **Vittoria.** Between the duomo and the church of San Francesco, this is a good place for a return to reality and an informal bite. Vittoria's thin-crust pizza with loads of fresh toppings is the star attraction, and locals praise it *molto.* But also try the pasta, maybe fusilli with tomatoes, zucchini, and mozzarella. Vittoria is pretty, too, with arches and tile floors. ✉ *Via dei Rufolo 3,* ☎ *089/857947. AE, DC, MC, V. Closed Tues. Nov.–Mar.*

$$$$ ✕🏠 **Palumbo.** Built in the 12th century as a palazzo, this famous hotel
★   has long been a stop for visiting Someones: Wagner, who composed here; Bogart, filming *Beat the Devil*; a young Jack and Jackie. Ancient marble columns, mosaic-tile floors, and museum-quality antiques combine to provide an elegant ambience throughout the hotel, while incredible views of the Bay of Salerno can be enjoyed from your own terrace or the lush gardens that sit below the hotel on the hillside. During the summer, guests have the option whisked down to a villa at sea level and being pampered in the hotel's coastal retreat. The classic yet innovative Continental cuisine—finish off your feast with lemon soufflé and Episcopio estate wine—is grandly served in the hushed 17th-century dining hall, or you can enjoy a view as delicious as the food atop the restaurant terrace. Most guest rooms display antiques and modern marble baths, except for those in the annex, though at just over half the cost you still have access to all the facilities of the main palazzo across the way. The lodging prices include both a sumptuous breakfast and a choice of either a gourmet lunch or dinner. ✉ *Via S. Giovanni del Toro 16, 84010,* ☎ *089/857244,* 📠 *089/858133,* 🌐 *www.hotelpalumbo.it. 21 rooms with bath. Restaurant, bar, air-conditioning, meeting room, parking. AE, DC, MC, V. Restaurant closed Nov.–Mar.*

$–$$ ✕🏠 **Salvatore.** Adjacent to the Hotel Graal and sharing the same glorious view, you enter by walking down into a small garden and then choosing between a large terrace or an indoor area for dining. The family creates classic Campanian cuisine, the service is friendly, and the over-look offers the best view of any inexpensive restaurant in the vicinity. Upstairs guest rooms are surprisingly upscale, with baths, TVs, air-conditioning, and balconies and with a price that makes them a great deal. ✉ *Via della Repubbliche 2,* ☎ FAX *089/857227. 6 rooms with bath. AE, MC, V. Restaurant closed Mon. in winter; hotel closed Nov.–mid-Mar.*

$$$$ 🏨 **Palazzo Sasso.** In this 12th-century home of the aristocratic Sasso family, Wagner penned part of his opera *Parsifal* in the 1880s, and in the fashionable 1950s, the Sasso hosted Ingrid Bergman and Roberto Rossellini. On reopening in July, 1997, after a 20-year hiatus, the hotel is still luring the glitterati—its first guests were Placido Domingo and his entourage. Ordinary mortals, too, can come to sightsee and peek at the gleaming marble atrium, glass elevators, two rooftop hot tubs, roaring waterfall, and bar (now one of Ravello's prime watering holes). Traditionalists might look askance (if not be totally horrified) at all this glitz in quaint old Ravello, but no one will complain about immacu-lately furnished guest rooms, with the latest computer-operated light-ing and air-cooling systems. The Rossellini restaurant is also not to be sniffed at. ✉ *Via San Giovanni del Toro 28, 84010,* ☎ *089/818181,* FAX *089/858900,* WEB *www.palazzosasso.com. 38 rooms, 5 suites, with bath. Restaurant, bar, café, air-conditioning, pool, outdoor hot tub, li-brary, solarium, meeting room. AE, DC, MC, V. Nov.–Feb.*

$$$$ 🏨 **Villa Cimbrone.** Suspended over the azure sea and set amid rose-laden
★ gardens, this magical place was once the home of Lord Grimthorpe and the holiday hideaway of Greta Garbo. Now exquisitely transformed into a hotel, the Gothic-style *castello* (castle) has guest rooms ranging from palatial to cozy (opt for the Peony Room, which has its own ter-race). Tapestried armchairs, framed prints, vintage art books, and other antiques which belonged to Viscountess Frost, the lord's daugh-ter, still grace the enchantingly elegant sitting room. Best of all, guests have the villa's famous gardens all to themselves once their gates are closed at sunset. The villa is a strenuous hike from the town center, but porters will carry your luggage and the distance helps keep this the most peaceful place on the Amalfi Coast. ✉ *Via Santa Chiara 26, 84010,* ☎ *089/857459,* FAX *089/857777,* WEB *www.villacimbrone.it. 19 rooms with bath. Library. AE, MC, V. Closed Nov.–Mar.*

$$$–$$$$ 🏨 **Caruso Belvedere.** Now closed for an on-going restoration (*possi-*
★ *ble* opening date: 2003), this is one of the most beloved hotels in the world, which in decades past has been a favored home-away-from-home for the likes of Virginia Woolf, Tennessee Williams, Graham Greene, the Khedive of Egypt, Margot Fonteyn, and Peter O'Toole. Legendar-ily old-fashioned, set in an 11th-century palazzo, overlooking an in-comparable panorama of the Bay of Salerno, with lush gardens and a grand salon that would have made even Napoléon feel comfortable, the Caruso Belvedere is now in limbo and "sotto sequesto," which basi-cally means all work has stopped: Rumor has it that the new owners thought they could make some radical changes to this historically listed building and were caught red-handed! Let us hope that the unique aura of this place will be retained and that the wonderful Caruso family will remain as presiding spirits. ✉ *Via Toro 52, 84010,* ☎ *089/857111.*

$$$–$$$$ 🏨 **Rufolo.** D. H. Lawrence worked on *Lady Chatterley's Lover* dur-ing his 1926 visit, so it might be fun to revisit the novel's groundbreaking love scenes while you're here. Rooms have mosaic or terra-cotta floors, and some have balconies to liven up the snug quarters with gorgeous sea and sky vistas framed by the palm trees of the Villa Rufolo, set just below the hotel. ✉ *Via San Francesco 1, 84010,* ☎ *089/857133,* FAX *089/857935,* WEB *www.hotel-rufolo.it. 34 rooms with bath. Restaurant, bar, air-conditioning, pool, meeting room, free parking. AE, DC, MC, V. Closed Feb.*

$$$ ☗ **Graal.** The name comes from the Holy Grail, as in Wagner's opera *Parsifal*, but this inn is more an operetta. It's much less grand that Ravello's famous hotels, with a modern decor that's a bit of a downer. Nevertheless, it reaches high-Cs for comfort, cleanliness, and contentment. Hovering over the water on the Via della Repubblica with a nearly unobstructed view of the bay, this hotel possesses one of the friendliest staffs around, a pretty pool area, and facilities for whirlpools and fancy baths. In the dining room, meals from a family kitchen are delivered to tables dressed in linen and set near large, arched windows. Most rooms are smallish, some are deluxe (especially No. 342, with a double whirlpool and a bed from which you can see the great view), but all offer tiled floors and balconies. ✉ *Via della Repubblica 8, 84010,* ☎ *089/857222,* FAX *089/857551,* WEB *www.graal.it. 35 rooms with bath. Restaurant, bar, air-conditioning, pool, meeting room, parking. AE, DC, MC, V. Restaurant closed Mon. in winter.*

$$$ ☗ **Villa Maria.** Fronted by a vast garden terrace, terra-cotta–color Villa Maria has more sunny warmth than most formal hotels in Ravello. Public areas have tiled floors, high ceilings, lace, and antiques. All but two rooms are standard, and there's an airy suite that has a large balcony overlooking the coast. If the hotel becomes too quiet, your hosts promote fun with dancing and music out on the terrace. Note that views here look out over the Vallone del Dragone, not the bay, but are memorable all the same. Also check out Maria's next-door sibling, the Hotel Giordano, a former 18th-century manor house, which shares facilities with the villa. The rooms are less desirable here, but the pool is closer. ✉ *Via Santa Chiara 2, 84010,* ☎ *089/858400,* FAX *089/857071. 17 rooms with bath. Restaurant, bar, air-conditioning, pool, parking. AE, DC, MC, V.*

$$–$$$ ☗ **Parsifal.** In 1288 this diminutive property was a convent housing an order of Augustinian friars. Today the intact cloister hosts travelers simply intent on enjoying themselves mightily. Ancient, ivy-covered stone arches and a tiled walkway looking out over the coastline lead to a cozy interior that still feels a bit like a retreat. Sun lounges, a garden, a fountain with reflecting pool, and alfresco dining all overlook the sea. Rooms are small (monk's cells, after all), so ask for one with a balcony; Numbers 20, 22, 23, 24, and 26 are best. The charming young manager just dotes on Americans. Half-board is often required at peak season. ✉ *Viale Gioacchino d'Anna 5, Ravello 84010,* ☎ *089/857144,* FAX *089/857972,* WEB *www.hotelparsifal.it. 19 rooms with bath. Restaurant, bar, free parking. AE, DC, MC, V.*

$$ ☗ **Toro.** Right off the ladder of steps which some consider akin to a main street, this little hotel with a big garden and lots of antiques has been in the Schiavo family for three generations. Even this modest inn once boasted visiting VIPs: Composer Edvard Grieg wrote in the guest book that he was *"molto contento"* and artist M. C. Escher also stayed here (his celebrated prints of spiraling staircases were inspired by those he discovered in Ravello and Atrani). If you don't mind spare rooms and enjoy simple, good food, you, too, will be content. ✉ *Viale Wagner 3, 84010,* ☎ FAX *089/857211. 12 rooms with bath. Dining room. AE, DC, MC, V. Closed Nov.–Mar.*

$–$$ ☗ **Villa Amore.** A 10-minute walk from the main Piazza Duomo, this hotel is family run, with a garden, and shares the same exhilarating view of the Bay of Salerno as Ravello's most expensive hotels. Rooms are small, with modest and modern furnishings. Full board is available here and may be required in the summer. Reserve ahead, and specify time of arrival if you need help with luggage from the parking lot or bus stop (you pay about €5 per bag). ✉ *Via del Fusco 5, 84010,* ☎ FAX *089/857135. 12 rooms with bath. Restaurant, bar. DC, MC, V.*

Nightlife and the Arts

Other than the concerts offered by the Fèstival Musicale di Ravello, there is little nightlife activity, unless you count moongazing. A few cafés and bars are scattered about, but the general peacefulness extends to evening hours. Hotels and restaurants may offer live music and can advise you about any clubs, but around these parts the sound is either soft and classical—or silence.

CONCERTS

Sublime music and views makes a nifty combo in Ravello, long host to the celebrated **Fèstival Musicale di Ravello** (Ravello Music Festival; ✉ Via Trinità 3, ☎ 089/858149, FAX 089/858249, WEB www. ravelloarts.org), held on the garden escarpments of the Villa Rufolo. Due to popular demand, this is no longer just a summer-only affair. In addition to the Wagner concerts held in July and the *concerti di mezzanotte* (midnight concerts, which actually begin at 11 PM) in August, many other concerts are performed from March through November and even later. The most unusual event is the *concerto all'alba* (dawn concert), when the entire town wakes up at 4:30 to watch the sun rise over the bay to the accompaniment of music from a full symphony orchestra; this event is usually scheduled for the second week of August. The Villa Rufolo concerts actually comprise a number of events through the year: the Concerti a Villa Rufolo, held in July and July; the Concerti di Mezzanotte and Genius Loci/Musicians from Campania, in August; the International Weeks of Chamber Music, in September; the Autumn Season, from October to December; and the Winter and Spring concerts, from January to May. Most evening concerts are held at 9:30, with occasional performances starting at 6:30. Note that the 9:30 concerts begin well after the sunset hour, so come earlier if you want to catch the evening glow. Annual concert schedules are posted outside Villa Rufolo and may also be picked up at tourist information offices on the Amalfi Coast.

Shopping

Bric-a-Brac (✉ Piazza Duomo 16, ☎ 089/857153) has some 19th-century antiques, including historic crèche scenes; in the front of the store is a fine selection of books and antique prints about Ravello—a must for history and art lovers. **Camo** (✉ Piazza Duomo 9, ☎ 089/857461), a coral and cameo studio, sells jewelry from simple to overwrought, crafted from shells and coral. Hillary Rodham Clinton is among those who have dropped by. Behind the shop is the town Museo dei Corallo, with some elaborate and antique coral concoctions on exhibit. **Ceramiche d'Arte** (✉ Via dei Rufolo 16, ☎ 089/857303) ships its good stock of Vietri-made and other hand-painted ceramics all over the world. Bargaining may reward you with a 10% discount, maybe more if you have a talent for it. There are also opportunities for gaining hands-on experience at their showroom and workshop a three-minute walk away in a courtyard at Via Roma 20. **Episcopio Winery** (✉ Via Giovanni a Toro, across from Hotel Palumbo) offers selections of fine Ravello vintages. **Gruppo Petit Prince** (✉ Via San Francesco, ☎ 089/858033) has a nice selection of stationery, prints, and artworks. **Ravello Gusti & Delizie** (✉ Via Roma 28, ☎ 089/857716) is stocked to the ceiling with *prodotti tipici e naturali della costiera Amalfitana*; this is the place for foodstuffs, as well as delicacies and wines from all over Italy. Sun-dried-tomato pasta, olive oil, and other treats are available, but most intriguing are the lemon products—candles and soaps, and even lemon honey, gathered and bottled by a town police officer.

Close-Up

A STROLL IN SWELLO RAVELLO

FROM THE CATHEDRAL in the the main square of the Piazza Duomo, head up the stepped Via Wagner, to the right of the church, then turn left on Via San Giovanni del Toro and take in the magnificent view of the Belvedere di Principessa di Piemonte. Proceed past San Giovanni del Toro, past the 13th-century convent of St. Augustine (now the Hotel Parsifal) to the Fontana Moresca fountain (near here is a good starting point for trails leading up to the chestnut forests above Ravello). Head back toward the main square via Viale Parco della Rimembranza to the Church of Santa Maria a Gradillo, opposite the famous step path which leads down to Atrani, along Via Roma to the Piazza Duomo. Explore the great Villa Rufolo, then return to its entrance and make a sharp left turn onto Via dei Rufolo and left again down Via Nevile Reid to the exquisitely picturesque Santissima Annunziata church. Backtrack 100 yards to pick up Via San Francesco, found off the northwest corner of the main square, to head past the underwhelming Convento di San Francesco, continuing upward until you hit Via Santa Chiara to reach the breathtaking Villa Cimbrone, thereby leaving the best until last. Tour the famous gardens, then return to the town center. Of course, few people ever really "leave" the Villa Cimbrone—you, as most visitors seem to do, will probably leave a part of your soul here.

Scala

 1½ km (1 mi) northwest of Ravello; 45 km (28 mi) east of Sorrento.

Scala is the country cousin to more sophisticated Ravello, and is a mere five-minute drive across the Vallone del Dragone. A tranquil farming center of vineyards and groves, it was once part of the Amalfi Republic, on a par with Ravello, and a few remaining traces reflect those days of grandeur. Possibly the first coastal town to be settled by the fleeing Romans, around the 4th century, the village was a bishopric until 1818 and the site of numerous convents, including the first Benedictine monasteries in southern Italy. A few churches remain from among more than 100 that were built in the tiny parishes which once threaded through its terraced hills.

The cathedral, consecrated to St. Lawrence, dates from the 12th century, as its belfry, basilica shape, and Romanesque portal show; the interior was completely remodeled in the 17th century. The glazed-tile floor is lovely, and the pulpit is decorated with colorful tesserae (tiny mosaics). A grateful Charles I of Anjou donated an enameled miter in 1270 after successfully repulsing a Saracen attack; other noteworthy items include 13th-century wood carvings above the altar depicting the crucifixion, and an elaborate ceiling, painted in 1748. The 13th-century crypt holds tombs of the Coppolas, a seignorial family of the town.

Among Scala's ruins is a Romanesque courtyard built by the wealthy Sasso family; Friar Gerardo da Sasso ran a hostel for pilgrims and later, in 1118, founded the Order of the Ospedalieri, an offshoot of the Knights of St. John. Scala has one distinction with which famed rival Ravello can't hope to compete: a panoramic view of Ravello.

Lodging

$$$ 🏨 **Marmorata.** Between Ravello and Minori, set in the township of Castiglione directly below clifftop Ravello, this former paper mill has been recycled into the most stylish, unusual hotel in this east-of-Amalfi stretch of lackluster lodgings. Originality, historic vibes, stucco-coved ceilings, gulf views, Oriental rugs, and guest rooms with minibars and TVs make this a most evocative and comfy hotel overlooking the gulf. It can be reached off Statale 163. Half-board is often required at peak season. ⊠ *Strada Statale per Amalfi, 84010,* ☎ *089/877777,* FAX *089/851189,* WEB *www.marmorata.it. 40 rooms and 2 suites with bath. Restaurant, bar, pool, dock, meeting room, free parking. AE, DC, MC, V.*

$ 🏠 **La Margherita.** Seeming more like a New England B&B than a Campania hotel—except perhaps for the view of the Bay of Salerno below and the sounds of spoken Italian—this charming little lodging above the Valle del Dragone has a pool in which you seem to be swimming across the valley to Ravello. The parlor is especially cozy, with Oriental rugs and antiques. Compact rooms have private showers and, most important, balconies on which to laze and gaze. Breakfast and a cold lunch are served on the terrace. The delightful young signora's parents own a restaurant down the road, and her pappa sometimes comes over to play the piano in the evening. The hotel is a five-minute walk south of Scala's center. ⊠ *Via Torricello, 84010,* ☎ *089/857106,* FAX *089/857219. 9 rooms with bath. Pool, meeting room. MC, V.*

Minori

㉟ *6 km (3½ mi) east of Ravello; 2 km (1 mi) west of Maiori.*

Minori can be traced to Roman times and functioned as a garrison outpost for the forces of the Amalfi Republic. Its gray-sand beach (along with neighboring Maiori's) is the widest and longest on the coast: tree-lined, level, with a promenade, a kids' amusement park, and scads of sunning locals. These two towns are much more modern than their neighbors due to 20th-century mountain floods that wiped out many historic buildings. However, there is the Romanesque (rebuilt 19th-century) **Basilica of St. Trofimena** and, in the western part of town, a 1st-century **Roman villa.** The latter was discovered (officially) in the 1932, and its ground-floor remains show that it incorporated a *viridarium* (garden) with a swimming-pool design—something like what an upscale vacation house would have today. Regrettably this area is currently roped off and only visitable by prior appointment, although you get a fairly good idea of the complex from the upper floor near the entrance. Built on the first floor and incorporating part of the baths structure is the Antiquarium. Inside (first room on the left) you can see the stubs of original *suspensurae* (small pillars) from the hypocaust system, stuccoed walls and part of the mosaic floor, as well as amphoras from various ages in antiquity, confiscated from over-enterprising antiques dealers. Information panels are all in Italian, so ask for the helpful English brochure available at reception. ⊠ *Via Santa Lucia,* ☎ *089/852893.* 🎫 *Free.* 🕙 *9–hr before sunset.*

Dining and Lodging

$$–$$$ ✗ **Capo d' Orso.** The pasta with ricotta and lemon is named here to honor Roberto Rossellini, who, in 1948, directed Anna Magnani and a young Federico Fellini in a film called *Il Miracolo (The Miracle),* right here at this very tower on the last really gorgeous point along the Amalfi Drive. Views are to both Capri and Salerno. A buzzy restaurant with a terrace and a glass-walled main room, it's run by three of the grandsons of the nonno who opened the place in 1950—they really know how to market, cook, and serve. They even won the Gold in the Salzburg Butter Competition for their sculpture of a coach and two horses, perhaps another miracle. The restaurant is in the Torre Nor-

manna, just past Maiori, which lies beyond the township of Minori. ✉ *Via D. Taiani 48, Maiori*, ☎ *089/877022*, FAX *089/852360. AE, DC, MC, V. Closed Nov.*

$$ ✕ **Ristorante L'Arsenale.** *Specialità marinare* is the focus at this little 13th-century arsenal-cum-restaurant, with stucco walls, two levels, an open kitchen, arched ceilings, and pretty plates and ceramics. It's a block from the expansive beach and a couple of blocks from the Roman villa. The citrus risotto with shrimp and prosciutto is to live for, and for something dolce, the young, ambitious brothers who have run the place since 1992 just opened a stylish coffee bar, L'Beccio, across the street. ✉ *Via S. G. a Mare 20*, ☎ *089/851418. AE, DC, MC, V. Closed Jan. and Mon. in winter.*

$$$ 🏨 **Hotel Villa Romana.** The nearby Roman villa inspires this family-run, low-key, in-town hotel. Rooms are being upgraded (some with whirlpools) to create a more attractive ambience. A solarium looks over the picturesque coastline and up to the heights and the lights of nearby Ravello, and room balconies overlook either the street or a quieter garden courtyard and the pool. A short walk takes guests to the sea. If you like the beach, don't need sophisticated surroundings, and want to be close to Ravello, this will suit you. ✉ *Corso Vittorio Emanuele 90, 84010*, ☎ *089/877237*, FAX *089/877302*, WEB *www.emmeti.it/villaromana.html. 53 rooms with bath. Restaurant, bar, air-conditioning, pool, meeting room, parking. AE, DC, MC, V.*

The Arts

Concerti di Mezza Estate (☎ 089/877135) presents music, ballet, and opera in July and August.

En Route After passing through Maiori, look up to see the twin turrets of the perfectly preserved Abbey of Santa Maria de Olearia, founded by the Benedictines in 973, now a private dwelling. You then round the cape, going eastward, under an imposing gray cliff carved into natural spires, towers, and pinnacles—locals accord some of these fanciful shapes descriptive titles, such as Horseback Rider. Descending from Monte Finestra to Capo d'Orso, the ridgeline runs between Valle dei Tramonti and Valle di Cava de' Tirreni; rock climbers face a challenge in this part. You may also hire a boat to take you to the Pandona Grotto, whose iridescence is similar to the Blue Grotto in Capri.

Marina di Erchie

36 *7 km (4½ mi) southeast of Minori; 3 km (2 mi) south of Cetara.*

With a looming Norman tower on the cliff above, the curving beachfront hamlet of Erchie is as romantic as can be, especially when it's just your party and the fishermen who haul in their catch in the pink sun of early morning. The little village of Erchie is built around a 10th-century Benedictine abbey destroyed and abandoned in the 12th century; Salerno took over the town in the 15th century. By the 1960s the abbey was restored in neo-Renaissance style, with a portal constructed in dark tufa and stone, and the little village was discovered by city dwellers in Salerno, who now flock here to windsurf along the cove and laze the day away.

Cetara

37 *3 km (2 mi) northeast of Erchie; 4 km (2½ mi) southwest of Vietri.*

Tourists tend to take a pass on the village of Cetara because of the hairpin turns off the main road. A quaint and quiet fishing village set below orange groves on Monte Falerzo, it was held in subjugation to greater powers, like most of these coastal sites, throughout much of its history. From being a Saracen stronghold in the 9th century, it became the final holding of Amalfi at the eastern edge of the republic, which all through the 11th and 12th centuries tithed part of Cetara's fishing catch, *ius piscariae*—the town's claim to fame. It is rumored that the village's Latin name comes from this big catch—*cetaria* (tuna net), but the town haul is most famous for its anchovies—thousands of years ago, salted and strained, they became a spicy liquid called *garum*, a delicacy to the rich of ancient Rome (it can still be purchased at local grocery stores here). After the Middle Ages, the village came under the dominion of the Benedictine abbey of neighboring Santa Maria di Erchie and then became the port of the abbey of Cava, above the coast, which traded with Africa and exchanged pilgrims with other abbeys and extracted anchorage dues. In 1534 the Turks, led by the tyrant Sinan Pasha—on the invitation, no less, of Prince Ferdinando Sanseverino of Salerno—enslaved 300 Cetaran villagers, spiriting them away in 22 galleys and executing those who would not cooperate. A few survivors fled to Naples, which immediately ordered a watchtower to be raised in Cetara to ward off future raids. This is one of the many landmarks that remind tourists that there were coastal perils previous to the one of driving on Statale 163. Beneath the tower is a rocky little beach, and a small park overlooks the harbor, where fishermen mend their nets and paint their boats. They often are away from home for months, fishing in deep waters. Other than the scenic charm of the waterfront, there are no main sights here, other than the Church of San Pietro, near the harbor.

Dining and Lodging

$ ✕ **Acqua Pazza.** Locals along this part of the coast rave about this tiny restaurant tucked on the main street. It is a modest environment—a spare interior with a few tables—its raison d'être being remarkably fresh seafood. ✉ *Across from church of San Pietro and a 3-min walk to the harbor. No credit cards. Closed Mon.*

$$$$ 🏨 **Cetus.** Cetara's leading hotel is set in a white-stucco building that seems to have grown right out of the living rock. The natural theme is continued within. A summer-light restaurant has floors of marble tile, a window-wall, and terraces. A steep walk leads to the hotel's private beach and "American" bar. Shutter doors open onto broad, stone-flagged spaces, with umbrella tables, casual seating, overflowing flower boxes, and close-up sea views. ✉ *Right off Amalfi Drive, just outside Cetara, 84010,* 🕿 *089/261388,* FAX *089/261388,* WEB *www.hotelcetus.it. 40 rooms with bath. Restaurant, 2 bars, air-conditioning, meeting room, beach, free parking. AE, DC, MC, V.*

Vietri sul Mare

38 *5 km (3 mi) northeast of Cetara; 3 km (2 mi) west of Salerno.*

Vietri sul Mare is rich in history. Founded in a river valley by the Etruscans, who called it Marcina, it was ransacked by the Samnites, became a prosperous Roman fishing outpost, and was then destroyed by the Vandals, all before 455. Then the Lombards made it a stronghold, the Saracens attacked regularly, and, in 1648, a French fleet pillaged the town. Perhaps to brighten their troubles, Vietrians have created renowned handcrafted and fired faience work and majolica ceramics since the beginning of the Middle Ages, when the craft was sponsored by the abbey at Cava de' Tirreni. In 1086 there were already 50 kilns blasting away, and the output decorates buildings and churches all along the coast, including the town's own 18th-century San Giovanni Battista and Confraternità del Rosario. Dozens of shops in town, and hundreds throughout the region, feature Vietri's colorful designs. For a complete rundown on Vietri's celebrated majolica and faience work, visit the **Museo della Ceramica Vietrese** (Ceramic Museum), housed in an eye-popping tile-covered edifice built in 1922, the former home of King Victor Emmanuel during the Salerno government of World War II. Exhibits range from medieval and Renaissance urns to the German-influenced ceramics of the 1950s, along with today's modern style, all painted with the traditionally colorful and fanciful designs based on the folklore, flora, and fauna of the Amalfi Coast. ✉ *Torretta di Villa Guariglia (Raito),* ☎ *089/211835.* 🎟 *Free.* ⊗ *Tues.–Sun. 9–1 and 4–7. Closed Mon.*

Vietri is the end, or the beginning, of the Amalfi Coast, and drive, depending on how you look at it—a busy, bustling town, with an older section by the sea and an upper area filled with factories, shops, and that mundane sign of the encroachment of civilization: traffic lights. It may be a manufacturing center, but the residents are keenly aware of aesthetics. Recently, the town imploded a modern building, which they felt blighted the beauty of the region. "It was like a nose job," said an official.

Lodging

$$$ 🏨 **Lloyd's Baia Hotel.** A short walk from the Museo della Ceramica Vietrese, this modern hotel has a restaurant with a wraparound sea view, a candlelit piano bar, and alfresco dining on the roof overlooking the sea. An elevator delivers guests to the bottom of a cliff, where they will find one of the most beachlike swimming areas of any hotel on the coast. There are two pools, practically in the gulf, a nice strip of sandy shore, cabanas, lounge chairs, umbrellas, and a restaurant. Sea sports and boating can be arranged from the beach. Guest rooms have sea views, small writing tables, TVs, and sitting areas, and some have balconies. Owned by Soglia Service, a local chain, it welcomes large groups. ✉ *Via De Marinis 2, 84019,* ☎ *089/7633111,* ﬔ *089/7633633,* ⓦⓔⓑ *www.lloydsbaiahotel.it. 121 rooms with bath. Restaurant, air-conditioning, pool, shops, convention center, free parking. AE, MC, V.*

Shopping

Dozens of shops purvey the exuberance, light, and color of the region captured in Vietri vases, dishes, statues, wall and floor tiles, and artworks. The most famous manufacturer is **Solimene Ceramica** (✉ Via Case Sparse at Fontana Vecchia, ☎ 089/210188), with a huge selection and established shipping. You can also visit the **factory** (✉ Via XXV Luglio 17).

OFF THE   **CAVA DE' TIRRENI** – Set in green hills inland from the coast (✉ 3½ km
BEATEN PATH   [2¼ mi] northwest of Vietri) is the modern town of Cava de' Tirreni—population about 50,000—reached by an easy turn off Highway A3, to or from Sorrento, Naples, or Rome. Cava was first a Roman settlement and later a major element in the Kingdom of Naples, famous for its silk tapestries. The old section has porticoed streets similar to those of Bologna, for centuries a leading importer of the local merchandise. The most picturesque area is Borgo Scacciaventi, named because its winding lanes block the winds and protect goods held beneath the porticos. The immensely rich abbey, the Abbazia della SS Trinita, was founded here in 1011 by a nobleman from Salerno and its church, monastery, cloisters, and museum hold many interesting treasures, including sarcophagi, paintings, pulpits, and 15th- and 16th-century majolica tiles from Vietri.

Salerno

③ *3 km (2 mi) southeast of Cetara; 50 km (31 mi) east of Sorrento.*

Salerno, the provincial capital creeping along its namesake gulf, lies just east of the Amalfi Coast, below the Monti Picentini (Picentini Mountains). Founded by the Etruscans in the 6th or 5th century BC, it later became a Roman colony, and the famed Salernitan medical school was established here around the 10th century, making it perhaps the oldest in Europe. Salerno's golden age was under the Lombards and Normans in the 9th–12th centuries, while others like the Swabians, Aragonese, and Spaniards fought hard over the territory, as did the Allied forces during World War II.

Salerno has a plethora of ports, parks, boulevards, and great old buildings, but also significant noise and air pollution thanks to its eternally congested streets and various kinds of urban blight—realities easily forgotten if you're coming from the idyllic Sorrento Peninsula and the Amalfi Coast. Nevertheless, Salerno is an important transportation, shopping, entertainment, and tourist-board hub, from which you can connect by bus, train, or boat to all major points in Italy. The Autostrada del Sole superhighway whisks you up toward Sorrento in as little as 40 minutes, a minor miracle for those who just spent hours on winding Statale 163 to cover the same distance. To get to Paestum, you just take the continuation of the highway south (E45) and exit at Battipaglia.

The city has made little capital out of its fine archaeological and historical pedigree: signposting to key monuments is generally poor, scooters still whiz through traffic-restricted zones, and the scenic network of footpaths leading from the medieval quarter up to the early medieval **Arechi castle** is very poorly maintained. Some would say this is part of the city's fascination, its many lights being seemingly hidden under compressed layers of bushels. If pushed for time, visit the grand 11th-century **Duomo** (⊠ Piazza Duomo, ☎ 089/231387. ☉ Daily 10–1:30 and 3–6). Founded in the mid-9th century and substantially rebuilt by Robert Guiscard in 1076–1085, the scene is set by the doorway—see the marble lions at the base—giving into a spacious atrium. The Cosmatesque ambos-pulpits rival Ravello's for elegance, while ornately carved marbled sarcophagi reinforce the cathedral's stately pedigree.

In addition, the **Museo Archeologico Provincale,** sited atmospherically in part of the medieval Benedictine abbey, has interesting displays of ancient artifacts from the region, with many of the higher quality finds consisting of grave goods from the Greco-Etruscan necropolis in what is now the suburb of Fratte. Some fine Attic and Corinthian vases are on display on the upper floor, though the show-stealer is the 1st-century BC bronze head of Apollo, fished out of the Gulf of Salerno in 1930. ⊠ *Via San Benedetto 28,* ☎ *089/231135.* ▨ *Free.* ☉ *Daily 9–5:30.*

Dining and Lodging

$$ ✕ **Alla Brace.** Stuffed peppers, potato soufflé, ravioli, and special fish dishes are well loved at this Salerno landmark near the waterfront. It's an especially convenient spot if you're staying at the Jolly Hotel. ⊠ *Lungomare Trieste 13,* ☎ *089/225159. AE, DC, MC, V. Closed Sun.*

$$ ✕ **Portacatena.** Occupying a centuries-old vaulted cellar midway between the opera house and the Duomo, this eatery labels itself as a mere trattoria but offers far more: try the *scarola imbottita* (escarole stuffed with capers, olives, and anchovies) or *tortina di carciofi* (artichoke pie). Half-portions or *assaggi* are thankfully encouraged here, so there are no agonizing decisions about what dishes to skip. ⊠ *Via Portacatena*

28–34, ☎ 089/235899. AE, DC, MC, V. Closed Aug. 10–20 and Sun. eve., Mon.

$$–$$$ 🏨 **Jolly Hotel.** Big, modern, and situated at one end of the waterfront promenade—near the major tourist sites—this lodging radiates the atmosphere of a business hotel. A member of the international Jolly chain, it is Salerno's finest: comfortable, indeed, but rather dull. Specify a sea-view when booking a double room, which also tend to be quieter. (Singles just get the town view.) The hotel is handily close to the port terminal for ferries plying the Amalfi Coast. ⊠ *Lungomare Trieste 1, 84100,* ☎ *089/225222, 800/2212626, or 800/2471277,* ☏ *089/237571,* WEB *www.jollyhotels.it. 103 rooms with bath. Restaurant, air-conditioning, parking. AE, DC, MC, V.*

$$ 🏨 **Hotel Plaza.** Guests can easily walk to the harbor, shops, and transportation from these clean no-frills lodgings, right across from the train station and tourist board. Though a period building, furnishings are contemporary in style, with all the paintings produced by the owner's artistic family. When booking, ask for a room on one of the upper floors, which tend to be quieter—or a room at the back overlooking the courtyard. ⊠ *Piazza Vittorio Veneto (Piazza Ferrovia), 84123,* ☎ *089/224477,* ☏ *089/237311,* WEB *www.plazasalerno.it. 42 rooms with bath. Bar, breakfast room, air-conditioning, free parking. AE, DC, MC, V.*

Nightlife and the Arts

Near the train station and along main streets in the waterfront area there are many clubs. One such is **Movida** (⊠ Via Generale Clark), the place to hear the latest disco music; ask at your hotel for the most up-to-date information about other nightspots. Cultural events are scheduled throughout the year, among them the **Festival Internazionale del Cinema** (International Film Festival; ☎ 089/254404) in October. The **Salerno Festival** (☎ 089/224744) offers major concerts July through September. Salerno's municipal summer arts season, **Viva l'Estate** (☎ 089/224744), is held from July to September.

Paestum

★ ⑩ *42 km (26 mi) southeast of Salerno, 99 km (62 mi) southeast of Naples.*

One of Italy's most majestic sights lies on the edge of a flat coastal plain: the remarkably well-preserved **Greek temples** of Paestum. The S18 from the north has now been rerouted via the train station (Stazione di Paestum), which is about 800 yards from the ruins. Access can be gained through the perfectly preserved archway **Porta Sirena,** or—if motorized—through the northern gate of **Porta Aurea.** The ruins are part of the ancient city of Poseidonia, founded by Greek colonists in the 7th century BC. When the Romans took over the colony in 273 BC and its name was latinized to Paestum, they changed the layout of the settlement, adding an amphitheater and a forum. Much of the archaeological material found on the site is displayed in the helpfully labeled **Museo Nazionale,** and several rooms are devoted to the unique tomb paintings discovered in the area, rare examples of Greek and pre-Roman pictorial art. About 200 yards from the museum (in front of the main site offices), framed by banks of roses and oleanders, is the **Tempio di Nettuno** (Temple of Poseidon), a magnificent Doric edifice with 36 fluted columns and an extraordinarily well-preserved entablature (area above the capitals), which rivals the finest temples in Greece. On the left of the temple is the so-called **Basilica,** the earliest of Paestum's standing edifices; it dates from very early in the 6th century BC. The name is an 18th-century misnomer, for the structure was in fact a temple sacred to Hera, the wife of Zeus. Behind it an ancient road leads to the **Foro**

Romano (Roman Forum) and the single column of the **Tempio della Pace** (Temple of Peace). Beyond—on the north side of the site—is the **Tempio di Cerere** (Temple of Ceres), thought to have originally been dedicated to the goddess Athena. From the thankfully pedestrianized road which runs past the site—actually it cuts the site in half—you can view the temples in the late afternoon or early evening, when the light enhances the deep gold of the limestone. *Via Magna Grecia,* ☎ *0828/811023.* ⌗ *Site €4.25, museum €4.25, combination ticket €6.35.* ⊙ *Excavations daily 9–1 hr before sunset; museum daily 9–6:30. Museum closed 1st and 3rd Mon. of each month.*

Lodging

$$ ⌗ **Azienda Agricola Seliano.** This working farm-with-a-difference is about 2 mi from the temples and consists of a cluster of 19th-century baronial buildings. The Baronessa Cecilia herself presides over all, with sons Ettore and Massimino handling visitor logistics. Top priority once you have settled in to your refurbished rooms is to make friends with all the farm dogs, who will then be your faithful companions on country walks past apricot orchards and fields of artichokes. Opt for half-board terms as most of the food is home-produced, including the rich buffalo stew, fresher-than-ever mozzarella, and more elaborate dishes brought with relentless regularity from the kitchens; you'll be seated, as is the tradition, with other guests around a large banqueting table. For those without transport, transfers can be arranged from Paestum main-line station while bicycles may be borrowed on a first-come, first-served basis. ✉ *Via Seliano, Paestum 84063, about ½ mi down a dirt track west off the main road from Capaccio Scalo to Paestum,* ☎ *0828/723634,* FAX *0828/724544,* WEB *www.agriturismoseliano.it. 9 rooms with bath. Restaurant, pool, horseback riding, bicycles. DC, MC, V. Nov.–Feb. (except Dec. 23–Jan. 7).*

$$ ⌗ **Helios.** Directly across the road from the Porta della Giustizia and only a few steps from the temples, the Helios has cottage-type rooms, each with a minibar, in a garden setting. Suites are also available. A pleasant restaurant serves local specialties and seafood. The home-produced ricotta and mozzarella are especially recommended. ✉ *Via Principe di Piemonte 1, Zona Archeologica, 84063,* ☎ *0828/811020,* FAX *0828/811600. 30 rooms with bath. 2 restaurants, minibars, pool. AE, DC, MC, V.*

SORRENTO AND THE AMALFI COAST A TO Z

AIR TRAVEL
CARRIERS
You can fly directly to Capodichino airport in Naples from Rome on Alitalia.

➤ AIRLINES AND CONTACTS: **Alitalia** (☎ 848/865641, WEB www.alitalia.it).

AIRPORTS
The nearest major airport is Capodichino in Naples. Autolinee Curreri Service runs the bus from Naples airport to Sorrento, leaving and arriving in Sorrento four times daily. Most hotels in the area will arrange transfers from the airport for an extra fee.

➤ AIRPORT INFORMATION: **Autolinee Curreri Service** (✉ Piazza Tasso, ☎ 081/8015420, 081/8015766, WEB www.curreriviaggi.it). **Capodichino Airport** (☎ 081/7896111).

BOAT AND FERRY TRAVEL

Ferries and hydrofoils run year-round but most frequently in high season. To get to smaller towns or to take private boats, you can make arrangements with private boat companies or independent fishermen. Seek out people who are recommended by the tourist office or your hotel.

In Alfami, ferries operated by Alicost, Cooperativa Sant'Andrea, and Linee Maritime Partenopee sail from Salerno to Positano (about €5), Capri (about €12), and from Amalfi to Salerno (€3.20); ticket booths are on the docks and on Lungomare dei Cavalieri. Hydrofoils are available in summer, but on an infrequent schedule.

In Positano the ferry and hydrofoil ticket office is in the Tabacchi Carpineto; ferries to Amalfi, Sorrento, Salerno, and Capri are available at a dock on Via Positanesi d'America, near the public beach in the center of town. Services are provided by Linee Maritime Partenopee and F.lli Grassi, which is located at the pier—look for the logo of a blue-and-white whale.

In Salerno, ferries to Amalfi and Positano leave from the main port at Piazza della Concordia; ferries continuing to Capri and Ischia leave from the west end of the waterfront at Molo Manfredi. A typical schedule is an early-morning departure and a late-afternoon return; the EPT office has current information, or call the Cooperative Sant'Andrea. Hydrofoil service is available in summer to Amalfi, Positano, Capri, and Sorrento.

In Sorrento, ferries and hydrofoils are operated by Alilauro, Caremar, Linee Lauro, Linee Marittime Partenopee; services—and fares—have been stepped up to Capri and there are frequent sailings of a variety of fast and slow craft (hydrofoil €8.50, ferry €6.50). Sorrento to Naples costs €10 and to Ischia Porto €12, with Salerno, Amalfi, and Positano served in the summer from June to September.

FARES AND SCHEDULES

➤ BOAT AND FERRY INFORMATION: **Alicost** (☎ 089/871483). **Alilauro** (☎ 081/8071430). **Caremar** (☎ 081/8073077). **Cooperativa Sant'Andrea** (☎ 089/873190, WEB www.coopsantandrea.it). **F.lli Grassi** (☎ 089/811620). **Linee Lauro** (☎ 081/8072009). **Linee Maritime Partenopee** (☎ 089/873301 in Amalfi; 089/875092 in Postiano; 081/8073024 in Sorrento). **Positano ferry and hydrofoil ticket office** (✉ Via del Brigantino, ☎ 089/875092).

BUS TRAVEL

Although some travelers opt for cars when touring the Amalfi Drive, most use the convenient and inexpensive SITA Blue Line buses. For best views on board, sit on the sea side of the bus (on your left as you board the bus if you're starting in Sorrento, on your right if you begin in Amalfi). The trip between Sorrento and Amalfi generally takes 80 minutes. The major bus stops, in order after departing from Sorrento's bus depot are: Sant'Agnello, Piano di Sorrento, Meta, Positano (the bus stops at the Chiesa Nuovo in the upper town, then a second—and the main—stop at Sponda, in the lower town), Praiano (in the township of Vettica Maggiore), Conca dei Marini, and then Amalfi, ending at the bus hub on Piazza Flavio Gioia. The bus driver will stop anywhere on the main route as long as you inform him of your destination, be it hotel or fork in the road, when boarding.

You can best enjoy the scenery if you leave the helm to drivers and bus power. Besides, the mighty elevation of bus seats high atop the road offers an even better perch to take in the passing show.

AMALFI

You can purchase SITA Blue Line bus and coach tickets prior to boarding at Bar Sita or any port-side bar, travel agency, or tobacco shop displaying a SITA sticker; all SITA buses leave Amalfi from Piazza Flavio Gioia. The special express bus to Naples departs many mornings at 8 AM (€3.65); catching this bus makes for an easy and scenic ride back to the city, allowing you to bypass a transfer from bus to the Circumvesuviana Railway in Sorrento.

POSITANO

Purchase SITA Blue Line bus and coach tickets prior to boarding at Tabaccheria. The Blue Line bus stops here are at Chiesa Nuova and Sponda. SITA buses pass through Positano almost hourly on the run from Amalfi to Sorrento, 7 AM–7:30 PM (later on weekdays). From Sorrento to Amalfi, 9 (earlier on weekdays)–9:30 PM (later on weekdays). In addition to the tobacconist listed above, check around for cafés and additional tobacconists selling SITA tickets.

In Positano, local Orange Line buses regularly ply even the smallest roads and make more stops than the SITA buses. Look for the orange sign and wait there for a pickup. Taxis and boats are usually by the harbor, or ask at the tourist office, travel agency, or your hotel. Service on most Orange Line runs begins at 7:50 and ends at 9; departures are usually every half hour on the main lines.

RAVELLO

ATACS (Orange Line) municipal buses make the run up and down the mountain between Ravello and Piazza Flavio Gioia in Amalfi, from where you can connect to the main Amalfi Drive run to Sorrento. You can purchase SITA Blue Line bus and coach tickets prior to boarding at Bar San Domingo, Bar Calce, and Tabaccheria. Buses run almost hourly.

SALERNO

SITA buses run hourly to Sorrento, three times per hour to Naples, and once or twice an hour to Amalfi. Purchase tickets for preboarding at the SITA office or at tobacco shops displaying the SITA sticker; ATACS (Orange Line) buses run locally through the city, while ATACS and SCAT buses, departing from the Salerno train station, run frequently to Paestum.

SORRENTO

SITA Blue Line buses and coaches depart hourly from Sorrento to Amalfi. Before boarding, purchase SITA tickets at the newspaper stand in the train station, or at Bar Tonino in the Piazza Lauro. For trips leaving from Sorrento and heading southward into the coastal towns of the Sorrentine Peninsula, the main run stops at Massa Lubrense, Sant'Agata, and Torca. Service usually begins at 5 AM and lasts until 10:30 PM, with varying schedule for weekends and holidays. The Sorrento–Nerano line at Piazza Tasso and Piazza Lauro (main destination: Termini and Marina del Cantone) either goes through Sant'Agata or through Massa Lubrense. Contact Azienda Turismo for complete information. Circumvesuviana buses are used for local Sorrento runs (€1–€2.25). In Sorrento, the main local Orange Line bus stops are in Piazza Lauro, Piazza Tasso, and down at Marina Piccola. You can also use Circumvesuviana buses (€1–€2.20) for local Sorrento runs.

➤ Bus Information: **Azienda Turismo** (☎ 081/8074033, FAX 081/8773397). **Circumvesuviana** (☎ 081/7722444, WEB www.vesuviana.it). **Orange Line** (☎ 089/811895, FAX 089/811896). **SITA** (✉ Via Irno 2–4, Salerno, ☎ 089/791660, FAX 089/796820; WEB www.sita-on-line.it).

SITA Blue Line tickets (✉ Bar Sita, Piazza Flavio Gioia, Amalfi, ☎ 089/871016, www.sita-on-line.it; Tabaccheria, ✉ Piazza dei Mulini, Positano; ✉ Circumvesuviana train station, Sorrento, ☎ 081/5934644; Bar San Domingo, ✉ Piazza Duomo, Ravello, ☎ 089/857142; Bar Calce ✉ Via Roma, 2, Ravello, ☎ 089/857152; Tabaccheria, ✉ Via dei Rufolo, 4, Ravello; WEB www.sita-on-line.it). **Sorrento bus depot** (✉ Circumvesuviana railway station near Corso Italia).

FARES AND SCHEDULES

SITA buses make the trip along the coast 22 times daily between 6:30 AM and 10 PM (festival, Sunday, and bank holiday schedules vary from weekday schedule). Wallet-size SITA bus schedules are available at ticket vendors, regional tourist offices, and from hotel concierges, or contact SITA in Salerno. If you're traveling along the coast by SITA bus, be sure to get a schedule, as it proves invaluable to planning your day. Schedules are also posted at the Sorrento train station and at the SITA bus office at Bar Sita, Piazza Flavio Gioia. One-way ticket prices range from €2 to €3.35. An express Amalfi–Naples line includes stops in Sorrento, Colli S. Pietro, Positano, and Praiano, with the return in reverse. This bus runs daily, except Sunday and bank holidays, usually leaves at 8 AM, and takes 2½ hours.

PAYING

Tickets must be purchased in advance (remember to time-stamp your ticket in the machine at the front of the bus as you board because conductors often make spot checks). You'll find ticket vendors in many cafés, bars, and newsstands area-wide; heading south, the Sorrento train station newsstand is where most people stock up, but between noon and 4, when it's closed, head for the cafés on the square two blocks to the south; heading north from Amalfi, Bar Sita, at Piazza Flavio Gioia in Amalfi, is the place to buy tickets.

CAR RENTAL

If flying into Naples, you'll find that the major car rental firms have offices there. Avis Car Rentals is located at all major airports and in major towns; they allow one-way rentals, including drop off in other countries. AutoNet International Car has rentals for Italy: drop-off and pickup in other countries is available. Try AutoEurope Car rentals for AAA-like service.

➤ MAJOR AGENCIES: **AutoEurope Car** (✉ 39 Commercial St., Box 7006, Portland, ME 04112, ☎ 800/2235555 or 207/8422000, FAX 800/2356321 or 207/8422222). **AutoNet International Car** (☎ 888/8808999). **Avis Car Rentals** (☎ 0641999; 167801180 emergency).

CAR TRAVEL

Running between the Sorrentine peninsula and Salerno, Statale 163 (or State Highway 163) is better known to Americans and Brits as the Amalfi Drive and to Italians as the Via Smeraldo (Emerald Road). It can be reached from Naples via the A3 Autostrada to Castellammare di Stabia, then linked from there to Sorrento via Statale 145. Most people travel from Naples, heading southeast, but others prefer to drive directly to Salerno via the A3, then return northwest using the Amalfi Drive, a concrete ribbon which rewards visitors with mountain-meets-sea views and panoramas unfolding at every turn. If bound for Ravello and traveling by car, exit the A3 Autostrada at Angri, and approach Ravello from the north via the pass called Valico di Chiunzi.

EMERGENCY SERVICES

➤ CONTACTS: **Road Assistance** (Italian Auto Club) (☎ 116).

PARKING

Parking is a major problem, with spaces in Positano and Amalfi costing per day almost as much as a three-course meal, so you should factor in this additional cost.

ROAD CONDITIONS

Driving the scenic and often hairpin roads of the Sorrentine Peninsula and the Amalfi Drive is both a joy and a challenge. Medium-size cars are a good compromise, and turns will be easier with automatic transmission. The round reflecting mirrors set along major curves in the road intend to show if others are coming around a bend; they may help, but remain ever alert. Honk before narrow curves to let oncoming traffic know about you, and listen for honks from oncoming curves. Buses and trucks will sometimes require you to back up; if there's a standoff, take it in stride, as it goes on all the time.

Driving will be on winding two-lane roads except for the A3 highway to and from Salerno. Although (and perhaps because) driving here requires total concentration, accidents occur surprisingly infrequently.

EMERGENCIES

➤ COUNTRYWIDE EMERGENCY NUMBERS: **Police** (☎ 112). **Emergency Police Help** (☎ 113). **Fire Department** (☎ 115). **Emergencies at Sea** (Coastguard) (☎ 1530). **International Inquiries** (☎ 176). **Medical Emergencies** (☎ 118). **Phone Directory Assistance** (☎ 12).

➤ AMALFI: **Police** (☎ 089/871633). **Ambulance** (✉ Piazza Municipio, ☎ 089/872785).

➤ POSITANO: **Police** (✉ Loc. Chiesa Nuova, ☎ 089/875011). **Ambulance** (✉ Via G. Marconi, ☎ 089/811444).

➤ RAVELLO: **Police** (✉ Via della Marra 4, ☎ 089/857498). **Ambulance** (✉ Piazza Fontana 9, ☎ 089/867248).

➤ SORRENTO: **Police** (☎ 081/8073111 or 081/8781010). **Ambulance** (☎ 081/5331111).

➤ HOSPITALS: **Ospedale Civico** (✉ Corso Italia, Sorrento, ☎ 081/5331111). **Ospedale San Giovanni di Dio** (✉ Via San Leonardo, Salerno, ☎ 089/671111).

➤ PHARMACIES: **Amalfi** (✉ Piazza Duomo 42, ☎ 089/871045). **Positano** (✉ Viale Pasitea 22, ☎ 089/875863). **Ravello** (✉ Piazza Duomo 14, ☎ 089/857189). **Salerno** (✉ Via Mercanti 62, ☎ 089/253965). **Sorrento** (✉ Via L. De Maio 19, ☎ 081/8781349; ✉ Corso Italia 66, ☎ 081/8781174).

MONEY MATTERS

ATMS

Almost all banks now have ATM machines, which provide the quickest currency exchange, of course with bank commission. Hotels have the worst exchange rate but are convenient for small change and last-minute needs.

CURRENCY EXCHANGE

In Salerno, banks line Corso Vittorio Emanuele; the Salerno train station information window is open 9–7. In Sorrento, the Ufficio Cambi is open daily 9 AM–10:30 PM. The Sorrento Post Office has better rates than town banks.

➤ EXCHANGE SERVICES: **Bank Ufficio Cambi Spot** (✉ Via Roma 38, Ravello, ☎ 089/858086). **Banca Popolare di Salerno** (✉ Via Roma 15, Ravello, ☎ 089/857872). **Banco di Napoli** (✉ Piazza Duomo, Amalfi, ☎ 089/871005). **Deutsche Bank** (✉ Via dei Ferrari 1, Amalfi, ☎ 089/873050; ✉ Via Cristoforo Colombo, Positano, ☎ 089/811066, FAX 089/811045). **Sorrento Post Office** (✉ C. Italia 210, Sorrento, ☎ 081/

8781495). **Ufficio Cambi** (✉ Piazza dei Mulini, Positano, ☎ 089/ 875864; ✉ Via Luigi de Maio 21, Sorrento).

TAXIS

Taxis are at stands by the main piazzas and harbors and can also be rented through hotels and restaurants. The following are the major taxi services in the area. Positano Car & Limo Service offers car and driver rentals, tours, excursions.

➤ TAXI COMPANIES: **Amalfi** (✉ Piazza Flavio Gioia, at pier, ☎ 089/ 872239). **Autoservizi Flavio Gioia** (✉ Via Cristoforo Colombo 91, Positano, ☎ 089/811895). **Positano Car & Limo Service** (✉ Via Cristoforo Colombo 2, Positano, ☎ 089/875541). **Ravello** (✉ Piazza Duomo, ☎ 089/857917). **Rent-A-Car** (✉ Viale Pasitea, Positano, ☎ 089/ 811777). **Salerno** (✉ Piazza XXIV, Maggio, ☎ 089/229171). **Sorrento** (✉ Piazza Lauro, ☎ 081/8782204; ✉ S. Agnello, ☎ 081/8781428). **Sorrento Rent a Scooter** (✉ C. Italia 210–A, ☎ 081/8781386, WEB www.sorrento.it).

TOURS

Private boat tours are available to the Emerald Grotto, Capri, and isolated beaches through F.lli Grassi in Positano. GoldenTours International in Sorrento offers excursions to Capri, Ischia, Positano, Amalfi, Ravello, Pompeii, Herculaneum, Paestum, Naples, Cassino, Rome; car rentals, limo services; package tours; and train, boat, and air tickets.

➤ FEES AND SCHEDULES: **Divina Costiera** (✉ Piazza Flavio Gioia 3, Amalfi, ☎ 089/872467). **F.lli Grassi** (✉ Spiaggia Fornillo, Positano, ☎ 089/ 811620 or 089/811403). **GoldenTours International** (✉ Corso Italia, 38–E, ☎ 081/8781042, FAX 081/8071745, WEB www.goldentours.it). **Wagner Tours** (✉ Via Trinità 4, Ravello, ☎ 089/858416, FAX 089/858914).

TRAIN TRAVEL

The two main train stations serving the Amalfi Coast are Salerno and Sorrento. Conveniently, the stations are also hubs for cheap, efficient bus services radiating towards the major tourist destinations along the coast and inland.

State Railways trains stop in Salerno on the Milan–Reggio Calabria line. Trains leave from Salerno for Pompei town (the archaeological site of Pompeii is 15 minutes' walk away) once or twice each hour; Naples twice an hour, €3.60. The station here is also an excellent starting point for buses to the Amalfi coast.

The Circumvesuviana departs from the Circumvesuviana train station and runs approximately every half hour from Sorrento to Naples; some trains are express, only stopping at major stations, returning in the reverse order. Round-trip fares are €6 for Sorrento to Naples and €3.20 to Pompeii. In Sorrento the train station is opposite Piazza Lauro and a five-minute walk from Piazza Tasso.

➤ TRAIN INFORMATION: **Circumvesuviana** (☎ 081/7722444, WEB www.vesuviana.it). **State Railways** (✉ Piazza V. Veneto, ☎ 848/ 888088, WEB www.fs-on-line.it).

TRAVEL AGENCIES

Divina Costiera in Amalfi also rents scooters (€70 per day). Golden Tours offers boat tours to Grotta dello Smeraldo (Emerald Cave) from Amalfi docks. The American Express representative in Sorrento is Acampora Travel.

➤ LOCAL AGENTS: **Acampora Travel** (✉ Via Correale 20, Sorrento, ☎ 081/5329711, WEB www.acampora.it). **Arechi Viaggi** (✉ Via Sichelmanno 17, Salerno, ☎ 089/759353, FAX 089/759341). **Divina Costiera** (✉ Pi-

azza Flavio Gioia 3, Amalfi, ☎ 089/872467, ☎ FAX 089/871254).
Faito Travel (✉ Via G. Marconi 344, Positano, ☎ 089/811802).
Golden Tours (✉ Corso Repubbliche Marinare 23, Amalfi, ☎ FAX
089/871301). **Positour** (✉ Via Cristoforo Colombo 69, Positano, ☎
089/875012, FAX 089/811045, WEB www.positour.com). **Ravello International** (✉ Via Roma 38, Ravello, ☎ FAX 089/858086).

VISITOR INFORMATION
Azienda Autonoma di Cura, Soggiorno e Turismo in Amalfi is open
weekdays 8:30–1:30 and 3–5; Saturday 8:30–1; in Sorrento the office
is open Monday to Saturday, summer 8–8, winter 8:30–2:30 and 3:20–
6:30.

In Positano the Azienda Autonoma Soggiorno e Turismo is open Monday–Saturday 8:30–2, and June to September, it is also open from 3:30–
8. In Ravello, the office is open Monday to Saturday 8–8 in summer
and 8–7 in winter.

In Salerno, the EPT office is open Monday–Saturday, 9–1 and 3–8.

Centro di Cultura e Storia Amalfitana is open Tuesday, Thursday, and
Saturday 9–1; Monday, Wednesday, and Friday 4–8.
➤ TOURIST INFORMATION: **Azienda Autonoma di Cura, Soggiorno e Tur-
ismo** (✉ Corso Reppubliche Marinare 29, Amalfi, ☎ FAX 089/871107;
✉ Via Luigi di Maio 35, Sorrento, ☎ 081/8074033, FAX 081/8773397,
WEB www.sorrentourism.it). **Azienda Autonoma Soggiorno e Turismo**
(✉ Via del Saracino 4, Positano, ☎ 089/875067, FAX 089/875760; ✉
Piazza Duomo 10, Ravello, ☎ 089/857096, FAX 089/877977, WEB
www.ravello.it/aziendaturismo). **Centro di Cultura e Storia Amalfitana**
(✉ Via Annunziatella, Amalfi, ☎ 089/873143). **EPT Office** (✉ P. Vit-
torio Veneto 1, Salerno, ☎ FAX 089/231432, WEB www.crmpa.it/ept).

5 BACKGROUND AND ESSENTIALS

Portrait

Map of Campania

Map of Italy

Smart Travel Tips A to Z

Italian Vocabulary

NAPOLI EVER AFTER

The acute stages are easy to diagnose: the symptoms cry out. Utter the words *Bay of Naples, Positano,* or *Capri,* and patients will close their eyes and sigh—or roll their eyeballs and moan. If it's an advanced case, they will embark on a monologue in which you will be able to discern such phrases and fragments as ". . . the lure of the Mediterranean," ". . . the magic of the Southern sun," ". . . water that outsapphires the jewels at Tiffany's," ". . . the song of the sirens." Every ailment—physical, mental, or social—reflects a need. Acute and widespread Campania mania—the hopeless infatuation with Campania and its myriad sun-wreathed resorts and starlighted isles—simply proves (with or without spots) that there is something in the organism, blood, and mental makeup of every modern-day escapist that requires a good dose of this relentlessly romantic corner of the world.

It has been this way ever since the Roman emperors escaped overheated Rome by building pleasure palaces around the Bay of Naples—and, in the process, inventing the very idea of the vacation. Back then, some Roman travel agent urged his countrymen to "See Naples and Die." Ever since, up to today, this pithy phrase has been interpreted in contrasting, equally viable ways. Lovers of Naples, asking what there is on earth that you can't find here, get the slogan's true meaning. The hard-liners, noting the murderous traffic, Mafia doings, ever-present threat of Vesuvius erupting, and the region's earthquakey history, say, "See Naples and die." As it turns out, the saying originally advised travelers to visit the city on the bay, then check out the nearby town of Mori (Latin for "to die"). And it is in this sense that this guidebook proceeds. It is simply a given that you must first explore this relentlessly fascinating city, then move on to the rest of Campania, a province that stacks snazzy resorts, grandly Baroque palaces, Edenic gardens, the most satisfying hundred miles of coastline to be found in tourist Europe, and some of the oldest ruins this side of Constantinople into one mammoth must-see sandwich.

However, if you limit your tour to Sorrento, Ravello, Capri, Ischia, Positano, Pompeii, and Amalfi, you will "see" Campania, but you won't understand it. To do that, you must get to know Naples itself. Most guidebooks approach this capital of Campania with a degree of circumspection, treating her as the cousin who would be presentable if only she toned down her makeup, watched her mouth, and didn't try to palm her date's wallet. But it could also have something to do with the array of things to see in Naples: the supreme, sun-drunk, natural setting with Dame Vesuvius tapping her feet across the Bay of Naples; the richest museum of Greco-Roman antiquities in the world; one of the finest collections of Renaissance paintings; outstanding examples of architecture from medieval to modern; and a kaleidoscope of colorful vignettes. But you don't come to Naples to see things, as such; you come to Naples to *be.* Naples is a kinetic gust of 3-D garlic-and-basil aromatherapy for the soul, a vital and revitalizing splash of reality; Naples is rediscovering the "simple things" and finding them exalted into ecstasies of complication; Naples is fluidity among stasis, fertility spawning misery, infinite intelligence circumventing colossal stupidity. Naples is intense, and intensely poetic. Naples doesn't need defending—it does that quite well by itself, thank you. And it is not rational, despite the many grids that various rulers vainly laid down to tame it. Naples is about falling in love, not blindly—that wouldn't last long, in any case—but instead by having your senses and sensibilities shamelessly charmed into full bloom.

It's not only the scenery that will incessantly engage your senses; it's also the Neapolitans themselves. More so than in any Italian city, the engine driving Naples is its people. Sophia Ponti, *née* Loren, the most famous living Neapolitan (okay, so she's from the suburb of Pozzuoli) recently confided that her *concittadini* "had many virtues: fantasy, sincerity, generosity, boastfulness, a sense of humor . . . Neapolitans do not have defects . . . or at least I've never noticed any." Not everyone has been so complimentary: Throughout history foreigners of all stripes have sustained a positively unseemly orgy of righteous indignation and disdain for the Neapolitans and their anarchic and passionate approach to morality. Already in ancient times, the entire Neapolitan area (of Baia in particular) was notorious as a fleshpot. The goings-on in the court of Joan I in the 14th century make that old 1980s soap opera *Dynasty* look like an unimaginative Romper Room model of treachery and lust. Naples's reputation for sexual permissiveness was sealed when the French troops of Charles VIII, chased out of Naples, took back with them an epidemic they later termed "the Neapolitan disease": syphilis. Epidemiological historians still argue over the origins of the disease in Europe, but the damage was done. The very Victorian philosopher Walter Benjamin simply dismissed Naples as "a lost city."

Yes, contrary to native daughter Sophia, others have looked upon the Neapolitans with a less generous eye, put off by their robust earthiness, their physicality, their volatility. The truth is, on deeper acquaintance, the mannerisms of the Neapolitans are found to be merely the prickly nettles that must be navigated before reaching the ripe center. Their mode of life is simply an inextinguishable belief that the art of living lies in enjoying what surrounds you, not passively, but with enthusiasm—be it the sun-

shine, a glass of wine, romance, a scam, a prayer, a song, an argument, a traffic jam. Sublime artists of existence, Neapolitans are skilled players in the larger, more serious world. And yet, far from being bitterly cynical, they take the same delight in the ingeniousness, the virtuosity as it were, of a crook as they do of an artist. They are free of cynicism and loaded with courage (Naples was the only city in World War II to rout the Nazi occupiers in a spontaneous revolt).

Naples is almost as old as Rome, and the main components of the historically constructed mentality are Greek and Spanish—testimony to the city's ancient Greek founders and its 16th-century Spanish rulers—rather than Italian as such. Greek was commonly spoken in Naples, even under the Roman Empire, and Naples was considered an outpost and living remnant of Greek culture in Italy, much as New Orleans retained its Frenchness in 19th-century America; the Neapolitans' brilliant, argumentative, and impossibly charming nature is ancient Greek, and a number of words in the widely spoken present-day dialect retain concepts of the founders. To this have been added Spanish pride and an intransigent sense of honor.

Once experienced deeply and openly, Naples remains a reference point while exploring the rest of Campania—at once a grounding in reality and a glimpse into the stratosphere of fantasy. There are a fair number of sights to see in this region, but many visitors find such pursuits beside the point, for they look upon Campania as a playground, a school, a way of life that insists on having its way with you. Who but the Neapolitans could have invented *dolce far niente*—the sweetness of doing nothing? But fulfillment under the Campanian sun comes in various guises. The legions of honeymooners, Main Streeters, and deadline slaves could be lounging in the very sand once trod by Nero, Tiberius, and Hadrian. Virgil's *Georgics* and Wagner's *Parsifal* came to life in view of these waters. Passion—pairs on the scene have included Admiral Nelson and Lady Hamilton and Elizabeth

Taylor and Richard Burton—has a way of percolating under these skies. Numerous great and once-great names spent time here, writing, painting, philosophizing, or just drinking in the grand scenery.

Like them, you will want to depart Campania with that final sense of beauty unparalleled, with the echoes of Capri's grottoes still resounding in your ears and the perfume of the flowers of Ravello still in your nostrils, with the austere classicism of Paestum oddly blending in your mind with the Cave of the Cumaean Sibyl, and with the panorama from your window in Naples, with its splendid bay and ever-threatening volcano, all comprising one vast picture in your mind. If you're lucky, that celebrated Neapolitan vista will be yours to enjoy from your hotel room on a spring morning when the sun is just warm enough to be comfortable. Step out onto your balcony for the first time, and drink in the panorama. Everyone does. Down below your balcony will

be the Bay of Naples, with its gently curving shoreline, docks, and palm-lined avenues. Farther along will be the Castel Nuovo of Charles I of Anjou, its eternal and primitive shape contrasting sharply with far more modern buildings near it. Follow the bay with your eyes to the horizon and Vesuvius itself. Look to your right to see a little islet that seems to spring directly out of the bay. This is Capri. Ischia is probably a little out of your vision's range, as are Pozzuoli and Cumae, but no matter. Far below you the bay is shimmering blue. In the distance gentle little waves fleck it with white. The air is fragrant with flowering vines and trees. A violently purple bougainvillea cluster clings to the hotel trellis within a few feet of your head. It would be pleasant just to sit there in the warmly comfortable sun and relax for the rest of the day—maybe for a week or so. That's what a Neapolitan would do. But we haven't time.

— Gregory W. Bailey

Portraits

Formia

Sessa
Aurunca

Teano

Dragoni

S372

Carinola

A2

S7

Caiazzo

S87

Mondragone

Capua

Caserta

Volturno

Grazzanise

S264

Castel Volturno

S75

Maddaloni

S7

Villa Literno

Aversa

Caivano

Acerra

A2

S30

Giugliano in C.

Casoria

Pomigliano

Cumae

A16

Lago d'Averno

Napoli
(Napies)

S268

Vesuvius

Pozzuoli

Ercolano

Solfatara

Baia

Herculaneum

Pompeii

Scafati

Casamicciola
Terme

Ischia
Porto

A3

Lacco
Ameno

Forio

Ischia

Golfo di Napoli

S18

Spiagga
di Citara

Ischia
Ponte

Sant'Angelo

Castellammare

G

S145

Sorrento

Positano

Gro
de
Smera

Grotta
Azzurra

Marina
Grande

Anacapri

Capri

Capri
Town

Marina
Piccola

Tyrrhenian Sea

N

ITALY

KEY

Ferry

0 _____ 10 miles

0 _____ 15 km

Guardia
Sanframondi

Telese

S87

S87

S88

S372

S88

Buonalbergo

Savignano
Irpino

Cervaro

S90

S90

Benevento

Ariano Irpino

Montesarchio

S7

Castello d. Lago

A16

S88

Paternopoli

Baiano

A16

S164

Lioni

S7

Nola

Avellino

S91

Sarno

Solofra

Mercato

A30

Nocera

S91

Sele

ragnano

Campagna

Vietri sul Mare

S88

Ravello

S163

Amalfi

Salerno

A3

S91

Battipaglia

Eboli

otta
ello
do

Golfo di Salerno

S18

S19

A3

Paestum

Capaccio

Agropoli

Italy

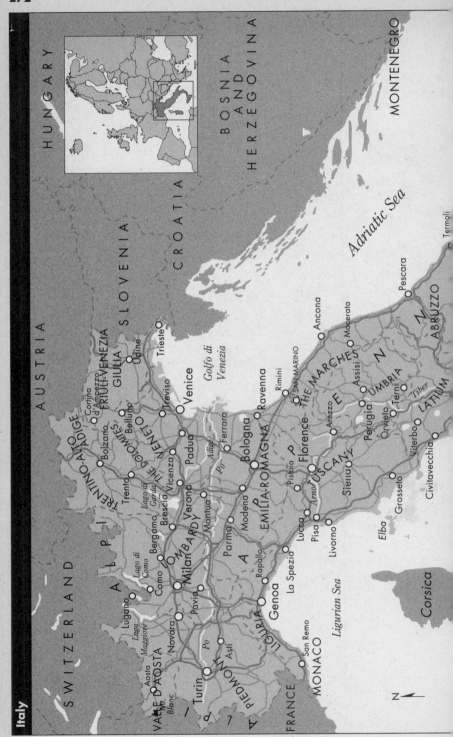

HUNGARY

BOSNIA AND HERZEGOVINA

MONTENEGRO

CROATIA

SLOVENIA

AUSTRIA

Adriatic Sea

Termoli

Pescara

Ancona

ABRUZZO

Macerata

THE MARCHES

San Marino

SAN MARINO

Assisi

UMBRIA

Rimini

Trieste

Udine

FRIULI-VENEZIA GIULIA

Cortina d'Ampezzo

Belland

Golfo di Venezia

Treviso

Venice

Ravenna

Perugia

Terni

Tiber

LATIUM

Arezzo

Orvieto

Viterbo

Civitavecchia

Bolzano

TRENTINO-ALTO ADIGE

Trento

THE DOLOMITES

THE VENETO

Vicenza

Padua

Ferrara

Bologna

EMILIA-ROMAGNA

Florence

TUSCANY

Pistoia

Arno

Siena

Grosseto

SWITZERLAND

Lago di Garda

Brescia

Verona

Mantua

Modena

Lucca

Pisa

Elba

Corsica

A L P I

Bergamo

Lago di Como

Como

LOMBARDY

Milan

Parma

Rapallo

La Spezia

Livorno

Ligurian Sea

Lugano

Lago Maggiore

Pavia

Novara

Aosta

Mt. Blanc

VALLE D'AOSTA

Turin

Po

Asti

PIEDMONT

LIGURIA

Genoa

San Remo

MONACO

FRANCE

N

ESSENTIAL INFORMATION

Half the fun of traveling is looking forward to your trip—but when you look forward, don't just daydream. There are plans to be made, things to learn about, serious work to be done. The following information will give you helpful pointers on many of the questions that arise when planning your trip. In addition, the organizations listed in this section will supplement the information in this guide book. Note that some of the information in this section is Italy-wide; for all the specific details about the various topics covered below *within* Campania itself, consult the A to Z sections at the end of each regional chapter in this book.

AIR TRAVEL TO
AND FROM NAPLES

BOOKING

When you book **look for nonstop flights** and **remember that "direct" flights stop at least once.** Try to avoid connecting flights, which require a change of plane. For more booking tips and to check prices and make on-line flight reservations, log on to www.fodors.com.

CARRIERS

When flying internationally to Italy, you must usually choose between a domestic carrier, the national flag carrier of the country, and a foreign carrier from a third country. You may, for example, choose to fly Alitalia to Italy—as the national flag carrier it has the greatest number of nonstops. Domestic carriers, such as Air One, AlpiEagles, AirEurope, and Meridiana, may have better connections to smaller destinations as well as a slight price advantage.

No international carrier makes a transatlantic flight to Naples, but Alitalia offers an extensive and varied schedule of flights connecting Naples with Rome and Milan and numerous other Italian and European cities. They continue to offer more nonstop flights to Italy from the U.S. than any other airline, including a nonstop flight from San Francisco to Milan's Malpensa Airport. Alitalia recently merged with KLM, making the company the largest airline outfit based in Europe. Among the cities that Alitalia connects with Naples (often with daily flights) are Amsterdam, Bologna, Cagliari, Genoa, Milan (both Linate and Malpensa), Palermo, Paris, Rome, Turin, and Venice. Alitalia's North American gateways are Boston, Chicago, Los Angeles, Miami, San Francisco, New York City, Montreal, and Toronto. The main sales offices for the airline in the U.S. is in New York City, with other offices in Washington, D.C. and San Francisco; the main reservations number and sales office numbers are listed below. For further information about schedules, special fare promotions, and Italiatour—their tour-group agency—visit their Web sites: www.alitalia.com or www.alitaliausa.com.

Many other carriers link European capitals with Naples—for instance, British Airways offers a direct route between London-Gatwick and Naples, Air France offers a direct route between Paris and Naples, and Sabena offers a direct route connecting Brussels and Naples. Mediterranean country-hoppers will find Olympic Airways connections with Marseilles and Athens particularly convenient, while Air Littoral flies between Naples and Nice. Internet bargain-hunters are appreciating the cut-price fares from London-Stansted to Naples with the carrier Go. Milan and Rome are also served by Continental Airlines, Delta Air Lines, and TWA. American Airlines, United Airlines, and Northwest Airlines fly into Milan. US Airways serves Rome. Lower-priced charter flights to a range of Italian destinations are available throughout the year.

► To and From Italy: **Air France** (☎ 800/237–2747; within Italy 848/884466, WEB www.airfrance.com). **Air Littoral** (☎ 06/841–8120; within Italy, 848/878510). **Alitalia** (☎ 800/223–5730; 020/760–27111; 0990/448259 in Britain; 848/865641 within Italy, WEB www.alitalia.it; individual sales offices in the U.S.: ☎ 212/903–3300 New York; 310/568–5941 Los Angeles; 312/644–0404 Chicago; 617/267–2882 Boston). **American Airlines** (☎ 800/433–7300, WEB www.im.aa.com). **British Airways** (☎ 848/812266, WEB www.britishairways.com). **Continental Airlines** (☎ 800/231–0856, WEB www.continental.com). **Delta Air Lines** (☎ 800/241–4141, WEB www.delta.com). **Go** (☎ 848/887766, WEB www.go-fly.com). **Lufthansa** (☎ 800/247–9297; 06/6568–4004 in Rome, WEB www.lufthansa.it). **Meridiana** (☎ 0171/839–2222; 800/555092 in Italy, WEB www.meridiana.it). **Northwest Airlines** (☎ 800/225–2525, WEB www.nwa.com). **Olympic Airways** (☎ 081/7649593 within Italy, WEB www.olympic-airways.gr/). **Sabena** (☎ 848/801616 within Italy, WEB www.sabena.com). **TWA** (☎ 800/892–4141, WEB www.twa.com). **United Airlines** (☎ 800/538–2929, WEB www.united.com). **US Airways** (☎ 800/428–4322, WEB www.usairways.com).

► Around Italy: **AirEurope** (☎ 848/824425 within Italy). **Air One** (☎ 06/488800; 848/48880 within Italy). **Alitalia** (☎ 06/65621; 06/65643 in Rome; 02/24991 in Milan; 848/865641 within Italy). **Alpieagles** (☎ 081/5992351 in Naples). **Meridiana** (☎ 06/478041; 800/555092 within Italy).

CHECK-IN & BOARDING

Assuming that not everyone with a ticket will show up, airlines routinely overbook planes. When everyone does, airlines ask for volunteers to give up their seats. In return, these volunteers usually get a certificate for a free flight and are rebooked on the next flight out. If there are not enough volunteers, the airline must choose who will be denied boarding. The first

to get bumped are passengers who checked in late and those flying on discounted tickets, so **get to the gate and check in as early as possible,** especially during peak periods.

Always **bring a government-issued photo I.D. to the airport;** even when it's not required, a passport is best.

CUTTING COSTS

The least expensive airfares to Italy must usually be purchased in advance and are non-refundable. It's smart to **call a number of airlines,** and when you are quoted a good price, **book it on the spot**—the same fare may not be available the next day. Always **check different routings** and look into using different airports. Travel agents, especially low-fare specialists (☞ Discounts & Deals), are helpful.

Consolidators are another good source. They buy tickets for scheduled international flights at reduced rates from the airlines, then sell them at prices that beat the best fare available directly from the airlines, usually without restrictions. Sometimes you can even get your money back if you need to return the ticket. Carefully read the fine print detailing penalties for changes and cancellations, and **confirm your consolidator reservation with the airline.**

► Consolidators: **Cheap Tickets** (☎ 800/377–1000). **Discount Airline Ticket Service** (☎ 800/576–1600). **Unitravel** (☎ 800/325–2222). **Up & Away Travel** (☎ 212/889–2345). **World Travel Network** (☎ 800/409–6753).

ENJOYING THE FLIGHT

All flights within Italy are smoke free. Smoking is allowed on an ever-dwindling number of international flights; **contact your carrier about its smoking policy.** For more legroom, **request an emergency-aisle seat.** Don't sit in the row in front of the emergency aisle or in front of a bulkhead, where seats may not recline. If you have dietary concerns, **ask for special meals when booking.** These can be vegetarian, low-cholesterol, or kosher, for example. On long flights, try to maintain a normal routine, to help fight jet lag. At night,

sleep. By day, **eat light**
drink water (not alcohol), and
around the cabin to stretch
legs. For additional jet-lag tips
nsult *Fodor's FYI: Travel Fit &*
Healthy (available at bookstores
everywhere).

FLYING TIMES

Flying time to Rome is 8½ hours
from New York, 10–11 hours from
Chicago, 11½ hours from Dallas (via
New York), 11½ hours from Los
Angeles, 2 hours from London (to
Milan), and 12½ hours from Sydney.

HOW TO COMPLAIN

If your baggage goes astray or your
flight goes awry, complain right away.
Most carriers require that you **file a**
claim immediately.

➤ AIRLINE COMPLAINTS: U.S. Depart-
ment of Transportation **Aviation**
Consumer Protection Division (✉
C-75, Room 4107, Washington,
DC 20590, ☎ 202/366–2220, WEB
www.dot.gov/airconsumer). Federal
Aviation Administration Consumer
Hotline (☎ 800/322–7873).

AIRPORTS & TRANSFERS

Located just outside Naples, **Aero-**
porto Capodichino serves the Campania region. It handles domestic and
international flights, including several
flights daily between Naples and
Rome (flight time 45 minutes). The
airport is currently run by the local
handler GESAC with some logistical
assistance from BAA (British Airports
Authority), the majority stakeholder.
From May to September there is a
direct **helicopter service** (☎ 081/
5841481 or 081/7896273) between
Aeroporto Capodichino and Capri,
Ischia, Praiano (near Positano), and
Sorrento. The major gateways to Italy
include Rome's **Aeroporto Leonardo**
da Vinci, better known as **Fiumicino,**
and Milan's **Aeroporto Malpensa**
2000 (MXP). Smaller, minor gateways are served by domestic and
some international flights.

➤ AIRPORT INFORMATION: **Aeroporto**
Capodichino (✉ Via Umberto Maddalena, 5 km [3 mi] north of Naples,
☎ 081/7896111, WEB www.gesac.it).
Aeroporto Leonardo da Vinci
or **Fiumicino** (✉ 35 km [20 mi]

southwest of Rome, ☎ 06/65953640,
WEB www.adr.it/it/fiumic/fiumic-00.
html). Aeroporto Malpensa 2000
(✉ 45 km [28 mi] north of Milan,
☎ 02/74852200, WEB www.
sea-aeroportimilano.it/malpensa).

Bologna: **Aeroporto Guglielmo Mar-**
coni (✉ Borgo Panigale, 7 km [4½
mi] from Bologna, ☎ 051/6479615,
WEB www.bologna-airport.it). Genoa:
Aeroporto Cristoforo Colombo
(✉ 6 km [4 mi] west of Genoa,
☎ 010/6512577, WEB www.airport.
genova.it). Milan: **Aeroporto Linate**
(✉ 10 km [6 mi] east of Milan, ☎
02/74852200). Palermo: **Aeroporto**
Falcone–Borsellino (✉ 32 km [20 mi]
west of Palermo, ☎ 091/591698,
WEB www.gesap.it).Turin: **Aeroporto**
Caselle (✉ 15 km [9 mi] north of
Turin, ☎ 011/5676361, WEB www.
turin-airport.com).Venice: **Aeroporto**
Marco Polo (✉ Tessera, about 10 km
[6 mi] north of Venice, ☎ 041/
2609260).

DUTY-FREE SHOPPING

As of July 1999 duty-free shopping in
airports was eliminated in Italy (and
European Union countries); you can
still make in-flight duty-free purchases
however.

BOAT & FERRY TRAVEL

As one of the great harbors of the
world, Naples offers a wide array of
boat, ferry (*traghetti*), and hydrofoil
(*aliscafo*) services between the city, the
islands of the bay, the Sorrentine
peninsula, and other Mediterranean
destinations. The main station is at
the Molo Beverello—the port of
Naples opposite the Castel Nuovo—
along the waterfront of Piazza Municipio. Here, hydrofoils and ferries
run by Caremar, Linee Lauro, SNAV,
and Alilauro connect Naples with
Sorrento, Capri, Ischia, and Procida.
More hydrofoils depart for Capri,
Ischia, and Procida, as well as the
further-flung islands of Ponza and
Ventotene to the northwest and the
Aeolian islands off Sicily's northern
coast, from the Mergellina harbor (a
short walk from the Mergellina train
station) at the far western end of the
Riviera di Chiaia; the trip to Ischia
and Procida is shorter and cheaper if
you use the ferry that departs from

Pozzuoli harbor (the nearest metro station is on the Cumana line at Pozzuoli). Next to the Molo Beverello is the Stazione Marittima (Molo Angioino), where larger ferries make trips to Ponza, the Aeolian islands, Sicily, and Sardinia. The most comprehensive coverage of services is found in the local paper *Il Mattino*, which features a *Per chi Parte* ("For Those Departing") section every day which lists schedules for Naples–Rome trains, flights from Capodichino Airport, long-distance bus services, and complete ferry and hydrofoil listings. *Qui Napoli*, the helpful monthly English-language periodical for visitors to Naples, also lists ferry and hydrofoil schedules. As there are substantial seasonal variations, double-check departure times and days, especially when traveling further afield on low-frequency services. Alternatively, consult the excellent Web site, www.campaniatrasporti.it, a helpful overview of most public transport lines in Campania.

The hydrofoil service is generally twice as fast as ferries and almost double the price. The service is considerably more frequent during the summer months. For specific information about boat, ferry, and hydrofoil travel between Naples and other destinations on the Bay of Naples and the Amalfi Coast, *see* the A to Z sections at the end of each regional chapter. Car ferries operate to the islands of the Bay of Naples, but advance reservations are best.

➤ BOAT & FERRY INFORMATION: **Alilauro** (☎ 081/7614909, WEB www.alilauro.it). **Caremar** (☎ 081/ 5513882, WEB www.caremar.it). **Linee Lauro** (☎ 081/5522838, WEB www. lineelauro.it). **Navigazione Libera del Golfo** (☎ 081/5527209, WEB www. navlib.it). **SNAV** (☎ 081/7612348, WEB www.snavali.com). **Siremar** (☎ 081/5800340, WEB www.siremar.it). **Tirrenia** (☎ 8408/99000 or 081/ 7201111, WEB www.tirrenia.it).

BUS TRAVEL AROUND
CAMPANIA

Campania's bus network is extensive and in some areas buses can be more direct (and therefore, faster) than local trains, so it's a good idea to **compare bus and train schedules.** Bus services outside cities are organized on a regional level, and often by private companies. Campania has three main bus companies, listed below. ANM handles buses within Naples, CTP usually handles medium- and long-distance routes out of Naples, while SITA services the Amalfi Coast. Taking buses from Naples requires both research and patience, since there is no central bus station as such: Different bus lines leave from different city squares, with the situation being compounded by recent traffic reorganization in Piazza Garibaldi. For more specific information, *see* the A to Z sections at the end of each regional chapter or ask at a tourist information office.

➤ BUS INFORMATION: **CTP** (✉ Via Sannio 19, Napoli, ☎ 081/7005091). **ANM** (✉ Piazza Garibaldi, main Servizio CTP bus stop, Napoli, ☎ 081/7632177, WEB www.anm.it). **SITA** (✉ Via Pisanelli 3, just south of Piazza Municipio, Napoli, ☎ 081/5522176 or 081/5934644, WEB www. sita-on-line.it).

PAYING

Tickets are not sold on board buses so you must purchase your tickets in advance by machine, at newsstands, or at tobacconists. Remember to time-stamp your ticket after you board as conductors often make spot-checks. Keep in mind that many ticket sellers close for several hours at midday, so it's always wise to stock up on bus tickets when you have the chance.

BUSINESS HOURS

BANKS & POST OFFICES

Banks are open weekdays 8:30 to 1:15 and 2:45 to 3:45.

Post offices are open Monday through Saturday 9 to 1; central and main district post offices stay open until 6 PM weekdays, 9 to 2 on Saturday.

MUSEUMS & SIGHTS

A major revolution in visiting times for Naples's museums occurred in 2000: After decades of afternoon closures, the main museums, such as Museo Archeologico Nazionale, Museo di zzo Reale, and San ... open through to the ... many smaller ...s are only open from 9 ... PM. The opening times of ...cal sites are subject to ...variations, with most sites ...an hour before sunset. When ...ook refs to summer hours, it ...s approximately Easter to Octo-...; winter hours run from November ... Easter. Most museums are closed one day a week, often on Monday. Always check locally.

Most churches are open from early morning until noon or 12:30, when they close for three hours or more; they open again in the afternoon, closing about 7 PM or later.

SHOPS

As in most European countries, shop opening times vary according to the retail sector. Clothing shops open from 10 to 1:30 and from 4:30 to 8, Tuesday through Saturday. They are generally closed on Monday mornings, but open regular afternoon hours, except from July to mid-September when they close Saturday afternoons and open on Monday mornings. *Alimentari* (grocers') and *panifici* (bakeries) open as early as 8 AM every day except for Sunday, but are closed on Thursday afternoons and Sundays. Barbers and hairdressers, with some exceptions, are closed Sunday and Monday. On Sundays the *pasticcerie* (cake shops) do a roaring trade, as most southern Italians like to round off their luncheon ritual with a calorie-rich *pasticcino* (little cake). The smaller shops in town will usually close for a week either side of Ferragosto (August 15th), when most larger urban areas are transformed into ghost towns and city-dwellers flock to seaside or mountain resorts.

CAMERAS & PHOTOGRAPHY

The *Kodak Guide to Shooting Great Travel Pictures* (available at bookstores everywhere) is loaded with tips.

➤ PHOTO HELP: **Kodak Information Center** (☎ 800/242–2424).

EQUIPMENT PRECAUTIONS

Don't pack film and equipment in checked luggage, where it is much

more susceptible to damage. X-ray machines used to view checked luggage are becoming much more powerful and therefore are much more likely to ruin your film. Always **keep film and tape out of the sun.** Carry an extra supply of batteries, and **be prepared to turn on your camera or camcorder** to prove to security personnel that the device is real. Always **ask for hand inspection of film,** which becomes clouded after repeated exposure to airport X-ray machines, and **keep videotapes away from metal detectors.**

CAR RENTAL

Renting a car in Italy is helpful when exploring the off-the-beaten-track countryside, but not necessary, as the bus system throughout Campania is excellent and far-flung. Signage on country roads is usually pretty good, but be prepared for fast and impatient fellow drivers. Major car-rental companies have boxy "utility" cars and Fiats in various sizes that are always in good condition.

➤ MAJOR AGENCIES: **Alamo** (☎ 800/ 522–9696; 020/8759–6200 in the U.K., WEB www.alamo.com). **Avis** (☎ 800/331–1084; 800/879–2847 in Canada; 02/9353–9000 in Australia; 09/525–1982 in New Zealand; 0870/ 606–0100 in the U.K., WEB www.avis. com). **Budget** (☎ 800/527–0700; 0870/156–5656 in the U.K., WEB www.budget.com). **Dollar** (☎ 800/ 800–6000; 0124/622–0111 in the U.K., where it's affiliated with Sixt; 02/9223–1444 in Australia, WEB www.dollar.com). **Hertz** (☎ 800/654– 3001; 800/263–0600 in Canada; 020/ 8897–2072 in the U.K.; 02/9669– 2444 in Australia; 09/256–8690 in New Zealand, WEB www.hertz.com). **National Car Rental** (☎ 800/227– 7368; 020/8680–4800 in the U.K., WEB www.nationalcar.com).

CUTTING COSTS

Most major American rental-car companies have offices or affiliates in Italy, but the rates are generally better if you make a reservation from abroad rather than from within Italy. To get the best deal, **book through a travel agent who will shop around.** Also **price local car-rental companies,** although the service and maintenance may not be as good as those of a major player. Remember to ask about required deposits, cancellation penalties, and drop-off charges if you're planning to pick up the car in one city and leave it in another. If you're traveling during a holiday period, also make sure that a confirmed reservation guarantees you a car.

Do **look into wholesalers,** companies that do not own fleets but rent in bulk from those that do and often offer better rates than traditional car-rental operations. Payment must be made before you leave home.

➤ WHOLESALERS: **Auto Europe** (☎ 207/842–2000 or 800/223–5555, FAX 207/842–2222, WEB www.autoeurope. com). **Europe by Car** (☎ 212/581–3040 or 800/223–1516, FAX 212/246–1458, WEB www.europebycar.com). **DER Travel Services** (✉ 9501 W. Devon Ave., Rosemont, IL 60018, ☎ 800/782–2424, FAX 800/282–7474 for information; 800/860–9944 for brochures, WEB www.dertravel.com). **Kemwel Holiday Autos** (☎ 800/678–0678, FAX 914/825–3160, WEB www. kemwel.com).

INSURANCE

When driving a rented car you are generally responsible for any damage to or loss of the vehicle. Before you rent, see what coverage your personal auto-insurance policy and credit cards provide.

Before you buy collision coverage, check your existing policies—you may already be covered. However, collision policies that car-rental companies sell for European rentals usually do not include stolen-vehicle coverage. Note that in Italy, all car-rental companies make you buy theft-protection policies.

REQUIREMENTS & RESTRICTIONS

In Italy your own driver's license is acceptable. An International Driver's Permit is a good idea; it's available from the American or Canadian automobile association, and, in the United Kingdom, from the Automobile Association or Royal Automobile Club. These international permits are universally recognized, and having one in your wallet may save you a problem with the local authorities. In Italy you must be 21 years of age to rent an economy or subcompact car and at least 25 years of age to rent a bigger car.

SURCHARGES

Before you pick up a car in one city and leave it in another, **ask about drop-off charges or one-way service fees,** which can be substantial. Note, too, that some rental agencies charge extra if you return the car before the time specified in your contract. To avoid a hefty refueling fee, **fill the tank just before you turn in the car,** but be aware that gas stations near the rental outlet may overcharge.

CAR TRAVEL

There is an extensive network of *autostrade* (toll highways), complemented by equally well-maintained but free *superstrade* (expressways). The ticket you are issued upon entering an autostrada must be returned when you exit and pay the toll; on some shorter autostrade, mainly connecting highways, the toll is paid upon entering. Viacard cards, on sale at many autostrada locations, make paying tolls easier and faster, though if you are just using the car on local autostrade within Campania you may find yourself with substantial surplus credit on your card at the end of your trip. A *raccordo* or *tangenziale* is a ring road surrounding a city. *Strade statali* (state highways, denoted by S or SS numbers) may be single-lane roads, as are all secondary roads; directions and turnoffs are not always clearly marked.

AUTO CLUBS

There are two major automobile clubs operative in Italy: ACI (Automobil Club D'Italia), which is in fact less of a club and more of a vehicle ownership registration service which also provides breakdown assistance coverage; subscription to the TCI (Touring Club Italiano) provides motorists with maps and logistical assistance when planning journeys and holidays, besides taking an active interest in Italian heritage preservation.

➤ IN AUSTRALIA: **Australian Automobile Association** (☎ 02/6247–7311, WEB www.aaa.asn.au).

➤ IN CANADA: **Canadian Automobile Association (CAA,** ☎ 613/247–0117, WEB www.caa.ca).

➤ IN ITALY: **Automobil Club D'Italia** (☎ 081/5931301, WEB www.aci.it). **Touring Club Italiano** (☎ 02/5359971, WEB www.touringclub.it).

➤ IN NEW ZEALAND: **New Zealand Automobile Association** (☎ 09/377–4660, WEB www.aa.co.nz).

➤ IN THE U.K.: **Automobile Association (AA,** ☎ 0870/600–0371, WEB www.theaa.com). **Royal Automobile Club (RAC,** ☎ 0990/722–722 for membership; 0345/121–345 for insurance, WEB www.rac.co.uk).

➤ IN THE U.S.: **American Automobile Association** (☎ 800/564–6222, WEB www.aaa.com).

EMERGENCY SERVICES

ACI Emergency Service offers 24-hour road service. Dial 116 from any phone, 24 hours a day, to reach the ACI dispatch operator.

GASOLINE

Gas stations are generally open Monday through Saturday from 7 AM to 7 PM with a break at lunchtime. Many stations have automatic self-service pumps which usually accept bills of €5, 10, or 20. Gas stations on autostrade are open 24 hours. Gas costs about €1.20 per liter. Almost all rental cars take so-called *benzina verde* (unleaded fuel known as green gasoline).

PARKING

Parking space is at a premium in Naples and most towns, but especially in the *centri storici* (historic centers), which are filled with narrow streets and restricted circulation zones. It is often a good idea (if not the only option) to park your car in a designated (preferably attended) lot. Parking in an area signposted ZONA DISCO (disk zone) is allowed for limited periods (from 30 minutes to 2 hours or more—the limit is posted); if you don't have the cardboard disk (inquire at the local tourist office) to show what time you parked, you can

use a piece of paper. The *parcometro,* the Italian version of metered parking in which you purchase prepaid tickets (from a newsstand or tobacconist's) that you scratch to indicate time and date of arrival and leave on the dashboard, has been introduced in some cities, including Naples. Within Naples, it is advisable to **leave your car only in designated parking areas,** usually marked out by blue lines. A red sign with a horizontal white stripe through it means do not enter; a blue circular sign with a red slash or an X means no parking, as do the signs VIETATO SOSTARE, DIVIETO DI SOSTA, and NON PARCHEGGIARE.

ROAD CONDITIONS

Autostrade are well maintained, as are most interregional highways. The condition of provincial (county) roads varies, but road maintenance at this level is generally good in Italy. Street and road signs are often challenging—a good map and patience are essential. Italians drive fast and are impatient with those who don't. Tailgaiting is the norm here—the only way to avoid it is to get out of the way.

RULES OF THE ROAD

Driving is on the right. Regulations are largely as in Britain and the United States, except that the police have the power to levy on-the-spot fines. In most Italian towns the use of the horn is forbidden in certain, if not all, areas; a large sign, ZONA DI SILENZIO, indicates where. Elsewhere, according to the Italian Highway Code, horns can only be used in situations where there is "immediate and real danger." Some drivers interpret this as covering every sharp bend on the Amalfi Coast, though an alternative noise-free technique is to slow down and keep a foot hovering over the brake pedal. Speed limits are 130 kph (80 mph) on autostrade and 90 kph (55 mph) on state and provincial roads, unless otherwise marked. Fines for driving after drinking are heavy, including the suspension of license and the additional possibility of six months' imprisonment.

CHILDREN IN ITALY

Although Italians love children and are generally very tolerant and patient with them, they provide few amenities for them. In restaurants and trattorias you may find a high chair or a cushion for the child to sit on, but rarely do they offer a children's menu. Order a *mezza porzione* (half-portion) of any dish, or ask the waiter for a *porzione da bambino* (child's portion).

Discounts do exist. Always ask about a *sconto bambino* (child's discount) before purchasing tickets. Children under a certain height ride free on municipal buses and trams. Children under 18 who are EU citizens are admitted free to state-run museums and galleries, and there are similar privileges in many municipal or private museums.

If you are renting a car, don't forget to **arrange for a car seat** when you reserve. For general advice about traveling with children, consult *Fodor's FYI: Travel with Your Baby* (available in bookstores everywhere).

FLYING

When booking, **confirm carry-on allowances** if you're traveling with infants. In general, for babies charged 10% of the adult fare you are allowed one carry-on bag and a collapsible stroller; if the flight is full, the stroller may have to be checked or you may be limited to less.

Experts agree that it's a good idea to use safety seats aloft for children weighing less than 40 pounds. Airlines set their own policies: U.S. carriers usually require that the child be ticketed, even if he or she is young enough to ride free, since the seats must be strapped into regular seats. Do **check your airline's policy about using safety seats during takeoff and landing.** And since safety seats are not allowed everywhere in the plane, get your seat assignments early.

When reserving, **request children's meals or a freestanding bassinet** if you need them. But note that bulkhead seats, where you must sit to use the bassinet, may lack an overhead bin or storage space on the floor.

LODGING

Most hotels in Italy allow children under a certain age to stay in their parents' room at no extra charge, but others charge for them as extra adults; be sure to **find out the cutoff age for children's discounts.**

SIGHTS & ATTRACTIONS

Places that are especially appealing to children are indicated by a rubber-duckie icon (🐥) in the margin.

CONCIERGES

Concierges, found in many hotels, can help you with theater tickets and dinner reservations: a good one with connections may be able to get you seats for a hot show or prime-time dinner reservations at the restaurant of the moment. You can also turn to your hotel's concierge for help with travel arrangements, sightseeing plans, services ranging from aromatherapy to zipper repair, and emergencies. Always, **always tip** a concierge who has been of assistance (☞ Tipping).

CONSULATES & EMBASSIES

➤ AUSTRALIA: Australian Consulate (✉ Via Alessandria 215 00198 Rome, ☎ 06/852721, WEB www.australian-embassy.it).

➤ CANADA: Canadian Embassy (✉ Via Zara 30, Rome, ☎ 06/445981, WEB www.canada.it).

➤ NEW ZEALAND: New Zealand Embassy (✉ Via Zara 28, Rome, ☎ 06/4417171.

➤ UNITED KINGDOM: British Consulate (✉ Via Dei Mille 40, Napoli, ☎ 081/4238911, WEB www.ukinitalia.it).

➤ UNITED STATES: U.S. Consulate (✉ Piazza della Repubblica 2, at west end of Villa Comunale, Napoli, ☎ 081/5838111, WEB www.usembassy.it).

CONSUMER PROTECTION

Whenever shopping or buying travel services in Italy, **pay with a major credit card,** if possible, so you can cancel payment or get reimbursed if there's a problem. If you're doing business with a particular company for the first time, **contact your local Better Business Bureau and the attorney general's offices** in your state and (for U.S. businesses) the company's home state as well. Have any complaints been filed? Finally, if you're buying a package or tour, always **consider travel insurance** that includes default coverage (☞ Insurance).

➤ BBBs: **Council of Better Business Bureaus** (✉ 4200 Wilson Blvd., Suite 800, Arlington, VA 22203, ☎ 703/276–0100, FAX 703/525–8277, WEB www.bbb.org).

CUSTOMS & DUTIES

When shopping, **keep receipts** for all purchases. Upon reentering the country, **be ready to show customs officials what you've bought.** If you feel a duty is incorrect or object to the way your clearance was handled, note the inspector's badge number and ask to see a supervisor. If the problem isn't resolved, write to the appropriate authorities, beginning with the port director at your point of entry.

IN AUSTRALIA

Australian residents who are 18 or older may bring home $A400 worth of souvenirs and gifts (including jewelry), 250 cigarettes or 250 grams of tobacco, and 1,125 ml of alcohol (including wine, beer, and spirits). Residents under 18 may bring back $A200 worth of goods. Prohibited items include meat products. Seeds, plants, and fruits need to be declared upon arrival.

➤ INFORMATION: **Australian Customs Service** (Regional Director, ✉ Box 8, Sydney, NSW 2001, Australia, ☎ 02/9213–2000, FAX 02/9213–4000, WEB www.customs.gov.au).

IN CANADA

Canadian residents who have been out of Canada for at least seven days may bring home C$750 worth of goods duty-free. If you've been away fewer than seven days but more than 48 hours, the duty-free allowance drops to C$200; if your trip lasts 24–48 hours, the allowance is C$50. You may not pool allowances with family members. Goods claimed under the CS750 exemption may follow you by mail; those claimed under the lesser exemptions must accompany you. Alcohol and tobacco products may be included in the seven-day and 48-hour exemptions but not in the 24-hour exemption. If you meet the age requirements of the province or territory

through which you reenter Canada, you may bring in, duty-free, 1.14 liters (40 imperial ounces) of wine or liquor *or* 24 12-ounce cans or bottles of beer or ale. If you are 19 or older you may bring in, duty-free, 200 cigarettes and 50 cigars. Check ahead of time with the Canada Customs Revenue Agency or the Department of Agriculture for policies regarding meat products, seeds, plants, and fruits.

You may send an unlimited number of gifts worth up to C$60 each duty-free to Canada. Label the package UNSOLICITED GIFT—VALUE UNDER $60. Alcohol and tobacco are excluded.

➤ INFORMATION: **Canada Customs Revenue Agency** (✉ 2265 St. Laurent Blvd. S, Ottawa, Ontario K1G 4K3, Canada, ☎ 204/983–3500 or 506/636–5064; 800/461–9999 in Canada, WEB www.ccra-adrc.gc.ca).

IN ITALY

Of goods obtained anywhere outside the EU or goods purchased in a duty-free shop within an EU country, the allowances are: (1) 200 cigarettes or 100 cigarillos or 50 cigars or 250 grams of tobacco; (2) 2 liters of still table wine or 1 liter of spirits over 22% volume or 2 liters of spirits under 22% volume or 2 liters of fortified and sparkling wines; and (3) 50 ml of perfume and 250 ml of toilet water.

Of goods obtained (duty and tax paid) within another EU country, the guidance levels are: (1) 800 cigarettes or 400 cigarillos or 400 cigars or 1 kilogram of tobacco; (2) 90 liters of still table wine plus (3) 10 liters of spirits over 22% volume plus 20 liters of spirits under 22% volume plus 60 liters of sparkling wines plus 110 liters of beer.

➤ INFORMATION: **Italian Customs** (Dipartimento delle Dogane e Imposte Indirette, ✉ Via A. de Gasperi 20, Naples, ☎ 081/2527111, FAX 081/5528234).

IN NEW ZEALAND

Homeward-bound residents 17 or older may bring back $700 worth of souvenirs and gifts. Your duty-free allowance also includes 4.5 liters of wine or beer; one 1,125-ml bottle of spirits; and either 200 cigarettes, 250 grams of tobacco, 50 cigars, or a combination of the three up to 250 grams. Prohibited items include meat products, seeds, plants, and fruits.

➤ INFORMATION: **New Zealand Customs** (Custom House, ✉ 50 Anzac Ave., Box 29, Auckland, New Zealand, ☎ 09/300–5399, FAX 09/ 359–6730, WEB www.customs.govt.nz).

IN THE U.K.

If you are a U.K. resident and your journey was wholly within the European Union (EU), you won't have to pass through customs when you return to the United Kingdom. If you plan to bring back large quantities of alcohol or tobacco, check EU limits beforehand.

➤ INFORMATION: **HM Customs and Excise** (✉ St. Christopher House, Southwark, London, SE1 OTE, U.K., ☎ 020/7928–3344, WEB www.hmce. gov.uk).

IN THE U.S.

U.S. residents who have been out of the country for at least 48 hours (and who have not used the $400 allowance or any part of it in the past 30 days) may bring home $400 worth of foreign goods duty-free.

U.S. residents 21 and older may bring back 1 liter of alcohol duty-free. In addition, regardless of your age, you are allowed 200 cigarettes and 100 non-Cuban cigars. Antiques, which the U.S. Customs Service defines as objects more than 100 years old, enter duty-free, as do original works of art done entirely by hand, including paintings, drawings, and sculptures.

U.S. customs officials tend to be very tough on loose food imports, so think twice before trying to import that fennel-flavored Neapolitan salami sausage or the creamy buffalo *bocconcino di mozzarella* that tasted so much better than the equivalent back home. Such items usually end up being special treats for the sniffer dogs at some airport in the U.S.

You may also mail or ship packages home duty-free: up to $200 worth of goods for personal use, with a limit of one parcel per addressee per day (except alcohol or tobacco products or perfume worth more than $5); label the package PERSONAL USE and attach a list of its contents and their retail value. Do not label the package UNSOLICITED GIFT or your duty-free exemption will drop to $100. Mailed items do not affect your duty-free allowance on your return.

➤ INFORMATION: **U.S. Customs Service** (✉ 1300 Pennsylvania Ave. NW, Room 6.3D, Washington, DC 20229, WEB www.customs.gov; inquiries ☎ 202/354–1000; complaints c/o ✉ 1300 Pennsylvania Ave. NW, Room 5.4D, Washington, DC 20229; registration of equipment c/o Office of Passenger Programs, ☎ 202/927– 0530).

DINING

The restaurants we list are the cream of the crop in each price category. Properties indicated by a ✕🏠 are lodging establishments whose restaurant warrants a special trip. For price categories, *see* the price charts found under "Pleasures and Pastimes" in each regional chapter.

RESERVATIONS & DRESS

Reservations are always a good idea: we mention them only when they're essential or are not accepted. Remember that when dining out in a nice restaurant (that is, not a café or casual trattoria), most Italians will make an effort to smarten up: Even when you are in a low-key seaside location, blue-jean shorts and sandals can attract "can-only-be-a-tourist" stares, especially during the evening.

DISABILITIES & ACCESSIBILITY

Italy has only recently begun to provide facilities such as ramps, telephones, and rest rooms for people with disabilities; such things are still the exception, not the rule. Travelers' wheelchairs must be transported free of charge, according to Italian law, but the logistics of getting a wheelchair on and off trains and buses can make this requirement irrelevant. Seats are reserved for people with disabilities on public transportation, but few buses have lifts for wheelchairs. High, narrow steps for boarding trains create additional problems. In many monuments and museums, even in some hotels and restaurants, architectural barriers make it difficult, if not impossible, for those with disabilities to gain access.

Contact the nearest Italian consulate about bringing a Seeing Eye dog into Italy; this requires an import license, a current certificate detailing the dog's inoculations, and a letter from your veterinarian certifying the dog's health.

➤ LOCAL RESOURCES: The **Italian Government Travel Office** (ENIT; ☞ Visitor Information) can give you a list of hotels that provide access and addresses of Italian associations for travelers with disabilities.

RESERVATIONS

When discussing accessibility with an operator or reservations agent, **ask hard questions.** Are there any stairs, inside *or* out? Are there grab bars next to the toilet *and* in the shower/tub? How wide is the doorway to the room? To the bathroom? For the most extensive facilities meeting the latest legal specifications, **opt for newer accommodations.**

➤ COMPLAINTS: **Aviation Consumer Protection Division** (☞ Air Travel) for airline-related problems. **Civil Rights Office** (✉ U.S. Department of Transportation, Departmental Office of Civil Rights, S-30, 400 7th St. SW, Room 10215, Washington, DC 20590, ☎ 202/366–4648, FAX 202/366–9371, WEB www.dot.gov/ost/docr/index.htm) for problems with surface transportation. **Disability Rights Section** (✉ U.S. Department of Justice, Civil Rights Division, Box 66738, Washington, DC 20035-6738, ☎ 202/514–0301 or 800/514–0301; 202/514–0383 TTY; 800/514–0383 TTY, FAX 202/307–1198, WEB www.usdoj.gov/crt/ada/adahom1.htm) for general complaints.

TRAVEL AGENCIES

In the United States, the Americans with Disabilities Act requires that travel firms serve the needs of all travelers. Some agencies specialize in working with people with disabilities.

➤ TRAVELERS WITH MOBILITY PROBLEMS: **Access Adventures** (✉ 206

Chestnut Ridge Rd., Scottsville, NY 14624, ☎ 716/889–9096, dltravel@prodigy.net), run by a former physical-rehabilitation counselor. **CareVacations** (✉ No. 5, 5110–50 Ave., Leduc, Alberta T9E 6V4, Canada, ☎ 780/986–6404 or 877/478–7827, FAX 780/986–8332, WEB www.carevacations.com), for group tours and cruise vacations. **Flying Wheels Travel** (✉ 143 W. Bridge St., Box 382, Owatonna, MN 55060, ☎ 507/451–5005 or 800/535–6790, FAX 507/451–1685, WEB www.flyingwheelstravel.com).

DISCOUNTS & DEALS

Be a smart shopper and **compare all your options** before making decisions. A plane ticket bought with a promotional coupon from travel clubs, coupon books, and direct-mail offers or on the Internet may not be cheaper than the least expensive fare from a discount ticket agency. And always keep in mind that what you get is just as important as what you save.

DISCOUNT RESERVATIONS

To save money, **look into discount reservations services** with toll-free numbers, which use their buying power to get a better price on hotels, airline tickets, even car rentals. When booking a room, always **call the hotel's local toll-free number** (if one is available) rather than the central reservations number—you'll often get a better price. Always ask about special packages or corporate rates.

When shopping for the best deal on hotels and car rentals, **look for guaranteed exchange rates,** which protect you against a falling dollar. With your rate locked in, you won't pay more, even if the price goes up in the local currency.

➤ AIRLINE TICKETS: ☎ **800/AIR-4LESS.**

➤ HOTEL ROOMS: **Hotel Reservations Network** (☎ 800/964–6835, WEB www.hoteldiscount.com). **International Marketing & Travel Concepts** (☎ 800/790–4682, WEB www.imtc-travel.com). **Players Express Vacations** (☎ 800/458–6161, WEB www.playersexpress.com). **Steigenberger Reservation Service**

(☎ 800/223–5652, WEB www.
srs-worldhotels.com). **Travel Inter-
link** (☎ 800/888–5898, WEB www.
travelinterlink.com). **Turbotrip.com**
(☎ 800/473–7829, WEB www.
turbotrip.com).

PACKAGE DEALS

Don't confuse packages and guided
tours. When you buy a package, you
travel on your own, just as though
you had planned the trip yourself.
Fly/drive packages, which combine
airfare and car rental, are often a
good deal. In cities, ask the local
visitors' bureau about hotel packages
that include tickets to major museum
exhibits or other special events. If you
buy a rail/drive pass, you may save
on train tickets and car rentals. All
Eurail- and Europass holders get a
discount on Eurostar fares through
the Channel Tunnel.

ELECTRICITY

To use your U.S.-purchased electric-
powered equipment **bring a converter
and adapter.** The electrical current in
Italy is 220 volts, 50 cycles alternating current (AC); wall outlets take
Continental-type plugs, with two
round prongs.

If your appliances are dual-voltage
you'll need only an adapter. Don't use
110-volt outlets, marked FOR SHAVERS
ONLY, for high-wattage appliances
such as blow-dryers. Most laptops
operate equally well on 110 and 220
volts and so require only an adapter.

EMERGENCIES

Also see Emergencies *in* the A to Z
section in regional chapters.

➤ EMERGENCY SERVICES: **General
emergencies:** ☎ 113. **Police:** ☎ 112.
Naples's main police station (⌑ Via
Medina 75, ☎ 081/7941111) has an
ufficio stranieri (foreigners' office) at
⌑ Via Ferraris 131 (☎ 081/6064111)
that usually has an English speaker
on staff and can help with passport
problems.

Ambulance: ☎ 081/7520696. **Medical emergency** after 8 PM: ☎ 081/
7613466 (ask for an English-speaking
nurse). **Hospital:** Cardarelli (☎ 081/
7471111). If the *farmacia* (pharmacy)
in Stazione Centrale is closed, it will

post the address of one that's open;
the newspaper *Il Mattino* also prints a
list of pharmacies that are open nights
and weekends. **Car breakdowns and
emergencies:** ☎ 116.

ENGLISH-LANGUAGE
AND ITALIAN MEDIA

The Azienda Autonoma di Soggiorno,
Cura e Turismo publishes *Qui Napoli,*
an English-language monthly periodical for visitors to Naples listing all the
special events held in the city, along
with complete listings of train, bus,
subway, ferry, and hydrofoil routes
and schedules. In addition, there are
exhaustive listings of the city's libraries, theaters, cinemas, and sports
facilities. A gratis publication, it is
available at all visitor information
centers in Naples and at many hotels.

BOOKS

For Naples's largest selection of
books in English, head to **Universal
Books** (⌑ Corso Umberto 22, inside
a palazzo off Corso Umberto near
Piazza Bovio, ☎ 081/2520069,
unibooks@galactica.it).

NEWSPAPERS & MAGAZINES

Il Mattino (www.ilmattino.it) is the
leading newspaper of Naples, while
the national dailies, *Corriere della
Sera* (www.corriere.it), *La Repubblica*
(www.repubblica.it), and *La Stampa*
(www.lastampa.it) also offer multi-
page Naples sections in their local
editions. Other newspapers published
for Campania include *Ultimissime*
and *Roma.*

RADIO & TELEVISION

One of the main regional papers, *Il
Mattino,* lists the various local TV
stations in its entertainment pages.
Viewers are fed a fairly indigestible
diet of television auctions, dubbed B
movies from the U.S., soccer highlights, soft porn (after midnight), and
the odd tidbit of news. If you have a
smattering of Italian, watch the better-
quality state-funded RAI TRE station
with local news and weather coverage
at 2, 7, and 10:40 PM (approximately)
every day (www.rai.it). The main
private radio station is the curiously
named Kiss Kiss (103.0 MHz), which
broadcasts late-night music directly
from its own disco up on the Vomero

Hill, but also does a fair amount of handy traffic news for those on the move (www.kisskissnapoli.it). For a good blend of traffic news (a permanent topic of conversation), interviews, news, and music, the state-run ISO Radio broadcasts on 103.3 MHz and is designed for those using the Italian motorway network.

GAY & LESBIAN TRAVEL

In keeping with its reputation as a city of stark contrasts, Naples combines a macho heterosexual image with, however, a strong gay undercurrent. Several gay clubs—both for men and women—have sprung up in the past few years in various parts of town.

➤ LOCAL RESOURCES: Arci–GAY/ Lesbica (✉ Vico S. Geronimo 17/20, Napoli, ☎ 081/5528815 or 081/ 5518293, WEB www.gay.it); this is the main clearinghouse for information in Naples and the region. Ferdinand strasse (✉ Piazza Portanova 8, Napoli, ☎ 081/207390) is a meeting spot that provides a semi-intellectual background for encounters close to the university, accompanied by meat and fresh fish menus costing about €16. Freezer (✉ Via Lauria 6, Napoli, ☎ 081/7502457) is set in the thick of the post-modern jungle of the Centro Direzionale (Naples Business Center); this discobar has a northern European mix of sexual persuasions. A minimum of about €8 has to be spent on drinks.

➤ GAY- & LESBIAN-FRIENDLY TRAVEL AGENCIES: Different Roads Travel (✉ 8383 Wilshire Blvd., Suite 902, Beverly Hills, CA 90211, ☎ 323/ 651–5557 or 800/429–8747, FAX 323/651–3678, lgernert@tzell.com). Kennedy Travel (✉ 314 Jericho Turnpike, Floral Park, NY 11001, ☎ 516/352–4888 or 800/237–7433, FAX 516/354–8849, WEB www. kennedytravel.com). Now Voyager (✉ 4406 18th St., San Francisco, CA 94114, ☎ 415/626–1169 or 800/255–6951, FAX 415/626–8626, WEB www.nowvoyager.com). Skylink Travel and Tour (✉ 1006 Mendocino Ave., Santa Rosa, CA 95401, ☎ 707/546–9888 or 800/225–5759, FAX 707/546–9891, WEB www. skylinktravel.com), serving lesbian travelers.

GUIDEBOOKS

Plan well and you won't be sorry. Guidebooks are excellent tools—and you can take them with you. You may want to check out color-photo-laden Fodor's Escape to the Amalfi Coast, which highlights 20 unique experiences and is available at on-line retailers and bookstores everywhere.

HEALTH

The Centers for Disease Control and Prevention (CDC) in Atlanta caution that most of Southern Europe is in the "intermediate" range for risk of contacting traveler's diarrhea. Part of this risk may be attributed to an increased consumption of olive oil and wine, which can have a laxative effect on stomachs used to a different diet. The CDC also advises all international travelers to swim only in chlorinated swimming pools, unless they are absolutely certain the local beaches and freshwater lakes are not contaminated.

In 2001, about one-quarter of the coastline in the province of Naples was considered by local health authorities unfit for bathing. The main areas off-limits are on the Naples waterfront, by the port, and on the shoreline by the Vesuvian towns as far as Castellammare di Stabia— places where you wouldn't choose to swim anyway. Fortunately, this leaves a lot of coastal mileage for potential bathers, and many beaches in the area have received a clean bill of health.

Contaminated seafood is a risk in Naples as elsewhere, and if you are going to indulge in oysters or other raw seafood, choose your restaurant wisely. Resist the temptation of prying open and eating mussels, clams, or other delicacies on your platter. If the shell doesn't open on cooking, then it is best left alone.

In bars and cafés, especially around areas with heavy traffic like the Stazione Centrale in Naples or in the depressed areas around Vesuvius, you can ask for your espresso or cappuccino in a bicchiere monouso (non-reusable plastic cup), rather than opting to drink out of the local crockery. However, most mainstream bars and restaurants take hygiene ultra-seriously.

Thanks to the prevailing westerly winds, Naples does not suffer such acute air pollution as its Greek neighbor, Athens. However, when the winds drop, WHO safety thresholds are sometimes exceeded, especially for nitrogen oxides, while the excessive number of polluting two-stroke motorcycles can make the air thick with partially combusted hydrocarbons. As a general rule, for those who are highly sensitive to air quality, try not to linger in traffic-ridden areas like Piazza Garibaldi in Naples, and take a bus or metro to avoid direct exposure to pollutants.

Out in the country, health risks are minimal. There is no poison ivy or poison oak in the countryside around Naples, although if you stray off beaten paths you might become entangled in the smilax plant or in blackberry bushes, both of which have persistent thorns. The vast majority of the snakes you might meet will be harmless, and are likely to be far more frightened of you—and more innocuous—than vice versa.

➤ MEDICAL-ASSISTANCE COMPANIES: **International SOS Assistance** (✉ 8 Neshaminy Interplex, Suite 207, Trevose, PA 19053, ☎ 215/245–4707 or 800/523–6586, FAX 215/244–9617; ✉ 12 Chemin Rieantbosson, 1217 Meyrin 1, Geneva, Switzerland, ☎ 4122/785–6464, FAX 4122/785–6424; ✉ 331 N. Bridge Rd., 17-00, Odeon Towers, Singapore 188720, ☎ 65/ 338–7800, FAX 65/338–7611).

HOLIDAYS

National holidays include January 1 (New Year's Day); January 6 (Epiphany); Easter Sunday and Monday; April 25 (Liberation Day); May 1 (Labor Day or May Day); August 15 (Assumption of Mary, also known as Ferragosto); November 1 (All Saints' Day); December 8 (Immaculate Conception); and December 25 and 26 (Christmas Day and St. Stephen's Day) are also holidays. During these holidays many shops and restaurants are closed, while decisions about whether to open major museums and archaeological sites like Pompeii and Herculaneum are usually made at the eleventh hour.

The feast days of patron saints are observed locally in various towns and villages; some of the more famous festas are: San Costanzo, Capri, May 14; San Antonio, Anacapri, June 13; Sant'Andrea, Amalfi, June 25–30; San Pietro, Positano, June 29; Sant'Anna, Ischia, July 26; and San Pantaleone, Ravello, July 27. In Naples, two annual celebrations are held at the Duomo on the first Sunday in May and on September 19 to celebrate the Festa di San Gennaro, or the Liquefaction of the Blood of San Gennaro. For information on these and other holidays, *see also* Festivals and Seasonal Events *in* "When to Go."

INSURANCE

The most useful travel-insurance plan is a comprehensive policy that includes coverage for trip cancellation and interruption, default, trip delay, and medical expenses (with a waiver for pre-existing conditions).

Without insurance you will lose all or most of your money if you cancel your trip, regardless of the reason. Default insurance covers you if your tour operator, airline, or cruise line goes out of business. Trip-delay covers expenses that arise because of bad weather or mechanical delays. Study the fine print when comparing policies.

If you're traveling internationally, a key component of travel insurance is coverage for medical bills incurred if you get sick on the road. Such expenses are not generally covered by Medicare or private policies. U.K. residents can buy a travel-insurance policy valid for most vacations taken during the year in which it's purchased (but check pre-existing-condition coverage). British and Australian citizens need extra medical coverage when traveling overseas.

Always **buy travel policies directly from the insurance company**; if you buy them from a cruise line, airline, or tour operator that goes out of business you probably will not be covered for the agency or operator's default, a major risk. Before making any purchase, **review your existing health and**

home-owner's policies to find what they cover away from home.

➤ TRAVEL INSURERS: In the U.S.: **Access America** (✉ 6600 W. Broad St., Richmond, VA 23230, ☎ 800/284–8300, FAX 804/673–1491, WEB www.etravelprotection.com), **Travel Guard International** (✉ 1145 Clark St., Stevens Point, WI 54481, ☎ 715/345–0505 or 800/826–1300, FAX 800/955–8785, WEB www.travelguard.com).

➤ INSURANCE INFORMATION: In the U.K.: **Association of British Insurers** (✉ 51–55 Gresham St., London EC2V 7HQ, U.K., ☎ 020/7600–3333, FAX 020/7696–8999, WEB www.abi.org.uk). In Canada: **RBC Travel Insurance** (✉ 6880 Financial Dr., Mississauga, Ontario L5N 7Y5, Canada, ☎ 905/791–8700, 800/668–4342 in Canada, FAX 905/816–2498, WEB www.royalbank.com). In Australia: **Insurance Council of Australia** (✉ Level 3, 56 Pitt St., Sydney NSW 2000, ☎ 02/9253–5100, FAX 02/9253–5111, WEB www.ica.com.au). In New Zealand: **Insurance Council of New Zealand** (✉ Level 7, 111–115 Customhouse Quay, Box 474, Wellington, New Zealand, ☎ 04/472–5230, FAX 04/473–3011, WEB www.icnz.org.nz).

LANGUAGE

In Naples and the leading resorts, language is not a big problem. You can always find someone who speaks at least a little English; remember that the Italian language is pronounced exactly as it is written (many Italians try to speak English by enunciating every letter, with disconcerting results). You may run into a language barrier in the countryside, but a phrase book and close attention to the Italians' use of expressive gestures will go a long way. Try to **master a few phrases for daily use** (☞ Italian Vocabulary at the back of this book) and familiarize yourself with the terms you'll need to decipher signs and museum labels.

LANGUAGES FOR TRAVELERS

A phrase book and language-tape set can help get you started. *Fodor's Italian for Travelers* (available at bookstores everywhere) is excellent.

LODGING

The lodgings we review in this book are the cream of the crop in each price category. We always list the facilities that are available—but we don't specify whether they cost extra: When pricing accommodations, always ask what's included and what costs extra. Extra fees can be charged for everything from breakfast to use of parking facilities to air-conditioning. For price categories, consult the price charts found under Pleasures and Pastimes in Chapters 1, 2, 3, and 4.

Most hotels still operate on the Continental Plan, with a Continental breakfast daily provided in the room rate; however, expensive and bargain hotels are increasingly adding an extra charge for breakfast, so inquire when booking. Note that this region of Italy has many resort hotels and in peak-season months (usually, June to September), some of them require either half- or full-board arrangements, whereby your (increased) room tab includes lunch or lunch/dinner provided by the hotel restaurant. Properties indicated by a ✗☐ are lodging establishments whose restaurants warrant a special trip.

APARTMENT & VILLA RENTALS

If you want a home base that's roomy enough for a family and comes with cooking facilities, **consider a furnished rental.** These can save you money, especially if you're traveling with a group. Home-exchange directories sometimes list rentals as well as exchanges.

➤ INTERNATIONAL AGENTS: **At Home Abroad** (✉ 405 E. 56th St., Suite 6H, New York, NY 10022, ☎ 212/421–9165, FAX 212/752–1591, WEB www.athomeabroadinc.com). **Drawbridge to Europe** (✉ 98 Granite St., Ashland, OR 97520, ☎ 541/482–7778 or 888/268–1148, FAX 541/482–7779, WEB www.drawbridgetoeurope.com). **Hideaways International** (✉ 767 Islington St., Portsmouth, NH 03801, ☎ 603/430–4433 or 800/843–4433, FAX 603/430–4444, WEB www.hideaways.com; membership $129). **Hometours International** (✉ Box 11503, Knoxville, TN 37939, ☎ 865/690–8484 or 800/367–4668,

WEB http://thor.he.net/~hometour/).
Interhome (✉ 1990 N.E. 163rd St.,
Suite 110, N. Miami Beach, FL
33162, ☎ 305/940–2299 or 800/
882–6864, FAX 305/940–2911,
WEB www.interhome.com). **Vacation
Home Rentals Worldwide** (✉ 235
Kensington Ave., Norwood, NJ
07648, ☎ 201/767–9393 or 800/
633–3284, FAX 201/767–5510,
WEB www.vhrww.com). **Villanet**
(✉ 11556 1st Ave. NW, Seattle, WA
98177, ☎ 206/417–3444 or 800/
964–1891, FAX 206/417–1832,
WEB www.rentavilla.com). **Villas and
Apartments Abroad** (✉ 1270 Avenue
of the Americas, 15th floor, New
York, NY 10020, ☎ 212/897–5045
or 800/433–3020, FAX 212/897–5039,
WEB www.ideal-villas.com). **Villas
International** (✉ 950 Northgate Dr.,
Suite 206, San Rafael, CA 94903,
☎ 415/499–9490 or 800/221–2260,
FAX 415/499–9491, WEB www.
villasintl.com).

➤ ITALY-ONLY AGENTS: **Cuendet USA**
(✉ 165 Chestnut St., Allendale, NJ
07041, ☎ 201/327–2333; ✉ Suzanne
T. Pidduck, c/o Rentals in Italy, 1742
Calle Corva, Camarillo, CA 93010,
☎ 800/726–6702). **Vacanze in Italia**
(✉ 22 Railroad St., Great Barrington,
MA 01230, ☎ 413/528–6610 or 800/
533–5405).

➤ IN THE U.K.: **CV Travel** (✉ 43
Cadogan St., London SW3 2PR,
England, ☎ 020/7581–0851). **Magic
of Italy** (✉ 227 Shepherds Bush Rd.,
London W6 7AS, England, ☎ 020/
8748–7575).

B&BS

Increasing numbers of southern
Italians, especially Neapolitans, are
following the long-tried British for-
mula of bed and breakfast. Besides
the substantial cost savings, this may
be your only chance to peek into an
Italian home and experience *vita* (life)
as lived by the locals. When booking,
try to find out exactly what is on
offer: It could be a cramped room in a
faceless suburb with overly inquisitive
hosts, or you could strike it lucky
with a room with an 18th-century
fresco ceiling in a quiet city-center
location. For further information,
contact the local tourist information
office or one of the agencies below.

➤ NAPLES AGENTS: **Associazione Bed
& Breakfast** (✉ Cupa Camaldoli 18,
Napoli, napolibbnaples@tightrope.it,
WEB www.tightrope.it/bbnaples/index.
htm). **Rent a Bed** (✉ Vico San Carlo
alle Mortelle 14, Napoli, ☎ 081/
417721, WEB www.rentabed.com).

CAMPING

Camping is a good way to find
accommodations in otherwise overcrowded resorts, and camper rental
agencies operate throughout Italy;
contact your travel agent for details.
Make sure you **stay only on autho-
rized campsites** (camping on private
land is frowned upon), and get an
international camping *carnet* (permit) from your local camping association before you leave home. The
Touring Club Italiano publishes a
multilingual *Guida Camping d'Italia*
(Guide to Camping in Italy), available in bookstores in Italy for about
€17, with more detailed information
on sites. Camp rates for two people,
with car and tent, average about
€30 a day.

Well-appointed campsites within easy
reach of the areas covered in this
guide are found on the islands of
Ischia and Procida, close to the temples of Paestum, in Sorrento, and in
Pozzuoli. Unless you find a campsite
with a good provision of shade, try to
avoid July and August, when facilities
are crowded and the heat will force
you out of your tent uncomfortably
early in the morning. For a comprehensive list of campsites in the area,
consult the Web site www.camping.it.

➤ DIRECTORY OF CAMPGROUNDS:
Write to the **Federazione Italiana del
Campeggio e del Caravanning** (✉
Federcampeggio, Casella Postale 23,
50041 Calenzano, Firenze, FAX 055/
8825918) and request *Campeggiare
in Italia;* send three international
reply coupons to cover mailing. It's
also available through the ENIT
office in the United States and at
tourist information offices in Italy
(☞ Visitor Information and *in* individual chapters).

FARM HOLIDAYS &
AGRITOURISM

Rural accommodations in the *agriturismo* (agritourism) category are

increasingly popular with both Italians and visitors to Italy. This is where a little surfing on the Internet can pay dividends: Just call up a search engine and key in the words, say, "agriturismo." and "Campania," and see what gives. Though technologically literate, as yet few farms in the Naples area will accept credit cards, so remember to load up with cash before your stay.

➤ AGENCIES: **Italy Farm Holidays** (✉ 547 Martling Ave., Tarrytown, NY 10591, ☎ 914/631–7880, FAX 914/631–8831). **Agriturist** (✉ Corso Vittorio 101, 00186 Rome, ☎ 06/ 6852342, WEB www.agriturist.it). **Turismo Verde** (✉ Via Flaminia 56, 00196 Rome, ☎ 06/3611051, WEB www.turismoverde.it).

HOME EXCHANGES

If you would like to exchange your home for someone else's, **join a home-exchange organization,** which will send you its updated listings of available exchanges for a year and will include your own listing in at least one of them. It's up to you to make specific arrangements.

➤ EXCHANGE CLUBS: **HomeLink International** (✉ Box 47747, Tampa, FL 33647, ☎ 813/975–9825 or 800/638–3841, FAX 813/910–8144, WEB www. homelink.org; $106 per year). **Intervac U.S.** (✉ Box 590504, San Francisco, CA 94159, ☎ 800/756–4663, FAX 415/ 435–7440, WEB www.intervacus.com; $93 yearly fee includes one catalogue and on-line access).

HOSTELS

No matter what your age, you can **save on lodging costs by staying at hostels.** In some 4,500 locations in more than 70 countries around the world, Hostelling International (HI), the umbrella group for a number of national youth-hostel associations, offers single-sex, dorm-style beds and, at many hostels, rooms for couples and family accommodations. Membership in any HI national hostel association, open to travelers of all ages, allows you to stay in HI-affiliated hostels at member rates; one-year membership is about $25 for adults (C$26.75 in Canada, £9.30 in the U.K., $30 in Australia, and $30 in

New Zealand); hostels run about $10–$25 per night. Members have priority if the hostel is full; they're also eligible for discounts around the world, even on rail and bus travel in some countries.

In the Naples area, several hostels have opened since January 2001, including ones in the towns of Pompeii and Positano. In Naples itself, the youth hostel has a neat location in Mergellina and maintains high standards of food and accommodation. Italy's main hostelling association (AIG) has an exhaustive website giving all the hostels in the various regions, complete with facilities and prices.

➤ ORGANIZATIONS: **AIG Italy** (✉ Via Cavour 44, Rome, 00184, ☎ 06/ 4871152, FAX 06/4880492, WEB www.hostels-aig.org). **Hostelling International—American Youth Hostels** (✉ 733 15th St. NW, Suite 840, Washington, DC 20005, ☎ 202/783–6161, FAX 202/783–6171, WEB www.hiayh.org). **Hostelling International—Canada** (✉ 400–205 Catherine St., Ottawa, Ontario K2P 1C3, Canada, ☎ 613/237–7884; 800/663–5777 in Canada, FAX 613/ 237–7868, WEB www.hostellingintl. ca). **Youth Hostel Association of England and Wales** (✉ Trevelyan House, 8 St. Stephen's Hill, St. Albans, Hertfordshire AL1 2DY, U.K., ☎ 0870/8708808, FAX 01727/ 844126, WEB www.yha.org.uk). **Youth Hostel Association Australia** (✉ 10 Mallett St., Camperdown, NSW 2050, Australia, ☎ 02/9565– 1699, FAX 02/9565–1325, WEB www. yha.com.au). **Youth Hostels Association of New Zealand** (✉ Level 3, 193 Cashel St., Box 436, Christchurch, New Zealand, ☎ 03/379–9970, FAX 03/365–4476, WEB www.yha.org.nz).

HOTELS

Italian hotels are awarded stars (one to five) based on their facilities and services. Those with three or more stars feature bathrooms in all rooms. Keep in mind, however, that these are general indications, and that a charming three-star might make for a better stay than a more expensive four-star. During low seasons and whenever a hotel is not full, it is often possible to negotiate a discounted rate. In Naples, room rates can be on a par with other European capitals: Deluxe and four-star rates can be downright extravagant. In those categories, **ask for one of the better rooms**, since less desirable rooms—and there usually are some—don't give you what you're paying for. Except in deluxe and some four-star hotels, bathrooms usually have showers rather than bathtubs.

In all hotels there is a rate card inside the door of your room, or inside the closet door; it tells you exactly what you will pay for that particular room (rates in the same hotel may vary according to the location and type of room). On this card, breakfast and any other optionals must be listed separately. Any discrepancy between the basic room rate and that charged on your bill is cause for complaint to the manager and to the police.

Although, by law, breakfast is supposed to be optional, most hotels quote room rates including breakfast. When you book a room, specifically **ask whether the rate includes breakfast** (*prima colazione*). You are under no obligation to take breakfast at your hotel, but in practice most hotels expect you to do so. It is encouraging to note that many of the hotels we recommend are offering generous buffet breakfasts instead of simple, even skimpy "Continental breakfasts."

Hotels that we list as ($$) and ($)—moderate to inexpensively priced accommodations—may charge extra for optional air-conditioning; somewhat surprisingly, this is usually the case for luxury hotels in southern Italy. In older hotels the quality of the rooms may be very uneven; if you don't like the room you're given, request another. This applies to noise, too. Front rooms may be larger or have a view, but they also may have a lot of street noise—happily, many of Naples's finer hotels offer windows with double-pane glass to effectively silence the noise. If you're a light sleeper, **request a quiet room when making reservations.** Rooms in lodgings listed in this guide have a shower and/or bath, unless noted otherwise. Remember **to specify whether you**

care to have a bath or shower since not all rooms, especially lodgings outside major cities, have both. It is always a good idea to **have your reservation, dates, and rate confirmed by fax.**

Naples has no official off-season as far as hotel rates go, though outside the city some hotels do offer substantial discounts during the slower parts of the year. Major cities have hotel-reservation service booths in train stations.

➤ TOLL-FREE NUMBERS: Best Western (☎ 800/528–1234, WEB www.bestwestern.com). Choice (☎ 800/221–2222, WEB www.choicehotels.com). Clarion (☎ 800/252–7466, WEB www.clarionhotel.com). Comfort (☎ 800/228–5150, WEB www.comfortinn.com). Forte (☎ 800/225–5843, WEB www.forte-hotels.com). Four Seasons (☎ 800/332–3442, WEB www.fourseasons.com). Hilton (☎ 800/445–8667, WEB www.hilton.com). Holiday Inn (☎ 800/465–4329, WEB www.basshotels.com). Le Meridien (☎ 800/543–4300, WEB www.lemeridien-hotels.com). Marriott (☎ 800/228–9290, WEB www.marriott.com). Quality Inn (☎ 800/228–5151, WEB www.qualityinn.com). Radisson (☎ 800/333–3333, WEB www.radisson.com). Ramada (☎ 800/228–2828, WEB www.ramada.com). Sheraton (☎ 800/325–3535, WEB www.starwoodhotels.com). Westin Hotels & Resorts (☎ 800/228–3000, WEB www.westin.com).

MAIL & SHIPPING

Though much improved in recent years, the Italian mail system can still be slow, so allow up to 10 days for mail to and from the United States and Canada, about a week to and from the United Kingdom.

POSTAL RATES

Airmail letters and postcards (lightweight stationery) to the United States and Canada cost €0.80 for the first 20 grams and €1.60 up to 100 grams. Always stick the blue airmail tag on your mail, or write "airmail" in big, clear characters to the side of the address. Postcards and letters (for the first 20 grams) to the United

Kingdom, as well as to any other EU country, including Italy, cost €0.45. In 2000, the *Poste Italiane* introduced a new priority mail system, with postage about 50% higher but almost guaranteed delivery in Italy within 2–3 days. You can buy stamps for both standard and priority mail at post offices and tobacconists. To send urgent letters and papers to the U.S. and elsewhere, consider the *Posta Celere* (swift mail) system, which tends to be cheaper than having them couriered. This service is offered at several major post offices in Naples and in town post offices throughout the area.

RECEIVING MAIL

Correspondence can be addressed to you care of the Italian post office. Letters should be addressed to your name, "c/o Ufficio Postale Centrale," followed by "Fermo Posta" on the next line, and the name of the city (preceded by its postal code) on the next. You can **collect it at the central post office** by showing your passport or photo-bearing ID and paying a small fee. American Express also has a general-delivery service. There's no charge for cardholders, holders of American Express traveler's checks, or anyone who booked a vacation with American Express.

MONEY MATTERS

The days when Italy's high-quality attractions came with a comparatively low Mediterranean price tag are long gone. Italy's prices are in line with those in the rest of Europe, with costs in its main cities comparable to those in other major capitals, such as Paris and Madrid. As in most countries, prices vary from region to region and are a bit lower in the countryside than in the cities. Good value for the money can still be had in many places in Campania, especially in Naples and on the Amalfi Coast.

Here are some sample prices: Admission to the Museo Archeologico Nazionale is €6.5; the cheapest seat at Naples's Teatro San Carlo runs €17; a movie ticket is about €7. Going to a Naples nightclub might set you back about €12–€15. A daily English-language newspaper is €1.50–€2.50.

A Naples taxi ride (1⅓ km, or 1 mi) costs €6. An inexpensive hotel room for two, including breakfast, in Naples is about €75–€100; an inexpensive Naples dinner is €15–€25, and a ½ liter carafe of house wine, €4. A simple pasta item on the menu runs €5–€7, a cup of coffee €0.80, and a rosticceria lunch about €8. A Coca-Cola (standing) at a café is €1.50 and a pint of beer is €3.5.

Prices throughout this guide are given for adults. Substantially reduced fees are almost always available for children, students, and senior citizens. For information on taxes, *see* Taxes.

CREDIT CARDS

Throughout this guide, the following abbreviations are used: **AE,** American Express; **DC,** Diners Club; **MC,** MasterCard; and **V,** Visa.

➤ REPORTING LOST CARDS: **American Express** (☎ 336/668–5110 international collect). **Diners Club** (☎ 702/797–5532 collect). **MasterCard** (☎ 800/870866). **Visa** (☎ 800/819014).

CURRENCY

The unit of currency in Italy was the lira until January 2002, when it was replaced by the euro, currently adopted in 12 countries of the European Union (the only EU Member States not to adopt the euro were Britain, Denmark, and Sweden). From February 28, 2002, Italian banks no longer accept the old lira, but if you have some left over from a previous visit it can be changed at the Banca D'Italia in the center of Naples (✉ Via Cervantes 71, ☎ 081/7975111) until the year 2012. The new euro is printed in bills of 500 (practically impossible to change outside of banks), 200, 100, 50, 20, 10, and 5. Coins are €2, €1, 50 cents, 20 cents, 10 cents, 5 cents, 2 cents, and 1 cent. All coins have one side that has the value of the euro on it and the other side with each countries' own unique national symbol. Notes have the principal architectural styles from antiquity onwards on one side and the map and the flag of Europe on the other and are the same for all countries. When changing money, make sure you ask for small denomination notes, preferably of 50 euros and below, as retailers in Naples and the surrounding area are notoriously bereft of small change.

The euro has fluctuated considerably against other currencies since its introduction in 2000. At the time of writing the exchange rate was about €1.15 to the U.S. dollar; €0.78 to the Canadian dollar; €1.67 to the pound sterling; €0.60 to the Australian dollar; and €0.48 to the New Zealand dollar.

CURRENCY EXCHANGE

The U.S. dollar (and all other currencies that are not part of the EU community) and the euro are in direct competition—in fact, this is the reason why the euro was created in the first place, so it could box with the big boys. Therefore, you still need to pay attention to where you exchange your dollars—**shop around for the best exchange rates (and also check the rates before leaving home) when it comes to non-EU currencies, such as the U.S dollar, the Japanese yen, and the British pound.**

For the most favorable rates, **change money through banks.** Although fees charged for ATM transactions may be higher abroad than at home, Cirrus and Plus exchange rates are excellent because they are based on wholesale rates offered only by major banks; **get your money on the road through ATM machines, by far the easiest and most convenient way to replenish your supply of euros.** You'll find getting euros from an ATM in Positano just as easy as getting dollars from an ATM in Chevy Chase. Exchange rates are higher at exchange booths in airports or rail and bus stations, in hotels, in restaurants, or in stores, although you may find their hours more convenient than bank offices. To avoid lines at airport exchange booths, **order a bit of local currency from your local bank before you leave home.**

➤ EXCHANGE SERVICES: International Currency Express (☎ 888/278–6628 for orders, WEB www.foreignmoney. com). Thomas Cook Currency Services (☎ 800/287–7362 for telephone orders and retail locations, WEB www. us.thomascook.com).

TRAVELER'S CHECKS

Do you need traveler's checks? It depends on where you're headed. If you're going to rural areas and villages, go with cash; traveler's checks are best used in Naples, Capri, Ischia, Sorrento, and the more popular destinations along the Amalfi Coast, although most major retailers now happily accept credit cards. In the end, however, traveler's checks may be a thing of the past, as ATM transactions are by far the easiest way to keep your wallet replenished with cash. Lost or stolen checks can usually be replaced within 24 hours. To ensure a speedy refund, buy your own traveler's checks—don't let someone else pay for them: irregularities like this can cause delays. The person who bought the checks should make the call to request a refund.

PACKING

The weather is considerably milder in Italy than in the north and central United States or Great Britain. In summer, stick with clothing that is as light as possible, although a sweater may be necessary for cool evenings, especially in the Lattari mountains along the Amalfi Coast (even during the hot months). Sunglasses, a hat, and sunblock are essential. Contrary to myth, the sun does not shine 24 hours a day on Campania: Brief summer thunderstorms are common in Naples, while typhoonlike storms occasionally arrive along the Amalfi Coast, so an umbrella will definitely come in handy. In winter bring a medium-weight coat and a raincoat; winters in Naples can be both humid *and* cold. Even in Naples, central heating may not be up to your standards, and interiors can be chilly and damp; take wools or flannel rather than sheer fabrics. Bring sturdy shoes for winter, and comfortable walking shoes in any season.

In Campania, laid-back style is the way to go. However, even on sweltering days residents do not usually wear shorts unless they're somewhere close to a beach resort. Men aren't required to wear ties or jackets anywhere, except in some of the grander hotel dining rooms and top-level restaurants, but are expected to look reasonably sharp—and they do. Formal wear is the exception rather than the rule at the opera nowadays, though people in expensive seats usually do get dressed up, especially for "First Nights." A certain modesty of dress (no bare shoulders or knees) is expected in churches.

For sightseeing, **pack a pair of binoculars**; they will help you get a good look at Naples's wondrous painted ceilings and domes. If you stay in budget hotels, **take your own soap**; many such hotels do not provide it or give guests only one tiny bar per room.

In your carry-on luggage, **pack an extra pair of eyeglasses or contact lenses and enough of any medication** you take to last the entire trip. You may also ask your doctor to write a spare prescription using the drug's generic name, since brand names may vary from country to country. In luggage to be checked, **never pack prescription drugs or valuables.** To avoid customs delays, carry medications in their original packaging. And don't forget to carry with you the addresses of offices that handle refunds of lost traveler's checks. Check *Fodor's How to Pack* (available in bookstores everywhere) for more tips.

CHECKING LUGGAGE

How many carry-on bags you can bring with you is up to the airline. Most allow two, but not always, so make sure that everything you carry aboard will fit under your seat or in the overhead bin, and get to the gate early. Note that if you have a seat at the back of the plane, you'll probably board first, while the overhead bins are still empty.

If you are flying internationally, note that baggage allowances may be determined not by piece but by weight—generally 88 pounds (40 kilograms) in first class, 66 pounds (30 kilograms) in business class, and 44 pounds (20 kilograms) in economy.

Airline liability for baggage is limited to $1,250 per person on flights within the United States. On international flights it amounts to $9.07 per pound or $20 per kilogram for checked baggage (roughly $640 per 70-pound bag) and $400 per passenger for unchecked baggage. You can buy additional coverage at check-in for about $10 per $1,000 of coverage, but it excludes a rather extensive list of items, shown on your airline ticket.

Before departure, **itemize your bags' contents** and their worth, and label the bags with your name, address, and phone number. (If you use your home address, cover it so potential thieves can't see it readily.) Inside each bag, **pack a copy of your itinerary.** At check-in, **make sure that each bag is correctly tagged** with the destination airport's three-letter code. If your bags arrive damaged or fail to arrive at all, file a written report with the airline before leaving the airport.

PASSPORTS & VISAS

When traveling internationally, **carry your passport** even if you don't need one (it's always the best form of I.D.) and **make two photocopies of the data page** (one for someone at home and another for you, carried separately from your passport). If you lose your passport, promptly call the nearest embassy or consulate and the local police.

ENTERING ITALY

Travelers need only a valid passport to enter Italy for stays of up to 90 days.

PASSPORT OFFICES

The best time to apply for a passport or to renew is in fall and winter. Before any trip, check your passport's expiration date, and, if necessary, renew it as soon as possible.

➤ Australian Citizens: **Australian Passport Office** (☎ 131–232, WEB www.dfat.gov.au/passports).

➤ Canadian Citizens: **Passport Office** (☎ 819/994–3500; 800/567–6868 in Canada, WEB www.dfait-maeci.gc.ca/passport).

➤ New Zealand Citizens: **New Zealand Passport Office** (☎ 04/494–0700, WEB www.passports.govt.nz).

➤ U.K. CITIZENS: **London Passport Office** (☎ 0870/521–0410, WEB www. ukpa.gov.uk) for fees and documentation requirements and to request an emergency passport.

➤ U.S. CITIZENS: **National Passport Information Center** (☎ 900/225–5674; calls are 35¢ per minute for automated service, $1.05 per minute for operator service; WEB www. travel.state.gov/npicinfo.html).

SAFETY

Most of the destinations in this guide book are among the safest spots in Italy. Naples, like any modern metropolis, has had certain problems with crime, but great inroads have been made in the past decade and the city today is as safe as many other big urban centers in Europe. For special provisos, *see* Being Streetwise in Naples *in* Naples A to Z *in* Chapter 1.

SENIOR-CITIZEN TRAVEL

To qualify for age-related discounts, **mention your senior-citizen status up front** when booking hotel reservations (not when checking out) and before you're seated in restaurants (not when paying the bill). When renting a car, ask about promotional car-rental discounts, which can be cheaper than senior-citizen rates. To qualify for senior-citizen discounts in museums and at archaeological sites, you should be from a European Union Member State. This will entitle you on most occasions to free or reduced admission.

➤ EDUCATIONAL PROGRAMS: **Elder-hostel** (⊠ 11 Ave. de Lafayette, Boston, MA 02111-1746, ☎ 877/426–8056, FAX 877/426–2166, WEB www.elderhostel.org). **Interhostel** (⊠ University of New Hampshire, 6 Garrison Ave., Durham, NH 03824, ☎ 603/862–1147 or 800/733–9753, FAX 603/862–1113, WEB www.learn. unh.edu).

SHOPPING

The notice PREZZI FISSI (fixed prices) means just that; in shops displaying this sign it's a waste of time to bargain unless you're buying a sizable quantity of goods or a particularly costly object. Always try to bargain, however, at outdoor markets (except food markets) and when buying from street vendors.

For any purchase you make, you should receive a regular receipt, which will list the amount spent, the name and—importantly—the *Partita IVA* (tax code) of the business concerned. You should have the receipt on you when you leave the shop; if you are stopped by the *Guardia di Finanza* (Revenue Police) and cannot produce a receipt, then both you and the retailer will be subject to a hefty fine. In Naples, which has a "black" economy running at over 20%, the Guardia di Finanza has been known to swoop on unsuspecting clients as late as one in the morning, so it is definitely worth asking for *la ricevuta* (the receipt). For information on VAT refunds, *see* Taxes.

STUDENTS IN NAPLES

Italy is a popular student destination, and in Naples there are facilities (information, lodging) geared to students' needs, though they are not always easy to locate. Students with identification cards may obtain discounts at museums, galleries, exhibitions, entertainment venues, and on some transportation. The main faculties of the Università degli Studi di Napoli can be found in buildings extending the length of Via Mezzocannone, off Corso Umberto I, near the district of Spaccanapoli, and on Via Porta di Massa. Another university, the Orientale, is located on and around the nearby Piazza Bovio. Both universities sport areas with noticeboards with advertisements for lodgings, forthcoming events, private tutoring, etc., though facilities like university common rooms, student bars, and premises for university clubs and societies remain the stuff of pipedreams. For more structured information about university life, **buy a copy of the periodical Ateneapoli** (www.ateneapoli.it), available at newsstands.

LOCAL RESOURCES

If in Naples for a prolonged stay, you might want to join **CUS Napoli** (⊠ Cupa Poligono 5, ☎ 081/5512623, WEB www.cusnapoli.org), the university sports club which has extensive facilities in the west of town in Fuorigrotta. Apart from mainstream sports like soccer, tennis, and basketball, it also has a swimming pool, fitness center, and athletics track. The **Centro Turistico Studentesco** (CTS; ☞ Travel Agencies) is a student and youth travel agency with an office in Naples; CTS helps its clients find low-cost accommodations and bargain fares for travel in Italy and elsewhere, but to avail yourself of CTS's student discount you need to purchase a membership card (about €30). CTS is also the Rome representative for EuroTrain International. Dedicated to helping students, **Euro Study Travel** is a travel agency across from the central Naples university building near the heart of Spaccanapoli. The **Associazione Italiana Alberghi per la Gioventù** operates hostels for student members, including the famous Ostello Mergellina in Naples.

➤ STUDENT I.D.s & SERVICES: Associazione Italiana Alberghi per la Gioventù (✉ Salita della Grotta 23, Napoli, ☎ 081/7612346). Associazione Italo-Americana (**American Studies Center**) (✉ Via D'Isernia 36, Napoli, ☎ 081/660562, WEB www. usembassy.it/usa/amstudies/italy.htm). **British Council** (✉ Via Crispi 92, Napoli, ☎ 081/667410, WEB www. britishcouncil.it). **Centro Turistico Studentesco (CTS)** (✉ Via Mezzocannone 25, Napoli, ☎ 081/5527960, WEB www.cts.it). **Council on International Educational Exchange** (CIEE, ✉ 205 E. 42nd St., 14th fl., New York, NY 10017, ☎ 212/822–2600 or 888/268–6245, FAX 212/822–2699) for mail orders only, in the U.S. **Council Travel** (CIEE; ✉ 205 E. 42nd St., 15th floor, New York, NY 10017, ☎ 212/822–2700 or 888/ 268–6245, FAX 212/822–2699, WEB www.councilexchanges.org) for mail orders only, in the U.S. **Euro Study Travel** (✉ Via Mezzocannone 119, Napoli, ☎ 081/5520947). **Università degli Studi di Napoli** (✉ Via Mezzocannone, Napoli, ☎ 800/322020, WEB www.unina. it).

Travel Cuts (✉ 187 College St., Toronto, Ontario M5T 1P7, Canada, ☎ 416/979–2406 or 800/667–2887

in Canada, FAX 416/979–8167, WEB www.travelcuts.com).

TAXES

HOTEL

The service charge and the 10% IVA, or value-added tax, are included in the rate except in five-star deluxe hotels, where the IVA (10%) may be a separate item added to the bill at departure.

RESTAURANT

A service charge of approximately 15% is added to all restaurant bills; in some cases the menu may state that the service charge is already included in the menu prices.

VALUE-ADDED TAX

Value-added tax (IVA or VAT) is 20% on clothing and luxury goods. On most consumer goods, it is already included in the amount shown on the price tag, whereas on services it may not be.

To **get an IVA refund,** when you are leaving Italy take the goods and the invoice to the customs office at the airport or other point of departure and have the invoice stamped. (If you return to the United States or Canada directly from Italy, go through the procedure at Italian customs; if your return is, say, via Britain, take the Italian goods and invoice to British customs.) Under Italy's IVA-refund system, a non-EU resident can obtain a refund of tax paid after spending a minimum of about €160 in one store (before tax—and note that price tags and prices quoted, unless otherwise stated, include IVA). Shop with your passport and ask the store for an invoice itemizing the article(s), price(s), and the amount of tax. In most cases, you will be given a form called a Global Refund Cheque to take to the customs desk on departure from Italy, where the procedure for the tax rebate will begin. Although even small stores in resort areas and larger department stores in Naples will be familiar with this and similar procedures, you may find some retailers in Naples are wholly unversed in tax-free shopping.

Fortunately, a growing number of stores in Italy (and Europe) are members of the Tax-Free Shopping System, which expedites things by providing an invoice that is actually a Tax-Free Cheque in the amount of the refund. Once stamped, it can be cashed at the Tax-Free Cash refund window at major airports and border crossings; you can also opt to have the refund credited to your credit card or bank account, or sent directly home. To save a step at the airport or border, you can send the Cheque to a Tax-Free Shopping address.

There are also many business services that facilitate quicker refunds—for an extra fee; one of the largest network services is called Europe Tax-Free Shopping.

➤ V.A.T. REFUNDS: **Global Refund** (✉ 99 Main St., Suite 307, Nyack, NY 10960, ☎ 800/566–9828, FAX 845/348–1549, WEB www. globalrefund.com).

TELEPHONES

AREA & COUNTRY CODES

The country code for Italy is 39. Here are area codes for major cities: Bologna, 051; Brindisi, 0831; Florence, 055; Genoa, 010; Milan, 02; Naples, 081; Palermo, 091; Perugia, 075; Pisa, 050; Rome, 06; Siena, 0577; Turin, 011; Venice, 041; and Verona, 045. Essentially, the region from Naples to the islands (Capri, Ischia, Procida) and around the Bay of Naples to Sorrento uses the area code 081; the region along the Amalfi Coast from Positano to Salerno uses the area code 089. For example, a call from New York City to Naples would be dialed as 011 + 39 + 081 + phone number. From the U.K., dial 00 + 39 + 081 + phone number. When dialing an Italian number from abroad, you do not drop the initial 0 from the local area code. When dialing numbers within Italy, you must always use the area code (e.g. 081 for Naples) even if the number you're calling is just down the road. When dialing from Italy overseas, the country code is 001 for the U.S. and Canada, 0061 for Australia, 0064 for New Zealand, and 0044 for the U.K.

Mobile phone numbers can be easily recognized as they begin with the digit 3, and run up to about 10 numbers. (In June 2001 the zero was dropped from the front of mobile numbers.) The first three numbers indicate the service provider (for example, 347 is an OMNITEL prefix, 330 is TIM) and are followed by another six or seven digits. Both OMNITEL and TIM have good network coverage throughout the Naples area.

DIRECTORY & OPERATOR ASSISTANCE

For general information in English, dial 176. To place international telephone calls via operator-assisted service, dial 170 or long-distance access numbers (☞ International Calls).

INTERNATIONAL CALLS

Since hotels tend to overcharge, sometimes exorbitantly, for long-distance and international calls it is best to make calls from public phones using telephone cards. These can be purchased from newsstands and tobacconists (☞ Public Phones). You can **make collect calls from any phone by dialing 172–1011,** which will get you an English-speaking operator. Rates to the United States are lowest around the clock on Sunday and 10 PM–8 AM (Italian time) on weekdays.

From major Italian cities, you can place a direct call to the United States by reversing the charges or using your phone credit card number. When calling from pay telephones, insert a coin or a telephone card that will be returned upon completion of your call. You automatically reach an operator in the country of destination and thereby avoid all language difficulties.

LOCAL CALLS

For all calls within Italy—local and long distance—you must dial the area code (*prefisso*), which begins with a 0, as 081 for Naples, 089 for Amalfi, etc. If you are calling from a public phone you must deposit a coin or use a calling card to get a dial tone

LONG-DISTANCE SERVICES

AT&T, MCI, and Sprint access codes make calling long distance relatively convenient, but you may find the local access number blocked in many hotel rooms. First ask the hotel operator to connect you. If the hotel operator balks, ask for an international operator, or dial the international operator yourself. One way to improve your odds of getting connected to your long-distance carrier is to travel with more than one company's calling card (a hotel may block Sprint, for example, but not MCI). If all else fails, call from a pay phone.

➤ ACCESS CODES: AT&T USADirect (☎ 172–1011). MCI Call USA (☎ 172–1022). Sprint Express (☎ 172–1877).

PUBLIC PHONES

Pay phones that accept coins are gradually being phased out. Therefore **consider buying a *carta telefonica* (prepaid calling card).** Scheda phones are becoming common everywhere. You buy the card (values vary) at Telecom centers, post offices, and tobacconists. Tear off the corner of the card, and insert it in the slot. When you dial, its value appears in the window. After you hang up, the card is returned so you can use it until its value runs out.

TIME

Italy operates on a 24-hour clock. In other words, AM hours are listed as in the U.S. and Great Britain, but PM hours continue through the cycle (1 PM is 13, 2 PM is 14, etc.). Daylight-saving time begins on the last Sunday in March, when clocks are set forward one hour; on the last Sunday in October, clocks are set back one hour. When it's 3 PM in Naples, it is 2 PM in London, 9 AM in New York City, and 6 AM in Los Angeles.

TIPPING

The following guidelines apply in Naples and most areas in southern Italy, where tipping effectively subsidizes fairly low wages and may ensure good service on return visits. In restaurants a service charge of about 15% sometimes appears as a separate item on your check. A few restaurants state on the menu that cover and service charge are included. Either way, it's customary to leave an additional 5%–10% tip for the waiter, depending on the service. Tip checkroom attendants €0.25 per person, rest room attendants €0.10 lire (more in expensive hotels and restaurants). Tip €0.05–€0.10 for whatever you drink standing up at a coffee bar, €0.25 or more for table service in cafés. At a hotel bar tip €0.50 and up for a round or two of cocktails.

If your car is being looked after by that southern Italian institution, the *posteggiatore* (parking attendant), to be found outside many city restaurants, then a tip of €1–€1.5 will usually be sufficient. Before you leave your car, make sure it is properly parked, as you will be liable for any fines incurred.

Tip taxi drivers 5%–10% of the meter amount. Railway and airport porters charge a fixed rate per bag. Tip an additional €0.25 per person, more if the porter is very helpful. Theater ushers expect €0.50 per person, and more for very expensive seats. Give a barber €1–€1.50 and a hairdresser's assistant €1.50–€4 for a shampoo or cut, depending on the type of establishment.

On sightseeing tours, tip guides about €1.50 per person for a half-day group tour, more if they are very good. In museums and other places of interest where admission is free, and a museum official has opened up a display specially for you, a tip of €2 or more would be appreciated, though this must be done with discretion. Service station attendants are tipped only for special services, for example, €0.50 for checking your tires.

In hotels, some clients round up the bill when checking out or leave cash for *il personale* (the staff), say €10 depending on the establishment and the length of stay. For two people in a double room, leave the chambermaid about €0.50–€1 per day, or about €3–€5 a week, in a moderately priced hotel; tip a minimum of €0.50 for valet or room service. Double these amounts in a very expensive hotel. In very expensive hotels, tip doormen €1 for carrying bags to the check-in desk, bellhops €1.50–€2.50 for carrying your bags to the room and the same for room service.

TOURS & PACKAGES

Because everything is prearranged on a prepackaged tour or independent vacation, you spend less time planning—and often get it all at a good price.

BOOKING WITH AN AGENT

Travel agents are excellent resources. But it's a good idea to collect brochures from several agencies as some agents' suggestions may be influenced by relationships with tour and package firms that reward them for volume sales. If you have a special interest, **find an agent with expertise in that area**; the American Society of Travel Agents (ASTA; ☞ Travel Agencies) has a database of specialists worldwide.

Make sure your travel agent knows the accommodations and other services of the place being recommended. Ask about the hotel's location, room size, beds, and whether it has a pool, room service, or programs for children, if you care about these. Has your agent been there in person or sent others whom you can contact?

Do some homework on your own, too: local tourism boards can provide information about lesser-known and small-niche operators, some of which may sell only direct.

BUYER BEWARE

Each year consumers are stranded or lose their money when tour operators—even large ones with excellent reputations—go out of business. So **check out the operator**. Ask several travel agents about its reputation, and try to **book with a company that has a consumer-protection program.** (Look for information in the company's brochure.) In the United States, members of the National Tour Association and the United States

Tour Operators Association are required to set aside funds to cover your payments and travel arrangements in the event that the company defaults. It's also a good idea to choose a company that participates in the American Society of Travel Agents' Tour Operator Program (TOP); ASTA will act as mediator in any disputes between you and your tour operator.

Remember that the more your package or tour includes the better you can predict the ultimate cost of your vacation. Make sure you know exactly what is covered, and **beware of hidden costs.** Are taxes, tips, and transfers included? Entertainment and excursions? These can add up.

➤ TOUR-OPERATOR RECOMMENDATIONS: **American Society of Travel Agents** (☞ Travel Agencies). **National Tour Association** (NTA; ✉ 546 E. Main St., Lexington, KY 40508, ☎ 859/226–4444 or 800/682–8886, WEB www.ntaonline.com). **United States Tour Operators Association** (USTOA; ✉ 342 Madison Ave., Suite 1522, New York, NY 10173, ☎ 212/599–6599 or 800/468–7862, FAX 212/599–6744, WEB www.ustoa.com).

TRAIN TRAVEL TO
AND FROM NAPLES

Almost all Italian trains have first and second classes, the main exception being the airport shuttle train from Fiumicino to Roma Termini. On local trains the higher first-class fare gets you little more than a clean doily on the headrest of your seat, but on long-distance trains you get wider seats and more legroom and better ventilation and lighting. At peak travel times, first-class train travel is worth the difference. Remember to **always make seat reservations in advance,** for either class.

The fastest trains on the Ferrovie dello Stato (FS), the Italian State Railways, are the Eurostar trains, operating virtually the length and breadth of Italy, including Rome–Milan via Florence and Bologna; seat reservations and supplement are included in the fare. Some of these (the ETR 460 trains) have little aisle and luggage space (though there is a space near the door where you can put large bags). To avoid having to squeeze through narrow aisles, board only at your car (look for the number on the reservation ticket). Car numbers are displayed on their exterior. Next-fastest trains are the Intercity (IC) trains, for which you pay a supplement and for which seat reservations may be required and are always advisable. *Interregionale* trains usually make more stops and are a little slower. *Regionale* and *locale* trains are the slowest; many serve commuters.

Trains can be very crowded; it is always a good idea to make a reservation. To avoid long lines at station windows, **buy tickets and make seat reservations up to two months in advance** at travel agencies displaying the FS emblem. Tickets can be purchased at the last minute, but seat reservations can be made at agencies (or the train station) up until about five hours before the train departs from its city of origin. For trains that require a reservation (many Eurostar and some Intercity), you may be able to get a seat assignment just before boarding the train; look for the conductor on the platform.

All **tickets must be date-stamped in the small yellow or red machines near the tracks before you board.** Once stamped, your ticket is valid for six hours if your destination is within 200 km (124 mi), for 24 hours for destinations beyond that. You can get on and off at will at stops in between for the duration of the ticket's validity. If you forget to stamp your ticket in the machine, or you didn't make in time to buy the ticket, you must actively seek out a conductor and pay a €6 fine. Don't wait for the conductor to find out that you are without a valid ticket (unless the train is overcrowded and walking becomes impossible), as he might charge you a much heavier fine. You can buy train tickets for nearby destinations (within a 200-km [120-mi] range) at tobacconists and at ticket machines in stations.

Note that in some Italian cities (including Milan, Turin, Genoa,

Naples, and Rome) there are two or more main-line stations, although one is usually the principal terminal or through-station. Be sure of the name of the station at which your train will arrive, or from which it will depart. Naples has at least four main-line stations: If your train leaves from Piazza Garibaldi, it means you must take the escalator down to the level below Napoli Centrale (follow signs to the *Metropolitana*). Some trains to Rome leave from the classy station of Mergellina, four stops away from Piazza Garibaldi on the Metropolitana. Potential confusion can also arise in Pompeii, as the main-line station is a good 20-minute walk from the archaeological site. For this site, you need to take the Circumvesuviana network from Naples to Sorrento and get off at Pompei Scavi.

There is refreshment service on all long-distance trains, with mobile carts and a cafeteria or dining car. Tap water on trains is not drinkable.

➤ FROM THE U.K.: **British Rail** (☎ 0171/834–2345). **French Railways** (☎ 0891/515477); calls charged at 49p a minute peak rate, 39p all other times.

CUTTING COSTS

To save money, **look into rail passes.** But be aware that if you don't plan to cover many miles you may come out ahead by buying individual tickets.

If Italy is your only destination in Europe, **consider purchasing an Italian Railpass,** which allows unlimited travel on the entire Italian Rail network. The Italy Flexi Rail Card allows a limited number of travel days within one month: $239 for four days of travel in first class ($159 second class); 8 days of travel ($334 first class, $223 in second class); and 12 days of travel ($429 first class, $286 second class). Passes for travel on consecutive days are also available: 8 days ($299 first class, $199 second class); 15 days ($373 first class, $249 second class); 21 days ($433 first class, $289 second class); and 30 days ($522 first class, $348 second class).

The Italian Kilometric Ticket is valid for two months and can be used by as many as five people to travel a total of 3,000 km (1,800 mi). The price is $354 for first class and $256 second class.

Once in Italy, **inquire about the Carta Verde (Green Card) if you're under 26** (€22 for one year), which entitles the holder to a 30% discount on all first-class tickets and 20% on second-class. Those under 26 should also inquire about discount travel fares under the Billet International Jeune (BIJ) and Euro Domino Junior schemes. Also in Italy, you can **purchase the Carta d'Argento (Silver Card) if you're over 60** (€22 for one year), which also allows a 30% discount for first-class rail travel and a 20% discount on second-class travel. For further information, check out the Ferrovie dello Stato (FS) Web site (www.fs-on-line.com).

Italy is one of 17 countries in which you can **Eurailpasses,** which provide unlimited first-class travel in all of the participating countries. If you plan to rack up the miles, get a standard pass. Train travel is available for 15 days ($554), 21 days ($718), one month ($890), two months ($1,260), and three months ($1,558). You can also receive free or discounted fares on some ferry lines.

If your plans call for only limited train travel, **look into the Europass,** which costs less money than a Eurailpass and allows train travel in France, Germany, Italy, Spain, and Switzerland within a two-month period ($348 for five days of travel, $388 six days, $460 eight days, $528 10 days, and $688 15 days). Rail travel to Austria/Hungary, Portugal, Greece, and Benelux can be added for additional fees ($60 one country, $100 two countries). You can receive discounts for two or more people.

Please note that these fares are subject to change in 2002 and/or 2003.

In addition to standard Eurailpasses, **ask about special rail-pass plans.** Among these are the Eurail Youthpass (for those under age 26), Eurail Saverpass and Eurail Saver Flexipass

(which give a discount for two or more people traveling together), Eurail Flexipass (which allows a certain number of travel days within a set period), and the EurailDrive Pass, which combines travel by train and rental car.

Whichever pass you choose, remember that you must **purchase your Eurailpass or Europass before you leave** for Europe. You can get further information and order tickets at the Rail Europe Web site (www.raileurope.com).

Many travelers assume that rail passes guarantee them seats on the trains they wish to ride. Not so. You need to **book seats ahead even if you are using a rail pass.** Seat reservations are required on some European trains, particularly high-speed trains, and are a good idea on trains that may be crowded—particularly in summer on popular routes. You will also need a reservation if you purchase sleeping accommodations. Trains going from the north of Italy via Naples through to Reggio Calabria in the toe of Italy will be particularly tightly packed, especially around weekends and public holidays. If traveling on a Saturday evening or Sunday, it may be worth finding out about important soccer matches and steering well clear of local fans (usually very well behaved) by upgrading to first class or changing your schedule.

➤ INFORMATION AND PASSES: Eurail- and EuroPasses are available through travel agents and **Rail Europe** (✉ 226-230 Westchester Ave., White Plains, NY 10604, ☎ 914/682-5172 or 800/438-7245; ✉ 2087 Dundas E., Suite 105, Mississauga, Ontario L4X 1M2, ☎ 416/602-4195). DER Travel Services (✉ Box 1606, Des Plaines, IL 60017, ☎ 800/782-2424, FAX 800/282-7474). **CIT Tours Corp.** (✉ 342 Madison Ave., Suite 207, New York, NY 10173, ☎ 212/697-2100; 800/248-8687; 800/2487245 in western U.S.). Italian rail passes can be purchased through DER Tours or CIT Tours as well.

➤ TRAIN INFORMATION: The main train station in Campania is the

Stazione Centrale in Naples (✉ Piazza Garibaldi, ☎ 848/888088, WEB www.fs-on-line.it). The Ferrovia Circumvesuviana leaves for points east from the **Stazione Circumvesuviana** (✉ Corso Garibaldi, ☎ 081/7722244, WEB www.vesuviana.it); all trains also stop on the lower level of Stazione Centrale. Destinations include Ercolano (Herculaneum), Pompei Scavi–Villa dei Misteri (Pompeii), and Sorrento. Note that there are two Circumvesuviana stations in the town of Pompeii, served by different lines. For the archaeological site, take the Sorrento line. SEPSA manages two railway lines that leave from the **Stazione Cumana** (✉ near Montesanto Metro station, ☎ 081/7354111, WEB www.sepsa.it). Both end at Torregaveta, at the west end of the Bay of Naples; the Cumana line goes along the coast and stops at Pozzuoli and Lucrino (near Baia), among other places. **Salerno's train station** (✉ Piazza V. Veneto, ☎ 848/888088, WEB www.fs-on-line.it) is a stop on the Milan–Reggio Calabria line.

➤ UNIQUE GUIDEBOOK: *Italy by Train* by Tim Jepson (Fodor's Travel Publications, ☎ 800/5336478 or from bookstores); $16.

TRANSPORTATION AROUND NAPLES AND ITALY

Public transportation is the fastest mode of travel among Italy's cities. It is also relatively inexpensive in comparison to the costs of renting a car and paying for gas and tolls. Italy's cities are served by an extensive state railway system (FS; ☞ Train Travel), with fast service on main lines (Milan–Venice–Florence–Rome–Naples) that in some cases beats plane travel in time as well as cost. A complete schedule of all trains in the country and fares can be bought from most newsstands for about €4, or can be accessed via the Ferrovie Dello Stato Web site at www.fs-on-line.it.

Buses (☞ Bus Travel), somewhat less comfortable than trains and slightly less expensive, offer more frequent service to certain smaller cities and towns that are served only by secondary train lines or are inaccessible by train. Ferries and hydrofoils ply among the islands; some islands, such as Capri and Ischia, have helicopter service, a more expensive alternative.

Italy has an intricate network of autostrade routes, good highways, and secondary roads, making renting a car (☞ Car Rental) for travel among most cities a feasible but expensive alternative to public transportation (not to mention complaints of white-knuckle driving by those inexperienced with autostrade speeds). A car can be a good investment if you are interested in carefree countryside rambles, offering time to explore more remote towns. Having a car in Naples, however, often leads to parking and traffic headaches, plus additional expense in the form of garage and parking fees.

TRAVEL AGENCIES

A good travel agent puts your needs first. Look for an agency that has been in business at least five years, emphasizes customer service, and has someone on staff who specializes in your destination. In addition, **make sure the agency belongs to a professional trade organization.** The American Society of Travel Agents (ASTA)—the largest and most influential in the field with more than 26,000 members in some 170 countries—maintains and enforces a strict code of ethics and will step in to help mediate any agent-client disputes if necessary. ASTA (whose motto is "Without a travel agent, you're on your own") also maintains a Web site that includes a directory of agents. (If a travel agency is also acting as your tour operator, *see* Buyer Beware *in* Tours & Packages.)

➤ LOCAL AGENT REFERRALS: **American Society of Travel Agents** (ASTA; ✉ 1101 King St., Suite 200, Alexandria, VA 22314 ☎ 800/965–2782 24-hr hot line, FAX 703/739–7642, WEB www.astanet.com). **Association of British Travel Agents** (✉ 68–71 Newman St., London W1T 3AH, U.K., ☎ 020/7637–2444, FAX 020/7637–0713, WEB www.abtanet.com). **Association of Canadian Travel Agents** (✉ 130 Albert St., Suite

1705, Ottawa, Ontario K1P 5G4, Canada, ☎ 613/237–3657, FAX 613/237–7052, WEB www.acta.net). **Australian Federation of Travel Agents** (✉ Level 3, 309 Pitt St., Sydney NSW 2000, Australia, ☎ 02/9264–3299, FAX 02/9264–1085, WEB www.afta.com.au). **Travel Agents' Association of New Zealand** (✉ Level 5, Paxus House, 79 Boulcott St., Box 1888, Wellington 10033, New Zealand, ☎ 04/499–0104, FAX 04/499–0827, WEB www.taanz.org.nz).

VISITOR INFORMATION

➤ AT HOME: **Italian Government Tourist Board** (ENIT; ✉ 630 5th Ave., New York, NY 10111, ☎ 212/245–4822, FAX 212/586–9249; ✉ 401 N. Michigan Ave., Chicago, IL 60611, ☎ 312/644–0990, FAX 312/644–3019; ✉ 12400 Wilshire Blvd., Suite 550, Los Angeles, CA 90025, ☎ 310/820–0098, FAX 310/820–6357; ✉ 1 Pl. Ville Marie, Suite 1914, Montréal, Québec H3B 3M9, ☎ 514/866–7667, FAX 514/392–1429; ✉ 1 Princes St., London W1R 8AY, ☎ 020/7408–1254, FAX 020/7493–6695, WEB www.enit.it).

➤ TOURIST OFFICES IN ITALY: **Rome** (✉ Via Parigi 5, 00185, ☎ 06/48899255). **Naples** (✉ Piazzadei Martiri 58, 80121, ☎ 081/405311, WEB www.ept.napoli.it); for further listings of tourist offices in Naples and the Amalfi Coast, *see* the A to Z section at the end of each regional chapter in this book. Official sites of the Italian National Tourist Board (www.enit.it), the local region (www.regione.campania.it), and the provincial tourist boards (www.ept.it.) also provide fair coverage.

➤ U.S. GOVERNMENT ADVISORIES: **U.S. Department of State** (✉ Overseas Citizens Services Office, Room 4811 N.S., 2201 C St. NW, Washington, DC 20520, ☎ 202/647–5225 for interactive hot line, WEB http://travel.state.gov/travel/html); enclose a self-addressed, stamped, business-size envelope.

WEB SITES

Do check out the World Wide Web when planning your trip. You'll find everything from weather forecasts to virtual tours of famous cities. Be sure to **visit Fodors.com** (www.fodors.com), a complete travel-planning site. You can research prices and book plane tickets, hotel rooms, rental cars, vacation packages, and more. In addition, you can post your pressing questions in the Travel Talk section. Other planning tools include a currency converter and weather reports, and there are loads of links to travel resources.

➤ SUGGESTED WEB SITES: For more information specifically on Italy, visit www.initaly.com, a constantly updated Web site with good-quality cultural information as well. The site for Ferrovie dello Stato, www.fs-online.com, is a good source for train information and journey planning, although at a local level www.campaniatrasporti.it provides an easily downloadable overview of local transport networks. Two handy sites for Capri are www.caprinet.it and www.caprionline.com; the island of Ischia is now on the cyberspace map at www.ischiaonline.it and, for last minute travel bargains, www.lastminuteischia.com. Many hotels now have on-line reservation facilities and several restaurants have thoughtfully posted menus to whet the appetites of Internet surfers. Where known, the sites have been included at the end of the individual listing in the relevant chapter.

WHEN TO GO

Campania is not always at its best in high summer: Naples can become a sweltering inferno, the archaeological sites swarm, and the islands and Amalfi Coast resorts are similarly overrun with tour buses and bad tempers. Any other time of year would be preferable, including even winter, when the temperature rarely falls below the comfort threshold and rain is usually concentrated into a few days. Optimum times are May–June and September–October. Due to the temperate climate, you'll find many floral displays blooming through Christmas, while swimming is possible year-round, though you will only see the hardiest bathers out between November and April.

Summer is also the worst time for ascents to Vesuvius; the best visibility occurs around spring and fall. Watch the clock, however, as the days get shorter; excursions to Vesuvius, Pompeii, Herculaneum, and the islands all require some traveling, and it's easy to get caught with little daylight left. At most archaeological sites you are rounded up two hours before sunset, but by that time most crowds have departed—so late afternoon is an optimum time to enjoy Pompeii and Herculaneum in peace and quiet. Remember that a good number of hotels, restaurants, and other tourist facilities in Sorrento, the Amalfi Coast, and the islands close down from November until around Easter.

If you can avoid it, don't travel at all in Italy in August, when much of the population is on the move, especially around Ferragosto (August 15). This is the national holiday period, which begins about August 7 and generally extends to the end of the month; at this time, Naples is fairly deserted and many of its restaurants and shops are closed. Of course, with residents away on vacation, this makes crowds less of a bother for tourists. Avoid traveling to and from busy holiday destinations during summer weekends (the Naples–Salerno *autostrada* and Naples–Sorrento coast road are particularly notorious for traffic congestion), while train seats are worth booking well in advance.

CLIMATE

Weatherwise, the best months for sightseeing are April, May, June, September, and October—generally pleasant and not too hot. The hottest months are July and August, when humidity can make things pretty unpleasant. However, most of the places covered in this book lie along the seashore, if not actually in the sea (Capri, Ischia, Procida) which takes some of the curse off the heat. Winters are relatively mild but cold fronts can arrive and stay for days.

➤ FORECASTS: **Weather Channel Connection** (☎ 900/932–8437), 95¢ per minute from a Touch-Tone phone.

NAPLES

Jan.	53F	12	May	72F	22C	Sept.	79F	26C
	40	4		54	12		61	16
Feb.	55F	13C	June	79F	26C	Oct.	71F	22C
	41	5		61	16		54	12
Mar.	59F	15C	July	84F	29C	Nov.	63F	17C
	44	6		65	18		48	9
Apr.	65F	18C	Aug.	84F	29C	Dec.	56F	14C
	48	9		65	18		44	6

FESTIVALS AND SEASONAL EVENTS

Campania's top seasonal events are listed below, and any one of them could provide the stuff of lasting memories. It is revealing that the Italian *festa* can be translated either as "festival or holiday" or "party"—with food being a key feature of most Italian celebrations. For further information contact the **Italian Government Tourist Board** (☞ Visitor Information *in* Smart Travel Tips A to Z) and the **regional visitor centers**, listed in the A to Z section at the end of each chapter in this book.

➤ DEC.: **Christmas in Naples** (Natale a Napoli) is celebrated through December until January 6 (Epiphany). The season officially opens December 8 on the day of the Immacolata (Immaculate Conception), when the mayor lays wreaths on the Guglia dell'Immacolata and when the *Presepe* (crèche) shops of Via Gregorio Armeno are thronged by Neapolitans. Historic crèches are on view in many churches, including Santa Chiara, San Domenico Maggiore, and the Gesù Nuovo.

➤ DEC.–JUNE: The **Opera Season** is in full swing at Teatro San Carlo in

Naples. ✉ *Via San Carlo 101–3,* ☎ *081/7972412 (ticket office),* FAX *081/400902,* WEB *www.teatrosancarlo.it.*

➤ DEC. 31: Naples stages a rousing **New Year's Eve** celebration, with the focal point being the concert in Piazza Plebiscito, concluding with a public fireworks display over the bay and an open-air disco till dawn at the Stazione Marittima. At about 2 AM many Neapolitans pile into their cars and regroup for a *Veglione* (New Year's Eve party). The night winds up with a dawn espresso at the châlets in Mergellina or at other panoramic spots along the bay, as well as gridlock traffic along the waterfront and in San Martino. As a general rule, avoid walking the streets of residential areas from midnight to 1 AM: some Neapolitans still take their celebrations far too seriously and—despite police warnings and civic initiatives—continue to indulge in a variety of banned pyrotechnics from their windows and balconies, though the days of flying refrigerators are thankfully over. Fashionable merrymakers zero in on Capri, where islanders stir from their wintry pace to welcome hordes for days-long celebrations.

➤ JAN. 5–6: **Epiphany Celebrations** (Epifania). Roman Catholic Epiphany decorations are evident throughout Campania. Notable is the celebration in Naples when the Befana witch arrives on the Piazza Plebiscito; she generally performs a similar function to that of the more northern European Santa Claus, with "good" children being rewarded with sweets and "naughty" children being given lumps of coal. This is still a major occasion— perhaps even more important than Christmas—for the *popolino* (common people) in Naples and the surrounding area: Streets close to Piazza Garibaldi like Via Foria and Via Carbonara are lined for the January 5th and 6th events with a welter of market stalls selling toys and other goodies, and locals are busy making last minute purchases until the early hours of the morning.

➤ EARLY APR.: **Easter in Naples** (Pasqua a Napoli) is celebrated around Easter Monday (Pasquetta). Throughout the Settimana Santa (Holy Week), choral concerts are offered in churches. Sorrento hosts two torchlit Good Friday processions, one at 4 AM and the other on the evening of the same day, involving the local **Incappucciati** (Brotherhoods). Easter Monday sees a mass exodus from Naples for a *scampagnata* (day trip into the surrounding countryside) or a boat ride across to the islands in the Bay of Naples.

➤ END APR./EARLY MAY: **Maggio dei Monumenti** (Monuments of May) opens Neapolitan palazzi, churches, and landmarks usually closed to the public. This time also sees the **Notti d'Arte,** a series of concerts and performances in historic settings, such as the Capella Palatina of the Castel Nuovo, the Salone da Ballo of the Museo di Capodimente, and the Salone d'Ercole of the Palazzo Reale.

➤ EARLY MAY: In Naples the first of the two annual celebrations of the **Feast of San Gennaro** is marked on the first Sunday in May at the Duomo of Naples (the ceremony of the Liquefaction of the Blood begins at 9 AM, but arrive by 7 or you'll wind up far from the altar and the action). Unlike the similar festa held in September, this one includes a *Processione di San Gennaro*—a procession of the saint's relics—through the streets of Spaccanapoli to the Church of Santa Chiara.

➤ EARLY JUNE: The **Regatta of the Great Maritime Republics** (Regatta Storica dell Antiche Repubbliche Marinare) sees keen competition among the four former maritime republics—Amalfi, Genoa, Pisa, and Venice. The regatta is held every four years in Amalfi, with the next scheduled for the first Sunday in June 2005.

➤ LATE JUNE: On the fourth Sunday of every June, the **Festa dei Gigli** (Feast of the Lilies) is held in Nola, just to the north of Naples. Spectacular wooden floats, often bearing orchestras, celebrate the homecoming of Bishop Paolino from Africa in 394.

➤ LATE JUNE–LATE SEPT.: **Estate a Napoli** (Summer in Naples) is a summer-long schedule of concerts and performances. In general, entertainment in the summer months in Naples moves outdoors. Cinemas often close for their *riposo estivo* (summer break), while cultural associations stage shows and festivals in historical venues throughout Campania. In recent years, special events have included *concerti a mezzanotte* (midnight concerts, which actually start at 11 PM) in parks; baroque, Neapolitan, and jazz concerts at the Borgo Marinaro; and a Comedy Festival at the Castel Nuovo. During the last week of June the **Napoli Cinefest Film Festival** is held in the city, featuring some outdoor movies. The main Piazza D'Armi at the top of Castel Sant'Elmo in the Vomero, towering over the rest of the city, hosts open-air movies in the Rassegna Cinematographica festival and avant-garde theatre. The suburb of Fuorigrotta is another fulcrum for entertainment, with the Neapolis festival taking place in the San Paolo soccer stadium and the nearby Mostra D'Oltremare a good open-air movie venue throughout the summer.

➤ JULY 16: The Feast of the **Madonna del Carmine** is held on Naples's Piazza Mercato and is celebrated by the "burning" of the campanile of Santa Maria del Carmine with fireworks.

➤ JULY–AUG.: **Estate Musicale Sorrentina** is the summer music festival in Sorrento. Concerts are held in historic cloisters and churches.

➤ JULY–AUG.: The **Fèstival Musicale di Ravello** actually schedules concerts throughout most of the year (except Jan.–Mar.) at Ravello's spectacular Villa Rufolo, but the annual highlights are the operatic concerts scheduled during July to commemorate the 1880 visit of Richard Wagner to the villa's famous gardens. ✉ *Piazza Vescovado, Ravello,* ☎ *089/858149,* WEB *www.ravelloarts.org.*

➤ AUG. 15: The traditional beginning of the **Ferragosto,** the traditional vacation period in Italy, is marked by an exodus from Naples and many regional celebrations, including the Assunta, or Feast of the Assumption of the Virgin Mary, in Positano, which commemorates the defeat of the Saracens with a procession and mass held on the main beach.

➤ EARLY SEPT.: The first week in September usually sees the **Vittorio de Sica Film Festival** in Positano. The **Premio Leonide Massine** dance awards are held in Positano during September.

➤ MID-SEPT.: You can't see *Il Vesuvio* erupt on command, but many regional organizations sponsor dinner sunset cruises on the Bay of Naples, with a **fireworks display to re-create the eruption of Vesuvius.** One celebrates the Festa di S. M. del Lauro a Meta di Sorrento in mid-September, leaving from the Molo Beverello of Naples. For information contact: *Ascultur Campania,* ☎ *081/665532; Associazione Aliseo,* ☎ *081/5265780.*

➤ SEPT. 19: The main celebration of the **Feast of San Gennaro** is held at Naples's duomo on this day. *Il Miracolo* begins (hopefully) shortly after 9 AM, but the best seats are grabbed hours earlier. Once the blood of St. Gennaro liquefies, a ceremonial cortege is paraded from Piazza del Duomo to Piazza del Carmine. For details contact: *Comitato Diocesano S. Gennaro,* ☎ *081/446103.*

WORDS AND PHRASES

English	Italian	Pronunciation
Basics		
Yes/no	Sí/No	see/no
Please	Per favore	pear fa-**vo**-ray
Yes, please	Sí grazie	see **grah**-tsee-ay
Thank you	Grazie	**grah**-tsee-ay
You're welcome	Prego	**pray**-go
Excuse me, sorry	Scusi	**skoo**-zee
Sorry!	Mi dispiace!	mee dis-spee-**ah**-chay
Good morning/ afternoon	Buon giorno	bwohn **jor**-no
Good evening	Buona sera	**bwoh**-na **say**-ra
Good bye	Arrivederci	a-ree-vah-**dare**-chee
Mr. (Sir)	Signore	see-**nyo**-ray
Mrs. (Ma'am)	Signora	see-**nyo**-ra
Miss	Signorina	see-nyo-**ree**-na
Pleased to meet you	Piacere	pee-ah-**chair**-ray
How are you?	Come sta?	**ko**-may **stah**
Very well, thanks	Bene, grazie	**ben**-ay **grah**-tsee-ay
And you?	E lei?	ay **lay**-ee
Hello (phone)	Pronto?	**proan**-to
Numbers		
one	uno	**oo**-no
two	due	**doo**-ay
three	tre	tray
four	quattro	**kwah**-tro
five	cinque	**cheen**-kway
six	sei	say
seven	sette	**set**-ay
eight	otto	**oh**-to
nine	nove	**no**-vay
ten	dieci	dee-**eh**-chee
eleven	undici	**oon**-dee-chee
twelve	dodici	**doe**-dee-chee
thirteen	tredici	**tray**-dee-chee
fourteen	quattordici	kwa-**tore**-dee-chee
fifteen	quindici	**kwin**-dee-chee
sixteen	sedici	**say**-dee-chee
seventeen	diciassette	dee-cha-**set**-ay

eighteen	diciotto	dee-**cho**-to
nineteen	diciannove	dee-cha-**no**-vay
twenty	venti	**vain**-tee
twenty-one	ventuno	vain-**too**-no
twenty-two	ventidue	vayn-tee-**doo**-ay
thirty	trenta	**train**-ta
forty	quaranta	kwa-**rahn**-ta
fifty	cinquanta	cheen-**kwahn**-ta
sixty	sessanta	seh-**sahn**-ta
seventy	settanta	seh-**tahn**-ta
eighty	ottanta	o-**tahn**-ta
ninety	novanta	no-**vahn**-ta
one hundred	cento	**chen**-to
ten thousand	diecimila	dee-eh-chee-**mee**-la
one hundred thousand	centomila	chen-to-mee-la

Useful Phrases

Do you speak English?	Parla inglese?	par-la een-glay-zay
I don't speak Italian	Non parlo italiano	non **par**-lo ee-tal-**yah**-no
I don't understand	Non capisco	non ka-**peess**-ko
Can you please repeat?	Può ripetere?	pwo ree-**pet**-ay-ray
Slowly!	Lentamente!	**len**-ta-men-tay
I don't know	Non lo so	noan lo **so**
I'm American/ British	Sono americano(a)	**so**-no a-may-ree-**kah**-no(a)
	Sono inglese	**so**-no een-**glay**-zay
What's your name?	Come si chiama?	**ko**-may see kee-**ah**-ma
My name is . . .	Mi chiamo . . .	mee kee-**ah**-mo
What time is it?	Che ore sono?	kay **o**-ray **so**-no
How?	Come?	**ko**-may
When?	Quando?	**kwan**-doe
Yesterday/today/ tomorrow	Ieri/oggi/domani	**yer**-ee/**o**-jee/ do-**mah**-nee
This morning/ afternoon	Stamattina/Oggi pomeriggio	sta-ma-**tee**-na/**o**-jee po-mer-**ee**-jo
Tonight	Stasera	sta-**ser**-a
What?	Che cosa?	kay **ko**-za
What is it?	Che cos'è?	kay ko-**zay**
Why?	Perché?	pear-**kay**
Who?	Chi?	kee
Where is . . .	Dov'è . . .	doe-**veh**
the bus stop?	la fermata dell'autobus?	la fer-**mah**-ta del ow-toe-**booss**
the train station?	la stazione?	la sta-tsee-**oh**-nay
the subway station?	la metropolitana?	la may-tro-po-lee-**tah**-na
the terminal?	il terminal?	eel ter-mee-**nahl**
the post office?	l'ufficio postale?	loo-**fee**-cho po-**stah**-lay

Italian Vocabulary

the bank?	la banca?	la **bahn**-ka
the . . . hotel?	l'hotel . . .?	lo-**tel**
the store?	il negozio?	ell nay-**go**-tsee-o
the cashier?	la cassa?	la **kah**-sa
the . . . museum?	il museo . . .?	eel moo-**zay**-o
the hospital?	l'ospedale?	lo-spay-**dah**-lay
the first aid station?	il pronto soccorso?	eel **pron**-to so-**kor**-so
the elevator?	l'ascensore?	la-shen-**so**-ray
a telephone?	un telefono?	oon tay-**lay**-fo-no
Where are the restrooms?	Dov'è il bagno?	do-**vay** eel **bahn**-yo
Here/there	Qui/là	kwee-la
Left/right	A sinistra/a destra	a see-**neess**-tra/ a **des**-tra
Straight ahead	Avanti dritto	a-**vahn**-tee **dree**-to
Is it near/far?	È vicino/lontano?	ay vee-**chee**-no/ lon-**tah**-no
I'd like . . .	Vorrei . . .	vo-**ray**
a room	una camera	**oo**-na **kah**-may-ra
the key	la chiave	la kee-**ah**-vay
a newspaper	un giornale	oon jor-**nah**-lay
a stamp	un francobollo	oon-frahn-ko-**bo**-lo
I'd like to buy . . .	Vorrei comprare . . .	vo-**ray** kom-**prah**-ray
a cigar	un sigaro	oon see-**gah**-ro
cigarettes	delle sigarette	day-lay see-ga-**ret**-ay
some matches	dei fiammiferi	day-ee fec-ah-**mea**-fer-ee
some soap	una saponetta	**oo**-na sa-po-**net**-a
a city plan	una pianta della città	**oo**-na **pyahn**-ta day-la chee-**tah**
a road map of . . .	una cara stradaleldi . . .	**oo**-na **cart**-a stra-**tah**-lay dee
a country map	una carta geografica	**oo**-na **cart**-a jay-o-**grah**-fee-ka
a magazine	una rivista	**oo**-na rec-**voess**-ta
envelopes	delle buste	**day**-lay **booss**-tay
writing paper	della carta da lettere	**day**-la **cart**-a da **let**-air-ay
a postcard	una cartolina	**oo**-na car-toe-**lee**-na
a guidebook	una guida turistica	**oo**-na **gwee**-da too-**reess**-tee-ka
How much is it?	Quanto costa?	**kwahn**-toe **coast**-a
It's expensive/cheap	È caro/economico	ay **car**-o/ay-ko-**no**-mee-ko
A little/a lot	Poco/tanto	**po**-ko-**tahn**-to
More/less	Più/meno	pee-**oo**/**may**-no
Enough/too (much)	Abbastanza/troppo	a-bas-**tahn**-sa/**tro**-po
I am sick	Sto male	sto **mah**-lay
Please call a doctor	Chiami un dottore	kee-**ah**-mee oon doe-**toe**-ray

Italian Vocabulary

Help!	Aiuto!	a-**yoo**-toe
Stop!	Alt!	ahlt
Fire!	Al fuoco!	ahl **fwo**-ko
Caution/Look out!	Attenzione!	a-ten-**syon**-ay

Dining Out

A bottle of . . .	Una bottiglia di . . .	**oo**-na bo-**tee**-lee-ah dee
A cup of . . .	Una tazza di . . .	**oo**-na **tah**-tsa dee
A glass of . . .	Un bicchiere di . . .	oon bee-key-**air**-ay dee
Bill/check	Il conto	eel **cone**-toe
Bread	Il pane	eel **pah**-nay
Breakfast	La prima colazione	la **pree**-ma ko-la-**tsee**-oh-nay
Cocktail/aperitif	L'aperitivo	la-pay-ree-**tee**-vo
Dinner	La cena	la **chen**-a
Fixed-price menu	Menù a prezzo fisso	may-**noo** a **pret**-so **fee**-so
Fork	La forchetta	la for-**ket**-a
I am diabetic	Ho il diabete	o eel dee-a-**bay**-tay
I am vegetarian	Sono vegetariano/a	**so**-no vay-jay-ta-ree-**ah**-no/a
I'd like . . .	Vorrei . . .	vo-**ray**
I'd like to order	Vorrei ordinare	vo-**ay** or-dee-**nah**-ray
Is service included?	Il servizio è incluso?	eel ser-**vee**-tzee-o ay een-**kloo**-zo
It's good/bad	È buono/cattivo	ay **bwo**-no/ka-tee-vo
It's hot/cold	È caldo/freddo	ay **kahl**-doe/**fred**-o
Knife	Il coltello	eel kol-**tel**-o
Lunch	Il pranzo	eel **prahnt**-so
Menu	Il menù	eel may-**noo**
Napkin	Il tovagliolo	eel toe-va-lee-**oh**-lo
Please give me . . .	Mi dia . . .	mee **dee**-a
Salt	Il sale	eel **sah**-lay
Spoon	Il cucchiaio	eel koo-kee-**ah**-yo
Sugar	Lo zucchero	lo **tsoo**-ker-o
Waiter/Waitress	Cameriere/cameriera	ka-mare-**yer**-ay/ka-mare-**yer**-a
Wine list	La lista dei vini	la **lee**-sta **day**-ee **vee**-nee

INDEX

Icons and Symbols

★ Our special recommen-
   dations
✕ Restaurant
⊞ Lodging establishment
✕⊞ Lodging establishment
   whose restaurant war-
   rants a special trip
🦆 Good for kids (rubber
   duck)
☞ Sends you to another
   section of the guide for
   more information
✉ Address
☎ Telephone number
🕙 Opening and closing
   times
💷 Admission prices

Numbers in white and black
circles ③ ❸ that appear on
the maps, in the margins, and
within the tours correspond
to one another.

A

Abbazia della SS Trinita,
256
Abbazia di San Michele,
180, 181
**Abbey of Santa Maria de
Oleria,** 254
A' Cantinella do Cunvento ✕,
112
'A Canzuncella ✕, 68
Acqua Pazza ✕, 255
Acunzo ✕, 75
'A Fenestella ✕, 74
Agritourism, 289–290
Aida ⊞, 167
Airports, 276
Air travel, 274–276
Amalfi Coast, 259
carriers, 274
check-in and boarding, 275
with children, 281
complaints, 276
cutting costs, 265
discount reservations, 284
enjoying the flight, 275–276
flying times, 276
Naples, 95–96
Sorrentine Peninsula, 259
Albergo Sansevero ⊞, 81–
82
Alfonso a Mare ✕, 228
Al Grottino ✕, 165
Alla Brace ✕, 257
Al Pesce d'Oro ✕, 238
Amalfi, 232–243
dining, 238–239
exploring, 233–238

festivals, 241
nightlife, 241
Piazza Flavio Gioià, 237
Porta della Marina, 237
Ruga Nova Mercantorum, 237
shopping, 241–242
Amalfi Coast, 191–198
cities and villages, 214–259
dining, 193–194
emergencies, 263
exploring, 196–198
festivals, 194
itineraries, 196–197
lodging, 194–195
price categories, 194, 195
shopping, 195
when to tour, 197–198
Ambasciatori ⊞, 206
Ambulance service, 285
Amici Miei ✕, 67–68
Anacapri, 158–163
Anfiteatro, 129
Anfiteatro Flavio, 136
Anima e Cozze ✕, 69
Antica Trattoria da Ciuffello
✕, 137
**Antico Francischiello da
Peppino** ✕, 212
Antiques shops, 90, 93–94
Antro della Sibilla, 142
A. Paranza ✕, 243
Apartment rentals, 288–289
Aquarium, 60
Arco di Traiano, 95
Arco di Trionfo, 30
Arco Naturale, 154
Arsenale della Repubblica,
234–235
Art galleries and museums
Capri, 154
Naples, 30, 44, 55–56, 90–91
Sorrento, 202
Art in non-gallery settings
Capri, 147
Naples, 57, 61–62
*Naples (City Center), 29–30,
32–33, 34, 35*
*Naples (Spaccanapoli), 39,
41–42, 42–43, 44–45, 47,
48–49*
Vettica Maggiore, 226
Art shops, 93–94
A' Scalinatella ⊞, 243
Astoria ⊞, 206
Astroni, 137
'A Taverna 'e Zi Carmela ✕,
73
ATMs, 99
Atrani, 242–243
Attanasio ✕, 77
Aurora ⊞, 240
Aurora-'O Canonico ✕,
204
Ausonia ⊞, 83
Auto clubs, 279–280

Azienda Agricola Seliano ⊞,
259
**Azienda Agrituristica Il
Casolare** ✕ ⊞, 142

B

B & Bs, 289
**Bagni della Regina
Giovanna,** 204
Baia, 139–142
Banco di Napoli, 29
Bank hours, 277
Barano D'Ischia, 180
Bar Daniele ✕, 64
Baroque art and architecture,
40
Bar-Ristorante Bagno Teresa
✕, 178
Basilica (Paestum), 258
Basilica (Pompeii), 124–125
Basilica di Sant'Antonino,
201
Basilica of St. Trofimena, 253
Bay of Naples region, 105–
145
dining, 106–107
emergencies, 144–145
itineraries, 108–109
lodging, 107
Phlegrean Fields, 132–144
*Pompeii, Herculaneum, and
Vesuvius, 108–109*
price categories, 107
when to tour, 109
Beaches
Amalfi Coast, 192–193
Capri, 169
Naples, 87–88
Positano, 217, 218–219
*Sorrentine Peninsula, 192–
193, 213–214*
Bellevue Syrene ⊞, 205
Belvedere ⊞, 231
Belvedere of Infinity, 247
Benedictine abbeys, 254
Benevento, 95
Biancamaria ⊞, 167
**Biblioteca Comunale
Popolare Luigi Bladier,** 154
**Biblioteca Nazionale Vittorio
Emanuele III,** 33
Bicycling
Ischia, 185
Procida, 187
Blue Grotto, 160–162, 185
Boating and sailing
Amalfi Coast, 193
Positano, 218–219
Procida, 183
Sorrentine Peninsula, 193
Boat tours, 141–142
Boat travel, 276–277
Amalfi Coast, 260
Capri, 183–184
Ischia, 185–186

ABOUT OUR WRITERS

The more you know before you go, the better your trip will be. The area's most fascinating small museum (or its most popular handmade sandal shop or sumptuous pizzeria) could be just around the corner from your hotel, but if you don't know it's there, it might as well be on the other side of the globe. That's where this book comes in. It's a great step toward making sure your next trip lives up to your expectations. As you plan, check out the Web as well. Guidebooks have been helping smart travelers find the special places for years; the Web is one more tool. Whatever reference you consult, be savvy about what you read, and always consider the source. Images and language can be massaged to make places appear better than they are. And one traveler's quaint is another's grimy. Here at Fodor's, and at our on-line arm, Fodors.com, our focus is on providing you with information that's not only useful but accurate and on target. Every day Fodor's editors put enormous effort into getting things right, beginning with the search for the right contributors—people who have objective judgment, broad travel experience, and the writing ability to put their insights into words. There's no substitute for advice from a like-minded friend who has just come back from where you're going, but our writers, having seen all corners of Naples and the Amalfi Coast, are the next best thing. They're the kind of people you'd poll for tips yourself if you knew them.

Many months with his nose buried in art history books helped **Gregory W. Bailey** cast his Texas days aside and blossom as a full-fledged Italian after relocating to Rome in 1996. On a side trip, he discovered and fell in love with Naples, quickly learning to remain *sempre tranquilla* (always calm) when riding in a taxi that never bothered to stop for red lights or speeding buses. Even so, Gregory has decided to remain in much more tranquilla Rome, where he has contributed to publications such as *Saveur* and the *International Herald Tribune*. He wrote nearly the entire Naples chap-

ter and also the Chapter 6 essay, "Napoli Ever After."

Having earned his architecture degree at New York City's Cooper Union, **Frank Gerard Godlewski** landed a job in the Milan studio of famed designer Aldo Rossi in the early 1980s. Family connections—the Godlewskis were an important family in 19th-century Naples and helped found the city's celebrated Aquarium—led him to set up base in the Vesuvian city. Realizing that a country's beauty lies not in its monuments, not even in its pasta, but in its people, he was soon giving some of Naples's most talked-about (and written-up) parties. Along with helping to produce features for *Gente Viaggio* and *Elle Decor Italia,* Frank has given the benefit of his knowledge to the Nightlife and the Arts and Outdoor Activities and Sports sections of the Naples chapter; in addition, he helped craft the Essential Information chapter. Today, he curates special programs for the National Italian American Foundation.

Language editor, travel consultant, and naturalist, British-born **Mark Walters** has been able to practice French, German, *napolitano,* and on occasion even Italian for many years now from his base in Naples. He settled in the city by the bay as an English instructor for the British Council, but soon became a tour guide and naturalist specializing in Mediterranean wildlife. In between playing field hockey and dodging Italian motorcycles, Mark has dusted down his graduate studies in archaeology and now leads expeditions in Italy and Greece for such groups as the American Association for the Advancement of Science, the Commonwealth Club, and Betchart Expeditions. He wrote the chapters on the Bay of Naples and its islands and, for the second edition, updated each of the regional chapters and the Smart Travel Tips section.

Lea Lane covers the world in varied guises: She was a columnist at Gannett newspapers, managing editor of the newsletter "Travel Smart," author of a cruise book and a guide to New England inns, and a talking head on The Travel Channel. Having been to more than one hundred countries, she has a special place in her heart for Italy—after all, she spent two honeymoons there. She wrote and researched—kilometer by beautiful kilometer—the chapter on Sorrento and the Amalfi Coast.

All that studying of art and architecture paid off for editor **Robert L C. Fisher** on his frequent trips to Naples, especially when he accurately guessed the date of the Palazzo Donn'Anna based solely on its architectural ornament, which he viewed as he fell from the palazzo's terrace into the Bay of Naples (it's much saltier than he had imagined). Part of Fodor's full-color Escape series, his *Escape to the Amalfi Coast* (2nd edition, 2001) captures in text and color photographs twenty of the dreamiest destinations in Campania, from Greta Garbo's Villa Cimbrone to the sky-kissing Hotel Cappuccini Convento, and can serve as a

handy travel aperitif to the region. We extend special thanks to **Frank Gerard Godlewski** for his valued contributions to the first edition's Naples chapter.

Don't Forget to Write

Your experience—positive and negative—matters to us. We follow up on all suggestions, so be sure to contact the Naples editor at editors@fodors.com or c/o Fodor's, 280 Park Avenue, New York, New York 10017. Have a wonderful trip!

Karen Cure
Editorial Director

FODOR'S NAPLES, CAPRI, AND THE AMALFI COAST

EDITOR: Robert I. C. Fisher

Editorial Contributors: Gregory W. Bailey, Lea Lane, Mark Walters

Editorial Production: Taryn Luciani

Maps: David Lindroth, *cartographer*; Rebecca Baer, *map editor*

Design: Fabrizio La Rocca, *creative director*; Guido Caroti, *associate art director*; Jolie Novak, *senior picture editor*; Melanie Marin, *photo editor*

Cover Design: Pentagram

Production/Manufacturing: Colleen Ziemba

COPYRIGHT

Copyright © 2002 by Fodor's LLC

Fodor's is a registered trademark of Random House, Inc. All rights reserved under International and Pan-American Copyright Conventions. Published in the United States by Fodor's Travel Publications, a unit of Fodor's LLC, a subsidiary of Random House, Inc., and simultaneously in Canada by Random House of Canada Limited, Toronto. Distributed by Random House, Inc., New York.

No maps, illustrations, or other portions of this book may be reproduced in any form without written permission from the publisher.

Second Edition

ISBN 0-676-901174

ISSN 1527-4837

SPECIAL SALES

Fodor's Travel Publications are available at special discounts for bulk purchases for sales promotions or premiums. Special editions, including personalized covers, excerpts of existing guides, and corporate imprints, can be created in large quantities for special needs. For more information, contact your local bookseller or write to Special Markets, Fodor's Travel Publications, 280 Park Avenue, New York, NY 10017. Inquiries from Canada should be directed to your local Canadian bookseller or sent to Random House of Canada, Ltd., Marketing Department, 2775 Matheson Boulevard East, Mississauga, Ontario L4W 4P7. Inquiries from the United Kingdom should be sent to Fodor's Travel Publications, 20 Vauxhall Bridge Road, London SW1V 2SA, England.

PRINTED IN THE UNITED STATES OF AMERICA

10 9 8 7 6 5 4 3 2 1

IMPORTANT TIP

Although all prices, opening times, and other details in this book are based on information supplied to us at press time, changes occur all the time in the travel world, and Fodor's cannot accept responsibility for facts that become outdated or for inadvertent errors or omissions. So always confirm information when it matters, especially if you're making a detour to visit a specific place.

PHOTOGRAPHY

Robert I. C. Fisher, *cover. (Hotel San Pietro, Positano)*

Tibor Bognar, *4-5.*

Corbis, *3 bottom left.* Mimmo Jodice, *7C, 8A, 9D, 9E, 10B.* Sandro Vannini, *8C.*

DIAF: *Bruno Morandi, 6B, 7E, 10A, 12C. Giovanni Simeone, 12A, 12B. Daniel Thierry, 11D.*

Robert I. C. Fisher, *1, 7D, 13E, 14A, 14D, 14F, 16.*

Grand Hotel Excelsior Vittoria, *14C.*

Houserstock: *Dave G. Houser, 11E.*

The Image Bank: *R. Vignoli, 13D.*

Italian Government Tourist Board, *2 bottom center; 3 top right, 14B.*

Le Sirenuse, *14E.*

Richard T. Nowitz, *6A, 8B, 10C.*

PhotoDisc, *2 top left, 2 top right, 2 bottom left, 3 top left, 3 bottom right.*

Sorrento Tourist Board, *2 bottom right.*